D1629475

# COMPANION TO PSYCHIATRIC STUDIES

## Volume I

*Editorial Committee*

## DR J. W. AFFLECK

M.B., F.R.C.P. (Edinburgh and Glasgow), F.R.C.Psych.
*Physician Superintendent, Royal Edinburgh Hospital*

## PROFESSOR G. M. CARSTAIRS

M.A., M.D., F.R.C.P.E., F.R.C.Psych.
*University of Edinburgh*

## DR A. D. FORREST

M.D., M.R.C.P., F.R.C.P.E., M.R.C.Psych.
*Physician Superintendent, Gogarburn Hospital*
*Consultant Psychiatrist, Royal Edinburgh Hospital*

## DR N. KREITMAN

M.D., M.R.C.P.E., M.R.C.Psych.
*Director, Medical Research Council Unit for Epidemiological Studies in Psychiatry*

## DR E. E. ROBERTSON

M.A., M.B., F.R.C.P.E., F.R.C.Psych.
*Consultant Psychiatrist, Royal Edinburgh Hospital*

## DR J. R. SMYTHIES

M.Sc., M.D., M.R.C.P., F.R.C.Psych.
*Reader in Psychiatry, University of Edinburgh*

## PROFESSOR H. J. WALTON

Ph.D., M.D., F.R.C.P.E., F.R.C.Psych.
*University of Edinburgh*

# COMPANION
# TO PSYCHIATRIC STUDIES

## VOLUME I

Editor: Alistair Forrest

CHURCHILL LIVINGSTONE    EDINBURGH AND LONDON 1973

© LONGMAN GROUP LIMITED 1973

ISBN 0 443 00933 3

Printed in Great Britain by Bell and Bain Ltd. Glasgow

# CONTRIBUTORS TO VOLUME I

J. W. AFFLECK, M.B., F.R.C.P. (Edinburgh and Glasgow), F.R.C.Psych., *Physician Superintendent, Royal Edinburgh Hospital.*

R. C. B. AITKEN, M.D., M.R.C.P.E., M.R.C.Psych.

W. D. BOYD, M.B., F.R.C.P.E., M.R.C.Psych.

G. M. CARSTAIRS (Professor), M.A., M.D., F.R.C.P.E., F.R.C.Psych.

RUTH CLAYTON, M.A., *Department of Animal Genetics.*

A. J. DEWAR, M.A., M.Sc., Ph.D., *Department of Pharmacology.*

D. ECCLESTON, Ph.D., M.D., M.R.C.Psych., *Department of Pharmacology.*

A. D. FORREST, M.D., M.R.C.P., F.R.C.P.E., M.R.C.Psych., *Physician Superintendent, Gogarburn Hospital. Consultant Psychiatrist, Royal Edinburgh Hospital.*

N. KREITMAN, M.R.C.P.E., M.R.C.Psych., *Director, Medical Research Council Unit for Epidemiological Studies in Psychiatry.*

S. K. LITTMAN, B.A., M.B., M.R.C.Psych.

F. M. McPHERSON, M.A., Ph.D., *Department of Psychology, University of Dundee.*

I. OSWALD, M.A., D.Sc., M.D., M.R.C.Psych.

A. S. PRESLY, M.A., Ph.D., *Department of Psychology, University of Dundee.*

H. W. READING, B.Sc., Ph.D., *Department of Pharmacology.*

M. H. T. ROBERTS, B.Sc., M.Sc., Ph.D.

P. T. SHIELDS, B.A., *Department of Pharmacology.*

J. R. SMYTHIES, M.A., M.Sc., M.R.C.P., M.R.C.Psych.

J. D. SUTHERLAND, C.B.E., B.Sc., M.Ed., Ph.D., M.B., F.R.C.P.E., F.R.S.Psych. F.R.S.E., F.B.P.S.

H. J. WALTON (Professor), Ph.D., M.D., F.R.C.P.E., F.R.C.Psych.

SULA WOLFF, M.A., B.M., F.R.C.P., F.R.C. Psych.,

# PREFACE

Three years ago plans were already in being to petition the Privy Council in the hope that a Royal College of Psychiatrists could be established.

At that time with my colleagues in the Department of Psychiatry and the Royal Edinburgh Hospital, I began discussions on how best to compile a book on psychiatry based on contributions from those who taught preclinical subjects and those who taught clinical psychiatry at undergraduate and post-graduate levels.

An Editorial Committee was established and accepted the task of devising a book which would cover all the main topics which were then expected to be required information for the examination for Membership of the Royal College of Psychiatrists.

I hope, therefore, that this Companion will be a useful text for candidates for the M.R.C.Psych. and also that it will be of interest to candidates for the Diplomas in Psychological Medicine.

This is not a book primarily for undergraduates, though some may wish to consult it during their undergraduate course in psychiatry; likewise the community physician may find it a useful source of information.

The book is presented in two volumes. Volume I is essentially a preclinical textbook, though readers may feel that some of the content has direct application to clinical practice—I am thinking of chapters by Professor G. M. Carstairs (Chap. II, Vol. I), Dr J. D. Sutherland (Chap. X) and Drs I. Oswald and S. Wolff (Chap. XIX).

Volume II is essentially clinical, therapeutic and administrative. The first eight chapters relate to neuroses, personality disorders, illnesses in childhood and adolescence, alcoholism, sexual problems and group therapy. The theme running through these chapters is psychotherapeutic; that of change through relationship, insight and group experience. The theme of Chapters IX to XIV is essentially clinical and descriptive, but there is also considerable coverage of theories of aetiology (e.g. Chap. X) on schizophrenia and Chap. IX on affective disorders).

Finally in Chapters XV to XX can be found discussion of treatment methods, administrative psychiatry and rehabilitation procedures. The last two chapters (XIV and XX) relate to mental handicap and forensic psychiatry which have certain common social and legal interconnections.

The reader may ask what is the best way to use this book? I am afraid there is no single answer to that question.

Personally I would not read right through Volume I and then proceed to Volume II. I would rather link chapters, thus genetics (Chap. XVIII, Volume I) would go well with mental handicap (Chap. XIX, Volume II). Likewise the basic sciences (Chaps. XIV to XVI, Volume I) might be read before proceeding to the clinical chapter on affective disorders, schizophrenia etc. (Chaps. IX to XIII, Volume II).

Again Chapters IX to XII in Volume I might lead on to those chapters in Volume II which relate to personality, its growth in childhood, neurosis, sexual disorders etc. (Chaps. I to VII, Volume II).

Many readers turn first to the index to see what has been left out. The index is identical in both volumes and refers to both volumes. It comprises topics and authors when their contribution constitutes a topic. We have not listed 'further reading' as this is a book for postgraduates, but a generous number of references are to be found at the end of each chapter. Thus a specialist author is best looked for in the references after the appropriate chapter, while a 'generalist' like Sigmund Freud can best be picked up in the index.

This book, partly because of the large number of contributors, has taken three years and a lot of hard work to compile. I believe that the resulting 'mix' of attitudes, opinions and special expertise makes this Companion rather different from any other current textbook of psychiatry, and I can only hope that readers will share in this opinion.

Edinburgh, 1973                                          A. D. Forrest

# ACKNOWLEDGEMENT

The Editor would like to acknowledge his indebtedness to Mrs Nora M. Gloyne, who acted throughout as administrative secretary, and had the courage and tenacity to persuade the many contributors to present their copy.

# CONTENTS

## Volume I

# Chapter I

# HISTORICAL INTRODUCTION

## A. D. Forrest

Psychiatry has been defined (1) as 'The part of medicine which deals with the diagnosis, treatment and care of the mentally ill.' Another approach, emphasizing the social roots of mental illness, might describe psychiatry as that medical speciality which ascertains and treats those social deviants whose deviancy society considers to be a problem for the health services rather than the courts or other social agencies. The concept of mental illness itself has been expanded of recent years to embrace much of ordinary human unhappiness, and, although Professor Szasz (1962) (2) regards this extension as rendering the whole concept meaningless, it appears that each society as it becomes more affluent identifies more and more of the problems of human living as psychiatric illness. Whether this process will continue or not it is hard to judge, but certainly at the present time psychiatry in Western Europe and America enjoys an eminence it has never known before. Pride needs to be tempered with the humility occasioned by our ignorance, and a brief historical review of how different epochs and different psychiatric thinkers have seen and attempted to deal with the problems presented by their patients may help us to achieve perspective.

Most histories of psychiatry start with the Greeks (3) but while acclaiming the empirical approach of Hippocrates and admiring the careful advice on the management of mania given by Caelius Aurelianus (3) we must recognize that across this vast span of time we cannot be sure that we are talking about the same phenomena. We have literally not enough information to evaluate these early clinical reports but must record our respect for the humanitarian outlook of these physicians.

*The Middle Ages* saw the development of a distorted theological view of social deviancy and its literary expression in the handbook for witch hunters, the *Malleus Maleficarum* (4) published in 1486. This was a time when women seem to have been feared and hated by men in a way which contemporary man must find hard to understand. The authors of the *Malleus Maleficarum* give some good descriptions of abnormal psychiatric states and remarkable revelations of their own sexual psychopathology. Toward the end of this era, most social deviancy seems to have been labelled 'witchcraft'. The great majority were women and the treatment was burning at the stake. While many physicians in the Middle Ages appear to have concurred with the delusions of their time, there were some, such as Johann Weyer (1515–88) (3), who retained some objectivity. He denied that the supposed activities of the witches were real, but suggests that they were fantasies, though given to them by the devil. He seems to have had a shrewd clinical sense; he distinguished amongst the mentally ill those who were possessed and those who pretended to such experiences by which means they were made to feel important.

*The Renaissance* was slow in its effects on psychiatric thought, but gradually a more humane attitude to the mentally ill emerged. Important was the renewed emphasis on naturalistic explanation. Paracelsus (1491–1541) (5) stated in 'Diseases which lead to the loss of reason' that mental illness was not caused by spirits but was due to natural causes. Unfortunately the therapies he advocated were not so liberal and he favoured fasting, ducking and beating for some complaints.

The seventeenth century was marked by little improvement in the conditions or treatment of mental patients.

*In England, Thomas Sydenham* (1624–89) (6) described hysteria and gave his opinion that this condition constituted one-sixth of his practice. An Edinburgh physician, Cullen, coined the term neurosis (1769) (3) but advocated treatment in the form of the straight jacket. Physical methods of treatment were popular, such as the rotating chair invented by Erasmus Darwin (1731–1802) (3), but also there emerged the beginning of psychotherapy, then termed the moral treatment [Tissot (1782), Haslam (1798)] (3).

But the close of the eighteenth century saw the first decisive steps in the emancipation of the insane when Pinel (1793) and Tuke (1796) (5) began the process of liberation.

It might be opportune at this stage to outline the problems which had perennially faced physicians in their dealings with the psychiatric patient. Were the manifestations due to evil (i.e. witchcraft) or natural misfortune (i.e. illness)? Was the appropriate treatment humane (i.e. liberation and moral treatment) or punishment (ducking, rotating chairs, etc.)? The problem of whether the aim of the hospital was to be custodial care or treatment was not even formulated in these terms until the last few decades of the eighteenth century.

*The French School of Psychiatry* dominated the European scene for the first half of the nineteenth century and declared strongly for a naturalistic explanation of mental illness and a humane approach to its treatment.

*Philippe Pinel* (1745–1826) (5) seems to have been a shy, cultured physician who was raised by political events to high position and later cast down as suddenly as he had been raised. In 1793 he was put in charge of the Bicetre Asylum and quickly set about freeing his patients from their chains. In 1795 he was given charge of the Salpetriere (a year earlier he had been appointed Professor of Hygiene). His *Traite medico-philosophique sur l'alienation mentale* published in 1801 (7) reveals that he was aware both of environmental and hereditary factors. His task he saw as that of the mental scientist, to observe facts and bring some order into the current therapies. Pinel, like many another, mocked his predecessors, especially Cullen of Edinburgh, but he had sensible things to say about how mental hospitals should be administered; he emphasized the role of the nurses and the value of work as therapy.

*Jean Etienne Dominique Esquirol* (1772–1840) (5) joined Pinel in Paris in 1799. In 1811 he was appointed to the staff of the Salpetriere and soon demonstrated his ability as a teacher and a clinician. His aphorism 'Il ne faut jamais etre absolu dans la pratique' reflects his eclectic and empirical approach. He was enthusiastic about new ideas but critical in his evaluation. He was not, in fact, very enthusiastic about the colony for the insane which had been established at Gheel in Belgium. Likewise he studied mesmerism but seems to have discarded it in favour of more traditional remedies. Esquirol was interested in statistics and was of the opinion that any increase in mental disorder might be more apparent than real.

About the middle of the nineteenth century a new theoretical approach to mental disorders appeared in France. This was expounded by Morel (8) in his *Traite des Degenerescences Physiques, Intellectuelles et Morales de L'Espece Humaine*, published in 1857. Insanity seemed especially suited to this theory of an inherited tendency to degeneration and Magnan (1835–1916) (3) who had made a study of alcoholism took up and developed Morel's ideas. The degeneration theory offered little scope for therapeutic optimism as degeneration was subject to the 'law of progressivity' so that if neurosis characterized one generation, then the next would be psychotic and the third generation would be idiots; it was presumed that the line would then die out. Needless to say Darwin's theory of Evolution gave apparent scientific backing for the degeneration theory. But later additions such as the study by Lombroso (1836–1909) (3) of criminals makes the whole theoretical structure somewhat suspect. Lombroso regarded criminals as a sort of surviving primitive race and identified them by the presence of atavistic stigmata.

Naïve though the degeneration theory may seem today, it strongly influenced French psychiatry for several decades and also those German professors of neuropsychiatry who were to dominate the European scene for the second half of the century. Such was Griesinger (1817–63) (3) who, after holding the Chair of Medicine at Zurich, became Professor of Psychiatry and Neurology at Berlin in 1865. He seems to have been an exceptional clinician and also an eclectic. He recognized the significance of unconscious mental phenomena, emphasized the role of the ego in harmonizing the different traits in the individual, noted how symptoms have significance only against the cultural background and accepted that predisposition was probably based on heredity. Griesinger was regarded as the father of neuro-psychiatry (3), the effect of his textbook (*Pathologie und Therapie der Psychische Krankheiten*) (9) was to strengthen the growing belief that mental illness was cerebral disease, and yet he clearly recognized the importance of emotional upset in precipitating mental illness. He promoted the unitary theory of psychosis (Einheitspsychose) which still has interest today, but his organic bias made impact on his contemporaries, while his psychological insights seem to have been forgotten.

*Emil Kraepelin* (1856–1928) was, in the opinion of F. J. Fish (10) 'probably the most outstanding psychiatrist who has ever lived.' Kraepelin is out of favour with many British and American psychiatrists at present as they regard his nosographical attempts as sterile and deride him as leaving the patient as a person out of the picture. It might be salutary to remember that Pinel derided Cullen, Kraepelin was over critical of Griesinger and later Freud in effect denied any relationship between his ideas and those of earlier workers. There is no doubt that Kraepelin was a perceptive clinician and his *Kompendium der Psychiatrie* (1883) exerted a great influence for several decades. He held different Chairs of Psychiatry from 1886 until he retired from the Chair in Munich in 1922. He recognized the failure of 'brain psychiatry' (mental illness = cerebral disease) but he maintained the hope that physiological research would eventually illuminate the problem of cerebral localization (3). His major contribution was perhaps to under-score the importance of accurate clinical examination. He regarded it as essential to know the classical disease patterns and thought that this would only be achieved by intensive clinical work. He emphasized the importance of making a valid prognosis and emphasized prevention as the goal in mental hygiene. Kraepelin is celebrated for his separation of dementia praecox from manic-depressive illness in which he differed fundamentally from the views of Griesinger. Kraepelin was a clinician rather than a theoretician. His description of the classical disease patterns survive the passage of time, but he was pessimistic about treatment and made minimal reference to psychotherapy in his textbook.

*Bleuler* (1857–1939) (11) was one of the great Swiss psychiatrists. He was an able clinician and open minded enough to introduce many of Freud's ideas into orthodox psychiatry. He was Director of the Burgholzli and Professor of Psychiatry at Zurich for many years. His monograph *Dementia Praecox or the Group of Schizophrenias* (1911) was published in English translation in 1950 (11). Bleuler really began the process, at least as regards schizophrenia, of bringing the patient, as a person, back into the clinical picture.

But while in Germany and Switzerland psychiatrists were concerned with psychoses and alcoholism (both Kraepelin and Bleuler were active campaigners for abstinence), the great neurologists of France were turning their attention to hysteria.

*Charcot* (1825–93) is said to have made hysteria respectable by his studies and teaching at the Salpetriere (2). He believed it was an hereditary disease of the internal capsule—in public. In private, according to a conversation overheard by Freud (2), Charcot recognized the significance of sexual conflicts (*'C'est toujours la chose genitale'*). This anecdote may be revealing to those readers who have any tendency to deride our predecessors. They were, of course, anything but foolish. Charcot was an eminent neurologist and received at the most elegant Salons in Paris (2). It suited him, and perhaps his epoch, to regard hysteria as a neurological disease, just as it has suited us in Britain in recent years to regard the criteria for termination of pregnancy as primarily sociopsychiatric. Another epoch may emphasize the volitional aspect of 'hysteria' and perhaps decide that the women herself may choose whether to have this baby or not. The real criticism of Charcot was that he was too credulous, allowing his hypnotic demonstrations to be 'arranged' (i.e. faked) (12). Charcot was not really interested in therapy as such and it was left to Hippolyte Marie Bernheim (1837–1919), Professor of Medicine at Nancy, to develop the therapeutic applications of hypnosis. Previously called mesmerism [after Mesmer (1734–1815) (3), a Viennese practitioner] the method had already been practised in Nancy by a family doctor called Liebeault (1823–1904) (3). Bernheim developed Liebeault's ideas and published in 1884 his first edition of *Suggestion-therapy*. He believed that hypnosis was not an hysterical (i.e. pathological) state as maintained by Charcot, but rather a state related to natural sleep. He considered that in hypnosis the patient was under psychological influence, as opposed to the magnetism of Mesmer; also, Bernheim maintained that it was not the sleep but the suggestion which was the essential treatment factor.

*Pierre Janet* (1859–1947) (2) was another eminent French physician who studied hypnosis. He was initially distinguished as a Professor of Philosphy but later qualified in medicine and in 1889 became established as a neurologist. He made the important discovery that traumatic memories which the patient had forgotten could be recovered during hypnosis. He suggested that these traumatic memories had, in effect, caused the illness and that making them conscious once more could lead to cure of the symptoms. Although he found that many of these memories derived from sexual experiences he warned against drawing any general conclusion from these observations. Janet thought that the incidence of hysteria was diminishing; most neuroses were, he thought, based on exhaustion and he grouped them under the rubric 'psychasthenia' (13). Janet clearly was an insightful therapist—he realized early that symptom removal was not always a sufficient treatment. He found that many subjects were resistent to hypnosis and talked of 're-educating' his patients. The patient's confused life situation (3) must be clarified and he must be taught to live reasonably 'within his small psychological means'. Janet was concerned with conscious and interpersonal events. We regard him as a very modern psychotherapist, but he was an eclectic and had relatively little impact on British or American psychiatry.

*Sigmund Freud* (1856–1939) was, according to Ackerknecht (3), the most celebrated physician of the first half of the twentieth century. As a student and a postgraduate, Freud's interests and work lay in the fields of physiology and neuro-anatomy. He worked in a physiological laboratory from 1876 until 1882. Then, while running a general medical practice, he continued his neuro-anatomical investigations and in 1885 was appointed lecturer in neuropathology. He was then awarded a travelling scholarship and studied under Charcot in Paris. Returning to Vienna, Freud established himself in medical practice and collaborated with Joseph Breuer (1842–1925), a well known Viennese physician, in the study of cases of hysteria. They used hypnosis and the recall of unconscious traumatic memories as their method of treatment. They called this method catharsis and published their results as a book, *Studien uber Hysterie* (1895) (14).

Soon after that their association ended. Ernest Jones (15) reports that this separation was brought about by Breuer's unwillingness to follow Freud in his investigation of his patients' sexual lives, or rather, in the far-reaching conclusions Freud was drawing from it.

In 1896 Freud gave an address to the Society of Psychiatry and Neurology in Vienna entitled 'The aetiology of hysteria'. According to Freud, the papers met with an icy reception. Krafft-Ebbing, who was in the Chair, contented himself with saying 'It sounds like a scientific fairy tale' (15). At this time part of his account of the aetiology of hysteria was analogous to a 'fairy tale' because Freud believed in the accounts patients gave him of childhood seductions. Two years later, judging from a paper on 'Sexuality in the etiology of the neuroses' Freud had come to realize that his patients' seductions were mostly fantasies. In 1889 he visited Bernheim in Nancy, but he subsequently abandoned hypnosis and came to appreciate the significance of repression and the function of symptoms as substitute gratifications. He became even more convinced of the importance of sexual experience in childhood and gradually mapped out the oral, anal, phallic and genital phases of childhood sexual development (16).

Over the first decade of the twentieth century he was refining his ideas on the nature of the libido, the 'Oedipal complex' and the process of sublimation (17). Concurrently he was elaborating his technique of 'free association' and exploring the phenomenon of the transference as the power factor in therapy.

And yet between 1896 and 1906 Freud had stood very much alone, apart from his friendship with Fliess (15). Fliess was a physiologist turned mathematician (or numerologist) and his Magnum Opus *The Rhythm of Life* appeared in 1906. He had met Freud in 1887 and their friendship became quite intense about 1893. Thereafter for several years they corresponded once or twice a week and met for a 'Congress' every summer. Freud seemed to need Fliess as a 'censor', a substitute parent figure possibly and only relinquished the relationship when his own self analysis seemed to have progressed satisfactorily (i.e. about 1900). It is salutary to remember that Freud had no analyst apart from himself and his friend Fliess, who must at times have given him obscure advice (in the form of numbers). Freud went through a very difficult psychological period between 1897 and 1900 when he was much troubled by his phobic symptoms and had quite serious bouts of depression. But if Freud stood alone in these difficult years (1896–1906) it was for reasons that were partly of his own making by denying any connection between his ideas and those of earlier workers, and insisting publicly on the primacy and ubiquity of childhood sexuality. He managed to attract much hostile criticism. Perhaps because of his ethnic background and early struggles for recognition he expected rejection, and indeed provoked that critical response by his own pronouncements. As Ernest Jones (15) describes him, he was a remarkable man, at times a charming companion but not always an easy colleague.

Notwithstanding these problems Freud attracted many gifted pupils between 1906 and 1913, such as Ernest Jones, Eugen Bleuler, Carl Jung and Alfred Adler. Journals were launched and in 1910 the International Psychoanalytic Association was founded. These early days when Freud was at last winning the respect of like-minded colleagues must have been most stimulating, and Jones (15) gives an inspirational account of a meeting organized by Jung at Salzburg in November 1907. Freud read the first paper entitled 'Case history' and the paper and discussion lasted from 8 a.m. until 1 p.m. By 1910 Freud had gathered quite a number of adherents in Vienna, Zurich, Berlin and other centres in Europe; also in Britain and U.S.A. small groups were being established. But that same year Bleuler resigned from the International Association. The year 1911 brought the break with Adler and at the Munich Congress in September 1913 the final separation from Carl Jung occurred.

It is interesting in relation to this last separation that the overt grounds for disagreement lay in Jung's attempt to redesignate the concept libido as a general tension or drive and his contention that incestuous wishes were not to be taken literally but as symbols representing more complex ideas. Similarly, the overt difference with Adler lay in the latter's emphasis on the innate aggressiveness of man and his emphasis on conscious ego functions and the significance of the social context of living (15).

In trying to evaluate Freud's conceptual system and his contribution to psychiatric thought, we must express our agreement with Ackerknecht (3); Freud was the greatest physician of the first half of this century. While many of his ideas derived from earlier workers and many of the emphases in his work were misplaced according to contemporary thought, he succeeded over a period of 30 years in creating a psychological explanatory model for mental illness. It was essential that he be dogmatic and it was necessary that his psycho-analytic technique should be of benefit to patients. We should remember that at the end of the nineteenth century the somatic approach was arid, the descriptive work of Kraepelin had already been completed and psychiatrists, and particularly neurologists, were at a loss to know what therapy to offer their patients. It seems to us that his theories began to gain acceptance because his therapy offered hope rather than because they were effective. As a psychiatric theorist Freud was committed as Szasz (2) says 'to the contemporary scientific Weltanschuang'. Trained as a neuropathologist he never gave up the hope that mental illness must one day be comprehended in biochemical terms and become amenable to pharmacological remedies. Likewise he adhered strictly to the medical model in thinking about and attempting to treat his patients. They had symptoms (pains, amnesias, etc.) which led to a diagnosis (hysteria or obsessional neurosis) attributable to antecedent causes (conflict over libidinal attachments, etc.) and which required treatment, i.e. psychoanalysis. Freud was not much concerned with the wider social matrix or even the complex of interpersonal relationships with which the patient was involved. His interest was in intrapsychic phenomena. It is remarkable how much he achieved within the limits of this conceptual frame.

And yet we must note that some of the points made by Adler and Jung coincide with contemporary thought. Adler's emphasis on aggression would match our contemporary switch of emphasis from sexual conflicts to those relating to assertiveness, submissiveness and dependence–independence dichotomies. Jung emphasized the wider nature of libido, the symbolic significance of many sexual fantasies, sentiments which we would perhaps applaud.

We have devoted a lot of space to Sigmund Freud but there are yet two topics which ought to be noted as of particular interest to the general psychiatrist, (a) his analysis of the Schreber Case (18) and (b) his paper 'Mourning and melancholia' (19). The Schreber Case was an analysis of a case of paranoid schizophrenia based on documentary evidence. From this and other material Freud deduced the latent homosexuality that underlies the paranoid projection. Although Jones (15) claims that Freud was adequately trained in psychiatry this can hardly have been true as psychiatry at that time was firmly based in the mental hospital and the university clinics of neuropsychiatry. In fact, Freud was practising a modified form of what we now aspire to—psychiatry in the community. His 1917 paper gives a lot of insight into the relationship between loss of a loved object, grief and depression. Due recognition of our indebtedness to this early insight has been made in a recent publication by Bowlby (20).

Meanwhile, in America psycho-analysis was flourishing in spite of the wild behaviour of Rank (15), and largely because of the steady and consistent support given by A. A. Brill (15) and Ernest Jones (21). At Johns Hopkins, Adolf Meyer (1866–1950) (3) was promulgating his synthesis of traditional psychiatry and Freudian theory which he termed 'psycho-biology'. Meyer was Swiss, trained in Europe; he reacted somewhat against the schematization of Kraepelin and accepted into his theories some of the dynamic ideas of Freud. He emphasized the uniqueness of the personal history of each patient and was, in some ways, a precursor of Binswanger (3) and the Existentialists. Meyer was clearly a great teacher and insisted that his pupils consider the entire life experience of the patient in an attempt to understand the nature and causation of the pathological 'reaction' the patient was now manifesting. Meyer's view of mental illness was essentially what Brown (24) has termed the 'normalizing view', and implied that anyone, given this set of experiences, might react in this way. Lidz (22) and R. D. Laing (23) are more recent exponents on the 'normalizing view'. To be fair Meyer did not reject the influence of heredity. He had a great influence on his associates and also apparently on his patients. His writings are remarkably difficult to read but he succeeded in bringing the patient as a person back into the picture.

It would be apposite at this juncture to review the problems still facing psychiatry at this time, i.e. the third decade of this century. It was agreed by now, at least amongst the professionals, that mental illness was due to natural causes. The problems were whether the illnesses were genetically determined or the result of early environmental factors. It was agreed that the treatment be humane but custodial, but whether it should be predominantly psychotherapeutic or somatic was to engage most of the protagonists in discussion for the next few decades. New contributors to psychiatric thought were also appearing—the sociologists and the anthropologists. Data on their contribution can be found in Chapters II and III. What made the whole argument more complicated was that the somaticists suddenly produced treatments that worked. This will be discussed more fully in Volume II (Chapter XV), but briefly it began with Sakel of Vienna who introduced insulin coma therapy in 1933 (10). This was followed by the work of Ugo Cerletti on electroconvulsion therapy in 1938 (10) and the development of leucotomy by Lima and Moniz (1936). Phenothiazine drugs became available in Britain about 1954 and the tricyclic antidepressants about four years later.

Apart from this theme of somatic therapies there were significant advances in psychotherapeutic theory and practice which will engage us for the remainder of this chapter. Considering the American scene first it seems to us that three analysts, Karen Horney, Erich Fromm and Harry Stack Sullivan, have probably each made a significant contribution to psychiatric thought. Karen Horney (25) was initially an orthodox Freudian analyst teaching at the Berlin Psychoanalytic Institute. In New York as a staff analyst in the Institute she began to stress the significance of social factors and to question the biological bias of Freud and his orthodox followers. She came to believe that Freud had been very much a prisoner of the concepts of his time and that his biological orientation, his tendency to dualistic thinking and his mechanistic evolutionistic outlook were responsible for conceptual biases which needed redress. In her book *The Neurotic Personality of our Time* Horney suggested that Freud was too rigid in his insistence on constitutional factors and his evident belief that the oral, anal, phallic and genital phases were innately determined. His tendency to think of psychic factors as pairs of opposites (ego and id, life and death instincts, etc.) were regarded by Horney as mechanistic, conceived in terms of physical systems. She also criticized Freud's view that present manifestations (i.e. of personality or neurosis) are not only strongly influenced by the past (i.e. childhood) but contain nothing but the past. The possibility of growth of personality in adult life was not a tenet of Freud's who was, indeed, somewhat pessimistic about human nature. By contrast, Carl Jung (26) came to believe in the possibilities of develop, ment even in later middle age. To quote Horney regarding Freud's libido theory (25) : 'Any kind of affection becomes an aim inhibited expression of libidinal desires. Any kind of submissive attitude towards others becomes suspect of being an expression of a latent homosexuality.' Horney (27) defines a neurosis thus: 'A psychic disturbance brought about by fears and defences against these fears, and by attempts to find compromise solutions for conflicting tendencies.'

Horney regarded all true neuroses as based on disturbances of character and believed that the conflicts of the neurotic were based on the conflicts existing in society at that time.

*Erich Fromm* was a social psychologist and a Freudian analyst. He had worked in Berlin before coming to America where he met and worked with H. S. Sullivan. His book *The Fear of Freedom* (28) was a study of the psychology of authoritarianism. Fromm had been influenced by Marx and always emphasized the background of culture and social organization. Discussing Freud's concepts of human relations he commented '. . . the relationship to the other individual is always seen as a means to an end not an end in itself.' Fromm regarded 'human nature' not as something biologically given but something created over time by man himself. Discussing Freud's views on religion (i.e. that religion is a form of universal neurosis) Fromm suggested that neurosis is a form of private religion. Whereas a religion is a generally accepted frame of orientation and devotion, a neurosis is a personal non-socially patterned one designed by the individual in order to explain his relationship to 'life'.

*Harry Stack Sullivan* was an American psychiatrist who became known for his success in treating young schizophrenic patients. Sullivan was not a particularly clear writer, he used a lot of neologisms, but he was possibly the first exemplar of social psychiatry in action. His book *Conceptions of Modern Psychiatry* (29) makes clear that he is not much interested in formal diagnosis or in psychiatry as a medical discipline; he thought psychiatrists were, or should be, experts on the problems pertaining to interpersonal relationships. Like Horney he saw anxiety as a central problem and regarded much of human effort as devoted to security operations, i.e. keeping anxiety within bounds.

In regard to Freud's concept of the unconscious, Sullivan thought of it functionally in terms of selective inattention. Anxiety monitors out much perceptual material from the narrowed field of attention, but there are other memories and fantasies which are disassociated and to which the self refuses to grant awareness. He also implicates volition in these processes—it is not that a person is driven mercilessly and mechanically by the force of the unconscious, but rather that this set of feelings and fantasies has been relegated to the not-to-be-made-aware-of category. For this choice a price has to be paid in inexplicable anxiety or more complex symptom formations.

Sullivan was primarily a practical therapist and his books are filled with insights gained at first-hand work with patients. His book *The Psychiatric Interview* (30) gives a remarkable guide to the processes involved.

In Britain there were important contributions from the child psychiatrists, Anna Freud and Melanie Klein (25), but we believe that another group represented here by *Suttie, Fairbairn and Guntrip* may in the long term prove equally important in the moulding of psychiatric thought.

*Ian Suttie* was an eclectic and like H. S. Sullivan he was essentially a social psychiatrist. His book *The Origins of Love and Hate* (31) was important because Suttie focussed sharply on the basic human need to love and be loved. If Freud was authoritarian and patriarchal Suttie was democratic and matriarchal (25). Suttie saw the mother–child relationship as underlying the future cultural and social activities of the child on becoming adult.

*Ronald Fairbairn* worked in isolation in Edinburgh and yet perhaps this helped him to develop his own ideas. Basically he arrived at a theory of object relations elaborating on the work of Melanie Klein on the predicament of the depressive subject. Fairbairn contended that our need for objects (i.e. relationships with people) is a primary need; we do not relate to others simply to satisfy sexual or other requirements. Fairbairn also outlined the developmental arrest that led to what he called the depressive and schizoid position. The depressive unable to tolerate loving and hating the same object (i.e. the mother) represses the hate. The schizoid comes to feel that his love is as dangerous as his hate, in that he gets rebuffed whatever feeling he manifests, and concludes that it is better to avoid all relationships (32). Fairbairn's ideas have been extended and elaborated by Guntrip (33), who has made the important point that man's ultimate fear is not of the dangerous forces of the unconscious but of his own weakness.

It is necessary to mention here the contribution of *D. W. Winnicott* whose emphasis is on the role of the family in establishing the basis of healthy personality (34) (35). Winnicott, like Guntrip, believes that ego weakness is the result of a failure in mothering. The *I am* feeling, which is at the centre of certainty about self, depends he thinks, on the capacity of the mother to 'be' for her child. A baby, he says, 'needs one person to gather his bits together—bits of nursing technique and faces seen and sounds heard and smells smelt are only gradually pieced together into one being to be called mother'. As he pieces the object (mother) together so the child pieces himself together too.

To summarize the main themes to which this historical review has drawn attention: the early problem of whether the subject was wicked (i.e. possessed) or ill has been settled; the question of whether punishment (i.e. ducking) or treatment (medical/humane) has been decided, though future generations may indeed question our use of leucotomy and aversion therapy; the respective contribution of heredity and environment to mental illness has still to be answered for many illnesses, and may indeed be unanswerable unless we pose the question in a different form; similarly, within the humane/medical treatment field there are some who emphasize psychoanalytic psychotherapy and others who urge the primacy of physical methods (i.e. drugs); we should be sophisticated enough to recognize that these differences may simply reflect the personalities of different psychiatrists. The mental hospital, once essentially a custodial institution, has now been 'hospitalized' in

Britain (36); the dangers of long residence have been so emphasized that we are now in danger of discarding the true 'asylum function' of the hospital altogether. Developments in the field of community care are discussed in a later chapter (Chapter VI). We have discussed briefly the concepts of Freud, the ideas of Horney, Fromm and Sullivan in America, and Suttie, Fairbairn and Guntrip in Britain; we think these latter workers were important because they developed the inter-personal rather than the instrumental function of human contacts; also Horney, Fromm and Sullivan opened the path towards what we now call 'social psychiatry', the recognition and exploration of those family, social and cultural factors which lie behind the individual illness. More detailed expositions of the contribution of the social sciences are to be found later in this volume, likewise the law relating to mental illness and the organization of the mental health services are reviewed in Chapters IV (Volume I) and XX (Volume II).

We hope this Introduction will have given some idea of how far psychiatry has progressed, but also of how far it still has to go; we are now at least humane and naturalistic in our explanatory models. There are still very many problems awaiting solution, and later chapters in this *Companion* will indicate some of the areas where progress may be expected.

## REFERENCES

(1) *Hutchinson's Twentieth Century Encyclopaedia* (1964) p. 876. London: Hutchinson.

(2) SZASZ, T. S. (1962)   *The Myth of Mental Illness*. London: Secker & Warburg.

(3) ACKERKNECHT, E. H. (1959)   A short history of psychiatry. Trans. S. Wolff. London: Hafner.

(4) SPRENGER, J. & KRAEMER, H. (1928)   *Malleus Maleficarum.'* Trans. Rev. M. Summers. London.

(5) ZILBOORG, G. & HENRY, G. W. (1941)   *A History of Medical Psychology*. New York: Norton & Coy.

(6) SYDENHAM, T. (1680)   *Letter to Dr Cole*. Quoted in Ackerknecht (1959), ref. (3), p. 28.

(7) PINEL, P. (1801)   *Traite Medico-philosophique sur l'Alienation Mentale*. Paris.

(8) MOREL, B. A. (1857)   *Traite des Degenerescences Physiques, Intellectuelles et Morales de l'Espece Humaine*. Paris.

(9) GRIESINGER, W. (1862)   *Pathologie und Therapie der Psychische Krankheiten*. Trans. C. G. Robinson. London: New Sydenham Society Publications no. 33.

(10) FISH, F. J. (1964)   *An Outline of Psychiatry*. Bristol: Wright.

(11) BLEULER, E. (1950)   *Dementia Praecox or the Group of Schizophrenias*. Trans. J. Zinkin. New York: International Universities Press.

(12) GUILLAIN, G. (1959)   *J. M. Charcot 1825–1893 His Life—His Work*. Edited & trans. by P. Bailey. New York: Haeber.

(13) JANET, P. (1919)   *Les Medications Psychologiques*, vols I–III. Paris.

(14) BREUER, J. & FREUD, S. (1895)   *Studies on Hysteria*. London: Tavistock Press.

(15) JONES, E. (1961)   *The Life and Work of Sigmund Freud*. Edited by L. Trilling & S. Marcus. London: Hogarth.

(16) Freud, S. (1956)   *Collected Papers*, vol. I. London: Hogarth.

(17) FREUD, S. (1956)   *Collected Papers*, vol. II. London: Hogarth.

(18) FREUD, S. (1956)   *Collected Papers*, vol. III. London: Hogarth.

(19) FREUD, S. (1956)   *Collected Papers*, vol. IV. London: Hogarth.

(20) BOWLBY, J. (1969)   *Attachment and Loss*. London: Tavistock Press.

(21) JONES, E. (1938)   *Papers on Psycho-analysis*. London: Baillière, Tindall & Cox.

(22) LIDZ, T. (1964)   *The Family and Human Adaptation*. The International Psychoanalytic Library, no. 60. London: Hogarth.

(23) LAING, R. D. (1961)   *The Self and Others*. London: Tavistock Press.

(24) BROWN, G. W. (1967)   In *Recent Developments in Schizophrenia—A Symposium*. Edited by A. Coppen & A. Walk. London: R.M.P.A.

(25) BROWN, J. A. C. (1961)   *Freud and the Post-Freudians*. London: Penguin Books.

(26) JUNG, C. J. (1940)   *The Integration of the Personality*. London: Routledge & Kegan Paul.

(27) HORNEY, K. (1937)   *The Neurotic Personality of Our Time*. London: Routledge & Kegan Paul.

(28) FROMM, E. (1942)   *The Fear of Freedom*. London: Allen & Unwin.

(29) SULLIVAN, H. S. (1955)   *Conceptions of Modern Psychiatry*. London: Tavistock Press.

(30) SULLIVAN, H. S. (1954)   *The Psychiatric Interview*. London: Tavistock Press.

(31) SUTTIE, I. (1935)   *The Origins of Love and Hate*. London: Penguin Books.

(32) FAIRBAIRN, R. D. (1952)   *Psycho-analytic Studies of the Personality*. London: Tavistock Press.

(33) GUNTRIP, H. (1964)   *Healing the Sick Mind*. London: Allen & Unwin.

(34) WINNICOTT, D. W. (1958)   Primitive emotional development. In *Collected Papers*. London: Tavistock Press.

(35) WINNICOTT, D. W. (1967)   The minor role of the mother. In *The Predicament of the Family*. Edited by P. Lomas. London: Hogarth.

(36) BATCHELOR, I. R. C. (1969)   *Henderson & Gillespie's Textbook of Psychiatry*. Oxford University Press.

Chapter II

# SOCIAL SCIENCE IN RELATION
# TO PSYCHIATRY

## G. M. Carstairs

In the vigorous reappraisal of programmes for the training of psychiatrists, which has been going on in recent years in Europe and in America, reference has repeatedly been made to the need to pay greater attention to the study of 'behavioural science', the 'social sciences', and sociology and, in some instances, social anthropology. It is open to question, however, whether the proposers of these additions to the trainees' curriculum have really clarified in their own minds just what aspects of the behavioural and social sciences should be taught, and by whom. After all, it takes at least three years of study before a graduate can claim to be a psychologist, a sociologist or an anthropologist, and even then he is only on the threshold of his subject. There are a few psychiatrists who have been sufficiently interested to devote some years to one or other of these social sciences: but the great majority must content themselves with a much more superficial knowledge, focussed upon topics which have practical relevance to the practice of psychiatry.

Since psychology is treated in Chapter IX we shall concern ourselves here with *sociology*, the study of the social life of man, and with *social anthropology*, a particular branch of sociology which differs from its parent science in the methods of inquiry used and in its traditional concern with relatively small, isolated, often preliterate societies. The anthropologists' techniques of prolonged participant observation and global description are now increasingly being applied to investigations of 'subcultures' within large industrialized communities.

In addressing ourselves to the study of sociology we need not, and should not, lose sight of the biological basis of all human behaviour; that is, the genetically determined structure and function of our bodies and brains which are the end product of millenia of slow evolutionary development.

Every child is born with an array of genomes which is unique (unless shared with a monozygotic twin) but which varies only within the general pattern of his community's genetic population pool. The translation of genotype to phenotype is, however, the product of repeated interactions between the child's genetic potential and his experiences, particularly those which he encounters during his formative years.

Since man is a social animal, many of his behavioural characteristics are acquired and perfected only in social settings. He is not alone in this. Ethologists have compelled us to recognize that there are elements in the behaviour of many species—elements formerly regarded as purely instinctive—which can only be properly acquired in a context of social learning. For example, Harlow has shown that monkeys reared in isolation not only fail to learn certain key behaviour patterns—such as how to respond to threats from dominant members of their group, and how to take care of infants—but also seem unable to acquire such behaviours when they are introduced into a group of their own kind. It has been suggested that they have outgrown the maturational 'critical period' at which their nervous systems would have been responsive to such learning. There are certainly many well documented instances of deviations of instinctive behaviour patterns, and apparent fixations of faulty patterns, in the ethological literature. It is tempting, but dangerous, to indulge in extrapolations from animal behaviour (even that of the primates) to man: we can draw analogies, but we should be very cautious in inferring close similarities.

The biologist Lenneberg has suggested that a human child's ability to learn the rules of his native language comes with a rush at about the age of 18 months, because from this time his neuronal maturation quite rapidly achieves the level of organization necessary for this task. Some phonetic learning of an elementary kind has already been taking place. Up to the age of 6 months, the crying and babbling of babies from any ethnic background remains very much alike; but after this age, the child begins to respond to cues from its parents and other kin who offer models of 'baby-talk', and show their approval of some of his utterances, their indifference to others. As a result, long before they can talk, a Japanese and an English infant are already making sounds which, to a trained observer, are recognizably different. Each child is beginning to separate out from the wide range of noises which it can make, a relatively restricted array of 'meaningful sounds' which will constitute the phonemes of his language.

Since the development of symbolic speech is the feature which both distinguishes man from all other animals and has given him his extra-ordinary cognitive mastery over his physical surroundings, the study of language and its acquisition is fundamental to an understanding of human psychology. Among the pioneers of modern linguistics two men in particular, Edward Sapir and Benjamin Whorf, emphasized the functional interconnection between the vocabulary and formal structure of a people's language and their social organization, their value systems and their outlook on the world. Anyone who has mastered a foreign language really well knows that there are some expressions which are almost untranslatable, because they relate to experiences, or shared attitudes, which seem peculiar to the life of that community. Recently, Noam Chomsky has argued that beneath the obvious, culturally determined diversities of human languages there are underlying similarities of formulation and of comprehension which, in his opinion, are based on common patterns of neural organization in the human brain; but at the everyday level languages are a powerful means of emphasizing the shared characteristics of the in-group in contrast with the strangeness of all the others, the aliens. Even within societies, differences in speech underline the separateness of subgroups; for example the Arabic and Malay languages have quite separate forms for 'polite' and for 'popular' speech. Nearer home, there are differences not merely of accent, but also of syntax and vocabulary in the speech habits of middle class and working class persons. Basil Bernstein, who has amply documented these differences, believes that they are associated with underlying differences in the speakers' perceptions of their world, and of their own roles. Failure to recognize these unexpressed differences of outlook can hamper communication between speakers from different social classes, a situation which not infrequently occurs in a medical or psychiatric interview.

## SOCIAL CLASS

Already, we have encountered one of the most significant elements in human societies: the tendency for the community to become sub-divided into subgroups, arranged in hierarchical order. This tendency resembles the 'peck orders', or status hierarchies, found in many bird and animal species. Ethologists have even demonstrated a simple form of inherited social privilege in some primate colonies, in which there is a rank-ordering among the mates of the dominant male. Here, the offspring of low status females are liable to enjoy a lesser share of the available food, and to share with their mothers a greater number of threats and occasions for flight than is the case with the offspring of the 'number one' female.

In our own society, those born into lower class homes have a signifi-cantly higher likelihood of suffering from many forms of morbidity. While it is true that the rates for maternal and infant mortality no longer show the very marked differences by social class that were apparent right up to the second World War, these differences are still there. Although tuberculosis, rickets, rheumatic fever and other 'diseases of poverty' have been largely controlled there are still cumula-tive differences of 'sickness experience' in the less privileged sectors of our society. Epidemiological surveys of psychiatric illness carried out in Britain and in the U.S.A. have shown markedly higher rates for most forms of mental disorder among the lower classes.

How are these social classes defined? The most important distinguishing features are *income, occupation, years of education,* and *locality and type of residence.* Many sociologists, including A. B. Hollingshead of Yale, have devised scales which give differential weighting to each of these factors in determining the social class of an individual or a family: but the British Registrar-General has decided that for most practical purposes the occupation of the head of the household suffices to give a good indication of his social class.

The number of social classes which have been distinguished has varied widely. The Registrar-General has at times used as many as 100 occupational groups for statistical analyses; but it is virtually impossible to put these diverse groups into a precise rank-order. Hierarchical grouping can be simple dichotomies, of 'rich and poor', or 'educated and uneducated', using an arbitrary cut-off point to draw the distinction; or they may be threefold, as 'upper, middle and lower'. The American sociologist Lloyd Warner used such a categorization, but with each of the three levels subdivided again into upper and lower, so that his hierarchy ran from upper–upper, through upper and lower–middle, to lower–lower. There have also been instances of dividing a society into 7, 8, 14 or 20 ranked categories. By far the commonest in Britain, however, is the Registrar-General's categorization of all citizens in terms of their occupation.

This is carried out in a number of stages. At the decennial census (and the 10 per cent national sample census which takes place at the midpoint between censuses) every respondent's occupation is ascertained. An alphabetical check list helps the census clerks to assign one of 211 code numbers to the stated occupation. These 211 occupations are marshalled in 26 groups, with provision for an extra category: 'Inadequately described occupation'. Those who have no occupation at the time of the census fall into one of three additional groups: (1) retired, (2) students in educational establishments, (3) other persons economically inactive.

The manual on classification of occupations issued by the General Register Office (1966) explains the basis of the classification as follows. 'The main purpose has been to provide groups with at least one common characteristic. The basic common factor of all groups is the kind of work done and the nature of the operation performed. But if, by reason of the material worked in, the degree of skill involved, the physical energy required, the environmental conditions, the social and economic status associated with the occupation, or any combination of these factors, unit groups based solely on kind of work done seemed too comprehensive they were further broken down on the basis of these other factors in order to identify what are substantially separate occupations.'

Since the 1911 Census it has been the practice also to allocate the numerous units and groups of occupations to one of five broad categories, termed Social Classes, arranged in hierarchical order as follows:

I   Professional, higher managerial, landowners
II   Intermediate occupations (including nurses, radiographers, social workers)
III   Skilled occupations
IV   Partly skilled occupations
V   Unskilled occupations.

Although these five classes give only a very imprecise ordering of social groups, they can still be of value. They have revealed significant differences in the incidence or prevalence of certain forms of illness, or of particular types of behaviour, in the different classes. Many diseases, including rheumatic heart disease, bronchitis and cancer of the stomach occur with increasing rates of incidence as one descends the social scale: a few, including cerebrovascular disease and coronary thrombosis, have their highest incidence rate in social class I. Not surprisingly, antisocial behaviour of various kinds occurs most frequently in the two lowest social classes; but there is an interesting contrast in the findings for rates of suicide, which are higher at the upper end of the class scale, and those for attempted suicide which are highest in social class V (see Chapter III).

Persons who share a common employment are likely to share other attributes, such as level of income and of education and type of residence. Systematic surveys have shown that they are also likely, in varying degrees, to have other things in common: to read the same newspapers, to indulge in the same recreations and to share the same prejudices.

Shared attitudes and values can have a profound influence on the development of children born into different social surroundings. Dr J. W. B. Douglas (1966), who has been studying the life histories of a large random sample of children born all over the United Kingdom in March 1946, was able to show that when this cohort of youngsters approached the 'eleven plus' examination which determined their future educational careers, the performance at this exam was more highly correlated with their parents' attitudes towards education than with their own native ability as measured by I.Q. tests.

This observation is particularly important because the educational system, more than anything else, serves to perpetuate the segregation of British society into hierarchically ranked classes. The accident of being born into a family of manual workers is likely to have an even greater influence upon an individual's life pattern than whether the chance distribution of genes which he has inherited is loaded with positive or negative attributes.

Most people display throughout their lives the attitudes, expectations and mode of interacting with their fellows which prevailed in their parental home, and in its surroundings. In earlier times, one indication of these early influences was a person's accent, which often bore the stamp of his upbringing; and in a class conscious society, great attention used to be paid to nuances of accent. As George Bernard Shaw put it in his preface to *Pygmalion*: 'It is impossible for an Englishman to open his mouth without making some other Englishman hate or despise him.'

One of the benefits conveyed by the most all-pervasive of the mass media, namely television, has been to make available to youngsters all over the country a standard form of speech—south-eastern English— which has proved a much more compelling model than the remote, alien 'Oxford accents' of sound radio. (Another, of course, has been the demonstration by the Beatles and their successors that one can have an 'underprivileged' accent and still display outstanding talent: as a result, the present generation of adolescents reared on TV are able to mimic southern English without feeling ashamed of their own local dialect.)

It has to be remembered that the 13 to 14 per cent of British citizens who are born into social classes I and II are no less likely than their fellows to acquire many of the biases of their social background. This is especially important, because until very recently nearly all the major decisions in public policy, legislation, education, religion and medicine were taken by upper or middle class persons. Of course, they believed that their decisions were rational ones, reached after an objective study of the facts: but one has only to turn back a few pages in the social history of the present century to see how often these supposedly rational decisions only reflected the prejudices of their section of society.

In the practice of medicine in general, and of psychiatry in particular, communication between the doctor and his patient is of the utmost importance: and yet this is often very imperfectly achieved. The incompatibility of the doctor's and his patient's view of the illness which has led to a medical consultation may pass unnoticed; but it is less likely to do so if these conceptions are very different indeed, as will often be the case when a Western-trained doctor practises in a totally different culture. For example, when the writer treated illiterate villagers in a remote area of northern India, there were frequent episodes of mutual incomprehension until he learned enough about their ideas concerning illness (in which the influence of witches and demons played a prominent part) to be able to talk to them, in more senses than one, 'in their own language'.

Similar misunderstandings, though of less extreme degree, can happen in this country. It is easy for a young doctor, intent on reaching a diagnosis and formulating the correct line of treatment in terms of his scientifically-based medical training, to forget that his working class patient may have encountered very few of these particular ideas: instead, the patient's perception of what is the matter may be coloured by quite different, and quite unscientific, concepts current in his own milieu.

Some of the indications of illness are relatively unambiguous: particular forms of infection, of tumour, of injury to the bones or soft tissues give rise to the same signs and symptoms whether they occur in an Indian, or an African, a manual labourer or a lord. The same cannot be said of the great range of other forms of disease or malaise, in which both physical factors and the patient's emotional state are involved—that is, the psychosomatic disorders. When a patient complains of vague pains, and of being 'out of sorts', in the absence of any detectable organic pathology, his doctor has to pay attention to what's on his mind; but he can only do so if he is able to help the patient to bring out what is worrying or exasperating him. To refer again to the writer's experience in the Indian village, it was only when he was able to indicate to his patients that he knew about witches and demons, and about the prevailing beliefs concerning sickness and death, that they were sufficiently put at their ease to allow them to unburden themselves of their fears.

In the case of the functional psychiatric illnesses, the neuroses and the psychoses, this matter of socially shared expectations, beliefs and values becomes still more important, because the criteria for recognizing these conditions are very often judgemental. A patient's behaviour, or his or her expressed beliefs are categorized as 'abnormal'; but who is the arbiter of what is normal? Psychiatrists try to guard themselves against subjective bias by using two independent criteria. The first of these is to see whether the patient is willing and able to submit his ideas to 'reality testing', and to accept the verdict if they are not borne out. Unfortunately it is often difficult to apply a reality test to the patient's erroneous beliefs or perceptions; for example, that the earth is flat, that people round about him are detectives disguised as nurses, or that he is suffering from an incurable disease. In such cases, the psychiatrist has recourse to comparing the patient's ideas with those of other people who share his cultural background and level of education. Often, however, the psychiatrist takes a short cut, and assumes that *his own* perceptions and values represent the norm for his patient's social group, and this can be a dangerous assumption.

It will be apparent that, in dealing with matters of feeling, perception and values, a doctor needs to be very well informed about the cultural life of other classes in his society besides his own if he is to do his job efficiently. Anthropologists have recently been turning their attention not only to large communities of working people in our society, such as Yorkshire miners (Dennis, Henriques and Slaughter, 1956) or villagers in North Wales (Frankenberg, 1957), but also to a variety of groups of people within our society who share experiences, traditions, patterns of behaviour and values, some or all of which may be at variance with those of their fellows in the larger society: these groups have been described as 'subcultures' within the society.

As doctors, we are particularly interested in reaching as full an understanding as possible of the behaviour, ways of thought, and values of our patients, whatever their social background; but we can only do so by studying the impact upon their behaviour of certain key influences, namely those of the family, the peer group, 'norm bearers', education, work, politics, religion and recreation.

## The Family

In every society throughout the world, the family is the principal agent for 'socialization', that is, for encouraging the youngsters of each new generation to conform (more or less) to the traditions and expectations of their culture. Having said this it must be added that, although universal, the family takes many different forms in different cultures. Common variations include the *extended family*, in which all the descendants of a common grandfather live together under one roof, or in close proximity. This contrasts with the *nuclear family* consisting of two spouses and their unmarried children, which is the common form of household in the West. Extended families may be *matrilocal*, (in which the husband joins his wife's extended family) or *patrilocal*, or the spouses may live alternately in each other's family of origin. There are many societies in which polygamy is practised, and a few in which a group of brothers or male first cousins share a single wife. In quite a number of societies the father plays a relatively minor role in the disciplining, care and instruction of his own children; instead, he gives this attention to his sister's children, and his own children look to their mother's brother for guidance. In many West Indian communities, fathers appear to be almost peripheral to the family—if indeed they are there at all. The mother is the dominant, if not the only parent.

In general, it is the role of the father which shows the greatest variation. The biological dependence of a baby upon its mother requires her to care for him in the first months of his life; but even here there are great differences in the duration and closeness of the mother's caring for her baby and in the extent to which other family members (grandmothers, aunts, or older siblings) share in this task. The anthropologist Margaret Mead (1928, 1930, 1935, 1950) has shown with a wealth of documentation that the way in which a mother handles her young baby already conveys to the infant its first lesson in how it should behave when it grows up to become a member of that society.

There are variations, too, in patterns of family life and in child rearing practices between subgroups within our own society.

The principal (though still inevitably crude) antithesis is between the type of learning which takes place in a working class, as contrasted with a middle class family. Some observers, including Richard Hoggart (1958) and Basil Bernstein (1965), have stressed differences in cognitive experience and in the use of language. The latter contrasts the restricted command of verbal expression shown particularly by members of the lower working classes whose language is grammatically simple, often shows errors of syntax, uses frequent repetitions and emphasizes personal and immediate experience, with that of the middle class which shows more elaborate grammatical form, greater attention to syntax, and a more extensive vocabulary. The working class person is less able to express fine distinctions in matters of feeling, or in relationships.

It may be difficult for the reader to recognize the crude realities of everyday speech behind these formal descriptions; and yet the antithesis between 'vulgar' and 'genteel' modes of speech has been a mainstay of theatrical comedy. As Bernstein and others have pointed out, teachers, doctors, lawyers and most public officials use the more elaborate form of speech; as a result, working class children have to learn a new vocabulary and new ways of expressing themselves before they can compete on equal terms with children from middle class homes.

Children, of course, learn much more in their family life besides forms of speech. A hundred years ago, the young Dr Sigmund Freud realized that the processes which he was coming to recognize in the mental life of his middle class patients might have very different counterparts in other walks of life. He wrote, in a letter to his fiancée: 'One might show how the common people judges, believes, hopes and works quite otherwise than we do. There is a psychology of the common man which is somewhat different from ours.'

In recent years, experimental studies have provided data to substantiate Freud's hunch. Lower class subjects show less control over impulse, less ability to postpone gratifications, less ability to persevere at difficult tasks than middle class subjects; and when they fail, lower class subjects are more likely to blame others, rather than themselves. Group differences are most marked in the control of aggression: in a slum environment, children learn by experience that physical aggression and ruthless self interest are necessary to avoid physical and emotional assault. Not surprisingly, children from such environments are unlikely to cultivate sensitivity to their own or their fellows' finer feelings. It is a common clinical experience to find a working class wife or husband assessing his or her spouse's feelings towards them in explicitly concrete terms: 'He's always given me my wages, regular', or 'She always keeps a clean house', 'The children are always warmly dressed, she'll see to that'.

Until quite recent years, the respective roles of a working class husband and his wife were highly segregated, with clear distinctions between what was regarded as 'man's work' and what was 'woman's work'. Since the Second World War, there have been some changes; for example, young working class husbands have begun to take some share in looking after their infants. Still, however, most of the task of teaching children 'how to behave' is left to the working class mother, whereas in the middle class this is more often a shared undertaking.

One quite important difference in early learning is the greater emphasis on self awareness in the middle class family. In contrast, the working classes are very conscious of their physical satisfactions or distresses, and less apt to recognize their feeling state. During the First World War, when standards of popular education were still very low, the commonest form of psychiatric casualty among the 'other ranks' was shell shock, or conversion hysteria, whereas among officers anxiety states were more frequent; in World War II, perhaps because of a higher general level of education, crude conversion hysteria was relatively infrequent, but in war, as indeed in peacetime, patients from working class backgrounds were more likely to 'somatize' their anxiety, and to present with physical symptoms such as dyspepsia, or localized pain, for which they expected a physical remedy.

In spite of these biases inherited from their formative experiences, patients from working class homes are capable of learning how emotional factors, and disturbed personal relationships can influence one's sense of bodily well-being. Although less articulate than their better educated fellow-patients, they soon learn to recognize these factors and in therapeutic groups they often make contributions whose directness compensates for any lack of nicety in their expression.


### OTHER FORMATIVE INFLUENCES

Ideally, the most important agent in a child's socialization is his family; but there are a great many broken or incomplete families, and many others in which the parents are themselves so immature or neurotic that they fail in a few—or, in some cases, in many—aspects of their parental role. This is obvious in the case of severe 'problem families' in which parental drunkenness, inability to make ends meet, promiscuity, quarrelling and other forms of social pathology cloud their children's early years. Such children have not only been deprived of security and affection, which tends to undermine their self confidence; they have also lacked the role models which are normally provided by an admired parent of the same sex as the child, and this makes it harder for the child to achieve a sense of personal and sexual identity when he or she reaches adolescence.

In many families, an elder sibling may take the place of a missing or inadequate parent. In some cases, as shown dramatically in Emlyn Williams's play *How Green was my Valley*, and in documentary form by writers like Edward Blishen or Lyward, a child may find understanding and support from a schoolteacher which helps to make good what he has missed at home, but this is inevitably rare if only because of the large size of classes in our school systems.

Nearly every child in the course of development goes through a phase in which belonging to the group of his or her age-mates means a great deal. It is easy, indeed, for membership of 'the gang' or 'the crowd' to become overvalued: instead of being a playgroup in which ideas and skills can be practised, it can come to seem more important than the adult world itself. This is more likely to occur when the parents have not been able to provide security within the family.

An interesting, and not unexpected finding of the careful inquiry into teenage sexual behaviour by Michael Schofield, published in 1965, was that most parents still fail in the task of teaching their children the 'facts of life'. Most children still learn about sex from their age-mates, and much of the information acquired in this way is inaccurate. Schofield found that the commonest source of correct information about sex today is instruction given in the schools.

Among adolescents of both sexes, hero-worship and a tendency to follow leaders is very widespread. To some extent, leadership may be given by forceful individuals among the peer group itself; but increasingly the 'norm bearers', that is those who set the fashions in behaviour and in accepted values, tend to be television personalities, often quite young and with an ephemeral presence among the 'top twenty' of the pop record charts.

Here, there is an interesting contrast between our contemporary society on the one hand, and both primitive cultures and past civilization on the other; almost without exception, prowess in adult pursuits such as hunting, warfare, or some creative art was a necessary attribute of a norm bearer. In all such circumstances, young people could say to themselves: 'When I grow up, I'll be like him (or her).' Today, however, there has been a cult of youth, unencumbered by the tiresome necessity of learning complex skills or demonstrating outstanding achievement; as a result, the mass audience is able to identify directly with their relatively artless idols, and to say: 'I *am* like him (or her)'.

It remains to be seen whether the cult of adolescence, which has prevailed during the 1960's, will have a positive effect through heightening the self esteem of a generation of youngsters; or whether their instant, effortless assertion of independence will be followed by a setback when they come up against the realities of the adult world, in which rewards generally have to be earned with considerable effort.

There is a sociology of education because this is the institution with which society consciously tries to mould each new generation to the task of perpetuating its inherited values and relationships. Education both perpetuates these traditions, and, by encouraging the spirit of inquiry, generates forces of change. There are, thus, contradictory forces at work in the educational system. In a stable society, the conservative elements are likely to be strong; but in times of rapid technological and social change, such as we live in today, the tension between conservative and 'exploratory' tendencies in education can become acute. In recent years we have seen a great deal of student unrest. At times this has been somewhat chaotic and anarchic, an exuberant, and sometimes destructive, abreaction of feelings on the part of the young; but in several instances the unrest has been of a constructive kind aimed at the replacement of educational institutions which were felt to be outmoded by others more in keeping with the age. An example of this was the involvement of the medical schools of Paris and Brussels in the student revolt of 1968. In both centres, young teachers and research workers took an active part in reforms which aimed, among other things, at doing away with the arbitrary and autocratic powers of the life tenure 'patrons', the chiefs of clinical services, and heads of university departments.

Anyone who studies the stages of this and similar 'confrontations' cannot fail to observe how difficult it is to effect radical change in a large institution. This is not only due to inertia; institutions *actively* resist change because change necessarily means a period of uncertainty, and the many people who make up an institution are unwilling to lose the reassuring fixity of their place in the peck order, their performance of a familiar role.

This 'dynamic conservatism', as the 1970 Reith Lecturer Donald Shon has called it, can be seen at work not only in large institutions but also in quite small organizations, such as a Faculty of Medicine, a Hospital Committee of Management, a University department. From the point of view of the innovator, a new method of work, or a new system of administration can seem perfectly rational; but it may encounter violently irrational resistances, simply because it creates anxiety among those who are going to be involved in a period of uncertainty and change.

### SOCIOLOGY OF WORK

Sociologists have taken an interest in religion, and in sport and other forms of recreation. The study of politics is one of the earliest of the social sciences, and political science, of course, has international as well as national relevance. Perhaps the most important of all the applications of sociology, however, is its analysis of work situations—their organization, authority structure, decision making and rewards (or lack of satisfaction) for the participants.

We shall not, here, consider the wider applications of sociology to national industries, to the trade unions or the professions, although the social history and recent reorganization of the medical profession in Great Britain is something that every doctor should inform himself about. Instead, we shall consider what light sociologists have thrown upon the organization and even the content of psychiatrists' professional work. Sociologists' contributions to psychiatry have been, in the main, in two areas: (1) studies of therapeutic institutions, and of the roles of psychiatrists and other members of their staffs, and (2) studies centred upon patients, viewing 'sickness behaviour' as the outcome of a series of social experiences and communally shared expectations.

The latter area of study merits separate consideration, and we shall return to it below. The former represents an attempt on the part of sociologists to view the work of doctors in somewhat the same way that management consultants or 'organization and methods' experts examine the operations of either small businesses or large industrial concerns.

Such investigations can start at an extremely modest level, and still yield illuminating findings. For example, Ann Cartwright, a sociologist who sat in on a large series of patients' consultations with their general practitioners, was able to categorize the events which brought them to the doctor, and the nature of the doctor's action. She showed, among other things, that the G.P's therapeutic task had consisted of advice about health in 21 per cent, enlisting help of social agencies in 10 per cent and discussing attitudes to work and personal relationships or simple 'therapeutic listening' in 10 per cent of cases (Scott, Anderson and Cartwright, 1960). This study made explicit the extent to which—at least in Britain—the general practitioner is viewed as a main source of help not only in healing sicknesses, but also in many other primarily social difficulties. Doctors had, inevitably, been vaguely aware of this for many years, but it was only as the result of objective inquiries that the informed public realized the extent to which pleas for help in social crises were being directed to physicians, who were not trained in the knowledge and skills required to deal with such situations. The Seebohm Report (1968) and the Social Work Acts which soon followed its publication were the direct consequence of this type of applied research.

Here we have one example of the sociologists' ability to take a detached look at what one is doing and to show that the reality differs from what one thinks. Similar rethinking has resulted from sociological analyses of psychiatric hospitals.

In the early stages of such studies, sociologists asked themselves in what ways these hospitals resembled, or differed from, other familiar service institutions. They were likened to passenger ships, in which a highly differentiated crew took responsibility for the care of some hundreds of passengers, feeding and entertaining them during their journey to their chosen destination; they were also compared with industrial plants, again with a variegated work force, only here the 'raw material' of the plant was an inflow of sick people and the end product, hopefully, the same people in a fitter state. This comparison revealed an interesting contrast between factories and hospitals. In the former, it is the lowest status personnel, the workmen on the shop floor, who carry out the crucial operations on the 'raw material', while the high status managers and directors of the business are concerned exclusively with planning and organization; in the latter, it is the workers of highest status, namely the doctors, who are supposed to perform the key tasks in treating the patients, while all the other workers play an auxiliary role, much as the more numerous 'support troops' make it possible for an army's front line soldiers to do their job. Hospitals have also been likened to schools, with patients taking the role of pupils, and the treatment staff that of the teachers.

The merit of these analogies is that they make one think afresh about the task of the hospital, and about what the staff and the patients actually do from day to day. If it is a ship, then how many of its passengers are travelling voluntarily; how many know their destination, and is this the same destination that the 'crew' have in mind? If it is a factory, are the managers quite sure that the end product of their work is going to be in accord with public demand? If it is a school, then what is the curriculum and towards what goals of learning are the pupils being directed? Not surprisingly, the tacit assumption held by most hospital psychiatrists, that their patients are sick people who come to hospital for medical investigation, diagnosis and treatment, and then get better, has been shown in many cases to give only a partial, and even a misleading, account of what actually happened. This is especially true of mental hospitals which have suffered from political and economic neglect.

The sociologist Ivan Belknap (1956) studied one such hospital, typical of many underprivileged State hospitals in the U.S.A. (and not dissimilar, one suspects, from some of the less favoured large provincial mental hospitals in Britain). This hospital had suffered for many years from overcrowding, with constant shortages of staff. During the past 40 years, the mean term of office of its superintendents had been just over 18 months, and that of its resident medical staff had been $2\frac{1}{2}$ years. Because of difficulty in filling staff positions, these doctors were nominally looking after from 1 to 300 patients. There were few trained nurses;

most of the attendants were unskilled aides who seldom stayed longer than a few months in this employment.

This was, evidently, a poorly functioning institution. That it functioned at all was due to the existence of a core of senior nurses and aides, constituting less than 20 per cent of the staff, who continued in the hospital's employment for many years, and were the carriers of a shared set of values and expectations, the 'culture' of the hospital. However, Belknap found that their culture was in many respects at variance with that brought to their task by the transient succession of doctors. The medical staff tried, as best they could, to treat their patients on medical lines, assigning diagnoses and prescribing treatments; but the doctor's occasional visit was only a minor event in the routines of the large wards, where the senior nurses' culture prevailed. For them, patients fell into three categories: co-operative, compliant and troublesome. There was a very marked status differentiation between patients and staff; the patients were addressed by their first names, but were required to say 'Mister' when speaking to a nurse or aide. The menial tasks of the ward were carried out by the patients, under staff supervision, and obedient workers were rewarded by being given small privileges: any signs of rebellion against staff authority could be controlled in two ways, by denying access to the doctor on his infrequent rounds, or by reporting him as being 'disturbed' or paranoid, and putting his name on the list for electroconvulsion treatment.

This analysis was carried out in a conspicuously neglected institution; but at roughly the same time another sociologist, Erving Goffman, was engaged on field work in the wards of St Elizabeth's Hospital in Washington, D.C. This Federally-run 7000 bed hospital situated in the nation's capital had been much better off in terms of medical and nursing staff, of equipment and material resources; yet here too the detached observer was able to indicate wide discrepancies between the doctors' concepts of what happened in their wards and the patients' actual experiences. Goffman's observations formed the basis of his celebrated paper: 'Characteristics of total institutions' (1958). By total institutions he meant those which encompass either the whole, or a very large part, of the total daily experience of those who enter them. Among these are *shelters* for those, such as orphans, the blind or impoverished old people, who require care and are harmless to others; and shelters also for others such as the mentally ill or sufferers from contagious diseases whose presence may cause distress or harm to others; *prisons* are, of course, totally encompassing for their prisoners and very largely so for their officers. Other similarly encompassing life settings are seen in monasteries, convents, ships, boarding schools and, where these still exist, in the servants' hall of large country mansions.

Goffman drew attention to the antithesis between life in a domestic household and that in a total institution. In the latter, daily experiences are not diversified but confined to one place, ordered and repetitive. Inmates are relieved (or deprived) of the normal responsibility to work for their living. Instead, the essentials of food, clothing and shelter are provided, and opportunities for individual initiative are denied. Above all, there is an explicit, ever present differentiation between *inmates* and *staff* of the total institution, with a clear difference in status between the two.

When a new patient becomes an inmate of the mental hospital he undergoes, in Goffman's terms, a series of 'mortification processes' designed to rob him of his individuality and to teach him his place and role in this unfamiliar world. In order to adapt, he has in many ways to become child-like: Goffman points out that in normal society the rules of politeness protect us from being publicly coerced or rebuked, but these rules are waived in the case of children and mental patients.

Moving among the patients, the sociologist found that most reacted to this new environment in one of four ways: (1) by withdrawal into their inner phantasy life; (2) by rebelling against the staff; (3) by accepting the humble status and menial roles assigned to them, and becoming 'institutionalized' ; or (4) by undergoing a type of conversion experience, as a result of which they became overcompliant, echoing the terminology of their nurses and doctors. There were, however, quite a number who did not commit themselves exclusively to any of these modes of behaviour, preferring to 'play it cool' and trying to learn how they could expedite their release.

Goffman's account of the mental hospital as one form of total institution makes horrific reading, in part because he chooses deliberately loaded terminology and depicts the patients throughout as the victims of a series of rather degrading, dehumanizing experiences. His paper is frankly offensive to psychiatrists and nurses, who see themselves portrayed in an unfavourable light; but it has had a very salutary effect, by making hospital staffs look afresh at their routines, from the point of view of the new patient.

It is not only in the large, impersonal state hospital setting that sociological observations have proved illuminating. One of the most painstaking studies of this kind was carried out by Stanton and Schwartz (1954) in Chestnut Lodge, a small, very expensive private hospital devoted to the psycho-analytic treatment of wealthy psychotic patients. Here, just as in the other studies, the sociologist showed that the patient's daily experience was often at variance with the concepts of his doctors. The sociologist observer Morris Schwartz demonstrated that it was not only the patient's daily hour of analytic treatment, but also the events of the other 23 hours of the day which influenced changes, for better or worse, in his mental state. For example, he found that when two doctors (or a doctor and a senior nurse) were in conflict about the handling of a particular patient, that patient usually showed a worsening of his psychotic symptoms. He also showed that there was a tendency for physicians to rationalize their day-to-day decisions as being 'therapeutic' for the patient, although in some cases these decisions were clearly made simply to suit the doctor's convenience.

In yet another early study of the hospital milieu the social anthropologist William Caudill (Caudill *et al.*, 1952) became an inpatient at the Yale Psychiatric Institute, without informing his fellow-patients or the psychiatric staff (other than its director) that he was in fact carrying out field work. He decided, incidentally, that this type of subterfuge was both unethical and unnecessary, and has warned his successors not to emulate his experience. Nevertheless, he did succeed in entering very thoroughly into the subculture of the group of patients, and described very clearly how they organized their perceptions of the treatment experience, and how they created a miniature society with its own values and rules of conduct.

It must not be thought that all sociological research on the psychiatric hospital has been negative in character. One of the pioneers of social psychiatry during the post-World War II generation has been Dr Maxwell Jones (Jones, 1968). Although he would certainly not claim to be the only begetter of the 'therapeutic community'—a term first used by T. F. Main (1946) in his account of the regime at the Cassel Hospital, near London, and exemplified in the 1940 'Northfield Experiment' initiated by a group of British army psychiatrists including Foulkes and Bion—he has been its most eloquent proponent. Under his inspiring leadership, the Henderson Hospital in Surrey and Dingleton Hospital in Melrose became justly celebrated therapeutic communities which have inspired psychiatrists all over the world to emulate their mode of operation. Maxwell Jones's great contribution was to demonstrate that not only nurses and other paramedical workers, but also the patients themselves can be enabled to play an informed and creative role in the processes of treatment.

The sociologist Robert Rapoport (1960) spent more than two years studying the organization of the Henderson Hospital. In this, as in other therapeutic communities, there are daily group meetings in which patients and staff participate, addressing each other by their first names; there are also discussions among the staff members, in which they clarify their perceptions of what is going on in the large group. Maxwell Jones emphasizes that learning is a two-way process; in his communities no one pretends that the psychiatrist or the senior nurses always know best. The patient-staff community comes to share a system of values and expectations, the 'culture' of the ward. Rapoport was able to show, however, that there is a constant interaction between the 'ideal values' of the staff and of those patients who have identified with them, and the actual mood of the changing population of the group. This results in a series of cycles, punctuated by crises and by periods of doubt and discouragement as well as by spells in which the whole group succeeds in working together.

The great virtue of these therapeutic communities is that they liberate creative energies in group members who used to play only a relatively passive role in the formal hospital setting. A possible danger is that, in the excitement of participating in a succession of 'living-learning experiences' (to use a favourite Maxwell Jones expression) psychiatrists, nurses, psychologists and social workers may forget that they each have a *particular* skill which can play an important part in the whole treatment process. It must be said, however, that the example of the therapeutic communities has prompted the great majority of more orthodox psychiatric hospitals to make better use of the abilities of all ranks of their staff—and of their patients. They have also focussed attention upon the powerful influence of the group upon the mental and emotional state of the individual patient. In this respect, they are related to another series of sociological studies of psychiatric disorders, viewed not as illness but rather as particular forms of behaviour, determined by social forces.

A consistent theme in this literature has been a critical re-examination of the 'medical model' in terms of which psychiatric disorders are treated as 'diseases' on the analogy of the many physical diseases with a known aetiology, pathology, course and outcome. Traditional psychiatrists, who employ this model, readily admit that as yet very little firm knowledge exists about the functional psychoses, the neuroses and the psychosomatic disorders, that is, about the great majority of the conditions which psychiatrists are accustomed to treat, but they express their conviction that before long biological and behavioural science research will clarify the morbid processes underlying all of these conditions, just as has happened in other areas of medical practice.

In complete contrast, a number of sociologists, psychotherapists and social psychiatrists have advanced quite different interpretations of these illnesses. They argue that societies contain not only a multitude of positive, productive roles but also a number of more or less stereotyped 'deviant roles' for those who find themselves unable, for one reason or another, to fit into any of the available ranges of acceptable roles. These deviant roles are never purely idiosyncratic: they too are the products of tradition and embody an array of social expectations.

Performance of these atypical roles—such as that of the *berdache*, the transvestite role adopted by a young male Comanche who finds himself unable to play the part of a warrior and a hunter like the rest of his fellows—is learned by observation of others performing this role. When first adopted, it is performed imperfectly, but the actor grows into his part, until it becomes second nature to him.

Most doctors, whose training has been focussed upon the medical model of illness, are disconcerted when they encounter references to 'sick role behaviour' (as in Parsons, 1950; Parsons and Shils, 1952; Mechanic, 1961, 1962). It has never occurred to them that patients need any instruction in their role: surely the disease itself dictates what they will experience, and how they will behave?

In fact, however, observation has shown that the patient's idea of what is afflicting him can very powerfully influence his perception of his own malaise; and in this he can, of course, be open to very compelling suggestions from his therapist. This is particularly clear in a number of primitive societies, in which nearly all afflictions are ascribed to supernatural powers. There, the shaman, priest or medicine man will divine the source of the trouble, and in so doing will often prompt the patient concerning the type of pains he can expect to suffer and the type of behaviour he is expected to display.

Nearer home, Dr Michael Balint (1957) has argued that a great deal of minor, and yet partially incapacitating functional illness assumes its particular forms as the result of an involuntary series of 'negotiations' between the patient and his doctor. As he puts it: 'Some of the people who, for some reason or other, find it difficult to cope with problems of their lives resort to becoming ill. If the doctor has the opportunity of seeing them in the first phases of their being ill, i.e. before they settle down to a definite 'organized' illness, he may observe that these patients, so to speak, offer or propose various illnesses, and that they have to go on offering new illnesses until between doctor and patient an agreement can be reached resulting in the acceptance by both of them of one of the illnesses as justified.' This 'justification' of a functional illness, together with more or less inadvertent prompting in the way the patient should behave is described by Balint as the doctor's 'apostolic function'.

Explanations of patients' symptoms and behaviour in terms of suggestion, imitation and social learning is very readily applicable in the case of hysteria, where both suggestibility and secondary gain from adoption of the role of a sick person can often be demonstrated. The psychiatrist Thomas Szasz (1960) in his paper 'The myth of mental illness' used a number of illustrations from hysterical patients to good effect, in arguing that a role behaviour model was more appropriate than the medical model in explaining their disorder; but in his book of the same title (Szasz, 1961) and in a series of subsequent papers he strains credibility too far, with his insistence that *all* mental illness can be so explained. Even the most thoroughgoing of the attempts to reinterpret the behaviour of the mentally ill in terms of social deviance (that is, by the adoption of learned, socially defined patterns of behaviour which respond to some inner need of the deviant individual), which is elaborated by the sociologist T. J. Scheff (1966), contains the caveat: 'Since the evidence advanced in support of the theory was scattered and fragmentary it can only be suggested as a stimulus to further discussion and research'.

It is a rather striking fact that the two most extreme proponents of the sociogenesis of all functional mental illnesses are both medical men, and not social scientists. Dr Szasz in the U.S.A. and Dr Ronald Laing in Britain have in common an early training in psycho-analysis, a discipline from which they have diverged in their respective ways. Dr Szasz has become pre-occupied with the legality and morality of depriving any patient, however irrational, of his liberty of action. Unfortunately, this has led him not only to champion the cause of the patients undergoing compulsory treatment, but also to address extremely intemperate criticisms against the conduct and motives of his fellow psychiatrists.

Dr Laing's writings first began to command widespread interest with the publication in 1959 of his book *The Divided Self* which revealed his gift of conveying, in strikingly eloquent prose, the experience of a schizophrenic, as seen from within. Like Erving Goffman, Laing has become an impassioned champion of the psychotic, defending him against the stigma and degradation which can so easily add to his distress. He soon adopted the theory first advanced by Gregory Bateson and his co-workers (1956) that schizophrenia could be seen as a result of bewildering and often self contradictory communications from powerful figures in the patient's early environment, of which the 'double bind' (see Vol. II, Ch. X) is a prime example. In his later writings, however, (Laing, 1964, 1967) he has moved progressively further from his original clinically based observations, adopting an increasingly apocalyptic style in which he portrays the schizophrenic as the victim of 'outrageous violence perpetrated by human beings on human beings'. He now asserts that 'behaviour that gets labelled schizo-phrenic is a special strategy that a person invents in order to live in an unliveable situation'.

Laing goes even further, insisting that schizophrenia is not an illness, but 'a natural way of healing our own appalling state of alienation called normality'. He likens the experience of acute psychosis to a psychedelic 'trip', calling it a voyage into inner space and time.

The most appealing aspect of Laing's rhetoric is his defence of the dignity and personal worth of the psychotic, and his repudiation of the common tendency to belittle and stigmatize him; but it is open to question whether his strident insistence that schizophrenics are not ill—that they are in some way superior to ordinary people because of their inability to come to terms with normality—will really lead either schizophrenics or those who try to help them to a clearer understanding of their condition.

This is heady, not to say intoxicating stuff. It has been greeted with acclaim by the literary intelligentsia of Europe and America, particularly by those on its outermost anti-establishment, hippy fringe, but with increasing reserve by his more critical readers.

In striking contrast are the series of studies of social factors influencing the symptomatology, course and outcome of schizophrenia which have been carried out by members of the Medical Research Council's Social Psychiatry Research Unit, at the Institute of Psychiatry, London (Brown et al., 1966; Wing and Brown, 1970). Here, aetiological speculation is much more restrained, and where it occurs it is explicitly speculative. Instead, the investigators have painstakingly collected evidence about actual events, experiences and environmental factors (both material and interpersonal) in the lives of large numbers of patients who have suffered from schizophrenia. They have demonstrated beyond question that, whatever may eventually be shown to be the key factors in the aetiology of this condition, the patients' social milieu can exercise a powerful influence upon the course of their disorder.

The continuing work of this and similar research teams, such as that of Sainsbury and Grad (1963) in Chichester, of Kessel (1965), Kessel and McCulloch (1966) and Kreitman, Smith and Tan (1969) in Edinburgh, is beginning to amass a substantial store of research findings on the interaction between social factors and the presentation of psychiatric illness. It is to such stores of data that students of applied science will increasingly turn in the future, in order to seek empirical verification of the numerous challenging and thought-provoking speculations which have been, and continue to be, advanced. That social factors influence human behaviour, both normal and abnormal is now accepted as a truism: but just how such influences are exerted, and to what degree, are matters which call for sustained, scientifically rigorous efforts of empirical research in this field.

## REFERENCES

Balint, M. (1957)    *The Doctor, His Patient and the Illness.* London: Tavistock Press.
Bateson, G., Jackson, D. D., Haley, J. O. & Weakland, J. (1956)    Toward a theory of schizophrenia. *Behavioural Science,* **1,** 251.
Belknap, I. (1956)    Social problems of a State mental hospital. New York: McGraw-Hill.
Bernstein, B. (1965)    A socio-linguistic approach to social learning. In *Penguin Survey of the Social Sciences.* Edited by J. Gould. London: Penguin Books.

BROWN, G. W., BONE, M., DALISON, B. & WING, J. K. (1966)   *Schizophrenia and Social Care*. Oxford University Press.

CAUDILL, W., REDLICH, F. C., GILMORE, H. R. & BRODY, E. B. (1952)   Social structure and interaction processes on a psychiatric ward. *American Journal of Orthopsychiatry*, **22,** 314.

DENNIS, N., HENRIQUES, F. & SLAUGHTER, C. (1956)   *Coal is our Life*. London: Eyre & Spottiswoode.

DOUGLAS, J. W. B. (1966)   *The Home and the School*. London: MacGibbon & Kee.

FRANKENBERG, R. (1957)   *Village on the Border*. London: Cohen & West.

GENERAL REGISTER OFFICE (1966)   *Classification of Occupations*. London: H.M.S.O.

GOFFMAN, E. (1958)   On the characteristics of total institutions. In *Symposium on Preventive Psychiatry*. Washington: Walter Reed Army Medical Center. Reprinted in his book *Asylums*. New York: Doubleday (1961). London: Penguin Books (1968).

HOGGART, R. (1958)   *The Uses of Literacy*. London: Penguin Books.

JONES, MAXWELL S. (1968)   *Social Psychiatry in Practice*. London: Penguin Books.

KESSEL, W. I. N. (1965)   Self-poisoning. *British Medical Journal*, **ii,** 1265, 1336.

KESSEL, W. I. N. & McCULLOCH, J. W. (1966)   Repeated acts of self-poisoning and self-injury. *Proceedings of the Royal Society of Medicine*, **59,** 89–92.

KREITMAN, N., SMITH, P. & TAN, E. S. (1969)   Attempted suicide in social networks. *British Journal of Preventive and Social Medicine*, **23,** 116–123.

LAING, R. D. (1959)   *The Divided Self*. London: Tavistock Press.

LAING, R. D. & ESTERSON, A. (1964)   *Sanity, Madness and the Family*. London: Tavistock Press.

LAING, R. D. (1967)   *The Politics of Experience. Bird of Paradise*. London: Penguin Books.

MAIN, T. F. (1946)   The hospital as a therapeutic institution. *Bulletin of the Menninger Clinic*, **10,** 66.

MEAD, M. (1928)   *Coming of Age in Samoa*. New York: Morrow. London: Penguin Books (1943).

MEAD, M. (1930)   *Growing up in New Guinea*. New York: Morrow. London: Penguin Books (1942).

MEAD, M. (1935)   *Sex and Temperament in Three Primitive Societies*. New York: Morrow.

MEAD, M. (1950)   *Male and Female*. New York: Morrow. London: Penguin Books (1962, 1967).

MECHANIC, D. (1961)   The concept of illness behaviour. *Journal of Chronic Diseases*, **15,** 189–194.

MECHANIC, D. (1962)   Some factors in identifying and defining mental illness. *Mental Hygiene*, **46,** 66–74.

PARSONS, T. (1950)   Illness and the role of the physician. *American Journal of Orthopsychiatry*, **21,** 452–460.

PARSONS, T. & SHILS, E. (1952)   *Towards a General Theory of Action*. Harvard University Press.

RAPOPORT, R. N. (1960)   *Community as Doctor*. London: Tavistock Publications.

SAINSBURY, P. & GRAD, J. (1963)   Mental illness and the family. *Lancet*, **i,** 544.

SCHEFF, T. J. (1966)   *Being Mentally Ill*. London: Weidenfeld & Nicolson.

SCHOFIELD, M. (1965)   *The Sexual Behaviour of Young People*. London: Longman (re-issued by Penguin Books, 1968).

SCOTT, R., ANDERSON, J. A. D. & CARTWRIGHT, A. (1960)   Just what the doctor ordered. *British Medical Journal*, **ii,** 293–299.

SEEBOHM REPORT (1968) *Report of the Seebohm Committee on Local Authority and Other Personal Services.* London: H.M.S.O. [Cmnd. 1360.]

STANTON, A. & SCHWARTZ, M. (1954) *The Mental Hospital.* New York: Basic Books.

SZASZ, T. S. (1960) The myth of mental illness. *American Psychologist,* **15,** 113–118.

SZASZ, T. S. (1961) *The Myth of Mental Illness.* New York: Hoeber-Harper.

WING, J. K. & BROWN, G. W. (1970) *Institutionalism and Schizophrenia.* Cambridge University Press.

## Chapter III

# SOCIAL AND CLINICAL ASPECTS OF SUICIDE AND ATTEMPTED SUICIDE

## N. Kreitman

The psychiatrist is always under an obligation to consider the medical, psychological and social aspects of the phenomena with which he is concerned, but the value of this triple approach is nowhere illustrated more clearly than in the study of 'suicidal behaviour', a term generally used to embrace both suicide and so-called 'attempted suicide' or parasuicide. The two forms of suicidal behaviour are best considered quite separately, and each will be discussed in turn before the relationship between them is reviewed.

### SUICIDE

#### DEFINITION AND BASIC STATISTICS

The importance of suicide is persistently under-recognized. In most European countries it ranks among the 10 most frequent causes of mortality: in some age groups over 1 in 50 deaths is attributable to suicide. According to the Registrar-General, between 4700 and 5000 suicides are recorded annually in the United Kingdom (which is some 12 times the number of homicides). Such figures of course raise questions concerning the Registrar-General's definition of suicide. Official statistics are based on verdicts reached by coroners (or by the Crown Office in Scotland) and reflect a 'legal' decision in which the key element is that the deceased intended to take his own life. The legal authorities require unequivocal evidence of such intent before classifying a death as suicidal. Many psychiatrists have commented that such a restrictive definition leads to gross underestimation of the true extent of suicide, arguing instead that as with a clinical diagnosis a decision should be reached on the balance of probabilities. Certainly, studies in which psychiatrists have reviewed the decisions of the legal authorities and have reached their own conclusions, suggest a gross disparity, in the order of 30 per cent (Dublin, 1963) to 100 per cent (Kessel, 1965; McCarthy and Walsh, 1966) between the numbers included by 'legal' and 'psychiatric' definitions.

All such estimates refer only to deaths brought to the attention of the authorities. It is impossible to say how many further suicides are not notified by the general practitioner or are concealed from him by the patients' families.

The methods for ascertaining the cause of death and the precise legal definitions used vary considerably from country to country. The extent to which official statistics can be employed when comparing the rates from different countries is very much open to question. In general, opinion is that cross-national comparisons are hazardous in the extreme but that valuable information can be obtained by studying the *pattern* (e.g. the frequency by age and sex groups) displayed by different countries, or better still, by considering changes occurring within each country over time.

According to the Registrar-General, the crude suicide rate for men in England and Wales is approximately 11.7 per 100,000 and for women 8.1 per 100,000 (averages for 1966–68). Suicide rates by age and sex for England and Wales are shown in Figure 1. The form of the curves

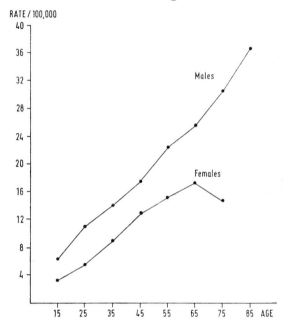

FIG. 1.    Suicide rates by age for England and Wales, 1966–68.

is similar to that of most western European countries and of the United States of America. It can be seen that for men the rate increases almost linearly with age, while for women the curve flattens out in the late fifties. For both sexes, however, suicide is evidently predominantly a problem of later life.

The corresponding figures for Scotland are somewhat lower, with crude rates of 9.3 per 100,000 and 5.9 per 100,000 for men and women respectively. The age-specific rates are illustrated in Figure 2. It is evident that the usual finding of increasing rates with increasing age, most obviously seen in men, does not obtain in Scotland, but why this should be so is by no means clear.

Marital status also has a marked effect upon suicide rates; after standardizing for age the divorced are the group with the highest rates followed by the single and the widowed, with married individuals coming lowest (Table 1). This pattern might reflect the stresses to which people in these different categories are exposed, but could also be due to the personality problems which the marital status categories may reflect.

In Britain, social class too has a marked effect on suicide rates, with the upper social classes having the highest mortality, but with the unskilled working class having higher rates than the middle class. This

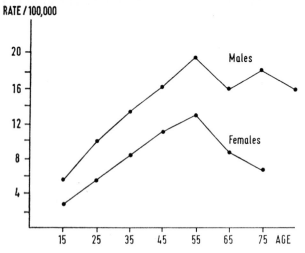

Fig. 2.    Suicide rates by age for Scotland, 1966–68.

relationship, however, may not be quite straightforward. Among men, for whom social class classification is less hazardous to apply than for women, it has been shown that upper class males have higher rates than lower class males at all ages up till about 65, at which point the pattern is reversed. Sainsbury (1961) has suggested that this might be because upper class men retire to relatively secure and enjoyable pursuits after their retirement, while lower class individuals face a period of economic uncertainty and stress. Certainly suicide rates and unemployment are also linked; Swinscow (1951) drew attention to the high correlation between deaths by suicide and unemployment levels in Britain over a 20-year period, while Sainsbury (1955) showed that the rates for those unemployed were markedly higher than for those in gainful employment.

Examination of the secular trends, i.e. changes over time, in suicide rates as illustrated in Figure 3 for England and Wales, shows two interesting features. Perhaps the most striking is the marked fall in the rates with the onset of each of the major wars in this century. It can be seen that this effect is clearly visible for both men and women, and that with the cessation of hostilities the rates climbed back to the pre-war levels and continued thereafter to follow the overall trend for the century. Interestingly, this pattern has also been reported from countries such as Switzerland which were not actually engaged in hostilities but in which considerable apprehension was experienced that the nation

TABLE I

*Mortality from Suicide by Marital Status and Age Groups Among Men and Women 15 Years and Over. United States, 1959*

| Age group | Total | Single | Married | Widowed | Divorced |
|---|---|---|---|---|---|
| MALES | | | | | |
| 15–24 | 7.4 | 6.8 | 8.4 | — | 19.7 |
| 25–34 | 14.5 | 23.2 | 11.1 | 95.8 | 66.7 |
| 35–44 | 20.5 | 29.8 | 16.7 | 81.7 | 112.6 |
| 45–54 | 30.3 | 39.0 | 25.6 | 53.3 | 111.7 |
| 55–64 | 39.1 | 58.3 | 32.4 | 65.0 | 89.4 |
| 65–74 | 45.5 | 82.0 | 33.6 | 79.6 | 152.5 |
| 75 and over | 54.6 | 85.3 | 34.5 | 79.2 | 140.0 |
| FEMALES | | | | | |
| 15–24 | 2.1 | 1.7 | 2.4 | — | 12.4 |
| 25–34 | 5.5 | 9.2 | 4.7 | 7.2 | 17.8 |
| 35–44 | 6.9 | 9.4 | 5.9 | 10.2 | 24.4 |
| 45–54 | 8.5 | 8.8 | 7.5 | 12.0 | 17.4 |
| 55–64 | 9.8 | 12.3 | 8.0 | 12.4 | 19.6 |
| 65–74 | 9.7 | 9.6 | 7.5 | 11.3 | 25.8 |
| 75 and over | 6.4 | 4.0 | 4.6 | 6.9 | 18.4 |

Dublin, L. (1963)   National Office of Vital Statistics, unpublished data.

might be involved in armed conflict. This dramatic effect of war might be explained by the fall in unemployment, which is usually a feature of a state of belligerency, but many writers have proposed that it owes more to the increased state of national cohesion, which gives people who might normally lack any clear role for themselves a definite and valued place in their society.

The other interesting feature to be noted is that apart from the effects of war, the crude rates for men have shown little change over the 50 years illustrated; subsequently they have fallen slightly. The rates for women have increased. More detailed examination of specific age and sex groups indicates that the fall in the crude rate for men is principally due to a decline of frequency of suicide in those in the later half of life, from among whose ranks most suicides are drawn. (Younger men have been much less affected, and indeed there is rather disturbing evidence which suggests that in the past 20 years or so the rates for young men have shown a marked increase.) For women the increasing rate is largely attributable to the increase in those aged 45 and over. In some parts of the United Kingdom the tendency towards parity of the sexes has already resulted in equal rates for the two sexes being reported. The social changes which presumably underlie these phenomena are still awaiting clear specification, though it is often suggested in a vague way that the increasing similarity of the social roles of men and women must be one of the major factors.

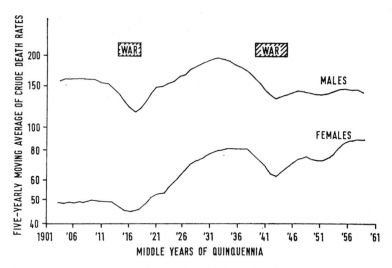

FIG. 3.    Suicide rates for England and Wales (Registrar-General, 1961).

The effect of general cultural changes of this sort can also be shown in other situations. For example, before the 1939 war Japanese society was largely organized in such a way as to attach particular value to the elderly, while many of the most acute social stresses tended to fall on the younger people. Age-specific rates for suicide showed a minor peak among individuals in their twenties with a marked decline in middle life and a second peak in the older age groups. However, after the war the American occupation of Japan profoundly affected the whole social fabric and many former institutions lost their efficacy. It is of great interest that the more recent suicide rates for that country show an approximation to the American pattern (Kato, 1969).

The sensitivity of suicide rates to social influences has for long excited the interest of sociologists, and indeed much of the fundamental work in sociology was done in the context of suicide studies. The problem that sociologists have attempted to answer is that of delineating more precisely what kinds of social relationships can explain variations in suicide rates between different social groups. The earliest theories were advanced by Emil Durkheim (1858–1917) whose views still dominate the field. Durkheim described a number of varieties of suicide, of which the major two he designated *anomic* and *egoistic*. The former refers to social situations in which the normative values of a community lose their force, and whose members therefore have no standards to guide them in times of stress. The second variety refers to a condition in which individuals become divorced from their social group and lose their sense of community involvement, ceasing to feel that social norms have any significance for them. Durkheim's distinction between these two varieties has often been confused by subsequent workers, and indeed his own account is not always explicit. Nevertheless his notions concerning the divorce of the individual from normative standards has been a major impetus behind subsequent studies. Sainsbury (1955), for example, was able to show in London the close correlation between suicide and social isolation of various kinds, including that attendant upon old age and the departure of offspring, physical handicap with its limitations of everyday activity, and the loss of family life consequent to divorce. Moreover, though Durkheim himself purported to be discussing processes of a purely social nature the subjective sense of loss of contact and loss of values are salient psychological processes attending many suicidal deaths.

Of the other sociological theories, that of status incongruity (Gibbs, 1967) may be briefly mentioned. In this view individuals are particularly susceptible to death by suicide when, although they are members of a well defined social group, they deviate from the other members on some salient characteristic. For example, in the southern United States being white is in general also associated with being relatively well-off and relatively well educated. A white man who is uneducated or poor is at a higher risk for suicide than other white men; similarly negroes who have risen to higher social levels are also at higher risk than those who have not. This interesting thesis lacks convincing empirical validation so far.

OTHER ASPECTS

It has long been known that suicide occurs more commonly in the spring and summer than at other times of the year (Fig. 4) and this seasonal variation occurs both in northern and southern hemispheres Various explanations have been proposed. Depression, as reflected in admissions to mental hospitals, is also commoner in spring and summer. Further it has been suggested that the depressed individual's sense of alienation is heightened in the spring, the rebirth of nature jarring with his own feelings of gloom and purposelessness. In line with this view is the fact that the spring peak is more evident in rural than urban communities. It is also true, however, that although unemployment falls in the spring the migration of labour increases and the stresses associated with migration may provide an alternative if less poetic explanation.

Discrepancies between the high rates for urban areas and low rates for rural districts have also been recognized for a long time, but there is no clear evidence that the rate of suicide increases with the size of the city. (Registrar-General, 1961). Possible but unproven hypotheses concerning the urban-rural difference are (1) that unstable individuals tend to migrate to cities, (2) that the stresses associated with immigrant status in the city are reflected in a raised suicide rate, and (3) that social cohesion is greater in country districts than in the more anonymous style of life in large cities.

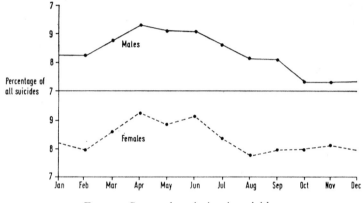

FIG. 4.    Seasonal variation in suicide.

Religious affiliation is often quoted as correlated with suicide, with low rates characterizing Catholic communities. As a general statement this is quite unfounded; the data, though highly conflicting, imply that although religious beliefs may provide both a social and an intellectual framework promoting the individual's sense of cohesion with others, nominal religion itself is without any major influence on suicide rates.

Similarly, much has been written alleging an inverse relationship between homicide and suicide (reviewed by Kendall, 1970). Most of the data supporting a negative correlation is based on cross-cultural comparisons, which in general illustrate a reciprocal pattern, though with numerous exceptions. Cross-cultural data of this kind are rarely a satisfactory basis for firm conclusions. Moreover, studies of rates between the different groups within a single society, and of fluctuations in homicide and suicide over time, show no evidence of any relationship (Lester, 1971).

## CLINICAL ASPECTS

The undoubted importance of social influences in determining the prevalence of suicide should not obscure the major role played by psychological illness in such deaths. Studies from the United Kingdom and Eire suggest that about 15 per cent to 30 per cent of suicides have been in contact with psychiatric services at some point in their lives, and the proportion may be expected to rise as increasing numbers of people seek psychiatric attention. Usually the contact has been shortly before their death. A further 25 per cent to 50 per cent of suicides can be recognized retrospectively to have suffered from a definable mental illness which contributed at least in part to the suicide itself: one American study quotes the proportion of mentally ill in a series of suicides as high as 94 per cent. (Robins *et al.*, 1959; World Health Organization, 1968, for other references). The three disorders of greatest importance are affective disorders, alcoholism and psychopathy.

### AFFECTIVE DISORDER

Patients treated by psychiatrists for manic-depressive psychosis and reactive depression have approximately 30 times the risk of dying by suicide than a member of the general population (Guze and Robins, 1970), and if such cases are followed through the rest of their lives there is good agreement that 15 per cent will die by suicide. The increased risk is most evident in the months or years following their initial treatment.

It is therefore important to be able to identify patients with affective disorders who are at high risk. Certain predictors will be those derived from what is known of the epidemiology of suicide in general, i.e. that men are at greater risk than women and the old rather than the young. Social isolation has already been mentioned, and will often be linked to being widowed, separated or divorced. The personal background of the patient is also relevant; a history of bereavement in childhood or of a broken home from other causes may indicate a heightened risk of suicide, though definite evidence on this point is lacking. Recent bereavements may also be of great importance; raised suicide rates have been shown both for those recently bereaved of their spouses and for only sons recently bereaved of their mothers (Bunch and Barraclough, 1972). Farberow, Shneidman and Neuringer (1966) have documented how patients with hostile passive-dependent relationships to their doctors seem to be another vulnerable subgroup. They persistently complain about their treatment and symptoms yet refuse to co-operate in the usually expected manner. These are very difficult patients to manage, yet they may be precisely those most likely to kill themselves. The risks attached to patients with a history of 'attempted suicide' will be discussed more fully later, but here it may be noted that such a history increases the risk of death by suicide to about 100 times that of the general population, and it seems very likely that among the depressive group such a history is also a predictor of a fatal outcome (McDowell *et al.*, 1968).

As mentioned above, the early months following psychiatric contact seem to be a particularly vulnerable period, which some authors, e.g. Slater and Roth (1969) ascribe to a lifting of psychomotor retardation at a time when mood has yet to improve, thereby increasing the risk that suicidal impulses will be put into operation. It is equally likely, however, that these early cases represent relapse after partial remission of the illness, presumably due to inadequate treatment.

The mental state examination sometimes fails to elicit suicidal ideas by a depressed patient who soon afterwards kills himself. This may be due to the patient's own reticence, but is often to be ascribed to reluctance on the part of the physician to probe fully through a misplaced fear that such enquiries may suggest suicide to a patient who has not previously entertained such notions. The expression of marked guilt feelings and ideas of unworthiness should also provide a warning, as should painful meditation by the patient about someone who has already died: fantasies of being reunited with departed relatives are a common theme in suicide notes. On the positive side obsessional features may afford some protection against a suicide outcome, as may hypochondriasis (Stenbeck, Achté and Rimon, 1965). It should be noted that the diagnostic label of endogenous or neurotic type of affective disorder has very little prognostic value.

### ALCOHOLISM

The risks of eventual death by suicide among alcoholics has been very variably quoted by different workers using different definitions of alcoholism, but a figure of 5 to 10 per cent over a 5-year follow-up for male alcoholics treated by a psychiatrist seems to be a modest estimate. Since treated alcoholics include many who are young or in middle life their mortality from suicide is very greatly in excess of that of members of the general population of comparable age. A noteworthy feature of follow-up studies on alcoholics is that the maximum risk appears to be within the first few years following contact with psychiatric services. However, attempts to distinguish from the remainder those within the group who eventually kill themselves have not been conspicuously successful, though it has been noted that of the eventual suicides nearly all relapse into heavy drinking after initial improvement (Kessel and Grossman, 1961).

PERSONALITY DISORDER

The association of personality disorder and suicide is difficult to document statistically in view of the notorious unreliability of the diagnosis. Moreover, many individuals with personality disorders present to the psychiatrists as alcoholics or as drug addicts and the effect of these associated factors is impossible to separate. Nevertheless, on clinical grounds there seems little doubt that individuals whose lives are fraught with problems of poor employment, inadequate inter-personal relationships, rage reactions, difficulties with the law, and possibly lowered intelligence are more likely than most to end their days by self-destruction.

## MANAGEMENT AND PREVENTION

The management of the patient judged to be an acute risk for suicide poses certain difficulties. In former times many hospitals employed a routine whereby the patient was closely supervised by a special nurse right round the clock, and who often went to great lengths to ensure that there was no conceivable means whereby the patient could harm himself. Such an oppressive regime probably caused more deaths than it prevented. Supervision of the acutely suicidal patients should be as unobtrusive as possible, though all staff must of course be alerted to the danger.

Perhaps the most salient point in the management of the patient is the vigorous therapy of the mental illness. All too often E.C.T. is withheld from depressed patients where indications for its use exist but instead time is spent in juggling the choice and dosage of anti-depressant drugs. It is equally important to persist in attempts to establish an effective psychotherapeutic relationship with the patient, even in the face of psychosis, in order to convince him that the therapist cares very much indeed whether he survives. Once the acute episode is past, patients who have been at high risk of suicide should be offered sustained follow-up attention to maintain the psychotherapeutic relationship and to monitor the course of the illness; frequently the resolution of a depressive episode takes much longer than either the patient or the therapist appreciate at the time, and a late relapse will sometimes lead to profound pessimism on the patient's part which may in turn prompt a suicidal act.

Many people who commit suicide communicate their intention to do so to others. Sometimes this is to a psychiatrist. A further proportion communicate their ideas to their relatives and to their general practitioners, or to some other physician. One cannot conclude from the fact that these individuals subsequently kill themselves that people in general and the medical profession in particular are insensitive to the receipt of such intimations from patients, or that they usually act ineffectively. One can, however, conclude that more effective attention to suicidal hints or threats by patients could make an appreciable impact upon the suicide rates of the nation. One of the main priorities in suicide prevention activities must be to increase the teaching of psychiatry to medical students and to general practitioners so that high risk cases can be recognized. The same is true for the education of social workers, lawyers, clergymen and others, who may be the people to whom the future suicide first turns, to emphasize that no threat of suicide should ever be dismissed as trivial.

In the United States well over a hundred suicide prevention centres have by now been established, and in this country the Telephone Samaritan organization functions in a broadly analogous manner. In both instances the aim is to reduce the frequency of suicide by providing a 24-hour service to which despairing individuals can turn for help. Anonymity is a key feature, and the telephone figures largely as a means of initial contact. The members of the Telephone Samaritan organization are non-professional volunteers who receive training in a counselling technique termed 'befriending' (Varah, 1965). It has been shown that the Samaritan organization does succeed in attracting the potentially suicidal, since there is evidence that those who are users of the organization are at higher than average risk for death by suicide (Barraclough and Shea, 1970). But it remains very difficult to evaluate the efficacy of these services despite the tremendous investment of money and energy they represent, although a study of Bagley (1968) can be interpreted as indicating that the Samaritan organization is effective in making an impact upon rates of suicide. Further critical evaluation of the work of such counselling services, and the way in which they might be improved, must be considered a research priority in this field.

Lastly there is the possibility of primary preventive action among defined groups of the population known to be particularly at risk for suicide. One such comprises the elderly and especially those who are living alone. The future may see the construction of 'at risk' registers of such people who are, of course, also at hazard for numerous other psychiatric and physical illnesses, and it is possible that by routine attention to such groups by social workers and general practitioners a number of suicides may be prevented. A second obvious group to whom special attention should be directed are those who have survived some form of self-injury or self-poisoning, and these will be considered in the next section.

## PARASUICIDE

The first problem that arises in the discussion of non-fatal self-destructive behaviour is that of terminology. Traditionally the term 'attempted suicide' has been used and for decades has led to confusion, especially by general practitioners and general physicians, as to just what is implied. Only too often patients are dismissed as having made purely histrionic 'gestures' and judged to be in little need of close attention since they were not in fact 'attempting suicide' in the sense of trying to kill themselves. Kessel (1965) proposed 'deliberate self-injury and self-poisoning' as an alternative. This is certainly preferable but can lead to difficulties if the patient has not in fact poisoned himself in the toxicological sense, and hence strictly speaking should exclude individuals who have taken a quantity of a substance which is pharmacologically safe but which in their mind represented a real hazard. Moreover, the term should logically include patients in states of acute alcoholic poisoning which are not normally regarded as part of the spectrum of suicidal behaviour. Further, by abandoning all reference to suicide the opportunity is lost to stress the real danger represented by such actions. For present purposes the term parasuicide (Kreitman *et al.*, 1970*a*) will be employed, as referring to any act deliberately undertaken by a patient which *mimics* the act of suicide, but which does not result in a fatal outcome. Parasuicide, then, is a self-initiated and deliberate act in which the patient injures himself or takes a substance in a quantity which exceeds the therapeutic dose (if any) or his habitual level of consumption, and which he believes to be pharmacologically active. (The term may also be used, according to context, for an individual who carries out a parasuicidal act.)

Although reliable data on the prevalence of parasuicide among the general population is difficult to come by there is little doubt that the number of patients being seen at hospitals is rapidly increasing not only in the United Kingdom but in other countries as well, including Czechoslovakia (Prokupek, 1969) and Australia (Oswald, 1966). A sizeable body of epidemiological information is now available and some of the findings will be briefly reviewed, with particular reference to Edinburgh which is particularly fortunate in its data collection facilities.

EPIDEMIOLOGICAL ASPECTS

The first point to note is that parasuicide is predominantly found among young people and appears to be commonest in the 20 to 24 age group (Fig. 5). In the first half of life it is distinctly commoner among women than men but there is little difference between the sexes after the age of 45. Parasuicide is very common in certain age groups. Among

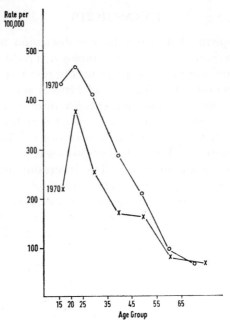

FIG. 5.   Patient rates (persons per 100,000) for parasuicide in
Edinburgh, 1970. o—o females; ×—× males.


TABLE 2

*Parasuicide Rates (Persons per 100,000) by Marital Status
(Edinburgh, 1969)*

|  | Males | Females |
|---|---|---|
| Divorced | 1368 | 564 |
| Widowed | 176 | 87 |
| Married—below 35 yr | 179 | 456 |
|     —35 yr and above | 107 | 136 |
| Single —below 35 yr | 262 | 371 |
|     —35 yr and above | 226 | 103 |

young women in Edinburgh, of the 20 to 24 age group, approximately
1 in 200 was admitted to hospital *at least once* for parasuicide during 1970.

Rates for different marital status groups (Table 2) show that the
divorced are most at risk for parasuicide, despite their relatively greater
age. Single men of all ages have higher rates than married men but the
converse is true among women.

Parasuicide rates also vary markedly with social class, being some eight times higher in social class V than in I and II (Table 3). This may be linked with high rates for two other variables, namely overcrowding and unemployment.

Less direct but highly suggestive associations have been demonstrated by ecological techniques whereby areas are ranked according to their rates of parasuicide and again for their rates (or similar indices) of other forms of deviant behaviour, and the rank orders compared (Philip and McCulloch, 1966). Areas with high rates of parasuicide have been shown to be characterized by high rates for juvenile delinquency and breaches of the peace, housing evictions and rent arrears, road accidents, cruelty to children, venereal disease, and illegitimate births. Such areas tend to be either the central disintegrating zones of the city or other sectors prominent for social pathology of diverse kinds (McCulloch and Philip, 1970).

TABLE 3

*Parasuicide Rates (Persons per 100,000) by Social Class, Overcrowding and Unemployment (Edinburgh 1968–70)*

|  | Males | Females |
|---|---|---|
| Social class I and II | 69 | — |
| III | 68 | — |
| IV | 195 | — |
| V | 493 | — |
| Overcrowding | | |
| (1.5+ persons per room)   present | 143 | 350 |
| absent | 88 | 107 |
| Employment   unemployed | 2444 | — |
| employed | 92 | — |

However, differences between city areas have been found to persist even when due allowance is made for discrepancies in the age-sex characteristics of the subpopulations and their differences in marital status, overcrowding, unemployment and social class (Buglass, Dugard and Kreitman, 1970). It has been suggested that these high risk areas might also be characterized by a culture in which parasuicide is viewed as a relatively acceptable form of behaviour. Within such communities it is possible to demonstrate that the individuals who carry out parasuicidal acts tend to be linked by personal acquaintance with greater frequency than would be expected by chance (Kreitman et al., 1970b). One can therefore envisage networks of individuals in which self-destructive behaviour is a recognized form of social behaviour and among whom the act carries a meaning which is culturally recognized.

It should be appreciated that all the data referred to so far concern admissions to hospital. Three studies have been carried out in the United Kingdom to determine the extent of the problem as seen at the general practitioner level (Parkin and Stengel, 1965; Hershon, 1968; Kennedy, 1971). These suggest that a further 20 to 30 per cent of cases are treated by the general practitioner without hospital admission, though the latter study indicated that most of the non-admitted patients are in fact referred to a psychiatrist sooner or later. It was also shown that the characteristics of patients seen at hospital were identical to those of patients not so referred, with the sole exception that self-injury appeared to be relatively more frequent in the non-referred cases and constituted approximately 10 per cent of all the cases known to the general practitioners. No-one can say how many further cases of self-poisoning or self-injury might occur which are not brought to the notice of medical services.

All studies in the United Kingdom agree that poisoning by the ingestion of drugs is by far and away the commonest mode of para-suicide, with self-injury, coal gas poisoning and other methods collectively accounting for only about 10 per cent of hospitalized cases. Among the drug group, preferences for one or other type of agent appear to vary somewhat according to age, barbiturates being more popular among older patients. A noticeable trend in the last decade has been the steady increase in the use of the newer psychotropic preparations at the expense of the barbiturates as a means of self-poisoning. This undoubtedly reflects changing prescription practices by general practitioners. At the same time it should be noticed that the increase in poisoning by aspirin, which is freely available without prescription, has exactly paralleled those for prescribed drugs. Thus there is no evidence that the prescribing habits of general practitioners are responsible for the increase in the *number* of self-poisonings in recent years, although the *types* of prescriptions issued will clearly be reflected in what drugs are to hand and are consumed.


PSYCHOLOGICAL ASPECTS

Much has been written concerning the various psychological motivations associated with parasuicidal activity and about the legitimacy of making inferences from what the patient himself is prepared to say. This latter point is one of some importance, since an appreciable number of patients are unable to express clearly after the act their reasons for performing it. Nevertheless it is possible to recognize a number of themes.

1. Some individuals describe a blind reaction in which some immediate relief from a stressful situation has been sought, or may clearly

say that they were seeking some form of 'interruption' (Shneidman, 1964) from an unendurable state of tension.

2. Others will reveal explicitly or implicitly that they were trying to secure the attention of other people in their immediate environment, often after more conventional means of doing so have failed. Such an account is commonly elicited from patients with marital difficulties or other kinds of family crisis, or may even be reported in connection with conflicts with authorites, as for example the police or the local housing department. For this group the parasuicidal act represents the 'cry for help' lucidly described by Stengel and Cook (1958).

3. Allied to them, but worth distinguishing, are those patients for whom the act has been a means of making others around them feel anxious or guilty and towards whom they may express aggressive feelings.

4. Another motive sometimes adduced, though often not very explicitly, is that of testing the benevolence of fate. Here the patient is replicating a primitive 'trial by ordeal' in which he stakes his life in a hazardous enterprise, interpreting survival as evidence that destiny intended him to live, and he may sometimes acquire from this a kind of self-satisfaction with his own capacities for taking desperate action, rather analogous to the dangerous pranks of the adolescent.

5. In yet another group it seems evident that the patient really intended to kill himself but was prevented from doing so either by his own ignorance of the required dosage or by chance intervention by others.

It is therefore possible to describe a variety of motives underlying parasuicide, but it would be mistaken to think that most patients show only one of the list just enumerated. In most parasuicides the motives are multiple, and may be mutually contradictory. Recognition of this has led to the ascription of marked 'ambivalence' to the act, usually an ambivalence between the wish to live and the wish to die. Such a formulation may be useful in describing the mental state of those who kill themselves, since there is evidence that many suicides had some wish to survive even if the death wish proved the stronger. But with parasuicides the concept of a simple antithesis of motives is naïve, and it is better to recognize that many motivations may co-exist. Many, perhaps most, parasuicides are carried out on impulse, with little opportunity for clarifying objectives. It is also important to appreciate that in half the male patients and a quarter of the women the act occurs under the influence of alcohol. It is scarcely surprising, therefore, that motivations are so often multiple and apparently confused.

Intensity of depressive affect has been shown to be related to the patient's expressed wish to die and the length of time spent contemplating the act. There is, however, *no* relationship between depth of depression and the amount of damage the patient inflicts upon himself, as indicated, for example, by the depth of coma (Birtchnell and Alarcon, 1971).

Lastly, it must be remembered that whatever the patient's expressed motivation most parasuicides occur in an interpersonal context, and as such will only be understandable if viewed from a sociocultural as well as an individual viewpoint. The full social significance of the act can only be grasped if the psychiatrist has some awareness of the norms and values of the group from which the individual comes.

Psychometric studies show that as a group parasuicides contain a high proportion of personality disorders, tend to be hostile to others and to themselves, and have high levels of anxiety (Philip, 1970a and b; Vinoda, 1966). These characteristics are also found in mixed groups of psychiatric patients, but the parasuicides have more extreme scores. Other tests have demonstrated traits such as impulsiveness, unpredictability and emotional immaturity, with those individuals who make repeated 'attempts' being particularly noteworthy in these respects.

Findings based on whole groups of parasuicides are relatively uninformative, and if further progress is to be made it will be necessary to identify and delineate the main subgroups. But they do serve to show that there is no such thing as a specifically 'parasuicide prone' personality.


PSYCHIATRIC DISORDERS

Most parasuicides have a recognizable form of psychiatric illness. Among young people minor reactive depressions are particularly common, the act often occurring in the context of domestic friction or some similar interpersonal stress. States of 'adolescent turmoil' are well represented, as are hysterical personality disorders among women and delinquency among young men, many of the latter being in difficulties with the police at the time of the act. Among the middle-aged, women show a preponderance of rather more severe depressive reactions, though the personality disorders are also commonly encountered. In this age range alcoholism becomes a major factor among men, and in some series appears to be the commonest diagnosis for parasuicide patients in middle life. Involutional depressions are also seen. The older age groups figure relatively infrequently but among them marked depressive reactions may be conspicuous. Such patients may also have considerable physical disability and be leading isolated lives. At all ages epilepsy and mental defect are represented more commonly than among the population at large.

Lastly, there is an appreciable minority of patients who show no evident psychopathology apart from their parasuicidal behaviour, and these are probably best regarded as basically normal individuals subjected to acute situational stresses.

## MANAGEMENT AND TREATMENT

All parasuicides must be taken seriously. One major consideration is, of course, the treatment of the patient's injuries or toxic state. The latter should be assessed and treated by a competent physician, ideally one with a particular interest in toxicology in view of the very large number of drugs now available. The patient's level of consciousness is itself a poor guide to the urgency of medical care; with poisoning by ferrous salts, for example, consciousness may be unimpaired until shortly before death from hepatic coma.

Secondly, all patients should be assessed by a psychiatrist (Ministry of Health, 1961) but only when any toxic effects that may have been present have completely subsided. It is not possible to make anything but the crudest provisional diagnosis if any degree of delirium persists.

Close collaboration between physicians and psychiatrists is thus essential and is optimally provided in regional poisoning treatment centres in which specialized resuscitation facilities can be concentrated, interdisciplinary collaboration fostered, and research activities carried out. Despite official recommendations regarding the establishment of such centres (Hill, 1968) few have so far appeared.

It is important to stress that the psychiatrists' judgement should not be influenced by the 'medical seriousness' of the act. It has been repeatedly shown that there is no association between the amount of injury or toxicity sustained by the patient and the severity of his psychological illness (Kessel, 1965; Rosen, 1970). A patient with agitated depression and intense morbid pre-occupation may be seen after he has taken half a dozen aspirins, while a young girl may be moribund through an overdose taken following a quarrel with her mother, yet with no evidence of psychopathology except for the act itself.

Appropriate therapy should be planned, bearing in mind that sometimes the crisis situation may itself be exploited to advantage, and that the psychiatric social worker often has a major contribution to make. More detailed consideration of treatment and management are given by Kessel (1965).

FURTHER SUICIDAL ACTIVITY

One of the outstanding difficulties in the treatment and management of parasuicides is the high repetition rate; various series report between 20 and 30 per cent of patients making further similar acts within 12 months (World Health Organization, 1968). It is likely that men are slightly more prone to repetition than women. The pointers to repetition are different for the two sexes. Among men a history of alcoholism and of violence received from or inflicted upon others in the recent past are all predictive of further episodes. Among women a previous parasuicidal act or an earlier history of psychiatric treatment, psychopathy or drug addiction, a high degree of residential mobility in the preceding few years, and the absence of either parent from the home when the patient was less than 10 years of age have all been identified as predicting further attempts (Buglass and McCulloch, 1970). It has been suggested (Bagley and Greer, 1971) that being widowed, divorced or separated is also a positive predictor of repetition. It is essential to realize that the apparent 'medical' seriousness of the act itself in terms of the amount of physical damage sustained by the patient is no predictor of the likelihood of a further attempt (Kessel and McCulloch, 1966; Greer and Lee, 1967; Bagley and Greer, 1971).

It is less easy to specify variables associated with a *suicidal* outcome. Studies on the risk of death by suicide among parasuicidal patients suggest that approximately 1 to 2 per cent will die from this cause over a 1- to 2-year follow-up period, and that thereafter the risk continues at a decreasing level; the period of greatest danger is in the few months following the parasuicidal act itself. These are small proportions of all those at risk, so that it is difficult for an investigator to amass enough cases for predictive criteria to be easily defined, except perhaps in rather special and atypical situations. So far as generalization can be risked, it seems that (1) male parasuicides are more likely to commit suicide than women. There is a further association with (2) age: Edinburgh data show that the risk for men aged 35 to 54 is about 5 times higher than for younger men. Other criteria include (3) being separated, widowed or divorced; (4) unemployed or retired; (5) living alone; (6) in poor physical health; (7) suffering from a specific mental disorder including alcoholism. Thus it seems that 'the more closely attempted suicides approximate completed suicides in personal and social characteristics, the greater the likelihood of death from a subsequent attempt' (Tuckman and Youngman, 1963).

To date there is little firm evidence concerning the best way of preventing either the repetition of suicidal behaviour or death by suicide among the parasuicidal group. Greer and Bagley (1971) report that patients who accept and co-operate with psychiatric treatment following the act do better than those who do not, and are inclined to interpret this as showing that therapy itself makes some difference. It is, however, difficult to exclude the possibility that patients with a better prognosis are also those who acquiesce most readily in the arrangements made for their psychiatric care. A study by Hicks and Chowdhury (1972) indicated that intensive aftercare of a group of repeaters made no difference to their rates of further repetition as judged against a control group who had received no special provision. Nevertheless, routine psychiatric attention certainly has some part to play in secondary prevention. It is noteworthy, for example, that depressed patients are among those with the best prognosis so far as repetition is concerned, presumably because depression will often yield to psychiatric intervention. For the remainder, prophylactic success may have to wait the advent of successful treatments for alcoholism and psychopathy. Meanwhile there is room for vigorous experimentation.

## PRIMARY PREVENTION

So much suicidal activity occurs in a setting of social pathology that prevalence rates are likely to be influenced primarily by changes in basic social conditions, including both short term fluctuations, such as unemployment, and more durable changes, such as the norms of marital behaviour or alcohol consumption. Any activities that can be undertaken by local authority social work departments or voluntary agencies to mitigate the consequences of adverse social factors deserve full support for this reason if no other.

It has been generally assumed that more direct preventative action is feasible for those individuals who are in distress and who might be influenced to seek assistance from an appropriate agency rather than proceed to parasuicide. The obvious agency of choice is the Telephone Samaritans, although the role of general practitioners and other social work groups is also a vitally important one. It has been shown, so far as the Samaritans are concerned, that their clientele does in fact approximate more to the population of parasuicides than of suicides (Chowdhury and Kreitman, 1971). Yet a study in which parasuicides were questioned regarding their choice of action revealed that it was not ignorance of the existence of help-seeking agencies which had dictated their behaviour. Instead, the patients variously cited a need for immediate relief, often coupled with the desire to make a dramatic impact on other family members, some disenchantment with the help they had already received from various agencies, or a reluctance to bring to the attention of strangers what seemed to them an essentially personal problem (Kreitman and Chowdhury, 1972). These attitudes, when viewed against the foreseeable consequences of their behaviour may not be logically consistent but they indicate some of the difficulties which primary prevention encounters in high risk groups.

Finally, it must be pointed out that although a proportion of parasuicides can be considered as failures of preventative care, nothing can be learned from such figures regarding the successes, that is to say, those individuals whom general practitioners, social agencies and others have successfully averted from parasuicidal action. It is to be hoped that the increasing dissemination of knowledge through the caring professions will highlight the importance of the early recognition of depressive illness and of alcoholism and increase sensitivity to the risks of para-suicide in these and allied conditions.


## THE RELATIONSHIP OF SUICIDE AND PARASUICIDE

When individuals who commit suicide are compared and contrasted with parasuicides certain differences and similarities emerge. It is important to define these points of contrast and overlap as closely as possible, though the task is not an easy one since no survey has yet appeared in which both forms of behaviour have been simultaneously studied in a single population using comprehensive criteria and case-finding techniques.


### PREVALENCES

The first point to note is the relative frequency of the two phenomena. Table 4 shows data from Edinburgh for parasuicide based on the total number of hospital-referred cases. These figures are higher than those quoted in most other studies, presumably because of a very liberal admission policy. Also shown in the Table are estimated rates derived from Kennedy's survey of general practice in the city (Kennedy, 1971). If these figures are typical of the whole United Kingdom they can then be compared with the Registrar-General's data for official suicide notifi-cations. The official figures are certainly minimal but it is evident that parasuicide is approximately 15 times more common for men and 30 times more so for women. Even if the 'true' suicide rate is assumed to be double the official figure (and this is probably an over correction) and these ratios are thereby halved, it remains evident that parasuicide is a vastly more frequent phenomenon: if all suicides were saved and reclassified as parasuicides it would make little difference to the prevalence of the latter.

Since age exerts such a marked effect on the rates of both forms of suicidal behaviour, it is clear that any assessment of their relative frequency based only on crude rates will obscure very marked differences for certain age groups. Thus, on the same basis of calculation as that used in Table 4, the relative excess of parasuicide to suicide among young women can be shown to be of the order of 190 times, while that for older men is about 4 times, both these being minimal ratios.

These somewhat arbitrary and very approximate indices merely exemplify the relative magnitudes, so far as they can be ascertained, of the two aspects of suicidal behaviour. A more direct link is established by considering the proportion of parasuicides who later kill themselves, and conversely the proportion of suicides who have earlier suffered some form of self-damage. It has already been noted that at short term follow-up studies on various samples, mostly from the United Kingdom, an estimated 1 to 2 per cent of parasuicides have been found to kill themselves within a 1- to 2-year period. This proportion is some 50 to 100 times the risk of death by suicide among the general population, and may be compared with ratios of 140 (Tuckman and Youngman, 1963) and of 80 to 100 (Motto, 1965), cited from the U.S.A. However, to determine the total contribution of parasuicide to suicide mortality one would require to know the life-time expectation of suicidal death. This data is not available although some authors have quoted an estimate of 20 per cent eventual mortality (Dorpat and Ripley, 1967).

TABLE 4

*Comparison of Annual Parasuicide and Suicide Rates*
*(Persons per 100,000 aged 15+)*

|         | Parasuicide (Edinburgh 1970) | | Suicide (United Kingdom 1969) | Ratio b/c |
|---------|------------------|--------------------|-------------------------------|-----------|
|         | Hospital referred | Total known to G.Ps |                             |           |
|         | (a)              | (b)                | (c)                           |           |
| Males   | 179              | 199                | 13.8                          | 14.4      |
| Females | 243              | 277                | 9.1                           | 30.4      |

Conversely, studies of suicide, usually defined in terms of coroners' verdicts, have reported figures for earlier parasuicidal activity. Excluding investigations based on very special groups, those studies which have relied solely on information contained in court records give figures of 10 to 20 per cent of all suicides having made an earlier 'attempt'. Those which have supplemented official records by more detailed enquiry cite proportions of 20 to 30 per cent. A recent study, which included deaths judegd by psychiatrists to be suicide (as distinct from the narrower legal definition) and also carried out additional enquiries into the deceased's background, reported a 40 per cent incidence (Ovenstone, 1972). Such figures relate, at least in theory, to a life-time history although one may well be sceptical about the accuracy of data concerning the years long preceding death:

nevertheless they suggest that most suicides are 'first attempts'. Among the minority with a positive history of parasuicide approximately half occur in the 12 months preceding death.

Though in the present state of knowledge it is not possible to build up a fully detailed picture, the data permit at least an outline to be constructed of the overlap and the differences between suicide and parasuicide.

QUALITATIVE DIFFERENCES

These have already been presented and may be summarized as follows.

TABLE 5

*Summary Comparison of Parasuicides and Suicides*

|  | Parasuicide | Suicide |
|---|---|---|
| Sex | Commoner in females | Commoner in males |
| Age group | Mostly below 45 | Mostly above 45 |
| Marital status | Highest rates in divorced and single | Highest rates in divorced, single and widowed |
| Social class | Higher in lower classes | Higher in upper classes (but age-related too) |
| Urban/rural | Commoner in cities | Commoner in cities |
| Employment status | Associated with unemployment | Associated with unemployment and retirement |
| Effects of war | ? | Lower in wartime |
| Seasonal variation | None evident | Spring peak |
| Broken home in childhood | Common | Common |
| Physical illness | No obvious association | Clear association |
| Psychiatric diagnosis | Situational reaction, depression, alcoholism | Depression, alcoholism |
| Personality type | Psycopathy common | ? |

MOTIVATIONAL ASPECTS

The two forms of suicidal behaviour can to some extent be distinguished from the motivational viewpoint. Among suicides the balance of motives is such that the wish to die emerges as stronger than any other desire while among parasuicides this is not usually the case, 'frustrated suicides' representing only a small minority. But as already mentioned, the pattern of motivations to be found within each group, and often indeed within a single individual, is a complex one. The suicide may simply wish to withdraw from life but may in addition have fantasies of reunion with predeceased loved ones, or of inflicting guilt and remorse for his death on other members of his circle.

Conversely, most parasuicides do not wish to terminate their lives but may seek an intermission of consciousness and be willing to gamble on survival. By means of a suicide ritual they too may try to achieve a state of remorse among their intimates or to arouse attention to their distress. Sometimes these interpersonal and manipulative aspects may dominate the clinical picture and such cases may appear to be quite distinct from the psychological viewpoint from completed suicides. The existence of such cases should not, however, lead to the neglect of the important overlap between the two classes of suicidal behaviour.

## REFERENCES

BAGLEY, C. (1968) The evaluation of a suicide prevention scheme by an ecological method. *Social Science and Medicine*, **2**, 1–14.

BAGLEY, C. & GREER, S. (1971) Clinical & social prediction of repeated attempted suicide: a multivariate analysis. *British Journal of Psychiatry* (in press).

BARRACLOUGH, B. & SHEA, M. (1970) Suicide and Samaritan clients. *Lancet*, **iii**, 868–70.

BIRTCHNELL, J. & ALARCON, J. (1971) Depression and attempted suicide: a study of 91 cases seen in a casualty department. *British Journal of Psychiatry*, **118**, 289–96.

BUGLASS, D. & McCULLOCH, J. (1970) Further suicidal behaviour: the development and validation of predictive scales. *British Journal of Psychiatry*, **116**, 483–91.

BUGLASS, D., DUGARD, P. & KREITMAN, N. (1970) Multiple standardisation of parasuicide ('attempted suicide') rates in Edinburgh. *British Journal of Preventive and Social Medicine*, **24**, 182–6.

BUNCH, J. & BARRACLOUGH, B. (1972a) Suicide following bereavement of parents. *Social Psychiatry*, **6**, 193–9.

CHOWDHURY, N. & KREITMAN, N. (1971) A comparison of parasuicides ('attempted suicide') and the clients of the Telephone Samaritan Service. *Applied Social Studies*, **3**, 51–7.

DORPAT, T. L. & RIPLEY, H. S. (1967) The relationship between attempted suicide and committed suicide. *Comprehensive Psychiatry*, **8**, 74–9.

DUBLIN, L. (1963) *Suicide: a Sociological and Statistical Study*. New York: Ronald Press.

DURKHEIM, E. (1951) *Suicide*. Trans. J. Spaulding & G. Simpson. Illinois: Glencoe.

FARBEROW, N., SHNEIDMAN, E. & NEURINGER, C. (1966) Case history and hospitalization factors in suicides of neuropsychiatric hospital patients. *Journal of Nervous and Mental Disease*, **142**, 32.

GIBBS, J. (ed.) (1967) *Suicide*. New York: The Macmillan Company.

GREER, S. & LEE, H. (1967) Subsequent progress of potentially lethal attempted suicide. *Acta psychiatrica et neurologica scandinavica*, **43**, 361–71.

GREER, S. & BAGLEY, C. (1971) Effect of psychiatric intervention in attempted suicide: a controlled study. *British Medical Journal*, **i**, 310–12.

GUZE, S. & ROBINS, E. (1970) Suicide and primary affective disorder. *British Journal of Psychiatry*, **117**, 437–8.

HERSHON, H. (1968)   Attempted suicide in a largely rural area during an eight-year period. *British Journal of Psychiatry,* **114,** 279–84.

HICKS, R. C. & CHOWDHURY, N. (1972)   Personal communication.

HILL, D. (1968)   Hospital treatment of acute poisoning. S.H.H.D. Report. London: H.M.S.O.

KATO, N. (1969)   Self-destruction in Japan. *Folia psychiatrica et neurologica japonica,* **23,** 291–307.

KENDALL, R. (1970)   Relationship between aggression and depression. *Archives of General Psychiatry,* **22,** 308–18.

KENNEDY, P. F. (1971)   An epidemiological survey of attempted suicide in general practice in Edinburgh. M.D. University of Leeds.

KESSEL, N. & GROSSMAN, G. (1961)   Suicide in alcoholics. *British Medical Journal,* **ii,** 1671–2.

KESSEL, N. (1965)   Self-poisoning. *British Medical Journal,* **ii,** 1265, 1336–40.

KESSEL, N. & McCULLOCH, W. (1966)   Repeated acts of self-poisoning and self-injury. *Proceedings of the Royal Society of Medicine,* **59,** 89 (1–4).

KREITMAN, N., PHILIP, A. E., GREER, S. & BAGLEY, C. (1970a)   Parasuicide. Corres. *British Journal of Psychiatry,* **116,** 460.

KREITMAN, N., SMITH, P. & ENG-SEONG TAN (1970b)   Attempted suicide as language: an empirical study. *British Journal of Psychiatry,* **116,** 465–73.

KREITMAN, N. & CHOWDHURY, N. (1972)   Distress behaviour: a study of selected Samaritan clients and parasuicides ('attempted suicide') patients (in press).

LESTER, D. (1971)   Suicide and homicide: bias in the examination between suicide and homicide rates. *Social Psychiatry,* **6,** 80–2.

MINISTRY OF HEALTH (1961)   Circular H.M.(61) 94. London: H.M.S.O.

MOTTO, J. (1965)   Suicide attempts: a longitudinal view. *Archives of General Psychiatry,* **13,** 516–20.

McCARTHY, P. D. & WALSH, D. (1966)   Suicide in Dublin. *British Medical Journal,* **i,** 1393–6.

McCULLOCH, W. & PHILIP, A. E. (1970)   The social prognosis of persons who attempt suicide. *Social Psychiatry,* **5,** 177–82.

McDOWELL, A., BROOKE, E., GREEMAN-BROWNE, D. & ROBIN, A. (1968)   Subsequent suicide in depressed in-patients. *British Journal of Psychiatry,* **114,** 749–54.

OSWALD, I. (1966)   Preventing self-poisoning. *British Medical Journal,* **ii,** 301.

OVENSTONE, I. M. K. (1972)   An epidemiological study of attempted and completed suicide in Edinburgh. M.D. University of Dundee.

PARKIN, D. & STENGEL, E. (1965)   Incidence of suicidal attempt in an urban community. *British Medical Journal,* **i,** 133–8.

PHILIP, A. E. & McCULLOCH, J. W. (1966)   Use of social indices in psychiatric epidemiology. *British Journal of Preventive and Social Medicine,* **20,** 122–6.

PHILIP, A. E. (1970a)   Traits, attitudes and symptoms in a group of attempted suicides. *British Journal of Psychiatry,* **116,** 475–82.

PHILIP, A. E. (1970b)   Personality and attempted suicide: traits related to having a prior history of suicidal attempts. *Applied Social Studies,* **2,** 35–39.

PROKUPEK, J. (1969)   Suicide recording in Czechoslovakia in 1963–68. M.S. publication.

REGISTRAR GENERAL FOR ENGLAND AND WALES (1961)   *Statistical Review,* part III, pp. 240–66. London: H.M.S.O.

ROBINS, E., MURPHY, G., WILKINSON, R., GOSSMER, S. & KEYES, J. (1959)   Some clinical considerations in the prevention of suicide based on a study of 134 successful suicides. *American Journal of Public Health,* **49,** 888.

ROSEN, D. (1970) The serious suicide attempt: epidemiological and follow-up study of 886 patients. *American Journal of Psychiatry*, **127,** 764–70.

SAINSBURY, P. (1955) *Suicide in London.* Maudsley Monograph 1. London: Chapman & Hall.

SAINSBURY, P. (1961) Suicide in old age. *Proceedings of the Royal Society of Medicine*, **54,** 266–8.

SHNEIDMAN, E. (1964) Suicide, sleep and death. *Journal of Consulting Psychology*, **28,** 95.

SLATER, E. & ROTH, M. (1969) *Clinical Psychiatry*, 3rd edn. London: Baillière, Tindall & Cassell.

STENBECK, A., ACHTÉ, A. & RIMON, R. (1965) Physical disease, hypochondria and alcohol addiction in suicides committed by mental hospital patients. *British Journal of Psychiatry*, **3,** 933–7.

STENGEL, E. & COOK, N. (1958) *Attempted Suicide.* Oxford: Oxford University Press.

SWINSCOW, D. (1951) Some suicide statistics. *British Medical Journal*, **i,** 1417–23.

TUCKMAN, J. & YOUNGMAN, W. (1963) Identifying suicide with groups among attempted suicides. *Public Health Reports*, **78,** 763–6.

VARAH, C. (1965) *The Samaritans.* London: Constable.

VINODA, K. (1966) Personality characteristics of attempted suicides. *British Journal of Psychiatry*, **112,** 1143–50.

WORLD HEALTH ORGANIZATION (1968) *Prevention of Suicide.* Publ. Hlth Paper, 38. Geneva: W.H.O.

Chapter IV

# COMPREHENSIVE MENTAL HEALTH SERVICES AND THE BRITISH MODEL

## J. W. Affleck

### INTRODUCTION

Mental health services cannot function in isolation. Their current developmental trends and relationships with other health, welfare, social work and educational services are discussed in this chapter. Epidemiological principles have rarely been applied in the planning of mental health services, which expand and contract with usage. Any excess beds are usually filled by patients whose need is marginal, or who properly should be looked after by other services, and in areas where beds are scarce, community services are organized which may or may not provide better results.

The psychiatrist must have adequate information about the social services which are available or needed in his area, otherwise he will be unable to advise his patient with full knowledge of the sources of help. He will have to work with social work colleagues on the planning or development of supportive services as well as with the Regional or Area Authorities on psychiatric services. A good understanding of the administrative mechanisms in which he is involved is therefore required and it will be advantageous to acquire some information about ways in which the problems are tackled by others.

### FACTORS INFLUENCING THE FORM OF THE SERVICE

#### HISTORICAL AND TECHNICAL DETERMINANTS

In Great Britain it was generally assumed, during the period 1850–1950, that admission to an institution would be the most efficient and appropriate solution to most severe psychiatric problems. The advent of the phenothiazine drugs, a more liberal outlook and the extension of outpatient services, however, has led to a review of opinion in favour of domiciliary and community services. A period of experiment and, one hopes, of evaluation, follows, during which the criteria determining hospital admission can be defined. The changes in the services so far, have involved increased contacts with patients suffering from personality disorder and neurosis in addition to psychosis and extensive application of new treatment techniques in both outpatient and inpatient departments. The inconveniences and inefficiencies of the large mental hospital distant from the population which it serves have been contrasted with the convenience of the district general hospital psychiatric unit which, of course, has its own limitations. The provision of a psychiatric hospital or unit can no longer be regarded as the creation of a mental health service, although the need for inpatient accommodation cannot be ignored. The historical delineation of the evolution of psychiatric thought and practice (Ch. I) is very relevant to the changes in services now being considered.

## CULTURAL INFLUENCES

National concepts of illness and health and treatment led many citizens of the U.S.A. to analytical psychotherapy, while in the U.S.S.R. the concept of such needs is not tolerated. The concept of social planning which included psychiatric services on the other hand, was first possible in Russia with the convenient removal of many historical influences which followed the 1917 revolution. Developing countries, once they have evolved their services for the mentally ill beyond the local prison stage, have the opportunity of a non-traditional approach—the Nigerian experiment of the extensive involvement of four large villages with the Aro hospital day patients and their families, illustrates this (Lambo, 1968). Official health services are moulded by the extent to which other sources of help are available in the community; religious organizations or private charities can dilute the need for supportive work whether or not under official surveillance.

The acceptance of services within each society tends to vary with citizens' ages and education. Examining a sample of the Edinburgh population, Maclean (1968) found that the younger and the better educated groups had opinions about psychiatric treatment which were more realistic than those expressed by the older generations. Hollingshead and Redlich (1958), in a more exhaustive study in which social class was defined in terms of locality of residence, education and occupation, showed that class-shared attitudes determined the quality of the patient-psychiatrist relationship and the extent to which the services of the profession were used. The high number of compulsory and forensic admissions from the lower income groups contrasted with the early treatment and the call for psychiatric help following brushes with the law, which were claimed by the affluent.

## SOCIAL AND DEMOGRAPHIC FACTORS

Family structure and demographic factors are of special relevance to psychiatric services. The small family, small house, family mobility, high divorce rates and women in work outside the home, expose the dependent geriatric and the subnormal to the possibility of lack of supervision and care and the need for institutional admission. The suburban family away from the supportive, though possibly slum neighbourliness, produces its own brands of separation neuroses (Martin, Brotherston and Chave, 1957) for which diagnostic and supportive services may be required. New towns, on the other hand, with adequate communal activities show no unusual pattern of psychiatric illness (Sainsbury and Collins, 1966). The less complex rural society can maintain larger numbers of the subnormal and the mildly demented than are usually tolerated in urban communities. Urbanization increases the need of services for the care and support of subnormal, schizophrenic and geriatric conditions and for the problems arising from alcoholism and drug abuse.

A high proportion of old people in any community produces extensive repercussions on all health and social services. Ineffective selection of the elderly when admission to institutional care is needed can produce serious loss of efficiency in the receiving organization and deterioration or death in the patient (Kidd, 1962). The admission of the confused elderly to the general or geriatric hospital where nursing of the restless can result in panic sedation, or the admission of the physically ill with deliria of types beyond the diagnostic resources of the mental hospital, are equally serious mistakes. The admission and retention of elderly with only mild degenerative conditions who can be looked after in domestic type establishments, or of the bedridden who do not require psychiatric nursing, produces unreasonable strain and overcrowding in many mental hospitals. It is of major importance to all general psychiatrists that adequate medical and social services for the old age pensioner are in operation in the community.

Where the proportion of young people is above average, ideal conditions would produce a corresponding increase in services for children, adolescents and forensic cases, but such services are noticeably deficient even in the most advanced countries.

POLITICAL AND FINANCIAL PRESSURES

The extensive influence of political and economic determinants will be observed in the description of the British National Health Service in its relationship to psychiatric practice.

PRINCIPLES AND OBJECTIVES

All health services provide treatment to which care of the incurable, rehabilitation and preventive services are added as they become more comprehensive. In the case of mental health services asylum was provided before treatment. The demand of society for protection from antisocial behaviour remains a matter of considerable importance and a burden which must be carried by the psychiatrist who is at the same time involved intensively with the welfare of the individual. The discovery and definition of successful methods of treatment and management, however, have provided new objectives.

Discussing the functions of the psychiatric hospital in the context of other mental health services, Jones (1963) adds to the asylum or sanctuary function the provision of a pattern of facilities for 'socialisation—the obverse of custodialism'. There should be links to day centres for the care and the employment of the chronically disabled and a range of services which will be provided in reponse to local concepts of need. The psychiatric service must be capable of responding to society's changing needs, currently illustrated by drug addiction problems and the great increase in self-poisoning episodes. The extensive manifestations of psychiatric morbidity revealed in general hospital wards and in surveys of general practice suggest that our ideas of comprehensiveness are still incomplete. Obviously psychiatric services must be part of a wider social and medical network. The comprehensive mental health service will also offer a major contribution to the modern needs of nurse training and to the training of other professions studying human relations and groups.

Rehabilitation and preventive services, especially in mental health services, require extensive involvement with social services. Comprehensive service planners require to give special attention to arrangements for integration, co-ordination and flexibility and to continuity of care to cover the patients' needs at all stages of illness. A full range of services has to be provided to meet the needs of the patient and his family and this implies the creation of a multidisciplinary organization.

INTEGRATION OF SERVICES

Integration is basically at staff relationships and communications level. The sharing of a common case record can be symbolic of an integrated service and, as the word implies, there should be unified management. The various professional, lay and voluntary groups are not usually so closely knit, however, and are often co-ordinated by sapiential direction rather than fully controlled.

When partially independent or geographically distant services function together, problems in co-ordination arise. If the service headquarters is not in the middle of its catchment area some inefficiencies must occur. The extent of this will depend on the distance from the clinic or hospital to the outlying parts. The importance of a close connection between hospital and community is the motivating concept behind the subdivision of large hospitals into two, three or four small but almost independent ones, each with its separate staff and segment of territory and population to be served. When a local 'agent' must be employed for more distant areas, there are advantages if he or she is 'one of the staff'. Apart from the benefits of easier holiday and sickness relief, fewer potential problems of confidentiality arise. The psychiatrist must have confidence in the individual at the periphery or his referrals diminish. If the agent is employed by a distant authority the psychiatrist is likely to feel that the patient's care is really beyond his influence. It is important that the patient does not suffer loss of confidence in his support by feeling that there has been an administrative handover within the service. This is usually avoided by pretransfer acquaintance with the new support. Adequate administrative mechanisms such as joint appointments and co-ordinating meetings must be arranged in these circumstances. Flexibility will be a measure of the success of co-ordination and communication and will be demonstrated in the ability to cross apparent administrative barriers for the patient's benefit.

CONTINUITY OF CARE

Continuity of care infers that the same team must be able to follow the patient both inside and outside hospital, in the outpatient clinic or the day hospital, and into the patient's home if necessary (May, 1968). This is accomplished through the co-ordinating leadership of the psychiatrist in charge of the patient and responsible for the overall treatment regime. A degree of flexibility must be injected into continuity of care systems. It may be thwarted in practice by legal systems, or set aside when subspecialization justifies this. Need for continuity is sometimes invoked by administrators wishing to maintain systems which are in other ways obsolescent, for example the involvement of all medical staff in short term/long term/one sex patient routines, rather than in a functionally planned organization. Larger services have the advantage of allowing change for mutual benefit of patient and psychiatrist.

COMMUNITY RELATIONSHIPS

Detailed consideration must be given to the ways in which the community can be made aware of mental health problems to ensure that people are referred on need, and that the sympathy is generated which is required to ensure modification of the community's attitudes and laws. Welfare, educational, forensic, social security and employment agencies must be involved and understanding sought from political and religious groups in which much voluntary effort originates.

The principle of organizing all services in a comprehensive way on an area basis is accepted in the United States Community Mental Health Centres Construction Act (1963). Central government funds are provided when private, voluntary and county or municipal organizations come together to plan a unified service. The State hospitals may be involved or, as in Denver, Colorado (Fort Logan), may comprise such a service independently (Glasscote *et al.*, 1964). The Federal regulations define comprehensiveness. The five items which are essential for financial support are inpatient treatment, outpatient treatment, partial hospitalization services, emergency services over the 24 hours and consultation and education services available to community agencies and professional personnel. Full comprehensiveness also includes rehabilitation, precare and aftercare (foster homes, halfway houses and home visiting), training, research and evaluation. The need to co-ordinate is recognized in other countries as in the Netherlands in which public health departments link services based on religious and ethnic groups as well as on municipalities and the state. In the U.S.S.R. the split between the mental hospital and the local or sector clinics is accepted and emphasis placed on adequate services locally. Epilepsy, speech defects and sexology are recognized sections of the larger clinics. There is emphasis on formal follow-up services and very adequate occupational and industrial therapy facilities which are integrated with local industry.

MANPOWER

The increase in urban living and in the level of the average citizen's education ensures that expansion of psychiatric services will be needed. Training needs and staff for operational research must be included in estimates for new services.

Medical, nursing, clinical psychology, social work and occupational therapy professionals operate in various ways—from single individuals to complex teams. Morale depends largely on appropriateness of the work done and on expectations. The incentives of training and career prospects must be recognizable. Intellectual stimuli should be provided by conferences and availability of research advice.

Where one profession is in extremely short supply the traditional roles may break down. Thus, members of staff who have not been appropriately trained may be found undertaking responsibility for psychotherapy with groups and with individual patients. Nurses may step in to undertake routine psychological testing or the organization of occupational therapy. Though blurring of roles may be favoured in certain settings as an alternative to status centred hierarchies, or may be accepted during staffing deficiencies, services functioning in these

D

ways are in danger of becoming oblivious of their lack of true specialist standards.

In the National Health Service the consultant in psychiatry expects to undertake domiciliary visiting with family doctors, to have facilities for his own inpatients, day patients and outpatients, contact with general hospital colleagues, the option of some private practice and time for a little research. Where a catchment area is served by two hospitals it is essential that at least some of the senior doctors and other senior professionals should work in both. This applies especially to general hospital/mental hospital linkages. The arrangement whereby two or three junior staff work with each consultant and groups of two or three such teams work together, allows reasonable service divisions to be formed. Each team may be completed by a half-time psychologist, a social worker, a nurse for community work and a nursing team under a unit nursing officer for inpatients, day patients and outpatients. Working in a team is a skill which has to be acquired and knowledge of the proper roles and skills of the other professions cannot be obtained without effort. It is not possible to define the exact amount of the work which will be undertaken as this will depend on local factors including time required for travelling, for study, and the extent to which other community services are available and used. As staff in the teams becomes available and consultation liaisons develop with social work services, opportunity can occur to investigate the possibilities of family therapy and marital problem services for which need has been long recognized.

The general practitioner must be regarded as part of the mental health team, even though he may choose to opt out. He provides the total treatment for the patients in whom he diagnoses psychiatric illness, apart from the 5 to 10 per cent he refers to psychiatrists. Geographically defined catchment areas allow meaningful relationships to develop. If he is involved and concerned, his knowledge of the patient's personality, the family and home and previous reactions to illness are invaluable. His knowledge of the locality may include the special stresses of the local industries and the customs and people in the local society likely to be involved in social disruption, marital discord, etc., items which may remain unknown to a professional who lives elsewhere.

The general practitioner working within the hospital must be posted according to his training or the extent to which he can acquire training in specialist practice.

DATA COLLECTION AND EVALUATION OF SERVICES

Services will organize the collection of statistics to help in evaluation and planning for the future. As pointed out by Brooke (1968) the necessary definition of available services can be a complex exercise. Conditions of 'entitlement' must be considered as in some services, beds may be occupied wrongly, e.g. by geriatric patients, by children, adolescents, or by the subnormal. Day patient places are sometimes omitted from official statistics, as are training centre places and hostel beds in services for the subnormal. Outpatient practice statistics are rarely broken down adequately. In assessing manpower needs, visits to medical and surgical ward patients in hospital may be equivalent to domiciliary visits, as are prison visits where no separate forensic service exists, and liaison visits to patients in other non-medical services.

The use of the services is monitored by admission, re-admission and waiting list statistics and for some services the geographical area of the patient's residence may be important. Discharges and deaths will be required to provide turnover figures. Where the day's work can include the completion of a proforma relating to each patient's admission, discharge or three-monthly chart, diagnostic studies and cohort studies with true re-admission rates, total time in hospital, movement to long stay care and use of rehabilitation and community services, can be arranged. Cohort studies must begin with a census of patient population concerned in the study. Punch card preparation and mechanically assisted sorting will be required and computer assistance may be utilized.

Evaluation of services usually requires a multidisciplinary approach involving statisticians and sociologists. It is often difficult to define the precise aims of individual items in a clinical-administrative programme. Sainsbury (1970) postulates that the primary objective of the evaluator is to define the social and clinical characteristics of patients and families who will do best within a particular service rather than that one service is 'better' than another. It should be possible to construct hypotheses predicting the type of facility in which outcome is likely to be favourable, and to test them. When innovations are introduced some attempt should be made to determine whether or not they meet the needs defined.

Statistics should be collected with specific objects in view, in addition to basic administrative requirements. A records system, in which a single clinical case record is available for all admissions and attendances and the contacts with each individual patient, is essential. This is required for any case register on which epidemiological studies can be undertaken and should be available in all hospitals in the first instance. Such registers have been extended to groups of hospitals, (Mitchell, 1877) to mental health services and to specified populations (Bahn, 1962). An essential aspect of psychiatric registers which are used for clinical as well as special epidemiological research, is the possibility of family records linkage. Such data banks increase in value with age as much information on psychiatric topics takes years to collect (Baldwin, 1970).

In addition to work based on a competent records department and the acquisition of quantitative data, operational research should include consideration of standards of care. This may be commenced by consideration of circumstances in which apparently similar groups differ in length of stay, or other measures of outcome. Work study investigations involve job analysis, consideration of the layout of facilities and time and motion studies, such as Morgan's account of his senior registrar duties (1967), though these investigations are usually indicated for functional groups rather than for individuals.

## THE ADMINISTRATION OF THE
## BRITISH PSYCHIATRIC SERVICES

The National Health Service is a complex structure by which a population of 50 million people are provided with comprehensive care and in which mental health services are an integral part of the general health services. The Scottish division serves five million and has variants of detail. It is a state service into which many safeguards are inserted to allow freedom of clinical practice and to ensure the elimination of political interference in the appointment of personnel. Doctors have the right to treat patients privately outside the state service if they do not undertake a full-time contract. The medical profession has an antipathy to hierarchies in administration and by the creation of a very large number of consultant posts, each with full clinical responsibility, such administrative patterns have been largely eliminated at senior medical level. In psychiatry the consultant is directly responsible for the patients in his wards to the hospital governors rather than to a superintendent. The inclusion of mental health services in the general medical service allows the extension of psychiatric services in general hospitals to take place relatively easily. The governing bodies in the regional and local organization of the service are composed of volunteers selected and invited to serve by the Secretary of State. The local government authorities which have responsibilities for the social work covering community care and aftercare of discharged patients are elected directly by the public, usually with political party support.

### THE CENTRAL ADMINISTRATION OF THE NATIONAL HEALTH SERVICE

The amount of money which is spent on all the social services and the share of this given to health services to be subdivided between hospital, local authority and general practice needs, is ultimately determined by the political party in power and the decisions of the politicians of the day. This, of course, is determined by the Ministers' interpretation of the economic state of the country. Long term programmes are under continuous scrutiny by the permanent Civil Service staff who advise the changing ministerial heads in turn and also propose subjects to be considered by the Standing Advisory Committees and Subcommittees composed of appropriate experts. The basic administrative relationships in the service are set out in Table 1.

The central bodies concerned overall with health services are the Department of Health and Social Security and the Scottish Home and Health Department. The Department of Education, the Home Office, and the Department of Employment are also related to the work of psychiatrists in child psychiatry, forensic psychiatry, and rehabilitation. Ministry officials with their medical, nursing, social work, architectural and other specialist advisers keep in touch through Regional Boards with hospital financial policy, developments and important day-to-day events usually arising as complaints.

The Department is subdivided for various purposes and includes a mental health planning division. It functions on Civil Service bureaucratic management principles in which decisions are made by administrators and politicians, and medical and other experts are in a strictly advisory capacity. Direct contact with the individual hospitals is limited. The most direct link was established by the inauguration of the Hospital Advisory Service in 1970, the members of which visit all long stay hospitals to obtain and report on evidence indicating deficiencies in the standard of care.

CONTROLLING MECHANISMS

Under separate financial headings provision is made for capital expenditure on new buildings, major alterations to existing premises and the increases in running costs. Alterations of major importance must receive prior approval by the Secretary of State and until this is obtained money will not be forthcoming. Ministerial and regional control of money is the cause of delay in the development of the service which is often regarded as unjustifiable at local level. Negotiations regarding staff salaries and conditions are undertaken by 'Whitley Councils'. These bodies meet regularly to cover all types of non-medical staff. Each Council has a number of representatives of the management, i.e. Ministry, Regional Boards and Hospital Management Committees and the members of appropriate representative organizations of the staff. In the case of the medical profession reviews of salary scales are re-examined regularly by an advisory review body which takes evidences from the British Medical Association and other sources.

TABLE 1

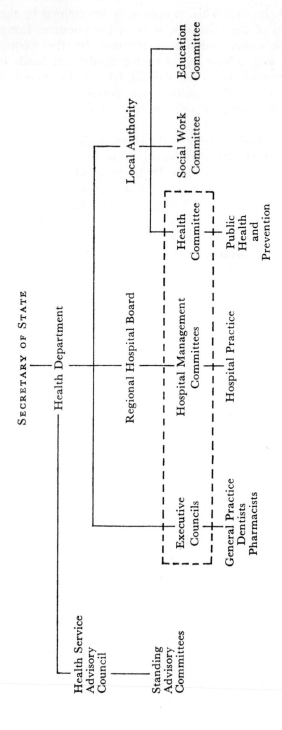

Dotted lines indicate the administrative bodies which will be fused to form 'Area Health Boards' in 1974. Teaching hospitals will be incorporated but will have special representation.

The 'question in Parliament' is of major importance in the British form of government. It is the ultimate safeguard of the citizen, the method by which the Secretary of State's responsibility for the National Health Service is openly acknowledged and declared. A Secretary of State cannot afford politically to give too many unsatisfactory answers to questions raised by Members of Parliament, and he is expected to demonstrate the wisdom of his priorities. Most matters of complaint and contention of dissatisfaction are dealt with at the level of hospital management or Regional Board and there is the possibility of recourse to the courts when questions of neglect arise. If, however, administrative matters, e.g. a local lack of beds or nurses, give rise to dissatisfaction, the citizen can bring the matter to the notice of his Member of Parliament who will probably write to the Secretary of State and receive a written explanation from him. Alternatively, it may be raised at question time in the House of Commons when it becomes a matter of open political debate.

The central administration has the responsibility for initiating and altering services in accordance with changes in statutes. This is finally effected by the issue of 'statutory intruments' or instructions which are legally binding on the bodies set up to implement the service concerned. The Ministry subsequently issues 'circulars' indicating policy with various degrees of compulsion, indicated by the use of the words 'must' or 'may' or 'should', and in addition 'memoranda' and letters are issued which usually give administrative advice rather than instructions. Regional Boards, and through them local Hospital Management Committees, are dependent on the Ministry for their allocation of funds on an annual basis for the maintenance of their services and therefore can be ultimately controlled by alterations in financial allocations and instructions with regard to expenditure.

*Research and Publications*

Standing Medical Advisory Committees, including one for mental health, review topics and situations which suggest need for policy change, e.g. the use of day patient care, services for alcoholism, etc. Their reports are usually reasonably comprehensive, concise and valuable. Annual statistics are collected from hospitals and other services and are reviewed in the reports and bulletins of the chief medical officers.

Money for operational research is provided from central, regional or local (hospital) annual budgets. Centrally controlled research is extensive and includes special units. Material collected from all the hospitals is available for analysis.

## REGIONAL ORGANIZATION

A basic concept in planning was that each region should be centred on a university and teaching hospital which is expected to provide leadership and to be a centre of progressive ideas and a source of postgraduate instruction and research. While most of the country could be fairly easily subdivided in this way, each Region having about three to four million population, the large number of teaching hospitals in London presented difficulties. Four Metropolitan Regions were created, each with a group of teaching hospitals in it. The present subdivision into 15 regions was accomplished in 1957 when the Wessex Board was established on the assumption that a university with a medical faculty would be established in Southampton. In Scotland there are five Regional Hospital Boards, of which only the Northern, based in Inverness, is without a university centre. Only the South-Western Board area covering Glasgow and the western area teaches the population dimensions of the English boards.

The Regional Hospital Boards provide their statutory service by employing specialists down to the grade of registrar and allocating money to Hospital Management Committees or Boards of Management throughout the region. In spite of the importance of the regional Teaching Hospital the great bulk of the work is, of course, undertaken in non-teaching hospitals in the various areas into which the region is divided. The standard of work accomplished in these areas determines the true efficiency of the hospital service.

Regional Hospital Board areas coincide with local authorities which look after the local government interests of populations varying from 50,000 to 1,500,000, though these are in process of reorganization. In such a situation co-ordination of hospital services with the many local authorities, which are expected to provide domiciliary health and social work services, can be a complex matter.

The number of Regional Board members who have a special interest in mental health services on the Regional Boards is small—only 2 members are expected to have special knowledge in this field among the total board membership of 18 to 24. Psychiatrists are sometimes invited to serve on Regional Boards, but special knowledge is more often represented by the chairman or members of a Mental Hospital Management Committee rather than by a professional person. The members with special knowledge cannot be expected to attend all meetings, nor even all meetings at which mental health matters are discussed. The technical needs and most urgent demands of the mental health services must be appreciated and emphasized where necessary by the permanent officers of the Boards—the Senior Administrative Medical Officer and his assistants, or the Board Secretariat. In practice mental health services in some regions have progressed much more than in others. For the first 10 years of the service some regions employed regional psychiatrists on the staff of the Senior Administrative Medical Officer with the special duty of advising Boards with regard to function and scope of services, deficiencies, forecasts of requirements and advice on priorities. Since 1958, however, the provision for advice of this type is by a consultant for a short time each week or when required. Boards were advised in a memorandum issued at the establishment of the service that they should have a Mental Health Committee to stimulate and monitor the running of these services. Advisory Committees usually formed by representatives of the Consultant Psychiatrists in the Region are also recommended.

## LOCAL ADMINISTRATION
(See page 81)

The National Health Service has three administrative authorities in each local area. The Executive Council appoints general practitioners to vacant practices, distributes payment to these doctors and to pharmacists and provides a supplementary ophthalmic service for the provision of spectacles. The second service is the health section of the borough or city council or county council. The third is the Hospital Management Committee (or Board of Management in Scotland.) These three elements, which will be fused into an Area Health Board (see p. 74), are sometimes referred to as 'tripartite administration'— a term also often applied to the intrahospital organization in which doctors, nurses and hospital administrators work together. In addition, psychiatrists will be in close touch with other services run by the local authority—the social work department, the probation department and the education department (see Table 2).

### HOSPITAL GOVERNMENT

The most suitable grouping of hospitals is still a controversial issue. When economies have to be made, or scarce resources have to be distributed, decisions have to be made by the Governors on the allocations to different types of medical and surgical services. Psychiatry has never had a high priority in this context and few members of Hospital management Committees in mixed groups of general and special hospitals have intimate knowledge or insight into mental health service needs. The kind of demoralization which can result from failure to maintain and improve the service when Governors and staff at hospital level fail to function closely, is demonstrated in the report prepared following complaints at the Ely Subnormality Hospital (Report of the Committee of Inquiry, 1969). When mental hospitals or mental deficiency hospitals

TABLE 2

*Administrative Organizations (with which the psychiatrist may be involved)*

| Central | Regional | Local |
|---|---|---|
| Department of Health and Social Security Scottish Home and Health Department | Teaching Hospital and University Hospital Regional Hospital Board Co-ordinating Offices of the Department of Health and Social Security | Board of Management or Hospital Management Committee Local Health Authority Social Work Departments Social Security Offices Executive Council (G.Ps) |
| Department of Education Scottish Education Dept. | | Local Education Authority |
| Department of Employment | Regional Offices Industrial Rehabilitation Centre (I.R.U.) Government Training Centre | Local Office with Disablement Resettlement Officer (D.R.O.) |
| Home Office Scottish (Home) Department | Remand Homes Prisons Young Offenders Institutions Detention Centres Borstal Training Centres | Approved Schools Probation Officer (England and Wales) |
| Voluntary Societies Headquarters | | Voluntary Associations |
| Medical Research Council | University Research Activities | Research Units |

are grouped together, however, there are fewer conflicting interests to choose from and confidence in appropriate distribution of resources can be more easily sustained. These matters may be of less importance where psychiatric services are based on new psychiatric units in general hospitals which should have been renovated and reasonably staffed at their inauguration. Administrative and management practices within hospitals will be considered in Chapter XVI, Volume II.

THE BASIC ORGANIZATION IN LOCAL AUTHORITIES

The members (councillors) of local authorities are elected, rather than selected by the Minister as in the case of Hospital Board members. Local politics, therefore, play an important part in the decisions of those authorities and this influences final decisions. A service may need to be expanded from the technical point of view, but the money to cover this must come from the local levy or rates. The result is that there is great variety in the standard of service provided, especially in regard to mental health services.

Local authorities work on a rather rigid system. The elected members are usually much more involved in detail than the public representatives in the hospital system. The Medical Officer of Health, the Director of Social Work and the Director of Education are the advisers and also chief executive officers, so the services often reflect their interests, experience and enthusiasms. All new proposals have also to pass through the full Council and the minutes of various committees making recommendations must be scrutinized by the Town or County Clerk who has the duty to ensure that the local authority fulfills its legal duty. Before any recommendation is passed, the Treasurer similarly scrutinizes it to report on its relationship to the money available.

The local authority serves one area only and it is sometimes disconcerting to find that the service stops at the city boundary with the result that citizens on the opposite side of the road cannot enjoy it. Such anomalies are often covered by co-ordinating arrangements. It is often possible for local authorities to use voluntary societies to cover some of their duties, e.g. some aspects of the mental health aftercare service. This can contribute to the varying standards of care provided.

*Health Services*

Public Health Departments, many of which were also welfare departments, have lost their mental health and social services by the Social Work Acts and their remaining functions will be taken over by Area Health Boards. Health visitors are involved predominantly with mothers and young children and with the aged, and district nurses are involved in psychiatric aftercare in some areas. Both are increasingly attached to general practices. The provision of systems for nursing psychiatric patients in the community is discussed in Chapter XVII, Volume II.

*Social Work Services*

The Social Work Departments have comprehensive powers to assist those in need. They are responsible for child care, the welfare of the handicapped including the mentally handicapped, the welfare of the aged, the needs of the homeless, etc. In Scotland the organization of Children's Hearings (instead of Juvenile Courts) and the probation, prison aftercare and parole services, have also been brought into these departments. Extensive residential services are included. The encouragement and co-ordination of voluntary effort in some of these fields is expected.

The philosophy of family centred case work by general purpose social workers, proposed as the ideal—as opposed to specialization, for example in the case of the mentally ill or subnormal—produces a conflict of priorities and interests. Local authorities are required to provide a mental welfare officer to take the place of relatives in the care of friendless psychiatric patients, and if they so wish they can reduce their 'specialist' services to this level. Many authorities, however, have extensive services providing hostels, clubs and specialist social workers available to advise the family, to help the patient to clinic or hospital, and to offer him support and guidance on his return home. Occupational Centres and Sheltered Workshops for all types of disabled are available in some areas.

*Education Services*

The Director of Education is the chief officer and executive of the local education authority while the Medical Officer of Health is usually the chief school medical officer. The education authority provides education for both children and adults. Many patients in suitably placed psychiatric and subnormality hospitals take part in adult classes either by attending special centres or having teachers seconded to groups. In most areas, educational psychologists serve within the school system. They should come to know the children whose difficulties are exhibited in the classroom and who are referred to the child guidance service by the teachers. Residential school facilities for children with emotional maladjustment can be provided. Special schools or classes for the educationally subnormal and occupational centres for the training/education of the subnormal children must also be provided by statute.

REGROUPING OF SERVICES

The National Health Service will be reorganized probably in 1974 by the creation of Area Health Authorities formed by the fusion of hospitals, general practice and public health departments. Each Area Authority in England will serve approximately 200,000 of the population and it is assumed that this will be associated geographically and functionally as far as possible with new local government sub-areas based on economical rather than historical factors. Social work services will remain separate administratively under local government so a local co-ordinative mechanism with medical services will be required. The Area Health Authorities will be co-ordinated with the central administration through Regional Health Authorities. In Wales and Scotland, where population, geographical and political requirements modify the situation, the central administrative offices will be in direct contact with the Area Authorities (called the Area Health 'Boards' in Scotland).

The mechanism for the provision of technical advice on psychiatric services in the context of the new administrative organization will evolve slowly. It may be provided by an Area Mental Health Service Council which should include representatives of the professions working in the psychiatric service with, in addition, general practitioners, geriatricians and observers from Social Work Departments.

ASSOCIATED ORGANIZATIONS

*For Research*

The Medical Research Council organizes research on its own initiative using a grant from the Privy Council. Projects for which M.R.C.

TABLE 3

*Voluntary Agencies*

| | |
|---|---|
| Education, information services, advisory services, hostels, etc. | National Associations for Mental Health<br>National Societies for Mentally Handicapped Children (originally associations of parents of the subnormal)<br>National Societies for Autistic Children<br>Ex-Service Men's Mental Welfare Association<br>The Mental After-Care Association<br>The Richmond Fellowship<br>The Simon and Cyrenian Communities |
| Research | The Mental Health Research Fund |
| General—with a bearing on mental health | Marriage Guidance Councils<br>Telephone Samaritans<br>The National League of Hospital Friends<br>The National Council for Social Service<br>The National Corporation for the Care of the Aged<br>The Nuffield Provincial Hospitals Trust<br>Associations for Welfare of Epileptics<br>The Salvation Army |

support is sought are passed to the Clinical Research Board which advises the Council on their quality and feasibility as well as possible duplication of work. Though the M.R.C. gives some personal grants it functions chiefly by setting up units consisting of teams of scientific research staff with a number of research fellows. Six psychiatric research units have been established covering social and clinical psychiatric research, brain metabolism and neuropsychiatry.

The Mental Health Research Fund attracts subscriptions from the public and is specially commended by the National Association for Mental Health. Smaller research projects are usually financed from charitable foundations and commercial sources. Other research funds are available within the universities.

### Voluntary Services

The headquarters of the main voluntary bodies undertaking working in the mental health field are usually located in London or Edinburgh. The services which they provide are essential for the completion of the total requirements of the services and are in many cases more appropriately provided in this way. The main organizations are listed in Table 3.

## REFERENCES

BAHN, A. K. (1962)   Psychiatric case register conference. *Public Health Reports*, **77**, 1071.

BALDWIN, J. A. (1970)   In *Psychiatric Epidemiology*. Edited by E. H. Hare and J. Wing, Ch. 7. London: Oxford University Press.

BROOKE, E. B. (1968)   Report on conference on *The Planning of Mental Health Services*. Copenhagen: W.H.O.

GLASSCOTE, R. N., SUSSEX, J. N., CUMMING, E. & SMITH, L. H. (1964)   *The Community Mental Health Centre*. Washington A.P.A.

HOLLINGSHEAD, A. B. & REDLICH, F. C. (1958)   *Social Class and Mental Illness*. London: Chapman & Hall.

JONES, K. (1963)   The role and function of the mental hospital. In *Trends in the Mental Health Services*. Edited by H. L. Freeman & J. A. Farndale, Ch. 6. Oxford: Pergamon.

KIDD, C. B. (1962)   Misplacement of the elderly in hospital. *British Medical Journal*, **ii**, 1491.

LAMBO, A. (1968)   In *Community Mental Health—an International Perspective*. San Francisco: Jossey-Bass Inc.

MACLEAN, U. (1968)   Scottish views on mental illness. *Scottish Medical Journal*, **13**, 211.

MARTIN, F., BROTHERSTON, J. H. F. & CHAVE, S. (1957)   The incidence of neurosis in a new housing estate. *British Journal of Preventive and Social Medicine*, **11**, 196.

MAY, A. R. (1968)   Report on conference on *The Planning of Mental Health Services*. Copenhagen: W.H.O.

MITCHELL, A. M. (1877) Contributions to the statistics of insanity. *Journal of Mental Science*, **22**, 261.

MORGAN, R. (1967) The work of a junior doctor in a psychiatric hospital. In *New Aspects of the Mental Health Services*. Edited by H. Freeman & J. Farndale, Ch. 20. London: Pergamon.

REPORT OF THE COMMITTEE OF INQUIRY (1969) into the allegations of ill-treatment at the Ely Hospital, Cardiff. London: H.M.S.O.

SAINSBURY, P. (1970) In *Psychiatric Epidemiology*. Edited by C. H. Hare & J. Wing, Ch. 6. London: Oxford University Press.

SAINSBURY, P. & COLLINS, J. (1966) Some factors relating to mental illness in a new town. *Journal of Psychosomatic Research*, **10**, 45.

# Chapter V

# HOSPITAL–COMMUNITY PRACTICE

## J. W. Affleck

### GENERAL PSYCHIATRIC SERVICES
### AND THEIR LOCATION

Psychiatric services can be provided for the patient in his home, in a local non-hospital clinic or private practice, in an outpatient department, in a general hospital or in a mental hospital.

The main arguments for preferring the general hospital services are that the stigma of the mental hospital or of mental illness can be reduced, and that the patient will benefit by his psychiatrist's involvement in the main stream of medicine. The atmosphere is also said to be more inclined to therapeutic optimism and there is less fear of transfer to long term wards. On the other hand, these arguments may foster the outlook that psychiatry is merely a variation of internal medicine or neurology. The extension of psychiatry into general hospitals in the U.S.A. was stimulated by the acceptance of mental illness as insurable sickness, and in Great Britain by McKeown's concept of the district hospital services as a balanced community incorporating all acute and chronic cases, and providing complementary services for all groups of patients (McKeown, 1965). The facilities currently available do not always provide district hospital services on one site however, but the arrangement by which psychiatrists give service at both general and mental hospitals is similar to those for other consultants moving between different hospitals and clinics.

The general hospital unit is equivalent to a small mental hospital. Where such a unit has responsibilities beyond observation and diagnosis, supporting community services must be provided. The services immediately required will include inpatient, day treatment and care, hostel wards or other facilities for patients returning to work before leaving hospital or becoming fully independent, and other industrial and social rehabilitation supports. The most elementary links between the hospital and the community are the outpatient clinic and the availability of staff to visit patients in their homes. These allow personal contacts to be made before admission or day patient attendance and for the planning of supportive treatment on discharge from hospital. The unit becomes a stimulant to the surrounding community. Local authorities and voluntary organizations must provide clubs, transport for day patients, hostels, etc. This pattern of changing hospital service and associated community response took place in the localities surrounding some larger mental hospitals which were suitably placed in the midst of their city catchment areas in the period 1945–55, e.g. in Nottingham under MacMillan and in York under Bowen.

The general hospital unit has usually the advantage of a relatively central site in its catchment area. Though its need for supporting services from local geriatric and social work services tends to strengthen its links in the community, staff philosophies can create a hospital which deals only (though effectively) with the patients who are referred. Preferably the psychiatric centre should be an organization which has a major or even a leadership role in the helping services. Such a position is not exclusive to the general hospital unit though the larger hospital with its larger staff may have to be subdivided to achieve it in the context of a wide commitment. Thus, under the influence of Maxwell Jones at Dingleton Hospital (400 beds), the Scottish Border Counties Committee for Co-ordination of Social Work and Mental Health was established, incorporating various statutory medical and social work services, family doctors and voluntary organizations. The hospital staff are subdivided to establish local connections with the three counties.

The 'large mental hospital in the country' has been rightly condemned as difficult to staff and failing in rehabilitative possibilities. It can only function fairly well if its professional staff undertake excessive travelling to and from the community and work in its general hospitals. Psychiatric units in general hospitals are regarded as efficient in comparison, but the true comparison is with the larger hospital (of not more than 1000 beds) within the community which it serves, which may have more potential and advantages in patient classification and staff training. The larger hospital will consist of a federation of teams each with its own territory and a central medical co-ordinating mechanism. The special units in the mental hospitals for the treatment of alcoholism, drug addiction, psychogeriatrics, rehabilitation and for adolescents, can be linked with the appropriate community organizations to form treatment services.

Variations in layout of these services are suggested in Table 1.

BED REQUIREMENTS

The minimum need for beds in a psychiatric service was the subject of much discussion in the 1960's. Tooth and Brooke (1961) estimated that as community services, including hostels, increased, the total need for psychiatric hospital beds might fall to 1.8 per 1000 of population. Discussing the 1956 statistics the authors pointed out that 0.34 beds per 1000 population covered the needs of the short term patient, i.e. those

TABLE I

*District Psychiatric Hospital Services*

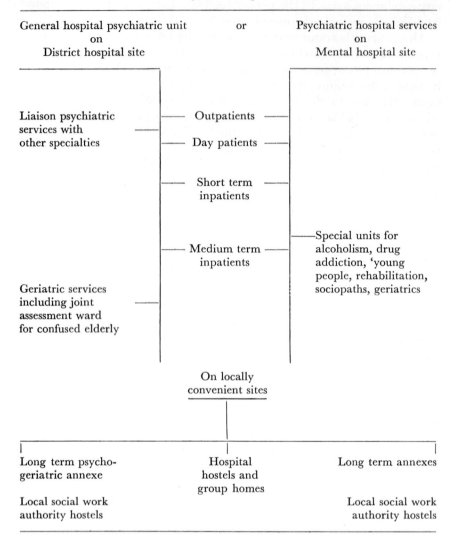

General hospital psychiatric unit         or         Psychiatric hospital services
on                                                              on
District hospital site                                    Mental hospital site

Liaison psychiatric services with other specialties

———— Outpatients ————

———— Day patients ————

———— Short term inpatients ————

———— Medium term inpatients ————

————Special units for alcoholism, drug addiction, 'young people, rehabilitation, sociopaths, geriatrics

Geriatric services including joint assessment ward for confused elderly

On locally convenient sites

Long term psycho-geriatric annexe

Hospital hostels and group homes

Long term annexes

Local social work authority hostels

Local social work authority hostels

leaving within 3 months, and 0.53 the needs of the medium term (who left within 2 years). It was noted that whereas in some areas admissions continued to increase in the subsequent years to 1959, in others increasing outpatient treatment, day hospital attendance and pre-admission screening appeared to have reduced admissions. Though the long term population resident in the mental hospital at that time were expected to have died in the subsequent 15 years, a projection for new long term patients (over 2 years in hospital) suggested a need for 0.89 beds per 1000 population for this group. Thus the total needs were about 1800 beds per million in the ratio of 2 men:3 women. Since then, the provision of extramural services has failed to materialize in different parts of the country and admission policies continue to vary. The number of admissions has not ceased to rise, though the rise is no longer steep, but the original long term residents have not fallen in numbers as quickly as anticipated. It has been demonstrated however, by Oldham (1969) in two London boroughs and in the district general hospitals of Lancashire (Downham, 1967) that 0.5 beds, or less, per 1000, has supplied the total psychiatric needs of the patients incepted by their services, given adequate day places and other support, though special units may have to be provided elsewhere in addition to facilities for the care of long term patients who were hospitalized before the inauguration of the new system and need continued treatment.

Hoenig and Hamilton (1969) have described the behaviour problems which prove a burden on the household when patients are maintained on this basis. While this study did not describe serious complaints arising from a maximum extramural organization, Grad and Sainsbury (1968) reported a comparison of two services with differing admission policies revealing that, on all the measures used, the service which favoured extramural care left the patients' families more heavily burdened.

In Scotland, where community geriatric services are less extensive and distances make day care difficult, the more empirical estimate of need of 3 beds per 1000 remains to be tested further. This is based on the proposal to have 0.5 beds per 1000 for short care (up to 3 month's stay), 1.25 beds per 1000 for medium term and rehabilitation (3 months to 2 years) and 1.25 beds for the longer term—including geriatric dementias. The removal of this last group would leave a total bed need at the Tooth and Brooke level. Describing the uses of day hospitals in 1968, the Ministry of Health stated that '. . . current policy is to base the hospital psychiatric services on the district general hospitals. If ideally constituted the psychiatric complex ought, for a catchment area of 250,000, to consist of an in-patient unit of 120 beds, and out-patient department and a day hospital with 150–160 places.' (H.M.S.O., 1969) This provides a psychiatric bed coverage of 0.48 beds per 1000 population. Hospitals separated from their catchments will remain with us for some time, however, and their problems are different. Travelling time will to some extent determine the needs. Carse, Paulin and Watt (1958), in the Worthing experiment, demonstrated the value of a satellite day hospital in a town some 20 miles away from the bed provision. The larger hospitals in cities of more than 250,000 population may find separate mental health centres useful. These function as filter and resettlement units with outpatient facilities (including E.C.T.) occupational therapy and accommodation for patient and professional groups. The Croydon centre is described by May, Sheldon and MacKeith (1962) and the work of the Plymouth Centre has been described and evaluated by Kessel and Hassall (1971).

SERVICES FOR NEUROSIS AND PERSONALITY DISORDERS

Reviewing the development of the psychiatric services in Great Britain since the commencement of the National Health Service in 1948, Hill (1969) points out the particular lack of facilities for patients with neurotic illness and personality disorder—adults and children. The psychiatric services in this country have evolved chiefly from the mental hospital, with major expansion into the community occurring when they established their own outpatient services. Psycho-analysis as such has been regarded as a disappointing treatment method and this has tended to create a suspicion of the psychotherapeutic approach—especially in the face of advances in drug therapy, etc. The result has been a paucity of enthusiastic or competent teachers of psychotherapeutic methods. Psychotherapy training for psychiatric trainees in Great Britain is thus still in its early stages. This contrasts with countries such as the United States in which many psychiatrists in private practice offer a few hours each week to teaching departments and hospitals for the supervision of trainees. The Tavistock Clinic and the Cassell Hospital were originally endowed for the treatment of outpatients and the inpatient treatment of neurotic patients, respectively. They have developed special postgraduate teaching responsibilities in psychotherapy and include methods of exploring family and marital problems. The training facilities of these centres have not yet been duplicated elsewhere.

Attempts to reformulate ideas on the nature of the neuroses have led to extension of group work of various kinds and intensive community methods stemmed from it. The creation of new types of clinical and administrative organizations are required, such as the sociotherapeutic networks of medical and social services based on a psychotherapy centre described by Sutherland (1968) (see Ch. VI). Such approaches are multidisciplinary and their success must therefore depend on the adequate theoretical and practical training of all the professionals involved. Few systematic training courses are available. Doctors and social workers have to seek posts in hospitals and clinics where a special interest is demonstrated. Systematic advanced courses on nursing and group dynamics such as those provided for four psychiatric nurses each year in the Royal Edinburgh and Dingleton Hospitals are also needed. Behaviour therapy departments based on learning theory approach have been established, often under the aegis of a clinical psychologist.

It is useful and convenient if one senior member of a hospital medical staff takes a special interest in the sexual disorders.

The Henderson Hospital of 40 beds at Belmont, Surrey, is probably the only non-forensic facility which sets out to tackle the problem of the severely disordered psychopath. It was established and developed by Maxwell Jones between 1948 and 1957 and intensively investigated by Rapoport (1960).

The problems of patients with personality disorders characterized by various forms of dependency were absorbed by the mental hospitals of custodial days by the acceptance of a certain number of 'settlers' who sought 'asylum' in the literal sense. Occasionally such provision may still be required. Many have been discharged to hostels of various types. General hospital units are usually too small to house them. Some form attachments to members of the staff, whether doctor, nurse or social worker, or manage with repeated visits to the ward, no matter whom they meet. In hospital or units which recognize the problem overtly and organize the visits, the nurse may be the person chosen and may be asked to carry the problem. If so, special training or instruction with regard to psychopathology and the phenomenology of the syndrome should be given. Often the patient is passed to 'new doctors' seriatim or informal 'tea and sympathy' clinics may be held. Other units insist on facing the failure and discharge the patient. The psychiatrist, of course, has also the consultation function of advising on the management of such patients by others in various circumstances without taking over management. Balint (1957) describes a method by which the psychiatrist can help a group of family doctors to deal more effectively with their difficult and manipulative patients.

## HOSPITAL-COMMUNITY SERVICE INTEGRATION AND PUBLIC EDUCATION

The provision of professional services by staff outwith the leading 'institution', whether hospital or not, and the encouragement of local professions to come into it, are frequent ingredients of successful services. If large or small units, day hospitals, hostels, etc., are provided by different authorities or societies, a co-ordinating or planning body is required. The Governors of the hospital and other services are the official links but important functional links can be forged by increasing the knowledge of and sympathy with mental health services by other 'helping' professions and the public. The organization of conferences and symposia can be initiated for invited groups or societies for discussion of selected topics.

The climate of public opinion in the community must be sympathetic to the mentally ill and subnormal if the finance necessary to provide the services is to be forthcoming and calls for restrictive measures are to be avoided when behaviour problems are brought to the Courts. The members of voluntary organizations helping within the hospitals or services are specially interested members of the public who play an important role in the spread of information. National and international Associations for Mental Health organize conferences, usually for professionals and for public representatives on governing bodies. They prepare publications and obtain publicity. Information services are developed extensively in some parts of the United States where many psychiatric units have their own information or public relations officer. It is not uncommon for the larger facilities to employ teachers and journalists and to hire radio or television time. Films and videotape are used extensively. At a simpler level the unit can increase public knowledge of its activities by encouraging visitors on open days or afternoons. A film can be shown and a member of staff give an orientation talk prior to visits in which the patients may be willing to act as guides. School leavers can be encouraged to attend and information on careers provided. Such contacts aim to familiarize the public with the 'open' practice of the psychiatric services, the simpler problems of treatment and basic aetiological concepts.

## SPECIAL SERVICES

### INTRODUCTION

In the majority of the services, which will be described from the administrative point of view, a group of hospital professionals link with organizations in the community to form a service. The extramural service, professional or voluntary, may offer continuing support, active treatment or advice and guidance towards treatment. Hospital staff may not be aware of the extent to which their patients are dependent on the community branch of the 'service' and may not communicate enough with them to allow co-ordination. In some instances the hospital aspects of the service are subsidiary to the community facilities.

#### SERVICES FOR SUICIDAL ATTEMPTS

Modern resuscitation procedures are medically complex and are best provided in special centres for self poisoning and self injury patients. Psychiatric examination on recovery is required and provision for this must be taken into account in the estimate of staff needs. The large numbers involved make it impossible for a consultant to undertake the assessment of each case. Stengal (1963) has listed the instructions to be left by the psychiatrist for nursing and medical staff on general medical and surgical wards whereby the relevant medical and social informa-

tion and items of psychiatric history can be obtained for his consideration, from the patient or his relatives.

Recent experience in the Edinburgh services suggests that about 20
per cent of such cases may require admission to a psychiatric inpatient
service and a further 30 per cent require psychiatric treatment. Though
some 40 per cent may be assessed as 'not suffering from formal psychiatric disorder', personality disorder is diagnosable in most. Social work
help and support are required by a large proportion. The patient who
makes repeated attempts at suicide, no matter how this is interpreted,
is in special risk of ultimate suicide. Methods of treating individuals with
this pattern of behaviour remain unsatisfactory.

The Telephone Samaritans (a voluntary organization) has branches
in most large towns. It has grown steadily throughout the world since
its commencement in London in 1954. Elementary training courses
giving instruction in social and legal matters and on the characteristics
of the suicidal to selected volunteers, are an essential part of the organization. A 24-hour availability of help is offered through a locally
advertised telephone number. Clients are defined as those 'in despair
or contemplating suicide'. Only some 20 per cent of those who make
the approach describe themselves as suicidal and they are obviously a
self selected sample. Medical and social differences between suicides
and attempted suicides have been delineated by Stengel (1964). Those
who threaten suicide no doubt constitute a third group, but Barraclough
and Shea (1970) have shown that the incidence of suicide after contact
demonstrates the validity of the Samaritans' claim that most of those
who consult them are suicidal. Their clients show a higher suicide rate
than outpatient psychiatric referrals generally. The results of such an
approach by a patient may depend on the availability of skilled help
in a genuinely emergency situation.

FORENSIC SERVICES

Even before psychiatric services were organized on modern lines,
medical men were asked to help the Courts to deal with people who
show signs of mental illness or subnormality. Some Regional Hospital
Boards have appointed consultants with specialist duties in the prison
in their areas. These consultants and the prison medical officers are
available to examine prisoners and advise the Courts with regard to
mental status and provide opinion on responsibility. In Scotland, prison
medical staff have general duties only but the Procurator Fiscal, who
has the duty of ascertaining that the prisoner is fit to stand trial, can ask
for consultant opinion. The assessment can be undertaken in hospital
in suitable cases. The defence have the option of producing evidence
also. In Scandinavian countries the Court takes over the assessment by

having a panel of experts to assess the evidence of the prisoner's mental state. In some American cities psychiatric clinics are established within the Court precincts leading to much closer co-ordination between psychiatric and legal professions.

In Great Britain, the Broadmoor and Mosside Hospitals receive prisoners who, before or after trial, are found to be mentally ill and also dangerous in behaviour and Rampton Hospital takes the subnormal. Carstairs Hospital in Scotland takes both categories. These hospitals are governed by the central authorities directly and separately from Regional Boards and are therefore called 'State' hospitals. Patients who are a danger to the staff or to other patients in other psychiatric hospitals, can be transferred to these hospitals. When serious mental illness is diagnosed following an offence and is liable to produce a recurrence of antisocial behaviour, the Court can issue an order restricting discharge without the necessity of State hospital detention. Such patients are not readily welcomed by hospitals as their presence disrupts the therapeutic atmosphere, and discharge, leave of absence, etc., has to be authorized by the Secretary of State. To reduce the adverse effects of such admissions the establishment of medium security units in each Region has been recommended.

Within the British prison service the psychiatrist's position is still experimental. He is available to the staff to discuss individual and prison community problems and to give guidance on counselling groups undertaken by prison officers. In some prisons individual and group psychotherapy is undertaken. The Grendon Underwood psychiatric prison, where a psychiatrist is Governor, is experimenting with therapeutic community methods. Reception centres for classification of prisoners are incorporated in modern penal systems but the management of the various groups is controversial. The California Department of Correction has made extensive experimentation on psychiatric lines (Jones, 1968). Expectancy scores from previous history have been followed by projects which seek to provide classification of prisoners according to maturity scales. This material may allow some evaluation of different forms of management. In Scandinavian countries various forms of partial imprisonment are in operation.

Juvenile Courts, even when they have family care, supervision, and support as a main objective, are beset with the difficulties arising from paucity of services. In many circumstances children must receive residential care and this is usually provided in schools approved by the Home Office. Psychiatric and psychological advice must be provided in these schools if they are to maintain an atmosphere in which behaviour can be approached scientifically.

The Scottish Social Work Act (1968) replaced court procedures for those under 16 by the establishment of 'Children's Hearings' at which panels of mature citizens, selected volunteers, who have had some training, are advised by social workers. Psychiatrists and psychologists can also attend.

The Portman Clinic in London and the Douglas Inch Forensic Clinic in Glasgow provide outpatient assessment and treatment for adults and children. University departments of forensic psychiatry can stimulate the organization of similar services. Referrals to such services or to hospital outpatient departments may be made by Courts as a condition of probation in lieu of sentence though this arrangement is often regarded as an unsatisfactory relationship between psychiatrist and patient. In many cases the psychiatrist can help by advising the probation officer who is working on the case.

SERVICES FOR THE TREATMENT OF ALCOHOLISM

Comprehensive services for alcoholics are not generally available though most Regional Boards have established units for the treatment of alcoholism. Mental hospitals take acute conditions and long term patients suffering from dementia and, to a lesser extent, will give asylum or support to some who do not suffer from organic complications. The management of alcoholics who move between 'skid row' and prison is attempted only by a few experimental hostel communities such as the Simon Communities, Cyraenians and by the Salvation Army. The need for a three-stage programme is observed by such organizations. A rescue station is required to make contact from which a hostel is offered for a period of stabilization to be followed by admission to more orthodox treatment and rehabilitation.

The provision of 'detoxification centres' is suggested in a survey of the needs of this group by a Home Office Committee (Report of the Home Office Working Party, 1971). Such centres would require some medical supervision and would expose underlying psychiatric and social problems and encourage further experiment and research in management methods.

Units for patients who are selected for treatment on the grounds of good prognosis usually provide group psychotherapy for inpatients and outpatients by staff who have special experience and develop techniques which assist the patient to acknowledge his problems and explore them (Ritson and Hassell, 1970). The poor overall results obtained by services which deal with the skid row types as well as those with better prognosis have been described by Freeman and Hopwood (1968) while McCance and McCance (1969) maintain that if the latter are considered as a group they may do well whether treated in a special unit or in a mental hospital. The special unit however, usually offers more intensive and exploratory types of treatment and more follow up and support and is more closely associated with community services. It is more readily accepted by new patients, and the staff are better placed to influence public opinion. This is usually effected by the establishment of a Regional Alcoholism Council which provides an advice centre for potential patients and relatives. Public education can emphasize early signs and recognized patterns of alcoholism and the availability of help.

Alcoholics Anonymous is a friendship club with its own rituals and 'games' in the social psychiatric sense (Berne, 1964). It gives extensive support to alcoholics in remission and also offers rescue services for those in relapse. The membership is largely self selective and differs considerably from the overall pattern of alcoholism (Edwards *et al.*, 1966). Branches may have their own shared philosophies and aetiological theories which may or may not correspond to those of the local psychiatrists. However, A.A. members are usually welcomed in psychiatric hospitals and special units where they can meet potential or recovering members and establish continuity of contact.

DRUG ADDICTION TREATMENT SERVICES

The Drug Addiction Treatment Act (1968) was passed to combat the epidemic of heroin and cocaine misuse which began in London in 1964. Powers of prescription were removed from the few doctors who had been distributing these drugs freely to addicts and the issue of heroin and cocaine to addicts was limited to named doctors, usually consultant psychiatrists, in designated treatment centres throughout the country. When an addict is initially dealt with in a treatment centre the consultation is notified to the Home Office so that a record can be kept of treatment provided and information readily obtained by any treatment centre subsequently visited. Notification involves no right to prescriptions, though addicts often make this assumption and demand. Treatment is given according to the judgement of the individual treatment centre doctor and can involve attempts to stabilize the patients on an outpatient basis by provision of drugs. The dangers of beginning such treatment in the new referral in the absence of previous inpatient or day patient assessment, have been demonstrated by Gardner and Connell (1970). Inpatient facilities are provided in psychiatric services which can be linked with rehabilitation hostels to remove the need to return to the drug 'scene'. Compulsory treatment for addiction without concomitant mental illness is not undertaken.

Treatment centres must have the necessary social work and supporting services and be associated, usually through a co-ordinating committee, with the other services in the area which are inevitably involved and concerned with the repercussions of addiction. This will include the police, Court and probation services, school and other educational services, youth clubs, parent-teacher associations, etc. Panels of experts are available to offer diagnostic help though they are rarely required. There is a Standing Advisory Committee to monitor the services.

The services of ex-addicts who are willing to work with addicts seeking help have been extensively used in the U.S.A. in such organizations as Synanon, Daytop and Phoenix Houses. They usually incorporate exploratory and abreactive activities and educational programmes.

The Treatment Centres have not taken over responsibility for treatment of addiction to non-narcotic drugs. These are not listed in the schedule of the Act which contains most of the morphine derivatives and tincture of cannabis. They are inevitably involved in such addiction problems however as so many addicts have multiple addictions.

SERVICES FOR CHILDREN AND ADOLESCENTS

The main work of the child psychiatrist is in the outpatient clinic with its emphasis on the family as the problem. New approaches are being explored. Play therapy is usually available. The clinics in Scotland are attached to paediatric departments of hospitals—usually teaching hospitals—in which close contact with paediatricians is maintained and to which general practitioners readily refer cases. Social workers and clinical psychologists are employed by the hospital. In England the major part of the service is based on the Local Authorities. Social workers and the school educational psychologists are joined by Regional Hospital Board consultants and sometimes also by health visitors from maternity and child welfare clinics of the public health department. The professionals have to overcome their multilateral origins and weld themselves into a team, often by excluding their administrators. As most of the sessions are held within social work or educational premises and the social worker or psychologist is responsible to his Director, the psychiatrist cannot assume team leadership until he has demonstrated his sapiential authority. Arrangements have to be worked out whereby the decision regarding family doctors' cases are reported back to him in the usual way. In both systems the School Medical Officer takes a regrettably small part. Links with the school emphasizes the need for remedial education and contacts with teachers, whereas hospital links encourage physical investigations, more liaison with the medical services and the easier establishment of medical staff training schemes.

Residential accommodation is chiefly outwith the hospital system and in residential schools which cater for small or large groups of maladjusted children, whether the school is approved by the Home Office or not. The psychiatrist must be engaged within the approved school system if the therapeutic programmes are going to be comprehensive and contain medical as well as educational and sociological components. The personal contacts which make patient transfers between services more satisfactory can be more readily achieved by such overlapping of staff.

When other services are markedly deficient, adolescents and even younger children find their way into the adult wards of mental hospitals. The Ministry of Health recommends 25 beds per million population for children under 12 years and a similar number for adolescents who require hospitalization. Hospital children's units are usually in a villa nearby, or part of a hospital. They bring in the nurse as a member of the team in the role of foster parent as well as therapist. Similar provision is recommended for adolescents requiring inpatient investigation and treatment. When the unit is run on therapeutic group principles and parents adequately involved, weekends at home are a useful linking arrangement. Day release or partial hospitalization when the adolescent is at school, college or work can be utilized.

## SERVICES FOR AUTISTIC CHILDREN

If current estimates of the number of autistic children are correct— 4.5 per 10,000 population, approximately the same as the number of blind children (Wing, 1971)—their special needs, when they are defined, will demand a considerable share of the resources. Currently, voluntary associations composed mainly of parents and professionals with special interest such as paediatricians, teachers, social workers and psychiatrists, press for extension of educational and training facilities and for money for research and have reported the existing deficiencies through the National Society (1970).

Education authorities can set up special schools or classes or provide an itinerant teacher. The strains in the home produce demand for admission to hospital, children's units, or failing this to subnormality or adult psychiatric hospitals. Undiagnosed adult cases must be present in these hospitals. Systems of relieving parents for holidays or to cope with other special circumstances are required, as in the services for the subnormal.

## PSYCHOGERIATRIC SERVICES

Prolongation of life increases the need for all medical and social services. Those provided for psychogeriatric problems have been organized separately and haphazardly in general medical, public health and social work departments and in association with mental hospitals. As a group, these patients hold a key position in mental health services and they must be identified and located in any overall study. If adequate provision is lacking they will have to be accommodated in wards or hostels earmarked for other groups whose services will be correspondingly diminished with serious effects on the morale of both staff and patients.

Within the mental hospital a decision will have to be made about the site of nursing patients with functional psychosis occurring in the aged. If such patients are mixed with those suffering from organic deterioration an increased turnover will be observed and this may boost morale. This arrangement is unusual, however, as the patients often suffer from recurrent illnesses which have made them known to the staff in the general psychiatric reception areas for some years and/or they may express preference for admission there.

The provision of a psychogeriatric assessment unit in each area (30 beds per half million population) has been recommended. The units suggested should be in general geriatric hospitals and the responsibility that of the geriatrician with the psychiatrist as adviser. An executive representative of the Social Work Department is also required—a social worker or medical adviser who can authorize the transfer of those who can use non-hospital accommodation. Adequate medical, psychiatric and social assessment is usually completed within a month. The majority of patients are usually accepted as the long term responsibility of the geriatrician (Morton, Barker and MacMillan, 1968).

The appropriate place for the care of ambulant dementias is controversial. The mental hospital has nursing expertise, day space, dining rooms and gardens—the other services usually lack at least one of these requirements. The occurrence of wandering or aggression makes such patients the responsibility of the hospital service while those who can be managed in domestic type circumstances should go to hostels. Foster home care is organized in some areas (Jones, Buchan and Beasley, 1970). Day hospital provision is essential for both functional and organic groups. This allows the continued maintenance at home for those for whom it is meaningful and it can also be used to help families to keep relatives in their care while waiting for admission when beds are scarce.

Though the elderly usually come to psychiatric services when their disorder is obvious, it has been shown that screening of the vulnerable part of the population can be effectively undertaken by health visitors working with general practitioners (Williamson, Lowther and Gray, 1966). Preventive clinics organized by the public health department can locate both functional and physical disorders (Anderson and Cowan, 1955). The occurrence of acute confusional states from toxic or nutritional diseases can be reduced by adequate general medical and social services. Housing authorities should provide sheltered housing, i.e. flatlets with some supervision and communal facilities for eating and conversation, to meet the needs of the more capable elderly who object to giving up their belongings and live in an institution, hostel or hotel. Home helps and district nursing services are provided as in a private domicile. Maintenance of the elderly person in his own neighbourhood or home, for as long as possible, is an accepted precept and recognizing the importance of this, the Severalls Hospital service in Essex organized an experimental emergency service in which hospital staff cared for elderly confused sick people in their homes for a few days to tide over a crisis and avoid removal (Barton and Whitehead, 1968).

Community services for the aftercare or precare of the psychogeriatric patient are shared with those with physical illnesses, supplemented possibly by social workers or nurses with special experience. The home help, chiropodist, meals-on-wheels service, voluntary visitors and the club organizer can contribute materially to the welfare of both functional and organic cases. The lunch club and work centre can be the equivalent of the day hospital care.

Reviewing the services for the elderly with mental disorder, a Scottish Committee (1970) recommended the maintenance of local registers of those at risk from information to be supplied by general practitioners, probably with the assistance of health visitors. The arrangements for support which can be made by general practitioners, health visitors, district nurses and social workers should suffice for most patients. Voluntary workers and street wardens should be available to supplement the professional services. Special hostels for the mentally infirm were recommended for 5 per 1000 of the population of 65 years and over, to which admission would be arranged after assessment.

To enable such services to be co-ordinated and extended, local professional and voluntary organizations must establish regular administrative conferences. There must also be an adequate information service for the family doctors, nurses and social workers and patients' relatives who will refer new patients to the services. This should be the duty of an area co-ordinating committee.


SERVICES FOR THE SUBNORMAL

About 70 per cent of the mentally subnormal in the British Isles live with their parents and relatives. The following items must be incorporated in comprehensive schemes: early identification, genetic guidance, complete clinical assessment by various experts, prompt treatment of biochemical conditions where indicated, parent guidance and support, training and education, occupation, periodic reassessment, and placement in suitable or special residential care. Even after Area Boards are established, a co-ordinating committee in each area seems likely to be needed to unite hospital plans with those of the local authority social work and educational departments, and with voluntary services.

Early identification and genetic advice are largely medical matters and can be provided by a clinic with a panel of experts including the geneticist, paediatrician, paediatric neurologist, psychologist and psychiatrist. The ophthalmologist, endocrinologist, general and orthopaedic surgeons, otorhinologist, psychologist, speech therapist and physiotherapist may be required for diagnostic and prognostic assessments and treatment. The family doctor has a guiding and supporting role to play with the family and will wish social work help at an early stage when a decision may have to be made regarding home or hospital care.

*Family Care*

Given assurance of support many families wish to bring up the child at home in spite of the physical, social and financial burdens which result. It has been estimated that about one-third of the severely subnormal, who usually have physical concomitant conditions, are living at home (Tizard, 1964). Parents find benefit from running their own voluntary association for mutual support. Those whose children have severe physical handicaps require special day centres for their care during week-days as well as accommodation for the child for holidays and periods of illness or additional stress in the family.

Occupational centres for children up to 16 years are provided by the educational service. Though it may contain elements of formal education, the day's activities are usually in the form of games, percussion music, eurythmics and speech training in groups, and the social training activities recommended by Gunsberg (1968). Special transport must be supplied. Occupation centres for the adult subnormal under the Social Work Department are an essential provision in each locality. For the reasonably stable older subnormal, hostels should be provided and linked with industrial centres and sheltered employment. Some defectives in residential jobs or at home can be in part supervised by social club attendance.

*Residential Care*

The facilities for assistance with domiciliary care of the subnormal are logically organized and valuable, though varying in availability according to local initiative. In contrast, the services for those who require residential care have been based on outmoded concepts and are also deficient in availability. Improved care resulting from the removal of the mentally defective from among the mentally ill was demonstrated by the creation of some notable institutions for defectives. This led to the 1913 Mental Deficiency Act making local authorities responsible for providing institutional care for their subnormals. The result was the creation of many large hospitals each serving populations of half to one million population. The medical and nursing patterns were taken from the parent mental hospitals. Those responsible for subnormals now are therefore faced with a system of care based on large institutions from which most of the higher grade well-behaved patients have been discharged. Staffing problems are widespread. Where the subnormal can be trained and helped in small groups on family care principles, and where industrial, social and physical rehabilitation provisions are adequate, the hospital may be able to maintain its reputation, but the hospital pattern is generally deplored and its deficiencies have been exposed in the review of eight such hospitals by Morris (1969).

Kushlick (1967, 1969) has outlined the clinical problems and needs for residential care faced by a Regional Hospital Board serving some three million people. Paediatric services and child care methods and sociological and psychological consultations regarding training, must obviously be introduced. Hospital accommodation for children is required to provide nursing for those with physical disablement and for the care and habit training of those whose incontinence, hyperactivity or generally prolonged infancy is beyond parental endurance. There are a large number of subnormals, however, whose requirements are, to borrow Kushlick's phrase, 'residential care only'. Depending on leadership, they might be accommodated in the equivalent of boarding schools or, alternatively, in hostels to which educational, training and occupational facilities are attached. These concepts are analogous to current British arrangements where the training of subnormal children living at home is undertaken by the education authority and that of the adolescent and adult by the Social Work Department.

The psychiatric contribution to the continued management of the groups so far mentioned is obviously minimal. At the same time the significance of a subnormal component in patients seen by child or adult psychiatrists in regard to antisocial behaviour, neurosis or psychosis, its relationship to physical factors and its significance regarding treatment, etc., makes experience in subnormality an important component of psychiatric training. Psychiatric supervision of the management of the behaviour disordered, antisocial or disturbed patient in the subnormality facility is obviously needed. It often happens that the psychiatrist is the only individual in the institution with adequate training and his direction is required for its general administration. Otherwise the medical care of the subnormal can be undertaken by general practitioners.

The ideal organization of residential accommodation for the subnormal is more likely to be achieved in a country with underdeveloped services than in Europe or America with their large institutions catering for a large number of severely subnormal people and the small number of high grade who have little in common with them. The well equipped and staffed Danish service contains, perhaps, the best examples of the larger composite institution, in which individual needs receive attention. Small units, some containing family type age and sex groupings, is one of the objectives in this situation, and hostels for some working groups within the larger institutions are readily organized. It would be possible for one of the local authorities in Great Britain to establish a model organization within the social work and education framework by establishing residential 'schools' and hostels for appropriate groups, but it seems currently unlikely that this will be regarded as a priority. Alternatively, an Area Board with smaller overall population problems than the present Regional Hospital Boards may find it possible to develop a service on similar lines, though under this authority the nursing structure which might otherwise be replaced by child care and educational service personnel, would probably be retained.

## Co-ordination of Services

Social work support and guidance is required for the families of the subnormal. In current social work concepts this would be available for those living at home through the general family casework service, with advice from a social worker with special experience within the same department. This consultant in social work could also advise hospital personnel, including community nurses whose help can be important in resettling patients who are leaving hospital. Social Work Departments which already have hostels, clubs, workshops and advice services will have the appropriate staff to assist the hospital with rehabilitation through liaison conferences. The hospital psychiatrist, obviously, should be the consultant to the local authority services.

### SERVICES FOR SCHIZOPHRENICS

The acute attack of schizophrenia will require full psychiatric services. Rehabilitation services (see Ch. XVII, Vol. II) must include the many social and occupational services required. Special resettlement units and day treatment facilities are useful (Bennett, Folkard and Nicholson, 1661). Follow-up studies suggest that continued supervision, day hospital support and the maintenance of drug regimes are important and that their absence results in increased likelihood of unemployment and re-admission to hospital (Renton et al., 1963). The commencement of community nursing services and the advent of depot phenothiazine administration, increases the possibility of successful follow-up systems. The supervisory services are somewhat analogous to those formerly provided for patients suffering from tuberculosis.

E

In geographically outlined areas without gross transport problems, follow-up services can be maintained without too much difficulty. A monitoring organization will be required to indicate the need to pay special attention to patients who fail to keep their contacts. A system of recall based on a computer, indicate that the patient is expected at the clinic or should be visited. This must be linked with a reliable reminder system and available staff who are free to make visits. If contact fails to occur, signals are repeated until a final decision is made on future policy. The community nurse is specially suitable in such a service as he or she is likely to have a good clinical experience and knowledge of symptomatology and drug effects. Collaborating with the general practitioner, she can give an injection at the patient's home or works' surgery or check the medicine bottle. An intramuscular drug clinic can extend into the evening to allow attendance outwith working hours. The specially relevant pathological family patterns and incidents can be observed and discussed with other professionals. A medical co-ordinator is required and the service must be linked with social work advice, access to hostels, supporting clubs, occupational and job hunting services as well as to the inpatient facilities.

EMERGENCY SERVICES

The emergency patient may present clinically with aggressive, suicidal, panic, hysterical or bizarre behaviour, or other manifestation of confusion or loss of control. Social emergencies may necessitate the intervention of the psychiatric team when the patient, surviving in the community with support, is suddenly bereft by death of his relative or landlady, or loss of the degree of tolerance required, perhaps following the occurrence of other stresses in the household. Administrative emergencies occur when the patient is recognized in a casualty department, the police station or other situations where there is 'other work' to be done or where he is found to occupy a bed required by another type of acutely ill patient. The diagnosis of 'emergency' in these situations may be technically misleading and the situation may require consultation only, rather than a psychiatrist's visit. Surveys of emergency and urgent referrals to hospital (Brothwood, 1965; Glasscote et al., 1966) reveal a high proportion of relapses in previously known patients and unexpected demands from those currently attending for treatment.

The maintenance of a good follow-up service can obviously reduce the number of emergencies in the schizophrenic and access to outpatient advice can be similarly effective for the depressive. The proposed detoxification centres might re-route some of the alcoholics but some medical screening and referral mechanism must be incorporated. In some areas the wandering geriatric is taken to the social work service emergency accommodation but the geriatric-psychiatric specialist assessment unit is more appropriate.

The emergency services available include the consultant's domiciliary visit, an urgent outpatient consultation, or similar services by non-medical members of the psychiatric team. Some situations may be dealt with on a consultation basis by advising another service. Admission to day hospital may cover the needs. The acceptance of responsibility by the psychiatric service may be enough to reduce the general tension. Where links with general practice are weak, 'walk-in' services may be indicated. If not officially provided by the psychiatric services they may be represented in the area by Telephone Samaritans, the police or other individuals who are known to be helpful and influencial. The Social Work Departments plan to encourage this type of service in their overlapping field.

An observation or diagnostic ward for short term admission can be of great value for the difficult diagnostic situation or the awkward socio-path who can create embarrassment for several medical and social services in one episode. The destructive effects of such individuals on the work of an admission/treatment unit has been described by Wood-side (1968). On the other hand the availability of an experienced psychiatrist with or without a social worker to attend at the site of the emergency can reduce the demand for admission.

The concepts of crisis intervention suggest that such situations produce states of disorganization and 'fluidity' in individuals and families in which the potential for change is greatly enhanced (Caplan, 1964; Brandon, 1970). The solution adopted may determine subsequent attitudes to a very important degree. As so many acute situations involve social aspects of the patient's life to which he is reacting or manipu-lating it is reasonable to assume that a social worker with psychiatric experience would be involved in emergency duties. This is not un-common practice in the U.S.A. where social workers are more numer-ous and may take more responsibility. The important task of assisting the family to adjust to the emergency situation tends to be omitted when the situation demands removal to hospital.

Emergency Services often consist of whatever service is available, or whoever is available, whereas competence and experience and a planned organization are of special importance in this field.

## REFERENCES

ANDERSON, W. F. & COWAN, W. R. (1955)    A consultative health centre for older people. *Lancet*, **ii,** 239.

BALINT, H. (1957)    *The Doctor, The Patient and his Illness.* London: Pitman.

BARRACLOUGH, B. M. & SHEA, M. (1970)    Suicide and Samaritan clients. *Lancet*, **ii,** 868.

BARTON, R. & WHITEHEAD, T. A. (1968)   A psychogeriatric domiciliary emergency service. *British Journal of Psychiatry*, **114,** 107.

BENNETT, D. H., FOLKARD, S. & NICHOLSON, A. (1961)   Resettlement unit in a mental hospital. *Lancet*, **ii,** 539.

BERNE, E. (1964)   *Games People Play*. New York: Grove Press.

BRANDON, S. (1970)   Crisis theory and the principles of therapeutic intervention. *British Journal of Psychiatry*, **117,** 627.

BROTHWOOD, J. (1965)   The work of a psychiatric emergency clinic. *British Journal of Psychiatry*, **111,** 631.

CAPLAN, G. (1964)   *Principles of Preventive Psychiatry*. London: Tavistock Press.

CARSE, J., PAULIN, N. E. & WATT, A. A. (1958)   A district mental health service—the Worthing experiment. *Lancet*, **i,** 39.

DOWNHAM, T. (1967)   The Burnley psychiatric service. In *New Aspects of the Mental Health Services*, Ch. 36. Edited by H. Freeman and J. Farmdale. London: Pergamon.

EDWARDS, G., HENSMAN, C., HAWKER, A. & WILLIAMSON, V. (1966)   Who goes to alcoholics anonymous? *Lancet*, **ii,** 382.

FREEMAN, T. & HOPWOOD, S. E. (1968)   Characteristics and response to treatment in an unselected group of alcoholics. *Scottish Medical Journal*, **13,** 237.

GARDNER, R. & CONNELL, P. H. (1970)   One year's experience in a drug dependence clinic. *Lancet*, **ii,** 455.

GLASSCOTE, R. M., CUMMING, E., HAMMERSKY, D. W., AZARM, L. D. & SMITH, L. H. (1966)   *The Psychiatric Emergency*. Washington: A.P.A.

GRAD, J. & SAINSBURY, P. (1968)   The effects that patients have on their families in a community care and a control psychiatric service. *British Journal of Psychiatry*, **114,** 265.

GUNSBERG, H. C. (1968)   Social competence and mental handicap. London: Baillière, Tindall & Cassell.

HILL, D. (1969)   *Psychiatry in Medicine*. London: Nuffield Provincial Hospitals Trust.

HOENIG, J. & HAMILTON, N. W. (1969)   *The Desegregation of the Mentally Ill.* London: Routledge & Kegan Paul.

JONES, A. P., BUCHAN, A. R. & BEASLEY, J. (1970)   Ten years boarding out in Somerset. *Lancet*, **ii,** 712.

JONES, M. (1968)   Social psychiatry in prisons. In *Social Psychiatry in Practice*. London: Penguin Books.

KESSEL, N. & HASSALL, C. (1971)   Evaluation of the functioning of the Plymouth Nuffield Centre. *British Journal of Psychiatry*, **118,** 305.

KUSHLICK, A. (1967)   Comprehensive service for the mentally subnormal. In *New Aspects of the Mental Health Service*. Edited by H. Freeman & J. Farndale, Ch. 38. London: Pergamon.

KUSHLICK, A. (1969)   Care of the mentally subnormal. *Lancet*, **ii,** 1196.

MCCANCE, C. & MCCANCE, P. F. (1969)   Alcoholism in N.E. Scotland—its treatment and outcome. *British Journal of Psychiatry*, **115,** 189.

MCKEOWN, T. (1965)   *Medicine in Modern Society*. London: Allen & Unwin.

MAY, A. R., SHELDON, A. P. & MacKEITH, S. A. (1962)   The future of district psychiatry. *Lancet*, **ii,** 1319.

MINISTRY OF HEALTH STATISTICAL REPORT, Series No. 7 (1969)   *A Pilot Study of Patients Attending Day Hospitals*. London: H.M.S.O.

MORRIS, P. (1969)   *Put Away—A Sociological Study of Institutions for the Mentally Retarded*. London: Routledge & Kegan Paul.

MORTON, E. V. B., BARKER, M. E. & MacMILLAN, D. (1968)   The joint assessment and early treatment unit in psychiatric care. *Gerontologia clinica*, **10,** 65.

OLDHAM, A. J. (1969)   Community psychiatry in London. *British Journal of Psychiatry*, **115,** 465.

RAPOPORT, R. N. (1960)   *Community as Doctor*. London: Tavistock Press.

RENTON, C. A., AFFLECK, J. W., CARSTAIRS, G. M. & FORREST, A. D. (1963)   A follow up of schizophrenic patients in Edinburgh. *Acta psychiatrica et neurologica scandinavica*, **39,** 548.

REPORT ON FACILITIES FOR AUTISTIC CHILDREN (1970)   London: National Society for Autistic Children.

REPORT OF SUB-COMMITTEE OF THE SCOTTISH HEALTH SERVICES ADVISORY COUNCIL (1970)   *Services for the Elderly with Mental Disorder*. Edinburgh: H.M.S.O.

REPORT OF THE HOME OFFICE WORKING PARTY (1971)   *Habitual Drunken Offenders*. London: H.M.S.O.

RITSON, E. B. & HASSALL, C. (1970)   *Management of Alcoholism*. Edinburgh: Livingstone.

STENGEL, E. (1963)   Attempted suicide: its management in the general hospital. *Lancet*, **i,** 233.

STENGEL, E. (1964)   *Suicide and Attempted Suicide*. London: Tavistock Press.

SUTHERLAND, J. D. (1968)   The consultant psychotherapist in the National Health Centre. *British Journal of Psychiatry*, **114,** 509.

TIZARD, J. (1964)   *Community Services for the Mentally Handicapped*. Oxford: Oxford University Press.

TOOTH, G. C. & BROOKE, E. B. (1961)   Trends in the mental hospital population and their effects on future planning. *Lancet*, **i,** 710.

WING, J. (1971)   Social psychiatry. *British Journal of Hospital Medicine*, **5,** 53.

WILLIAMSON, J., LOWTHER, C. P. & GRAY, S. (1966)   The use of health visitors in preventive geriatrics. *Gerontologia clinica*, **8,** 369.

WOODSIDE, M. (1968)   Are observation wards obsolete? *British Journal of Psychiatry*, **114,** 1013.

Chapter VI

# COMMUNITY AND PREVENTIVE SERVICES AND THE PSYCHIATRIST IN INDUSTRY

## J. W. Affleck and J. D. Sutherland

### COMMUNITY SERVICES

#### INTRODUCTION

In the description of services in Chapters IV and V it has been assumed that hospital and community services are essentially inseparable. The objective and possibility of providing effective treatment with a minimum of hospitalization results in an increasing number of patients being home based rather than hospital based. In these circumstances, it is desirable to examine the services available in the neighbourhood.

Where community services develop as an extension of hospital services they tend to deal with individuals rather than families. Community based services which do not originate as follow-up from hospital often approach the problems on a family basis on the lines of child psychiatric services. In the U.S.A., where the State hospital system still provides the majority of the psychiatric beds, psychiatric units in general hospitals and partial hospitalization services are always regarded as 'community services' and are increasingly brought together by the extension of the Community Mental Health Center policy. In Britain, the need to form one unified system to replace the hospital/local authority/general practitioner tripartite arrangement is recognized in the plans for Area Health Boards though social work services will be administered separately. The social worker is required both within and outwith the hospital but there are many precedents for joint appointments or secondment of social workers by local authorities to work with hospital staff. In Holland, the Amsterdam Service built up by Querido is administered in the Public Health Department (Querido, 1968). It is based on the availability of psychiatrists and nurse-social workers to respond to major and minor emergencies in the patient's home over the 24 hours with follow-up, supportive psychotherapy and social work.

MEDICALLY-BASED SERVICES

The general medical practitioner service is a cornerstone of the British system. The general practitioner is available to all and deals with the bulk of the psychiatric illness in the community. The possibility of dealing constructively with the problems arising from all the personality disorders and neurosis present, however, is beyond the scope of the family doctor even with the support of psychiatrists in Balint type groups. From an operational study using the Camberwell register, Wing and Wing (1970) conclude that to provide an individual psychotherapy service for adult patients only and limited to those under 45 years on current referral rates from general practice, an additional 450 to 500 consultant psychotherapists would be required in England and Wales. The extent to which the general practitioner makes psychiatric diagnoses and subsequently refers patients to specialists depends on his age, training and interests. The effect of the doctor's personality on his style of practice has been outlined by Walton (1968). In a rationalized system of group practice in which one general practitioner in five had special knowledge of psychiatry a more effective service might be provided.

The general practitioner can have specialist consultant help in diagnosis and for any appropriate treatment in the patient's home. The relative absence of specialist and supportive services must be accepted in rural life where the family doctor is usually aided only by a district nurse, midwife and health visitor (possibly one person) and social workers or psychiatrists visiting the county town. In urban areas, however, groups of practitioners working in health centres can expect to see an increase in services from social workers seconded from the Local Authority departments as well as visits from hospital specialists, though the best use of such visits has still to be assessed. In the larger towns and cities psychiatric day units (Chapter V) may increase in number.

The need for social workers in the service of psychiatric patients and their families has never been met on a large scale. The Mental Health Act duties of care and aftercare by Local Authorities were met in England in the 1960s by the creation of an establishment of Mental Welfare Officers in the Public Health Departments. Many recruits to these appointments came from the ranks of psychiatrically trained nurses who subsequently obtained special training courses in social work. This background provided expertise in giving support for the ex-patient and advancing treatment arrangements for new or old contacts. Following the passing of the Social Work Acts and the scarcity of social workers to man the more extensive service, many of the Mental Welfare Officers can obtain promotion or transfer to general as opposed to specialist social work. Some of the gaps in the provision of community care can be filled by a community nursing service.

Some progressive Local Authorities built up extensive mental health services within their Public Health Departments between 1948 and 1970. Describing the services in Newham (London), now taken over by the Director of Social Work, Kahn (1967) points out the initial need to define the area demographically and to describe the social patterns and problems in it. In addition to general services supporting the family when one of its members is admitted to hospital and subsequently providing aftercare, the child guidance service was organized and a range of residential services was recommended—for disturbed children, for the ex-hospital adult, for the elderly who require care but not hospitalization and for the child and adult subnormal. The consultative service provides help with mental health problems becoming apparent in non-psychiatric services. This is used by health visitors, school medical officers and school welfare officers, the probation service, housing officials and the Department of Employment, marriage guidance and other voluntary organizations. There is also a 'walk-in' advice service for adolescents and a co-ordinating committee for workers dealing with problem families. These services involve case work or counselling relationships and investigation of the problems of family functioning, occupational suitability and social life problems. Diagnoses are in terms of competence, role limitations and capacities, and family interactions.

Such arrangements were developed on the system of specialized services under medical leadership in which specialist social workers played a major part. Adequate psychiatric backing was regarded as essential in this setting. Under the Social Work Act, however, such activities have been taken over by the departments of social work which provide social work professional leadership and new patterns of administration.

SOCIAL WORK SERVICES

The social work services are in process of reorganization in Great Britain during the 1970s. This follows the recommendations of the committees which studied local authority and allied personal services—the Kilbrandon report for Scotland (1964) followed by a 'White Paper' on Social Work in the Community (1966) and the Seebohm Report (1968) for England and Wales. The subsequent Social Work Acts instructed the Local Authorities to set up Social Work Departments with the duty of discovering individual, family and community needs and organizing appropriate social work services. The previous services for children, the welfare of the homeless, the aged and handicapped persons including the mentally ill and subnormal, are therefore combined under a Director of Social Work. The new departments have responsibilities beyond those which they replace and have the objective of providing services according to social need in parallel to the National Health Service provision for medical need. The main responsibilities of the Departments are listed in Table 1.

TABLE I

*Responsibilities of the Social Work Departments*

| For children | Adoption procedures (optional)<br>Reception of homeless<br>Homes and foster homes<br>School welfare service<br>Remand homes<br>Residential (Approved) schools |
|---|---|
| General services | Family case work<br>Reception of homeless<br>Communication, travelling and recreational facilities for the disabled (Chronically Sick and Disabled Persons Act 1970)<br>Industrial centres<br>Sheltered Workshops<br>Blind welfare<br>Home help services |
| For the aged | Social worker advice and support<br>Home help services<br>Hostels for those requiring care and attention |
| Mental health services | Occupation Centres for subnormals over 16<br>Hostels<br>Social worker advice and support ('care and aftercare')<br>Social worker advice and support for families<br>Social centres (club activities)<br>Responsibility for certain steps in connection with compulsory admission or guardianship |
| Also probation, parole and prison aftercare in Scotland (only) | |

A main objective of social work departments is the creation of an adequate service for families, but the needs of those deprived of family support, especially children and the aged, must also receive special concern. Specialist advice by social workers, e.g. on mental health problems will be provided within the organization. The Director can request the advice of a psychiatrist in connection with the management of the difficult individual or in planning services for different groups. Hostel accommodation must be provided for people requiring care and attention as a result of old age or inability to look after themselves, including those who require care on account of mental illness or subnormality, but who do not need hospital admission. Sheltered employment *must* be provided for the blind and can be provided for other handicapped people including those with mental illness and subnormality who are unable to compete in industry. The service should be contacted and used either on social worker or medical advice or by self referral, when a need is recognized. When long term family needs can be met an element of prevention may be inferred. Meeting short term financial needs may be justified in some instances, for example, to prevent a family being split up by eviction.

The Social Work Departments have also responsibility for stimulating a sense of community in their various neighbourhoods by supporting and encouraging local groups and leaders to explore their 'village' needs.


## PREVENTIVE SERVICES

Preventive measures are often classified as primary—the prevention of the occurrence of new cases of a disease, secondary—the reduction of the effect of illness by early treatment, and tertiary—the reduction of disability and dependency in the established case. The services described in this and the preceding chapters incorporate elements of secondary and tertiary prevention. In a paper entitled 'Preventive psychiatry—is there such a thing?' Carstairs (1958) points out that primary prevention in psychiatry has stemmed from measures which are essentially medical. These have reduced parasyphilitic psychosis, dementia following pellagra, cretinism and phenylketonuric amentias, etc., while improved obstetrical and prenatal care minimizes brain injury and the effects of anoxia. Recent knowledge of chromosomal anomalies and increasing effectiveness in contraception increases primary preventive possibilities. Epidemiological methods include recognition of the natural history of a disease, the comparison of inception rates and point prevalence of subgroups and thus the recognition of vulnerable groups. Brooke (1968) illustrates the value of this approach by the recognition of the importance of psychiatric conditions in students—a subject discussed from the clinical and preventive angle by Ryle (1969).

The theory of the significance of crises in personality development and later adjustment (Lindemann, 1944; Caplan, 1964), has had considerable impact in the planning of mental health services in the United States. Crises provoke tension, and prolonged crisis seems likely to alter the homeostatic mechanisms associated with emotional experiences. Methods by which crisis can be dealt with can result in increasing personal confidence or, alternatively, confusion and maladjustment.

The individual or the family in crisis can be greatly influenced by others. Solutions based on fantasy or pathological mechanisms can be followed by persistent disability. Bereavement is a common crisis to be followed by mental illness in the absence of the normal mourning process, illustrated by Parkes's demonstration of the six times greater than expected admission rate in those recently bereaved of a spouse (Parkes, 1964). A series of major or minor critical points of life can be defined in advance but may occur by chance. Crisis theory suggests preventive intervention and anticipatory guidance. This can be expressed, for example, in the employment of social worker help for the recently widowed.

Bowlby's observations on the natural history of psychopathic delinquency and the development of the amoral personality, unable to relate to others, has led to extensive alteration in the practice of child care and recognition of the need to provide support for families from which the mother has been temporarily or permanently lost (Bowlby, 1951). The need to reduce the size of public homes (taking children deprived of normal home life) has been accepted, and arrangements for the continued contact of mother and child when one or other is in hospital have become official policy in Britain.

SOCIAL ADMINISTRATION AS A PREVENTIVE WEAPON

Such concepts from psychiatric observations and theory have been extensively adopted and adapted by other professions dealing with social problems from whom the citizen may seek help. The non-medical professions interested in the interaction of the individual and his environment are increasing their influence on society. Psychiatry has to redefine its role in relation to social administration as it moves from the era in which it cared for the community's rejects only. The psychiatrist will continue to see the most sick members of society—those who are failing to survive in the community—and will have to advise on and demonstrate methods of care for them. The psychiatrist will thus always be in a consultant role to those dealing with similar though relatively less severe problems. He will expect to plan with other professionals and with political leaders, the palliative, rehabilitation and preventive services which will reduce the numbers of social failures, as well as follow his research into the effects of treatment. At the same time he will be expected to examine the results of experiments in other fields and explore the constantly changing social scene.

Though leadership in social policy-making does not normally fall on the psychiatrist, many agencies involved directly or indirectly will look to psychiatry for guidance. The more neurosis and personality disorder is recognized as an unacceptable burden, the more people will seek help. The call for help is made to the family doctor, the clergy, the schoolteacher, the 'Samaritan' and the 'non-psychiatric' social worker. The first person to be asked to help may depend simply on the nature of the symptom, medical or social. The importance of the inter-connections between the various helping agencies or helping professions is thus obvious and a consultation system is indicated. This is the more necessary in view of the tendency towards rivalry and discord which may occur between the various agencies (professional or voluntary) which may have grown out of different philosophies and perhaps from objectives of a previous social structure. The production of a socio-therapeutic network involves knowledge of the aims and functions of each agency's work and philosophy as well as the limitations of indi-vidual resources. There must be acceptance of the help of the individual who has the appropriate knowledge and skills without the impulse merely to pass the buck. This happy situation can arise with under-standing but must be coupled with resources. The acquisition of the necessary funds and staff should be a common interest.

### Area Council

A potential network of social and medical services, with preventive possibilities in the secondary or tertiary sense, is available in the western societies. It can only be integrated by planned effort aimed at linking good rehabilitation services with enlightened referral and consulting arrangements. The psychiatric service may be expected to provide the leadership. The various organizations must have the unity provided by an Area Mental Health Council. This should be a broadly based organization which sponsors information for the public and in-service training for the staff of all the member organizations. The aim is to provide a network composed of people who can provide a thera-peutic relationship, defined by Sutherland (1960) as available, constant, understanding and tolerant of the acting out of repressed personal relationship need systems. Individuals in close transactional relation-ships, e.g. those with marital problems and interfamily problems may present opportunities for change by relief from certain internal sources of tension. Specialized training must therefore be provided for medical and social workers who are going to come into contact with these groups.

### Area Development

The physical association of social and medico-social workers with experience of all services (family and child care, probation, geriatric, etc.) in the same building as Local Authority housing officials and voluntary agencies, such as Citizens' Advice Bureau, Adoption Society,

Marriage Guidance Council, etc., to form a health, welfare and advice centre has been shown to be effective (Short, 1969), and can be the nucleus of a social or mental health council. Psychiatric services can fit in reasonably with such an organization (Ebie *et al.*, 1970), and can offer supportive collaboration and teaching in group methods as well as orthodox services.

The presence of such a group can act as a catalyst by giving opportunity and an organizational base for the discussion of locality problems. New relationships, with and among local leaders, are formed and the opportunity can be provided for a wider range of participants in the exploration of the needs of vulnerable groups. The extended network of communication may produce a demand for community planning beyond the concepts previously held by those holding official positions. The encouragement of local initiative towards recreational and cultural efforts requires expertise in the knowledge of getting things done administratively and in mobilizing all types of resources. This can be supplied by the professional who is able to attract financial grants otherwise unavailable. Help in identification of special needs and in achieving their rectification through non-professional leaders produces the recognition that a community exists. This can be the beginning of local involvement in area planning and of basic social change in under-developed localities.

## THE PSYCHIATRIST IN INDUSTRY

The psychiatrist in industry must work in close collaboration with the industrial psychologist as well as with management and the trades unions. In day-to-day work he will find himself a member of a group or conference discussing conditions and situations with the business administrator, foreman, personnel manager, industrial psychologist and work's doctor. Tredgold (1954a) has reviewed the function of the psychiatrist's role in industry and considers that four categories of work should be undertaken: (1) treatment, (2) selection and induction procedures, (3) education and (4) research.

### TREATMENT

In the setting where access to the work situation is readily available, it is possible to understand the patient's strains and difficulties much more readily than when the interview and investigation take place in a hospital setting. The work's doctor may ask the psychiatrist to see individuals who have recurrent psychosomatic illness, excess sick leave, 'fatigue' problems, those who react violently to difficult situations or become ill when criticized by departmental heads or on pressure of work. It may be possible to arrange changes in the worker's environment with immediate effect. The patient with the gross psychological disorder is not the main concern of the psychiatrist in industry and should be under treatment elsewhere. The psychiatrist will meet a large number of relatively minor illnesses in industrial settings—states of tension, anxiety, psychosomatic disorders, the effects of the obsessional character, etc. He will be able to help by defining the problems, serving as a 'neutral ear' and influencing the situation towards some change in the environment. Such treatment might be considered preventive at the simple level of allowing tensions to subside.

SELECTION AND PROMOTION

The psychiatrist can usefully take a place on selection boards or subcommittees which appraise people seeking employment or under consideration for promotion. Curran (1952) maintains that psychiatrists should keep to negative selection by stating that a certain individual is likely or unlikely to be able to withstand certain strains. Difficulties can arise when, as part of the selection procedure, a psychiatric interview is undertaken and the individual imparts information about himself which is likely to affect his chances of obtaining the position he seeks, but of which the remainder of the selection board would not be aware. No formal guidance can be offered to cover all cases, but industrial colleagues must accept the psychiatrist's ethical position even if only to preserve the procedure. The psychiatrist, of course, may be of help to the applicant in the re-examination of his own resources.

Psychiatrists may be asked to take part in selection board procedures involving groups. These are extensively used in the British Army Officer selection techniques (Vernon and Parry, 1949), in the Civil Service and by many firms for the selection of executives or in assessing applicants for promotion. Leadership qualities are defined and sought by observing the individual in his behaviour with others in various situations.

SOCIAL AND PSYCHOLOGICAL STUDIES

Industrial psychological research may be equated with studies of efficiency and hence regarded as of benefit to management as opposed to employees. No doubt there is some basis in this assumption because the management would be unlikely to agree to employ industrial psychologists unless they expected to obtain some recompense. However, the fact that work has importance as a function of society is becoming increasingly recognized. Sickness and absentee rates vary with different parts of the country and with age groups. Lloyd Davies (1954) demonstrated that more than 75 per cent of adolescents select their jobs for social reasons. Few had a definite desire to undertake a particular job. Reasons given for job acceptance included having friends or relatives at work, that the firm had a good reputation, good staff facilities, etc. Opportunities for promotion, security of employment or being near home were less frequently presented.

The work of Elton Mayo (Mayo, 1933) included the famous Hawthorne experiments in the Los Angeles factory where groups of girls assembling telephone relays received special study. Variations in the hours of work, the physical surroundings, the lighting, the heating, etc., were made with ever increasing output and reduction of absenteeism. The increase in output continued even when all the improvements were reversed and the original conditions reinstated. It was concluded that by making the girls feel their importance as a special group, morale and consequently efficiency, greatly increased.

*Stress*

The sources of stress arising from the individual's role in an organization can be complex and numerous. Kahn and Quinn (1970) offer a framework for analysis of role stress. They emphasize ambiguities and conflicts which arise from the expectations of the person holding the position or of those with whom he works. New posts, changing organizations and personal assistantships cause special difficulties and demand special capacities, especially if feedback regarding effectiveness is lacking. Stress will arise as the result of failure to match expectation with results, whether arising from the mistaken anticipations of others, the failure of resource provision, or inadequacies in the personality of the operative or work organization. The individual's evaluation of his own work and his personal standards will determine his personal suffering.

Stress occurring in industry may be a reflection of an unsatisfactory marital or domestic situation arising from working conditions or career factors. Excessive overtime, frequent changes of house to fit in with job changes and unexpected demands on the wife's personal resources may lead either party to seek counselling or psychiatric advice. The special problems of managers and their wives have been investigated by Pahl and Pahl (1971).

The concept of primary prevention might be invoked in regard to the work of selection committees where they are effective in preventing the appointment of an individual who will create stress in himself and others when attempting to play certain roles. Early rectification of stress indicated by interpersonal friction, marked inefficiency, excess absenteeism, etc., can be regarded as secondary prevention. Such signs and other 'job disruption indices' (Ross, Fowles and Winstone, 1965) can be spotted by non-professional observers. Providing the 'lame' individual with a restricted role is a frequently used mechanism for tertiary prevention.

Tension within and between various working and organizational groups is a potent source of stress requiring continual investigation. Its expression as aggressive behaviour has been surveyed by Tredgold (1954b). Stress can often be attributed to situations in which people are not treated as mature individuals. The offer of some responsibility can increase personal development. Low morale resulting in industrial schisms appears to follow situations in which groups are organized in ways in which mature behaviour is unnecessary. The break up of the job to suit the machine rather than the person contributes directly to such situations. The autonomous working group is more productive as well as more satisfying. The 'dehumanizing' of nursing procedures is an example of a similar process when services for the patient are broken up into parts which can be undertaken without human contact and in an atmosphere in which the nurse is not expected to require any emotional support (Menzies, 1960).

EDUCATION IN HUMAN RELATIONS

Technical success in industry often contrasts with failure in the social field. In his contacts with industrial staffs, whether on selection boards or in his attempts to understand the tensions arising from jobs or groups, the psychiatrist will be automatically educating others in his approach to problems, his methods and his views. It is, therefore, essential that his approach should be a commonsense rather than a doctrinaire one. It is assumed that more widespread understanding of the unconscious causes of hostility, the psychopathology of everyday life and elementary group dynamics, will be a preventive weapon if applied by those who have occasion to supervise the work of others.

In recent years psychiatrists have contributed substantially to new training methods for giving those who manage groups a greater understanding of the dynamics within large and small groups, and between groups. One approach (Rice, 1965), largely founded on the work of Bion (1961), confines the attention of the participant strictly to the group process.

Another pattern described as sensitivity or training groups ('T groups') endeavours to combine learning about group process with insight into personal responses to others (Bradford, Benne and Gibb, 1964). Psycho-drama is often incorporated. The extensive use of such groups in U.S.A. has been reviewed by Goldberg (1971).

MANAGEMENT CONSULTANCY

Management consultancy is usually the province of industrial psychologists and experienced industrialists. Psychiatrists as well as psychologists have been involved in social consultations in which the consultant's support is maintained while the reactions to change are taking place. These procedures have been described in publications of the Tavistock Institute of Industrial Relations (Rice, 1963; Trist, 1963). Industrial firms, educational bodies and hospitals have asked for advice regarding human relationship problems within their organizations. In one example quoted by Sofer (1961) in *The Organisation from Within*, an engineering firm asked for help in selecting a new company secretary. Preliminary information on the nature of the job suggested that conditions in the organization would lead to trouble no matter who was appointed. This led to a more detailed review of the principles on which the business was conducted and the relationship of the directors who were all members of one family, to the prospective secretary, to trainees and to one another. Suggestions were made to make promotion prospects fairer for all employees and trainees, whether family members or not. In another 'case' the relationship of a research unit to the remainder of a mental hospital was investigated and suggestions made to break down the rivalry and antagonism which threatened to impede progress in both.

POST-INDUSTRIALISM

The advent of automation and the potential leisure which follows, provides new fields of study. Discussing the transition to 'post-industrialism' Trist and Emery (1972) point out that great discrepancies may occur between the 'quality of life' available to various social groups. This is an important background in social segregation and conflict. The scientific study of welfare and political systems by sociologists must be of increasing concern to psychiatrists.

## REFERENCES

BION, W. R. (1961) *Experience in Groups*. London: Tavistock Publications.
BOWLBY, J. A. (1951) *Maternal Care and Mental Health*. Geneva: World Health Organization.
BRADFORD, L. P., BENNE, K. D. & GIBB, J. R. (1964) *T-Group Theory and Laboratory Method*. New York: Wiley.
BROOKE, E. (1968) Methods in determining needs for mental health services. In *Report of Conference on Mental Health Services*. Copenhagen: World Health Organization.
CAPLAN, G. (1964) *Principles of Preventive Psychiatry*. London: Tavistock Publications.

CARSTAIRS, G. M. (1958)   Preventive psychiatry—is there such a thing? *Journal of Mental Science*, **104,** 65.

CURRAN, D. (1952)   Psychiatry limited. *British Journal of Psychiatry*, **98,** 373.

EBIE, J. C., HICKS, R. C., LYTHE, G. & SHORT, R. (1970)   An integrated approach to community health and social problems. *Health Bulletin* (Edinburgh), **28**(2), 35.

GOLDBERG, C. (1971)   Group sensitivity training. *International Journal of Psychiatry*, **9,** 165.

KAHN, J. H. (1967)   The Newham Community Mental Health Service. In *New Aspects of the Mental Health Services*, Ch. 32. London: Pergamon.

KAHN, R. L. & QUINN, R. P. (1970)   Role stress: a framework for analysis. In *Mental Health and Work Organisation*. Edited by A. McLean, Ch. 3. Chicago: Rand McNally.

LINDEMANN, E. (1944)   Symptomatology and management of acute grief. *American Journal of Psychiatry*, **101,** 141.

LLOYD DAVIES, T. A. (1954)   Society and work. In *Mental Health and Human Relations in Industry*. Edited by T. M. Ling, Ch. 11. London: Lewis.

MAYO, E. (1933)   *The Human Problems in an Industrial Civilization*. Boston: Harvard University Press.

MENZIES, I. E. P. (1960)   A case study in the functioning of social systems as a defence against anxiety. *Human Relations*, **13,** 95.

PAHL, J. M. & PAHL, R. E. (1971)   *Managers and Their Wives*. London: Allen Lane.

PARKES, C. M. (1964)   Recent bereavement as a cause of mental illness. *British Journal of Psychiatry*, **110,** 198.

QUERIDO, A. (1968)   The shaping of community mental health care. *British Journal of Psychiatry*, **114,** 293.

REPORT OF THE COMMITTEE ON CHILDREN AND YOUNG PERSONS (SCOTLAND) (1966)   *The Kilbrandon Report*. Edinburgh: H.M.S.O.

REPORT OF THE COMMITTEE ON LOCAL AUTHORITY AND ALLIED PERSONAL SERVICES (1968)   (*The Seebohm Report*.) London: H.M.S.O.

RICE, A. K. (1963)   *The Enterprise and its Environment*. London: Tavistock Publications.

RICE, A. K. (1965)   *Learning for Leadership*. London: Tavistock Publications.

ROSS, W., FOWLES, W. & WINSTONE, W. (1965)   Secondary prevention of job disruption in industry. *Journal of Occupational Medicine*, **7,** 314.

RYLE, A. (1969)   *Student Casualties*. London: Pergamon.

SHORT, R. (1969)   A multidisciplinary approach to social and medicopsychological problems. In *Progress in Mental Health*. Edited by H. Freeman, Ch. 34. London: Churchill.

SOFER, C. (1961)   *The Organisation from Within*. London: Tavistock Publications.

SUTHERLAND, J. D. (1960)   In *Stress and Psychiatric Disorders*. Edited by J. M. Tanner, p. 105. London: Blackwell.

TREDGOLD, R. (1954a)   The place of the psychiatrist in industry. In *Mental Health and Human Relations in Industry*. Edited by T. M. Ling, Ch. 9. London: Lewis.

TREDGOLD, R. (1954b)   Aggression in industry. In *Mental Health and Human Relations in Industry*. Edited by T. M. Ling, Ch. 4. London: Lewis.

TRIST, E. L. (1963)   *Organisational Choice*. London: Tavistock Publications.

TRIST, E. L. & EMERY, F. E. (1972)   Towards a social ecology. (In press.)

VERNON, P. E. & PARRY, J. B. (1949)   *Personnel Selection in the British Forces*. London: London University Press.

WALTON, H. J. (1968)   Effect of the doctor's personality on his style of practice. *Journal of the Royal College of General Practitioners*, **16**, 113.

'WHITE PAPER', COMMAND 3065 (1966)   *Social Work in the Community*. Edinburgh: H.M.S.O.

WING, J. K. & WING, L. (1970)   Psychotherapy and the National Health Service— an operational study. *British Journal of Psychiatry*, **116**, 51.

# Chapter VII

## PSYCHIATRIC TRAINING FOR FOREIGN MEDICAL GRADUATES

### G. M. Carstairs

During the 1960s, and at the beginning of the subsequent decade, psychiatrists in Britain and in North America became increasingly aware of the fact that a substantial proportion of the training posts in their specialty were occupied by young doctors from other countries— and particularly from the developing countries. The figures speak for themselves: in England and Wales, in 1969, of all trainee psychiatrists holding posts as senior house officer, 71 per cent were from overseas; at the registrar level, 60 per cent were from overseas, and at the senior registrar level, 20 per cent.

In the U.S.A. and Canada, the nett annual inflow of foreign medical graduates almost equals the total output of all North American medical schools. The State Hospital systems depend very largely on immigrant doctors, and this is especially true of the less privileged regions. For example in 1970, out of 55 physicians working in the State Hospitals of West Virginia, no less than 53 were foreign graduates; at the beginning of 1971, 10 per cent of approved psychiatry residency training centres in the U.S.A. and Canada were training only foreign graduates.

At first sight these figures, though disconcertingly large, could be justified by the argument that the developing countries need many more trained psychiatrists, and that they have few, if any, facilities for training them at home. Their need for trained personnel is undeniable. At the close of the 1960s, India had 1 psychiatrist to 1.8 million of the population; Pakistan and Sudan 1 to 2 million; Malaysia and Indonesia, 1 to 3 million; Nigeria, 1 to 4 million. In these and other developing countries, the few psychiatrists tend to work in the large towns, remote from the rural masses of the population.

In contrast, the ratios of psychiatrists to population in some Western countries are approximately as follows: Czechoslovakia, 1 to 30,000; U.K. and U.S.S.R., 1 to 20,000; Denmark, 1 to 10,000.

Unfortunately, the presence in the West of trainees from the developing countries is doing little to redress this imbalance, rather, it tends to aggravate it still further for a number of reasons. Chief among these is the fact that the development of mental health services stands relatively low among the priorities of the Ministries of Health and other planning bodies in these countries, and as a result career prospects in psychiatry are uninviting. In most developing countries the ablest young medical graduates aspire to specialize in surgery or internal medicine, knowing that there are many opportunities in teaching, in senior hospital appointments, and in lucrative private clinics; whereas in psychiatry the few hospital posts available tend to be in understaffed, impoverished, low status mental hospitals. Academic departments of psychiatry frequently do not exist at all in their medical schools, and private psychiatric practice exists only in large cities, whereas in most of the developing world the population is still predominantly rural.

It is therefore not too surprising that only a minority of the foreign-born psychiatric trainees in the West made psychiatry their first career choice. Many more originally aspired to train as physicians or surgeons, but found it difficult to obtain suitable posts or to surmount the qualifying examinations for these specialties. The number who intend to return home to practise as psychiatrists is quite small. So far, little objective evidence has been gathered about this aspect of the 'brain drain', but studies in Canada showed that whereas in the early 1960s, 33 per cent of trainees in psychiatry from the Caribbean area returned there on completing their training in Canada, in the closing years of the decade this proportion had fallen to 25 per cent.

It has been estimated that there are today more Indian and Pakistani psychiatrists employed in the U.K. and in North America than in the whole of their respective countries of origin. The countries of the 'free world' pride themselves on their citizens' being able to move about at will—provided they have the money to do so. This is one aspect of a more general 'freedom' of the non-socialist countries, namely the recognition that every man should have the right to better himself financially, with the least possible governmental interference. An unfortunate byproduct of these freedoms is the fact that doctors, trained at great public expense in the developing countries where their services are badly needed, are migrating in large numbers to the U.K. and North America where even low status posts, e.g. as staff psychiatrists in outlying mental hospitals, offer them much better incomes than they could hope to earn at home.

Only political action can, in the long run, remedy these anomalies. Already India, for example, has taken steps to control the outflow of her medical graduates by requiring the deposit of substantial sums of money, which may be forfeited if the emigrant does not return. On the positive side, India has created a basic two-year postgraduate programme in each specialty, culminating in an M.D. degree, and has coupled this with promises of preferment for those graduates who acquire this M.D. instead of the British diplomas which have traditionally been the passports to advancement.

Because career opportunities in psychiatry are dependent upon a country's readiness to spend money on this branch of its health services, the advancement of this specialty, and its ability to attract good entrants, will also be determined by political decisions. In countries where infectious diseases, malnutrition, poor sanitation and lack of pure water supplies are still major problems, psychiatry tends to be assigned a low priority; but this situation may change within a few years' time. As the standards of living rise in the developing countries, we can expect a demand for improvement in their mental health care, and with it an increase in career opportunities for their emigrant psychiatrists.

Meanwhile, and for several years to come, a very substantial proportion of trainee psychiatrists in the English-speaking world will continue to be men and women graduates from developing countries. Their training presents a number of special problems, which can be considered under three headings: (1) problems shared by all trainees from non-English-speaking countries; (2) needs of foreign graduates who will make their careers in the U.K. or North America; (3) special needs of psychiatrists who intend to return to work in developing countries.

### PROBLEMS SHARED BY ALL FOREIGN MEDICAL GRADUATES

Psychiatry, more than any other branch of medicine, is intimately related to the language, culture and values of the society in which it is being practised. A surgeon or a physician can, with the help of an interpreter, elicit the symptoms and signs of the illnessess which will respond to his intervention; the biochemical and pathological investigations on which he relies are carried out in identical fashion in laboratories all over the world.

In part, this is also true of the work of the psychiatrist. Because all mankind shares largely similar anatomical and physiological characteristics; mental illnesses which are secondary to bodily diseases or injuries—particularly those affecting the central nervous system—present similar signs and symptoms wherever they occur. A careful neurological examination, or an analysis of the constituents of the cerebrospinal fluid, the blood, or the urine can be interpreted with equal confidence whether the patient be European, African or Chinese, but this still helps us only to identify the physical disease. Its psychological consequences can be assessed only by observing the patient's behaviour, by testing his mental state and by eliciting the history; and these observations, in turn, can be properly evaluated only when one knows the language, the values and the norms of behaviour of the patient's particular culture or subculture.

However, only a fraction of psychiatric disorders are associated with demonstrable physical pathology. Even the major psychoses, the schizophrenias and the affective psychoses, which occur all over the world, still have to be classed as 'functional'. It seems probable that biochemical research may soon provide objective indicators of their presence; but in the meantime their diagnosis is still dependent on first eliciting, and then evaluating evidence of speech and behaviour which departs from the cultural norm.

The same can be said of mental subnormality: there are a few conditions, such as Down's syndrome, phenylketonuria, cretinism or galactosaemia, which reveal themselves unequivocally, but there are many more in which the subnormality is not accompanied by gross organic defects, and can be recognized only as an inability to acquire manual and intellectual skills to the same degree as do others in the patient's cultural milieu.

The foreign medical graduate who comes to an English-speaking country faces many social problems. Foremost among these are problems of language. Even graduates of medical colleges in India, Pakistan, Singapore or Hong Kong, where instruction is given in English, find the speech and accents of their patients hard to follow; while those who come from non-English speaking countries face great difficulty in understanding their teachers and consultants as well. All encounter problems in adapting to unfamiliar foods, living quarters, customs and manners; even the relationships between doctors, nurses and patients, may be very different from those to which they are accustomed.

Among so much that is strange, it is perhaps comforting to the foreign graduate who has already practised psychiatry to recognize familiar conditions, such as chronic schizophrenia or manic-depressive psychosis; and for those new to the specialty to focus their attention on the psychiatric syndromes which most closely conform to the 'medical model' of symptoms, signs, diagnosis and treatment.

Most psychiatrists from overseas—and not a few of the home-bred ones—are content to settle for a relatively restricted range of competence, stressing drug therapy and E.C.T. They find this the easiest part of their new studies; but at the same time they have to contend with studying the sciences basic to psychiatry, handicapped in most cases by previous undergraduate teaching which may have dealt cursorily with the neurosciences and not at all with psychology, genetics or statistics.

It is hardly surprising that few foreign graduates succeed in acquiring a firm grasp of the contending theories of personality development, and fewer still progress to a real competence in group or individual psychotherapy. This, perhaps, is just as well; because the techniques of drug therapy, E.C.T. and behaviour therapy are not only easier to learn, but are also more likely to be applicable in another culture, than are those of psychotherapy.

## NEEDS OF FOREIGN GRADUATES WHO WILL MAKE THEIR CAREERS IN THE WEST

From what has been written above, it is clear that the foreign graduate runs a serious risk of becoming a second class citizen in the psychiatric services in his adoptive country. The less gifted among them, in particular, may settle for a relatively undemanding (and unrewarding) career in the peripheral mental hospitals, where they are denied the stimulus of having their work exposed to the scrutiny of their peers, or of younger students.

It would be extremely short sighted of their host countries to allow this to happen, because it would be detrimental not only to the foreign graduate's own professional development, but also to the standards of care in these hospitals which already rely so heavily upon immigrants to fill their staff positions.

The American Psychiatric Association and the Royal College of Psychiatrists have both begun to take a very active interest in the quality of training offered to new entrants to the profession, and both bodies have given special attention to the needs of foreign graduates. In both countries, the first step has been to take stock of where they go for their training, and what careers they follow thereafter. It has at once become evident that the foreign graduates tend, on the whole, to be involved in the weakest training experiences that each of these countries has to offer.

If this is to be remedied, either there will have to be a system of required rotation through the stronger training institutions, or else the quality of their tuition in outlying hospitals will have to be improved. For several years, the State of Nebraska has demonstrated how quite widely separated hospitals can share in clinical teaching disseminated from the academic centre by means of closed circuit television. In the near future, cassettes of half-inch Videotape will be readily available, enabling formal teaching, as well as clinical demonstrations, to be shared by even the most remote hospitals.

These are matters which concern the teaching institution. From the point of view of the foreign trainee, perhaps the first obstacle to overcome is the mental barrier of wondering whether he can ever compete on equal terms with his British or American colleagues. If he is fortunate, he may be helped in this respect by meeting some able and conspicuously successful immigrant colleagues; but equally, he may be discouraged by encountering others who appear to have given up the struggle, and to have settled for a modest level of professional attainment.

Undoubtedly, one of the foreign graduate's first tasks should be to ensure that he has a firm command of English. In our specialty, communication is the *sine qua non*: no matter how well read a psychiatrist may be, his book knowledge will be of little help to him if he is unable to put a patient at his ease, and to elicit a meaningful history.

Command of language is clearly a first step towards understanding the psychological factors contributing to a patient's illness. Of hardly less importance is the psychiatrist's knowledge of the customary forms of relationships, the accepted values and the behavioural expectations which obtain in different subsections of his adoptive society. This appreciation of his patient's cultural background cannot be taken for granted, but has to be cultivated by deliberate inquiry, reading and personal participation in the life of the community.

In future years, as the scientific basis of psychiatry becomes more firmly established, there will be an increasing field for subspecialization. The foreign graduate, like his indigenous fellow trainees, will aim first at acquiring a sound grasp of clinical practice, and of the scientific findings upon which this is based. During the later stages of his training, he would be well advised to select a particular area, such as child and adolescent psychiatry or forensic psychiatry, individual and group psychotherapy, or community psychiatry for more intensive study. It is assumed that a critial appreciation of the use of psychotropic drugs forms part of the basic training of all psychiatrists. Some may discover a special interest in pursuing research and should seek additional basic training in the field of their choice.

So long as the basic psychiatric qualification in Britain remained the Diploma in Psychological Medicine, which could be taken after a minimum of two years' approved experience, the dice were loaded against the average immigrant doctor's being able to compete on equal terms with his British colleagues. Now that the Royal College of Psychiatrists has come into being, its concept of a three-year period of basic training, followed by at least two years of increasing clinical responsibility offers a much more realistic time-span, closely akin to the requirements of North American Specialty Boards. During the span of five years, a foreign graduate has time to master the language and to familiarize himself with the new social environment, and hence to be able to deploy his own talents and abilities to full advantage.

Medical students themselves have recently drawn attention to the need for a better understanding of their own society, and of the various subsections of that society from which their patients are likely to be drawn. British and American students, in particular, have come to realize that they are drawn from a privileged minority of their respective societies, and have shown a lively interest in the very different living conditions and life experience of large underprivileged groups among their fellow countrymen. This interest is not purely academic, because both the prevalence and the perception of most forms of mental disorders are found to differ in different subgroups.

Social observers have noticed that, especially in rural areas, traditional healing practices survive for several generations after apparently more potent Western remedies have become available. A principal reason for this is that the doctor has failed to inspire confidence: his unfamiliar techniques do not carry the authority of traditional methods of healing.

This difficulty is not confined to developing societies. In the West, also, problems can arise when psychiatrists fail to appreciate that their patients may have quite different concepts of mental disorder, and of treatment, from those of the medical profession. Hence, teaching about the sociological analysis of 'sick role behaviour' and about the social role of therapists in our society is of great importance to foreign trainees, as it is also to indigenous candidates for specialization in psychiatry.

### Special Needs of Psychiatrists who Intend to Return to Work in Developing Countries

In the highly developed countries it has long been known that the minor degrees of mental and emotional handicap, which we diagnose as neurosis, psychosomatic disorders or personality disorders are much more numerous than either the functional or the organic psychoses. These 'minor' disorders—which can still be severely incapacitating—are believed to be determined only in small part by organic or constitutional factors, and in much larger degree by traumatic experiences in the patient's personal life. As such, they have at times been regarded as the results of faulty conditioning, or as the learning of maladaptive patterns of behaviour. Because vicissitudes of socialization (such as failures to come to terms with sexual, aggressive or dependency feelings) were frequently identified as contributing to these conditions, and because advanced societies make more severe demands on ther members, these disorders have been collectively termed 'diseases of civilization'.

This term reflects a widely held misconception, that neurotic disorders are rare or absent in technologically undeveloped peoples. For example, Benjamin Rush, the eighteenth century father of American psychiatry said that he had never seen cases of 'madness, melancholy or fatuity' among members of the Red Indian tribes. J. J. Rousseau's concept of the 'noble savage' undoubtedly coloured the perceptions of many generations of travellers and explorers; their superficial conclusion that emotional disorders were rare among primitive peoples was made easier to sustain because they seldom stayed long enough to gain an intimate knowledge of these peoples' language, customs and beliefs.

It has only been during the present century that some anthropologists—such as Ruth Benedict, Ralph Linton and Cora Dubois—have made the study of cultural factors in personality development a major element in their field work. Their reports have made it clear that every society, even the most primitive, imposes, during children's preparation for their adult role, restraints which can result in neurotic or psychosomatic symptoms.

The writer's own studies in villages of Rajasthan revealed that neurotic symptoms (which were recognizable only after he had become familiar with the full range of normal behaviour) were extremely common among his village informants. (Carstairs, 1953, 1956, 1957). These findings have been confirmed by systematic surveys of rural and urban populations in Taiwan (Lin, 1953; Lin et al., 1969) and in Nigeria (Leighton and Lambo, 1963).

The 'diseases of civilization' are present, it seems, in every human society. So long as the killing diseases, such as malaria, smallpox, tuberculosis, and leprosy are rampant, tackling morbidity due to emotional disorders occupies a low priority in the minds both of patients and of public health planners. As soon as these 'killers' are checked, and the news of modern psychotropic drugs begins to spread through the bazaars, patients appear at psychiatric clinics in the developing countries in rapidly increasing numbers. The need to be able to cope with large numbers of patients, with little in the way of clerical, nursing or social work help, is one of the major challenges awaiting the returning trainee.

A reproach frequently levelled against postgraduate training programmes in the U.K. or in North America is that while preparing the trainee for work in the psychiatric services of the host country they do not equip him to meet the very different requirements of practice in his home environment. Some of these young men (e.g. Dr Persad of Trinidad) have made it plain that in some ways their Western training was an obstacle to returing to work in their own localities. Dr Persad (1970) has described a double 'culture shock', occurring at the first encounter with North American standards of living and the relatively prodigal facilities of their teaching institutions and again when the trainee returns to his own country. After several years of becoming accustomed to practice in a Western setting, the rudest shock of all is the return to a situation of scarcity—scarcity of psychiatrists, of trained nurses, social workers, psychologists and even secretaries, and also limited premises, equipment, and access to psychiatric literature. There is, on the other hand, a superabundance of patients, which is positively overwhelming because the trainees soon despair of being able to practise the skills which they have laboriously learned, if they are to keep pace with these pressing clinical demands.

When these major practical difficulties are combined with insecurity of employment, low status in the medical profession of his own country and meagre financial rewards, it is not surprising that for many the outcome of this second culture shock is a precipitate return to one of the richer countries in the hope of finding more rewarding (and better rewarded) work there.

Speakers at International Workshops in Edinburgh and East Africa (Commonwealth Foundation, 1969) and in Montreal (Canadian Mental Health Association, 1970) have endorsed the principle which was so clearly stated by Professor Tsung-yi Lin of Taiwan in 1961: that future trainees in psychiatry should obtain their first introduction to clinical practice in their own country. Ideally, they will receive their basic theoretical training in their own, or in a neighbouring country; but where this is not possible they should take part in multinational seminars which will remind them of the nature of the tasks which they will have to undertake once they are fully qualified.

Put at its simplest, they will know, for example, that they will encounter a lot of general medical problems in their psychiatric practice: in developing countries, infectious, toxaemias and organic lesions of the C.N.S. are common accompaniments of psychiatric disorders. It would seem logical, therefore, that the examination for the Membership of the College of Psychiatrists, or for Specialty Boards, should contain a set of optional questions on tropical medicine, for the benefit of overseas trainees.

The writer has found that in many developing countries medical students and young doctors tend to become alienated from the very people they hope to serve and treat. Especially in countries such as India, Africa or South America, where illiteracy or semiliteracy is widespread, doctors educated in Western medicine are liable to forget that the great majority of their fellow countrymen still hold quite different concepts of illness and treatment. In order to be able to help them, the doctor must first be able to show that he understands these concepts, even though he may no longer share them, and he must try to explain his Western concepts of illness and treatment in language which will be intelligible to his patients. Western trained doctors will soon realize that they can cope with the flood of patients only by sharing their task with whatever paramedical assistance is available; and this will require the ability to teach simple procedures to their modestly qualified assistants and in general to act as leader of the mental health team, rather than as the personal therapist of each individual patient.

The concept of the 'psychiatric team' is already widely recognized and taught in the West: but this usually means a team of already highly trained persons each contributing in terms of his or her professional role. Under conditions of scarcity, there can be no such nice distinctions of role. Visitors to the highly organized urban and rural psychiatric services of the U.S.S.R. have been impressed by the fact that there nurses often 'double' the part of social workers, and psychiatrists, of necessity, acquire some of the skills of clinical psychologists.

In developing countries, flexibility of role has to be carried still further. In several countries, psychiatric wards, and even small mental hospitals are run entirely by nurses, with only remote and intermittent medical supervision. The task of the young psychiatrist, who may be the only specialist in his field serving a population of millions, is how best to delegate treatment functions, and how to distribute his own clinical involvement in the most economical way.

These are problems of which most teachers in the West have little or no experience; and hence there is no place for them in the curricula of Diplomas, Memberships or Specialty Boards in psychiatry. Clearly, however, this is a gap which should and can be filled. In every major training centre there are numerous trainees—in social work, psychology and nursing, as well as in psychiatry—who come from diverse cultural backgrounds, but who share the common experience of having to cope with large patient populations with relatively meagre resources. By assembling these trainees in multidisciplinary seminars it is possible to stimulate their thinking about new and better ways of coping with these situations. Sometimes experienced mental health workers from the developing countries are available to lead such seminars; not infrequently some of their Western teachers have themselves had experience overseas, but the principal source of learning probably lies in the discovery that they themselves may have something new to offer in the pioneering years of psychiatry in their respective countries.

Overseas students have frequently stressed the need to emphasize the social sciences, epidemiology and the techniques of planning and evaluating new community services as part of their specialist training. With much of this one can agree; record-keeping, statistics, survey methodology and operational research are all of immense practical value, and enable pioneers not only to explore new patterns of care but also to learn whether or not they are really efficacious. It is less easy to see what could be usefully learned from a short course in anthropology. The principles of social structure and the comparative study of institutions cannot be taught without a rather full analysis of a range of different societies, and there is clearly not going to be time for such study in depth during basic psychiatric training.

Two aspects of anthropology should certainly be considered for inclusion in the curriculum: (1) an introduction to the social anthropology of the candidate's own society, or of subcultures within that society, and (2) an introduction to studies of culture and personality.

In several developing countries (including Iran, the Federation of Arab Republics—formerly the United Arab Republic—some of the South American countries, and some of the Republics of the U.S.S.R.) medical students, like other university students, are expected to devote some time to practical work among less advanced groups of their own people. This confrontation with traditional ways of life can serve to quicken an interest in studying these communities systematically.

The obvious difficulty of introducing a highly differentiated series of studies of local cultures and subcultures as part of the psychiatrist's training is that in any one training centre there may be representatives of several quite different societies. This could be overcome by inviting a guest lecturer to give, say, three introductory talks about the subject matter and methods of inquiry of social anthropology after which each student could be instructed to read a monograph on a particular society in his own culture area, and to write a dissertation upon that society.

In contrast, the theme of culture and personality is one in which the whole class can join, because it is best taught by drawing illustrations from studies carried out in a number of contrasting societies. Here, the general theoretical principles and the methods of observation leading to the formulation and subsequent verification of hypotheses about particular aspects of personality development are most important, because once the student has grasped these principles and methods he can apply them himself in an examination of his own local culture.

Many able psychiatrists from Eastern or African countries have reported that the classical stages of personality development, as described by Freud and the post-Freudians, have only limited applicability in their own societies. This point was made by Malinowski (1927) who showed from observations made on the Trobriand islanders, that Freud's formulation of how the growing child acquires and internalizes the values of his society was not universally valid. For example, the role of the father, as exemplified in the Oedipus complex, was quite different among the Trobrianders. There, it was the mother's brother who acted as the surrogate for society's rules and sanctions; and it was he, and not the father, who appeared in this people's mythological counterpart of the Oedipus legend.

Another early classic work in this field was Margaret Mead's (1928) study of adolescence in Samoa, which showed that the emotional turbulence which Western students of personality regarded as inseparable from late puberty was not an invariable human reaction, but was a response to particular, and not universal, forms of social conditioning.

N. C. Surya (1969) and Takeo Doi (Doi, 1969) have severally pointed out that in Hindu and in Japanese culture the concept of dependency has quite different connotations from those associated with it in Europe and America. In the West, dependency is seen as an attribute of immaturity, which should be outgrown when the individual reaches adult stature; but in the East, it is accepted as a continuing trait to be manifested in certain relationships which continue well into old age. Dr Surya goes on to postulate that the Western emphasis on individual autonomy is also alien to Hindu ways of thinking; consequently, the Hindu patient does not feel at ease when offered the detached, impersonal guidance of a Western psychotherapist. Instead, he requires his therapist to assume the role of a *Guru*, or idealized father figure, and expects to receive the Guru's guidance and support in his search or a solution of his personal problems.

There will, in time, be as many variants of psychotherapy as there are major cultures; but only Africans, Chinese and Indians (or Europeans who have made a very prolonged study of these societies) will be able to identify the particular forms which personality development takes in each particular culture, and hence the different styles which therapists must adopt if they are to operate in accordance with th e various socially defined norms of personality.

This is a task for future generations of indigenous psychiatrists; but it is the responsibility of their teachers to alert them to the importance of this pioneering work, and to equip them with techniques of inquiry which will enable them to discover for themselves, and for their successors, the key themes of personality development, and its vicissitudes, in their respective cultures.

## REFERENCES

CANADIAN MENTAL HEALTH ASSOCIATION (1970) *Report of a Seminar on Mental Health in Developing Countries*. Toronto: CMHA.

CARSTAIRS, G. M. (1953) The case of Thakur Khuman Singh: a culture-conditioned crime. *British Journal of Delinquency*, **4**, 14.

CARSTAIRS, G. M. (1956) Hinjra and Jiryan: two derivatives of Hindu attitudes to sexuality. *British Journal of Medical Psychology*, **29**, 128.

CARSTAIRS, G. M. (1957) *The Twice-Born: A Study of a Community of High-Caste Hindus*. London: The Hogarth Press.

COMMONWEALTH FOUNDATION (1969) *Mental Health Services in the Developing World*. [Occasional Paper, No. 4.] London: Marlborough House.

DOI, T. (1969) Japanese psychology, dependency need, and mental health. In *Mental Health Research in Asia and the Pacific*. Edited by W. Candill & T. Y. Lin. Honolulu: East West Center Press.

LEIGHTON, A. H., LAMBO, T. A. et al. (1963) *Pyschiatric Disorder Among the Yoruba*. New York: Cornell University Press.

LIN, T. Y. (1953) A study of the incidence of mental disorder in Chinese and other cultures. *Psychiatry*, **16**, 313.

LIN, T. Y. (1961) Perspectives in the teaching of psychiatry. In *Teaching Psychiatry and Mental Health*. [Public Health Paper, No. 9.] Geneva: World Health Organization.

LIN, T. Y., RIN, H., YEH, E. K., HSU, C. C. & CHU, H. M. (1969) Mental disorders in Taiwan, fifteen years later. In *Mental Health Research in Asia and the Pacific*. Edited by W. Candill & T. Y. Lin. Honolulu: East West Center Press.

MALINOWSKI, B. (1927) *Sex and Repression in Savage Society*. London: Routledge & Kegan Paul.

MEAD, MARGARET (1928) *Coming of Age in Samoa*. New York: Morrow.

PERSAD, E. (1970) Some cultural factors in psychiatric training: a personal view. In *Report of a Seminar on Mental Health in Developing Countries*. Toronto: Canadian Mental Health Association.

SURYA, N. C. (1969) Ego structure in the Hindu joint family. In *Mental Health Research in Asia and the Pacific*. Edited by W. Candill & T. Y. Lin. Honolulu: East West Center Press.

# Chapter VIII

# RESEARCH AND STATISTICAL METHODS

## R. C. B. Aitken

### INTRODUCTION

In psychiatric practice, it should be our everyday concern to take account of recent research. We are required to make recommendations based on our understanding of whether some observation has led to a significant advance, or merely to a new opinion without foundation. From the conclusions of others, we are required to decide to what extent they can be applied to the patient under our consideration. We are exposed to a plethora of reports, which invite us to change our practice. Yet the history of our subject has been chequered with policies based on conclusions later found to be false. The key to advance in psychiatric practice lies in the appreciation of statistical and clinical significance: knowledge about the influence of chance and bias, and about applicability and relevance.

The aim of this chapter is to cover some points which will allow us to reach our own conclusions about the applicability of the findings obtained by others—points, which will allow us to judge the evidence better and so to change our practice more sensitively when that is indeed the correct approach. Better clinical management will be developed many times faster by more attention to these points than by more of us undertaking research. Nevertheless, a subsidiary aim of this chapter is to alert the unwary to pits into which he might fall, should he want to advance knowledge by contributing to it.

The practice of psychiatry is a clinical art based on knowledge in the biological and social sciences. It changes by progress in many subjects and its research uses many techniques. It is a clinical art because psychiatrists are concerned primarily to alleviate the distress in an *individual*. In recent times their responsibility has extended to additional members of society, particularly to the patient's family, as well as to a variety of features within each patient. To understand any psychiatric disorder, influences within and outwith the patient must be taken fully into account. Hence research in psychiatry involves a multitude of variables, but for measurement they have certain things in common.

### INDIVIDUAL DIFFERENCES

Most research involves understanding the differences between individuals—and even within individuals at different points of time—

F

in order to tease out the meaning of any common factors. Detecting a similarity is the hallmark of a contribution to knowledge, but it must be done in such a way that the probability of it being due to chance is appreciated simultaneously. Awareness of the differences allows the significance of an observation to be determined, and so whether the conclusions will also apply to another patient.

These similarities and differences may be so obvious that description in words should be sufficient to record them accurately. A literary account of a patient with florid Huntington's chorea can so graphically distinguish him from a healthy person that measuring indices of muscle movement or intelligence are superfluous. This distinction of pathology from normality is an example of a *nominal* measurement scale. But the halcyon days for the literary account are over in most psychiatric research. Interest now lies in the degree of abnormality—quantity is demanded, and the use of numbers is paramount. The number of muscle movements in unit time, and the score of the patient with Huntington's chorea on a test of intelligence need to be recorded on an *interval* scale in order to measure the rate of deterioration. Much thought has to be given to the appropriateness of the measuring instruments to the requirements of the study. For instance, there are reasons which make it more appropriate only to rank intelligence test scores, so converting them to an *ordinal* scale.

The information collected needs to be examined in such a way that its nature is capable of summary by mathematics. The use of numbers permits conciseness, precision and clarity, quite unavailable through words only. Powerful methods of calculation are available to achieve these desirable attributes, and so determine statistical significance in order to allow judgement on clinical relevance.

## Definition of Measurement

In its broadest sense, measurement is the assignment of numerals to events so that they represent the nature of the observations. To say that a phenomenon exists is to give it dimension, albeit perhaps in a unit that may be indefinable. Certain types of observation in psychiatry may at first seem beyond measurement, but it is the clear duty of the researcher to determine how to do so, however crudely. Perhaps the major problem in psychiatric research is that many of the dimensions have no acceptable units—and even when they have, the units may appear to change magnitude.

When interval scales are unacceptable, sometimes order of magnitude can be obtained, and hence data for an ordinal scale. The epidemiology of a disease with known cause can be ascertained considerably more precisely than one where differing criteria for diagnosis apply, such as in most of psychiatry. Commonly the measurement of more than one continuous dimension is required, but there is no universal index of what constitutes abnormality. The diagnostic process in all but a few psychiatric conditions, depends on establishing magnitude in a series of dimensions before defining taxonomy. Artificial categories—such as mild, moderate or severe—may have to be used in order to achieve communication, but fundamental deficiencies thereafter remain. Ideas must be postulated quite specifically as hypotheses, and then put to the test, somehow, by measurement of observations.

## VALUE OF VARIATION

Wide variability is usual for the multiple measurements required in psychiatry. The range of both normality and morbidity may be extensive, and there are few conditions which are qualitatively different. The first use of statistics is to provide techniques which will summarize data; to produce numbers which describe the central tendency and dispersion of the scores on an interval scale. The mean and median scores can be used to signify the former, and the standard deviation and range the latter (Statistic Example 1). As can be seen from Figure 1, it is informative to plot frequency histograms of the scores,

## STATISTIC EXAMPLE 1

The data analysed are nurses' observations of the duration (in hours) that patients slept while taking either placebo or hypnotic (nitrazepam). Distributions of the scores are shown in Fig. 1.

| Patients | Placebo | Hypnotic | Difference |
|----------|---------|----------|------------|
| A | 6.4 | 7.2 | 0.8 |
| B | 6.1 | 7.0 | 0.9 |
| C | 4.7 | 7.3 | 2.6 |
| D | 4.4 | 6.6 | 2.2 |
| E | 5.7 | 6.6 | 0.9 |
| F | 7.0 | 6.5 | −0.5 |
| G | 4.7 | 5.3 | 0.6 |
| H | 4.5 | 7.6 | 3.1 |
| I | 6.9 | 7.7 | 0.8 |
| J | 5.9 | 4.5 | −1.4 |
| K | 6.2 | 6.9 | 0.7 |
| L | 5.7 | 7.0 | 1.3 |
| M | 6.6 | 6.3 | −0.3 |
| N | 5.3 | 6.1 | 0.8 |
| O | 6.0 | 6.0 | 0 |
| P | 4.5 | 6.5 | 2.0 |
| Q | 4.9 | 6.3 | 1.4 |
| R | 7.2 | 8.3 | 1.1 |

Statistic Example 1—*contd.*

|  |  | Placebo | Hypnotic | Difference |
|---|---|---|---|---|
| Total score | $\Sigma X$ | 102.7 | 119.7 | 17.0 |
| Number of scores | $N$ | 18 | 18 | 18 |
| MEAN, $\bar{x}$ | $\dfrac{\Sigma X}{N}$ | 5.71 | 6.65 | 0.94 |
| Median (middle score occurring at 50 per centile) |  | 5.8 | 6.6 | 0.9 |

Let $x$ = deviation of a score from the group mean

i.e. $x = \dfrac{\Sigma X}{N}$

note: $\Sigma x^2 = \Sigma X^2 - \dfrac{(\Sigma X)^2}{N}$

|  |  | Placebo | Hypnotic | Difference |
|---|---|---|---|---|
| Sum of squared values | $\Sigma X^2$ | 600.55 | 809.23 | 36.76 |
| Correction factor | $\dfrac{(\Sigma X)^2}{N}$ | 585.96 | 796.01 | 16.06 |
| $\therefore$ Sum of squared deviations | $\Sigma x^2$ | 14.59 | 13.22 | 20.70 |
| VARIANCE, $S^2$ | $\dfrac{\Sigma x^2}{N-1}$ | 0.86 | 0.78 | 1.22 |
| STANDARD DEVIATION, $S$ | $\sqrt{\left(\dfrac{\Sigma x^2}{N-1}\right)}$ | 0.93 | 0.88 | 1.10 |
| STANDARD ERROR OF THE MEAN, $S\bar{x}$ | $\dfrac{S}{\sqrt{N}}$ | 0.22 | 0.21 | 0.26 |

## STUDENT'S '*t*' TEST

### A. RELATED SAMPLES

Let us consider that a pair of scores were obtained for the same patient on two occasions, the drugs having been given in alternate order, i.e. the samples were not independent.

$$t = \frac{\bar{d}}{S\bar{d}} = \frac{0.94}{0.26} = 3.62$$

A statistical table of the percentage points for the distribution of $t$ at $N-1$ (17) degrees of freedom (d.f.) reveals that this value of $t$ exceeds that found at a probability (P) of 0.01. That is, this difference in distribution could only have occurred due to chance on less than one occasion in every hundred.

Statistic Example 1—*contd.*

## B. INDEPENDENT SAMPLES

Let us now consider an analysis if the scores had been obtained independently from two groups of patients. In these circumstances differences between pairs are meaningless because they were unrelated.

The pooled variance between the two samples,

$$S^2 = \frac{\Sigma x_1{}^2 + \Sigma x_2{}^2}{(N_1 - 1) + (N_2 - 1)} = \frac{14.59 + 13.22}{(18 - 1) + (18 - 1)} = 0.82$$

The standard error of the difference between the two means,

$$S_{\bar{x}_2 - \bar{x}_1} = \sqrt{\left(\frac{S^2}{N_1} + \frac{S^2}{N_2}\right)} = \sqrt{\left(\frac{0.82}{18} + \frac{0.82}{18}\right)} = 0.30$$

$$t = \frac{\bar{x}_2 - \bar{x}_1}{S_{\bar{x}_2 - \bar{x}_1}} = \frac{6.65 - 5.71}{0.30} = 3.13$$

$$\text{d.f.} = (N_1 - 1) + (N_2 - 1) = (18 - 1) + (18 - 1) = 34$$

$$P < 0.01$$

such as the number of times that classes of different magnitude occurred.

If a histogram is symmetrical, it is likely to follow the Gaussian (or 'normal') distribution. Sixty-six per cent of the readings should lie within one standard deviation above or below the mean score. 2.5 per cent of the readings should lie beyond two (1.96 to be exact) standard deviations from the mean score in each direction. In other words, when a score lies beyond two standard deviations from the mean, it is *unlikely* to have occurred only by chance, though it could well have done so at that level of probability, i.e. on between two and three occasions out of every hundred.

Many distributions in biological variation are not symmetrical, for example, in the case of heart rate, experimental readings tend to be bunched toward the lower end with an upper tail. Should these frequency histograms be plotted against the logarithm of the dimension magnitude, such a skew distribution reverts to symmetry; in other words, normal distribution has been brought about by logarithmic *transformation*. When this is found to have occurred, the logarithm of each reading should be taken before calculating the summary statistics; the mean is then the *geometric mean*. For some measures, a different transformation will be required; when measuring proportions for example, the 'arcsin' is suitable (Snedecor and Cochran, 1967). Most parametric statistics, i.e. of implied, usually 'normal', distribution, are fairly robust to asymmetrical distribution, but this point and compar-

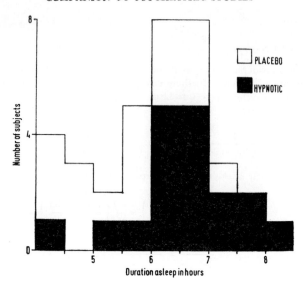

Fig. 1. (a) *Frequency histograms.* It should be noted that the observations are not symmetrically distributed, particularly while on placebo. This is not uncommon, but transformation as mentioned in the text is only required when the distribution is clearly skew. It can be seen that the proportion of observations while on hypnotic is increased towards longer duration of sleep.

ability of variation (homogeneity of variance) constantly require consideration.

The variation which produces distribution of the scores about the central tendency may be attributable to causes whose influence is known, e.g. age or social class to name only two of the more obviously relevant in psychiatry. The total variation found in any experiment can be apportioned in certain ways. Some can be due to influences between different groups of subjects; some to variation found between individuals in these groups; and when more than one reading is taken from each subject, to variation within individuals. Notwithstanding what can be accounted for, there will always be variation whose cause is not known; even if all influences have been standardized, there would still always be some variation due to unknown events, or what is generally termed the 'error' variation. This is likely to have occurred at random. Contrary to what might be imagined this is not irrelevant; it provides the index against which the possible variation introduced by the influence under test can be examined. Analysis of variance is a sensitive and elegant statistical technique for examination of these various influences, suitable for most experiments obtaining quantitative data, and essential if data is obtained from more than two groups.

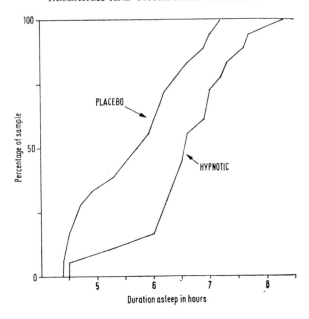

FIG. 1 (b). *Cumulative frequency histograms.* This display makes it clearer that the scores while on hypnotic are towards longer duration. It is now obvious that taking hypnotic ensures that few patients sleep less than six hours. For data normally distributed, the curves would be S shaped.

## SIGNIFICANCE OF ANY DIFFERENCE

Clearly, if there is an obvious central tendency for a measure, with little spread of the scores on either side, and if under another condition there is a distribution which does not overlap, then it is very likely that the condition influenced the magnitude of the measure. This result rarely occurs in psychiatry. More usually the central tendency is there alright, but the distribution is widespread and there is considerable overlap in scores found from the differing circumstances, as illustrated in Figure 1. The question at issue is whether the difference observed in the distributions could have occurred due to random irrelevant influences—or put more precisely, what was the probability that it might have occurred by chance?

The usual hypothesis in experiment will be the null one, i.e. the distributions were similar and occurred irrespective of the feature under study. It is customary that this will only be rejected when that could be inferred to have arisen purely by chance less than five times in a hundred occasions $(P < 0.05)$. Then the findings can be accepted as significant, and only then should be worthy of explanation and deduction of their meaning. This is statistical significance. The likelihood of this occurring for comparison of any distributions is affected by the numbers involved. Knowledge of the means, standard deviations and number of readings, allows calculation of the probability that any difference in the means could be accounted for by chance. This is illustrated using the Student's '*t*' test in Statistic Example 1. The smaller the probability that the difference could have occurred by chance, the greater the confidence that the altered circumstances were the relevant factor.

## STATISTIC EXAMPLE 2

The data given in Example 1 will now be analysed by nonparametric methods, the calculations being done on ranking of observed values. For simplicity, the corrections available for tied values will be omitted.

| Patients | Rank of values Placebo | Hypnotic | Rank of differences (ignoring direction) |
|---|---|---|---|
| A | 20 | 31.5 | 6 |
| B | 15.5 | 29 | 8.5 |
| C | 5.5 | 33 | 16 |
| D | 1 (shortest 4.4 hours) | 24 | 15 |
| E | 10.5 | 24 | 8.5 |
| F | 29 | 21.5 | − 2 |
| G | 5.5 | 8.5 | 3 |
| H | 3 | 34 | 17 (largest 3.1 hours) |
| I | 26.5 | 35 | 6 |
| J | 12 | 3 | − 12.5 |
| K | 17 | 26.5 | 4 |
| L | 10.5 | 29 | 11 |
| M | 24 | 18.5 | − 1 (smallest 0.3 hours) |
| N | 8.5 | 15.5 | 6 |
| O | 13.5 | 13.5 | — |
| P | 3 | 21.5 | 14 |
| Q | 7 | 18.5 | 12.5 |
| R | 31.5 | 36 (longest 8.3 hours) | 10 |
| Sum of values | 243.5 | 422.5 | |

Statistic Example 2—*contd.*

A. RELATED SAMPLES: *Wilcoxon Matched-Pairs Signed Ranks Test*

Ranking differences, $T = $ smaller sum of like-signed ranks

$$= 2 + 12.5 + 1 = 15.5$$

A statistical table of critical value of $T$ reveals a level of significance less than 0.01 for the difference between the samples.

B. INDEPENDENT SAMPLES: *Mann-Whitney U Test*

Ranking values, $U = N_1 N_2 + \dfrac{N_1(N_1 + 1)}{2} - R_1$

where        $R_1 = $ the larger sum of the ranks in one of the groups

and          $N_1 = $ the number in that group.

$$U = 18.18 + \frac{18(18 + 1)}{2} - 422.5 = 72.5$$

$$P < 0.01$$

For small numbers there are more simple ways to obtain levels of probability on which to judge the statistical significance of any observed differences (Statistic Example 2). The scores can be ranked by their magnitude. As previously mentioned, they then become an ordinal scale. These ranks have no quantity in a unit thereafter and are called non-parametric. No assumptions regarding the distribution of the scores need be met. Unfortunately it is tedious to rank more than about 20 values. There is a variety of tests available for examination of such ordinal data, the most appropriate of which should be selected on whether the samples were related or independent, and on whether the samples were two or more in number. The mathematical calculations required for these tests are remarkably simple to perform. A textbook by Siegel (1956) on this subject is recommended for its clarity. Non-parametric statistical methods are a little less powerful for detecting significance than parametric ones, but this matters rarely.

Clinical significance is something quite different and can only be assessed when previous experience is taken into account. Should some influence have been discovered to produce effects of statistical significance, i.e. unlikely to have been due to chance, then the next question that should arise is whether this matters. Was the increase in duration of sleep attributable to the hypnotic sufficient to be of clinical importance? It could have been found that an increase was of statistical significance (i.e. unlikely to have been due to chance), but insufficient in amount to be of clinical relevance.

This kind of question can also arise occasionally even without a statistically significant difference, but for a quite different reason.

When a percentage of patients improve with treatment A and the same percentage also improve with treatment B, it might be concluded that the treatments are equally effective. This could be fallacious. Should the condition under study have been anaemia—both megaloblastic and iron deficient—then clearly the individual people who would have responded to vitamin $B_{12}$ or iron would have been different with each treatment. In the treatment of agoraphobia, to take a psychiatric example, a similar proportion of patients respond to psychotherapy as respond to behaviour therapy. But are the respondents the same type of patient? This question on whether agoraphobics are a homogenous group requires an answer.

### Experimental Bias

It is wise to be sure that the only explanation for any observed difference is the one under investigation. It would be ludicrous to make the selection into experimental groups in some biased way so that any difference observed could have been due to the characteristic of the selection rather than any subsequent influence.

Virtually all research can be undertaken only on a sample of the population available with a specific feature—rarely can everyone with the feature be included. But if the conclusions are to have meaning, they must be capable of extrapolation to the members of the population not included. The selection must have been without sampling bias. It is sensible at least in simple experiments to have the groups comparable, except for the one actual influence under study. Subjects can be allocated to these quite at random, and theoretically when the numbers are substantial the various known and unknown, but unwanted influences will be evenly distributed, e.g. the same number of each sex will be in each group. On the other hand the selection can be stratified, so that by controlling allocation the factors which are thought likely to affect the results are *made* to be distributed evenly throughout the groups. These characteristics of the design should also assist homogeneity of variance; the shape of the distribution of the known and unwanted factors should be the same within each group as well as their average level being similar.

This draws attention to the need for control subjects; people who are exposed to the exact situation, but who receive an alternative treatment. They must be examined identically so that the same information is available on each. In the case of drug trials, they may be given placebo, because a certain proportion of patients with most psychiatric syndromes tend to respond to this with improvement; or they may be given the most effective treatment available, against which the unknown can then be contrasted. For this type of comparison there is much to be said for always having both these control groups, and then the effect of the influence under study can be placed along the spectrum of improvement expected for the variable being recorded. In psychiatric research a control group is quite essential, and should as far as possible be examined 'blind' because of the extensive influence of observer bias on almost any measure.

The judgement on the findings of a study should involve the efficiency of the matching or the randomness of the allocation. In phenomenology and epidemiology this advice is just as important as in therapeutic assessment.

The effect of unwanted variables is easier to control in prospective studies, and wherever possible this type of study is preferable. In retrospective research—usually on information gleaned from case-notes—measurement of the variables may not have been recorded at the time. It cannot be concluded that the factors were necessarily absent, randomly distributed or whatever the experimenter hopes should have occurred.

Sex and marital status of the subject are important sources of experimental bias which may influence findings, as may social class and age, as mentioned. In controlled investigation, factors which are known to influence outcome should be matched between groups. Depending on the experiment, body build, intelligence, duration in hospital, characteristics of diagnosis—nature, length and severity of symptoms and of treatment—side-effects, drug serum levels, patient's co-operativeness and the like, could all be relevant variables which might confound any conclusions by having introduced experimental bias. It is wise to check that any possibly relevant factors have been distributed randomly. In a large experiment, it may be better to have more than two groups regarding these variables (e.g. older and younger patients), and other variables (e.g. higher and lower dose of treatment given) stratified in blocks. If desired, the influence of main effects and their interactions on each other can be examined in a sophisticated way by analysis of variance.

The need for much of this attention to matching can be avoided by using the patient as his own control; treatments can be presented sequentially using a cross-over design. As psychiatric patients tend to improve most shortly after starting any treatment, it is important to present both treatments on the first occasion to the same number of patients. Unfortunately by using this design a new problem is introduced from carry-over effects. Improvement on the first treatment may continue into the second treatment's period; or on the other hand withdrawal of the first treatment may worsen the clinical state so upsetting the second treatment's effects, or even making that treatment appear to worsen the clinical state. This could have happened, for example, in the trial on the effect of hypnotic and placebo on sleep.

Should more than two treatment periods be used (e.g. placebo and one drug at two doses) the subjects within a group can be allocated to them evenly in all possible orders; this involves a block design called a Latin-square, so the effects of order can be under scrutiny unconfounded with effects of treatment.

TABLE I

*Example of Latin Square Design*

| Subjects | Treatment period | | |
|:---:|:---:|:---:|:---:|
| | 1 | 2 | 3 |
| 1 | A | B | C |
| 2 | A | C | B |
| 3 | B | A | C |
| 4 | B | C | A |
| 5 | C | A | B |
| 6 | C | B | A |

In most clinical trials it is usual for some of the patients to drop out before completion of the treatment period. Unfortunately this reduces the credibility of the results considerably, because it cannot be known whether these patients would have been the ones who might have done well, done badly or have been evenly distributed in both outcomes. Generally if the attrition rate is more than a third, the value of any subsequent assessment is spurious.

Prejudice in the observer is another source of experimental bias; should he know the treatment given, wittingly or unwittingly, his recording of results may be distorted. Similarly the patient is less likely to respond if he is told he is on placebo rather than some powerful treatment. Hence trials of treatment should always be carried out 'blind'. The term 'double-blind' is used when neither the patient nor the experimenter has any clue to the nature of the particular treatment the patient is on at any one time. Time and again in psychiatry, failure to acknowledge this principle has produced optimistic results later discarded because what was believed to have been the important influence was found to have been due to something quite different, not least being just the enthusiasm conveyed in the relationship with the experimenter.

## ASSOCIATION BETWEEN SCORES

In view of the breadth of relevant factors in psychiatry, and the extensive range of variation in each, it is unwise in research to rely on only one measure. As these measures are generally only indicative of the phenomena, none will provide the exact parameter. Nevertheless many of the phenomena are associated; for example, on intelligence, size of vocabulary correlates with capacity for object assembly; on emotion, heart rate with proneness to anxiety.

Correlation signifies degree of association. This can be examined by plotting the two scores against each other in a *scattergram*. If there is a clear slope then a statistical association exists between them. The mathematical function of this slope is the regression equation which best represents the relationship. Usually it will be in the form to give the amount of increment in the vertical measure ($y$ axis) for a standard unit in the horizontal measure ($x$ axis). The calculation can be extended to determine the distance from the regression line (the confidence limits) within which, say 95 per cent of all the values were likely to have occurred.

The correlation co-efficient lies between positive unity ($+1$) representing perfect agreement, through zero where the relationship between the two scores occurred at random, to negative unity ($-1$) representing perfect inverse association (Statistic Example 3).

The significance of any association is dependent on the number of observations. Though a result may achieve a level of probability indicating that it was unlikely to have occurred by chance, it may be still of relative unimportance if the number of observations has been extensive. Similarly the correlation may be quite high and yet not statistically significant if the number of observations was few. Only when a correlation is unlikely to be due to chance (i.e. statistically significant) should meaning of the association be considered. The proportion of the variation accounted for by a correlation is the square of the co-efficient; thus an $r$ of 0.5 implies that 25 per cent of the variance in one measure is accounted for by variation in the other measure.

## RELIABILITY AND VALIDITY

In behavioural science, perhaps because of the very nature of the subject, there is awareness that strict attention has to be paid to methodology; an awareness that is often sadly lacking in clinical studies. The tools of research are known to rely on human judgement, and thus indices of their accuracy should always be available. Two questions must be asked of any measure:

## STATISTIC EXAMPLE 3

At the same time as nurses recorded their observations for the data just analysed, the patients reported their feelings about the quality of sleep on a visual analogue scale with possible scores ranging from 0 (none) to 10 (perfect). Let us now look at the association between the patients' and nurses' scores while on placebo.

| Patients | Nurses' obser- vations $X$ | Patients' feelings $Y$ | Products $XY$ | Rank of nurses' obser- vations | Rank of patients' feelings | Differ- ence in rank $d$ | $d^2$ |
|---|---|---|---|---|---|---|---|
| A | 6.4 | 6.3 | 40.32 | 14 | 12 | −2 | 4 |
| B | 6.1 | 5.1 | 31.11 | 12 | 6 | −6 | 36 |
| C | 4.7 | 7.1 | 33.37 | 4.5 | 14 | +9.5 | 90.25 |
| D | 4.4 | 3.7 | 16.28 | 1 | 4 | +3 | 9 |
| E | 5.7 | 5.9 | 33.63 | 8.5 | 10 | +1.5 | 2.25 |
| F | 7.0 | 9.1 | 63.70 | 17 | 18 | +1 | 1 |
| G | 4.7 | 1.9 | 8.93 | 4.5 | 2 | −2.5 | 6.25 |
| H | 4.5 | 5.8 | 26.10 | 2.5 | 8.5 | +6 | 36 |
| I | 6.9 | 5.8 | 40.02 | 16 | 8.5 | −7.5 | 56.25 |
| J | 5.9 | 5.0 | 29.50 | 10 | 5 | −5 | 25 |
| K | 6.2 | 5.4 | 33.48 | 13 | 7 | −6 | 36 |
| L | 5.7 | 8.3 | 47.31 | 8.5 | 16 | +7.5 | 56.25 |
| M | 6.6 | 7.6 | 50.16 | 15 | 15 | 0 | 0 |
| N | 5.3 | 6.2 | 32.86 | 7 | 11 | +4 | 16 |
| O | 6.0 | 6.7 | 40.20 | 11 | 13 | +2 | 4 |
| P | 4.5 | 2.5 | 11.25 | 2.5 | 3 | +0.5 | 0.25 |
| Q | 4.9 | 0.8 | 3.92 | 6 | 1 | −5 | 25 |
| R | 7.2 | 9.0 | 64.80 | 18 | 17 | −1 | 1 |

$$\Sigma X = 102.7 \qquad \Sigma Y = 102.2$$

$$N = 18 \qquad N = 18$$

$$\Sigma X^2 = 600.55 \quad \Sigma Y^2 = 670.34 \quad \Sigma XY = 606.94$$

$$CF = 585.96 \quad CF = 580.27 \quad CF = \frac{\Sigma X \Sigma Y}{N}$$

$$= 583.11$$

$$\Sigma x^2 = 14.59 \qquad \Sigma y^2 = 90.07 \qquad \Sigma xy = 23.83 \qquad \Sigma d = 0 \quad \Sigma d^2 = 404.5$$

A. *Parametric*: PRODUCT-MOMENT CORRELATION COEFFICIENT

$$r = \frac{\Sigma xy}{\sqrt{(\Sigma x^2 \Sigma y^2)}} = \frac{23.83}{\sqrt{(14.59 \times 90.07)}} = 0.657$$

A statistical table of the significance of this correlation coefficient reveals that at $N-1$ (17) d.f. this value exceeds that significant at $P = 0.01$. That is, there is a highly significant association between the sets of scores.

Statistic Example 3—*contd.*

B. *Nonparametric*: SPEARMAN RANK CORRELATION COEFFICIENT

$$r_s = 1 - \frac{6\Sigma d^2}{N^3 - N} = 1 - \frac{6 \times 404.5}{18^3 - 18} = 0.583$$

A statistical table of critical values of $r_s$ (note: different table from that for product-moment) reveals also $P < 0.01$.

It should be noted that the values of the correlation coefficients differ when calculated by these two methods, though the significance of the association remains the same.

1. *Is it reliable?* How much can the technique be depended upon to obtain results consistently? A questionnaire for example, in order to be acceptable must have been found to produce comparable results when administered again in the same circumstances to similar people.

2. *Is it valid?* How much does the score represent the reality which it purports to measure?

Assessment of reliability is relatively straightforward; the test can be conducted twice, either on two occasions or by two observers, when the degree of association will give an index of consistency. Correlations of the former provides an index of test/retest reliability and of the latter inter-rater reliability.

Assessment of validity presents a more difficult problem, because so often there is no absolute criterion against which it can be judged. There can be no final arbiter on what the mood level of a patient was at a particular time. There can be no standard by which to judge the method of assessment, except another measure itself open to the same problems. The patient's view cannot always be accepted because it may be distorted by delusion or bias in communication. Validation can be accepted only if the measure *predicts* accurately some eventuality, if it is comparable to some *concurrent* assessment, if its *content* is readily applicable without extrapolation, or if its *construct* fits an acceptable theory. These four standards of validity should be applied to all investigations (Cronbach, 1960). In psychiatry it should not be enough to assign acceptable validity to an instrument only examined on groups of patients; the question should be asked on whether the score is valid for each patient alone. Rarely is the question asked to this standard.

## INDICANTS OF PSYCHIC PHENOMENA

Many phenomena in psychiatry, by their very nature are incapable of being measured directly. This applies just as specifically to the patient's statements reporting his feelings as it does to measurement of a biochemical metabolite. Reliance has to be placed on only *indicants* of the phenomena under observation. There are various types of indicants. Firstly the patient's view can be recorded by himself systematically using self-rating methods. Usually these are self-administered questionnaires, by which the patient selects the applicable reply from a choice provided for a particular question or statement. Not surprisingly this method is susceptible to distortion, wittingly or unwittingly by the patient, the amount of which remains beyond the knowledge of the experimenter. The Taylor Manifest Anxiety Scale (Taylor, 1953) and the Beck Depression Inventory (Beck *et al.*, 1961) are two examples in common use for the assessment of moods. Both have been shown to be valid.

An alternative method is to present the subject with a quantity, e.g. a 100 mm line, the ends of which are defined as the extremes of the variable; he can then apportion the quantity in some representative way (Aitken, 1969). This method has the advantage of giving the subject an analogue—rather than a series of categories—for the dimension under scrutiny, rather like a thermometer.

Osgood's semantic differential (Osgood, Suci and Tannenbaum, 1957) is a technique in which the subject allots a score (usually from seven categories) between a variety of two extremes on a particular concept, e.g. love: kind–nasty or strong–weak. Mean scores for groups can be determined, and the analysis also extended into aspects of their association.

Another variety of indicants relies on the judgement of an observer. He can record his interpretation of the patient's statements regarding a number of concepts, such as on the presence of delusional thinking and assign his judgement into a few categories—observer-rating methods. Hamilton (1959, 1960) has devised effective scales for recording the severity of depression and anxiety. These methods also depend on verbal communication from the patient. In addition, the observer can record his own observation of the patient's behaviour and take into account the relevance of non-verbal communication such as, for example, degree of agitation. A new source of error has been introduced in that any bias by the observer will effect the validity of the observation. This can be systematic and so distort conclusions, or be at random and so render the experiment insensitive. As this method has to rely on communication between two people, it seems inevitable that something must be lost. But something can also be gained in that the observer can bring to the situation his skill and knowledge. Observer-rating methods usually ensure systematic recording on all the possible features.

It is customary to record assessment into categories, each carefully defined beforehand for a variety of features known to be associated with the condition. It is common practice for these scores to be added in order to determine a total score; but in fact this practice is based on false logic as the scores are not in the same units. An additional global assessment into say a five category scale— absent, minimal, mild, moderate or severe—provides a valuable index for many situations. Again it is common practice to determine mean scores, but caution is required. No information may be available on the relative *magnitude* of the categories, or on the equivalence of the *distance* between them. Nevertheless such a method has produced results of considerable value.

Measurements can also be made of objective indices—ones that are beyond systematic manipulation by the patient or the observer. Physiological indicants such as heart rate, forearm blood flow, skin conductance or biochemical measures have been found to alter with mood. These are not measures themselves of the mood state, only indicants. Though objective indicants, they have not been measured without error. Experimental error, both systematic and random can still occur, and frequently so substantially that they become relatively insensitive as indicants. It must always be remembered that the stress of the investigative procedure itself may have altered the clinical state, producing experimental bias.

## EPIDEMIOLOGICAL STUDIES

Epidemiological studies provide examples where the unit of measure is usually frequency of events or persons (e.g., number of times patients with defined characteristics occur in a stated population). Rarely, if even possible or desirable, is the whole of the population examined; it is more usually just a sample. An exception might be a census of a particular institution, such as a hospital at a certain moment in time. The *point prevalence* of a disorder could then be ascertained for that population as the number of cases per 1,000 patients. The prevalence of a disease could be calculated by examining a random sample from the general population, and if required and justified it could be extrapolated to a rate of cases per 100,000 people in the whole population. Seldom is this justified without some conditional clause to indicate that the figures might still be in error, e.g. all the cases required might not have been identified or declared.

An absolute prevalence rate is rarely obtainable accurately and hence of limited use. What is of greater interest is a comparative prevalence when the methodology for examining samples has been identical. If the samples had been selected to have differed on only one criterion, e.g. age, then only that criterion should have produced any discrepancy in prevalence rates.

*Incidence* or *inception* is another epidemiological concept. It refers to the number of new cases emerging in a designated period and population. Again this is unlikely to be absolute, and comparative frequencies are more informative. One complexity in hospital studies is to distinguish between rates referring to the number of admissions and rates referring to the number of patients. These may be quite different as the same patient could have contributed disproportionately to the admission rate if he was readmitted on more than one occasion. It is usual to keep the rates for each sex separate.

Follow-up study of a *cohort* is a common requirement—a group of patients selected by some criterion and followed throughout a given period. Caution is required when there is selection over a period, e.g. a year, because the follow-up period will not be uniform if the closing date is the same; or on the other hand if the follow-up period is preferred to be the same, the closing date will need to be spread over another year related to the date of entry or time of treatment. It is unacceptable to examine proportions or mean scores for only a diminishing number of patients who have completed the necessary period.

Chi-square is a non-parametric test, designed to assess statistical significance of data such as this. It is based on comparison of the observed and expected frequencies when numbers of cases are allotted into categories, such as for example male/female or old/young into improved/unimproved by a certain treatment. The test can only be used when the expected frequency in any cell exceeds five.

PROBLEMS OF 'ERROR'

At this stage the reader may feel that the problems of 'error' in measurement have been over emphasized. But 'error' does not mean 'mistake' but rather variation attributable to a number of sources other than the one being examined, some systematic, others random, some at least always being irremediable or 'residual'. Understanding the problems of examining 'error' is the key to efficient methodology in research. Clearly it is advantageous to reduce this 'error' variation to as little as possible, by being able to account for as much as possible. For many observations it may be negligible such as in measuring weight, family size or duration of hospital stay, but even in the best experiment it is unlikely to be non-existent.

FALLACY OF CAUSALITY

It is imperative to appreciate that demonstration of association between scores gives no proof that the connection is causal; it may be due to associations with another common factor, and the association observed be only the result of this. This limits the usefulness of correlation as there must always be some reason for confidence in a unique logical theory before acknowledging meaningfulness. For example, in recent years there has been a steady increase in the number of admissions for self-poisoning; and also in the number of prescriptions for psychotropic drugs. The numbers have been found to correlate highly, and it is tempting to deduce that the one resulted from the other. Though this *could* be true, correlation would also have been found if there had been a similar change in another common factor, such as prevalence of distress in the community. If this had occurred, it is likely that there would be an increase in symptoms for which psychotropic drugs might be prescribed and also, but independently, in the frequency of attempted suicide. Causality cannot be implied only from the demonstration of association by correlation.

Yet should there appear to be a logical explanatory theory for a correlation found between two sets of data it is appropriate to act upon it; it would be foolish to ignore it. For example, in recent years there has been a decline in the number of suicides by carbon monoxide poisoning; and also in the concentration of CO in town gas. It seems very likely that the one can be attributed to the other, but causality cannot be deduced with certainty. Nevertheless it is wise to encourage the abolition of CO from town gas.

Another limiting factor in the usefulness of correlation is that demonstration of association must not be extrapolated beyond the limits of the data. For example, the duration of sleep falls from infancy to old age, the rate depending on the age range. If the rate of reduction in children is extrapolated to adults, the unwary might conclude that no sleep at all is required by a certain age. But demonstration of an association at one level of maturity provides no evidence whatsoever on the form of the relationship to be expected at another. The relationship is curvilinear, and hence the meaning of correlation can alter at a different range of scores.

There is no way to determine the significance regarding lack of association. False conclusions have been made frequently, because small correlations may have been statistically significant, but clinically meaningless. Repeated observation may fail to confirm association, but will fail to prove that association does *not* exist. More's the pity in psychiatry where the mass of data lies in the hinterland between interest in possible associations but lack of positive proof regarding their causal relationship.

FACTOR ANALYSIS

When a correlation matrix is constructed of all the possible correlations between a set of variables, their relative magnitude allows understanding of the likely features which go together. Clearly if the correlations were low, these measures were unlikely to share much in common. Factor analyses have been extended in sophisticated ways into 'principle components' analyses whereby a selection of variables can be taken into account each given a weighting factor, determined by the degree of association with the others. Associations emerge which can be interpreted into general concepts, like neuroticism for example. The proportion of variation accounted for can also be recognized, and hence the relative importance of the factors. Important ones are called high-order, which may even be correlations of correlations.

The use of Kelly's Repertory Grid technique in the assessment of an individual patient is gaining popularity, since Slater (1965), in association with the Medical Research Council, provided a computing service for its analysis. Basically the patient ranks a number of elements (e.g. people) on a series of constructs (e.g. amount of kindness or depression). A grid can thus be prepared which reveals the consistency and nature of his attitude. Correlations and factor analyses will allow testing of certain hypotheses regarding associations, and reveal how the patient's view on various matters relate to each other.

MULTIVARIATE ANALYSIS

When subjects are characterized by some specific criterion, e.g. diagnosis allotted, the relationship between the criterion and the score on any variable can be ascertained. As mentioned, generally in psychiatry there is overlap; not all, but only the majority of patients in one category have the variable extensively. In what way is it best to take into account the scores on all the variables in order to achieve the best separation for the specific criterion? With multivariate analysis a 'discriminant function' can be determined by assigning weighting scores to all the variables, and so providing the most effective division should it have been determined solely by the scores on the variables. The weights can then be used on a different group of patients whose scores on only the variables are known, in order to predict into which category they belong. If the correlation between any two variables has been perfect (i.e. unity), nothing will be gained by using more than one of them in the discrimination.

ANALYSIS OF COVARIANCE

As mentioned previously, analysis of variance is a technique by which the variation attributable to a feature of the experiment (e.g. type of treatment, or serial order of observation) can be examined in relation to all the variation found. This will leave residual variation unaccounted for, against which that due to the known feature is tested. As the residual is attributable to 'error', and assumed to have occurred at random, the probability of the variation being due to the feature and not to having occurred by chance can be ascertained.

It may be that the scores correlated with the scores on another feature, e.g. age. In analysis of covariance, the influence of this feature can be removed. The data can then be reanalysed to assess the effect of different treatments, ignoring the age effect. The same problem arises here as with simple correlations. Even if association can be demonstrated or there is a significant difference between scores after selection by some feature, the obvious connection may not be the only answer to explain causality. There may be an alternative explanation due to a common factor or introduction of systematic error. The unwary must keep an ever-watchful eye for this trap.

## DATA COLLECTION

In experimental work it is a golden rule that the design should allow the data to be ascertained numerically. As indicated, numbers can be used to count (interval), to label (nominal), or to rank (ordinal). Before any statistical analysis, the scores should be displayed to correspond with the questions asked of the data. The liberal use of graph paper for histograms, such as in Figure 1, or scattergrams is to be recommended. Should the quantity of data be substantial it is helpful to transfer it to punched-hole cards. These can then be sorted in order to provide the information for simple calculations on the data such as in the Statistic Examples. An additional advantage is that the numbers can be printed and listed for inspection, and this can be done as often as required. Checking is required at every stage where numbers are being transferred or changed by calculation. Once they are on punched-hole cards correctly, the opportunity for introduction of careless error is reduced.

### PRESENTATION OF EXPERIMENTAL RESULTS

Reading journal articles gives a clear indication of current convention; but attendance at meetings is frequently unrewarding because speakers rarely follow the correct manner for display of results. Each slide should have little more than one item of information on it. Lines drawn should be preferred to typed numbers. Legibility for the viewer, and audibility for the listener, are the responsibilities of the speaker.

### ETHICS OF CLINICAL RESEARCH

This is a topic on which there are as many opinions as there are moral philosophers, amateur or academic, but on which fear of litigation has had as profound an effect as any principle. Current practice in the United Kingdom has been encouraged to follow a statement of responsibilities in investigations on human subjects by the Medical Research Council (1963).

There is a clear distinction between procedures which will contribute to the benefit of an individual patient, and those in which he only assists by participating in an experiment which will lead to a finding for the ultimate benefit of all. The former, which includes some standard drug trials, requires only the standards of good clinical care, but the latter requires special co-operation, as the investigations are purely experimental. The individual has rights that the law protects and nobody can infringe those rights for the public good.

A patient should not be included in an experimental procedure without his informed consent. That it is both considerate and prudent to obtain the patient's agreement before using a novel procedure is no more than a requirement of good medical practice. Investigations that are of no direct benefit to the individual require that his true consent to them shall be explicitly obtained. Exactly what constitutes informed consent may involve legal issues when referring to certain types of psychiatric patient. For experimental procedures, the patient must be told the nature of any risks involved.

The experimental design need only be explained in general terms, and should include, for example, the information that a drug prescribed could be placebo. Clearly any clinical research is unjustified if it involves unwarranted risks to the patient, unless the advantage to him could be substantial. Rarely in psychiatry does this apply.

A controlled trial is only required when there is a prima facie case that a new treatment may be effective. Benefit may have been suspected during a simple clinical trial, or just by theory; a carefully controlled investigation must then follow. On the other hand, controlled trials are only justifiable when doubt remains as to which of two treatment procedures is the better—when the null hypothesis has not yet been rejected. The null hypothesis cannot be discarded by an uncontrolled trial, because it would produce no evidence on whether any changes could have resulted from another aspect of the treatment procedure than the drug prescribed. When such a trial is investigating the choice between two treatments, one of which is placebo, it follows that there must be genuine doubt on the effectiveness of any drug treatment for that condition.

An important safeguard, both legally and professionally, has been introduced recently in many hospitals by the surveillance of clinical research by a medical committee. This encourages the experimenter to consider the ethical implications of his research, and provides him with some assurance of their acceptability to colleagues who are aware of the local situation and the ability of the research worker. Informed consent for example, can be accepted as what colleagues agree to be responsible and reasonable. All who have been concerned with medical research are aware of the impossibility of formulating any detailed code of rules which will ensure that irreproachability of practice which alone will suffice when investigations on human beings are concerned.

# REFERENCES

AITKEN, R. C. B. (1969) Measurement of feelings using visual analogue scales. *Proceedings of the Royal Society of Medicine*, **62**, 989–993.

BECK, A. T., WARD, C. H., MENDELSON, M., MOCK, J. & ERBAUGH, J. (1961) An inventory for measuring depression. *Archives of General Psychiatry*, **4**, 561–571.

CRONBACH, L. J. (1960) *Essentials of Psychological Testing*. 2nd edn. New York: Harper.

HAMILTON, M. (1959) The assessment of anxiety states by rating. *British Journal of Medical Psychology*, **32**, 50–55.

HAMILTON, M. (1960) A rating scale for depression. *Journal of Neurology, Neurosurgery and Psychiatry*, **23**, 56–62.

MEDICAL RESEARCH COUNCIL (1962–63) Responsibility in investigations on human subjects. Report (Cmnd. 2382), pp. 21–25.

OSGOOD, C. E., SUCI, G. J. & TANNENBAUM, P. H. (1957) *The Measurement of Meaning*. University of Illinois.

SIEGEL, S. (1956) *Nonparametric Statistics for the Behavioral Sciences*. New York: McGraw-Hill.

SLATER, P. (1965) The use of the repertory grid technique in the individual case. *British Journal of Psychiatry*, **111**, 965–975.

SNEDECOR, G. W. & COCHRAN, W. G. (1967) *Statistical Methods*. 6th edn. Ames: Iowa State University Press.

TAYLOR, J. A. (1953) A personality scale of manifest anxiety. *Journal of Abnormal and Social Psychology*, **48**, 285–290.

## Chapter IX

## SOME ASPECTS OF PSYCHOLOGY

### F. M. McPherson

#### INTRODUCTION

This chapter is intended as an elementary introduction to some aspects of psychology. The topics selected are those which seem to be among the most relevant to psychiatry, i.e. they are often referred to in psychiatry textbooks or articles, and psychologists are frequently asked about them by their psychiatrist colleagues.

Clearly, in a chapter of this length, some drastic oversimplification has been necessary, and many important aspects of the topics considered have had to be ignored. For this reason, further reading will frequently be recommended; a particularly useful, and inexpensive, general textbook of psychology is Wright and Taylor (1970).

The term 'psychology' is used in psychiatry in several distinct ways. Psychological medicine is used synonymously with 'psychiatry'. Medical psychology can refer to the study of abnormal behaviour, but can also be used to refer to the theories and practices of various psychodynamically orientated therapists such as Freud, Jung and Klein. Psychological treatment is usually taken to mean the various forms of psychotherapy, as opposed to physical methods such as drugs and E.C.T. Psychological (or psychic) symptoms are disorders of thinking and feeling, as opposed to physical (or somatic) complaints. Finally, there is the scientific, or experimental, psychology with which this chapter deals. This is the discipline which University Departments of Psychology teach and study, and of which clinical psychology is an applied branch. What, then, is scientific psychology?

#### DEFINITION

Most psychologists would accept that psychology is the scientific study of the behaviour of man and other animals.

Scientific study is specified because it is not only psychologists who study behaviour. Each of us continually tries to understand and predict our own thoughts and behaviour and those of other people. Many people, e.g. salesmen, make use of this understanding in their daily work. What distinguishes psychologists is not that they study behaviour, but that they do so using the methods of science.

Psychology had modelled itself on the natural sciences, and attempts to describe, explain, predict or control behaviour. An aspect of behaviour may be studied by observing it as it occurs naturally, but wherever possible—practically or ethically—psychologists tend to carry out experiments, in which elements of the situation are systematically altered so that a causal connection may be established between the behaviour and the events which influence it. Frequently, although not always, psychologists measure and quantify the behaviour which they study, and use statistical methods to analyse the results (see Vol. I, Chap. VIII).

## Scope and Content of Psychology

Behaviour for the psychologist has a much wider meaning than for the layman. It includes not only those actions which are overt and directly observable, such as social interaction or speech, but also many aspects of subjective experience such as perceptions, thoughts, and feelings. The main technical problem of psychology is to devise methods by which 'private' experience can be made public and observable, and so be investigated scientifically.

Among the most important areas of behaviour which psychologists study are (1) cognitive and symbolic processes, which are those to do with acquiring and using information about the world around us, and include the processes of attention, perception, learning, retention, thinking and communication; (2) motivation, which refers to the forces which drive and direct behaviour, such as thirst, hunger, fear and aggression, and social motives such as the 'needs' for affiliation and achievement; (3) personality, which is usually taken to refer to the attitudes, beliefs, traits, and other typical and relatively stable modes of reacting which distinguish one person from another; (4) social interaction, which is about how people interact with, and influence one another in dyads and small and large groups; (5) abnormal behaviour, i.e. the nature and causes of abnormalities and disorders of psychological functioning; (6) animal behaviour, which is studied by psychologists because it is 'behaviour', interesting in its own right, but also because of the light which it can throw on human processes.

## Explanation in Psychology

A confusing feature of psychology is that very many different concepts, techniques and theories are used by psychologists. One reason for this is that psychologists differ in the sorts of explanation of behaviour which they attempt. The same facet of behaviour can be explained in several different ways, all of which are equally valid, although they may differ in their usefulness.

Thus, for example, the immediate causes of the behaviour can be studied, as can the more long-term historical influences, its purpose and function, its genetic basis and its relation to structures and processes of the nervous system.

Some psychologists are less concerned with why behaviour occurs than with whether it can be predicted, or controlled or modified. Other psychologists are more concerned with description, e.g. in describing and measuring the main ways in which people differ from one another.

Because of this, psychology appears very fragmented, with empirical investigations in many areas proceeding almost independently of the remainder of psychology. There are few concepts or principles which can be applied throughout psychology and no general theory of behaviour to which all psychological investigations can be related.

## PURE AND APPLIED PSYCHOLOGY

In psychology, as in other sciences, a distinction is sometimes made between pure and applied study. The main types of applied psychologists are (1) occupational psychologists, concerned with vocational selection and guidance, the design of equipment, communication and morale within factories etc., (2) educational psychologists, concerned with the treatment of learning disorders, with educational guidance, devising and evaluating teaching methods etc., and (3) clinical psychologists, who apply psychological findings and techniques to the investigation and treatment of psychiatric illness.

## LEARNING

### DEFINITION

Learning can be defined as: any relatively permanent change in behaviour which is brought about as a result of past experience. 'Past experience' is specified in order to exclude changes due to maturation, senility, injury or illness.

'Relatively permanent' draws attention to a crucial distinction between learning and the performance of what is learned. Only the latter can be observed and measured directly, and learning must be inferred from performance. However, performance is not always an accurate index of learning because it can be influenced by other factors, such as motivation; day-to-day fluctuations may occur in how a learned habit is expressed in behaviour.

The 'learning' with which students are most familiar is the 'learning-by-heart' of facts before an exam., or the learning of skills such as driving or typing. However, it is obvious from the above definition that, for the psychologist, learning has a much wider meaning.

THE STUDY OF LEARNING

As there is hardly a facet of human or animal behaviour which is not affected in some way by learning, a great deal of experimental psychology is about learning, its effects and what influences them. Psychologists are interested both in the basic processes of learning and in how these can be applied in practical situations.

Many psychologists believe that by studying simple learning in animals and humans it will be possible to establish the fundamental laws which govern learning in more complex situations, and hence to develop general theories of behaviour. One of the simplest forms of learning is conditioning, and numerous studies have been carried out of conditioning both in animals and in man. Several elaborate theories of behaviour, of which the best known is Hull's (1943), have been developed on the basis of conditioning studies. Although few psychologists now consider these general theories to be adequate, conditioning is still used to explain the development of many aspects of behaviour.

A second major area of interest for psychologists concerned with establishing fundamental laws of learning is verbal learning, which is about how we acquire and retain symbolically represented material, such as words, sentences and numbers. Rote-learning, or learning facts 'by heart', is one aspect of this. Many of the terms and concepts of conditioning are employed in the study of verbal learning, although information theory (see Brown, 1964; and Chap. 5 in Foss, 1966) is increasingly influential. A third area of interest is social learning, which concerns learning in an inter-personal situation such as an interview, or parent–child interaction. The concepts of simple learning are used here also, but in addition, 'social' forms of learning have been described and investigated, e.g. imitation, identification and introjection (see Wright and Taylor, 1970, Chap. 21).

Among the studies of the practical applications of learning of most interest to psychiatrists are those of behaviour therapy, or behaviour modification. This is the general name given to a number of techniques whose aim is the removal or reduction of symptoms or distress in patients, and whose rationale derives from conditioning (see Vol. II, Chap. XVIII; and Beech, Chap. 18, in Foss, 1966). A second practical application of fundamental studies of conditioning is programmed learning. The basic approach to the development of teaching machines and programmed texts, which are having a considerable impact on teaching methods, was formulated by Skinner (1954) on the basis of his earlier work on simple learning in pigeons (see Kay, Chap. 16, in Foss, 1966). A third topic is learning difficulties as the cause of backwardness in school subjects such as reading and counting. Some studies concern the nature of these difficulties, and relate them to cognitive processes, while other psychologists try to devise remedial methods of teaching and training for children (and adults) with particular difficulties (see O'Connor, Chap. 17, in Foss, 1966).

Obviously it is not possible in this section to deal with all these aspects of learning, so only conditioning will be discussed.

FEATURES OF CONDITIONING

CLASSICAL AND INSTRUMENTAL CONDITIONING SITUATIONS

It is usual to distinguish between classical conditioning and instrumental or operant conditioning (or learning).

Classical conditioning is associated with early Soviet psychologists such as Pavlov (1927) and Bekhterev (1932). The main effect of classical conditioning is to increase the number of stimuli which are capable of eliciting a given response. The starting point is a stimulus which 'naturally' elicits a response or reflex—respectively termed the Unconditional (or Unconditioned) Stimulus, abbreviated to US, and the Unconditional Response, UR. If a second stimulus, which does not 'naturally' elicit the UR, is paired with the US, so that it occurs immediately before the US on several occasions, this second stimulus will acquire the power to elicit the UR in the absence of the US. When it does so, it is termed the Conditional Stimulus, C.S., i.e. its power to elicit the response is *conditional* upon its having been associated with the US. The response, when elicited by the CS instead of by the US, is termed the Conditional Response, CR. It usually differs slightly from the UR, e.g. by occurring more slowly or being of smaller magnitude. For effective conditioning to occur, the CS must precede the US. The length of time between the presentation of the CS and of the US is important. If it is too great, no conditioning will occur; the optimal time interval is different for particular CS–US combinations, and subjects, but is often less than 1 sec.

Much of Pavlov's work was with dogs which were trained, for example, to salivate to the sound of a bell by having meat powder (US) placed in their mouths, causing them to salivate (UR), immediately after the bell (CS) was rung. Very many human responses have been conditioned. The eyeblink reflex is frequently used in research, the US being a puff of air directed into the eye, and the CS being a tone or buzzer.

Instrumental conditioning has been studied most comprehensively by Skinner (1938) and his colleagues. The aim of this form of learning is to select the class of behaviour, from among many alternatives, which the learner will habitually give in a particular stimulus situation. In a typical operant learning experiment, a rat is placed in a box which has a lever on one wall. When the lever is pressed, a pellet of food is sent into the box. After exploring the box for some time, the rat will accidentally press the bar and obtain the food. This may happen several times before any noticeable change in the rat's behaviour occurs, but gradually it begins to press the bar more frequently, until eventually it spends much of its time pressing. In other words, the behaviour of the rat has been modified and, from the whole range of possible actions which it could perform in the box, it has learned to perform one.

There are three main types of operant situation: (1) reward training, in which the learned behaviour or habit allows the organism to obtain a 'reward', such as food or water; (2) in escape training, the learned behaviour allows the animal to escape from a noxious stimulus, e.g. a rat on an electrified grid can learn to escape by running to another part of the cage as soon as the shock begins; while (3) in avoidance training, the animal learns to avoid the noxious stimulus entirely, e.g. by running to the non-electrified part of the cage whenever it hears a bell, which is rung a few seconds before each shock begins (see Stretch, Chap. 15, in Foss, 1966).

SOME PRINCIPLES AND CONCEPTS OF CONDITIONING

There are some obvious differences between the classical and instrumental situations. For example, in the former, the US produces directly, in the learner, the response which is to be conditioned; hence it is sometimes referred to as respondent conditioning. In instrumental conditioning, on the other hand, the learner must emit the response 'spontaneously'. It is not clear whether classical and instrumental conditioning are distinct types of learning, or whether classical conditioning is merely a special case of the latter. Certainly, many of the same features and processes appear to be involved in both. Some of these will now be outlined.

*Acquisition of learned habits*

Learning typically proceeds gradually and erratically, with periods of rapid improvement being interspersed with 'plateaux' when no change in performance is observable. Learning may occur as the result of a single reinforcement (one-trial learning) but many reinforcements are usually necessary for stable learning.

*Extinction of learned habits*

Learned responses do not last forever, and in the absence of reinforcement they tend to disappear. Thus, a dog which has been trained to salivate (CR) to a bell (CS) will gradually cease to do so unless the CS–CR connection is reinforced occasionally by the US being presented immediately after the CS. However, extinction, like learning, may not be permanent and after a period during which a habit has apparently been completely extinguished, it may reappear briefly (spontaneous recovery).

## Higher-order conditioning

In classical conditioning, once a CS–CR connection has been established, the CS can serve as a US in the conditioning of a connection between a *new* stimulus and the response. For example, if a dog had been trained to salivate at the sound of a bell, a light could be paired with the bell until the light alone elicits the salivation—although the light had never itself been associated directly with the original US, the food in the mouth. Higher-order conditioning is similar in many ways to the secondary reward or reinforcement which can operate in an operant conditioning situation (see below).

## Stimulus generalization and discrimination

An animal which has been conditioned to respond to a given stimulus will also tend to respond to other stimuli which are physically similar to it: this is stimulus generalization. The tendency to respond is greatest for stimuli which are most similar to the original: this is known as the gradient of generalization. Response generalization also occurs. The opposite of stimulus generalization is stimulus discrimination, shown when the learner responds to one stimulus but not to another which differs from it in some way.

Motivation and learning interact in two main ways. First, as noted above, the performance of learned behaviour depends upon the initial learning but also upon the motivation for performance. Day-to-day fluctuations in an individual's performance can often be accounted for by variation in motivation or drive-level. Thus, a rat which has learned to run through a maze to reach food will run more quickly when hungry than when not.

Second, while some motives derive from basic, physiological needs, such as hunger or thirst (primary drives), others appear to be learned or acquired (secondary drives). The most closely studied of these in humans is anxiety or fear. The needs for affiliation, achievement, power and money are frequently mentioned as being important 'secondary drives' in humans (see Argyle, 1967, Chap. 1).

### REINFORCEMENT

This is a central concept in many theories of behaviour.

#### DEFINITION

Several definitions of reinforcement are used, a common one being that a reinforcing stimulus is one which increases the probability of occurrence of that class of response that immediately precedes it. The presentation of a reinforcing stimulus is a reinforcement. In classical conditioning, the US is said to reinforce the CS–CR connection: in operant learning, the bar-pressing is reinforced by its consequences, e.g. the food-pellets.

TYPES OF REINFORCEMENT

Very many different stimuli have been used as reinforcers. One distinction is between positive and negative reinforcers. These are respectively, stimuli which, when *added* to a situation, and which when *removed* from it, increase the probability of occurrence of a class of behaviour. Food and water, are often used as primitive reinforcers in animal studies, and electric shock as a negative reinforcer.

Another distinction, somewhat arbitrary, is between primary and secondary reinforcement. Some reinforcers, such as food and water, seem to be effective 'naturally' (primary reinforcers) whereas others appear to be effective only because of a specific history of conditioning (secondary reinforcers), i.e. a previously neutral stimulus, repeatedly presented just before a primary reinforcer, can itself acquire reinforcing properties.

The stimuli which have been shown to be effective in modifying behaviour vary from organism to organism, and from learning situation to learning situation. They range from food and drink, and escape from a noxious stimulus, to electrical stimulation of the brain (e.g. Olds and Milner, 1954) and expressions of approval or disapproval by the experimenter.

SOCIAL REINFORCEMENT

From human conditioning experiments there is clear evidence of the effectiveness of social reinforcers, i.e. one individual can serve as a source of meaningful stimuli which alter, direct and maintain the behaviour of someone else. For example, studies of verbal conditioning have shown that, by using a variety of reinforcing stimuli (such as verbal expressions of approval and disapproval, apparent interest or lack of interest, etc.), experimenters can influence what interviewees say during an interview, e.g. increasing or decreasing the frequency with which the interviewee uses certain classes of words, such as plurals, or references to their symptoms. Often, this seems to occur without the interviewee being aware that his verbal behaviour is being affected.

Some of the most interesting work in this area has been by Salzinger and his colleagues (see Inglis, 1966, Chap. 7). For example, Salzinger and Pisoni (1958) increased the frequency with which schizophrenics used affect statements, e.g. 'I like him' and 'he enjoyed it', in interviews by having the interviewer say 'mm-hm', 'I see', 'Yeah' and so forth every time the schizophrenic used an affect statement. Salzinger, Portnoy and Feldman (1964) have pointed out the relevance of findings of this sort for psychotherapy. Therapists of different orientations may inadvertently, by showing interest etc., reinforce in their patients the kind of statements and insights they think should be produced. For example, the non-directive form of psychotherapy described by Rogers (1951) has much in common with a verbal conditioning situation.

NATURE OF REINFORCEMENT

Because so many different reinforcers have been described, it is very difficult to discover what they have in common which might indicate why reinforcement has its effect. Some reinforcing stimuli clearly satisfy primary biological needs, while others have in the past been associated with the satisfaction of such needs. Some, however, particularly in human learning, seem merely to draw the attention of the learner to one aspect of the situation, as the 'mm-hm' drew attention to the affect statement. Still others appear to give the learner knowledge of the results of his behaviour, e.g. when using teaching machines, the learner knows immediately whether his answer was correct or incorrect (see Kay, Chap. 16, in Foss, 1966).

REINFORCEMENT AND LEARNING

While some learning may occur in the apparent absence of reinforcement (see Exposure Learning, below, p. 167), the performance of learned habits is greatly influenced by reinforcement conditions. For example, the resistance of learned behaviour to extinction increases with the number of reinforcements. The reinforcement schedule is also important; a class of behaviour which, when it was being learned, was reinforced only intermittently (partial reinforcement) is particularly resistant to extinction (see Stretch, Chap. 15, in Foss, 1966).

## CONDITIONING AND PERSONALITY

One example of how complex human behaviour can be accounted for in terms of simple learning, is Eysenck's theory of the development of personality and of neurotic symptoms.

SOCIALIZATION

Eysenck (see Eysenck and Rachman, 1965, Chap. 1) follows Mowrer (1950) in regarding socialization, or the development of socially desirable behaviour, as being based on a two-stage process of conditioning, involving a learned (secondary) drive, fear. The first stage is when a child behaves in a way of which his parents, teachers, peers, etc. disapprove. The act (CS) will be followed by verbal or physical punishment (US) leading to pain and fear (UR) until eventually the act itself will evoke fear or anxiety (CR). Generalization and higher-order conditioning ensure that a range of similar acts, and even thinking about them, will arouse fear and anxiety in the child. In the second stage, the fear which is evoked by the punished act functions as a secondary drive, and reinforces any behaviour which reduces the fear, such as avoiding or escaping from the fear-producing situation. The child who has been punished for taking his sister's toy will feel anxious when he does so, but the anxiety will be reduced when he hands it back, so that the handing back will be reinforced (escape training); alternatively, not taking it in the first place will lead to avoidance of the anxiety and will also be reinforced (avoidance training). Classical conditioning is thus involved in the first stage and operant conditioning in the second. In this way the child's behaviour becomes acceptable to those around him and eventually he develops a 'conscience' (Eysenck, 1964).

DEVELOPMENT OF NEUROTIC SYMPTOMS

Eysenck and Rachman distinguish between two general types of neurotic behaviour. The first, 'dysthymic' disorders, e.g. phobias, anxiety states, obsessional disorders, are regarded as being learned in the same way as most human behaviour. However, unlike the socially approved behaviour described above, dysthymic symptoms are maladaptive, i.e. they serve no useful purpose to society or to the patient, although they may be of short-term benefit in allowing him to avoid anxiety temporarily.

Phobias, for example, are held to be the result of a traumatic event (US) producing fear (UR) which becomes associated with a previously neutral stimulus (CS), e.g. a cat, a street, a motor car, which then evokes the fear (CR) on its own. Avoidance of the CS, e.g. by remaining indoors, is anxiety reducing and so is reinforced and repeated. This avoidance has the advantage to the patient that it prevents him from encountering the feared object (CS) and so becoming anxious. However, the disadvantage is that it also prevents the acquired fear (CR) from being extinguished; extinction will tend to occur if the CS is encountered on several occasions in the absence of the traumatic event (US) and hence in the absence of reinforcement.

Two examples of the second type of disorder are sociopathic behaviour and euresis. Here, the disorder results from the failure of appropriate conditioned responses to occur, either because of faulty training procedure or because the patient has been unable to benefit from normal training. Thus, sociopaths or psychopaths are regarded as

G

lacking many of the conditioned anxieties which control the behaviour of normals. They therefore act antisocially or asocially. In enuresis, the failure of conditioning is more specific; the patient lacks the normal conditioned connection between the physical sensations of a distended bladder (CS) and waking up and inhibiting micturition (CR).

Treatment of disorders of the first type takes the form of extinguishing the excessive, maladaptive habits; with the second type, treatment involves establishing adaptive habits.

## INDIVIDUAL DIFFERENCES

What determines who will develop neurotic illness, and what type of illness they will have?

Eysenck postulates that individuals differ in the number of adaptive, learned responses which they acquire and that this is related to differences in conditionability, which in turn is related to personality characteristics. Eysenck (1947) factor-analyzed ratings and other psychiatric data, questionnaire responses and objective test results, obtained for many hundreds of psychiatric patients and normals. The factor-analysis suggested that many of the important differences in people's personality could be summarized in terms of their differing along two main independent dimensions, introversion–extraversion, and neuroticism. People at the extreme introversion pole of the introversion–extraversion dimension are quiet and reserved, plan ahead and dislike excitement, control their feelings and are reliable. The extreme extravert is sociable, craves excitement, expresses his feeling readily, and is not always reliable. Everyone can be placed somewhere between these two extremes. The neuroticism dimension distinguishes people who are emotionally labile from those who are stable and calm (see Eysenck and Rachman, 1965, Chap. 2). People who are high on the neuroticism dimension over-react to stressful situations and are therefore predisposed to develop neurotic behaviour. Regarding the type of illness which people develop, Eysenck's theory (1957) was influenced by Pavlov's (1927) theory of experimental neurosis, which was based on the concepts of excitation and inhibition. Eysenck postulates (see Eysenck and Rachman, 1965, Chap. 3) that individuals differ in the speed with which cortical inhibition is produced and dissipates. Individuals in whom it generates quickly and dissipates slowly are prone to develop extraverted patterns of behaviour. Those in whom inhibition generates slowly are introverted and develop dysthymic disorders in the event of breakdown.

The link between cortical inhibition, and personality and neurosis, is conditioning. Individuals in whom inhibition builds up slowly are said to condition quickly and so acquire many adaptive responses, i.e. they are introverted. They also run the risk of acquiring many maladaptive responses and of thus developing disorders of the first type. Individuals in whom cortical inhibition generates quickly may not acquire a sufficient number of adaptive responses and may therefore behave psychopathically (see Eysenck and Rachman, 1965, for their account of the development of specific conditions).

### DISCUSSION

Eysenck's formulation has run into many difficulties, e.g. there does not seem to be a unitary trait of 'conditionability', and the relationship between introversion and speed of conditioning seems to hold only under certain conditions. It is also often argued that learning theory accounts of neurosis are simplistic in that they ignore, for example, cognitive factors such as what the patient thinks about his illness, and also interpersonal factors such as the disturbed relationships which neurosis typically involves. However, Eysenck and Rachman argue that learning theory accounts for some of the most important aspects, and in particular those which are most relevant to treatment. The adequacy of conditioning models of neurosis and of complex behaviour in general, and the question of whether behaviour therapy is, as claimed, rigorously derived from learning theory, is discussed by Breger and McGaugh (1965, 1966), and in the replies of Rachman and Eysenck (1966) and Wiest (1967), and in Vol. II, Chap. XVIII.

### EXPOSURE LEARNING

This may be a special case of conditioning or may be a different type of learning.

### LATENT LEARNING

Some studies seem to indicate that while the performance of a learned habit seems to depend upon reinforcement, the initial learning may sometimes occur in the apparent absence of reinforcement. Thus, in a typical latent learning situation, an unmotivated, unreinforced animal is given the opportunity to explore a maze; its behaviour (performance) gives no indication that it has learned anything about the maze. However, it must have done, because when it is later motivated and reinforced, it learns to run the maze more quickly than animals without the previous experience, so indicating that something must have 'carried over' from the exploration.

### MODELLING

Another apparent example of unreinforced learning is modelling. The subject merely observes another (the model) performing some behaviour and then later repeats it, without seemingly having been reinforced in any way. Bandura (Chap. 15, in Krasner and Ullman, 1966) argues that modelling is particularly important in the development of new behaviour. Reinforcement, as used in operant conditioning studies, is an efficient and reliable method of strengthening or modifying behaviour which already exists in the behavioural repertoire of the learner. However, much of the behaviour that humans learn cannot be elicited directly by a stimulus, or is not emitted 'spontaneously' so that it can be reinforced. Of course, it is possible to produce some very odd and 'unnatural' behaviour, such as pigeons playing 'table tennis', by the method of 'shaping' or successive approximations, in which behaviour increasingly similar to the required behaviour is reinforced (see Stretch, Chap. 15, in Foss, 1966). However, this is a cumbersome and inefficient method and Bandura suggests that it is unlikely to account for the development of much new behaviour in real life.

MODELLING IN THE DEVELOPMENT OF SOCIAL BEHAVIOUR

Bandura (Chap. 15, p. 314, in Krasner and Ullman, 1966) claims that: 'much (human) social behaviour is fostered by exposure to real life models who perform, intentionally or unwittingly, patterns of behaviour that may be imitated by others'. These patterns may actually be demonstrated by the model, or may be described verbally, shown in pictures, etc.

In a typical experiment, Bandura, Ross and Ross (1963) showed that children who had watched a film of adults (models) behaving aggressively towards plastic dolls themselves later behaved in the same way towards the dolls. Children who had seen a film in which the adults were subdued and inhibited were themselves subdued when later playing with the dolls. Bandura suggests that exposure to aggressive models disinhibits aggressive responses which are normally inhibited and also teaches specific ways of behaving aggressively. If modelling is an important determinant of aggressive and other types of behaviour, the practical implications for child upbringing, the treatment of delinquency and of deviant behaviour in general (and for television) are considerable (see Bandura, Chap. 15, in Krasner and Ullman, 1966; and Wright and Taylor, 1970).

COGNITIVE PROCESSES

Those psychologists who study simple learning are mainly concerned with establishing relationships between environmental conditions and stimuli, and the response of organisms to them. They are less concerned with what goes on 'in the head' of the learner. Other psychologists, however, are interested in exactly this—in the processes involved in the acquisition of knowledge of our environment, and in manipulating and using this knowledge. These processes are usually referred to as the cognitive processes, from the Latin cogito, I know. They are sometimes also termed mediating processes, because they mediate our response to the environment.

Cognitive processes, for the most part, cannot be observed directly. What can be observed are only the environmental conditions and the information from the environment which is potentially available to an individual, and how he responds to these conditions—what he does, says, etc. Thus, the psychologist studying memory can observe only what information is presented to an individual, and what of it he can subsequently remember. The various cognitive processes are hypothetical processes invented by psychologists to account for observed relationships between stimuli and responses. A construction such as 'short-term memory' has therefore been invented to describe one of these hypothetical stages suggested by the empirical findings.

For convenience, psychology text-books usually discuss cognitive processes under the general headings of attention, perception, thinking, memory and communication. However, these should not be regarded as distinct and independent. Thus, the processes of attention merge into those of perception and of memory, and the decision as to whether a particular finding is considered under the heading 'attention', 'perception', etc. is often arbitrary. Moreover, processes at all stages of cognition interact with one another, e.g. unless we attend to something we cannot later remember it, while to some extent what we attend to in a particular situation is influenced by what we remember about similar situations in the past.

The following sections will outline some of the processes involved under three of these headings—attention, memory, and thinking.

SELECTIVE ATTENTION

*Introduction*

The first of the cognitive processes involved in the series of events between stimulus and response are those of selective attention. Clearly, it is only *via* our sense organs that we are in contact with the environment and are influenced by it. Any information that we think about, remember and react to, must first have been transmitted in some form by our sense organs. We are able to 'take in' only a very small proportion of the sensory information potentially available to us in the environment. What we do 'take in' is not decided randomly. To a considerable extent we select from among the available stimuli.

Psychologists use the term 'attention' in other ways also. Sustained attention, or vigilance, refers to performance on tasks in which someone has to watch, or listen, over long periods of time for occasional signals to occur.

'Attention' is used in connection with the level of arousal, or state of alertness, of the organism. Another aspect of attention is *set*, which can refer to a predisposition of the organism, often voluntarily maintained, to behave in a certain way. It is not clear how these various 'types' of attention relate to one another, or whether similar processes are involved in all of them.

Selective attention, vigilance, arousal and set have all been studied in psychiatric patients (see McGhie, 1969). However, most studies have been of selective attention. This reflects the prominence of this topic in general experimental psychology in the last decade, and also the importance of distractibility as a psychiatric symptom; distractibility is often described as a failure of the processes of selective attention. This section therefore deals only with selective attention; most of the research in this area has been on selective listening.

## Limited Capacity

As noted above, there is a strict limit to the amount of information which we can 'take in' at any one time. If we are required to deal with more than that amount, our performance breaks down.

This is demonstrated in studies employing Cherry's (1953) shadowing technique. To 'shadow' a spoken prose passage is to repeat it out loud, staying as close 'behind' the speaker as possible. If two prose passages are presented simultaneously, through head phones, with one message being transmitted to one ear and the other to the other ear, a listener can usually distinguish between them and can 'shadow' one passage while ignoring ('rejecting') the other. With the listener attending to one message, how much of the other does he 'take in'? Can he, for example, listen to both simultaneously? Cherry reported that very little of the 'rejected' message is 'taken in'. The listeners are aware only of its simple physical characteristics. They may recognize it as speech but may not identify individual words. If the language of the 'rejected' message changes from English to German and back again, they may not notice the change; neither may they realise if the message is sometimes played backwards, although they usually notice whether the message is spoken by a male or female.

In other words, we are able to attend to only one source of information at a time; while looking at or listening to something, we can 'take in' very little else. The limits to what we can 'take in' seem to depend less on the capacity of the sense organs than on the speed with which the brain can process incoming sensory stimuli. This, in turn, is influenced by the information content (predictability) of the input (see Brown, Chap. 5, in Foss, 1966). If the input is familiar and predictable, and so requires little conscious attention, it can be dealt with while leaving some capacity free to 'take in' other sensory input.

Thus, in the 'shadowing' experiment, if instead of unfamiliar prose passages well-known nursery rhymes are used, the listeners can often pick up quite a lot of the 'rejected' message. Welford (1958) suggests that one effect of learning a complex skill thoroughly is that it becomes 'automatic' and so requires less attention. If, on the other hand, the input is unfamiliar and cannot be predicted, so that more intense concentration is required, only one sensory 'message' can be coped with at a time.

## Broadbent's 'Filter' Model

The starting point of most modern research into selective attention is the very influential model of attention proposed by Broadbent (1958).

According to this, information enters the organism over many parallel sensory pathways from the eyes, ears etc. This input is dealt with in two stages. At the first, the brain identifies the general physical properties of the input, e.g. whether a voice is male or female, loud or soft, where it appears to be coming from. At the second stage, a central decision channel identifies and evaluates the input, e.g. it discovers what words the voice is speaking. However, the capacity of this second stage is much smaller than that of the first, and to prevent it being 'swamped' by incoming sensory messages, a selective system or 'filter' blocks off many of them.

The 'filter' operates so as to ensure that the total information of the input reaching the second stage does not exceed its capacity. It can select or reject sensory 'messages' on the basis of any feature which can be identified at the first stage, and to some extent which ones are selected is under voluntary control. Thus, someone may 'choose' to select a female voice rather than a competing male one. The 'filter' is said to be biased towards input which is novel, and intense, and toward the ear more than the eye.

The selection is not carried out peripherally, i.e. the 'rejecting' of a message is not done by 'turning off' the appropriate ear. This was demonstrated by Treisman (1964) who simultaneously transmitted three messages of equal loudness through two headphones—one message to each of them alone, and the third to both at once. This third message was heard by the listener as coming from the middle of the head. Listeners could 'shadow' this third message while ignoring the other two. Obviously they did not 'switch off' both ears, so that the selection mechanism must be located more centrally than the peripheral parts of the afferent pathways.

Input which is selected is transmitted immediately to the decision channel for analysis and identification, and may be responded to and/or integrated with memories in the 'long-term memory store'. If the input does not pass through the 'filter' immediately, it is stored for a very short time in a memory store which receives all the information direct from the sense organs.

Broadbent's 'filter' model has given rise to a considerable amount of research and controversy. Several studies have tried to demonstrate the minimum time required to switch attention from one channel to another, but no firm conclusions have yet been reached (see Moray, 1969). Another controversy has been about what happens to those sensory messages which are not selected by the 'filter'. Broadbent's original model suggested an all-or-none block, with rejected messages never being able to pass through the 'filter' to be analysed. However, later studies showed that under some circumstances even rejected messages may make an impression on the individual (see Treisman, Chap. 4, in Foss, 1966). Treisman proposed that rejected messages are attenuated rather than blocked entirely and that their content (e.g. which words they are) may still be noticed by a specifically attuned decision channel. A 'dictionary unit' in the brain has the task of recognizing all incoming words. The test which this 'dictionary unit' applies when identifying words may be less strict with some words, e.g. those which we are expecting or which are important to us, than with others. These words will be recognized on the basis of less evidence than other words, and even after attenuation will still be 'picked up'. Attenuated, but unimportant, words will not be recognized, although the listener will be aware of their physical characteristics, e.g. male *versus* female voice.

ATTENTION AND PERCEPTION

So far, the emphasis has been upon the mechanisms which enable us to select some sensory input while rejecting others. However, as well as selecting, we also identify and impose meaning on our sensory input; this is the task, for example, of Treisman's 'dictionary unit' and of Broadbent's limited capacity decision channel. The term perception is used to refer to the processes involved in the interpretation and organization of what we attend to.

When we look at something, the sensory input is a pattern of light rays, continually shifting and bearing little resemblance to the objects which give rise to them or to the experience which we will have of these objects. From this pattern, we are able to distinguish objects from their background, to detect whether objects are moving or stationary, near or distant etc. In addition to this primitive organization of sensory data, we give them more complex meanings. We recognize an object not merely as being distinct from its background, but as being a car, or house. We understand the meaning of what a voice says to us. Clearly, this more complex organization depends upon our past experience, i.e. upon learning. However, there is also evidence that at least some aspects of the more primitive organization of sensory input are not innate, but develop as a consequence of early learning (see Wright and Taylor, 1970, Chap. 9 and 10; and Dixon, Chap. 2 and Gregory, Chap. 3, in Foss, 1966).

DISORDERS OF SELECTIVE ATTENTION

Clinicians have noted that some psychiatric patients are very distractable, a disorder often described as an 'inability to attend selectively' or an 'inability to select relevant information'. In a typical experimental demonstration of distractability, McGhie and his colleagues (see McGhie, 1969, pp. 56–64) required patients to attend to, and report, a series of rapidly presented digits or letters, while being distracted by a similar series being presented simultaneously. McGhie found that schizophrenics, particularly hebephrenics, were unable to ignore the distracting series, so that their reporting of the required series was poor. These schizophrenics seem to be particularly poor at attending to visual stimuli, even in the absence of specific distractions. McGhie also suggests that the communication difficulties of many schizophrenics may be related to an inability to attend selectively to the speech of other people. Normal speech is usually too quick for us to be able to attend to every word, so that we learn to attend only to the important ones. The schizophrenic, unable to direct his attention, 'takes in' many redundant and unimportant words in place of relevant ones, so that the information which he obtains from, for example, a conversation is greatly reduced.

McGhie interprets his findings in terms of a breakdown in the normal 'filtering' process, postulated by Broadbent. The defect is greatest when the patient has to cope with a great deal of information, and the decision channel has no 'spare capacity'. Payne, Mattusek and George (1959) also interpreted distractability ('perceptual over-inclusion') and 'overinclusive thinking' in terms of defective 'filtering', although later research (Payne, Hochberg and Hawks 1970) suggests that distractability and 'overinclusiveness' are not related. There is no general agreement as to why any such breakdown of 'filtering' should occur, although some writers relate it to levels of cortical or autonomic arousal (see McGhie, 1969, pp. 75–83). It should be stressed that the 'filter' is a hypothetical construct; all we know about distractable patients is that they appear to be attending to stimuli which the clinician or experimenter (and possibly they themselves) think ought to be ignored.

Distractability has also been studied in neurotic patients, where it seems to be due to their being preoccupied with their own thoughts and feelings rather than to their being distracted by external stimuli, as with schizophrenics (McGhie, 1969, pp. 28–29). Organic patients, e.g. brain-injured children and adults, also appear to be distractable (McGhie, 1969, pp. 105–148).

## MEMORY

### INTRODUCTION

The term memory is used by psychologists to refer to the processes involved in the retention of information in the brain over a period of time, and its subsequent retrieval and use.

Because 'memory' is used in everyday speech in several different ways, psychologists tend to substitute terms such as remembering, forgetting, recall, retention, etc. which are somewhat more specific and refer to aspects of 'memory'. Retention has been studied over periods as short as a second or so, and as long as many years, but recent work has tended to concentrate on retention over relatively short periods—seconds or minutes. Most recent studies have been of the retention of relatively simple, verbal or other symbolic material such as words, digits or phrases. However, a wide range of other situations, from the recall of real-life events to the reproduction of motor skills such as writing or typing, have also been investigated.

### PHASES OF REMEMBERING

The following phases or stages can be distinguished in the sequence of events by which an item of information is remembered. The item must (1) be attended to and perceived, after which, (2) it is retained briefly in a 'short-term memory store', while (3) it is converted into a more long-lasting memory, and (4) then retained in a 'long-term memory store', from which (5) it is recovered, and (6) used. This account is influenced by Broadbent's (1958) two-stage model of memory. Some psychologists telescope these six phases into three: acquisition or registration (1–3), retention or storage (4), and reproduction or retrieval (5–6).

### Attention and Perception

As noted above, before information can be remembered it must first have been attended to and perceived, so that logically the processes of attention and perception should be considered along with those of the other aspects of 'memory'. In practice, however, the study of memory is usually confined to those stages following perception, i.e. it deals with the retention of identified and organized information (see Talland, 1968, pp. 34–37).

### Short and Long-Term Memory

Some information to which we attend is retained only briefly before being forgotten, e.g. if we look up a telephone number we may remember it long enough to dial successfully, but some minutes later cannot recall it. When retention lasts only seconds or minutes, short-term memory is said to be involved. When information is recalled months or years after it was first learned, as when we recall some childhood event, long-term memory is said to be involved. Some writers use immediate memory to refer to retention for a few seconds, e.g. as measured by the digit-span test, and short-term memory for retention up to about 30 min; others use short-term for the former and medium-term for the latter. Short-term memory is sometimes also used to refer to the retention for a second or less of all sensory input which does not immediately pass through the 'filter', i.e. to *pre*perceptual retention.

Psychologists disagree as to whether short-term and long-term retention are different 'kinds' of remembering, involving different processes and obeying different laws. Some writers, e.g. Broadbent (1958) and Atkinson and Shiffrin (1968), have postulated two independent, although overlapping memory 'stores'. According to this view, all sensory input which is identified, etc. (perceived) enters a 'short-term store' where it is retained briefly. Some of this information is processed so that it passes into a 'long-term store' where it is retained for a longer period, perhaps permanently. Information which is not made more permanent in this way drops out of the 'short-term store', and is forgotten very quickly. Some psychologists, e.g. Melton (1963), do not accept that there are two separate 'stores', and argue that short-term retention are aspects of the same process, sampled at different points in time (see Brown, 1964).

### Transfer from Short-to-Long-Term Retention

Some items of information which we perceive are forgotten very quickly while others are remembered for a long time. What determines how long an item will be retained? Very important seem to be repetition and rehearsal.

In general, repeated presentation (repetition) of an item results in its being recalled better after any length of time. The study of verbal learning has to do with problems in this area, such as the effects of the number of repetitions, of the meaningfulness of the information, the effects of the repetitions being spaced out in time rather than grouped together, the effects of previous learning etc. (see Kay, 1964). However, items which are presented only once, and not repeated, may still be retained for a long time if they are rehearsed, i.e. if the learner recalls the information to himself, either silently or out loud, deliberately or involuntarily. Indeed, a problem in studying short-term retention is that it is difficult to prevent someone rehearsing information which he has just been given and which he knows he will later be asked to recall. It can be done by keeping his attention occupied with something else, e.g. with subtracting numbers (out loud, so that the experimenter can be sure that he is doing it!). If a few words or digits are presented, and rehearsal is prevented, they are forgotten very quickly—within a few seconds. The likelihood that an item of information will subsequently be recalled increases with the amount of time available for rehearsal (Waugh and Norman, 1965). In general, the effects of rehearsal seem to be similar to those of repetition. However, the properties and characteristics of this rehearsal process have not yet been defined (see Talland, 1968, pp. 37–40).

### Retention and Reproduction

Most psychologists distinguish between the retention (or storage) of information and its subsequent reproduction (or retrieval), although the former can only be inferred from the latter. The distinction draws attention to the possibility that information may be 'forgotten' because, although it has been retained, it cannot be retrieved when required.

As a great deal of information is stored in the 'long-term store', a major problem of remembering is to find the required item of information from among all the other items. Clearly, some filing or index system must operate. Broadbent (pp. 167–171, in Talland and Waugh, 1969) uses the analogy of the main shelves of a library where books (items of information) are stored under appropriately indexed labels. The contrast is with storage in the 'short-term store', which is similar to the recent acquisition shelves, with items stored in the order in which they arrived, regardless of 'author' or 'subject'. Important, unresolved questions remain concerning the number and nature of the storage and retrieval systems (Keppel, 1968; Talland, 1968, pp. 40–47).

Information can be reproduced in several ways, the two main ones being recall, in which it is recreated from memory, and recognition, in which it is responded to as being familiar (*ibid* pp. 66–75).

### FORGETTING

We are often far more aware of what we have forgotten than of what we can remember. Why do we forget?

### Inattention

One important reason for our 'forgetting' a fact or event is that we did not attend to it in the first place. This is an obvious point, but is worth making because the 'poor memory' of which many psychiatric patients complain sometimes appears to be due to their being so preoccupied with their own thoughts and feelings that they notice little of what goes on around them.

*Forgetting in Short-Term Memory*

Most of the information which is perceived is forgotten quite quickly. This is not always a disadvantage, since there are many things which we require to remember only for a short time. Thus, when we look up a telephone number we usually need to retain it only until we have finished dialling.

Why is unrepeated, unrehearsed information forgotten so quickly? One sort of explanation postulates that memory traces decay and that, purely as a function of the passage of time, spontaneous changes occur in traces which lower their effectiveness. For one type of decay, Brown (1964) uses the analogy of a weather-beaten signpost. Another sort of explanation is in terms of interference by other stimuli. For example, the 'short-term store' is assumed to have a very limited capacity, i.e. it can hold very few items of information simultaneously. When the capacity is reached, incoming items displace those already in the 'store'; the analogy here is with a leaky bucket. The present evidence does not allow a decision to be made between the two theories (Brown, 1964).

*Forgetting in Long-Term Memory*

Even information which has been repeated and/or rehearsed, and which has been recalled correctly over short periods, will eventually tend to be forgotten. As with short-term memory, explanations invoke either the decay of 'unused' memory traces, or interference from other stimuli, or both. Whereas decay explanations emphasize inadequate retention of information, interference theories give more weight to difficulties in reproducing information which cannot be retrieved when required.

There have been very many investigations of the effect which learning one set of items, e.g. a list of words, has on the ability to recall a second set. The effects of activities which precede the events to be recalled (proactive inhibition), or which follow them (retroactive inhibition), have both been investigated. The results of these studies cannot be summarized briefly; they have been reviewed by Postman (pp. 195–210, in Talland and Waugh, 1969). However, the relevance of these laboratory studies to forgetting in everyday life is not clear (see Talland, 1968, pp. 55–66).

Another type of 'interference' is illustrated by the temporary effects of emotional arousal on the retrieval of information, e.g. the well-known phenomenon of forgetting facts during an exam which were recalled perfectly before and afterwards. Longer-term effects have been studied under the heading 'motivated forgetting', of which repression may be an example. Repression refers to Freud's notion that ideas or events which have unpleasant or threatening connotations may be 'expelled' from memory although continuing to influence behaviour. Experimental evidence for this notion is flimsy and although 'pleasant' events have been found to be recalled better than 'unpleasant' events, several explanations are possible (see Talland, 1968, Chap. 5).

RECALL OF EVERYDAY EVENTS

There have been relatively few studies of our ability to remember meaningful verbal material, e.g. stories or events which we have witnessed as opposed to lists of words.

*Reconstruction in Recall*

The investigations of Bartlett (1932) are particularly important because they indicate that we do not reproduce past events in the way that a tape-recorder replays what was originally recorded. Recall of meaningful events is a much more active process and involves a large element of reconstruction. What happens when we are asked to describe an event which we witnessed some time before, e.g. a football match? Clearly, we will be unable to remember every incident which we observed at the time. Instead, we will be able to recall only a 'skeleton' or outline of the game with, perhaps, a few 'incidents' which have served to identify and specify the game and to distinguish it from the other events stored in our memory. In some cases we may be unable to recall any specific event and the 'skeleton' with which we are left may only be a general impression of the game, e.g. 'It was fast and exciting and Celtic won'. This 'skeleton' may not be wholly accurate. Separate incidents may be 'telescoped' together and be recalled as a single event; some incidents of another game may be recalled as having happened in this one.

This 'skeleton' is then filled out and we reconstruct the game in as plausible and coherent a way as possible. On the basis of what we know about football, about the teams involved etc., we bridge the gaps between the incidents which we have recalled. Incidents may be invented, or 'imported'; the sequence of events may be altered. In other words, we actively attempt to make our recall as meaningful and sensible as possible.

Our original perceptions of the game will have been highly selective and distorted (e.g. rival supporters convinced that they saw the ball cross, or not cross, the line), and this 'effort after meaning' in recall will have added considerably more distortion and inaccuracy. Accuracy can be influenced by the prompting of a questioner, e.g. 'Do you remember Johnstone's goal?' and by leading questions, e.g. 'Johnstone did score, didn't he?'. (For further discussions see Hunter, 1964, Part IV.)

*Recall of Medical Data*

Psychiatrists and other clinicians place considerable weight upon what patients, and their relatives, recall of the patients' personal and medical history. How accurate are case-histories likely to be? Wenar (1961, 1963) discusses the reliability of mothers' accounts of their children's development. One study showed that 40 per cent of mothers forgot that their babies had ever crawled, and another found that half of the child's minor illnesses, e.g. measles and chickenpox, and one-third of his major ones, e.g. pneumonia and tuberculosis, were later forgotten! Recall of child-rearing practices and interpersonal relationships is particularly inaccurate. The emotional content of the events is important, and those which touch upon mothers' feelings or attitudes seem to be particularly liable to be distorted (see Wenar, 1963).

It is not only mothers whose recall is poor; psychiatrists' recall of therapeutic interactions is also inaccurate (see, for example, Walton and McPherson, 1968).

DISORDERS OF MEMORY

Disorders of memory have been studied mainly in connection with the effects of traumatic head injury and of cerebral disease.

It is usual to distinguish between anterograde amnesia and retrograde amnesia.

*Anterograde Amnesia*

This refers to difficulty in learning new skills, or in recalling events occurring after the onset of the illness or injury. Following traumatic head injury, patients are frequently unable to remember events which occurred some time after they regained consciousness. Russell (1959), in his review of 1029 cases, reported that the modal duration of amnesia was between 1 and 24 hours.

Much more long-lasting effects are found in patients with cerebral disease. Talland's studies of patients with Korsakoff's psychosis (see Inglis, pp. 101–107, in Costello, 1970; and Talland, 1968, pp. 121–128) showed that, although they had no major perceptual abnormalities, they were grossly disorientated in place and time. This was because their memory was virtually nil for every event occurring after the onset of their illness. Studies of their ability to learn lists of words, narrative material, etc., showed that they required very many more repetitions than a control group to reach a criterion of success, such as three accurate repetitions, i.e. they were almost unable to acquire new information. To some extent, however, this disability varied with the task, and although the patients were very poor at learning verbal material, or puzzles, they sometimes managed to learn manipulative skills.

Their ability to retain what they had learned was also poor and seemed to be particularly susceptible to distraction between the initial learning and the recall.

In his studies of elderly people, Kral (see Kral, pp. 41–48, in Talland and Waugh, 1969; and Inglis, pp. 108–110, in Costello, 1970), distinguishes between benign, or normal, memory dysfunction, in which details of events in the remote past are forgotten, although the events themselves can be recalled; and malignant dysfunction in which the events themselves, even in the recent past, are forgotten. 'Benign' dysfunction seems to be a disorder primarily of retrieval, since facts forgotten on one occasion may later be recalled. 'Malignant' dysfunction seems to involve inability to acquire or to retain information or both, and it often leads to disorientation.

The ability of patients with senile dementia to learn new verbal material seems to be particularly bad and some of the most useful psychological tests for diagnosing 'brain damage' require the patient to learn lists of words (see Kendrick, Parboosingh and Post, 1965). In a series of studies, Inglis (see Inglis, pp. 110–117, in Costello, 1970) demonstrated an apparent defect in the short-term storage of information in some 'memory-disordered', elderly patients.

*Retrograde Amnesia*

This is a defect in recalling events which occurred before the onset of the illness or injury. After traumatic head injury it appears to be common, Russell (1959) reporting it in over 80 per cent of his patients for whom records were available, although in the majority of cases it was of under 30 min duration. Sometimes, although not always, memories return in an orderly way, with the most remote ones returning first and those for the period immediately before the injury returning last, if at all (see Williams, 1970, pp. 40–45; and Talland, 1968, pp. 117–119). Retrograde amnesia following E.C.T. has also frequently been reported (see Williams, 1970, pp. 45–50; and Talland, 1968, pp. 119–121). This evidence of retrograde amnesia due to trauma illustrates the vulnerability of memories in the few minutes after they have been acquired.

Talland reported widespread forgetting of personal and public events in Korsakoff patients, although they retain well-practised skills such as spoken and written language, and the special skills of a trade. The 'malignant' dysfunction described by Kral (1969) involves retrograde amnesia. It has been claimed that, just as the return of memory following trauma is orderly, so too is the forgetting in amnesic patients. Ribot's Law of Regression (1885) is that amnesic disturbance extends from recent to more distant and then to remote memories. Recall for events in the far past is therefore said to be better than for recent events.

While the law seems broadly to be valid, prolonged retrograde amnesia often appears somewhat 'patchy', with 'islands of memory' occurring (see Talland, 1968, pp. 135–136).

## THINKING

### INTRODUCTION

The term 'thinking' is used in many different ways (see Thomson, 1959, Chap. 1). McKellar (1957) makes a useful distinction between Type A and Type R thinking. Type A is thinking which is dominated by processes of the fantasy kind, rather than being geared to reality; it thus includes autistic thinking, dreams and hallucinations. Type R is thinking contained by concern with observable facts and characterized by connections of a logical kind; scientific thinking and logical reasoning is of this type.

Experimental psychology has mainly been concerned with Type R, i.e. with reasoning, or 'mental problem-solving'. As Thomson (1959) points out, many different activities can be included under the heading of Type R thinking, or reasoning. Solving a mathematical problem, understanding this chapter, making a diagnosis, writing an examination answer, are all examples of reasoning, but involve very different skills. What they have in common is that they involve the use of symbols, e.g. words, numbers, images which are manipulated internally, i.e. 'in the head'. It should be noted that when clinicians describe a patient as 'thought-disordered' it is often because of his abnormal language. However, while disordered thinking is probably always reflected in abnormalities of language, the latter may not always be due to disordered thinking.

Psychologists have devised many techniques by which some of the processes involved in reasoning can be externalized and hence studied objectively. The three main aspects of reasoning which have been investigated are the development of reasoning processes in children, problem solving and concept usage in adults. Some psychologists consider human problem-solving to be a complex kind of learning and relate it to the simpler kinds of learning, such as classical and operant conditioning. Much of their work is with animals (see Thomson, 1959, Chap. 2). Other psychologists treat human problem-solving in relative isolation from simpler processes. They study humans solving anagrams, geometrical problems, technical problems in medicine, etc. (see Thomson, 1959, Chap. 3). Recently, computer models and analogies have been widely used (see Wason, Chap. 6, in Foss, 1966).

However, it is the other two areas which have most influence on psychiatry, and the following sections will therefore consider in some detail the development of reasoning in children, and the use of concepts by adults.

## Development of Reasoning: The Work of Piaget

Some studies of the development of reasoning in children aim to establish normative standards and patterns of growth. Typically, standard tests or measures are applied to large numbers of children of various ages so as to describe the level of reasoning behaviour of which the average child of that age is capable, and the range of behaviour shown by different children of the same age. Important normative studies of cognitive development in very young children have been carried out by Gesell (1940) and Griffiths (1954).

Other studies are less concerned with quantifying the skills of the average child than with examining the processes underlying these skills. The most influential work of this sort has been by the Swiss psychologist Jean Piaget. The scope of Piaget's writings is enormous, and this section will consider only his views on the development of reasoning.

### PIAGET'S METHODS OF INVESTIGATION

The methods and techniques by which Piaget studies reasoning are very different from those of most contemporary psychologists. His is a qualitative approach which shuns statistical analysis and rigorous research design. He is not at all interested in obtaining normative data. Instead, he tries to discover why children behave and think as they do. His usual approach involves the detailed investigation of a very few children—often his own three—and has rightly been termed a 'clinical' method. It may involve the close observation of a child as it lies in its cot, or plays in the nursery, thus:

'Observation 27—Jacqueline, at 0:4 (27) and the days following, opens her mouth as soon as she is shown the bottle. She only began mixed feeding at 0:4 (12). At 0:7 (13) I note that she opens her mouth differently according to whether she is offered a bottle or a spoon . . .' (Piaget, 1952, p. 60).

Sometimes, small experiments will be carried out, as far as possible in the child's natural setting. The following example demonstrates the child's ability to infer a cause, after having observed only its effect:

'At 1:1 (4) Laurent is seated in his carriage and I am on a chair beside him. While reading and without seeming to pay any attention to him, I put my foot under the carriage and move it slowly. Without hesitation Laurent leans over the edge and looks for the cause in the direction of the wheels. As soon as he perceives the position of my foot he is satisfied and smiles.' (Piaget, 1954, p. 296).

After the child has learned to talk, Piaget and his co-workers may engage in long conversations with the child, to discover why he holds particular opinions, rather than to test whether the opinions are correct or incorrect.

DYNAMICS OF THE SYSTEM: ASSIMILATION AND ACCOMMODATION

Central to Piaget's account of cognitive development is the notion of schemata. A schema is a well defined sequence of physical or mental actions. Piaget observed that very soon after birth, babies appear to begin to organize their behaviour, so that habitual actions develop. Thus, for example, a child's tendency to grasp whatever touches the palm of his hand might develop into a habit of clasping and unclasping his hand. During the early months of life, the child has schemata only in connection with its perceptual and motor behaviour (sensori-motor schemata). However, later the child develops the ability to let one thing 'stand for', or be represented by, another, e.g. he lets an image of an object 'stand for' the object itself. Eventually, words, numbers and other symbols are also used in this way so that representational schemata are constructed. In some ways schemata are similar to concepts and, in particular, to personal constructs (see below, pp. 190–192).

Accommodation is the modification of schemata as a result of new experiences. Assimilation is the incorporation of new objects and experiences into existing schemata. Piaget considers these two complimentary processes as being basic to thinking, each being one aspect of adaptation to the environment. We are continually acting on the environment trying to make sense of it. We organise, interpret, modify, distort (assimilate) environmental stimuli so that they are compatible with, and fit into, our existing conceptual system. At the same time, our environment acts on us, constraining us, rewarding some actions, punishing others and so forcing us to modify (accommodate) our conceptual system and ways of behaving. Accommodation is an active process which often involves questioning, trial-and-error and exploration.

Piaget suggests that, in the early stages of life, assimilation is more dominant, so that the child is less well adapted to reality, interpreting new events solely in terms of his own point of view (egocentricity). As the child grows older, accommodation increases until a balance (equilibrium) is reached around the age of 12. However, at any age there may be disequilibrium in favour of assimilation or accommodation. If the former, the child (or adult) is characterized by autism and egocentricity, by excessive fantasy and by an inability to differentiate self from environment. When accommodation predominates, there may be excessive imitative behaviour. Effective intellectual behaviour, on the other hand, requires a state of equilibrium between the two processes. As Flavell (1963) writes:

'... (equilibrium) is a functional state in which potentially slavish and naïvely realistic (in the epistemological sense) accommodations to reality are effectively held in check by an assimilatory process which can organize and direct accommodations, and in which assimilation is kept from being riotously autistic by a sufficiency of continuing accommodatory adjustments to the real world. In short, intelligent functioning, when equilibrium obtains, is made up of a balanced recipe of about equal parts of assimilation and accommodation. Through this fine balance, a both realistic (accommodation) and meaningful (assimilation) rapport between subject and object is secured' (p. 65).

STAGES OF COGNITIVE DEVELOPMENT*

One of the main characteristics of human, adult reasoning and problem-solving is that it occurs 'in the head'. A small child asked to add one and one will require to move two objects physically together before calculating the answer. It is only gradually that it can perform this action mentally. Imagery, and later words—and later still mathematical symbols—replace the physical activity. Actions which have been internalized in this way are termed operations and much of Piaget's work on cognitive development is about the development of operations, i.e. about the gradual replacement of physical actions by mental, or psychological, actions.

Piaget distinguishes four main stages in this development. (It should be emphasized that the ages attached to each stage in the following account, are *very* approximate.)

1. *The Sensorimotor Stage (Age 0 to $1\frac{1}{2}$ or 2 Years)*

The behaviour of the newborn indicates that he cannot distinguish between himself and the outside world, and that he does not yet recognize objects as existing apart from his own activities, and as being permanent. He is born with a set of built-in reflexes, for example the sucking reflex. These become modified as a result of functional exercise so that after a few days the infant finds the nipple more easily and feeds with more assurance. Fortuitous, accidental behaviours, for example thumb sucking, are repeated for their own sake and develop into systematically pursued activities, or 'habits'. At first the infant behaves as if the object he sees is not the same as the object he grasps or sucks. Then comes a time when he will reach out for an object he sees (vision and prehension become coordinated) but only if he can see both his hand and the object at the same time. If his hand is out of sight he behaves as if he had forgotten it and does not reach out even for a desirable toy. This is followed by a stage when he will invariably reach out for anything he sees wherever his hand is. He discovers that he can make things happen. Accidentally his hand hits a row of rattles strung across his pram and he now deliberately repeats the activity (the 'circular reaction') to produce the interesting spectacle and noise. Even when the child has detached himself and his actions from the object 'out there' recognizing it as the same object whether he looks at

*Contributed by Dr S. Wolff.

it, grasps it, or sucks it, (at around 4 to 5 months, coincidentally with his development of discriminatory smiling), he still behaves as if the universe consisted of 'shifting and unsubstantial 'tableaux' which appear and are then totally reabsorbed'. When a child of 5 to 7 months is about to seize an object and this is covered with a cloth, he will withdraw his hand and cry. For him the object he does not see has disappeared. At 9 to 10 months he behaves quite differently, searching for the hidden object and removing the interfering obstacle. His behaviour now indicates that for him the object does not cease to exist when it disappears from view.

During the sensorimotor stage, in which the child becomes upright and mobile, he builds up inner representations of himself and of permanent outer objects, of practical relationships between objects in space and time, of simple causal relationships, and of his own effects on the objects and people around him.

## 2. *The Stage of Animism and Precausal Logic (Age $1\frac{1}{2}$ to 7 Years)*

Sensorimotor mechanisms are prerepresentational. Symbolic functions begin only during the second year of life. Now for the first time one can observe deferred imitation, that is imitation starting after the disappearance of the model; symbolic play; verbal evocations of events not occurring at the time; and later, drawing. The child rapidly acquires an increasing vocabulary and changes from a creature of action to one of words and thoughts. His thinking and reasoning are however quite different from those of adults and, as a result, he misinterprets his environment. Just as the infant cannot distinguish between himself and the world around him so the animistic child cannot as yet detach words from the objects they symbolize nor his own thoughts from the things thought about.

There are four principal characteristics of this stage: egocentrism, animism, precausal logic and an authoritarian morality. Under seven, children are egocentric and cannot imagine another person's point of view. They talk more in each other's company but there are few shared topics. Instead one observes what Piaget has called the 'collective monologue', each child talking about his own concerns. Children see themselves literally as the centre of the universe, believing that as they walk along the street the sun by day and the moon by night actually follow them. Explanations for events in the physical world are animistic. Everything is alive and has feeling and thoughts, resembling those of the child himself. Explanations are psychological in terms of motivation and every event occurs by intent. There are no impartial, natural causes and the notion that some events happen 'by chance' cannot be grasped.

Reasoning is precausal, that is non-scientific. It is based not on observations but on the child's internal model of the world. Children at this stage are insensible of contradictions and accept false explanations that others or they themselves may offer even if these are in conflict with their observations. This is the stage at which babies can be bought in shops and Father Christmas delivers presents the world over. When liquid is poured from a short, wide container into a long, narrow one it becomes 'more' because the level of water rises.

The child's authoritarian morality reveals itself both in his notions about the rules of games, which are believed to be sacrosanct even if they are incompletely understood, and in his ideas about crime and punishment. Under seven, children believe that bad events are punishments, that the punishment must fit the crime and that bad deeds are inevitably followed by retribution.

Piaget himself points out that this cognitive stage coincides on the social-emotional level with the genesis of duty, that is with a unilateral sense of obligation, and later with the development of conscience and guilt. Perhaps it is not surprising that the fears and phobias of childhood are commonest in the animistic stage.

### 3. The Stage of Concrete Operational Thought (Age 8 to 12 Years)

Children now lose their egocentrism, their animism, and their authoritarianism. In Piaget's terms a 'decentering' of thoughts from objects and from the subject himself occurs. This enables the child to differentiate between co-ordinate multiple perspectives, to argue logically on the basis of observations (accurate deductions, for example, relating to number, to the conservation of weight and volume and to other physical relationships can now be made in an experimental situation with objects) and to engage in co-operative activities with others. Justice is now a more central concept than obedience.

### 4. The Stage of Abstract or Propositional Thought (Age 12 to 15 Years)

The child now succeeds in freeing himself from the concrete and is capable of logical operations using thought alone. In the preceding stage logic was tied to actual observations of objects, to their observed interrelationships and to counting them. The final transformation of cognitive schemata consists of the differentiation of form from content so that the individual becomes capable of reasoning correctly in the realm of pure hypothesis. He can now draw conclusions from truths which are merely possible and this, Piaget thinks, constitutes the beginning of formal or hypothetico-deductive thought.

Piaget stresses the interaction at each stage of cognitive and emotional processes. Social and affective experiences foster exploration of the environment and constitute 'the energetics' or motives of cognitive behaviour. On the other hand affectivity and the nature of social relationships are dependent on the child's cognitive level. Similarly the affective changes characteristic of adolescence, the pre-occupations with ideologies, future life styles and social change, reflect the cognitive transformation achieved at this stage from concrete operational logic to abstract thought. (For more detailed discussion of Piaget's views, see Butcher, 1968, pp. 182–198).

CLINICAL APPLICATIONS

Although Piaget's work has had a considerable influence on educational and developmental psychology, its influence on child psychiatry in the U.K. has been slightly disappointing, possibly because British child psychiatry is still dominated by psycho-analytic theory. However, as Anthony (1956) states: 'It is not a system we can afford to ignore in our clinical practice today'.

One application of Piaget's methods and theories was Woodward's (1959) investigation of the repetitive hand mannerisms of severely defective children. At first sight purposeless and unlike the behaviour of normal children, these mannerisms were shown to be similar to those described by Piaget as being present during the sensorimotor stage of development of the normal infant, during the first two years of life.

## CONCEPT USE IN ADULTS

A major topic in the psychology of thinking is how concepts are formed and used. Studies of concept use can give information about the role of abstraction and generalization in reasoning. They are also frequently employed in the investigation of thought-process disorder and of aspects of personality.

DEFINITION OF CONCEPT

A concept is: a learned response to a class of events, or a grouping of things into a single category on the basis of some feature, or features, which they share.

A typical concept attainment experiment might require the subject to discover what several objects have in common (abstraction) and then to indicate which of some other objects also share this attribute (generalization). When we conceptualize, or categorize, we respond to discriminably different things as though they were equivalent, i.e. we respond to their class membership rather than to their unique features; things conceptualized as similar are therefore not identical to each other in all respects.

The same object, event, etc., can be conceptualized in many different ways, e.g. Mr Smith is a man, a father, a bus-driver, fair-minded, bald, living, etc.

Concepts may differ from one another in several ways. Affective, functional and formal concepts or categories can be distinguished.

Affective concepts are those which group together those people, places, objects, ideas, events etc., that produce a similar emotional response in the person using the concept, e.g. 'not very nice', 'beautiful'. Functional concepts group together things which are equivalent in their purpose or use, e.g. 'cooking utensil'. Formal concepts refer to the logical, mathematical, scientific, etc., properties of the things, e.g. 'triangle', 'heavier', 'equivalent'. Some concepts are conjunctive, i.e. are defined by the presence of features $x$ and $y$ and $z$, whereas others are disjunctive and are defined by the presence of $x$ or $y$ or $z$. Concepts differ in the number of features which define them. They also vary in their range of applicability, some being applicable to a large number of things, e.g. 'animate', whereas others refer to only a few, e.g. 'king'.

Typically, a concept is labelled with a word or phrase, and all nouns and adjectives label concepts. However, some concepts are unverballized, e.g. a baby which is able to recognize its mother has formed a concept although it may not be able to add the label 'mama' until later. Some concepts are taught formally, e.g. at school ('A triangle is defined as . . .'), others are taught informally, e.g. by parents ('No, that's not a dog, it's a cat'), or are acquired by trial and error.

FUNCTION OF CONCEPTS

What advantages are there to us in categorizing? Among those suggested by Bruner, Goodnow and Austin (1956) are that concepts help us to reduce the complexity of the environment. Many human beings are able to discriminate seven million different colours. Clearly, if we responded to each of these as being unique, labelling each one, etc., we would have time for little else. Therefore, we group them into 'reds', 'blues', etc., and only make finer discriminations when it is important to do so. Categorization is also the means by which we identify objects in the world around us, and know their properties. Thus, if we know that a concept is defined by a certain number of properties, e.g. that a particular illness has six main symptoms, and we encounter all of them, then we can be more confident that we have made the correct identification. We can often predict what some of the properties of a concept will be before we actually encounter them, e.g. if we know that a liquid is 'poison' we know what would happen if we drank it and so can take appropriate action. The predictive nature of concepts is emphasized particularly in Kelly's (1955) theory of personal constructs (concepts).

VALIDATING CONCEPTS

Many concepts are not taught but are learned through experience, by trial-and-error. What criteria do we use when validating our concepts?

Sometimes, we have recourse to an ultimate criterion, e.g. we can validate our provisional classification of something as 'hot' by touching it. At other times, we can assess whether our provisional classification is consistent with the context in which it was made. Concensus—what other people think—is frequently used to validate 'psychological' concepts; we learn from our family and peer-group what behaviour is generally considered to be 'kind' and what 'honest'. Some concepts are confirmed by affective congruence; the person 'feels sure' that it is correct (as with many paranoid delusions).

CONCEPTS AND REASONING

Two very important series of studies of the function of concepts in reasoning are those of Piaget on concept formation and of Bruner *et al.* (1956) on concept attainment.

Piaget and his colleagues have carried out very many investigations of the development of some of the specific logical and mathematical concepts which are necessary for effective reasoning, e.g. concepts such as 'equivalence', 'reversibility' and 'causality' (see Thomson, 1959, Chap. 5). Bruner *et al.* (1956) analysed the strategies adopted by subjects when attempting to discover a concept determined by the experimenter. They described four systematic strategies, each one deriving from a different general plan, and showed how people's ability to use these strategies was influenced by the type of concept to be discovered, e.g. conjunctive *v.* disjunctive, the nature of the material, e.g. meaningful *v.* abstract, etc. (see Thomson, 1959, Chap. 4).

CONCEPTS AND PERSONALITY

*Individual Differences in Concept Use*

Concepts have also been studied for the light which they throw on cultural and personality variables.

The particular concepts which someone uses will depend partly upon general, environmental factors that are similar for all humans, e.g. everyone finds it useful to develop concepts of weight and temperature. Another influence will be the cultural and social groups to which he belongs, e.g. Eskimos have many more concepts relating to snow than the English do, reflecting the relative importance of snow in the Arctic and in England.

As well as general environmental and social factors, the unique experiences of an individual will influence which concepts he normally uses. Presumably, we tend to use those concepts which have, in the past, proved to be most helpful to us, e.g. in predicting events. Concepts which enable us to anticipate events successfully will be used in preference to those which are frequently invalidated.

Moreover, the specific meaning attached to a concept will vary from person to person. Each concept has both a public (extensional) and private (intensional) meaning to the user, the former being much the same for everyone but the latter varying from person to person, reflecting the unique experiences of each. Thus, while everyone agrees that a dog is a four legged animal with a bark, etc., the definition of one person might also include 'affectionate' and 'lovable', while that of another might include 'vicious' and 'dangerous'.

Discovering which particular concepts an individual uses when construing certain situations, people, etc., as well as exploring the private meanings which he attaches to the concepts, can give important information about his past experiences and about how he now views the world. Several theories of personality are centrally concerned with the personal meaning of concepts; the best developed and most influential of these is Kelly's (1955) theory of personal constructs.

PERSONAL CONSTRUCT THEORY

Kelly describes man as a 'scientist'; we continually try to understand, predict and control our world. To enable us to do this, we invent a unique system of concepts, or personal construct system, which acts as a set of 'goggles' through which we perceive the world. 'Constructs' differ from 'concepts' in being, by definition, bipolar, e.g. 'kind–cruel', 'black–white', but are similar in most other aspects. Personal construct theory is about how personal construct systems develop, change and are organized, and how they are related to other aspects of behaviour. The main features of the theory are described by Bannister (1966). Personal construct theory is, in effect, a general theory of behaviour although it is particularly concerned with interpersonal relationships, and how people conceptualize one another. Thus, emotion is the awareness of the fact that our construct system is in a state of change or transition; anxiety is the awareness that the events with which one is confronted lie mostly outside the range of convenience (i.e. of applicability) of one's construct system; hostility is the continued effort to extort validational evidence in favour of a type of social prediction which has already been recognized as a failure (see Bannister, pp. 367–369, in Foss, 1966).

Kelly (1955) developed repertory grid technique to enable the construct systems of individuals to be analysed and described precisely and quantitatively. This is not a standardized test which is presented in the same form to everyone, but a highly flexible technique which enables people, objects etc., relevant to the particular person being tested to be rated in terms of concepts provided by the person himself, rather than by the tester. Repertory grid technique is widely used in clinical personality assessment (see Bannister, 1965a, and Chap. 19, in

Foss, 1966; and Bannister and Fransella, 1971 for examples and detailed discussion).

## DISORDERS OF CONCEPT USE

There have been very many attempts to relate psychiatric signs and symptoms to underlying disorders of conceptualization. Three groups of studies will be discussed, those deriving from Goldstein's work on concreteness, Payne's on overinclusive thinking and from personal construct theory.

### CONCRETENESS

Forming a concept involves abstracting a common feature from a group of objects, items, etc. Goldstein and Scheerer (1941) argued that brain damaged patients, schizophrenics and other psychiatric groups are unable to abstract. They operate at a concrete level, and, for example, cannot group together common objects according to features which they share. This, Goldstein and Scheerer claimed, results in a variety of cognitive and personality disorders, e.g. inability to assume a mental set voluntarily, to account for acts to oneself, to hold in mind various aspects of a situation, to plan ahead ideationally etc. More recent studies confirm that many patients with dementia show clear evidence of 'concreteness' (see Williams, 1970, p. 131), as do some schizophrenics (see Payne, pp. 62–68, in Costello, 1970). It seems to be related to low intelligence and may underly the impoverished vocabulary of these patients.

Clinically, 'concrete thinking' has been measured in a variety of ways, the interpretation of proverbs being often used. A proverb is a concrete example of a general principle and whereas normals can explain this principle, 'concrete' patients cannot go beyond the specific words, e.g. 'still waters run deep'—'Yes, deep rivers are often like that'.

### OVERINCLUSIVENESS

Several writers (see Payne, pp. 67–77, in Costello, 1970) have claimed that some psychiatric patients are unable to preserve the boundaries of their concepts, which thus become abnormally vague and ill-defined, with features which are normally only remotely related to a concept being integrated into it.

There have been a variety of tests purporting to measure 'overinclusive thinking' but they have usually been found to be unrelated to one another, so that it is not clear how it should be measured or even whether 'overinclusiveness' is a single, unitary disorder (see Price, 1970). 'Overinclusiveness' is sometimes said to be the abnormality underlying thought-process disorder but this has not been established (Foulds et al., 1967a). Payne's work suggests that 'overinclusiveness' is mainly a disorder of acute schizophrenia, although other workers have reported it also in chronic schizophrenia (Foulds *et al.*, 1967*b*).

PERSONAL CONSTRUCTS

The structure of the construct systems of thought-process disordered schizophrenics has been investigated by Bannister (Bannister, 1960; Bannister and Fransella, 1966). Bannister and Fransella (1966) showed that thought-process disordered schizophrenics have abnormally loose and inconsistent construct systems. Subjects rank eight photographs of people according to six constructs, e.g. 'kind', 'honest', 'mean'. In people without thought-process disorder, the different rankings are closely related, being either positively related (e.g. 'kind and honest') or negatively related (e.g. 'kind' and 'mean'), i.e. they tend to use 'kind' and 'honest' in much the same way, but 'kind' and 'mean' in opposite ways. However, the rankings of thought-process disordered schizophrenics show little relationship to each other (looseness) and the pattern of relationships is highly unstable (inconsistent) over short periods of time. Bannister regards these disorders as being a consequence of the schizophrenic's concepts having been frequently, and arbitrarily, invalidated. Schizophrenics react to this by 'loosening' their construct systems, a loose system being one which generates vague and imprecise predictions. A loose system has the advantage that it is difficult to invalidate, but it is also much less useful in prediction and description than a 'tight' concept system, whose meaning is more precisely defined. Some evidence for this view was presented by Bannister 1965*b*).

McPherson and his colleagues have been more interested in the content of the construct systems of schizophrenics, and in particular in the use made of 'psychological' constructs, i.e. those to do with personality, emotions and abilities, e.g. 'kind'–'cruel', 'happy'–'sad', 'clever'–'stupid'. Some schizophrenics make abnormally little use of 'psychological' terms when construing other people, and this is related to the presence of the clinical signs of thought-process disorder, flattening of affect, and certain delusions and hallucinations (McPherson, Buckley and Draffan, 1971).

INTELLIGENCE

INTRODUCTION

Scientific psychology involves not only the study of those basic laws of functioning which apply to everyone, but also the description and measurement of differences between people. Research into intellectual activity is an example of the latter: 'If people did not differ from one another, concepts such as intelligence would not exist' (Foss, 1968, p. 40).

The various processes of cognition which have been discussed above—those of attention, perception, memory, concept attainment, problem-solving, etc.—interact with one another in enabling individuals to acquire information about the environment and to store, manipulate and use this information so as to adapt to the environment. 'Cognition' thus refers to a purposeful series of activities, aimed at providing solutions to the problems posed by our day-to-day activities. People differ in the efficiency with which they solve these problems. Some people may be more likely than others to arrive at correct solutions, or to provide original and imaginative answers to problems; people may differ in the speed with which they are able to produce solutions. Intelligence tests are intended to summarize and quantify these differences.

The scientific value of intelligence tests has been greatly reduced by their having developed almost independently of the remainder of experimental psychology over the last 70 years. The items used in most intelligence tests have little in common with the tasks and situations used in the investigation of cognitive processes, such as concept attainment and problem solving. Traditional intelligence testing has also paid too little attention to the influence of personality variables such as persistence (see Butcher, 1968, pp. 9–39). Eysenck (1967) has argued convincingly that the study of basic processes and of individual differences should be integrated.

Despite these scientific limitations, may—although not all—psychologists consider that intelligence testing of the traditional type is of considerable practical value. Intelligence tests are widely used in the clinical, educational and vocational assessment of individuals, and they have been frequently shown to have many advantages over alternative methods of assessing intelligence, e.g. by interview. In research, intelligence test performance has been found to be related to a very wide range of variables of importance to psychiatrists and clinical psychologists. There are many different approaches to intellectual assessment. The one described here is the traditional British approach, based on the statistical technique of factor analysis, which is the one with which British psychiatrists are most likely to come into contact (see Butcher, 1968, pp. 9–39, for references to other approaches).

FACTOR-ANALYTIC APPROACH

*Factor-analysis of Performance*

If a wide selection of tests involving mental skills is given to a representative sample of people, the test scores are usually found to be positively correlated. One statistical method of interpreting a pattern of intercorrelations is factor-analysis (see Chap. VIII). The results of a factor-analysis are influenced by which particular tests are used, the type of factor-analysis employed, etc. However, most British psychologists accept that the typical pattern of intercorrelations among mental test scores indicates that intelligence can be regarded as hierarchical, with a general factor, or ability, which is present in all tests; several group factors, or abilities, each of which influences performance on one group of tests; and specific factors, or abilities, which are found only in individual tests. The general factor—'g' as it is sometimes labelled—is what is usually meant by general intelligence.

### Definitions of 'g'

There have been many attempts to express in words what this general ability is, e.g. 'the capacity to benefit from experience', or 'the ability which is involved in every kind of cognitive skill'. Eysenck (1967) has recently argued that mental speed may be the general factor which underlies differences in performance. This failure to agree upon a definition is hardly surprising in view of the many different ways there are of behaving intelligently (and unintelligently).

### The Group Factors

Two commonly described group abilities are: an abstract one, defined by performance on tests involving verbal, numerical and educational material, such as tests of word knowledge, general information and mental arithmetic; and a practical one, relating to mechanical, spatial and physical material, e.g. tests involving understanding diagrams, arranging patterns etc. These two major group abilities can be analysed further into several minor abilities (see Butcher, 1968, Chaps. 1 and 2, for further discussion).

### MEASUREMENT OF INTELLIGENCE

The study of intelligence mainly centres around the development and use of intelligence tests. Although early experimental psychologists such as Galton (1870) attempted to measure individual differences in mental capacity, intelligence testing as we know it today started with the construction by Binet and Simon (1908) of a test for the measurement of mental levels in subnormal children.

### Content of Tests

Intelligence tests differ very considerably in the items which they include. One reason is that they may differ in the abilities which they assess. Some psychologists, in constructing tests of general intelligence, begin with a definition of 'g' (e.g. as the ability to discern relations) and devise a single test intended to measure this ability. In other tests, a variety of different subtests is presented, covering a wide range of material (verbal, numerical, etc.) and processes (memory, visual perception, inductive reasoning) in the hope that an individual's average performance on these is a measure of his general ability. Other tests are concerned only with particular aspects of intelligence, e.g. verbal-educational, and contain only items relevant to those aspects.

Tests differ in respect of the age of the people with which they are intended for use; in whether they are administered individually, or to a group of people; in whether they are timed or untimed; and in many other ways.

These differences are not arbitrary but reflect the various purposes of intelligence tests. While it is convenient in everyday life to refer to someone's 'intelligence', when a test is used professionally it is essential to specify the areas of intellectual ability which the test measures, and how it does so. Great care must be taken when comparing performance on two tests, since different facets of intelligence might be assessed by each.

### Reliability and Validity

Intelligence tests, like all objective measures, should have adequate reliability and validity for the purposes for which they are used. The notions of reliability and validity are discussed in detail below (see also Chap. VIII), so that only two points need be made here. Validity is the extent to which the test fulfils its purpose. However, as most intelligence tests have more than one purpose, there is no single criterion against which they can be validated and it is probably better to talk about the validities of a particular test (see Butcher, 1968, Chap. 8). Second, tests should only be used for the purposes for which they have been validated.

### Standardization

Knowing someone's score on an intelligence test is useful only if it can be compared with the scores of other people—where does he stand in relation to others of his age? Clearly, it is seldom possible to test everyone in a given population, e.g. all British adults, or all students. Instead a standardization sample is selected and tested, and their scores serve as the norms of the test, with which the performance of other people can be compared. There are several ways of selecting a sample. For example, the Wechsler Adult Intelligence Scale (WAIS) was standardized (Wechsler, 1958) on a sample of 1700 people, aged 16 to 64, drawn from the general U.S. population. As intelligence is influenced by age, separate norms were obtained for age groups

16 to 17, 18 to 19, 20 to 24, 25 to 34 etc.; as education also influences intelligence, the sample was selected so as to have the same proportions of various occupational groups as existed in the general population. In so far as a sample is representative of the population from which it is drawn, then—within known limits of error—it is possible to assume that the same distribution of scores exists in the population as a whole, as in the sample. Thus if someone has a score better than, e.g. 90 per cent of the normative sample, he would also have scored better than approximately 90 per cent of the population—only 'approximately' because various sorts of error reduce the confidence with which we can interpret a test score (see Chap. VIII). Strictly, the norms of a test are valid only for people who belong to the population from which the sample was drawn, so that the norms of WAIS are not applicable to British adults (rather than American), or to U.S. adults of 1971 (rather than of 1958). In practice, tests are used with populations on which they have not been standardized, provided there is no strong reason for believing that the norms are misleading. All these factors limit the confidence with which a test score can be interpreted.

## Comparison with Norms

There are several ways in which the standing of an individual's test score, relative to the test norms, can be expressed. The one with fewest disadvantages is that of percentile ranking, e.g. 'his score places him at the eightieth percentile', i.e. he is superior to 79 per cent of the standardization sample. In some children's tests, I.Q's are calculated based on the child's Mental Age (M.A.), i.e. the age at which the average child scores the same as he does. The I.Q. is this M.A. expressed as a percentage of the child's real, or chronological, age (C.A.). Because laymen appear to like using 'I.Q.', some adult tests convert percentile scores into I.Q., e.g. a percentile score of 50 is converted to an I.Q. of 100, etc.; WAIS uses this method, which has little to recommend it.

## Factors Affecting Test Performance

Intelligence, like learning, can be measured only through performance. Many factors may cause an intelligence test performance to be a misleading estimate of an individual's intellectual ability. Some of these factors are controlled by having standard instructions, examples and testing procedures, which are used for all subjects. Other factors which might affect performance include low motivation, high anxiety, fatigue, and a hostile attitude towards testing. Individual testing (one subject, one tester) has the advantage over group administration that the tester can often minimize these effects, or can estimate their consequences for the test performance, so that the subject's score can be interpreted in that light. Many of these factors are discussed in Sattler and Theye (1967).

Having reliable, quantitative measures of intelligence allows many facts about intelligence and its relation to other variables to be established.

*Intelligence and Ageing*

The exact relationship between intelligence test scores and ageing is influenced by many factors, including the abilities which the test measures. With vocabulary and many other verbal tests, scores increase until age 20 or 30 and thereafter remain stable until age 50 or 60 when a decline begins. With tests involving reasoning, however, the decline begins shortly after age 20 and continues rapidly after 30 or so; in one study, the average score at age 55 was the same as that of the average 10-year-old. Of course, the above ages are very approximate, and big differences are found between people in the rate at which their ability develops and declines. Test scores seem to increase for longer, and to decline less rapidly, among the most intelligent.

*Social Influences on Intelligence*

There is ample evidence that intellectual development can be severely affected by poor environment, i.e. by the lack of the intellectual stimulation which is provided by contact with adults, adequate schooling, access to toys and books etc. The harmful effects of poor environment are greater for older than for younger children, and for bright than for dull children. Older and brighter children require more intellectual stimulation in order to develop their potential, and an environment which provides adequate stimulation for a 5-year-old may be inadequate for a 10-year-old. Kellmer Pringle's (1965) studies of children suggest that intellectual development is usually affected by institutionalization and that the effects on intellectual performance seem to be related more closely to the age at which the child was separated from its mother than to the length of time spent in the institution. Of course, where the home environment has been particularly deprived, an institution can provide more stimulation and so may enhance intellectual development. Finally, the greatest effects of deprivation do not always seem to be shown on the verbal–numerical–educational aspects of intelligence, as might have been expected; mechanical–spatial–physical aspects can be affected as much or even more (for further discussion see O'Connor, Chap. 17, in Foss, 1966).

H

INTELLECTUAL DEFICIT

Because some psychotic patients have been found to show disorders of attention, memory, conceptualization and other aspects of cognition, it is reasonable to expect that these disorders will be reflected in their scores on intelligence tests. Very many studies have attempted to demonstrate this, especially with schizophrenia, but there are few unambiguous conclusions.

The only satisfactory way of establishing that a patient is showing evidence of intellectual deficit is to compare his current score on a test with his pre-illness score on the same test. Fortunately, the routine testing of school-children, and of men entering the armed forces, has made available the pre-illness scores of large numbers of people who subsequently developed psychiatric illness.

There is strong evidence, e.g. from the careful studies of school records by Albee, Lane and their colleagues (e.g. Heath, Albee and Lane, 1965), that even long before their illness has appeared clinically, the process/hebephrenic/simple groups of schizophrenics perform less well on intelligence tests than their siblings and peers. Paranoid schizophrenics seem not to differ from their peers. Various U.S. Army studies (Kingsley and Struening, 1966) suggest that schizophrenics as a group suffer a sharp decline in test scores soon after the signs and symptoms of schizophrenia appear. Although the evidence is not unanimous, it seems that verbal as well as non-verbal aspects of intelligence may be affected. There seems to be no great difference in the deficit shown by the various subcategories of schizophrenia. The evidence is ambiguous as to whether the deficit is progressive, i.e. whether it increases as the illness continues. However, there is considerable agreement that the deficit is reversible, i.e. that patients who are judged clinically to have recovered from schizophrenia show significant improvement in their scores, compared with their scores while ill (Haywood and Moelis, 1963). It is not clear, however, whether this is sufficient in most cases to make up all the deficit. There is some evidence for the clinical observation that low intelligence is a poor prognostic sign in schizophrenia, possibly because of the association of low intelligence and the process/hebephrenic/simple subcategories.

It is not possible to summarize adequately the results, often conflicting, of the large number of studies of the effects of 'brain damage' on intelligence test scores. The amount of deficit appears to be influenced by the locus, magnitude and nature of the damage, the suddenness with which it occurred, the age of the patient at the time of the injury, the 'chronicity' of the damage, the interests and skills of the patient etc. Generalized damage, as in senile and presenile dementia, multiple sclerosis, etc., usually seems to result in intellectual deficit, although the evidence is conflicting as to whether the amount of cerebral damage is related to the degree of deficit. Left-sided lesions appear to result in greater deficit than right-sided damage, and deficit also seems to be greater with posterior than with anterior lesions (see Piercy, 1964). It is often claimed that left-sided lesions produce greater deficit in verbal than in non-verbal intelligence, while the opposite is true with right-sided damage, although the evidence is conflicting (see Smith, 1966).

In conclusion, three points should be made about studies of intellectual deficit. First, it should be emphasized that there are very big differences between patients in the effects of pathology, and that even if a particular group, e.g. schizophrenics, exhibits deficit, not every patient of that type does so. Second, few intelligence tests have been devised specifically to detect intellectual deficit, so that they are often insensitive to the effects of brain damage and other pathology. This may account for some of the negative results. Finally, even if deficit is detected, the reason for it is often unclear. Intelligence tests involve several different cognitive processes, and disorder of any one might result in reduced scores; non-cognitive factors, including poor motivation, might also be involved.

## REFERENCES

ANTHONY, E. J. (1956) The significance of Jean Piaget for child psychiatry. *British Journal of Medical Psychology*, **29**, 20–34.

ARGYLE, M. (1967) *The Psychology of Interpersonal Behaviour*. London: Penguin Books.

ATKINSON, R. C. & SHIFFRIN, R. M. (1968) In *The Psychology of Learning and Motivation: Advances in Research and Theory*. Vol. 2. Edited by K. W. Spence and J. T. Spence.

BANDURA, A. (1966) In *Research in Behaviour Modification*, Chap. 15. Edited by L. Krasner and L. P. Ullman, New York: Holt, Rinehart & Winston.

BANDURA, A., Ross, D. & Ross, S. A. (1963) Imitation of film-mediated aggressive models. *Journal of Abnormal and Social Psychology*, **66**, 3–11.

BANNISTER, D. (1960) Conceptual structure in thought-disordered schizophrenics. *Journal of Mental Science*, **106**, 1230–1249.

BANNISTER, D. (1965a) The rationale and clinical relevance of repertory grid technique. *British Journal of Psychiatry*, **111**, 977–982.

BANNISTER, D. (1965b) The genesis of schizophrenic thought disorder: retest of the serial invalidation hypothesis. *British Journal of Psychiatry*, **111**, 377–382.

BANNISTER, D. (1966) In *New Horizons in Psychology*, chap. 19. Edited by B. M. Foss. London: Penguin Books.

BANNISTER, D. & FRANSELLA, F. (1966) A grid test of schizophrenic thought disorder. *British Journal of Social and Clinical Psychology*, **5**, 95–102.

BANNISTER, D. & FRANSELLA, F. (1971) *Inquiring Man*. London: Penguin Books.

BARTLETT, F. C. (1932) *Remembering: A Study in Experimental and Social Psychology*. Cambridge: University Press.

BEECH, H. R. (1966) In *New Horizons in Psychology*, chap. 18. Edited by B. M. Foss. London: Penguin Books.

BEKHTEREV, V. M. (1932) *General Principles of Reflexology*. New York: International Publishing Co. Inc.

BINET, A. & SIMON, T. (1908) The development of intelligence in the child. *Année psychologique*, **14**, 1–90.

BREGER, L. & McGAUGH, J. L. (1965) Critique and re-formulation of 'learning theory' approaches to psychotherapy and neurosis. *Psychological Bulletin*, **63**, 338–358.

BREGER, L. & McGAUGH, J. L. (1966) Learning theory and behaviour therapy: a reply to Rachman and Eysenck. *Psychological Bulletin*, **65**, 170–173.

BROADBENT, D. E. (1958) *Perception and Communication*. Oxford: Pergamon Press.

BROADBENT, D. E. (1969) In *The Pathology of Memory*, pp. 167–171. Edited by G. A. Talland & N. C. Waugh. New York: Academic Press.

BROWN, J. (1964) Short-term memory. *British Medical Bulletin*, **20**, 8–11.

BROWN, J. (1966) In *New Horizons in Psychology*, chap. 5. Edited by B. M. Foss. London: Penguin Books.

BRUNER, J. S., GOODNOW, J. S. & AUSTIN, G. A. (1956) *A Study of Thinking*. New York: Wiley.

BUTCHER, H. J. (1968) *Human Intelligence*. London: Methuen.

CHERRY, E. C. (1953) Some experiments on the recognition of speech with one and with two ears. *Journal of the Acoustical Society of America*, **25**, 975–979.

DIXON, N. F. (1966) In *New Horizons in Psychology*, chap. 2, Edited by B. M. Foss. London: Penguin Books.

EYSENCK, H. J. (1947) *Dimensions of Personality*. London: Routledge & Kegan Paul.

EYSENCK, H. J. (1957) *The Dynamics of Anxiety and Hysteria*. London: Routledge & Kegan Paul.

EYSENCK, H. J. (1967) Intelligence assessment: a theoretical and experimental approach. *British Journal of Educational Psychology*, **37**, 81–98.

EYSENCK, H. J. & RACHMAN, S. (1965) *The Causes and Cures of Neurosis*. London: Routledge & Kegan Paul.

FLAVELL, J. H. (1963) *The Development Psychology of Jean Piaget*; Princeton, N.J.: Van Nostrand.

FOSS, B. M. (ed.) (1966) *New Horizons in Psychology*. London: Penguin Books.

FOSS, B. M. (1968) In *Psychopharmacology*, chap. 2. Edited by C. R. B. Joyce. London: Tavistock.

FOULDS, G. A., HOPE, K., McPHERSON, F. M. & MAYO, P. R. (1967a) Cognitive disorder among the schizophrenias: I. The validity of some tests of thought-process disorder. *British Journal of Psychiatry*, **113**, 1361–1368.

FOULDS, G. A., HOPE, K., McPHERSON, F. M. & MAYO, P. R. (1967b) Cognitive disorder among the schizophrenias: II. Differences between the subcategories. *British Journal of Psychiatry*, **113**, 1369–1374.

GALTON, F. (1870) *Hereditary Genius*. New York: Appleton.

GESELL, A. (1940) *The First Five Years of Life*. New York: Harper.

GOLDSTEIN, K. & SCHEERER, M. (1941) Abstract and concrete behaviour, an experimental study with special tests. *Psychological Monographs*, **53**, No. 2.

GREGORY, R. L. (1966) In *New Horizons in Psychology*, chap. 3. Edited by B. M. Foss. London: Penguin Books.

GRIFFITHS, RUTH (1954) *The Abilities of Babies*. London: University Press.

HAYWOOD, H. C. & MOELIS, I. (1963) Effect of sympton change on intellectual function in schizophrenia. *Journal of Abnormal and Social Psychology*, **67**, 76–78.

HEATH, E. B., ALBEE, G. W. & LANE, E. A. (1965)   In *Proceedings of 73rd Annual Convention of the American Psychological Association*, pp. 223–224. Washington: A.P.A.

HULL, C. L. (1943)   *Principles of Behaviour*. New York: Appleton–Century–Crofts.

HUNTER, I. M. L. (1964)   *Memory*. London: Penguin Books.

INGLIS, J. (1966)   *The Scientific Study of Abnormal Behaviour*. Chicago: Aldine.

INGLIS, J. (1970)   In *Symptoms of Psychopathology*, chap. 4. Edited by C. G. Costello. New York: Wiley.

KAY, H. (1964)   Human learning. *British Medical Bulletin*, **20**, 3–7.

KAY, H. (1966)   In *New Horizons in Psychology*, chap. 16. Edited by B. M. Foss. London: Penguin Books.

KELLY, G. A. (1955)   *The Psychology of Personal Constructs*. New York: Norton.

KENDRICK, D. C., PARBOOSINGH, R.-C. & POST, F. (1965)   A synonym learning test for use with elderly psychiatric patients: a validation study. *British Journal of Social and Clinical Psychology*, **4**, 63–71.

KEPPEL, G. (1968)   Verbal learning and memory. *Annual Review of Psychology*, **19**, 169–202.

KINGSLEY, L. & STRUENING, E. L. (1966)   Changes in intellectual performance of acute and chronic schizophrenics. *Psychological Reports*, **18**, 791–800.

KRAL, V. A. (1969)   In *The Pathology of Memory*, pp. 41–48. Edited by G. A. Talland & N. C. Waugh. New York: Academic Press.

McGHIE, A. (1969)   *Pathology of Attention*. London: Penguin Books.

McKELLAR, P. (1957)   *Imagination and Thinking*. London: Cohen and West.

McPHERSON, F. M., BUCKLEY, F. & DRAFFAN, J. (1971)   'Psychological' constructs and delusions of persecution and 'nonintegration' in schizophrenia. *British Journal of Medical Psychology*, **44**, 277–280.

MAIR, J. M. M. & CRISP, A. M. (1968)   Estimating psychological organization, meaning and change in relation to clinical practice. *British Journal of Medical Psychology*, **41**, 15–29.

MELTON, A. W. (1963)   Implications of short-term memory for a general theory of memory. *Journal of Verbal Learning and Behaviour*, **2**, 1–21.

MORAY, N. (1969)   *Listening and Attention*. London: Penguin Books.

MOWRER, O. H. (1950)   *Learning Theory and Personality Dynamics*. New York: Ronald Press.

O'CONNOR, N. (1966)   In *New Horizons in Psychology*, chap. 17. Edited by B. M. Foss. London: Penguin Books.

OLDS, J. F. & MILNER, P. (1954)   Positive reinforcement produced by electrical stimulation of septal area and other regions of rat brain. *Journal of Comparative and Physiological Psychology*, **47**, 419–427.

PAVLOV, I. P. (1927)   *Conditional Reflexes*. Oxford: University Press.

PAYNE, R. W., MATTUSEK, P. & GEORGE, E. I. (1959)   An experimental study of schizophrenic thought disorder. *Journal of Mental Science*, **105**, 627–652.

PAYNE, R. W. (1970)   In *Symptoms of Psychopathology*, chap. 3. Edited by C. G. Costello. New York: Wiley.

PAYNE, R. W., HOCHBERG, A. C. & HAWKS, D. V. (1970)   Dichotic stimulation as a method of assessing disorder of attention in overinclusive schizophrenic patients. *Journal of Abnormal Psychology*, **76**, 185–193.

PIAGET, J. (1952)   *The Origins of Intelligence in Children*. New York: International University Press.

PIAGET, J. (1954)   *The Construction of Reality in the Child*. New York: Basic Books.

PIERCY, M. (1964)   The effects of cerebral lesions on intellectual function: a review of current research trends. *British Journal of Psychiatry*, **110,** 310–352.

POSTMAN, L. (1969)   In *The Pathology of Memory*, pp. 195–210. Edited by G. A. Talland & N. C. Waugh. New York: Academic Press.

PRICE, R. H. (1970)   Task requirements in tests of schizophrenic overinclusion. *British Journal of Social and Clinical Psychology*, **9,** 60–67.

PRINGLE, M. L. K. (1965)   *Deprivation and Education*. London: Longman.

RACHMAN, S. & EYSENCK, H. J. (1966)   Reply to a 'critique and reformulation' of behaviour therapy. *Psychological Bulletin*, **65,** 165–169.

RIBOT, T. (1885)   *Diseases of Memory*. London: Kegan Paul.

ROGERS, C. (1951)   *Client-Centred Therapy: Its Current Practice, Implication and Theory*. Boston: Houghton Mifflin.

RUSSELL, W. R. (1959)   *Brain, Memory, Learning: A Neurologists's View*. Oxford: University Press.

SALZINGER, K. & PISONI, S. (1958)   Reinforcement of affect responses of schizophrenics during the clinical interview. *Journal of Abnormal and Social Psychology*, **57,** 84–90.

SALZINGER, K., PORTNOY, S. & FELDMAN, R. S. (1964)   Experimental manipulation of continuous speech in schizophrenic patients. *Journal of Abnormal and Social Psychology*, **68,** 508–516.

SATTLER, J. M. & THEYE, F. (1967)   Procedural, situational and interpersonal variables in individual intelligence testing. *Psychological Bulletin*, **68,** 347–360.

SKINNER, B. F. (1938)   *Behaviour of Organisms*. New York: Appleton.

SKINNER, B. F. (1954)   The science of learning and the art of teaching. Harvard Ed. Rev., **24,** No. 2.

SMITH, A. (1966)   Verbal and non-verbal test performance of patients with 'acute' lateralized brain lesions (tumors). *Journal of Nervous and Mental Diseases*, **141,** 517–523.

STRETCH, R. (1966)   In *New Horizons in Psychology*, chap. 15. Edited by B. M. Foss. London: Penguin Books.

TALLAND, G. A. (1968)   *Disorders of Memory and Learning*. London: Penguin Books.

THOMSON, R. (1959)   *The Psychology of Thinking*. London: Penguin.

TREISMAN, A. (1964)   The effect of irrelevant material on the efficiency of selective listening. *American Journal of Psychology*, **77,** 533–546.

TREISMAN, A. (1966)   In *New Horizons in Psychology*, chap. 4. Edited by B. M. Foss. London: Penguin Books.

WALTON, H. J. & McPHERSON, F. M. (1968)   Phenomena in a closed psychotherapeutic group. *British Journal of Medical Psychology*, **4,** 61–72.

WASON, P. C. (1966)   In *New Horizons in Psychology*, chap. 6. Edited by B. M. Foss. London: Penguin Books.

WAUGH, N. C. & NORMAN, D. A. (1965)   Primary Memory. *Psychological Review*, **72,** 89–104.

WECHSLER, D. (1958)   *The Measurement and Appraisal of Adult Intelligence*. Baltimore: Williams and Wilkins.

WELFORD, A. T. (1958)   *Ageing and Human Skill*. Oxford: O.U.P.

WENAR, C. (1961)   The reliability of mothers' histories. *Child Development*, **32,** 491–500.

WENAR, C. (1963)   The reliability of developmental histories: summary and evaluation of evidence. *Psychosomatic Medicine*, **25,** 505–509.

WIEST, W. M. (1967)   Some recent criticisms of behaviorism and learning theory. *Psychological Bulletin*, **67,** 214–225.

WILLIAMS, M. (1970)  *Brain Damage and the Mind.* London: Penguin Books.

WOODWARD, M. (1959)  The behaviour of idiots interpreted by Piaget's theory of sensori-motor development. *British Journal of Educational Psychology*, **29**, 60–71.

WRIGHT, D. S. & TAYLOR, A. (1970)  *Introducing Psychology.* London: Penguin Books.

## Chapter X

# A PSYCHODYNAMIC APPROACH TO THE UNDERSTANDING OF THE PERSON

### J. D. Sutherland

#### INTRODUCTION

Just as the pathology of various organs and systems in the body was the main origin of our knowledge of organic functions in health and disease, so it has been with our understanding of the development and functioning of the person. It is for the relief of suffering that people collaborate with the doctor in the investigations and procedures he has to use. Only under this motivation is it possible to explore the depths of the inner worlds of people and to gain insights into those forces whose nature as well as their origins are often unrecognized by the individual, yet which determine the course of his development, his future well-being and his effectiveness—or the converse.

Patients seeking help for psychological suffering come with a bewildering range of complaints—all the phenomena grouped under the headings of the psychoneuroses, character or personality disorders and the borderline and functional psychoses. Unlike the clinical pictures arising from identifiable pathological agents in the body, psychological symptoms often show within the same individual fluctuations in intensity and changes in pattern. They can remit for varying periods, at times for no apparent reason, though on other occasions, changes are clearly related to events in the life of the individual. Much disturbance is painfully intractable, either constantly or in its liability to recur.

As careful histories have been accumulated, presenting symptoms are revealed to be end-products of disturbances deeply rooted in the development of the person. The irrational behaviour emerges as having *meaning*, i.e. it is linked with past experiences and has its own function for the person in expressing a part of his self that has failed to become integrated into the more unified person he would like to be. When Freud published his studies on hysterical patients about eighty years ago, he demonstrated how painful experiences could be split off from awareness and how, far from remaining inert, they operated with a dynamic of their own which preserved, for example, the hysterical paralysis in spite of the suffering it caused. In the early investigations of these puzzling phenomena, it seemed that what was segregated in the mind was a relatively limited experience, albeit an intolerably distressing one, and that the bringing of it back into consciousness resolved the trouble. Further work showed the situation was not so simple. Fresh symptoms would appear associated with other, often earlier, experiences; and to confound matters, the painful feelings frequently emerged linked, not to actual events, but to fantasies, i.e. to situations in the imaginative life of the person. Even more complexity entered when it was recognized that the symptoms of conflict within the person were markedly affected by the culture within which he lived. Thus, when the grosser manifestations of hysterical processes became widely recognized after the first World War, they began to disappear. Similarly with other symptoms, so that in recent years complaints have focussed more and more directly on feelings about the nature of the individual's quality of personal life, and especially in his relationships with himself and others. Underneath or alongside the various specific symptoms, which may occupy a dominant place in consciousness, he feels divided within himself, unable to find satisfaction in one or more areas of living. He is beset with fears or vague anxieties that cripple him from achievement in work, in making good relations with others or from gaining enjoyment or enrichment from his leisure.

The fact that so much psychological suffering and incapacity resists the struggles of the person to overcome it inevitably leads us to the view that the person in the course of development becomes organized into dynamic structures or systems in varying degrees of conflict. It is as though he acquires more than one sub-self constantly ready to realize its own goals, while his central self, the self he would most wish to be, battles against the others with fluctuating success or failure in the task of controlling or reconciling incompatible aims. The drive towards integrating the conflicting parts is a persistent one, fostered from within the person by the need to feel a unified 'somebody' within the social setting in which he lives and reinforced by the satisfying responses he gains from others. The balance, however, in the management of conflict may remain precarious. When it has to be maintained by restricting the 'life space', for example, by an over-dependent relationship with another member of the family or a colleague at work, or by a dependent attachment to some activity or part of the physical environment, then the loss of these supports quickly exposes the instability that may hitherto have been concealed. Again, the restriction may consist in the active denial of a part of the self as in the 'intellectual' who tries to dissociate himself from much of his instinctive and emotional self. If he has not managed to come to terms with these needs in a profound way, then he is prone to find he is confronted in midlife with a progressive and eventually overpowering sense of emptiness which leads to breakdown.

*Psychotherapy* must rest on an adequate understanding of the nature and origin of these conflicts in the person. Moreover, because all the available evidence suggests that the more severe psychological disorders, i.e. those conditions which come to the psychiatrist, stem from very early anomalies in the growth of the personality, our understanding must encompass as far as possible an appropriate view of these beginnings. We are at once in a dilemma. Inferences about what is happening at the personal level in the infant must be speculative. Nevertheless, in the first two years of life the baby advances from a stage in which the word 'person' makes little sense, to becoming a toddler with obvious indications of complex structuring within the personality. We have only to observe the spontaneous play of a child in the third year of life to see richly imaginative activity at work, of responses to people and things that show that these can assume highly personal significances for him. Behaviour such as transient phobias and many other responses point to the close connection between what is going on in his inner world and his interactions with the outer one. Within another two years, he can tell us of dreams and nightmares, as well as fantasy play, which reflect unmistakably elaborate processes in his inner world.

The relevance and status of our knowledge in this whole area is currently in debate and it is important that the psychiatrist does not adopt prematurely a standpoint that may preclude him from making any sense of much of the disorder that he has to treat. The most controversial issue concerns its position as 'scientific'. A full consideration of this matter is clearly outwith the scope of this chapter and so only a few points will be made. First, if we are to deal with what is most 'personal', most vital, in helping the individual to gain more understanding of himself, then *we have to deal specifically with what he presents at the personal level.* There are many ways in which people can be helped to achieve some degree of relief from psychological suffering and disorder, from the wide range of psycho-tropic drugs to the giving of support, reassurance and counselling. These measures are being provided increasingly by less specialized sources such as the general practitioner and the expanding personal service agencies. As a specialist source of help, the psychiatrist has got to understand, for example, how the following difficulties can arise and be ameliorated.

*Case* 1. A young man, ambitious and successful in his career as an engineer, married a young woman to whom he was greatly attached. With only the flimsiest foundation, mainly an attempt on the part of one of his wife's employers to have an affair with her before their marriage, he became obsessed with what occurred between his wife and the older man. He persecuted her with resentful questioning for days after which he would feel great contrition and would try to make up to her. His work began to be interfered with during these spells of compulsive pre-occupation. Though weeping in distress at the dangerous threat his behaviour represented to his marriage and his advancement, he remained powerless to alter himself.

*Case* 2. An attractive, intelligent, and sociable student after a successful first year at University found herself unable to carry out the tasks set by her tutors. She failed her second year and in the further period granted to her, she was about to fail again. Despite the fact that she faced the termination of the career on which she had embarked with high hopes, she could not get herself to work. She became convinced that her teachers thought 'she was no good'. At the same time, she began to make demands on various people, general practitioners and others, for 'something' to get her out of her difficulties.

Both of these patients had found drugs to be of some help at first and then to provide no relief. Both had had a great deal of sympathy and encouragement, and both sought psychiatric help in desperation, although in each case with the proviso that this help was to be kept secret.

These two people are mentioned not to illustrate any particular pathology but to highlight the powerful reality of the forces that threatened them with grave consequences, and in face of which they were helpless, and which they were reluctant to reveal. The conflicting forces are highly personal, they concern attitudes to themselves and to others. Furthermore, these forces express themselves in specific forms. Are they to be adequately understood in any terms which 'reduce' them to 'simpler', or what are thought to be more 'real' processes such as the physiological; or are they to be studied as expressions of some obscure personal needs built into their inner worlds? To pursue the latter kind of inquiry entails our entry into these subjective realms. We have no instrument with which the forces, despite their powerful and enduring nature, can be readily identified and measured. Yet they are of the very stuff with which people's lives are run as well as making their dreams. From the point of view of science as it is commonly regarded, the situation is even worse because the therapist as investigator in trying to find out with the patient what is going on is also using his own highly subjective responses. Notwithstanding these intimidating barriers to the gaining of communicable knowledge, we must not act as if such knowledge cannot be obtained.

The situation in fact is not devoid of scientific grace, for as a second consideration in our approach to this subjective world, we have a vast range of data. The psycho-analytic method, the most widely used and best described instrument for investigating the nature and origins of the conflicting forces in the person, has been applied during three quarters of a century to an increasingly diverse range of personalities, from non-patients in the form of analytic candidates, through the full range of the neuroses and character disorders to severely ill hospitalized psychoses. A consensus of broad findings has emerged paralleled by theories of the growth of the personality as an essential part of this work. While Freud's contribution towers over this whole field, many advances have been made which have amplified and expanded his formulations. Major sources of new data have been made available since Freud's main work. The retrospective theories of child development have been strongly reinforced by psychoanalytic studies of young children from their spontaneous fantasy productions in play with toys as well as their verbalizations. Such work permits us to watch the changing role of the imaginative world in the formation of many features of the person. Supplementing these endeavours has been the great amount of research on the interaction between mothers and infants carried out by psychologists and others and using objective aids to observation.

The evidence on which we can construct at least a tentative outline of the development of the person to give some order to the range of normal and pathological functioning is thus broadly based, if still in the category of 'soft' according to the prevailing scientific values. The student has to decide for himself whether such 'harder' data as we can obtain by taking samples of restricted psychological processes really enables him to understand and to treat *persons*. In the following account, the basis is chiefly the work of some of the most penetrating psychoanalytic thinking of the last few decades. It draws on the contributions of many, but above all on those of Melanie Klein (1932, 1948, 1957); Fairbairn (1952); Winnicott (1957, 1958, 1965, 1965a); Balint (1952, 1959, 1968); Guntrip (1961, 1964, 1968) and Erikson (1950, 1959, 1964). The aim here is to introduce a theoretical approach that is directly related to what the normal functioning of the person involves at the personal level and to a therapy based on an understanding of psychological conflicts.

## THE PHASE OF INFANTILE DEPENDENCE

Winnicott has rightly stressed that in imagining what goes on at the start of the baby's extra-uterine life, we must take the baby with his mother as the relevant unit of study. He has suggested that the mother is prepared towards the end of her pregnancy by the emergence of a state of maternal pre-occupation to provide an enveloping empathic care for the baby which bridges the intra- and the extra-uterine worlds. At birth, the baby is equipped with a number of response systems which are rapidly added to in the course of maturation and the role of these innate potentials has been richly illuminated by the work of the ethologists (see Bowlby, 1969). We cannot but assume that conscious-

ness is present at birth and whether or not this fundamental psychological property has begun in the foetus remains an open question.
Several psychoanalytic investigators have encountered responses from
adult patients indicating that events at birth have been 'recorded' in
memory even though they did not become part of organized experience.
By the time the smiling response is evoked, after a few weeks, it would
be hard to resist the conclusion that the baby is experiencing pleasurable states. Engel (1962) describes well the cycles during the early
weeks of sleep, alert inactivity, alert activity and states of discomfort
with crying.

Two kinds of interaction with the mother, the appetitive and the
reactive, can be separated for consideration although these are closely
linked in their effects. In whatever initial matrix of consciousness there
may be, it seems that the need to suck and feed plays a prominent part,
possibly through a particularly vivid quality in the affective experience
that accompanies the activities of incorporation. Its instinctive equipment prepares the baby to suck and very soon to seek the nipple. When
in a state of needing to be fed, tension grows, as seen in heightened
activity and frequently going on to crying. The ordinary good mother is
equipped by nature to respond to these states so that undue distress
seldom arises. The baby's responses show that learning of a simple
kind proceeds rapidly. We can readily imagine that as tension rises, an
anticipation of the nipple is present. No clear awareness of the self as
internal and the mother as an external figure would be likely at the
start. As Winnicott has put it, in such a state of need and with well-
timed response from the mother, the baby could have a feeling of
having 'created' this wonderfully satisfying state of having the breast.
When the feeding response grows in vigour, in keeping with the
expanding aliveness in other sensori-motor areas, the quality of exciting
satisfaction must be vivid. A good feeding relationship would therefore
provide one of the basic ways in which a feeling of trust in the environment develops.

The other kind of interaction, while not perhaps so intense emotionally because more diffused in time, concerns the rest of the stimulation
the mother provides for the reacting systems of the baby. Although this
kind of interaction was given little attention in the past in comparison
with the feeding one, we now know it is crucial for the baby's development. It includes all those factors in the good mothering relationship
apart from feeding, that treat the baby as a loved person, e.g. being
fondled and rocked, being smiled at and hearing mother's voice
speaking and crooning, and all the contacts around nappies and bath-
ing. That the baby needs this wide sensory input is indicated by the
fact that what stops crying and goes on to smiling can be a certain kind
of interaction with the mother. Spitz (1946, 1965) in his classic study of

institutionalized babies, showed that adequate feeding without the usual amount of 'mothering' interaction proceeding simultaneously led to serious developmental failures in the form of 'depressed' states, though later described by Engel more accurately as states of 'depression–withdrawal'.

For our present purposes, the chronology of early development is taken in very general terms. By about the end of the first six months, the baby is beginning to be specifically attached to his mother and to a lesser degree to other family figures. He now tends to resist the attempts of strangers to do what mother does. In short, we can assume that by this time, mother has become represented in his mind in a much more organized way than hitherto. He is also acquiring ways of responding to inner needs, and his expressive motor activities suggest he is starting to show the characteristics of becoming a person.

When we turn to what is going on in the inner world of the baby in the first year of life, we are led to assume several developments. Experiences of good mothering provide a basis for the development of a good self-feeling. At first this feeling must rest on the pleasurable experiences during good and loving care. Mothers who are inhibited by anxiety or other adverse emotions from responding warmly while caring for their babies induce an anxious inhibited state in them (see Engel). In the earliest stages, the body and the embryonic self-feeling appear to be closely interdependent. The framework of care which the mother supplies leads to a progressively internalized and organized imago of this good mother. 'Good' and 'bad' describe what feels good or pleasurable and with which contact is sought, and for what feels painful or unpleasurable and from which the baby seeks to rid itself, e.g. by turning or pushing away or by spitting out. Just how we can describe some of the differentiating mental activities at this stage is understandably a difficult matter but there is value in adopting the term *fantasy*. With this term we can cover, for example, the notion that in a period of anticipating the breast, the infant could have a fantasy about it as good. Such a fantasy would be difficult to maintain if mother did not appear within a certain period. The infant's state would then be one of distress with reactive 'angry' or aggressive protesting responses. Such feelings give rise to fantasies of a 'bad' breast-mother with destructive impulses towards it. In postulating such contrasting fantasies, we do not have to assume that they are accompanied by highly developed imagery; we are merely trying to describe an embryonic *relationship* as reflected in consciousness. Although we commonly focus attention on feelings, emotions are the affective accompaniments of response systems, i.e. of relationships. We are not just angry or aggressive; we are angry or aggressive with someone or something for not doing something we wish or doing something we do not wish. It is the pattern of this relationship with the imagined object and its specific feelings that the term *fantasy* covers.

In the main area of self-feeling, within which the differentiation of structure takes place, the overall interaction with the mother gives an affective tone of pleasure, trust and confidence if things go well. When the mother communicates a general input of loving care and a sense of her enjoyment in her interactions with the baby, there is a sound foundation for the development of a more defined and secure self-feeling, a sense of being, or of 'I-ness'. Expanding cognitive abilities going hand in hand with increasing motor skills permit a recognition of the mother as external and the self as internal to become more clearly established. The organization of this adaptive central area constitutes the ego. The relationship between the ego and the matrix of self-feeling is complex. Given a good balance of experience, the activities of the ego can incorporate into one central system the bodily experiences and the more intense excitements associated with the main instinctual needs as well as the characteristic ways of responding to the mother and to the external environment. Under these circumstances, the ego is 'strong', i.e. there is a confident enjoyment in relating to the outer world of people and things. Naturally, much is assimilated from the mother by identification with her. The individuality of the infant, however, in asserting and creating its own self becomes manifest. In this process the close background presence of the mother paradoxically permits more independence. As Winnicott puts it, the 'capacity to be alone' grows successfully only when the mother is felt to be *there*. Her 'holding' or supporting function permeates an *ego-relatedness* for the developing potential to feel secure while enriching the inner world. The formation of the ego can only take place over time and its capacity to remain integrated derives from the security of the mother's consistent responsiveness. The major part of the self-feeling can then become invested in all the opportunities that the maturation of the ego capacities offers—soon to include mobility, other motor and perceptual skills, and language as enormous resources for play. With this foundation, 'others' and the external world can become exciting and more fulfilling than the satisfactions from fantasy and autoerotic play.

No infant can grow without periods of frustration and indeed it is a function of good mothering to dose this frustration to initiate the growth to independence. The inevitable painful experiences, especially those from unmet needs, lead to a certain amount of splitting within the systems beginning to organize experience. We have to keep in mind, too, that the mothering environment may fail the infant in many respects. Basic needs for food and physical care may be met but with the much more personal interaction required for good self and ego development missing. Such a depriving mother induces a feeling that various activities and needs are 'bad' because their expressions are unwanted by her. There is a cohesion of those negatively toned aspects into a segregated part of the self which withdraws into a hidden or secret core.

A substantial degree of *splitting* in the self through withdrawal seems to be established by deprivation of the mother's interaction with the early stages of the activity of the infant's response systems. The central ego then seeks to diminish the general sense of insecurity and dependence by remaining relatively apathetic or by a more anxious conformity with the mother. With the lesser degrees of this kind of deprivation, the chief effects appear to be the tendency to feel a part of the self as secret, realizable only in fantasy and other self-bounded satisfactions. When appetitive needs are frustrated within a mothering relationship which is not depriving of the stimulus satisfaction the developing ego requires, then the responses are of an entirely different character. The impulses towards the frustrating object are of destructive rage, of biting and tearing to pieces. Such feelings, when the infant tries to reject them, create an inner situation as though he were being persecuted or attacked by dangerous 'objects' inside his mind—by imagos of mother or parts of her possessed by the same kind of violence, i.e. which will bite and tear him to pieces. To free himself, he attempts to 'project' them, i.e. to regard them as 'outside'; and if this process occurs too intensively, then an unduly anxious or phobic reaction may be established to parts of the environment. A hitherto accepted part of his cot or a familiar toy may become frightening through its association with the inner imago. The earliest persecutors are felt almost entirely in terms of primitive violence. When he can later describe them, only the wildest and most savage animals can express for the child the nature of the attacks he fears in his fantasies. Much of the intensity of these early fantasies diminishes though some remains permanently in varying degrees. The outcome is a system in which a part of the self becomes identified with the threatening attacker especially when needs arise. This system is thus the precursor of the later super-ego, the term used for the inner inhibiting parent imago after the sexual identity has become established.

In using the word 'system' for these organizations within the mind, we describe an inner situation in which a part or state of the self acquires a consistent way of responding to an inner 'object'. And when a system goes into action with a part of the external world, the latter is reacted to as though it had the properties of the inner object.

The lessening of persecutory fears takes place within the mothering relationship by a process of 'projection' and 'introjection'. That is to say, if the infant is under the sway of a persecutory system, it will react to the mother as though she were a frightening attacker, e.g. it may desperately try to get rid of her. The persistence of the mother in offering comfort soon reinstates her good status which is then taken inside again, i.e. it is introjected. Where the effects of persecutory anxiety are not ameliorated in this way the infant retains a frightened attitude to parts of its world and so its general development may be impeded.

The effects of a persecutory system are also eased by the development of a system of satisfying inner objects for frustrated needs. An intensely needing self at one pole relates to an inner 'object' at the other, this imago being created out of the fantasies of what would satisfy the needs. These fantasy relationships include a wide range of patterns—from the self securing exciting satisfaction to the coupling of such excitement with intense anger and destructiveness to the needed object. In the earliest layers of these frustrated needs, the most prominent patterns of meeting them are incorporative, i.e. the child wants to make up for the frustrated 'empty' feelings, by taking a mother or a part of her inside his mind, a fantasy which can be reinforced for a time by sucking a finger or other object. The total experience of the infant makes many fantasies possible, e.g. by linking inner objects with various parts of the external environment or of the body, especially those capable of erotic sensation.

The first major qualitative change in the movement away from the high degree of dependence of the first six months occurs when the mother begins to be separated as an external whole person. This growing awareness confronts the baby with the dilemma that the mother he fantasies as so good is the same figure he can at other times hate for not responding to his needs. This ambivalence is normally overcome by the processes of introjection undoing the effects of projecting bad objects. The mother who has become bad because she is perceived and reacted to in terms of anger, ordinarily 'contains' this projection. As she continues to provide her care, she becomes 'good' again and so she is re-introjected. This learning prevents the infant feeling that mother's frustrations are being 'caused' by his hate. He is not beset with fantasies of having damaged her, an inner situation which is now capable of evoking the affective response we can only describe as depressive guilt.

The successful mastery of this danger can be seriously impeded if mothers are unable to accept these angry reactions, or if some external break in the mother-infant relationship occurs so that the mother is not there to provide the opportunity for removing the fantasy of having damaged her. Such infants then tend to avoid the use of the ordinary aggressive assertions that are necessary for the ongoing impetus to independence.

This phase, the *depressive position* as Melanie Klein called it, is closely related to the process of weaning, the first experience of a sustained effort from the mother to withhold what had previously been freely available.

To go through this phase requires a sufficient development of trust and security in the earlier experiences, and then the continuation of the good mothering which accepts the anger and rage of frustrated spells. It is from this phase that the foundations of concern for others and the capacity to feel guilt are laid down. It also enables the person to grieve and mourn the loss of a good object, an emotional task that cannot be accomplished if the individual's response to his loss contains too much anger or too little interaction with the mother. It then has to be split off into a system in which it realizes itself by attacking the individual from within—a division in which one part of the self reproaches or persecutes the other with a resultant state of guilt and depression.

It is readily understandable that a system with an inner object which arouses fear and anxiety should be segregated from the central ego. A frustrated *need system* becomes segregated because it increasingly embodies needs whose satisfaction is felt to be disallowed by mother. Its activity thus tends to evoke the persecutory system—mother becomes 'angry' or rejecting because the infant has expressed its needs in certain ways.

The broad structuring of the person during the phase of infantile dependence thus contains the following main systems:

(1) *The Central Self and Ego* associated with the imago of the good mother;

(2) *A withdrawn Self* of varying proportions associated with being 'bad', empty, isolated, helpless, or terrified;

(3) *A segregated sub-self* containing frustrated needs and an associated inner exciting object which fulfils these needs;

(4) *A second segregated sub-self* beginning to be identified with the inner object which threatens the needing self by attacking it.

The divisions (2), (3) and (4) can be viewed as deriving from experiences incompatible with the positive 'good' relationship needed with the mother and sought by the main self. Their evolution represents the most primitive defence processes at work and occurs through the innate properties of the affects whereby 'bad' or painful states must be avoided by fight or flight responses. In their formative stages, these systems are fluid and closely inter-related. If the experience of good mothering is grossly inadequate in this period, the main part of the first year, then the splitting appears to have the most serious consequences as it impairs the capacities for the further interaction which might lessen some of its severity even when later care is, by ordinary standards, good.

THE TRANSITIONAL PHASE

By the time infants pass to the toddler stage, the resources they have for outgrowing infantile dependence fill much of their play. Walking gives a new sense of mastery and the possibility of exploring and expanding the world. Having one's own possessions has already become important, especially the favourite comforting object which can be held on to when mother leaves, a 'transitional object' as Winnicott termed it. Games of dropping things or of peek-a-boo provide a recurrent experience for mastering the giving up of the constant presence of the familiar figures with the excitement of re-finding them. Speech and language provide new ways of retaining imagos through the additions they make to the use of symbols, and so greatly increase the capacity to bridge needs and satisfactions. The exploration of the body is engrossing and new kinds of auto-erotic pleasures become available. Relations with mother around toilet training also make for fresh powers. The child can now defy or assert himself by refusing or acceding to mother's requests. Excreta acquire symbolic value for they can be 'gifts' which delight mother or they can be bad things which are destroyed and expelled. For Freud, the particular pleasure associated in the course of maturation with the excretory processes and organs was held to be a critical factor. Later work suggests that the prominence of this 'anal behaviour' may be more associated with its symbolic value at this stage of development, when 'power' and 'self-assertion' are central emotional issues, than with the kind of pleasure it provides. The greater richness of the intellectual processes (see Piaget 1937) with the associated resources in fantasy, certainly give the excretory processes and the excreta a much greater meaning. Dangerous objects in the inner world can be imagined as the faeces which has been got rid of, though this may make faeces and dirt dangerous retaliators which can destroy. When parental demands for toilet training are too severe or are premature, instead of the child being trusted to develop control at his own natural pace, the excretory patterns of relating to objects become excessive. Control of others against these demands for what he feels to be part of his personal content assumes a major importance for the child both in his inner world and in his external relationships with people and things. It was from the study of this phase of development that the whole phenomena of obsessional behaviour became understandable, above all the morbid obstinacy, the excessive pre-occupation with cleanliness and tidiness as a reaction to the underlying wish to make a mess in defiance, and the interest in hoarding and collecting. The excretory act also gives a basis for sadistic relations with its ready combination of pleasure and destruction of the inner object.

The father and other members of the family take on new significance as the child moves to greater inner autonomy. Parsons (1955) in his analysis of the socializing of the person within the family, suggests that the phase of infantile dependence establishes the child emotionally. As he moves from this phase to the acquisition of instrumental powers, intellectually and physically, and with the accompanying drive away from his dependence on the mother, the father becomes a necessary 'model' additional to the mother for the stimulation and encouragement of the powers which facilitate separation from the mother.

In the second and third years, the marked activity of the inner world is seen in his animistic way of responding to objects; his toys and other articles have the same feelings as himself. The greater range and significance of other relationships, mainly within the family, enrich his ego by the new identifications he makes with these other figures and his inner world enlarges with new imagos. The basic role of the mother, however, is not far to seek. She remains the comforter in distress and if his relationship with her is disturbed, as in separation, then the effects can be far-reaching (see Bowlby). Appropriate and consistent care throughout this phase, with the encouragement of his own emerging identity, maintains his security and confidence in the task of coming to terms with the demands and needs of others.

THE DEVELOPMENT OF SEXUAL IDENTITY

In their fourth and fifth years, most children begin to manifest behaviour indicative of the maturation of sexual instinctive patterns. The genitals are explored and masturbation becomes almost universal. Sexual curiosity about the parents is openly expressed and sexual games with other children start. In the boy, erections compel his interest. The biological maturation creates new behaviour and, although knowledge of sexual intercourse is normally absent, the sexual colouring to much of this new behaviour is obvious. He begins to want mother to admire his penis and he becomes more interested in her body. His play assumes a more assertive and aggressive character; 'penetrating' activities with knives, tools and weapons begin to dominate. Father is challenged directly and in fantasy; stories of the boy hero saving the good princess or other female figure from the bad man are favourites. The conflicting fantasies around both parents are normally resolved without undue difficulty. For though in fantasy the boy may fear father will retaliate and remove his penis for wanting to take mother away from father—a fear which can be reinforced by his awareness of the sex differences—his good relationship with father leads eventually to the repression of the oedipal situation, as it is now universally known, with the parents. Mother, too, furthers this process for, while she may accept the boy's feelings, she does not permit him the intimacies he unconsciously seeks nor does she abandon her special relationship with father.

The internal processes of these few years from the fourth onward create major changes in the dynamic systems formed earlier. These systems were profoundly influenced by the incorporative behaviour characteristic of the dependent period. While the anal phase contributes many new patterns of managing the conflicts of this phase with its new kind of relationship with mother and others, the start of sexual forces within the child brings a resurgence of needs for intimate contact with others. The earlier oral patterns, however, are gradually replaced by genital interests. When previous development has gone on within good family relationships this change does not create an unduly difficult task. The ego has now a highly developed capacity to respond to dangers, whether in fantasy or external, with fear or anxiety. Anxiety over the loss of the good relationship with the father, or from the fantasied danger of his becoming a castrator, plays a central part in coming to terms with this new situation. Understandably, the earlier system containing the frustrated needs and the exciting object forms a pre-established pattern which is again aroused. Under its influence, fantasies arise that the sexual relationship between the parents is an oral one, e.g. in which they feed each other with their genitals. This influence recedes with the repetition of phallic activity and masturbatory experience. The fact that the boy cannot achieve intercourse and the prohibitions around his sexual interests re-invokes the earlier persecutory system which adds intensity to what he fears father may do as a retaliator. Thus, a not uncommon castration fantasy, in play or in anxiety dreams, is of a man or animal coming to bite him or his penis.

As these oral elements recede, the earlier systems take in more of the characteristics of the oedipal triangle. The good mother who formed the supporting imago to the central ego is now superseded in part by the good father. The boy wishes to be like this powerful male and he assimilates many of his attributes. At the same time, the rejecting figure he fears also changes to take on much from those aspects of father which frighten him. The frustrated need system retains the mother as its exciting object but now as the sexual woman rather than the earlier breast-mother. The internalization of the prohibiting father into the mind was the process Freud described as the establishment of the super-ego. The further work on early development in no way replaces this concept: what it does is to fill out the structuring that precedes the formation of the super-ego and to explain some of its characteristics that at times are difficult to account for in terms of the experiences at this stage. Thus, the acute anxiety and the savagery of the super-ego in some children are much more understandable when we realize that fantasies of attack stem from more primitive violent imagos.

The much greater awareness of the parents as external figures makes for strong feelings of guilt as well as anxiety when the sexual interests of the boy create hostile feelings and fantasies to his father. The effects of both these painful emotions along with the real relationship lead to this sexual interest in the mother being banished from consciousness. This banishment does not occur by the primary process of splitting but by the more developed mechanism of repression in which the ego and super-ego play a more active role.

For the girl, the early sexual maturation proceeds differently. The clitoris is excited in masturbation and while the new drive to others draws her back to mother at first, it is not long before her behaviour shows a new attraction to father and a corresponding negative streak to mother. Again the normal parental acceptance of these mani-festations, coupled with a manifestly good relationship between the parents, enables the girl to adopt her femininity. She too internalizes father into her ego-ideal, the good parental imago of her central ego, while its precursor, the rejecting persecuting mother, becomes modified by new and less severe internalizations of her parents to form her super-ego.

Successful adaptive growth through the oedipal phase is of the greatest importance for the establishment of a secure sexual identity. The capacity in later life to make a good hetero-sexual relationship in marriage and to be a good mother is made or marred in this period. In Western Societies, overt sexual play is prohibited in the so-called latency period, i.e. from ages six to seven to the emergence of adoles-cence. The underlying sexual forces are not as quiescent as they were formerly assumed to be and their apparent diminution is probably a cultural effect. Much of the sexual drive in these years is dispersed in fantasy and play. Many new activities and relationships absorb the ego and greatly multiply its resources. School takes the child into a new world with new attachments to others. Over-attachment to parents with the risk of undue anxiety and guilt from the underlying sexual fantasies is thereby reduced. Development is normally smooth enough though strain in working through the sexual pressures may show in regression or reversion to earlier modes of behaviour, e.g. in minor outbreaks of anal patterns with transient loss of excretory control, in nightmares of being attacked, or in transient phobias. Boys and girls begin to reinforce their sexual identity by becoming more separate in their play, the girls going on to 'being mothers' and the boys to being the tough and powerful fathers of their fantasies.

The ego with its much greater readiness to respond to the dangers of the sexual drives by anxiety and guilt now institutes a range of defences against these pressures—the familiar defence mechanisms so fully described by Freud and later amplified by Anna Freud (1937). According to the particular defences most used, and the pattern adopted is greatly determined by earlier experience and parental attitudes, so the character traits are formed.

As pre-adolescence approaches, peer groups and other adults provide many models for adding to the parental ones. Gang membership for boys reinforces their masculinity into adolescence and releases a great deal of assertive aggression. When the increasing sexual drive takes them into sexual encounters, the support of gangs is used until more serious pairing begins. For girls, friendships with others fulfil the same functions.

The psychology of adolescence is a topic which is dealt with separately in Chapter IV, Vol. II. In short, the attachment to parents has to be given up and their controlling function replaced by the young person acquiring his own morality. The turmoil of this phase, the task of finding a new identity which comes from a feeling of being significant for others outside the family has been well described by many writers (see Erikson and Anna Freud).

## The Functioning of the Normal or Mature Adult

The personality of the adult retains the divisions we have outlined, although these acquire much more content from experience and changing biological needs. They also become more complexly inter-related. They are:

(1) *The Central Ego system*

(2) *Frustrated need systems* whose activity is inhibited by (1) and by

(3) *A primitive control system.*

Additionally, we have noted that alongside the central ego there is a residue split off from it and which has been referred to as the *withdrawn ego.*

### THE CENTRAL EGO

The self and the ego, as has been indicated, are complexly related. The self is used to describe the primary matrix of the individual's experience of being and which, for most people, preserves a continuity of being throughout the life cycle. At the start, there is presumably only a generalized quality of feeling. This phase precedes any Cartesian 'I think therefore I am' and may be described as that in which 'the "I" is the first reality—I am real, therefore the world is real'. (Weisman 1965). The ego develops within this matrix as the adaptive organiser of experience. Hartmann (1964) made clear that the ego is not tied to appetitive instinctual experience; it draws on the many autonomous processes connected with the maturation of motor, perceptual, and intellectual capacities, but its successful evolution is dependent on the input from good mothering.

Instinctual experience within the framework of a good environment enriches and enlarges the boundaries of the ego so that its adaptive range manages effectively a relatively full satisfaction for the person as a whole. The normal person comes to include sexual needs as part of his self with a lessened feeling of them as foreign bodies to be subdued. The role of the instincts or innate response patterns in supplying the drives of the person to action are obscure. Apart from the sexual and parental drives which retain their specific goals, other action systems appear to be absorbed into the generalized life aims of the individual in the process of socialization. These needs are grouped into broad patterns with their 'programs' or goals organized within the ego which then operates as the main dynamic system for the person. The functioning modes of the ego are thus very much conditioned by the culture in which the person is reared.

The ego's activities are characterized by consciousness and constant adaptation. As a dynamic system its strength and cohesion has to be maintained by adequate transactions with the environment—in personal relationships, in the psychosocial activities of work, and in leisure. Relationships and activities are mediated by the imagos of the good parental figures and others from later experience. These imagos constitute a pattern for the person of what feels 'ideal' for him and so when nearly matched by others give rise to satisfying emotional qualities in relationships. In adulthood, they are not so much fixed imagos of particular figures as more generalized representations containing the good feelings attached to earlier figures. The conduct associated with these earlier figures creates a set of values or 'ego-ideals'.

THE SEGREGATED SYSTEMS

These incorporate relationship goals that are incompatible with the central ego. As described, these systems have at one pole a part of the self in a relationship with an internal object. Although their segregation precludes them from the degree of learning and adaptation that occurs in the central ego, they are modified in the course of maturation. Thus in the earliest stage, the inner object of the frustrated need system is predominantly the exciting breast-mother who gives unconditional satisfaction. The sexual instincts later add the forbidden sexual parent or a sexual organ into the system. Correspondingly, the early persecuting or rejecting object acquires the features of the prohibiting parents of the oedipal phase.

Derived from experience with external figures, inner objects as structures within the mind are also parts of the self. Fantasy, conscious and unconscious, leads to their elaboration and multiplicity under the impact of various inner reactions, e.g. hate, triumphing, controlling, or fusions of these with erotic needs in sadistic or masochistic relationships. The affective similarities within systems also permit needs from different phases to combine in forming imagos such as the vagina with terrifying teeth or the penis which is to be sucked as a breast. The structuring in these dynamic systems is thus 'three-dimensional', for each has its component layers from the various developmental phases, with the most recent layer usually forming the one nearest consciousness.

Segregated systems operate with varying degrees of 'distance' from the consciousness of the ego, this distance being governed by the intensity of the anxiety associated with their activity. Many of their original aims become actively disguised. Experiences from the earliest phases tend to remain excluded from recognition with the most powerful barriers. This exclusion is not due solely to their early occurrence but also to their being associated with the frightening, and often terrifying, anxiety of these stages in which annihilation is a basic dread. Resistance to awareness of later experiences, say at the oedipal phase, is less difficult to overcome as a rule. These differences are indicated by the concepts of the earlier segregation arising from primitive splitting processes compared with the more organized process of repression induced by the super-ego.

Internal object-relationship systems find much of their activity in fantasy, but there is always the tendency to seek an appropriate figure in the outer world who is then coerced in varying degrees into the role of the inner object. The inner object thus serves at times as a scanning apparatus to detect suitable figures to match its properties. Relationships with others, because the systems are virtually closed ones, do not permit much individuality to the other, and hence, such relationships are difficult to maintain. Others do not ordinarily tolerate being restricted to what the individual wants them to be. This instability can lead to a reversal of relationships by the process which Melanie Klein called 'projective identification'. This reversibility is made possible by the fact that the object pole as a structure within the mind can also become part of the self. Thus, residual needs to gratify infantile dependence may seek one or more adults to fulfil the role of the inner object as a good breast-mother. To realize this need may be felt by the central ego as too childish and it may also lead to anxiety by the unconscious evocation of the inner rejecting object. To avoid these pressures, the needing self may then be projected into another person, e.g. a dependent child, with whom this part of the self is then identified. The individual may now act out freely his own needs by mothering the other in the way he wishes for himself. This reversibility is commonly manifest in sadomasochistic relationships. For instance, the man who may at one time treat a woman sadistically in the role of the sexually exciting object (in this case erotic needs are combined with aggressive vengeful aims because of the frustration over the inner object's original rejection) may at other times identify with her. She then has to be the sexualized attacker. Again, when the primitive control system is unduly strong, this may set up a more or less constant pressure to get oneself victimized, punished, or rejected.

The activity of unduly strong segregated systems is experienced by the central ego as neurotic or pathological conflict. The individual 'cannot help himself' when he comes under their sway. If an unconscious need is operating powerfully, he is compulsively driven by it to 'act out' the inner relationship with varying amounts of disguise. In contrast, when primitive control fantasies are too prominent, the individual feels bereft of the drive and energy he requires to achieve what he wants. When the strength of the segregated systems is more normal, then the integrative capacity of the ego can manage their activity by restricting it to fantasy or drawing it into acceptable areas of living through the use of the defence mechanisms and other processes. Additional resources of energy and power then become available to the ego. Synthesis of this kind underlies the interest in particular occupations, as when dependent needs are carried over to caring for others. Frequently, repressed needs are successfully channelized into creative leisure pursuits and their absorption into the activities of the central ego may be attained with stability in the person as a whole. An underlying precariousness, however, may suddenly be revealed when the external environment upsets the equilibrium that has been achieved. A housewife, for example, may cope well for years with unconscious needs to defy and hate mother by messy anal behaviour through her reaction formation of being very orderly and tidy. This successful equilibrium may be shattered if her home is suddenly made filthy by some external disaster, e.g. flooding. Her inner world can then no longer maintain the feeling that she has stopped her buried hate and she passes into a depression, the state induced by the destruction of her good inner object.

Maturity or normality in the individual means that in his relations with others and with the physical environment he has become in large measure able to perceive them as they are instead of imposing inner requirements upon them in an unrealistic way. For him, the activities of the ego incorporate most of his self-feeling and so 'who he is' is virtually 'what he thinks and does'. To maintain this identity, then, as has been mentioned, he needs an appropriate social and physical environment. The structuring of the person, like that of the body, has to have its own 'metabolism'—a psychosocial one. The equilibrium the ego seeks to maintain is constantly vulnerable. Changes within the dynamic systems, e.g. from biological variation as at adolescence, the menopause, or from loss of intellectual capacities through brain damage, or those from alteration in the facilities of the external environment, have to be dealt with by a persistent integrative effort. Times of marked change commonly produce disruption, the reactions to 'crises' emphasized by Lindemann (1953) and Caplan (1964). Most people manage these upsets through the support of those with whom they share their experiences. Without such help they may be unable to 'pull themselves together' again in which case various disorders appear the characteristics of which are determined by the properties of the segregated systems. That even highly stable persons disintegrate if the environmental deprivation becomes severe has been vividly demonstrated in recent years by the sensory-deprivation experiments. The fluctuations of the integrative effort of the central ego in face of the conflicting pressures from within and without is also seen in the tendency of psychoneurotic behaviour to be managed over time. The underlying situation does not disappear, however, and symptoms are liable to recur whenever the balance is upset.

The typical functioning of the mature person required to maintain the stability and enrichment of the ego throughout the life cycle can be summarized as follows:

Relationships with people and activities with the physical environment give satisfying feelings of an 'investment in living'.

Close mature relationships in marriage and the family, in which the individuality of others is fully accepted, enrich the ego. In such relationships all parties influence each other in a mutually constructive way.

The bringing up of children is an important experience for the adult in that the residues of some of his own childhood conflicts, embodied in his segregated self-systems, can be greatly reduced.

Good object–relationship systems facilitate the use of experience by reducing distortions in the perception of reality induced by the sub-selves. Participation in the shared social tasks of work give a social acceptance which maintains an ongoing self-realization.

For progressive growth, particularly throughout later stages, the significance of his life needs a degree of satisfaction from a concern with the general human values expressed in such fields as what will happen to future generations, social progress, religion, the arts etc.

Spontaneous involvement in living and in the world under these inner conditions removes serious self-doubts. There can then be an acceptance of one's own assets and liabilities and a realistic confrontation of the conflicts inherent in living while preserving an overall enjoyment.

## REFERENCES

BALINT, M. (1952)  *Primary Love and Psychoanalytic Technique*. London: Hogarth.
BALINT, M. (1959)  *Thrills and Regressions*. London: Hogarth.

BALINT, M. (1968) *The Basic Fault: Therapeutic Aspects of Regression*. London: Tavistock.

BOWLBY, J. (1969) *Attachment and Loss*. London: Hogarth.

CAPLAN, G. (1964) *Principles of Preventive Psychiatry*. New York: Basic Books.

ENGEL, G. L. (1962) *Psychological Development in Health and Disease*. London: Saunders & Co.

ERIKSON, E. H. (1950) *Childhood and Society*. London: Penguin.

ERIKSON, E. H. (1959) *Identity and the Life Cycle*. New York: International Universities Press.

ERIKSON, E. H. (1964) *Insight and Responsibility*. London: Faber & Faber.

FAIRBAIRN, W. R. D. (1952) *Psychoanalytic Studies of the Personality*. London: Routledge.

FREUD, A. (1937) *The Ego and the Mechanisms of Defence*. London: Hogarth.

GUNTRIP, H. (1961) *Personality Structure and Human Interaction*. London: Hogarth.

GUNTRIP, H. (1964) *Healing the Sick Mind*. London: Unwin.

GUNTRIP, H. (1968) *Schizoid Phenomena Object-Relations and the Self*. London: Hogarth.

HARTMANN, H. (1964) *Essays on Ego Psychology*. New York: International Universities Press.

KLEIN, M. (1932) *The Psychoanalysis of Children*. London: Hogarth.

KLEIN, M. (1948) *Contributions to Psychoanalysis*. London: Hogarth.

KLEIN, M. (1957) *Envy and Gratitude*. London: Tavistock.

LINDEMANN, E. (1953) In *Interrelations Between the Social Environment and Psychiatric Disorders*. Milbank Memorial Fund, New York.

PARSONS, T. & BALES, R. F. (1955) *Family, Socialization and Interaction Process*. Glencoe, Illinois: Free Press.

PIAGET, J. (1937) *The Construction of Reality in the Child*. London: Routledge.

SPITZ, R. A. (1946) Anaclitic depression. *Psychoanalytic Study of the Child*, **2**, 313.

SPITZ, R. A. (1965) *The First Year of Life*. New York: International Universities Press.

WEISMAN, A. D. (1965) *The Ego and the Existential Core of Psychoanalysis*. Boston: Little, Brown & Co.

WINNICOTT, D. W. (1957) *The Child, The Family and the Outside World*. London: Penguin.

WINNICOTT, D. W. (1958) *Collected Papers*. London: Tavistock.

WINNICOTT, D. W. (1965) *The Maturational Processes and the Facilitating Environment*. London: Hogarth.

WINNICOTT, D. W. (1965a) *The Family and Individual Development*. Paperback, London: Tavistock.

# Chapter XI

# INTERVIEW METHODS

## H. J. Walton and S. K. Littmann

### INTRODUCTION

The interview is the basic technique in all medical work. The dyad concerned is the clinician and the patient, who engage in a verbal interaction. In addition, both participants communicate by non-verbal means, their facial expressions, gestures, body posture and eye contact all serving to modulate and colour the words exchanged.

In the practice of medicine generally, regardless of the patient's complaint, the clinician interrogates the patient and listens to his communications before proceeding to any physical examination. Indeed, the chance given to the patient to unburden himself of his concern, in many cases contributes greatly to the relief experienced by patients who consult for primarily physical ailments.

In the practice of psychiatry the potentially therapeutic role of an interview is not in question. The clinician at the same time elicits the information he requires for his diagnostic task and also initiates his treatment interaction with the patient. This is not to say that an interview is invariably helpful. It may on the contrary operate as a psycho-noxious influence.

Psychiatrists use interviews for three main purposes: as a diagnostic procedure, as a treatment method and as a research tool.

### THE DIAGNOSTIC INTERVIEW

The psychiatrist systematically pursues relevant information in predetermined biographical and behavioural sectors. This is not to imply that when face-to-face with the patient he follows a stereotyped course—the competent interviewer even at this initial stage leaves the patiently relatively free to scan his ideas and experiences. However, when interrogation and listening cease and the interview is ended, the psychiatrist will have:

*Taken a history* of the present illness, a family history, a personal history, and he will have data about the previous personality and previous illnesses.

He will have *examined the mental state*, i.e. he will have evaluated the patient's speech and behaviour for qualitative deviations from normality in all the following psychological sectors: general behaviour; mood;

talk; thought (delusions); perceptions (hallucinations); ideation (obsessions); orientation; memory; attention and concentration; information; intelligence; insight. Where circumstances prevent the clinician from appraising one or more of these sectors, he will remain aware of the need to return for closer inspection in a subsequent interview. In certain cases a series of interviews will be required before the clinician is in a position to move to the next stage.

*Diagnosis*: the first diagnostic requirement is *nosological*, i.e. to name (1) any illness considered present on the basis of a syndrome, a cluster of symptoms and signs, disclosed during the examination; (2) any deviation from normality in the personality itself (see Chapter XII, Vol. I).

The second diagnostic task is the *psychodynamic formulation*, a statement setting out the factors which explain why that particular patient became ill in that particular form at that point in time.

### THE THERAPEUTIC INTERVIEW

The clinician makes himself available as an active participant to improve the patient's well-being, the chief ingredient being a verbal exchange, which occurs in the context of a relationship. This comes about, in a mode which can be predicted and specified, when the patient meets certain requirements and the clinician on his part discharges responsibilities of a technical and subjective nature.

Interview methods is the field of discourse comprised of the various extensions and detailed considerations called for in the above statement. The field is not to be equated narrowly with psychotherapy, for the reason that a range of technical interventions also need to be included which collectively may be referred to as 'behaviour modifying techniques' (see Chapter XVIII, Vol. II). Nor is it to be equated with any theoretical or doctrinal account of the various schools of medical psychology, although it is of course highly likely that each prominent psychotherapeutic theorist will have suggested important technical procedures of which the clinical interviewer may need to be aware, some of which he will want to incorporate in his own interviewing approach, at least in certain circumstances with particular patients.

### INTERVIEWS IN CLINICAL RESEARCH

An account of interview methods will not be complete without attention to the use of interviews in clinical research. So that the same stimuli can be offered to each subject, the interview may be *structured* and all subjects asked an identical series of questions in unvarying form. Certain responses may be taken as an indication for extended questioning in that sector (*semi-structured interviewing*). Another method in use is the *focussed* interview (Merton and Kendall, 1946; Merton,

Kendall and Fiske, 1952): it has a fixed schedule of questions, but the interviewer is also allowed freedom to have the subject expand on any topic he may raise of particular relevance to the investigation.

An interview is regarded as structured or standardized when the questions have been decided on in advance, and are put with the same wording and in the same order to all the subjects in the sample which is being investigated. The interviewer is not given the freedom to re-word questions, nor to alter their sequence, nor to introduce new ones. In contrast, an unstructured interview varies with the individual subject (Maccoby and Maccoby, 1954).

AIMS IN INTERVIEWING

The interviewer needs to be clear about his purposes when talking to a patient, because the form of the interview will vary with his aim. Interviewing can be carried out with four ends in view:

1. To get objective facts from the subject which—as informant—he knows about but the interviewer does not (as in social surveys).

2. To get information about behaviour which the informant is not able to observe.

3. To assess personality and the mental state, as in the psychiatric interview.

4. To change a person's behaviour, as in psychotherapeutic interviewing.

## The Fact-Finding Interview:
### a Contribution of Kinsey

When the interview is used for research purposes as a fact-finding method, the interviewer has a defined aim, and the subject being interviewed complies in achieving this aim. The data being sought is obtained by means of the verbal interchange between an interviewer and his subject in a face-to-face encounter. In particular, the procedure permits the interviewer to obtain knowledge about behaviour he cannot observe. The first major empirical study of human sexual behaviour (Kinsey, Pomeroy and Martin, 1948) was based on interview data*.

*Sexual Behaviour in the Human Male* reports findings from 12,000 interviews carried out by Kinsey, Pomeroy and Martin (and three other investigators). Kinsey himself did 7,000 (58 per cent) of these interviews.

The aim was for the interviewer who saw the subject only once to get a sexual history. A small payment (one to two dollars) was made to very poor people for the few hours an interview took, and also to those professionally involved in sexual activities, and to those who spent a

* Subsequent investigators have also observed sexual behaviour directly, rather than relying on informants to describe it—see Masters and Johnson, 1966.

great deal of time on behalf of the investigation. Kinsey's method exemplifies a survey using the standardized interview. All subjects were asked a uniform range of pre-worded questions.

The steps taken with each subject were the following. First, the interviewer selected the informant and persuaded him to be included in the sample. Second, rapport was established, by making the subject realize that no moral judgement was being exercised—he could say anything without shocking the interviewer—and that the confidences of the record would be kept inviolate. Security was ensured by never writing down any words in the subject's presence. A code was used to record information, devised with the help of a cryptographer. Kinsey and his colleagues never published any case histories; when quoting examples in lectures, they were careful to make cases composite.

The *technical methods* used by the interviewers are clearly described, and an indication given of the sequence in which procedures were deployed.

1. Every interview took place in private without fear of interruption.

2. The subject was put at ease by general conversation.

3. The interviewer showed interest in the subject as a person, by looking him straight in the eye, and giving minimum attention to any notes being made.

4. A preordained sequence of topics was discussed, starting from subjects least emotionally charged and ending up with the most disturbing matters. The sequence was not the same for all subjects, because tension varied with social class. College men most readily dealt with a sequence beginning at questions regarding nocturnal emissions, masturbation, premarital petting, premarital intercourse, then moving to consider premarital intercourse with prostitutes, raising questions about animal contacts only near the end of the interview, and ending with homosexuality. Those who left school before the 10th grade, on the other hand, could discuss premarital intercourse early in the interview without corresponding embarrassment.

5. The interviewers assessed a subject's intellectual status—they did not interview if the I.Q. seemed below 50.

6. They practised 'systematic coverage', i.e. every subject was asked at least 300 questions. Those with a full range of sexual experiences were asked as many as 521 questions, all listed in the code sheet.

7. The interviewer always put 'the point of the question', but varied the words used for different individuals. For the less educated, the venacular was used. The question was then further clarified until the interviewee grasped it. If the subject was at a loss, the interviewer indicated the range of answers from which he might choose, in scrambled order: e.g. when dealing with frequency of intercourse, the alternatives were: once a week/3 or 4 times a week/once a month/

every day. They found it important not to be squeamish. No 'polite' words were used. Masturbation was spoken of as such, and not as 'touching yourself'.

8. The burden of denial was put on the subject. The interviewers assumed all subjects had engaged in every type of sexual behaviour. They did not ask, 'Do you do so and so?', but 'When did you begin doing so and so?'

9. They avoided multiple questions, placing only one idea before the subject at a time. 'Do you feel emotionally aroused by seeing nude males or females?' This question simultaneously puts two questions, enabling men to confine comment to their heterosexual arousal, and to evade saying whether they feel emotionally roused by seeing nude males.

10. Rapid-fire questioning was used both to save time, and not give the subject time to fabricate an answer.

11. Interlocking questions were carefully planned, e.g. in approaching homosexuality 12 questions were first asked before the direct one about homosexual activity, i.e. 'build-up' was used. The subjects were also softened up by slipping in a word from the venacular, e.g. prostitutes were asked: 'How long have you been in the life?'

12. To 'prove an answer' a question was deliberately asked a second time when an answer was provided which the interviewer did not believe.

13. The interviewer did not point out that a subject contradicted himself if he was inconsistent, accepting the last statement the subject made.

14. Cross-checks on accuracy were made by such statements as, 'Now give it to us straight', looking the subject squarely in the eye.

15. The interviewer 'forced the subject' when he believed the subject had come out of curiosity, dismissing him when impressed that he was untruthful.

Many clinical interviewers who have carried out surveys will recognize from this technical inventory some steps which they themselves took, perhaps not always as consciously or in as planned a fashion as the Kinsey team. Their requirements were to get factual information about overt sexual behaviour. They did so by enquiry from all subjects about a predetermined area dealing with a defined range of experiences. They exerted themselves to maintain security, and to preserve their reputation for integrity. Finally, the interviewers took steps to establish their *reliability*, i.e. the amount of agreement between different interviewers examining the same subject. Reliability indicates the extent to which interview data are public and objective. It is possible to train interviewers so that those similarly experienced have a high degree of reliability. Such control is necessary

J

to deal to an explicit extent with the known difficulty that people say different things to different interviewers.

Another requirement when examining the accuracy of interviews is to determine their *validity*, by comparing the interview data against an external criterion. For example, Freud believed his patients were telling him accurately about their sexual traumata during childhood, but on checking up he later discovered that the reports of seductions by fathers were fantasies, made up by patients who falsified their past (Jones, 1953).

## CLINICAL MEDICINE AND INTERVIEWING: THE CONTRIBUTION OF MICHAEL BALINT

Estimates put the proportion of patients asking help for emotional disturbances from their general practitioners or from hospital out-patient departments at 10 per cent. The senior levels of the medical hierarchy hardly ever see the patient alone. Consultants and Senior Registrars are usually accompanied by a junior doctor and a nurse or two. There are very few hospital wards where a doctor may talk to his patient, safe in the knowledge that their confidential conversation will not be overheard. The situation is a little better in the outpatient departments (Balint, 1961).

An attempt can be made to understand the patient's problems only if a special kind of relationship between the patient and the doctor is allowed to develop. This is called the psychotherapeutic relationship. In such a context sharing of responsibility is not feasible—the whole therapy must be carried out by one doctor. He must enter into a personal relationship with his patient, because it is this which creates and maintains the psychotherapeutic process. In psychotherapy the doctor's personality is his tool. A psychotherapist in training must learn how to use his own personality. If a person wants to learn the technique of psychotherapy he has to learn it in the psychotherapeutic situation; this learning calls for a change in the doctor's personality.

Psychotherapy is a two-person relationship involving considerable intensity of emotion. If a student is to learn how to conduct the psychotherapeutic relationship, all communications must be concentrated between him as therapist and his patient. Such a relationship allows no delegation of responsibility and no part-duties. There are three requirements:

1. The clinician should maintain a continuous therapeutic relationship with his patient, which presupposes that he has reached a stage at which the patient can be entrusted to him.

2. He should be supervised, and his supervisor should watch his development very closely, so as to intervene and help him whenever necessary.

3. He should be able to watch the supervising consultant and other consultants at work.

Balint's writings have illuminated the gap between the practice of general medicine and skill in psychotherapy. Medical training turns the doctor into an authority. He perceives it as his task to diagnose and then to treat the patient's disorder, a programme effective with many physical illnesses, but not necessarily so, however, with emotional disorders. Now the doctor needs to concede that hidden but crucial knowledge is locked up in the patient, who must remain the active and creative participant if resolution is to be achieved. Psychotherapeutic training thus calls on the doctor to unlearn his authoritative role for certain purposes, to undergo a small but necessary personality change. Balint has given particular emphasis to this somatic-psychic chasm in the practice of medicine by expounding his concepts of the doctor as a drug, the patient's offering, and the apostolic mission of the doctor.

CONCEPT OF THE DRUG 'DOCTOR'

The most frequently used 'drug' in general practice is the doctor himself. Yet there is a striking lack of information about the ways this particular drug is prescribed, when and how often it should be administered, when it is safe to stop, and what the side-effects of this 'drug' are.

The way this drug is presented, in other words, the way the doctor 'administers' himself to his patients, is a matter of individual choice, and is left to the doctor's often intuitive judgement.

THE PATIENT'S OFFERING

In a clinical interview, events occur at two levels. The most obvious is the overt content, the easily observable verbal interaction. Not so evident is the so-called hidden agenda, the covert negotiations proceeding between doctor and patient. The pair meet, as it were, at a negotiating table. The doctor, whether he is aware of it or not, possesses healing powers which bring patients to him, and which derive only in part from his special skills. Much of his professional charisma is attributed to him by those who come to him for help. Patients are sometimes in awe of their doctors, and often invest them with special powers. Some of their expectations are reasonable and some quite irrational.

The patient has a presenting complaint. Balint has referred to this as the 'offering'. By making an offering the patient enters into the healing circle of the doctor. Each doctor has his relatively individual ways of dealing with patients. He has expectations, for example, of how sick people ought to behave. What is more, each doctor has his way of dealing with offerings. Some are inclined to look upon symptoms according to the 'set' of their particular speciality. Thus, a neurosurgeon would be more likely to link headache with intracranial pathology whereas a psychiatrist is more used to thinking in terms of tension headaches. Another difference among doctors is that some want to achieve 'closure' at an early stage while others are quite prepared to tolerate ambiguity (Walton, 1968). Thirdly, doctors vary to the extent to which they are prepared to acknowledge the role of psychological and emotional factors in the causation of somatic complaints. From the doctor's point of view, he is quite prepared to help the patient (or to promise healing) provided the patient accepts the doctor's 'creed'.

This creed comprises the following factors: how to behave when ill; whether to pay attention to more intimate (i.e. emotional) factors; the need to arrive at clear-cut answers; the need to fit symptoms into conceptual systems according to specialty; the right (one could say 'divine right') to expect adherence and obedience from patients and many others; and the relative emphasis to be placed on either drug treatment or on a psychological treatment approach. Unless the patient is prepared to become a convert to his doctor's creed he is unlikely to reap the full benefits of the doctor's healing powers. Most patients learn their family doctor's peculiarities, i.e. they soon know what approach to use with a particular doctor, what offering to make, in order to get the healing activity directed to one or another body site or personal concern.

It is this quasi-religious interaction which has been designated the doctor's apostolic function (Balint, 1957).

### THE APOSTOLIC MISSION

By exercise of the apostolic function doctors train the population from childhood onwards what to expect and what not to expect when they go to the doctor. Apostolic function stems from doctor's urge to prove to the patient, to the world, and to himself that he is good, helpful, and considerate. This may lead, for example, to an excessively strong urge to help the patient at all costs ('furor therapeuticus').

Every doctor has a vague but firm idea of the way a patient should behave when he is ill. This idea is subject to wide individual variations among different doctors. The patient has to accept his doctor's 'faith and commandments' and be converted at least superficially, or else reject them and change to another doctor.

This conversion of the patient to the doctor's view of the illness, and to the unique atmosphere of the individual practice, depends on the doctor being regarded by the patient as kind and good. Further, apostolic function always implies a degree of infallibility. Infallibility can however be a defense which the doctor uses against self-examination. He takes up and sometimes maintains a position of infallibility in the clinical relationship as a means of masking his own problems in relation to patients. The doctor sometimes behaves as if he has 'received' knowledge, as if it is not necessary for the patient to take the initiative and convey the detailed personal information—without which proper diagnosis is in fact not possible. The doctor's assumption of superior wisdom may cause him to proceed in the absence of adequate knowledge and understanding of the case. The result can be shot-in-the-dark treatment. Balint's dictum is: no treatment without diagnosis.

If the dictum were followed, no therapy, e.g. reassurance, would be administered before it became known what was wrong with the patient. The need for such cautious delay the doctor accepts intellectually, but on account of his apostolic function he has difficulty in carrying it out. To be witness to anxiety or other anguish, without doing anything about it, is viewed as cruelty, inhumanity or unhelpfulness. The doctor resorts to premature comforting in order to relieve his own professional conscience.

The patient may enter into conspiracy. One man (Balint, 1955; case 26) attended each week, took his prescription remarking that it would do him no good, but departed from his doctor greatly cheered. He felt the doctor was on his side. They were agreed that his illness would not be helped by anything the doctor did. The arrangement continued 16 years.

Doctors are trained at teaching hospitals in an hierarchical system, with the result that when he sets up on his own the doctor feels a kind of exile and, when he refers a patient to a specialist, still keeps the teacher-pupil relationship. In hospitals there is a dilution of responsibility. Enacting God-like behaviour is the senior consultant at the top, with the junior doctors and other ancillary staff at the base.

Balint, in examining the wide differences among doctors in their ability and willingness to deal with psychological problems of patients, directs attention to difficulties that may impede the clinician. When a doctor examines the heart sounds he knows that he is not going to do much harm. He does not feel on such safe ground when he is called upon to enquire into the intimate details of the relationship of husband with wife, or any other 'psychological' problem. There are many reasons for his diffidence. He may lack the skills: when examining a person psychologically, a personal relationship has to be established different in nature from that necessary for performing a physical examination. Another reason for distancing oneself from a patient is conventional 'respect' for a person's intimate life.

Only by learning technical methods for carrying out psychological enquiries, and by demonstration that such intervention is necessary and effective, can clinicians add psychotherapeutic skills to their professional abilities, and become willing to deal with emotional issues. A preliminary step is to help clinicians become aware of their stock responses to patients, and to identify their patterns of administering themselves to patients. Study of the apostolic function is one direct way in which a doctor can set out to clarify his effect on patients, and to replace automatic idiosyncrasies by flexible responsiveness.

INSIGHT PSYCHOTHERAPY:
THE CONTRIBUTION OF FINESINGER

Psychotherapy has to be a planned, consistent, repeatable and teachable procedure, if it is to obtain the status of a clinical method. The subjectivity and perceptual distortions of the clinical interviewer need to be brought under control before psychotherapy can become a rational treatment procedure with specifiable goals. A serious weakness in much contemporary practice and reporting is that narrative accounts of psychotherapists are assumed to reflect accurately what transpired in treatment sessions. This is manifestly not the case: clinicians are variously responsive to different segments of a therapeutic session, and differ in the emphasis they place on patients' statements. A psychotherapist who gives a narrative account of a treatment session inevitably provides a highly subjective and personal report, which cannot be regarded as a reliable or valid description of the clinician-patient interaction (Walton and McPherson, 1964). Such variable responsiveness and selective inattention may not seriously impede therapeutic progress, but negate the acceptability of narrative reports either for purposes of training a therapist, or for scientific study of processes occurring in psychotherapeutic interviews.

The essence of the technical procedure advocated by Finesinger (1948) is that the interviewer is required to make verbatim notes during the course of each session, setting down everything the patient says and also every comment he himself makes. This requirement is often strenuously repudiated by clinicians learning psychotherapy. They protest that they cannot then attend to the patient with proper concentration, that an artificial atmosphere is generated, and that they themselves become stilted in their reactions. These objections can of course be countered by arguments that in time the clinician's writing becomes an integral part of his technique, that psychotherapy is in fact a highly contrived procedure, and that major damage results from excessive activity on the part of the clinician. In time the clinician will perceive that certain elements in his behaviour while successful socially are contraindicated in interviewing. Indeed, a second major emphasis in Finesinger's approach is the drastic curb that is placed on the clinician, who is required to consider in advance the degree of activity he may appropriately show at any point in a treatment session. His restraint promotes activity on the part of the patient.

When the psychotherapist in training reports his sessions to his supervisor he does so by reading his verbatim records. He is not asked to convey impressions or inferences, nor to summarize or paraphrase his material. What is wanted is an exact account of the verbal events in the interviewing session. The supervisory discussion thus centres on the raw data in the record. From this material the problems are identified that call for resolution in subsequent sessions. By reviewing the verbatim records to extract the patient's chief problems the interviewer progressively develops his skills in observation; the supervisory sessions also serve as a method for sensitivity training. As the interviewer reports his own comments, he can study the influence on the patient of his own attitudes and social values.

The frame of reference adopted is a scientific one. An objective approach is adopted to the process whereby facts are obtained and validated. Intensive data collection occurs over the course of a sequence of interviews.

A usual duration of insight therapy is 20 to 40 interviews. Finesinger considers it only rarely necessary to expose a patient's deeply repressed memories or fantasies. He does not advocate emphasis being placed by the interviewer on any dream material the patient may relate, nor on the transference.

The questions raised with the interviewer in the supervisory sessions are focussed on technical matters, i.e. what the clinician must do under varying conditions. These procedures are laid down precisely, and are based on the principle that the clinician has to maintain the patient's communication through use of the minimal intervention which will achieve this aim. Only when this relative inactivity fails does the clinician promote the flow of material by proceeding to the more pointed interventions discussed below.

There are four general principles:

## I DEVELOPMENT OF AN EFFECTIVE DOCTOR–PATIENT RELATIONSHIP

The treatment relationship provides the patient with support and adds tension to the interaction. Both are necessary for treatment to progress. The clinician adjusts the emphasis on either support or tension at different phases in treatment, depending on the emotional tone which is considered most appropriate. Thus, while the transference of the patient to the clinician is not a matter for comment in the sessions, its technical importance in the course of treatment is not overlooked. The treatment relationship and the patient's communications are the main ingredients of therapy.

## II GOAL-DIRECTED PLANNING AND MANAGEMENT

The *ultimate* goals of treatment are threefold: (1) To remove or alleviate symptoms; (2) to achieve a better personal and social adjustment by the patient; (3) to have the patient make improved use of his abilities.

However, treatment proceeds by defining and promoting *intermediate* goals, which are decided upon by the clinician in advance of the corresponding interview, e.g. he may undertake to explore the relationship the patient had with his mother, and focus the interview accordingly (see below).

1. *Production of material*: the patient is encouraged to provide a detailed description of his current symptoms and personal problems; his recurring patterns of behaviour are examined; the effect which his behaviour patterns and their repetitiveness have on his current adjustment are examined. The historical development of these behaviour patterns is traced, and the function they serve for him is explored.

2. A leading intermediate goal is *the adjustment of the doctor-patient relationship*, as required at various stages of treatment.

## III FOCUSSING ON TOPICS RELEVANT TO GOALS

The clinician repeatedly focusses the patient's efforts on material relevant to the goals pre-set for that particular interview; he does so by altering the degree of interest he shows as the patient deals with successive topics. When he wants the patient to drop a topic he gives signs of diminished attention, and shows interest—perhaps by leaning forward slightly—when material relevant to the session's goals is produced.

## IV MINIMAL ACTIVITY

This principle calls on the therapist to keep his activity as low as is consistent with the session's goals and the treatment plan. There are clear reasons for minimal activity. Random interference by the clinician tends to bring about a social type of relationship rather than a therapeutic one. The less the clinician contributes the more the patient is allowed to project his own behaviour patterns into the relationship. In addition, when the onus for speaking is on the patient, he is enabled to talk more freely about experiences meaningful to him. If the clinician fails to observe the principle the patient develops persistent dependence and management difficulties arise.

## PROCEDURES IN INTERVIEWING

The hierarchy of interventions available to the clinician make it possible for him to select the least active gesture or statement which will set the patient talking again when a halt occurs.

1. *Low activity* aims to help the patient gently at points of hesitation or embarrassment:

(*a*) The clinician can articulate syllables with a rising vocal inflection: e.g. 'so . . .', 'well . . .', 'hmm . . .'

(*b*) He can repeat the patient's last word: e.g. 'upset?', 'your heart?'

(*c*) If these assistances fail, he can elaborate the patient's last phrase or statement: e.g. 'you mentioned pain . . .?'

(*d*) The next intervention available is the use of a mild command: e.g. 'Please tell me more about this.'

(*e*) Finally, the interviewer can put general questions aimed at the topic he wants pursued: e.g. 'What do you mean by nervous?'

2. *Moderate activity* is used when the clinician intends to focus the patient's attention on a topic about which he has difficulty in speaking:

(*a*) Repeat statements made by patient which need elaboration.

(*b*) Direct questions to the patient's personal associations: e.g. 'Perhaps you could tell me what is going on in your mind?'

(*c*) Put questions relating to the difficulty which has arisen in communication with the therapist: e.g. 'Could you tell me why it is hard to talk about this?'

(*d*) Mild encouragement to talk about difficulties in communication: e.g. 'I know it is not easy to talk about this.'

(*e*) More active encouragement can next be used: e.g. 'I really wish you could talk about this.'

3. *Marked activity* is used, sparingly and with caution, when the above procedures are likely to be ineffective, or have been unsuccessfully tried:

(*a*) Prompting by provision of a suggested reason for the patient's reticence, e.g. 'I wonder if the reason you are not talking is because you feel I can't help you.'

(*b*) Provocative and dramatic interpretations can be attempted which are based on the physician's guess or hunch. The psychoanalyst T. Reik (1948) describes a woman patient who was evasive in an interview for which she arrived late, having cancelled preceding ones. She first in an abstracted way pointed out to the therapist that a book on his shelves was upside down; then she mentioned a visit to a dentist for an extraction. Reik surmised what she was concealing, and asked her why she withheld that she had had an abortion.

(*c*) An emotional response can be provoked in the patient by a number of procedures. The clinician can use rapid probing; he can focus on transference material, e.g. 'you are angry with me, and your silence is your way of showing displeasure'; he can force material by insistence; he can show negative feeling to the patient, e.g. impatience.

(d) The final steps the clinician can take comprise active participation. These steps include: active reassurance; sharing experience with the patient; gratifying the patient's demands; and allowing a shift towards a social relationship.

The techniques and the interpretation schema provided by Finesinger constitute a well-tried method for training clinicians in psychotherapy, and a pioneering attempt to monitor the treatment interaction. Above all, this approach emphasizes that psychotherapy requires to be planned, the overall outcome and also the step-by-step goals for the patient clearly specified in advance.

## PSYCHOANALYTICALLY-ORIENTED PSYCHOTHERAPY: THE CONTRIBUTION OF COLBY

Many clinicians who find the Finesinger approach unacceptable will respond more positively to the procedure advocated by Colby (1951), in his highly readable and justly celebrated introduction to psychotherapy. The interview method he advocates is not as systematized as Finesinger's.

Colby regards psychotherapy as not only a science but as an art also. The progress and outcome of psychotherapy depend both on the patient and on qualities of the clinician. These can be specified in general terms. The clinician must be knowledgeable about his culture and in touch with it. He must have mastered a theory of psychotherapy, having at his command a logical system in terms of which to organize his clinical observations. He should be experienced in human affairs. He should be psychologically-perceptive, 'intuitive'. Finally, he has to be self-aware, understanding his own wishes, desires and psychological defences. The clinician is both human and expert. His qualities as a human may have led him into psychiatry and motivated him to satisfy personal drives by intense treatment associations with his patients. As an expert, his task is to help the patient verbalize 'unconscious' thoughts and feelings. He is not called on to offer himself as a model, to offer love, etc.

Colby's view about the way the clinician should behave towards the patient conflicts with Finesinger's in important respects. He advocates that the psychotherapist should avoid acting a part, behaving as consistently as possible with his own personality. Nevertheless, he is to be gentle, kind, friendly, constant and non-judgemental. The patient should know as little about his personal life as possible: encumbering the patient with the clinician's private life, as would occur were the latter to accept phone calls from friends or relatives during sessions, is not desirable. Good physical health is also necessary, and to conduct interviews when ill is unwise. The clinician need not have been psychoanalyzed to carry out this form of psychotherapy effectively, but ongoing self-analysis is always a useful practice, and an analytical attitude towards oneself a necessity.

## THE PATIENT

The patient seeking psychotherapy has hopes and fears which need to be considered, some of them not necessarily clear to the patient. (Colby makes extensive use of the concept of an 'unconscious' mind.) They may dread that treatment will make them dependent on the clinician, that their neurosis will become more crippling, or that they will be exposed as insane or perverse.

Equally unrealistic can be the hopes with which some patients enter psychotherapy. They may hope for spontaneous change, or for some magical transformation to be effected by the clinician. Some patients enter treatment with the prime intention to engage in duels, or to have masochistic punishment meted out to them. Others seek friendship or even marriage with the clinician.

As a pre-requisite for uncovering or explorative therapy Colby requires good ego function; if psychotherapy is undertaken in default of ego strengths it should be of supportive or covering form, i.e. defense-adding, especially if the patient suffers from 'latent' or 'ambulatory' schizophrenia (the book is written within a U.S. context). Special emphasis is thus given to the need for assessing prospective patients carefully before engaging them in psychotherapy. Appraisal of three separate areas is required:

1. *The patient's organism,* which subsumes his capabilities and his physical state of health;

2. *His ego,* his capacity for and mode of relating to his environment;

3. *His environment,* which includes his relatives (and the extent to which they are an asset or a liability), his work, and his social situation.

## TECHNICAL PROCEDURES

The clinician's task is seen as helping the patient to become aware of his underlying conflict. Psychotherapy is realistically regarded as repair work, not a means of effecting a psychological rebirth or a complete re-organization of the patient's personality. The clinician helps the patient become aware of his underlying conflict. He does so by enabling the patient to verbalize his thoughts and feelings. These the clinician then interprets, disclosing to the patient what it is that he is refusing to acknowlege about himself. Neurotic symptoms are viewed as conflicts between forbidden wishes and the defenses against such wishes.

They are cured or relived by modifying the defense in the wish-defense conflict. In consequence the wish is allowed greater gratification.

A clinical example cited (p. 87) is the case of a homosexual man with an anxiety neurosis. His great fear is of being ill-treated by brutal, stronger men. This is interpreted as a defense, in the form of projection onto sturdy men of hostile impulses. What the patient protects himself from perceiving by this defense is a wish to be treated like a woman by powerful men.

In Colby's view, inner conflict is signalled by two main areas of behaviour during the session:

1. resistances (i.e. hesitations, pauses)
2. transference reactions (e.g. anger at the clinician, demands for affection or for active assistance, etc.)

The clinician intervenes during sessions to point out resistances, to enquire about unusual behaviour (e.g. late or early arrival for the interview), to offer interpretations which clarify the patient's resistances and transference reactions, and at all times he offers the patient his full and undivided attention.

In psychoanalytically-oriented psychotherapy, as distinct from psycho-analysis, sessions lasting 45 to 50 minutes once to three times weekly are used. The patient may sit upright, especially if covering therapy is being used, but Colby advocates use of a couch if possible. His reason is Freud's: 'It is unbearable to be stared at for eight hours a day.'

Another contradiction to Finesinger thus emerges; Colby evidently does not want the patient scrutinizing him for changes in his level of interest or for alterations in his posture. Neither does he recommend note-taking during the session itself.

The verbal exchange desired is conversation and association to topics raised by the patient, not free association as in psychoanalysis. Exploration of childhood events and dream analysis are also not particularly sought after. The transference is not developed to intense degree, the clinician operating at a more supportive level than in psychoanalytic treatment.

Clearly, as its name signifies, this interviewing method derives directly from psycho-analysis, and sets out to make its benefits available to the many sufferers for whom intensive analysis is not a feasible (if indeed a desired) treatment approach. Psychoanalysts for various reasons frequently themselves advocate and apply treatment along the lines Colby describes.

## THE CONTRIBUTION OF FREUD: PSYCHOANALYSIS

No psychiatrist in his use of interviews for treating patients will fail to draw upon the technical innovations of Freud, whether or not he does so knowingly. Moreover, all psychotherapists are influenced by the theoretical system devised by Freud and added to by subsequent psychoanalytical theorists. They use, for example, the terms for designating three sectors of the mental 'apparatus':

1. The *Id*, biologically grounded, represents the unorganized subjective content of the 'unconscious', mainly repressed sexual and aggressive urges.

2. The *Ego* is conscious, and subserves the person's ongoing exploration of sensory stimuli, attention, relations with other people and memories.

3. The *Superego* is the aspect of self which has to do with conscience functions, and is learned from the parents.

The three principles which control behaviour are those relating to:

1. *Pleasure*: tension is reduced and distressing ideas or experiences are repressed.

2. *Reality*: immediate satisfactions are postponed, precedence being given to organized behaviour which meets present and future goals.

3. *Repetition*: many actions are stereotyped reiterations of early behaviour.

The first two principles are often in conflict, as when a person debates within himself whether to invest in a necessary task at a time when relaxation is also feasible, and the third is an explanation of the fact that much neurotic behaviour is monotonously repetitive.

A psychoanalyst, who need not be a psychiatrist, has had a personal (training) psychoanalysis, is certified as qualified by a recognized psychoanalytical institute, and subscribes to a body of psychoanalytic theory of one of the standard schools (e.g. Freudian, Kleinian, Jungian, etc.).

The aims of psychoanalysis are to help the patient discover the nature of his repressed conflicts and the responses related to them (Ford and Urban, 1964). A basic assumption is that the conflict and the defenses secondary to it are in the 'unconscious' and inaccessible to the patient (e.g. as the result of repression). They are therefore not readily or directly available to scrutiny. Psychoanalytic technique is basically a method for altering conditions in such a way that in the interview the patient is enabled to appraise himself and experience himself without constant need to make excessive use of defense mechanisms (repression, denial, projection, sublimation, etc.).

Analyst and patient meet regularly, traditionally for one hour on five days per week. Interviews take place with the patient reclining on a couch, the analyst all but out of sight, seated at the patient's head. An analysis lasts several years.

The patient is instructed to express verbally his thoughts and feelings in a completely unrestricted, uncensored and random manner. He is told that no thought is to be regarded as too private or trivial for utterance. This method, whereby a person allows himself to communicate his inner life to another as it pursues a relatively free course, is known as free association. It is not any easy procedure for the patient and requires discipline.

The analyst maintains a serious and neutral attitude to his patient. He listens with undivided attention; he does not select from the material verbalized nor is he entitled to discard from it. He does not criticize and he does not openly reciprocate any of the patient's feelings. The behaviour of the analyst consists in the main of: (1) Identifying and uncovering resistances; (2) Offering interpretations; (3) Focussing (when appropriate) on the patient/doctor relationship (transference).

Resistance is an avoidance response of the patient which operates whenever anxiety reaches too threatening a level. It often manifests as a difficulty or block in continuing free association. Treatment cannot satisfactorily progress unless each resistance is dealt with as it occurs. The analyst's task is to identify resistance when it comes about. For example, if a patient's free flowing associations suddenly cease, and the patient reports that his thoughts have dried up, the analyst surmises that a significant memory has activated marked anxiety, and is dealt with by an avoidance response, i.e. silence. Resistance can also manifest as sudden changes in topic, joking, yawning, etc.

Interpretations are comments interjected by the interviewer about aspects of the patient's experience which are under discussion. Thus, a patient who has been recounting his numerous angry interactions with teachers and with employers at a succession of offices might be told by his analyst that his real conflict seemed to be with those in authority, indicating that he had been jealous of his father; alternatively, the analyst might suggest that the patient was warning the analyst (as an authority figure) to be careful with the patient. Interpretations constitute hypotheses which the analyst derives from the patient's reported behaviour. They often are inferences or even intuitions, and require to be tested against later material, and usually repeatedly introduced before the patient can make use of them in a meaningful manner. An interpretation's value can be gauged by the emotional response provoked by it, by the insight resulting, or by the further new material it evokes.

Much time is devoted to dreams and their analysis. Freudian dream interpretation relies on the patient's associations to elements in the dream and their symbolic meanings.

The origins of conflicts are ultimately located in the individual's early years, particularly in his association with his parents and others close to him. Behaviour patterns or attitudes originally linked to significant family figures as analysis progresses, become recreated and 'transferred' to the analyst, who is thus the recipient of considerable emotion. Great technical emphasis is placed on the exploration of the resulting transference relationship.

Countertransference is the term used by psychoanalysts to designate the feelings and attitude of the analyst for his patient. The analyst is required at all times to take countertransference into consideration but, as in psychoanalysis generally, he keeps his personal thoughts and feelings to himself.

Psychoanalysis is not widely available, for evident reasons. It is expensive, not simply because payment for service is an integral part of the method, but also because analysis is a lengthy procedure. Patients must therefore be independent (in the sense of being self-supporting, with the exception of children), and they must be prepared to invest a portion of their financial means in the treatment procedure.

The majority of patients in psychoanalysis are not seriously ill psychiatrically. Adequate ego function is required. Psychotic patients are usually not treated by this method. It relies heavily on the verbal ability of the patient, so adequate intelligence is required. An analyst would not treat relatives or close friends.

From this outline will emerge many technical features of considerable relevance to all clinicians practising psychotherapy. They will require, therefore, to acquaint themselves with this complex approach to intensive clinical interviewing, a difficult task because often the very detailed case material elicited from patients is transformed in the technical literature into the special terminology of the author's particular psycho-analytic school.

## THE CONTRIBUTION OF SULLIVAN: INTERPERSONAL PSYCHIATRY

The particular contribution of Sullivan (1953) is the emphasis he placed on the patient's behaviour to other people, i.e. on patterns of interpersonal relationships. He dismissed the view advanced in psychoanalytic theory that internal events determine behaviour. He thus theorizes little about subjective impulses or wishes. Instead, regarding behaviour as situationally produced, he attends to communication. He regarded thought as a person's communication with himself, and speech as communication with others.

Of considerable importance, in addition to his focus on behaviour in interpersonal situations, is his emphasis on observable phenomena. Inferences by the therapist, assumptions about inner states of covert type in the patient, receive scant respect. The Sullivanian interviewer thus sets out to get a clear view of the patient's social transactions, and particularly of interferences in the patient's communications with others or in his efforts to relate to them. Anxiety is the reason for such interferences.

It follows that the circumstances for any observed behaviour have always to be stipulated by the interviewer. 'She becomes embarrassed and belittles herself whenever the interviewer appears likely to approve of her actions.' 'He becomes angry when his statements are questioned.'

Recurrent patterns of behaviour typical of the patient in his relations with other people are termed 'dynamisms', e.g. a lust dynamism or a fear dynamism may be particularly prominent. Regard is also given to the avoidance measures, 'security operations', by which the patient seeks to protect his self-esteem; their drawback is that they are perseveratively employed, and prevent the person entering new learning situations.

In his book *The Psychiatric Interview* (1954) Sullivan defines the procedure: 'A primarily vocal communication in a two-group, voluntarily integrated, on a progressively unfolding expert–client basis for the purpose of elucidating characteristic patterns of living of the subject, person, patient or client, which patterns he experiences as particularly troublesome or especially valuable, and in the revealing of which he expects to derive benefit.'

The psychiatrist derives his income and status from competence in his particular field of service to others. He should avoid using the patient in any way to support his prestige. He should not collect examples of odd behaviour, nor set himself up as a connoisseur of strange people; excessive curiosity about his patients is also to be avoided. His attitude to the patient should be polite seriousness.

The patient's initial attitude to the interviewer can set the direction of the preliminary enquiries. He expects the psychiatrist to be in relation to him as an expert. The patient's symptoms and signs may only become intelligible when his personality is understood. Difficulties in his current personal relationships will be found to derive from his past experiences.

An essential goal of the interview is that the patient leaves with some increased clarity about himself and his mode of relating to other people. If the patient realizes the interview is useful, he may be willing to divulge information which he fears may be detrimental to him, e.g. mentioning that he has embezzled money. The psychiatrist is not detached and neutral, but is personally involved and therefore a 'participant observer'. He is constantly aware of the cultural handicaps under which the patient labours, a series of popular misbeliefs. People are taught that they 'ought not' to need help, and should be independent. They are taught that they should 'know themselves'. They are expected to have 'good natural instincts' and be governed by 'logic'.

People feel ashamed if they have not risen above the limitations of their past misfortunes, mistakes and handicaps.

The psychiatrist is constantly aware of the transference situation, which implies that the patient is misperceiving some events in the interview. He should also remain aware of his own personal handicaps.

The interview may be of various types—such as diagnostic, therapeutic, or with the aim to advise some organization about the interviewee—but regardless of the type, it is fundamental that the interviewer should convey to the patient a sense of greater capacity, of adequacy to go on living, and of doing better in consequence of the interview.

As in Finesinger's approach, the interviewer consciously employs transitions in the session to change topics. A smooth transition minimizes anxiety, e.g. 'Well, now that brings us up to the topic of so-and-so'. An accented transition allows a pause in which to introduce a new topic, e.g. 'Well, the world is about to undergo some mild change.' An abrupt transition, where a topic is introduced at an awkward point in the interview, is not recommended unless one is trying to avoid dangerous anxiety or trying to provoke some anxiety because the interview is not proceeding adequately. Unlike Finesinger, Sullivan does not advise more than a few notes; he recorded changes of tone and body movements as well, and on occasion used a tape-recorder.

The interviewer seeks to promote integration, mutual involvement between the patient and himself. They become integrated by 'coincident reciprocal motivation'. He notes particularly any occasion when material which might reasonably be expected does not come forth.

The interview is divided into four *stages*:

THE FORMAL INCEPTION

The interviewer should familiarize himself with any facts he can get in advance about the patient. Not to do so conveys that the interviewer is not interested in the patient. He should invite the patient to come into the interviewing room and point out where the patient should sit, never leaving him in a state of uncertainty as he enters. He should tell the patient what he knows about him. (Very disturbing implications may be excluded.) This gives the patient a chance of correcting any initial misunderstandings. The end of the first stage comes when the patient has made a statement which he feels gives the psychiatrist some idea of his problem and himself. In general this statement should come from within the interview and not from outside information.

THE RECONNAISSANCE

This may last from twenty minutes to fifteen hours. It is essentially a rough social sketch of the patient and would include the family history, the personal history, previous illnesses, and previous personality. At the end of the reconnaissance, the psychiatrist summarizes aloud what he knows and he points out to the patient what he considers to be the problems. He then asks the patient to amend his summary. This may take up to ten minutes in a one-and-a-half hour interview. The patient is thus enabled to see his past history in a meaningful fashion, and to gain hope; he is also motivated to reveal more about himself.

## THE DETAILED ENQUIRY

This is an attempt to find the real problem and consists of improving on earlier approximations or revising the total impression of the patient. Because anxiety is intolerable to the patient, who is constantly attempting to diminish it, he will use every possible manoeuvre to impress the psychiatrist. 'He seeks to know what the psychiatrist thinks of what is being disclosed.' Anger is one of the commonest responses for dealing with anxiety, but there are many verbal techniques for avoiding or minimizing anxiety. 'This vast system of operations, precautions and alertness could perfectly properly be called the *self system*—that part of the personality which is born entirely out of the influences of others upon one's feeling of well-being.' Any disapproval or imagined disapproval by the psychiatrist brings about security operations to protect the self system from an increase in anxiety or a fall in euphoria. This is what leads the patient often to 'walk around the obvious' in an attempt to put his best foot forward and maintain his self esteem. The degree of anxiety a patient can tolerate will depend upon how much benefit he thinks he will get from the interview.

The psychiatrist should note when the patient changes his behaviour in the interview, for that implies that an attitude has altered. When communication improves it may be because the patient has perceived the psychiatrist as an understanding person, as motivated to do a competent job, or as an expert in interpersonal relations. Deteriorating communication may mean either that the psychiatrist was wrong in appraising it as good in the first place, or that the psychiatrist has unwillingly reacted to the patient's expressed attitudes by some restrictive tone, gesture or words.

From the detailed enquiry, the psychiatrist should know the following points about the 'personified self' of the patient:

1. What does the patient esteem and what does he disparage about himself?

2. To what experiences is the patient's self-esteem particularly, perhaps unreasonably, vulnerable?

3. What are the characteristic security operations which appear after the patient has been made anxious?

4. How great are the patient's reserves of security? Are there secret sources of shame or enduring regret?

TERMINATION OF THE INTERVIEW

In this stage the goal is to consolidate the progress made, using four technical steps:

The summarizing statement consists of all the relevant data presented in such a way as to show the patient possible future action to his own benefit. Even in poor prognoses, one should try 'never to close all the doors to a person.'

The second step is to provide a prescription for action to be taken by the patient in the future.

The final assessment consists of a hopeful picture within the limits of reality given to the patient as an idea of the future if the patient adopts the prescribed action.

Lastly, the formal leave taking. This should be a clean-cut, respectful finish that does not confuse that which has been done, avoiding at all costs a slow disentanglement.

## THE CONTRIBUTION OF CARL ROGERS:
### CLIENT-CENTRED PSYCHOTHERAPY

In this form of non-directive therapy the interviews are client-centred inasmuch as all material is introduced by the patient. They are non-directive in that the therapist does not engage in the customary psychotherapeutic procedures of probing, interpreting or analyzing.

Rogers has proposed a Self-theory (Rogers, 1959) in which *self* is defined as a person's own concept of himself. This self image is constructed gradually through one's interaction with the environment and in particular with the expressed values of other people. The way one responds to other people is dependent upon this self-concept. Any new experience can be reacted to in three different ways: (1) it can become incorporated into one's self-concept; (2) it can be ignored; or (3) it can be responded to by distortion. The latter two reactions are liable to occur in the presence of new experiences which are not consistent with one's self-concept, or which are actually seen as threats to it.

People with very rigid self-concepts may thus encounter great difficulties in adapting to novel situations. Client-centred psychotherapy is a procedure which, according to Rogers, creates an enabling situation in which the person feels less (internal) pressure to distort or deny experiences that do not readily fit in with an aspect of his self-concept, which is designated 'the ideal self'.

The aims of a Rogerian psychotherapist are thus:

1. To provide the patient with an accepting, uncontrolled environment in which he has no need to distort his perceptions.

2. To be non-directive so that the patient is able to behave in any way that he wants to, i.e. to act in accordance with his real self.

The goal of treatment is to help the patient perceive his real feelings and attitudes more accurately and to make it possible for him to modify his concept of his ideal self. The latter goal is akin to reduction in strength of the superego.

Underlying Rogers' technique is the belief that patients are capable of finding their own solutions. Rogers believes that change will occur without any specific intervention of the therapist. Therefore the main activity of the clinician is to *reflect and clarify feelings associated with what the patient is saying*. But above everything else Rogers looks to the clinician for the creation of the type of interview climate in which the patient does not feel threatened. This climate depends for its generation not on the technical skill or training of the therapist but on present certain attitudes in the therapist which he communicates to, and which are perceived by the patient. Rogers emphasizes the following three essential attitudes of the therapist:

## Congruence or genuineness

This means that the therapist is his actual self during his encounter with his patent, without any social facade. Not that he discloses his total self all the time, nor that he overburdens the patient with an overt expression of feeling, but Rogers wants the therapist to experience any *persistent feelings* that exist in the relationship and to let these be known to the patient.

## Unconditional positive regard

The therapist at all times communicates to his patient a deep and genuine caring which is uncontaminated by evaluations of the patient's thoughts or feelings. Rogers is, however, prepared to be more conditional when dealing with very immature or regressed patients.

## Accurate empathic understanding

Rogers wants the therapist to be completely at home in the patient's universe.

While the therapist communicates the above attitudes to his patient he refrains from doing many things that other types of therapist customarily do. He thus avoids:

1. giving information and advice
2. using reassurance and persuasion
3. asking direct questions
4. offering interpretations
5. giving criticisms.

As already mentioned constructive change during Rogerian psycho-therapy is judged to be largely independent of the following attributes of the therapist:

1. professional qualifications
2. theoretical knowledge
3. orientation
4. interview techniques
5. skill in making interpretations.

## EXISTENTIAL PSYCHOTHERAPY

This form of psychotherapy makes use of certain concepts of existen-tial philosophy but the actual interview procedure is marked by the absence of any standard technique.

The human condition is seen the state of *being* (or *becoming*) with in addition an awareness of the threat of *non-being* (or *dying*) (May, 1959). To take note of the fact that I am alive now also entails that I shall cease to be alive in the future. The individual in the modern world copes with such a threat by essentially denying its existence. This denial, according to existential therapists, can only be achieved by the individual turning away from the world of inner experience.

The aim of existential psychotherapy, rather like Rogerian therapy, is to provide the patient with a profound affective experience. How this is achieved matters little. Indeed, existential therapists believe that any technical procedure can be used. The clinician should not behave as a technician but a human being. He should not be clever but under-standing. He is (in essence) no longer a therapist or expert in the customary sense but more like a close friend. He is not entitled to any preconceived ideas about the patient. Indeed, in order to fully under-stand the patient the therapist is expected to be greatly empathic and the desired degree of empathy can only be achieved by the therapist 'putting the world into brackets'. In other words, the encounter between therapist and patient is above all a highly personal one in which the patient discovers denied aspects of himself. Fromm-Reichmann has referred to the patient needing an experience, not an explanation.

In an existential interview the techniques employed therefore vary, not only from patient to patient but also from one phase to another. According to 'where the patient is' the therapist may use any tech-nical procedure deemed appropriate, such as interpretation, analysis of resistence, reassurance, challenge, etc. The approach is exceedingly flexible and versatile. Transference is seen as a real event in a real relationship and not as a (dehumanizing) technical happening.

## DETERMINANTS OF OUTCOME

A review of interview methods would not be complete without a brief mention of some of the important variables which determine the outcome of psychotherapy.

1. *Therapist variables* (Betz, 1963; Whitehorn and Betz, 1961) include personality attributes, the capacity for accurate empathy, an ability to foster hope in patients and the competent adherence to *some* kind of theoretical framework. The ability to tolerate ambiguities and a readiness to carry out self-scrutiny have also been emphasized as necessary qualities in psychiatrists who undertake psychotherapy.

2. *Patient variables* include the degree of suffering experienced and the expectations of relief to be gained (Frank, 1961, 1968). The degree of motivation has been found of importance, and also the patient's attitudes towards the clinician.

3. *Therapy variables* include the setting, the actual number of the interviews and the technical approach used.

4. *Situational variables*: A patient may get better or worse in psychotherapy for reasons other than events in the interview. A disastrous marriage relationship, the death of a parent, an occupational setback, etc. can cause the patient to deteriorate. Such events outside the treatment have therefore always to be considered when evaluating the effectiveness of an interview method.

## REFERENCES

BALINT, M. (1955)  The doctor, his patient, and the illness. *Lancet*, **i**, 683–688.

BALINT, M. (1957)  *The Doctor, His Patient and the Illness*. London: Pitman Med. Publ. Co.

BALINT, M. (1961)  The pyramid and the psychotherapeutic relationship. *Lancet*, **ii**, 1051.

BETZ, B. J. (1963)  Validation of the differential treatment success of 'A' and 'B' therapists. *American Journal of Psychiatry*, **119**, 883 & 1090.

COLBY, K. M. (1951)  *A Primer for Psychotherapists*. New York: Ronald Press.

FINESINGER, J. E. (1948)  Psychiatric interviewing. *American Journal of Psychiatry*, **105**, 187.

FORD, D. H. & URBAN, H. B. (Eds.) (1964)  *Systems of Psychotherapy*. New York: John Wiley. pp. 161–178.

FRANK, J. D. (1961)  *Persuasion and Healing*. London: Oxford University Press.

FRANK, J. D. (1968)  Influence of patients' and therapists' expectations on the outcome of psychotherapy. *British Journal of Medical Psychology*, **41**, 349.

JONES, E. (1953)  *Sigmund Freud: Life and Work*. Vol. I. London: Hogarth Press.

KINSEY, A. C., POMEROY, W. B. & MARTIN, C. E. (1948)  *Sexual Behaviour in the Human Male*. Philadelphia: Saunders.

MACCOBY, E. E. & MACCOBY, N. (1954)  The interview: a tool of social science. In G. Lindzey (ed.): *Handbook of Social Psychology*, Vol. I. Cambridge, Mass.: Addison–Wesley Publishing Co. Inc.

MASTERS, W. H. & JOHNSON, V. B. (1966)  *Human Sexual Response*. Boston: Little, Brown and Co.

MAY, R. (1959)  The Existential Approach, In *American Handbook of Psychiatry* (ed. Arieti) vol. II, Ch. 66.

MERTON, R. K. & KENDALL, P. L. (1946)  The focussed interview. *American Journal of Sociology*, **51,** 541.

MERTON, R. K., KENDALL, P. L. & FISKE, M. (1952)  *The Focussed Interview*. Columbia University, N.Y.: Bureau of Applied Social Research.

REIK, T. (1948)  *Listening with the Third Ear*. New York: Farrer, Strauss and Co.

ROGERS, C. R. (1959)  Client-centred Psychotherapy. In S. Koch (ed.) *Psychology, a study of Science*. Vol. III.

ROGERS, C. R. (1959)  Client-centred Psychotherapy. In *American Handbook of Psychiatry* (ed. Arieti) III, Ch. 13.

SULLIVAN, H. S. (1953)  *Interpersonal Theory of Psychiatry*. London: Tavistock Publications.

SULLIVAN, H. S. (1954)  *The Psychiatric Interview*. London: Tavistock Publications.

WALTON, H. J. & McPHERSON, F. M. (1964)  Clinicians as observers of psychological events. *Journal of Psychosomatic Research*, **8,** 167.

WALTON, H. J. (1968)  Effect of the doctor's personality on his style of practice. *Journal of the Royal College of General Practitioners*, **16,** 113.

WHITEHORN, J. C. & BETZ, B. J. (1961)  Further studies of the doctor as a crucial variable in the outcome of treatment with schizophrenic patients. *American Journal of Psychiatry*, **117,** 215.

## Chapter XII

# THE DIAGNOSTIC PROCESS

## W. D. Boyd

### INTRODUCTION

Many changes have occurred in psychiatric practice in recent years. The importance of assessing the patient in the context of his social setting and of involving the 'psychiatric team' in his care has been rightly emphasized (Jones, 1968), and the need to look at the psychiatrically disturbed individual as the 'presenting patient' with a disordered family in the background has been discussed. (Howells, 1968).

With the development of Social Work Departments and other community services the psychiatrist finds himself frequently working as one member of a group of professional people dealing with an ill patient, and may at times be placed in the role of adviser to others who are working in more intimate contact with the disturbed individual.

However, the psychiatrist in Britain to-day still spends a considerable amount of his time in the out-patient clinic or the in-patient psychiatric unit, whether attached to a general hospital or to a psychiatric hospital, and in this setting, usually under considerable pressure of time, he is expected to examine individual patients referred to him by other medical practitioners, to give an opinion about their mental state and to formulate a policy about their further care. Decisions which may have far-reaching results for the patient and his relatives are made on the basis of this confrontation; it is the intention in this chapter to comment on the process by which the psychiatrist comes to these decisions regarding the diagnosis and management of his patient's disturbance.

### THE NEED FOR DIAGNOSIS

Diagnosis, in its narrowest sense, refers to the way in which the clinician distinguishes certain discrete areas of disease. But, more usefully, it is seen as an attempt to understand all the complex factors causing the patient to be ill, and to fit his illness into a recognizable pattern which will allow a logical treatment to be instituted. It may be looked on as 'a problem-solving activity directed towards the classification of a patient for the purpose of relating experience with past patients to him and of assessing the therapeutic and prognostic implications of his condition' (Gorry, 1970). Since it is sometimes suggested that diagnosis in psychiatric illness is less relevant than in physical medicine, it is helpful to examine the diagnostic process as it is used in the field of general medicine.

## THE MEDICAL MODEL

The medical student learns to take a history from a patient, to make a physical examination in which certain signs are elicited, to carry out further investigations which seem necessary, and to use his theoretical background of medical knowledge and his practical experience of other patients in order that he may make a confident diagnosis of the disorder and institute appropriate treatment. The attaching of a diagnostic label will also allow him to discuss the condition with his colleagues, to undertake research among similarly labelled cases, to gather statistical information about the frequency of the disorder, and to compare different methods of treatment. On the post-graduate scene, however, it has to be admitted that diagnosis tends to become less well-defined and less clear-cut. The successful hunches of the experienced clinician give credence to the view that medicine is an art, while the fallacies of confidently-made diagnostic assertions are sometimes made explicit by the findings of the pathologist at post-mortem.

It is not surprising, therefore, to find increasing pressure on clinicians to examine closely the way in which they reach their decisions, the cues they recognize, the possibilities which they weigh up before dismissing one aspect of the case and retaining another.

With the recent developments in computer science, probability theory and decision theory, teachers of clinical medicine are being urged to clarify the process of diagnosis so that it can be taught more logically to undergraduates (Gorry).

## THE PSYCHIATRIC MODEL

If it is difficult to give a logical description of the diagnostic process in the field of internal medicine, it is still more so in the area of psychiatry. The discrepancies between observers in their recognition of psychiatric syndromes have often been reported (Beck, 1962; Foulds, 1955; Kreitman, 1961; Sandifer, et al., 1968), and have been discussed fully in a review of the psychological assessment of acute psychiatric patients by Ley (1970).

For the moment, however, the psychiatrist is faced with the dilemma where he either provides a diagnostic formulation which is virtually specific to the individual patient and without relevance to more general psychiatric experience, or he makes use of psychiatric classifications which include syndromes still poorly differentiated in terms of strict scientific basis.

Yet the purposes of diagnosis in psychiatry are exactly the same as those in general medicine, and if present classifications are unsatisfactory they must be replaced by improved versions as knowledge increases, rather than discarded as meaningless.

It is true that some aspects of the psychiatric examination can be made more objective by means of questionnaire or inventory, but other important aspects remain difficult to assess. For if some uniformity in the description of depressive states or of personality may be reached by making use of appropriate scales, it is still difficult to qualify the degree of rapport between doctor and patient, or to measure the 'flatness' in the affect of a young man suffering from schizophrenia. Attempts are being made to bring greater objectivity to such aspects of the psychiatric examination (Macpherson, *et al.*, 1970) but for the most part they remain poorly defined, yet of enormous importance in building up the total picture of the patient, his problems and his diagnosis.

Furthermore, these cues which are so difficult to make explicit are available from the moment that initial and formal contact is made with the patient, continue to be picked up during the reception of the patient at the clinic, become more apparent still during the psychiatric interview, and are vital in reaching a decision about future care and treatment.

## PRELIMINARIES TO THE PSYCHIATRIC INTERVIEW

### THE INITIAL CONTACT

The first contact commonly comes from the patient's own family doctor, by telephone or by letter. Sometimes, however, the referral is arranged by Police, Social Work Department, or a voluntary group such as Telephone Samaritans. It is always worth considering why the referral has come at this particular moment. Has the patient been planning to take this step for many months, or has the family doctor seized an opportune moment to persuade him that a psychiatric consultation is desirable? Has the family doctor reached the end of his tolerance in coping with a disturbed and demanding family or is he sending the patient along only because the family has insisted that 'something must be done'? Is this someone who is seeking help as a last resort and as an alternative to a suicidal attempt or is it someone who feels that a psychiatric interview might prove useful in his impending Court case? Whatever the answer may be, it is possible that it will throw considerable light on the immediate needs of the patient.

Some comment should also be made about the referring agents and their attitude to psychiatric disorders. Some doctors, for example, only seem to refer cases with psychotic illness; sometimes it is assumed that people who have had a psychiatric illness in the past are still psychiatrically ill if they have come into conflict with the law; and sometimes social incompetence is equated too readily with illness, perhaps in hope that the malaise will respond to a specific psychiatric treatment.

Important information should be available about the medical intervention which has already been made. This may have involved medication of the patient with specific drugs, or unsuccessful attempts to help him by altering his environment or by supporting him in his difficulties. Medical referral letters are perhaps too often constricted by the model acceptable in referral of patients with physical illness; and the informed family doctor may have a detailed knowledge of the family interactions which only becomes apparent in a telephone conversation after the interview.

## ARRIVAL AT THE CLINIC

It is advisable that careful preparation is made for the reception of the patient. Not infrequently people complain of the attitude of receptionists in the consulting-rooms of family doctors or in hospital out-patient departments. At a time when the patient is flustered, embarrassed, or perhaps angry at being sent along for a psychiatric interview, it is essential that the first contact should be a helpful one, and that the receptionists should be welcoming, sensitive to the different needs of individual patients and capable of responding to them. Given that there is a satisfactory and stable arrangement for introducing the patient to the clinic, his attitude at this stage is useful to observe. Is he suspicious? Does he respond aggressively to questions about himself? Does he appear to be over-dependent on accompanying relatives?

## DOMICILIARY VISIT

Although the majority of patients are seen at out-patient clinics, examination of the patient in his own home—the domiciliary visit—deserves mention. This arrangement is time-consuming and in the British National Health Service may only be carried out by consultant psychiatrists when the health of the patient makes it impossible for him to come to the hospital. Yet the experience of seeing him in his own home can be of extraordinary value in assessment. Away from the hospital, the family relationships, the physical surroundings, the social pressures, and their effect on the patient, can be seen in a few minutes and can provide the examiner with knowledge which may take a long time to build up in the consulting-room.

## BASIC INFORMATION

The observant psychiatrist will not disregard the initial information which is provided in the patient's case-notes, for even such basic details as surname, address, age, or religion, may immediately demonstrate the possibility that the patient is in a cultural or social situation of particular stress.

## THE PSYCHIATRIC INTERVIEW

Once the preliminary reception of the patient has been completed and the letter from the referring doctor, along with any other relevant information, has been studied, the patient will be invited to enter the consulting-room. He may well be uncertain of the name of the doctor he has come to see, and the psychiatrist should introduce himself clearly. The fact that there is considerable pressure of time makes it all the more important that the interview is carried out with freedom from interruptions by telephone or by the ubiquitous 'bleep' of a hospital call-system. In this connection it may be of interest to mention the case of a patient who became convinced during several interviews that she was being exposed to electrical stimuli in the consulting-room. She felt unable to admit her fears to the psychiatrist, but fortunately her anxiety was allayed when it became apparent to her that her hearing-aid was responding to the impulses of the call-system!

The value of telling the patient, in general terms, what is already known from the referring agent has been advocated by Sullivan (1954); such an arrangement allays the fears of the patient that something is being kept from him.

### THE PATIENT AND THE INTERVIEW

The attitude of the patient to his psychiatric referral is of considerable importance in the process of diagnosis. Without the full co-operation of the patient it will be impossible to elicit many aspects of his difficulties, and if therefore he does appear to be unco-operative then this problem must be examined urgently and often made explicit to him. Has he been persuaded to come to the clinic by his family doctor, or his relatives, and has this been against his own judgement? Does he feel desperately threatened by the involvement of a psychiatrist? Does he have a worry that he may be detained compulsorily in hospital? Does he suspect that the dictating-machine on the desk is a recording-apparatus? Does he have fears regarding the confidentiality of the interview?

Conversely, it is possible to find the very co-operative patient who has exaggerated expectations of magical powers of the psychiatrist. Does he think the psychiatrist can read his mind or is hypnotizing him? Does he see the psychiatrist as an ally against family or employer? Does he assume that one interview will be sufficient to sort out all his problems?

Unless the examining psychiatrist is sensitive to these possibilities he may easily misinterpret the attitude of the patient in front of him. He must remember that the patient coming to his consulting-room may have very stereotyped ideas about psychiatry which could seriously complicate his attempts to express feelings and thoughts which he has never before put into words. Every effort must be made, therefore, to avoid superadded anxiety engendered by an unsatisfactory interview situation.

## THE DOCTOR AND THE INTERVIEW

An understanding of the interactions involved in psychotherapy has made us aware of the complicated factors which govern the therapeutic relationship and the importance in successful treatment of the attitude which the doctor himself holds towards the patient (Goldstein, 1962. Also see Chapter XI, Vol. I).

In the diagnostic interview, the opportunity for a complicated and carefully-structured relationship is of course limited, yet this very limitation means that the doctor must be particularly aware of his own attitudes and of the pressures affecting him at the time of his interview. The shortage of beds for in-patient care, the knowledge that a severely disturbed psychotic patient is demanding attention in the waiting-room, or even an interest in the trial of a new psychotropic drug could so easily colour his attitude to the patient in front of him. It is inevitable and necessary that, in reaching the point in the diagnostic process where further management is being considered, he should consider environmental factors which might be relevant. At least he must be aware of the attitudes which are governing his decisions. He should also have insight into his own personality traits and the responses which he normally arouses in other people.

It is worth reiterating that throughout the diagnostic process the patient is more likely to provide the essential clues which will allow the psychiatrist to help him if he is relaxed and at ease, confident that he has an interested professional listener who is able to understand his difficulties and who is not passing judgement on him.

## THE RELATIVES AND THE INTERVIEW

The patient is often accompanied by a relative who may be very keen to provide information and opinion about the patient's condition and who may wish to enter the consulting-room with him. Sometimes the patient himself asks that the relatives should be allowed to come. Without decrying the enormous value of the family interview as a way of observing and improving pathological family interactions, it is advisable that the patient should always be seen on his own in the first instance—unless he is totally disorganized as a result of serious psychotic illness—and a relative will usually accept a firm invitation to remain in the waiting-room. This arrangement is particularly important in the case of a young person, who must feel that there is interest in his own account of his problems if he is going to develop confidence in any treatment which may be offered him. Furthermore, an apparently supportive relative may turn out to be the most disturbing influence on the patient as the case unfolds.

After seeing the patient, and with his consent, the relative should then be interviewed whenever the opportunity arises. It must be common experience to find that where circumstances have made it impossible to interview a family member some very useful information has been missed and has then been produced at a much later and more inopportune moment.

## THE DIAGNOSIS

Having stressed the relevance of the preliminaries to the interview and of the attitudes of the participants it is now appropriate to examine the general plan by which a diagnosis may be reached and followed by the further steps of management and treatment.

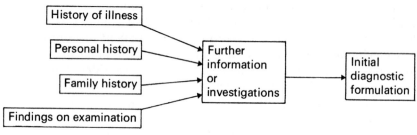

FIG. I

As we go through the history-taking and examinations of the patient, we look at certain areas, namely, history of illness, family history, personal history, and mental state on examination; we add to the information from these sources the results of any immediate investigations or further information which may be obtainable and come to some preliminary diagnostic formulation (Fig. 1) following which we make plans for the patient's further management. These plans will include the possibilities of out-patient or in-patient care, referral to another specialist, referral for further investigations, and arrangements for specific methods of treatment, whether these be the use of drugs, psychotherapy, electro-convulsant therapy or some other regime (Fig. 2). A decision must also be made regarding the need for admission as a recommended patient in terms of the Mental Health Act. (See Chapter XX, Vol. II).

A suggested scheme of case-taking is set out below. But it should be pointed out that much of the information obtained formally under the heading of 'Mental State' has already been observed during the taking of the history. Thus, orientation and memory have been assessed in obtaining information about the patient's past and present history. Behaviour is apparent in the way in which the patient reacts to the examiner. Mood has been demonstrated as the patient has described relationships and feelings within the family, and intelligence has been gauged by an account of school career and recent work capacity. Nevertheless, the short-cuts which the experienced examiner may make, or be forced to make, in coming to a speedy decision about his patient, are acceptable only when based on a sound knowledge of the detailed system of examination of the mental state.

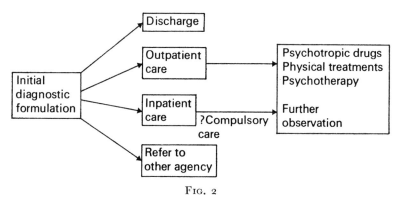

FIG. 2

CASE-TAKING

An outline for psychiatric case-taking is given below:

*History*

1. *Description of Patient.* (1) Name, (2) Age, (3) Occupation, (4) Marital Status, (5) Address, (6) Source of Referral.

2. *Reason for the Examination.* Circumstances leading up to the patient's presentation to the psychiatrist.

3. *Present Illness.* The illness is described from the onset and a chronological account of each of its manifestations is given.

4. *Family History*
   (*a*) Parents: patient's own description of their individual personality, their attitudes to each other and their respective influence in the family.
   (*b*) Siblings: listed in order of birth and with their progress and characteristics.
   (*c*) Atmosphere in the home.

(*d*) Mental illness in the family, including emotional instability and alcoholism.

5. *Personal History*
    (*a*) Circumstances of birth.
    (*b*) Infancy.
    (*c*) Childhood, including any neurotic sysmptoms.
    (*d*) Schooling, and further education.
    (*e*) Adolescent development.
    (*f*) Occupation (set out in order).
    (*g*) Sexual development and experience.
    (*h*) Marital history.
    (*i*) Details of children.

6. *Previous Illnesses*
    (*a*) Physical (accidents, operations and illnesses, in order of occurrence).
    (*b*) Psychiatric, including treatment by G.P.

7. *Previous Personality.* Patient's relationships with other people in the home, at work, and in social situations. Reactions in the interview situation. Interests, character traits, fantasy life, habits, misuse of alcohol or drugs.

## The Mental State

Appearance and behaviour; thought process; sample of talk; mood; delusions and misinterpretation; hallucinations; obsessions; orientation; memory; attention and concentration; general information; intelligence; insight and judgement.

## Physical Examination

It is essential that facilities are available in the Out-Patient Department to allow a full physical examination to be carried out. It is justifiable to make a physical assessment of all older patients and of younger patients where history and examination of mental state suggest that a physical component may exist.

## Diagnostic Formulation

From the information obtained in the interview, it should be possible to provide a formulation of the case which includes two aspects, namely nosological and psychodynamic.

1. *Nosological.* This is the diagnostic label appropriate for the symptom complex presented by the patient. It should be in accord with the International Classification of Diseases, Injuries and Causes of Death (1965).

2. *Psychodynamic.* A concise statement is made about the multiple factors which are considered to have interacted to bring about the patient's disorder.

DIAGNOSTIC CATEGORIES

Some of the more specific points which the psychiatrist observes and makes use of as he makes his way through the diagnostic process will now be described.

Broadly, the patients presenting to the psychiatrist will fall into one of the following diagnostic groups:

1. Psychiatrically healthy.
2. Neurosis.
3. Personality disorder.
4. Psychosis.
5. Organic brain disorder.

The schemes already described in arriving at the appropriate care of the patient (Fig. 1 and Fig. 2) may be related to these different groups.

In the paragraphs which follow, the features commonly associated with individual psychiatric illnesses will be described. It is evident that while there is much overlap there are also features which stand out most often in association with certain conditions. It is therefore valuable, in the diagnostic interview, to use this information as a very general discriminating tool.

1. *Psychiatrically Healthy*

It has already been explained that patients are referred by various agencies, and that these may be more or less experienced in their awareness of psychiatric disorders, and may be requesting a psychiatric assessment before taking further action themselves. Thus, it may be extremely difficult to determine whether the agitated young man on the door-step of the Telephone Samaritans is suffering from a depressive illness, is reacting to the knowledge that he is two weeks behind with his rent or is simply looking for a free bed for the night. Or referral of a case from a general physician may be more in hope that the psychiatrist will provide an answer to a difficult diagnostic problem rather than as a result of any particular psychological aspect, and the psychiatrist should be careful not to give a positive psychiatric diagnosis unless there are real grounds for doing so, for this may simply give a false sense of security that a 'label' has been attached. Follow-up of patients where 'hysteria' was diagnosed has demonstrated that physical pathology may later emerge (Slater and Glithero, 1965). Conversely, however, it should be remembered that some patients suffering from a hypomanic illness may present themselves as being within the normal

K

range of cheerful optimism until the history from a relative emphasizes the marked change in the individual when compared with his usual behaviour.

### 2. *Neurosis*

Patients suffering from Neurosis form the majority of the attenders at the out-patient clinic. They are less likely to present as emergencies than those with psychotic illness or with disorders of personality, and instead are more often seen by appointment after being referred by their family doctor.

(*a*) *Family History.* Personality difficulties or neurotic traits in the parents or siblings will be of special relevance here.

(*b*) *Personal History.* Disturbances in early childhood, broken home, school career, especially ability to mix with other children, will be relevant. Information about sexual development and relationships with the opposite sex, stability in work-record, or perseverance in any particular interest, will all be of especial interest as evidence of the degree of maturity reached. Long absences from school due to physical illness can produce later difficulties and will be enquired for.

(*c*) *Recent History.* The development of acute symptoms of neurosis is often seen as an additional burden on someone who is already vulnerable, already anxiety-prone, already emotionally labile, or already rigid and houseproud.

(*d*) *Examination.* The patient describes symptoms clearly to the examiner. While agitation, tension and tearfulness may be apparent, these symptoms are relevant to what the patient is describing and are not likely to persist throughout the interview. Fears of memory disturbance or of 'going mad' are recognized as the result of poor concentration or agitation.

(*e*) *Further Information.* The referring agent may express considerable frustration that the patient has not improved, or irritation at his importuning. The family may be totally involved in the patient's difficulty, and may have made enormous sacrifices to support him emotionally. Alternatively they may be rejecting, angry, taking the familiar view that 'he needs a good shaking' or 'he should pull himself together'.

(*f*) *The Conclusion of the Interview.* It may be necessary occasionally to admit a patient with a neurotic disorder to hospital as an emergency, but much more usually it will be possible to undertake his further management as an out-patient. Drugs will be prescribed or formal psychotherapy or behaviour therapy instituted. These patients form the bulk of the out-patient referrals to a psychiatric out-patients clinic. It is particularly important, therefore, that the degree to which the patient is motivated towards treatment is assessed and that wherever possible the arrangements for further care are discussed fully, so that the psychiatrist and the patient come to an understanding of their respective expectations and of the contract which they are making with each other.

3. *Personality Disorder*

This group of patients form a large number of referrals, and frequently present themselves as emergencies.

(*a*) *Family History*. As with neurosis, there is likely to be considerable disturbance in early home circumstances, with parents themselves abnormally disturbed, separated or divorced.

(*b*) *Personal History* is often a long recitation of unhappy events throughout childhood, adolescence and adult life. Either in terms of physical or emotional environment there will probably be major disturbance.

(*c*) *Present History*. Referral to hospital will frequently follow a crisis involving family relationships, impulsive self-poisoning, alcohol abuse, or social ineptitude.

(*d*) *Further Information*. This is often lacking at the time of referral. The family doctor has perhaps only known the patient for a short time, or his desperate plight brings him as a direct referral from a social agency. Not infrequently, the long saga of distress, of previous psychiatric involvement, of massive help from social agencies, or of entanglement with the law only emerges at a later date and after an initial plan for management has been decided upon.

(*e*) *Examination*. Often the patient is referred at the urgent request of another agency and with some coercion. In such a situation the patient may deny symptoms entirely or react aggressively to the questions of the examiner. He may be frankly paranoid and refuse to consider further help. At other times, he is clearly distrubed in his affect, or is suffering from secondary problems such as alcoholism or drug abuse.

(*f*) *Conclusion of the Interview*. These patients deserve a particularly careful decision about their treatment. It is evident that only a minority of this group are going to be helped by any intensive involvement in treatment, yet a great deal can be done to help them in the crisis, not necessarily by removing them from their problems, but by helping them to cope with them. Temporary admission to hospital may be useful, but more often appropriate help can be given as an out-patient. The acute symptoms of tension or depression may respond to medication and should not necessarily be withheld because of the impulsiveness or unpredictability of the patient, or because he strains the credulity of the examiner. Day-Patient attendance or daily visits to the hospital to obtain prescribed medication may act as a useful measure to help the patient. Again, motivation is of paramount importance in deciding on appropriate treatment.

## 4. *Pyschosis*

This group includes the patient suffering from schizophrenia and from manic-depressive illness. Referral is arranged because of the increasing distress of relatives or of the patient himself. Those involved in the referral will probably have little doubt that the patient is 'ill'.

(*a*) *Family History* is relevant here in terms of enquiry whether similar illness may have been suffered by other members of the family. The effects of early parental-loss, and of parental attitudes is more debatable and of less relevance to the immediate treatment goals but deserves enquiry.

(*b*) *Personal History.* The development of the patient is less significant than in the understanding of neurotic disorders, but is of relevance in assessing how the patient will cope with his psychosis, especially during the phase of recovery and rehabilitation.

(*c*) *Further Information.* It may be vitally important to hear from relatives or others about behaviour in the home. At interview, the patient may be guarded in manner, and may succeed in covering up his disturbed thinking. He may oppose the request of the psychiatrist to see his relatives, and the doctor will have to weigh up carefully the benefit of confirming his own views against the dangers of disrupting an already disturbed family immediately after the interview, knowing that any schism could have serious consequences.

(*d*) *Examination.* The mental state of the patient is of particular relevance. Change in mood, whether it be elation, depression, or the flatness and incongruity which is so significant, will be apparent to the experienced examiner. Behaviour may be inappropriate, and dress may be bizarre. Special note will be taken of the thought-processes.

(*e*) *Conclusion of the Interview.* The decision about further treatment will include the question of in-patient care. The patient may be potentially suicidal, or his behaviour may be intolerable to society and dangerous to himself or others. If he refuses to accept admission informally, the need for compulsory detention will be considered. It is important to remember the long-term implications of the decision, taking into account all the aspects of the patient's background. The sensitive individual may be greatly distressed by the implications of admission as a Recommended Patient and may be in the hands of informed relatives who can be relied on to behave sensibly in the situation. Should the psychiatrist feel it necessary, however, he should not hesitate to insist to the patient, in front of the relatives, that he come into hospital. Frequently the patient accepts this without the need for legal restraint.

5. *Organic Brain Disorder*

Cases of organic brain disorder may present as an acute problem of confusional state or with a more insidious onset.

(*a*) *Family History*. The relevance of family history of disease may be considerable in certain organic conditions, from the clear genetic picture in Huntingdon's Chorea to the less clear correlations in senile dementia or in epilepsy. Certainly these factors should be looked for.

(*b*) *Personal History*. The previous medical history is of particular importance in the Organic Brain Disorder, since there may be evidence of head-injury, diabetes, or hypertension prior to the onset of psychiatric symptoms. There may also be evidence of excessive consumption of drugs or alcohol, or of a life-style where veneral infection might have been likely.

(*c*) *Further Information*. While the acute brain syndrome is a fairly easily identified disorder, the onset of the more chronic disorder may be extremely insidious. A single oddness of behaviour may usher in the organic disorder, or a relative who has not seen the patient for a long period of time may be the first to observe the changed behaviour.

(*d*) *Examination*. In the organic disorder the formal examination will be of particular importance. Changes in orientation, in memory, in level of consciousness will all be assessed. Lability of emotions, irritability, or lack of concentration may be demonstrated.

(*e*) *Conclusions of Interview*. The diagnostic process in a patient where organic pathology is suspected will attempt to demonstrate more precisely, in terms of organic pathology, the nature of the disorder and the possibility of improvement. Investigations may require hospital admission and further neurological assessment. If the patient lacks insight into his condition, it may be necessary to invoke legal measures for his own care and for the safe arrangement of his financial committments.

## FURTHER STEPS IN THE DIAGNOSTIC PROCESS

It will be clear that the material discussed in this chapter relates to the initial contact with the patient and to the decisions which must be made, often after one interview in the out-patient clinic, as to his further care.

The more intricate and elaborate details of diagnosis will follow as the case unfolds and as the psychiatrist builds up a complete picture of all the factors which relate to a particular patient. This process may involve many sessions of psychotherapy or much observation in the ward. There is no alternative to the building up of confidence and rapport between doctor and patient over a period of time, the careful elucidation of facts not at once apparent, and the assistance of other professional staff—nurses, clinical psychologists or occupational therapists—whose skills may add new dimensions to the first impressions. The purpose of this chapter, however, has been to indicate some of the ways in which the psychiatrist working in the hurly-burly of clinical practice may use the information available to him and the cues presented to him in a way which is of value to himself and to the patient. Only if the initial confrontation is satisfactory can the further working through of the case be successful.

## REFERENCES

BECK, A. T. (1962)   Reliability of psychiatric diagnosis. Pt. I. *American Journal of Psychology*, **119,** 210–216.

FOULDS, G. (1955)   The reliability of psychiatry and the validity of psychological diagnosis. *Journal of Mental Science*, **101,** 851–862.

GOLDSTEIN, A. P. (1962)   *Therapist-Patient Expectancies in Psychotherapy.* Oxf. M.D.: Pergamon Press.

GORRY, G. A. (1970)   Modelling the diagnostic process. *Journal of Medical Education*, Vol. 45, No. 5.

HOWELLS, J. G. (1968)   *Theory and Practice of Family Psychiatry.* London: Oliver & Boyd.

JONES, M. (1968)   *Social Psychiatry in Practice.* London: Penguin Books.

KREITMAN, N. (1961)   The Reliability of Psychiatric Diagnosis. *Journal of Mental Science*, **107,** 876–886.

LEY, P. (1970)   *Assessment of Adults: Acute Psychiatric Patients. The Psychological Assessment of Mental and Physical Handicap.* Edited by P. Mittler. London: Methven & Co. Ltd.

MACPHERSON, F. M., BARDEN, V., HAY, A. J., JOHNSTON, D. W. & KUSHNER, A. W. (1970)   Flattening of affect and personal constructs. *British Journal of Psychiatry*, **116,** 39–43.

SANDIFER, M. G., MODERN, A., TIMBURY, G. R. C. & GREEN, L. M. (1968)   Psychiatric diagnosis: A comparative study in North Carolina, London and Glasgow. *British Journal of Psychiatry*, **114,** 1–9.

SLATER, E. T. O. & GLITHERO, E. (1965)   A follow-up of patients diagnosed as suffering from 'hysteria'. *Journal of Psychosomatic Research*, **9,** 9.

SULLIVAN, H. S. (1954)   *The Psychiatric Interview.* New York: Norton.

Chapter XIII

# AN INTRODUCTION TO CLINICAL PSYCHOLOGY

## F. M. McPherson and A. S. Presly

### INTRODUCTION

In his clinical work, the psychiatrist cooperates with members of several different professions. Effective cooperation depends in part upon the psychiatrist having a clear idea of the roles, responsibilities and skills of these colleagues. One profession which is closely involved with psychiatry is clinical psychology, and clinical psychologists are employed in many psychiatric hospitals and specialist units. A doctor joining a clinical team of which a clinical psychologist is also a member will want to know what he may expect of the psychologist and what, in turn, the psychologist is entitled to expect of him. This chapter aims to help psychiatrists to cooperate effectively with their clinical psychologist colleagues. It will attempt to indicate the range of roles and activities open to psychologists, and will discuss some of the most common problems which can reduce the effectiveness of cooperation.

### CLINICAL PSYCHOLOGISTS AS APPLIED PSYCHOLOGISTS

Although several roles are open to psychologists working in the hospital service, the authors of this chapter consider that clinical psychologists should function as *applied scientists, whose general clinical task is to make available to the hospital service the relevant findings and methods of scientific ('experimental') psychology.*

All clinical psychologists have a basic training in experimental psychology which, as discussed in Chapter IX, Vol. I, is the study of areas of behaviour such as learning, thinking, memory, perception, personality, emotion and social interation. As Shapiro (1967) points out, much of the work carried out in psychiatric hospitals also has to do with these areas. For example, psychiatric patients may have abnormalities or disorders of perception, memory or thinking and psychiatrists observe and classify these disorders and attempt to modify them. Occupational therapy, and rehabilitation programmes, are designed so that patients can learn new skills, or re-learn forgotten ones. Nurses and social workers are concerned with the effects on patients' behaviour of social factors in the wards and in the community. The clinical psychologist in a psychiatric hospital must cooperate with his colleegues in these other professions to ensure that, whenever behaviour is observed, assessed or modified, it is done as effectively as possible.

In attempting to do this, the psychologist has three sorts of knowledge at his disposal. First, there are the *facts and theories* of psychology, some of which may be directly relevant to clinical problems. Secondly, the psychologist knows about the *techniques* which have been devised for observing, measuring and changing individual and group behaviour, i.e. techniques such as mental and personality tests, psychophysiological measures and operant learning procedures. Thirdly, the psychologist has been trained to apply the general methods of science to the understanding of human activities. Scientific method is not something remote from clinical practice. It is a set of rules and procedures which scientists have formulated and adopted because they are useful in helping to reduce the sorts of errors which scientists are liable to make, e.g. mistakes in observation and in drawing inferences from evidence. It is important that clinicians also should avoid these errors, and the application of scientific method can enable them to do so.

Thus, the clinical psychologist differs from other clinicians in that he aims to use in his clinical work only scientifically valid information and methods; he differs from other psychologists in that he aims to apply scientific psychology to the benefit of distressed patients. He is not solely employed to administer tests routinely, or to do behaviour therapy, or to calculate t-tests—although most clinical psychologists are able to do all three.

Meehl (1960) states:

'If there is anything that justifies our existence . . . it is that we think scientifically about human behaviour and that we come from a long tradition, going back to the very origins of experimental psychology in the study of human error, of being critical of ourselves as cognizing organisms and of applying quantitative methods to the outcomes of our cognitive activities' (pp. 26 to 27).

In addition to their clinical responsibilities, clinical psychologists have obligations to *general experimental psychology*. The observation of abnormalities of behaviour can often throw light on the processes involved in normal functioning, and clinical psychologists must ensure that such observations are made, and brought to the attention of their colleagues in other branches of psychology. This is an important function, but is outside the scope of the present chapter.

## FUNCTIONS OF CLINICAL PSYCHOLOGISTS IN THE HOSPITAL SERVICE

There are many ways in which scientific psychology can be applied to clinical problems. The activities of any particular psychologist will be influenced by his own training, interests and attitudes, and by those of his colleagues, as well as by the requirements and facilities of the unit in which he is employed. However, not every clinical activity open to a psychologist is equally useful, and the present authors consider that clinical psychologists should concentrate on *those activities which are relevant to the prevention or reduction of psychological distress or dysfunction.* This does not mean that psychologists must necessarily engage in therapy themselves, although this is a legitimate activity for them. Often, from the point of view of the effectiveness of the clinical team as a whole, they can contribute more usefully in other ways, such as by helping their colleagues in other professions with the formulation of clinical problems; by assessing the psychological functioning of patients; by advising their colleagues, formally and informally, about psychological findings and methods; and by undertaking evaluation studies and research. Of course, no clear distinction can be made between these activities, and a psychologist's contact with a patient often involves them all.

This section will outline these activities, and will concentrate particularly on the functions of the psychologist working in *adult psychiatric and mental subnormality units.* However, it should be emphasized again that many clinical psychologists work outside these areas, but there is no reason to suppose that the approach outlined in this chapter would not be equally applicable to their activities.

FORMULATION OF PROBLEMS

One function of the clinical psychologist is to help psychiatrists and other colleagues to clarify and formulate clinical and research problems so as to render them more readily soluble.

Clinicians, in their daily work, are continually being confronted by problems which require immediate solution, e.g. a patient whose distress and dysfunction must be relieved; a ward whose efficiency appears to need improving; or a new drug which may, or may not, be more effective than an existing alternative. In the process of decision-making, the clinician usually attempts, first of all, to formulate the problem so that he may then decide what information should be collected and how it should be evaluated. As more information becomes available, the initial formulation may have to be modified several times until a solution can be attempted—which, if unsuccessful, will require the problem to be reformulated, and so on. Good clinical practice, like good research, depends upon the right questions being asked at appropriate times.

However, formulating the problem is often very difficult and a clinician may not know what are the most important questions to ask. Cooperation between a psychologist and psychiatrist can be most useful at this stage, with the psychologist contributing in two ways.

Because of his training as a behavioural scientist, he may have some skill in isolating those parts of a total problem which are most relevant to its solution; he might therefore be able to advise on which variables should be assessed and manipulated. Secondly, because psychologists have an orientation and background which is very different to that of psychiatrists, their view of the problem is also likely to differ. Sometimes the psychologist's conceptualization might indicate opportunities for investigation or modification which were not apparent from the psychiatrist's standpoint. When a psychologist does contribute to the specification of a problem in this way, he may then continue to carry out the procedures suggested by the formulation. Alternatively, this may be done by the psychiatrist or by a colleague in another profession.

## Assessment of Psychological Functioning

Psychological assessment is the *'systematic collection, organization, and interpretation of information about a person and his situations, and the prediction of his behaviour in new situations'* (Gwynne Jones, 1970).

The measurement of behaviour is central to scientific psychology, and the assessment of 'problem cases' is one of the traditional activities of the clinical psychologist. Psychiatrists frequently refer patients for an assessment to be made of some aspects of their functioning, such as their intelligence, personality or specific symptoms. Clearly, during a clinical interview, a psychiatrist can make a rough estimate of this, but the aim of a psychological assessment is to provide an estimate that is more *objective* and *valid* than one based on clinical judgement alone (see Chapter IX, Vol. I). 'Objective' means that the method is 'as independent as possible of the clinicians' changing moods and experience. Standard situations and standard methods of evaluating responses are necessary' (Shapiro, 1951). A procedure is 'valid' if inferences can be drawn from it which can be shown empirically to be correct. Assessment procedures which are unreliable and invalid have no advantages over uncontrolled clinical judgement and their use is rejected by the more scientifically rigorous clinical psychologists.

### METHODS OF ASSESSMENT

There are two main ways in which psychologists can describe and investigate the psychological features and disorders of patients— *standardized tests* and *ideographic and experimental methods*.

A 'standardized test' is a device from which an objective, quantitative score is obtained, which permits the person being tested to be compared with other people. *Standardization* implies that the test has been given to a representative sample of the population with which it is intended for use (e.g. British men aged 18 to 60, or all depressives) so that test *norms* are obtained (see Chapter IX, Vol. I). The score of someone tested subsequently can be compared with the scores of the sample and, e.g., the 'abnormality' of his performance can be assessed, within specifiable limits of error.

Of course, such a comparison is valid *only* if the test is administered exactly as it had been to the people in the normative sample. For this reason, tests usually have detailed instructions for their administration and scoring. It is an important part of the training of a clinical psychologist to learn to administer tests in accordance with the instructions, while at the same time obtaining the cooperation of disturbed patients (Shapiro, 1967).

Very many standardized tests have been developed, but Shapiro (1967) concludes that only a few of them are sufficiently objective and valid for large-scale routine use. He continues: 'Among these are a few intelligence tests, a few scholastic attainment tests, and a few vocational interest inventories'.

However, frequently in clinical work, the information required about a patient cannot be obtained from standardized tests. Suitable tests may not exist; or if they do, they may be designed for general use with a range of patients, and so do not allow sufficiently detailed investigation of the unique features of that particular patient. In these cases, the psychologist might devise and construct a test specifically for the patient. For example, a patient might complain of forgetting the names of friends. In the absence of an adequate standardized test, the psychologist could assess whether this forgetting was abnormal, i.e. greater than would be expected in a person of the patient's age, by devising a test and then giving it to the patient and to a specially collected control group of people of the same age. In other cases, an experiment might be carried out with variables thought to influence the patient's condition being varied systematically. Thus, a patient who experienced sudden attacks of panic while at the dentist was assessed to discover which features of the total situation were most important in triggering-off the anxiety. While the patient recorded her subjective level of anxiety on a rating scale, various stimuli such as the sight of the dental instruments and the sound of the drill were presented singly and in combination. It was found that she could tolerate the drill being used, provided that she did not hear it.

Various questionnaires and rating scales can be used to record and analyse the specific content of a patient's illness. The *Personal Questionnaire* (Shapiro, 1961) comprises statements made by the patient himself about his illness and recorded in his own words. *Repertory Grid* technique (see Chapter IX, Vol. I) elicits and analyses the ways in which the patient describes and discriminates among people known to him.

In addition to these two objectives approaches to psychological assessment, clinical psychologists, like any clinicians, should be skilled in obtaining information by observing and interviewing patients. The psychologist's uncontrolled observations might help in the formulation of hypotheses which can be tested later by more rigorous methods.

SPECIFYING THE PROBLEM

As discussed earlier, it is essential that the problem to which the assessment is relevant should be clearly specified. The problem as it appears to the psychiatrist may often have to be redefined before it can be approached usefully by the psychologist. For example, psychologists are often asked to assess a patient's intelligence. At first sight, this might appear to be a simple matter, easily dealt with by the routine use of a standardized test. However, research (see Chapter IX, Vol. I) shows that intelligence can be assessed in several different ways, e.g. by verbal and by non-verbal tests, by tests of verbal memory and of verbal reasoning, and by tests of mental speed as opposed to those which reward persistence. These various tests may give different estimates of 'intelligence', and are related to different 'real-life' activities. Before deciding how to assess a patient's intelligence, the psychologist must therefore know for what purpose the estimate will be used. For example, discussion with the referring psychiatrist might reveal that what he wanted to know was whether the patient was intelligent enough to complete a university course in civil engineering. Once the problem has thus been specified, the psychologist's task is to decide which aspects of intelligence are most relevant, and what minimum level of performance is required. Often, this information can be found in published research reports or in test standardization data. If it is not available, the psychologist might have to test a group of successful engineering students at the local university and compare their scores with those of the patient. Of course, the review of research findings might show that intellectual level was a less efficient predictor of success than, e.g., attainment in mathematics, or some feature of personality; these would therefore have to be assessed. In other words, the problem would be continually respecified, and the psychologist would carry out a very different, and more useful, assessment than that implied by the original request for 'I.Q. please'.

Similarly, the assessment of personality can be undertaken only in connection with defined problems. The procedures which would help to clarify the patient's attitudes to his parents are very different from those which would help to predict his response to behaviour therapy.

Psychologists are frequently asked for help in establishing a patient's *diagnosis*. There is disagreement among psychologists as to whether this is a legitimate activity. Foulds (e.g. 1968) argues that it is, and much of his work has been directed towards improving psychiatric classification by means of psychological tests and questionnaires (see Foulds, 1965). On the other hand, Payne (1957) thinks that diagnosis should be left to the psychiatrist and that the task of the psychologist is to provide a detailed description and analysis of the patient's symptoms.

It is essential that psychologists who accept diagnostic referrals recognize that several different questions are involved, which must be dealt with separately. For example, the question: 'Is this patient suffering from a presenile dementia?' can be subdivided into *descriptive* questions such as 'Is there evidence of general falling off from a previously higher level of performance?' and: 'Is there evidence of some specific deficits, such as aphasia or memory disorder?'; *aetiological* questions, such as: 'Does the nature of the deficit allow any conclusions to be drawn about the type and locus of the brain damage responsible?'; and *prognostic* questions, such as: 'Can any inferences be drawn about whether the patient's condition is likely to deteriorate over the next year?'.

It does not follow that, because a test permits valid descriptions to be made, it also has valid aetiological or prognostic implications. As Payne and Inglis (1960) state:

'... aetiological implications ... must themselves be proven before the test results can be used to make inferences about causation. A similar argument may be put forward concerning prognosis. Valid descriptive characteristics are not necessarily valid prognostic indicators and the psychologist can and must tackle this problem in its own right (p. 1137).

Discussion with the referring psychiatrist might show that what he was mainly interested in was the patient's prognosis, so that various decisions could be made about the patient's management. The problem having been thus reformulated, more appropriate assessment methods could then be used, i.e. ones which had been validated against prognosis. At present there are very few tests which have been validated in this way, so that, in practice, the investigation would probably stop at this point. However, some indication of what is possible is Inglis' (1959) finding that a word learning test was a better predictor of outcome in elderly, brain-damaged or depressed patients than was the initial psychiatric diagnosis.

PURPOSE OF THE ASSESSMENT

Clinically, what is the purpose of carrying out a psychological assessment of a patient? What general sorts of information should an assessment attempt to provide?

Psychological assessment is time-consuming, and hence expensive, and is thus not justified unless the results have, potentially at least, some practical implications for the patient. Many psychologists would agree with Gwynne Jones (1970) that the goal of assessment is: 'the devising and application of procedures designed to modify the client's reaction to situations or, by appropriate manipulation of the environment, to modify the actual situations, i.e. with treatment in the broadest sense'. In other words, the assessment must be directed towards the treatment or management of the patient.

Experimental methods of assessment are particularly appropriate in this connection, since—as in the example of the dentist phobia cited above—they often specify the particular features of a patient's situation which are relevant to his illness, and may indicate how these features can be manipulated so as to eliminate his symptoms. Many vocational guidance assessments also have implications for management, e.g. determining which skills remain to a patient following a severe head injury, with a view to retraining and rehabilitation. On the other hand, personality assessment and diagnostic testing is often of no value—not because the methods used are inadequate (although they often are) but because the wrong questions have been asked, and no practical consequences follow from the assessment. These and other aspects of assessment are discussed in Williams (1965) and Gathercole (1968). Many of the tests used by clinical psychologists are described by Gathercole.

MODIFICATION OF BEHAVIOUR

The term 'modification' is used here to refer to a wide range of activities, including treatment of patients individually, or in groups, by behaviour therapy or psychotherapy; rehabilitation and training; and work relating to management and administration.

Until recently, most clinical psychologists were reluctant to become involved in any form of therapy. However, the situation has changed markedly within the last decade, and a survey carried out in 1967 (Desai, 1969) found that therapy of some sort was practised in two-thirds of National Health Service psychology departments. This proportion is very likely to be even greater now.

*Behaviour Therapy*

This is the name given to a group of techniques whose primary aim is the modification of specific aspects of behaviour, such as signs and symptoms, and which are derived from psychological theories of learning (see Chapter IX, Vol. I). Although the ideas underlying these techniques have a long history, the systematic investigation of them, and their widespread application to the problems of psychiatric patients, has occurred only in the last 15 years. However, now it is the method most widely used by psychologists, particularly in the treatment of phobias (by systematic desensitization), and of behaviour problems in areas such as toilet training, social interaction and the production of speech (by methods based on operant learning, see Chapter XVIII, Vol. II), and in the elimination of socially undesirable behaviour, such as excessive drinking and sexual deviance (by aversion methods). Many psychologists reject the use of aversion therapy, both because of the specific techniques employed, and because of the more general ethical issues (see Smail, 1970). The present authors agree with Shapiro (1965) that the aim of therapy should be 'to help people to increase their ability to exercise their own judgements freely, and with maximum efficacy, concerning questions affecting their own interests', and that 'one should not carry out forms of treatment aimed at giving people socially acceptable reflexes or conditioned attitudes of obedience to certain persons or authorities'.

## Psychotherapy

Individual psychotherapy is one of the traditional activities of clinical psychologists in the U.S., but in Britain it has been confined mainly to a small group of child psychotherapists. Recently, Bannister (1969) has argued that psychologists should be more concerned with psychotherapy than they have been. He noted that psychotherapy has to do with psychological change and that 'the understanding, induction and guidance of such change is properly speaking the province of those who are trained in psychology, and in no sense the appropriate province of the medically trained' (p. 300).

Some psychologists who accept behaviour therapy as one of their tasks will not become involved in psychotherapy because it is an 'unscientific' procedure. Bannister replies:

'The essence of an applied science approach in psychotherapy is that the psychologist should be continually concerned to work from a general theoretical framework, in terms of which he derives a specific rationale for the individual case; he should be concerned to try and monitor changes in the course of psychological treatment; he should hinge his treatment on specific predictions which are checked against outcome. Such an approach would certainly preclude him from undertaking general chat or vague 'tender loving care' types of psychotherapy, but it does not preclude psychotherapy as such' (1969, p. 299).

In particular, it does not preclude therapeutic methods derived from personal construct theory (see Bannister and Fransella, 1971), or from small group psychology (see Walton, 1971), and both approaches have recently become more widely used by psychologists.

## Rehabilitation and Training

Psychologists who work with the mentally or physically handicapped, or with brain-injured, or chronic psychiatric patients, often organize and take part in programmes designed to teach communication, social or vocational skills (see Chapter XIX, Vol. II). In child psychiatry, psychologists often undertake remedial teaching of children with severe reading and counting difficulties (see Chazan, 1967).

## Management and Administration

There are many ways in which psychological methods and findings can be applied to improving the therapeutic effectiveness of wards or hospitals. 'Token economies', or other methods based on operant learning, are used to control disruptive behaviour and to teach social skills to groups of patients in mental subnormality and chronic psychiatric wards. Various findings of industrial and occupational psychology are relevant to the design of equipment, or to the implementation of incentive schemes, in occupational therapy or rehabilitation programmes. Some findings and methods of social psychology can be applied to the solution of problems of ward management, such as improving communication between staff and patients, and ensuring that the ward 'atmosphere' is conducive to therapetuic progress. For example, in a study supervised by the present authors, Gray (1971), using a Repertory Grid method investigated the ways in which patients construed a psychotherapy day hospital. The results of the investigation had important implications for the future organization of such a unit. Of course, these 'social psychological' activities may extend beyond the hospital, and the psychologist might contribute to community mental health programmes, or might be involved in hostel or sheltered workshop schemes.

It should be emphasized that, as yet, very few methods of psychological treatment have been adequately validated. They ought not therefore to be applied routinely and when a psychologist undertakes modification of any sort it should usually be in the context of a research investigation designed to evaluate the effectiveness of the procedure.

### CONSULTATION WITH COLLEAGUES

The clinical psychologist also has the task of communicating to his colleagues in other professions any psychological information which might help them in their work. Many psychology departments are responsible for formal courses of lectures and seminars to psychiatrists, nurses and occupational therapists.

However, possibly more useful teaching is that which is given informally at ward rounds, or over coffee. A psychologist should not wait to be asked for advice, but should be sufficiently aware of his colleagues' activities and problems to know when and how he can contribute. The contribution might be to report and interpret relevant research findings. It might be an offer to teach psychiatrists and nurses to administer and score certain psychological tests, or how to apply and evaluate behaviour modification techniques. Cooperation in research is another way in which psychologists can make their colleagues aware of psychological methods. In all these cases, of course, the psychologist must ensure that his advice represents an accurate distillation of current psychological knowledge and practice, and that it is understood and acted upon by his colleagues.

## EVALUATION AND RESEARCH

In the present state of our knowledge of psychiatric illness, the most useful clinical activity open to psychologists is to undertake systematic evaluation and research, either on their own, or in cooperation with colleagues in psychology or in other professions.

### Evaluating Effectiveness of Psychological Procedures

It has been emphasized above that few of the assessment techniques, and perhaps none of the methods of modification, used by psychologists have been so well validated that they can be applied routinely.

A great deal more needs to be found out about standardized tests and other assessment procedures. Their *validity* must be established. Tests which claim to measure thought disorder, or short-term memory deficit, must be shown to do so. Tests intended to help in vocational guidance must be shown to predict performance in the real-life work situation. Little is known about the short- or long-term *stability* of most tests. Very few tests permit estimates of the patient's *prognosis* to be made. The complex problem of making decisions on the basis of test scores also requires much more investigation.

Similarly, modification techniques must be evaluated, both from the point of view of improving the effectiveness of the techniques themselves, and from that of comparing their effectiveness with that of alternative treatments (see McPherson, 1971). A systematic approach to teaching would also require some evaluation of the students' progress in relation to the stated goals of the course of instruction.

Data relevant to questions of this sort, in the amount required, can only be obtained if it is collected routinely by every hospital psychology department in the course of their normal clinical work. Clearly, individual departments may not be able to collect sufficient data to carry out an evaluation study on their own; but data from several departments, if they were collected and recorded in the same way, could be pooled.

It is important to stress that evaluative research is not in the least 'academic' or 'ivory tower'; nor is it an intrusion into clinical work. Rather it is a way—the most efficient way—of helping psychologists to perform their clinical duties more effectively. Evaluating the effectiveness of the procedures which one uses is as fundamental to clinical practice as it is to science. A clinical psychologist who fails to do this, and who continues to employ techniques whose validity is unknown, is a poor psychologist and a worse clinician.

## Cooperative Research

An important clinical commitment of psychologists is to assist colleagues to evaluate, and improve the effectiveness of *their* procedures. Psychologists are often the only people working in a psychiatric hospital who have a training in scientific method. They are therefore often asked by psychiatrists—and also by nurses, occupational therapists or social workers—to help in the design and execution of research investigations, e.g. by helping to formulate the problem, design the study, select and possibly administer assessment measures, and by analysing the results. Drug trials are among the most common of these cooperative, evaluative studies.

## More Basic Research

Some of the clinical research undertaken by psychologists has less immediate relevance although, in the long term, it may have consequences for prevention or treatment. Investigations aimed at clarifying the exact measure of the psychological dysfunctions produced by various conditions, or at isolating the environmental variables associated with the onset of some illness, are of this type.

Basic research can follow directly out of a psychologist's other activities, such as assessment and modification. Shapiro (1963) and Chassan (1967) have both demonstrated that, by careful experimental design, findings of fundamental importance can be obtained from the study of individual patients undergoing psychological treatment. Even if the research requires groups of patients to be studied, a psychologist can often collect the necessary data routinely, merely by recording systematically information which is in any case potentially available to him.

This section has described some of the ways in which clinical psychologists can function as applied scientists, bringing the methods and findings of experimental psychology to bear on clinical problems. How effective the contribution of a particular psychologist is, depends partly upon his ability as a clinician and scientist, but also upon his working relationships with his psychiatrist colleagues. The next section will discuss some aspects of this cooperation.

### Some Practical Issues

#### CLINICAL RESPONSIBILITIES OF PSYCHOLOGISTS

The present situation in National Health Service hospitals is that ultimate clinical responsibility almost always resides with psychiatrists, and it is only with their agreement that a psychologist undertakes assessment, modification or research with a patient. It is the responsibility of the relevant psychiatrist to assure himself that the psychological procedures will contribute to the patient's clinical wellbeing, or in the case of research, will at least not have detrimental effects. On the other hand, as the member of the clinical team who is the expert in the application of psychological procedures and the interpretation of their results, the psychologist is entitled to expect that his advice on these matters will normally be followed.

Arguments have been advanced for giving psychologists greater clinical responsibility for patients, in particular those whose condition can be construed more logically in social and psychological, rather than in medical, terms—such as some of those with behaviour disorders and mild neuroses, and most of the mentally subnormal. However, the present situation is likely to continue into the foreseeable future, although particular groups of colleagues might agree to different arrangements.

ASSESSMENT

*The Referral*

When, and how, should a psychiatrist refer a patient for psychological assessment? This can be time-consuming, and even a routine intellectual assessment can take three or four hours. Patients should therefore be referred only if there is a clinical situation in which the objective and valid measurement of some aspects of psychological functioning is relevant to an important practical decision being made about the patient, preferably one which has implications for treatment or management. Referrals should not be made routinely, or 'for the record', or as a substitute for a careful psychiatric examination.

When referring a patient, the psychiatrist is not expected to specify the assessment procedures which the psychologist must use. Instead, his task is to define, in as great detail as possible, what he considers to be the clinical problem with which the psychologist's help is required. If the psychologist considers that he cannot make a useful contribution, he is entitled to decline to accept the referral, although he should give reasons for doing so. More usually, he may wish to reformulate the problem, so as to make it more amenable to psychological investigation, in which case, the referring psychiatrist must ensure that the reformulation remains clinically relevant.

In its final form, the referral should thus be the end product of a period of collaboration between psychologist and psychiatrist. It is never satisfactory for patients to be referred by letter without discussion, and, whenever possible, this should not be done.

It is useful for the psychiatrist to mention to the patient that he will be seen by a psychologist. The psychiatrist should explain that he will remain the patient's doctor (patients are often confused about this) but that he wants some advice about some aspects of the patient's condition. Sometimes, between assessment sessions, a patient may become distressed because he had 'done the tests badly'. It is important that the psychiatrist or nurse should not reassure him by belittling the importance of psychological assessment; this does not make subsequent assessment easier.

## The Report

The psychologist will usually report the results of his assessment verbally to the referring psychiatrist. A written report is also prepared but this should serve only as a record, and not as a substitute for the verbal report.

Since the main purpose of a psychological assessment and report is to influence decisions made by the psychiatrist, it is essential that he should understand fully the conclusions of the report, and the recommendations based on them. The psychiatrist must, in particular, be clear about which of the psychologist's conclusions are based on the evidence of objective and valid measures, and which derive from his clinical judgement. It is quite legitimate for a psychologist to 'go beyond' his data, in particular if he is an experienced and sensitive clinician, but his colleagues must know when he has done so. In general, the psychiatrist must know how much weight to place on particular findings and conclusions, and this information can come only from detailed discussion of the report with the psychologist.

In some cases, e.g. vocational guidance problems, the psychologist will discuss his findings with the patient; in others, this is more appropriately done by the psychiatrist. The important point is that there must be agreement beforehand between the psychologist, psychiatrist and any other member of the clinical team, such as nurses or social workers, who might be involved, about whether or not the assessment is to be discussed with the patient, and if so, what he is to be told.

### BEHAVIOUR MODIFICATION

The two most important issues relating to psychologist–psychiatrist cooperation in treatment are those of clinical responsibility and whether therapy should be a routine activity of psychologists. Both are usually discussed in relation to behaviour therapy.

## Behaviour Therapy by Psychologists or Psychiatrists?

Some clinical psychologists take the view that, as behaviour therapy is a treatment which derives from psychological theory, only psychologists have the training necessary to carry it out. They envisage psychologists being the behaviour therapy specialists in a hospital, in the way that some psychiatrists specialize in group or individual psychotherapy. All potential behaviour therapy cases in the hospital would therefore be referred to the psychology department.

Other psychologists hold that their role should be mainly a research one, concerned with the development and evaluation of new techniques. If and when these techniques become sufficiently well validated to warrant their being used routinely, then responsibility for doing this should be handed over to psychiatrists; the psychologist's role would then be to instruct psychiatrists in these methods, as well as dealing with any 'problem' cases which might require the development of new techniques.

This issue has not yet been resolved. However two points are relevant. If a treatment is effective, it must be used as widely as possible, and there will be too few psychologists trained in the foreseeable future for them to be able to treat more than a small fraction of those patients who might benefit from behaviour therapy. Secondly, the question of the routine use of behaviour therapy does not yet arise, as at present it has not been sufficiently well validated to be used outside a research context, except in a few rare conditions, such as monosymptomatic phobias (Marks, 1969).

*Clinical Responsibility*

The issue of whether psychologists should have full clinical responsibility for the patients they treat was mentioned above. The survey by Desai (1969) found that the attitudes of psychiatrists to psychologists undertaking treatment ranged from 'enthusiastic' and 'wholly favourable' to 'definitely hostile'. The degree of responsibility in relation to the treatment of patients varied very widely, and seemed to depend largely on the interpersonal relationships between psychologists and consultant psychiatrists.

No matter how this issue is resolved in general, it is of course crucial that in individual cases the psychologist and psychiatrist should agree about their responsibilities, and that their colleagues, and the patient, should be made aware of their decision.

RESEARCH

Psychiatrists will usually be involved in psychologists' research, at least to the extent of being asked for permission to investigate patients under their care. Possibly they may be asked also to rate some aspect of a patient's illness, such as the degree of thought disorder shown.

Psychologists are sometimes put under pressure by their psychiatrist colleagues to spend their time on routine assessment rather than on research. This pressure should be resisted, and it is up to the psychologist to justify his research and show that it is not an optional extra, but is an essential part of his *clinical* work.

Regarding what was termed above 'cooperative research', initiated by the psychiatrist, the most important point is that the psychologist should be brought into the planning at as early a stage as possible. There are many examples of hours of painstaking work being wasted because the data were collected in the wrong way or because inappropriate measures were used.

## CONCLUSIONS

The role of the clinical psychologist which this chapter has described is that of an applied scientist, who uses the methods and findings of psychology in the interests of patients. This is a very difficult task, and despite the excellent work of scientific clinicians such as Foulds, Shapiro and Bannister, the contribution of clinical psychology to psychiatry over the last 20 years has been disappointing. Some psychologists, faced with the problem of being both scientific and useful, have engaged in what Smail (1970) describes as 'the flight into experimental activity . . . an obsession with technique, so that technical and technological achievements have become an end in themselves rather than a means'. Others have ceased to be scientists, and use unvalidated procedures. Both solutions are inadequate. What psychologists must do instead is to ensure the relevance of their work through close and continuous contact with their colleagues in other professions. Instead of jettisoning their scientific training they must, in Bannister's (1969) words 'simply become scientists who are working harder than usual'.

## REFERENCES

BANNISTER, D. (1969)   Clinical psychology and psychotherapy. *Bulletin of the British Psychological Society*, **22,** 299–301.

BANNISTER, D. & FRANSELLA, F. (1971)   *Inquiring Man*. London: Penguin.

CHASSAN, J. B. (1967) *Research Design in Clinical Psychology and Psychiatry*. New York: Appleton–Century–Crofts.

CHAZAN, M. (1967)   The effects of remedial education in reading: a review of research. *Remedial Education*, **2,** 4–12.

DESAI, M. M. (1969)   The functions of clinical psychologists in relation to treatment. *Bulletin of the British Psychological Society*, **22,** 197–199.

FOULDS, G. A. (1965)   *Personality and Personal Illness*. London: Tavistock.

FOULDS, G. A. (1968)   Where's the bloody horse? *Bulletin of the British Psychological Society*, **21,** 167–169.

GATHERCOLE, C. E. (1968)   *Assessment in Clinical Psychology*. London: Penguin.

GRAY, A. (1972)   *Consumer Evaluation of a Therapeutic Milieu: a Repertory Grid Study*. Unpublished M.Sc. dissertation, University of Edinburgh.

GWYNNE JONES, H. (1970)   Principles of psychological assessment. In *The Psychological Assessment of Mental and Physical Handicaps*, edited by P. Mittler, Ch. 1. London: Methuen.

INGLIS, J. (1959)   On the prognostic value of the Modified Word Learning Test in psychiatric patients over 65. *Journal of Mental Science*, **105,** 1100–1101.

McPHERSON, F. M. (1971) Some research topics in group psychotherapy. In *Small Group Psychotherapy*, edited by H. J. Walton. London: Penguin.

MARKS, I. M. (1969) *Fears and Phobias*. London: Heinemann Medical.

MEEHL, P. E. (1960) The cognitive activity of the clinician. *American Psychologist*, **15,** 19–27.

PAYNE, R. W. (1957) Experimental method in clinical psychological practice. *Journal of Mental Science*, **103,** 189–196.

PAYNE, R. W. & INGLIS, J. (1960) Testing for intellectual impairment—some comments reconsidered. *Journal of Mental Science*, **106,** 1134–1138.

SHAPIRO, M. B. (1951) An experimental approach to diagnostic psychological testing. *Journal of Mental Science*, **97,** 748–764.

SHAPIRO, M. B. (1961) A method for measuring psychological changes specific to the individual psychiatric patient. *British Journal of Medical Psychology*, **34,** 151–155.

SHAPIRO, M. B. (1963) A clinical approach to fundamental research with special reference to the study of the single patient. In: *Basic Research Techniques in Psychiatry*, edited by P. Sainsbury & N. Kreitman. Oxford: O.U.P.

SHAPIRO, M. B. (1965) An approach to the social responsibilities of the clinical psychologist. *Bulletin of the British Psychological Society*, **18,** 31–36.

SHAPIRO, M. B. (1967) Clinical psychology as applied science. *British Journal of Psychiatry*, **113,** 1039–1042.

SMAIL, D. J. (1970) Values in clinical psychology. *Bulletin of the British Psychological Society*, **23,** 313–315.

WALTON, H. J. (1971) *Small Group Psychotherapy*. London: Penguin.

WILLIAMS, M. (1965) *Mental Testing in Clinical Practice*. Oxford: Pergamon Press.

Chapter XIV

# NEUROANATOMY IN RELATION TO PSYCHIATRY

## J. R. Smythies

### THE FUNCTIONAL ANATOMY OF THE BRAIN

When the curricula leading to the post-graduate degrees in Psychiatry (D.P.M.) were being planned in the early years of this century, it was felt important that the psychiatrist should receive an extensive training in neurology. This was not because the continental concept of the neuropsychiatrist—a physician actively practising in both fields—ever took root in Britain. The reasons were otherwise. Although the psychiatrist was not meant to treat patients with neurological disorders it was felt that patients with such disorders might be referred to him by the general practitioner, and he should know enough neurology so as not to treat a case of brain tumour with psychotherapy for example. Furthermore, since psychiatry dealt with disorders of the brain, it was felt that practitioners should know the basis of cerebral activity no matter how 'functional' their attitude was likely to become.

Thus neuroanatomy and neurophysiology became a part of the curriculum for the post-graduate degree in Psychiatry, and a major hurdle in the Part I examinations. Unfortunately the historical reasons for this inclusion became obscured during the years and students came to regard this segment of the course as dealing with material quite foreign to their real interests, no more relevant to today's needs than the teaching of Latin and Greek in primary schools. Firstly neurology has no claim to a special relationship to psychiatry. The psychiatrist should certainly know enough neurology so as not to make mistakes, but this applies with equal or greater force to many other branches of medicine—endocrinology, for example. Secondly, the type of neuroanatomy and neurophysiology taught dealt mainly with the 'lower' functions of the nervous system of no great relevance to psychiatry. For example, a detailed knowledge of the spinothalamic pathways, or the mechanisms controlling muscle tone are of clear and obvious importance to the neurologist or neurosurgeon—they are, however, of little importance to the psychiatrist.

The psychiatrist deals with the higher functions of the central nervous system. He is interested in people's perceptions, emotions, motivation, thought processes, dreams, conditional reflexes, etc. However, until very recently, very little was known of how the brain organizes these functions, and so the traditional training was maintained. Over the last few years this situation has changed.

Psychiatrists, neurophysiologists, neuroanatomists, biochemists and people in all the interrelated and interlocking disciplines that make up the neurosciences have become interested in the role of the brain in controlling behaviour. It is of course too early to be able to state that a great deal is as yet *known* in this field; but there is no shortage of experiments nor of ideas and this work is engaging the interest of increasing numbers of brain scientists, including neuroanatomists. However an important feature of this new work is that the traditional boundaries between the disciplines are becoming blurred. Neuroanatomy, for example, is no longer content merely to describe the nuclei and fibre tracts of the brain in terms of simple descriptions and wiring diagrams. The chemical identification of neurones by the fluorescent techniques developed in Sweden in terms of which amine (adrenaline, dopamine or serotonin) is used as a transmitter has enabled us to add colour codes, as it were, to the wiring diagram. The development of more powerful electron microscopes has enabled the anatomist to observe and describe events at greater levels of resolution, currently reaching down to the molecular level itself. The development of computer technology allows the anatomist to ask sophisticated questions about the possible meaning of the complex wiring diagrams in the brain that his techniques help to unravel.

Therefore there is now a strong case for the reorganization of the basic training given to psychiatrists in training. In place of separate courses of neuroanatomy, neurophysiology and neurochemistry given in terms of the 'lower' functions of the nervous system, an integrated neurosciences course is needed, which should concentrate on what is known about the higher functions of the brain and of brain function in relation to behaviour. This chapter will therefore be devoted to several aspects of this with particular attention to the limbic system. I will first deal with some relevant topics from developmental anatomy: then a quick review of some basic gross anatomy: the brain mechanisms relevant to psychiatry with emphasis on chemical factors: the microanatomy of neurones and finally a discussion of the possible relevance of all this to the practising clinical psychiatrist.

## Brain Development

Two points of general interest to psychiatrists emerge—one concerns the basic layout and the other the extent of post-natal growth of the brain.

### BASIC LAYOUT

Most students start, and may finish, a course in neuroanatomy, with a feeling that the brain is an enormously complex and quite confusing tangle of neurones, nuclei and fibre traits running in all directions. However, the basic brain plan is really rather simple and is illustrated in Figure 1.

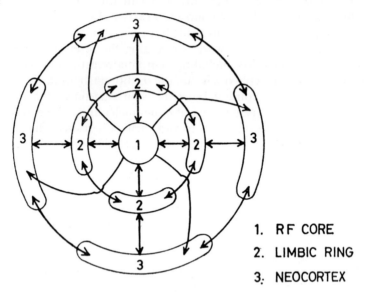

1.  R F CORE

2.  LIMBIC RING

3.  NEOCORTEX

FIG. 1.  The basic brain plan: (1) central reticular core (2) limbic system (3) cortex.

(*Reproduced by courtesy of Blackwell Scientific Publications Ltd.*)

There is a central core—the reticular formation—which houses the central switching and meta-organizational systems. Any complex computer requires that part of its machinery does the actual computing (the organizational system) and the rest operates on this system to switch on this or that subsection when required, to see that proper sequences are followed and so on. This is the meta-organizational system, and in the brain this is represented mainly by the reticular formation in the brain stem and thalamus. Around this core there is a ring which organizes the basic behavioural mechanisms. This is the limbic system whose main parts are the hippocampus, amygdala, septum, and hypothalamus. Lastly there is the cortex which appears to be there to deal with complexity and to provide certain specialist functions. This functional division is mirrored in their anatomical arrangements but this is obscured by the distortions that visit the brains of higher mammals consequent on the marked growth of the cortex and its related fibre traits.

The brain develops from a simple tube—the neural tube. Early in development this puts out two buds from its top end—the cerebral vesicles, that grow out on either side in the manner shown in Figure 2. In these vesicles some cells stay on the surface to form the future cortex and some stay around the wall of the lateral ventricle to form the future corpus striatum and septal nuclei as shown in Figure 3.

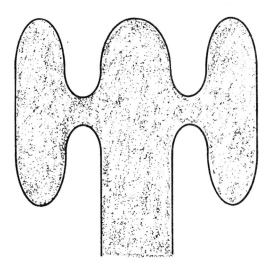

FIG. 2.    The primitive cerebral vesicles growing out from the neural tube.

In the midbrain, some cells stay close to the central canal—the future reticular formation—whereas the walls in other places develop local thickenings of which the thalamus and hypothalamus are examples. The future hippocampus is merely a part of the vesicle wall joining the primitive olfactory cortex to the future neocortex as shown in Figure 3.

The amygdala develops as the most posterior part of the corpus striatum. Thus at this stage all the elements of the future limbic system are close together and simply related. For example the embryo fornix runs a short path from the hippocampus in the roof of the primitive cerebral vesicle to the nearby septal nuclei in the side of the medial wall, as shown in Figure 3. From here the fibres run across the isthmus joining the vesicle to the central neural tube and enter the hypothalamus. The fibres merely take the shortest and most direct route. The equivalent fibres from the amygdala—the stria terminalis—likewise run directly from the posterior end of the corpus striatum to the adjacent septal nuclei and thence to the hypothalamus.

This simple arrangement is distorted by two factors, the enormous growth of the cortex and of its fibre tracts—the corpus callosum and the pyramidal tracts. The growth of the cortex pushes the hippocampus over from its primitive position in the roof of the vesicle, to its most medial portion (Fig. 4). The olfactory cortex hardly grows at all and becomes reduced to a very small area in the base of the brain.

This shift occurs only on the surface and the deep structures. The corpus striatum and septal nuclei stay in their original positions on the lateral and medial walls of the vesicle respectively.

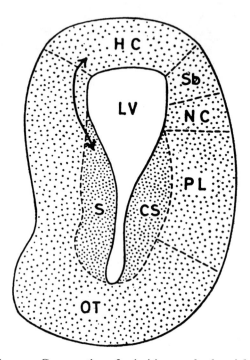

FIG. 3.    Cross-section of primitive cerebral vesicle.

| LV | lateral ventricle | NC | neocortex |
|----|-------------------|----|-----------|
| HC | hippocampus | PL | pyriform lobe |
| Sb | subiculum | CS | corpus striatum |
| OT | olfactory cortex | S | septum |

The arrow indicates the fornix.

*(Reproduced by courtesy of Blackwell Scientific Publications Ltd.)*

Now, in addition to this expansion that pushes the hippocampus medially, the continued growth of the neocortex pushes the posterior pole of the brain at first backwards, then downwards and then forwards, in the manner of opening a fan, so that this pole—the temporal pole—ends up tucked under the frontal lobe, and the occipital lobe, which used to be on top, becomes the new posterior part of the hemisphere. This backward growth carries the hippocampus and amygdala with it. Thus the hippocampus, which was located in the *roof* of the lateral ventricle becomes located in the *floor* of this new development that forms the inferior horn of the lateral ventricle. Likewise the corpus striatum is located in the floor of the lateral ventricle (main body) and so is located in the roof of the inferior horn, in the form of the amygdala. Their fibre tracts, the fornix and stria terminalis are pulled out, as it were, by this growth and retrace the path of migration of their nuclei. The septum remains in its primitive position in the lower part of the medial wall of the vesicle and fuses with the overlying cortex to become the subcallosal gyrus in the human, the gyrus on the most medial aspect of the frontal lobe tucked up under the sweep of the rostrum of the corpus callosum.

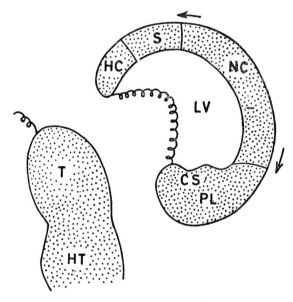

FIG. 4.   A later stage of brain development.
T    thalamus                        HT   hypothalamus

*(Reproduced by courtesy of Blackwell Scientific Publications Ltd.)*

Lastly, in higher mammals, the enormous growth of the corpus callosum runs across from one cerebral hemisphere to the other, in between the fornix and the hippocampus. The former remains intact running under the corpus callosum, but this part of the hippocampus (the dorsal hippocampus in lower animals) is reduced to a vestigial remnant—the indeum griseum. Thus the human hippocampus is the analogue of the ventral hippocampus in lower species. Lastly the growth of the pyramidal tracts sticks the medial side of the cerebral vesicle to the lateral surface of the old central tube along the line of the internal capsule (which divides the corpus striatum, derived from the cerebral vesicle, from the thalamus). This provides a new route for fibres running from the old cerebral vesicle to central structures and many fibres running from the hippocampus and amygdala to the hypothalamus and other central structures go by this new direct route rather than the old circuitous route via the fornix or stria terminalis. This new route forms a diffuse projection running through the subthalamic area under the thalamus to enter the hypothalamus from the side.

Thus the simple brain plan shown in Figure 1 becomes distorted into the apparent complexity of the adult human brain, but the complexity derives mainly from quantity, and the topological distortions that the differential growth of some parts in relation to others entails. Figure 5

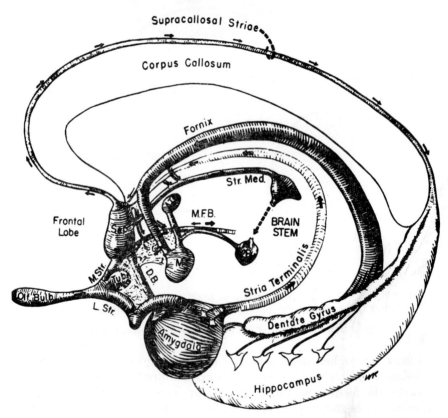

FIG. 5. Diagram of the limbic system.

M    mamillary body          MFB    medial forebrain bundle

*(From Himwich and Maclean, reproduced by courtesy of Blackwell Scientific Publications Ltd.)*

shows the main elements of the limbic system in the adult human brain. The basic functional simplicity remains—for clearly it makes engineering good sense to locate the meta organizational system in the centre of a complex computer, and to locate the most complex and specialized banks of computers in the periphery, with the basic functional mechanisms in between.

THE POST-NATAL DEVELOPMENT OF THE BRAIN

The fact that very little neuronal growth is possible in the brain capable of repairing injuries, has led to the assumption that little brain growth of significance occurs after birth. However, recently Altman (1967) and others have shown that this is not the case. At birth the human brain looks very different from the adult brain and continual neuronal growth goes on until the age of two. At birth the brain possesses the full complement of large pyramidal cells but the dendrites have only a few branches and the incoming axons likewise have sparse terminal arborizations. There is also lacking a full complement of small round cells. After birth new small round cells are formed by division of ependymal cells, and these cells migrate up into the cortex. When they pass a pyramidal cell they may put out an axon which attaches to that cell. The small cell may then continue its migration spinning out its axon behind it. The neurones themselves cannot divide, but the dendrites continue to grow to form extensive arborizations as do the incoming axons. Thus clearly adverse nutritional, or hormonal—including stress hormones—influences may have a permanent effect during the first two years of life by modulating this growth process.

## Some Basic Anatomy

In so far as the psychiatrist is dealing largely with functional changes in the brain, and even in organic lesions, with the functional consequences of such lesions (he does not for example have to know his way around the temporal lobe in order to remove a glioma or tie a bleeding artery), a 'black box' description of the parts of the brain concerned could suffice. For even in those organic lesions of the limbic system, such as Korsakoff's psychosis, it is sufficient to know there are haemorrhagic lesions in certain basic circuits, without being able to picture the exact shape or connections of the circuits concerned. Nevertheless some knowledge of what the black boxes actually look like is useful and of interest (Fig. 5). The *hippocampus* is a sheet of primitive cortex. It consists essentially of only three layers for its large pyramidal cells are packed into one dense layer and all their apical dendrites run in the same direction and their basal dendrites and axons in the other. This sheet is continuous on the lateral side with the cortex of the temporal lobe. On the medial side, it is capped by a small portion which becomes separated—the dentate gyrus, and then runs into the choroid plexus, the neurone-free true medial wall of the cerebral hemisphere. In its anterior half the hippocampus forms a wavy plate, the digitations, in the floor of the inferior horn of the lateral ventricle whereas the posterior half is rolled into the ventricle in the form of the familiar little sea-horse. The axons of the pyramidal cells collect on the ventricular surface as a sheet of white matter, the alveus, which in turn gives rise to the fornix. The fornix carries fibres in both directions to and fro between the hippocampus and the septal nuclei, hypothalamus and reticular formation. Another important connection comes from the adjacent temporal lobe cortex. These two projections go to different places, the former axons ending wrapped around the main trunk of the apical dendrites of the pyramidal cells and the latter going to the ends of the apical dendrites. The possible functional significance of this arrangement will be discussed later.

The *amygdala* consists of a collection of nuclei located in the roof of the inferior horn of the lateral ventricle in the depths of the anterior end (medial aspect) of the temporal lobe. On top its nuclei are continuous with temporal lobe cortex (in the vicinity of the uncus). It consists of two quite distinct portions. The medial and cortical nuclei are parts of the olfactory apparatus and the much larger lateral and basal nuclei are parts of the limbic system. There is a very widespread input to the amygdala from the surrounding temporal cortex as well as fibres running up from the septal area and hypothalamus. The output goes to the same locations. There is a particularly strong connection with the hypothalamus in the area of the medial forebrain bundle.

The *septal nuclei* consists of a slab of primitive cortex on the medial surface of the frontal lobe. It should not be confused with the largely neurone-free septam pellucidum. It has important connections with the hippocampus and amygdala upstream, the adjacent orbitofrontal cortex, and the hypothalamus and reticular formation downstream.

The anatomy of the *hypothalamus* is more familiar. It consists of a number of small nuclei densely packed in the lateral wall of the lower part of the third ventricle. The fornix forms a prominent tract running through it to terminate in the mamillary body, and the tract of Vicq d'Azyr forms another running from the mamillary body to the anterior nucleus of the thalamus. The important medial forebrain bundle runs in an anterior posterior direction through the lateral side of the hypothalamus.

The *reticular formation* consists of two portions. The part in the brain stem surrounds the central canal of medulla, pons and midbrain and the cells receive a very widespread input. The sensory incoming fibres send a collateral branch into the reticular formation and many fibres run down from the cortex. A large input from hippocampus, amygdala, septal nuclei and hypothalamus runs to the so-called 'limbic area' of the reticular formation in the midbrain. The output runs to the entire cerebral cortex, as well as to all the hypothalamic nuclei, the septum, hippocampus and amygdala, as well as a projection to lower centres and spinal cord. The thalamic reticular formation consists of certain nuclei in the midline, and the diffuse neurones in between the larger more specialized nuclei (reticular nucleus). This is connected to the rest of the reticular formation, the other thalamic nuclei and the cerebral cortex.

The *limbic circuits*. The above account makes it clear that the limbic system is arranged in a series of circuits. One is the famous Papez circuit, named after one of the originators of our thinking about the functions of the limbic system. This runs—hippocampus—fornix—mamillary body—anterior nucleus of the thalamus—cingulate gyrus—cingulum—hippocampus. Another important circuit runs hippocampus—fornix (or direct route)—septal nuclei—hypothalamus—reticular formation—cortex—hippocampus. The amygdala circuits are very similar except that the stria terminalis (or again the direct route) is used in place of the fornix. This circuit formation is shown in Figure 1 and is consonant with the required layout of a central integrating and meta organizational mechanism.

Thirty years ago 'central integration' was regarded as a function of the cortex and only of the cortex. Hughlings Jackson's doctrine of levels indicated that all 'mental' functions, which were clearly of the highest level, must be a function of the cortex. The information was supposed to be fed into the sensory cortex whence it was fed to the association cortex, perhaps directly or via the specific thalamic nuclei. Here all the higher mental functions took place and the result was fed to the motor cortex and action and behaviour resulted. The limbic system was known in those days as the rhinencephlon and its function was thought to be concerned with the sense of smell.

Then in 1942 Moruzzi and Magoun discovered the function of the reticular formation, which acts, as it were, as the major switching mechanism in the brain, turning on and turning off the entire cortex, and through its thalamic portion, selected regions of the cortex. Thus it subsumes the functions of the cerebral basis of consciousness and selective attention (see Chapter XVII, Vol. I).

More recently, people have come to realize that the limbic system is an essential part of the cerebral mechanisms underlying memory formation, conditioned reflexes, emotional reactions, motivation and in fact all the basic mechanisms controlling behaviour. Moreover the realization has grown that this kind of function cannot be localized in any rigid sense. For any one particular function, the laying down of permanent memories for example, the integrated activity of many different nuclei, cortical centres and tracts may be necessary, the

L

removal or destruction of any one of which may disrupt the entire mechanism. Therefore the results of ablation experiments need to be interpreted with caution. To use Gregory's simile—if we remove a valve from a radio set, a melancholy wail may result—but the function of that valve is not to suppress the wail.

The next section will deal with the functional anatomy of various psychological functions.

## The Anatomy of Memory

It has been known for many years that Korsakoff's psychosis is associated with haemorrhagic lesions in the mamillary bodies, mid-brain reticular formation and hippocampus. Thus memory formation must in some way be a function of these structures. Memory itself is of two varieties, *primary memory* which is effervescent and attention dependent, the kind of memory we use for dialling telephone numbers after looking them up in the book, and developing from this, *permanent memory*. The main lesion in Korsakoff's psychosis is the inability to turn the former into the latter. Meissner (1968) has recently made an important analysis of the basic lesion in Korsakoff's psychosis. He classifies normal memory function into three parts.

1. *Primary memory*, which can relate $n$ elements of a simple input so long as $n$ is not greater than 2. An item can only spend a limited time in this slot and must either be transferred to the secondary memory or be erased by the never-ceasing flood of sensory input.

2. *Secondary memory*. The new input considered important is transferred here and consolidated by rehearsal. The storage depends on a complex coding and integrating mechanism involving a sequential organization of the efficient laying down and recall of complex memories. Complex items can be stored in secondary memory but their recall depends on the effective operation of the sequencing mechanisms. Thus secondary memory is not a place—not a simple pigeon-hole where memories are stored—but it is a function of the memory stores plus the complex sequencing mechanisms that put in and take out specific memories.

3. *Tertiary memory*. Elements in the tertiary mechanism have achieved a level of sequential integration and consolidation such that active recall does not need any sequential reconstruction. The only input into the tertiary memory is via the secondary memory.

The function destroyed in Korsakoff's psychosis is (2) the sequencing devices that allow memory to be consolidated in the permanent memory store. Material in this store is not affected by the lesion, but no new material can be added.

Likewise the primary memory is still intact.

Now it is likely that the primary memory is a function of the primary sensory cortex and the permanent memory banks would seem to be diffusely distributed throughout the cortex perhaps stored on holographic or holophonic principles. But the main brain work would appear to be concerned with the secondary memory. Although the lesions in the limbic system that produce the common kind of Korsakoff's psychosis are secondary to vitamin deficiencies in alcoholism, the syndrome can also occur following bilateral vascular lesions of the hippocampus alone. Thus the human data suggests that the hippocampus is particularly concerned in this function. Animal data is more equivocal. It is difficult to think up a behavioural task that the animal must learn whose disruption can unequivocally be attributed to the disruption of memory formation. In the case of the laboratory animals we do not have the verbal reports that tell us why the subject is no longer pressing the lever or traversing the maze properly. The task may be interfered with in a number of possible ways.

For example, a great number of experiments have been conducted where both hippocampi have been removed and the resulting defect investigated. Stepien, Cordeau and Ramussen (1960) noted that many tests for 'recent memory' used previously really did not test recent memory at all. So they tested monkeys with a test, Konorski's compound stimuli test, that they claimed really did so. In this the monkey is presented with two stimuli, e.g., two discs of different colour—Sx and Sy—presented consecutively with a five-second gap in between. The meaning of the compound stimulus is given by whether the two are the same or different. That is the animal can be trained to associate Sx followed by Sy with 'food' and the sequence Sx–Sx with 'no food' and to respond accordingly. Hippocampal ablations abolished the ability to perform this task although it did not affect the animal's ability to perform well on tasks of equal complexity where there was no need to hold one stimulus for a period of time in order to compare with a second in order to determine the meaning of the stimulus. However, as Douglas (1967) pointed out in an important review, many similar experiments indicate that a basic difficulty for the animal with a hippocampal ablation is to *inhibit* a previously learned response. If for example a rat is taught that red means 'food' and blue means 'pain' and then these signals are reversed, the lesioned rat will go on reacting as though 'red = food' and 'blue = pain' and finds it very difficult to reverse his responses, although his learning capacity in the other learning tasks of equal complexity but not requiring response reversal is not affected. Now, it was further pointed out that in Konorski's compound stimulus task the monkey must inhibit the correct response to 'Sx + Sx' in order to emit the correct response to 'Sx + Sy' if the latter stimulus is presented. Moreover a check of the original data of Stepien et al. (1960)

revealed that the errors were all of commission and none of omission, that is the animal responded to too many negative signals (Sx + Sx) but did not miss any positive ones, suggesting that it could remember the first stimulus alright to compare with the second but could not inhibit the unwanted response. This interpretation was confirmed by Correll and Scoville (1965) who used a different task—the delayed matching test—which does not entail the inhibition of a previously learned response.

In this test the monkey is shown a coloured thread and some seconds later two threads and he is rewarded for touching the matching thread. Hippocampal lesions do not affect the ability to do this task.

However, other tests suggested that the learning disability following hippocampal lesions was really due to an excessive emotional response to frustration (Rabe and Haddad, 1968): or because an important function of the hippocampus is to categorize sensory data (Wincour and Salzen, 1968), or to adjust the motivational state (Crossman and Mountford, 1964).

However, a most important factor was pointed out by Drachman and Ommaya (1964), which was that the animal psychologists and the clinicians were using the word 'short-term memory' in different ways. The former were really studying 'primary memory' in Meissner's sense whereas Korsakoff's psychosis is a defect in laying down permanent memories. In a later paper (Drachman and Arbit, 1966), this group showed that patients with bilateral hippocampal lesions had a normal digit span (memory for digits presented only once) but their total digit storage capacity (for digits repeated up to 20 times) was 8·6 as compared with a normal of 20.

Of course the hippocampus may have a number of functions. It is known for example to maintain a tonic inhibitory control on the hypo-thalamic–pituitary stress mechanisms. Moreover these apparent functions may derive from a common more basic function.

The wiring diagram of the hippocampus referred to briefly above shows that the main input from the environment (cortex) runs to the ends of the apical dendrites of the pyramidal cells, whereas the main input from the hypothalamus, perhaps signalling the visceral state of the organism, e.g. 'hungry', 'food just arrived in stomach', etc., runs to the main shaft of these dendrites. It is also known that the former input cannot fire the hippocampus cells by itself but needs concommitant activity in the latter input. Thus this wiring pattern suggests that the hippocampus could act as a valve. The processed pattern of neural impulses coding the state of the external environment could be fed from the sensory cortices, via the temporal lobe cortex to end on the tips of the apical dendrites of the hippocampal pyramids.

Incorporation in the permanent memory requires that the pattern coding a particular experience can pass this valve, and this can only occur if a signal is also received from the hypothalamus coding 'pain' or 'pleasure' (or negative or positive reinforcement). As the latter always come after the former, some complexity in the hippocampal circuits may be interpreted as providing delay circuits from the former.

Electrical stimulation of the hippocampus does not yield any information of interest, largely because of its very low epileptogenic threshold and the consequent ease of provoking temporal lobe seizures.

### THE STORAGE OF PERMANENT MEMORY

If we now turn to the cellular level, there has been much work in recent years on the problem of what can be the physiochemical change in brain neurones that carries the permanent memory trace. The theory that was generally accepted until recently ran something like this. Short term memory is based on feed-back loops and closed circuits forming nerve nets in the cortex around which the pattern of impulses representing a stimulus continue to circulate for some seconds. Permanent memory storage depends somehow on the change of properties of individual synapses, so that a synapse frequently used becomes more effective in firing its neurone or possibly new synapses may grow under such conditions. The effects of E.C.T. on recent memory was regarded as evidence for the former and phenomena like post-tetanic potentiation as evidence for the latter. However, this theory has recently been severely criticized. It has been pointed out that mere repeated use of a circuit leads not to learning but to habituation and so no theory of learning is any good unless it provides an explanation for the mechanism of reinforcement. Secondly it has been shown (Nielson and Fleming, 1968) that the memory loss due to E.C.T. is an example of state specific learning and is not due to wiping out circulating patterns of nerve impulses. One effect of E.C.T. on the brain is to raise its threshold for direct electrical stimulation some fivefold and this takes some four days to return to normal. If this change in brain excitability is controlled for by using previous E.C.T. so that the *learning* occurs at the same state of brain excitability as the *recall*, then E.C.T. does not lead to any amnesia at all.

Recently attention has been directed to possible chemical mechanisms underlying the formation of the permanent memory trace. It has been shown that protein synthesis is necessary in that inhibitors of protein synthesis such as acetoxycycloheximide, if present in the brain at the time the stimulus is received, or for up to five minutes afterwards, can inhibit permanent, but not recent, memory formation. If a synapse is frequently fired, the presynaptic neurone will synthesize more of the enzymes synthesizing the transmitter (say acetylcholine) by the usual feedback control. The increased activity of the postsynaptic neurone will also lead to alterations in local protein synthesis. But this process by itself, for reasons we saw above, would not lead to learning, rather to habituation.

There is now a possibility that the mechanisms underlying learning are chemically coded. The arrival of positive reinforcement in the brain may be signalled by the widespread release of a particular transmitter. Poschel and Ninteman (1963) have suggested that the positive reward mechanism uses noradrenaline and it has been suggested that the negative reward mechanism is based on excessive release of acetylcholine. The bulk of the noradrenergic neurones in the brain have their cell bodies in the locus coerulus in the medulla and pons. From here the axons sweep up in the medial forebrain bundle to be distributed all over the brain. The serotonin-containing neurones are likewise concentrated in the raphe nuclei in the pons and medulla and their axons pursue a similar course. One of the actions of noradrenaline and serotonin may be to modulate the firing of cholinergic synapses. The following mechanism may be proposed. The normal traffic of information in the brain may be carried by non-aminergic transmitters such as acetylcholine or various amino acids. Positive reinforcement may be signalled by the widespread release of noradrenaline and perhaps serotonin, in that any neurones active at the time will be rendered more effective by some biochemical mechanism initiated by these chemicals. Likewise the excessive release of acetylcholine mediating painful responses will tend to make the target neurones less likely to fire next time. This action of the aminergic transmitters may be mediated by stimulation of protein synthesis in the target synapses and it would explain why lack of these transmitters would lead to the manifold symptoms of depression (see Chapter XV). The lack of the positive reward signalling transmitters would lead to feelings of depression, lack of desire and motivation, and poor learning capacity. The link with sleep mechanisms would be based on the postulated role of 5HT and noradrenaline-containing neurones in sleep and the suggested role of sleep in brain protein synthesis. Depressed patients lose their appetite but do not become thirsty—the brain mechanisms controlling the former are adrenergic and the latter cholinergic. The topic of the chemical anatomy of the brain will be returned to later.

These amines are also closely related to mood (see Chapter IX, Vol. II) In addition norepinephrine is widely released in the brain during rage reactions. Eleftheriou and Boehlke (1967) have shown that the level of monamine oxidase activity increases for one to two days in the brain of mice which have been defeated in fights with trained fighter mice. This suggests that the increased enzyme has been induced to deal with the excess amines produced. Observations of profound psychiatric importance have been made on the effects of altering the levels of these hormones in pregnant rats. Severe stress (conditioned anxiety, overcrowding, or injections of adrenaline) lead to permanent changes in the later behaviour of their offspring, which became less emotional and fearful. Injections of hydrocortisone or noradrenaline on the other hand, resulted in more fearful and emotional offspring.

## THE AMYGDALA AND ITS ROLE

One of the features of the Klüver-Bucy Syndrome is the tameness and loss of aggression induced in the animals. Likewise stimulation of the amygdala can induce aggressive outbursts, as well as widespread autonomic reactions. These reactions seem to stem from the major role of the amygdala in the higher control of the hypothalamus. Egger and Flynn (1963) used placid laboratory cats who normally took no notice of a live mouse placed in the cage. Electrical stimulation of the lateral hypothalamus led to an immediate lethal attack on the mouse. Simultaneous stimulation of the basal nucleus of the amygdala inhibited this response whereas stimulation of the dorsolateral part of the lateral nucleus facilitated it. The 'rage-aggression-defence' reaction is not organized solely from the amygdala but seems to involve a circuit that includes the hypothalamus and reticular formation.

The amygdala also seems to play a role in learning and conditioned reflex formation. A major input to the amygdala comes from the viscera and stimulation in humans gives rise to a large variety of visceral sensations as well as autonomic responses. Experiments have shown that the amygdala is concerned in mechanisms determining the reinforcing value of stimuli. Animals with lesions in the amygdala find it difficult to discriminate between positive and negative stimuli. More subtle effects were noted by Schwartzbaum (1960). Monkeys, trained to press levers for food reward, will normally press a lever more quickly to get a large reward than a small one. Monkeys with lesioned amygdalae show much less of this modulation. Thus the amygdala would seem to be the main centre feeding visceral data into the limbic circuits informing the brain as to the motivational state of the organism, i.e. 'hungry', 'satiated', 'arrival of food in stomach' or 'pain in paw', etc.).

The amygdala is also a part of the reward mechanism in that it is a positive reward centre in Old's technique. These positive reward areas are quite extensive in the brain and include the amygdala, septum and hypothalamus, particularly the area of the medial forebrain bundle. Negative areas (whose local stimulation is adversive) include the posterior hypothalamus and the reticular formation.

## THE SEPTUM

Lesions of the septum induce in both humans and animals a characteristic syndrome—emotional irritability with outbursts of aggression.

This effect seems to be mediated via the hippocampus. The important 'visceral' inflow to the latter passes via the septal cells, and the well-known theta rhythm depends on the septal cells as pacemakers. Thus the septum normally would appear to exert a tonic calming effect on behaviour, mediated via the hippocampus and the pituitary-adrenal stress mechanism. This irritability is abolished by subsequent lesions of the amygdala, suggesting that the symptom is due to the overactivity of the latter.

However, one cannot conclude from this that the primary function of the septum is emotional control. Evidence suggests that it cooperates with the hippocampus in motivation mechanisms, response inhibition and evaluation of reinforcement contingencies.

THE ROLE OF THE HYPOTHALAMUS

The more familiar functions of the hypothalamus are concerned with autonomic, homeostatic and metabolic processes, however it also plays an essential role in higher nervous processes. Primitively organized and relatively undifferentiated patterns of behaviour can be organized by the hypothalamus and reticular formations alone. These patterns are elaborated and integrated by the limbic system and in turn are modulated by finer cortical control. Thus the hypothalamus may be concerned with reorganizing, recoding and redistributing instructions received from the amygdala and hippocampus in terms of 'fright', 'flee', 'eat', 'approach gingerly' into the appropriate outflow of sympathetic, parasympathetic and pituitary-adrenal signals for such behaviour. There is no sympathetic/parasympathetic differentiation in the amygdala or hippocampus.

The hypothalamus also plays an important role in learning and conditioned reflex formation. Lesions can lead to disruption of a conditioned reflex leaving the unconditioned reflex intact. Moreover the hypothalamus can exert direct control over motor responses. MacDonnell and Flynn (1966) have shown that touching the lip of a cat, which does not normally lead to any marked response, results in rapid jaw opening if applied during hypothalamic stimulation. Touching the muzzle leads to a head turning response under similar circumstances.

ROLE OF THE LIMBIC, MIDBRAIN AND THALAMIC AREAS

The more familiar functions of the reticular formation are concerned with consciousness (see Chapter XVII). However, the midbrain limbic area has other important functions concerned with learning, conditioned reflexes and limbic activities in general. It is a part of the 'rage-fear' mechanism. Recent memory is disrupted by stimulation. For example if a rat receives an electric shock at its food cup and then the reticular formation is stimulated, it immediately returns to the cup. Stimulation can abolish one conditioned reflex and facilitate another. The effects of lesions are hard to evaluate owing to the coma that results from extensive lesions.

The thalamic reticular formation is also closely concerned with conditioned reflex formation. Stimulation will evoke a conditioned response but only if the relevant drive is present. Furthermore the particular response evoked can depend on which drive is present. Kopa, Szabo and Grastyan (1962) trained cats in a conditioned avoidance response. If the nucleus centrum medianum was stimulated while the cat was on an electrified grid expecting shock, it became agitated and restless and the avoidance reflex was activated. On the other hand if this nucleus was stimulated whilst the animal was on the bench where it had never been shocked, it curled up and went to sleep.

The dorso-medial nucleus, familiar to psychiatrists as the target for thalamotomy and leucotomy (when its connections with the frontal lobe are severed) is an adversive area in Old's sense. Lesions in the anterior thalamic nuclei can induce altered states of consciousness or a marked reduction in the emotional response to noxious stimuli. This links in with Papez' theory that the circuit which bears his name, and of which this nucleus is a part, is concerned with the higher control of emotion.

ROLE OF THE LIMBIC CORTEX

In between the primitive cortex of the hippocampus, septum and the amygdala (cortical nucleus) and the neocortex proper, there extends a zone of intermediate or juxtallocortex, which has important limbic functions. Its major parts are the cingulate gyrus, the hippocampal gyrus and the orbito-insular-temporal cortex (which covers the insula in the depths of the lateral fissure, the orbital surface of the frontal lobe and the uncal region of the temporal lobe). Stimulation of these regions leads to a wide variety of visceral responses, e.g. changes in blood pressure, gastric motility, pupillary responses, piloerection, salivation, etc. Stimulation of the anterior cingulate region gives inhibition of all spontaneous movement and sleep.

The cingulate region seems to be concerned with the higher control of emotional responses and particularly with the motor and visceromotor aspects of emotion, as though it represented a sort of visceromotor cortex. Another view (Kimble and Gostnell, 1968) is that the cingulate cortex is primarily concerned in organizing temporal sequences of complex behaviour patterns. The most convincing evidence comes from the studies carried out by Slotnick (1967) who studied the effects of anterior cingulate lesions on maternal behaviour. The operated rats showed all the normal items of maternal behaviour but they were carried out in an irregular and confused manner. Pups were carried in and out of the cage and frequently dropped anywhere. Little nursing was done and one or two pups might be fed but the rest were ignored. The mothers spent much of their time sniffing about the cage. The defect did not seem to be due to indifference but to inappropriate although well-motivated responses to pups and nesting material.

## THE ANATOMY OF THE CONDITIONED REFLEX

A good way to study the role of brain structures in behaviour is to follow the development of a conditioned reflex with intracerebral recordings. The path taken by a sensory input in the brain can be followed either by tracing the resulting evoked potentials or by putting a tracer label on the stimulus. This may be done by using a flickering light as the conditioned stimulus. The resulting cerebral activity can be traced for it will 'follow' the flicker frequency. When a wholly novel stimulus is presented the arousal reaction takes place. The input must constantly be scanned by its sensory cortex and if a novel stimulus (S) is detected a signal is sent to the reticular formation which switches on all the relevant computers in an attempt to further categorize S. This is shown in the E.E.G. by widespread cortical and E.E.G. desynchroniza-tion and the evoked potentials are large and distributed widely over the cortex. The amplitude of the later secondary waves are more closely related to the significance of S than is the amplitude of the primary wave. Using a flickering light as the CS, John and Killam (1959) were able to show following in the lateral geniculate, superior colliculus, visual cortex and hippocampus. A little following also occurred in the reticular formation, septum and amygdala. If the S is repeated without reinforce-ment, these responses quickly habituate and disappear in the reverse order, i.e. amygdala first and geniculate body last.

During the initial responses to a new S the animal evinces the 'arousal response'. It turns its head towards S, pricks up its ears and scans the neighbourhood, behaviour designed to gain the maximum information about S. This response is organized by the reticular forma-tion. During this phase the thalamic reticular formation becomes pro-gressively more active and serves to switch on selective areas of the cortex that turn out to be specifically concerned with S and to switch off those areas not so concerned. This is accompanied by a diminution and change of form of the evoked potentials outside the primary projection area concerned.

If, however, S is now reinforced by associating it with say food or shock, it evokes anew behavioural arousal and cortical desynchroniza-tion. Activity now appears strongly in the reticular formation–septum–hippocampus complex but not, with an avoidance response, in the amygdala. As soon as the conditioned reflex is established these potentials die away and a new rhythm, at 40 c per s (Hz), appears in the amygdala.

In another experiment the animal was trained to associate 'food' with a 10 c per s flash and 'no food' with 6 c per s. The animal then received a long series of 6 c per s to which it habituated. This was suddenly switched to 10 c per s. At this moment the new 'environmental' rhythm appeared in the visual cortex and midbrain reticular formation but the old 6 c per s rhythm still appeared in the hippocampus and thalamic reticular formation. As soon as the animal 'woke up' to the new situation and responded correctly the 'internal' rhythm switched to 10 c per s. There is some evidence that food reflexes and avoidance reflexes are handled differently by these mechanisms.

Thus the limbic system is involved in the mechanisms establishing conditioned reflexes and there is evidence that it can mediate a pattern representing what the organism is expecting, as though it was carrying some sort of taped programme which was directing behaviour. Behaviour is only changed when there is a mismatch between this programme and the sensory input. The wiring diagram of the hippocampus presented above suggests how it could act as a matching device between a circulating pattern of impulses representing the real environment and another representing the appropriate (expected) environment for the pattern of behaviour being emitted at that time. It is of psychiatric interest that the 40 c per s rhythm of the amygdala is evoked under conditions of stress and difficulty and it may be associated with the rapid switching on of the pituitary-adrenal stress mechanism mediated by the amygdala.

THE CHEMICAL ANATOMY OF THE BRAIN

It has been known for a long time that there are very important chemical differences between different neurones in the brain. The work of Weiss, Gaze and others on the regeneration of cut nerves in amphibia indicates that cut sensory fibres will grow back to their proper terminals in the brain even if the eye is put back upside down. Thus in the developing embryo the nerves make the correct connections because they carry a chemical code on their surfaces which entail that the nerve endings can only make a synapse with the correct neurones that carry on their surfaces the complementary code. Since the surface of the neurones is covered with mucopolysaccharides it is thought that this code may take the form of a complex mosaic of mucopolysaccharides attached to the protein surface of the neurone. These mosaics are genetically determined and ensure that the basic wiring of the brain is carried out correctly.

Moreover, this pattern may be subjected to dynamic influences. We saw earlier how the formation of the permanent memory trace is dependent on protein synthesis and how the factors that determine which synapses are 'successful' and go to form permanent engrams and which become reabsorbed may be chemical. However, one great difficulty in all such theories is that they lead inevitably to a 'connectivist' theory, i.e. that the memory is based on the re-evocation of activity in a particular set of neurones, as in an ordinary computer the memory is located in a fixed stack of units.

However, there is a good deal of evidence (Lashley, 1934; John, 1967) that memory is stored in the brain in a statistical manner, that is it is stored in the form that requires a particular pattern of nerve cells to be fired and not any one set of particular cells, i.e. the pattern can be evoked in any of the neurones in the memory bank and as long as the pattern is the same, the same memory will be evoked. This can be based on a holographic or holophonic mode of operation (Longuett-Higgins, 1968; Longuett-Higgins, 1970). Clearly it is very difficult to base such a theory on the facilitation of events at particular synapses. It can be concluded that we are still a long way away from understanding the cerebral basis of memory.

In classical anatomy, neurones were linked together in a class because their cell bodies were located in the same place. The proper subject of discourse was held to be the properties of the nucleus. For example the anterior nucleus of the thalamus might be ascribed certain functions based on its connections and the effects of ablation, stimulation, clinical lesions, etc. Currently, however, a tendency has grown to link neurones into functional units on the basis of their chemical properties. The development of fluorescence histochemical techniques by the Swedish School has transformed our notions about the relation between structure and function.

In the section on learning, the distribution of aminergic neurones in the brain was described and a possible link between them and the mechanism of memory was suggested.

The main cholinergic patterns so far delineated in the brain, are the arousal system, and the septal-hippocampal pathway. However, the main inputs into the hippocampus (from the temporal lobe and from the hippocampus of the other side) are not cholinergic. The cholinergic arousal system consists of the dorsal tegmental pathway which runs from the midbrain tegmentum to the thalamus (particularly the geniculate bodies, the thalamic reticular formation and the anterior nucleus) and the ventral tegmental pathway which runs to the lateral hypothalamus and the basal forebrain area which is rich in cholinergic neurones. Other cholinergic pathways connect the globus pallidus, caudate and all forebrain cortical areas; and the posterior and lateral hypothalamus with the septum and amygdala. The cholinergic cells in these areas closely resemble the cells of the reticular formation and

Shute and Lewis (1967) call the entire system the 'ascending cholinergic reticular system'. Stimulation of a sensory nerve or of the reticular formation leads to widespread release of acetylcholine from the cortical surface, but to an even greater release of glutamic acid, which thus may also be involved in cortical arousal. The main action of morphine and related compounds is to inhibit the release of acetylcholine from the presynaptic terminal. This fits in with the theory that pain is a function of excessive release of acetylcholine.

The contrasting role of noradrenaline and acetylcholine is also shown in the mechanisms controlling eating and drinking. Carbachol injected into the dorsomedial and lateral hypothalamus induces drinking, and norepinephrine in the same areas induces eating, indicating that the former is controlled by a cholinergic and the latter by an adrenergic mechanism. Likewise carbachol injected into other hypothalamic areas induces a general fearful reaction. Over-stimulation of arousal mechanisms generally leads to fear and rage reactions, whereas adrenaline induces sleep. Injections of carbachol into the dorsomedial nucleus has been reported to induce exploratory behaviour (arousal) whereas adrenergic stimulation gives playful behaviour.

The role of the dopaminergic neurones in the corpus striatum and substantia nigra and their relation to Parkinsonism is well known. In all these formulations the possibility of species differences should be borne in mind. In some animals, for example, catecholamines lower and 5HT raises the body temperature; in other animals these effects are reversed.

## FEATURES OF THE MICROANATOMY OF THE BRAIN OF RELEVANCE TO PSYCHIATRY

Healthy mental function depends on the proper operation of the 10 billion neurones of the brain and so the psychiatrists should know some general principles of importance for the maintenance of this function. Many psychiatrists, when thinking about the brain, tend to picture it in static terms as though the neurones and their axons and dendrites had a permanent structure like the wires and transistors of a computer. However the reality is rather different and the entire brain is in a perpetual state of metabolic flux. The basic structural components—proteins and lipids—are continually being renewed and broken down. The DNA in the nucleus is continually forming RNA by the action of the enzyme RNA polymerase, and the RNA exported to the cytoplasm in turn gives rise to proteins by the action of the ribosomes. This protein moves down the axon in a steady stream—the 'axon flow' which includes the enzymes that will form the transmitter. These enzymes synthesize the transmitter which is then stored inside special vesicles which may be seen on electron micrographs. When the transmitter is released following an action potential, the vesicles are disrupted. The synthetic enzymes in turn are also broken down by intracellular proteases to be replaced by the protein synthetic machinery. This protein has also to supply the membrane of the cell which constitutes its major component.

The cytoplasm of the neurone is packed with special organelles, each of which is a specialized chemical factory. The mitochondria contain the enzymes supplying the energy for the rest of the cell. The inner surface of each membrane is packed with organized arrays of enzymes. A single mitochondrion will have about 15,000 complexes of respiratory chain enzymes, each complex containing a dozen or more separate enzymes. These enzymes catalyse both respiration and phosphorylation. Mitochondria contain their own DNA and the replication of mitochondria takes place independently of the cell nucleus, the local DNA coding for the local enzymes. The theory has been advanced that the mitochondria were originally free living bacteria that very early on in the evolution of single celled organisms became engulfed in the cytoplasm and took on a symbiotic relationship with their hosts, ending up finally as a part of the structure. The ergastoplasm (or Nissl substance) is composed of banks of ribosomes lined up in the walls of systems which are continuous with the microtubule system of the neurone that may play a role in the transport of macromolecules. The Golgi apparatus is now known to be a specialized factory for the production of glycoproteins and similar substances.

The part of the neurone of the most interest to psychiatrists is the synaptic region, as many psychiatric disorders seem to be connected with malfunctions of transmitter function. The end of an axon usually forms a small swelling—the bouton termineau—which is applied closely to the side of the dendrite, cell body, or even the preterminal axonal region of the post-synaptic neurone. Each of these 3 portions contains special structural features. The axon terminal is packed with synaptic vesicles and with mitochondria. The former contain the transmitter bound to some macromolecular complex. These vesicles are of two varieties, 'dense core' vesicles thought to contain aminergic transmitters and smaller vesicles with clear centres, thought to contain acetylcholine and perhaps amino acid transmitters. The post-synaptic membrane often has specialized features, a subsynaptic 'fuzz', in some cases quite a complex 'subsynaptic apparatus' and many axons end on special projections from the post-synaptic membrane—the 'dendrite spine'.

Another assumption commonly made by psychiatrists is that one person's brain is very much like another's. This may be true in terms of gross anatomy, and even in terms of anatomy available to the microscope. But it is very possible that different personality types and structures may have as their biological basis different patterns of development of the anatomy of the brain at the macromolecular and chemical level. The key enzymes that determine patterns of behaviour have been shown to include the enzymes responsible for the synthesis and degradation of central transmitters and differences in the level of function of these enzymes, due perhaps to genetic and to environmental factors, may determine whether a person is prone to anxiety or to aggressive reactions, or his tolerance for stress and so on.

Thus anatomy is reaching down to further levels of resolution and is entering a phase in which the *structure* concerned is the macromolecular structure of neurochemical mechanisms in the brain underlying behaviour. Already molecules such as DNA have been photographed by electron microscopy and molecular models enable us to visualize and analyse the microstructure of the cell. For the structure of neurones as seen by the light and electron microscopes is nothing more than an overview of the seried and organized racks of structural macromolecules, each of which has a precise form. The patterns that these molecules take up in relation to their neighbours are determined by their physiochemical properties; shape, charge distribution, the precise location and orientation of binding groups, capacity to form lipophilic interactions and quantum chemical properties. These relationships in turn determine the shape of the membrane, of the enzymes, and of all the components of the cell which in their turn determine the shape, nature and function of the cell, all of which form a system of hierarchically arranged complexes or holons of almost incredible complexity.

## The Relevance of Functional Neuroanatomy to Clinical Psychiatry

It may be wondered how a knowledge of brain structure and function may be useful in everyday clinical psychiatry. One obvious field of application lies in an understanding of the symptomatology of organic conditions. The memory defect of Korsakoff's Psychosis becomes of greater interest when it is seen in its context of a defect of secondary memory than as an isolated symptom to be remembered as associated with a specific disorder. Likewise the manifold psychiatric disorders seen in epilepsy become intelligible in the context of ictal phenomena of the limbic system.

However it would also be of great value if our understanding of the functional psychoses could be similarly advanced. The main focus of current interest in these conditions lies in the field of synaptic biochemistry, depression being linked to a deficit of brain amines, particularly noradrenaline and serotonin and schizophrenia to some possible disorder whereby serotonin mechanisms are blocked by some endogenous psychotoxic substance. In this context the anatomical distribution of these aminergic neurones and their possible function becomes directly relevant.

The limbic system may be seen as largely concerned with the continuous sifting of the sensory inflow so that items of importance to the organism may be detected. Then a strategy must be developed for dealing with this item in terms of the immediate and long-term needs of the organism. If the biochemical mechanisms mediating these functions go awry, then functional breakdowns at different levels may be expected to result. We have reviewed earlier how the classical symptoms of depression, depressed mood, loss of interest in things, loss of appetite and drive, disturbed sleep, etc., can all be seen as secondary effects of decreased levels of the transmitters operative in the central mechanisms mediating positive reinforcement. Likewise, features of delirium, such as clouding of consciousness, may be seen as resulting from disturbances of the cholinergic arousal mechanisms. But the layout of the limbic system suggests answers to other kinds of question. For example it is legitimate to ask why depressed patients develop delusions. In clinical psychiatry this is merely represented as a basic fact about depressive illness for which no explanation is available. However, it is possible that these delusions may be generated by the disordered brain mechanisms, as follows. We have seen how the great integrated limbic circuits form the means of evaluating and integrating experience, evolving programmes directing behaviour and finally laying down relevant items in the permanent memory and discarding the irrelevant. We have also seen how the amygdala seems to be concerned largely with visceral phenomena and the hippocampus with the environment. Now the system may be supposed normally to work by the schemata (patterns of neuronal excitation), coming from the environment, generating the beliefs and emotional responses partly by virtue of the fact that the circuits of the amygdala and the hippocampus are so closely interwoven. Thus news that the person is ruined normally evokes a biochemical storm in the amygdala and hypothalamus that is the neural basis for an acute grief reaction. But if a similar biochemical storm is evoked by some metabolic lesion, 'depression-laden' abnormal schemata may be circulated around the limbic system and this causal mechanism comes to be operated in reverse so that the abnormal affects now generate the belief that a disaster has occurred of the type that would normally have led to the evocation of such effects. 'In other words the anatomical substrate for the close link between affect and belief may be in part the fact that the amygdala and the hippocampus share the great limbic circuits, that these circuits are responsible for blending affect and ideation into a conjoined programme for behaviour. Major upsets in the emotional system impose schemata on the ideational system that represent the kind of events that might have been expected to cause, in the normal course of events, feelings of despair and dejection. Minor upsets in the emotional system do not, as it were, spill over into the ideational system but once the threshold for overspill is reached delusions, and the vicious circle of depression that these delusions engender, develop' (Smythies, 1970).

If we turn to schizophrenia we can suggest that many of the disturbances are due to a strictly mechanical interference with normal mental processes. Very similar patterns of disruption can be found in the 'bad trips' induced by hallucinogenic drugs. The perceptual illusions so characteristic of both conditions would seem to be due to a fairly low level disruption of serotonergic sensory mechanisms, the hallucinations perhaps with cortically evoked disturbances, and the typical disorders of meaning and significance with temporal lobe and particularly limbic system disruption. Likewise the thought disorder of schizophrenia is of a kind to suggest that the endogenous toxins are literally disrupting the delicate mechanisms on which thought depends, presumably on circuits involving the speech areas, and basic limbic structures. These formulations are of course in no sense antagonistic to, or competitive with, formulations of the genesis of these disorders made at a psychological or a psychodynamic level—they are complementary. However, in the final analysis what we say and think and feel and do is determined *directly* by the physiochemical events in our brains and *indirectly* by the nature of the input into the system. However in terms of explanatory value different types of disorder require a different emphasis on different *levels* of explanation.

The neuroses are most readily understandable in psychological and psychodynamic terms and in physiological terms as a function of conditioning and learning theory. In the psychoses the emphasis shifts to a consideration of abnormal brain biochemistry and the disorders in the function of brain mechanism that result. The psychological aspect is still powerfully represented by the consideration that the brain is not programmed from birth but must learn its own basic rules on how to handle and deal with its own data. The organic disorders may be understood in terms of actual structural damage, epileptic foci, etc.

However, this is only a matter of emphasis. In all conditions many of these factors may play a significant role.

## REFERENCES

ALTMAN, J. (1967) In *The Neurosciences*. Edited by G. C. Quarton, T. Melnechuck & F. O. Schmitt. New York: Rockefeller University Press.

CORRELL, R. E. & SCOVILLE, W. B. (1965) Performance on delayed matching following lesions of medial temporal lobe structures. *Journal of Comparative and Physiological Psychology*, **60**, 360.

CROSSMAN, S. P. & MOUNTFORD, H. (1964) Learning and extinction during chemically induced disturbance of hippocampal functions. *American Journal of Physiology*, **207**, 1387.

DOUGLAS, R. J. (1967) The hippocampus and behaviour. *Psychological Bulletin*, **67**, 416.

DRACHMAN, D. A. & OMMAYA, A. K. (1964) Memory and the hippocampal complex. *Archives of Neurology*, **10**, 411.

DRACHMAN, D. A. & ARBIT, J. (1966) Memory and the hippocampal complex II. Is memory a multiple process? *Archives of Neurology*, **15**, 52.

EGGER, M. D. & FLYNN, J. P. (1963) Effects of electrical stimulation of the amygdala on hypothalamically elicited attack behaviour in cats. *Journal of Neurophysiology*, **26**, 705.

ELEFTHERIOU, E. & BOEHLKE, K. W. (1967) Brain monoamine oxidase in mice after exposure to aggression and defeat. *Science*, **155**, 1693.

JOHN, E. R. (1967) In *The Neurosciences*. Edited by G. C. Quarton, T. Melnechuck & F. O. Schmitt. New York: Rockefeller University Press.

JOHN, E. R. & KILLIAM, K. F. (1959) Electrophysiological correlates of avoidance conditioning in the cat. *Journal of Pharmacology and Experimental Therapeutics*, **125**, 252.

KIMBLE, D. P. & GOSTNELL, D. (1968) Role of cingulate cortex in shock avoidance behaviour of rats. *Journal of Comparative and Physiological Psychology*, **65**, 290.

KOPA, J., SZABO, I. & GRASTYAN, E. (1962) A dual behavioural effect from stimulating the same thalamic point with identical stimulus parameters in different conditional reflex situations. *Acta physiologica Academiae scientiarum hungaricae*, **21**, 207.

LASHLEY, K. S. (1934) Nervous mechanisms in learning. In *Handbook of General Experimental Psychology*. Edited by C. Murchison, Worcester, Mass: Clark University Press. pp. 456–496.

LONGUETT-HIGGINS, C. (1968) The non-local storage of temporal information. *Proceedings of the Royal Society, B*, **171**, 327.

LONGUETT-HIGGINS, C. (1970) Series of associative recall. *Quarterly Review of Biophysics*, **3**, 223–244.

MACDONNELL, M. F. & FLYNN, J. P. (1966) Control of sensory fields by stimulation of hypothalamus. *Science*, **152**, 1406.

MEISSNER, W. W. (1968) Learning and memory in the Korsakoff Syndrome. *International Journal of Neuropsychiatry*, **4**, 6.

NEILSON, H. C. & FLEMING, R. M. (1968) The effect of electroconvulsive shock and prior stress on brain amine levels. *Experimental Neurology*, **20**, 21.

POSCHEL, B. P. H. & NINTEMAN, F. W. (1963) Nor-epinephrine: a possible excitatory neurohormone of the reward system. *Life Sciences*, **1**, 782.

RABE, A. & HADDAD, R. K. (1968) Effect of selective hippocampal lesions in the rat on acquisition, performance, and extinction of bar pressing on a fixed ratio schedule. *Experimental Brain Research*, **5**, 259.

SCHWARTZBAUM, J. S. (1960) Changes in reinforcing properties of stimuli following ablation of the amygdaloid complex in monkeys. *Journal of Comparative and Physiological Psychology*, **53**, 388.

SHUTE, C. C. D. & LEWIS, P. R. (1967) The ascending cholinergic reticular system: neocortical, olfactory and subcortical projections. *Brain*, **90**, 497.

SLOTNICK, B. M. (1967) Disturbances of maternal behaviour in rat following lesions of the cingulate cortex. *Behaviour*, **29**, 204.

SMYTHIES, J. R. (1970) *Brain Mechanisms and Behaviour*. Oxford: Blackwell.

STEPIEN, L. S., CORDEAU, J. P. & RAMUSSEN, T. (1960) The effect of temporal lobe and hippocampel lesions on auditory and visual memory in monkeys. *Brain*, **83,** 470.

WINCOUR, G. & SALZEN, E. A. (1968) Hippocampal lesions and transfer behaviour in the rat. *Journal of Comparative and Physiological Psychology*, **65,** 303.

# Chapter XV

# TOPICS IN NEUROCHEMISTRY

## A. J. Dewar, D. Eccleston, H. W. Reading and P. J. Shields

### Energy Metabolism in the Central Nervous System

The second law of thermodynamics, a fundamental law of the physical universe, states that 'systems in isolation spontaneously tend towards states of greater disorganization'. This may be expressed mathematically as:

$$\Delta F = \Delta H - T \Delta S$$

where $\Delta F$ is the change in free energy, $\Delta H$ is the change in heat content or enthalpy, $T$ is the absolute temperature and $S$ is the degree of disorganization or entropy.

On the basis of this law, the existence of life would appear to be thermodynamically improbable. However, the above equation does imply that if free energy is supplied to a system the state of organization of that system will increase. The main property of living cells is that they are effective transducers of chemical potential energy into other forms of energy which can be used to maintain their organized structure. The cells of the human body are, from the chemical viewpoint, an unlikely collection of essentially unstable compounds dissolved in, or surrounded by, a salt solution of precisely controlled composition and maintained, generally, above the temperature of their surroundings. Each cell must expend chemical energy merely to prevent its disintegration. It follows that an organ of such organizational complexity as the human brain will require a plentiful supply of chemical energy in order to maintain its structural integrity. Over and above this, further energy is required for the performance of its endergonic physiological functions, synthetic processes, active transport systems, etc. It is not surprising, therefore, that the central nervous system has a high metabolic rate and accounts for approximately 10 per cent of the total energy expenditure of the whole body at rest. The oxygen consumption of the brain is nearly 25 per cent of the total oxygen consumption of the body at rest. The brain, like the rest of the body, obtains its chemical energy by the oxidation of foodstuffs and the capture of energy released in the form of high energy phosphate bonds in adenosine triphosphate (ATP).

The primary energy source of the central nervous system is glucose and in this the brain differs from other tissues which are able to utilize lipids and, to a lower extent, protein. There is little storage of either lipid or glycogen. Thus the metabolism of the brain cannot be sustained by its carbohydrate reserves and is consequently dependent on a constant blood-borne supply of glucose. Under normal conditions, the brain utilizes approximately 16 to 20 $\mu$mol glucose per g brain per h and cessation of the blood supply of glucose and oxygen results in irreversible brain damage within minutes.

In nutritional studies a commonly used index for estimating the proportion of fat and carbohydrate being utilized is the respiratory quotient (RQ).

$$RQ = \frac{\text{Volume of } CO_2 \text{ produced}}{\text{Volume of } O_2 \text{ consumed}}$$

The RQ for fat oxidation is 0·71 and that of carbohydrate oxidation 1·00. The RQ calculated for the adult brain is 0·99. Moreover, *in vivo* under normal conditions, the amount of oxygen consumed in the brain is equivalent to that of the glucose removed from the blood, as indicated by studies of the arteriovenous difference between the two substances.

The normal arterial blood glucose concentration is approximately 80 mg per 100 ml. In hypoglycemia, brain glucose consumption is reduced more than its oxygen utilization and the total $CO_2$ produced by the brain is increased to twice the basal level. Isotope experiments have shown that this increased $CO_2$ production is due to the oxidation of non-carbohydrate substrates, probably amino acids and lipid. As a result, hypoglycemia causes marked neurological manifestations including convulsions. Coma can result from insulin induced hypoglycemia where the blood glucose concentration can be as low as 8 mg per 100 ml. Under these conditions, the reduced production of ATP is inadequate for normal brain function.

Nervous tissue contains all the enzymes and metabolic intermediates of anaerobic and aerobic carbohydrate metabolism and is also able to utilize lipid and protein *in vitro*. The dependence of the brain on glucose as its primary energy source is due to the fact that the availability of other substrates is severely limited by the set of diverse homeostatic mechanisms known as the blood brain barrier. Whereas glucose has an unimpeded entry from the blood into the brain and rapidly reaches tissue levels adequate for maintaining normal metabolism, the entry of fructose, lactate, pyruvate, succinate and glutamate is restricted and tissue levels comparable to those achieved by glucose are not reached.

The manner in which the potential chemical energy of glucose is employed for the synthesis of ATP is broadly similar to that in other tissues and is achieved in three main stages. In the initial stage, glucose is converted to pyruvic acid in the cell cytoplasm by the glycolysis or Embden Meyerhof pathway. Although the glycolytic pathway is the main pathway of glucose utilization, the pentose phosphate pathway also functions in brain, but its relative significance is not clearly known. Its main function is to produce reduced co-enzymes for use in biosynthetic pathways. In the second stage, pyruvic acid is oxidized in the mitochondria to $CO_2$ via acetyl CoA and Kreb's tricarboxylic acid cycle. In the third stage, the electrons produced by the Kreb's cycle are provided for the electron transport chain (flavoprotein-cytochrome system) where they are used in the reduction of oxygen, coupled with the generation of ATP. This process is known as oxidative phosphorylation.

A general scheme of glucose metabolism in brain is shown in Figure 1. In the course of the complete oxidative breakdown of glucose to $CO_2$ and water, there is a net synthesis of 38 ATP molecules. Since each high energy bond has a bond energy of approximately 7600 calories (0·032 MJ) the 38 new bonds represent 288,800 calories (1·21 MJ). Since one molecule of glucose contains of the order of 686,000 calories (2·88 MJ), the capturing of 288,800 calories represents an efficiency of 42 per cent. In glycolysis, direct transfer of high energy phosphate from 1,3 diphosphoglyceric acid and phosphoenolpyruvate to ADP results in the formation of 2 ATP. Under anaerobic conditions, therefore, there is a net synthesis of 2 ATP molecules since glucose breaks into two triose molecules and 2 ATP molecules were used in the formation of glucose-6-phosphate and fructose-1, 6-diphosphate. Under aerobic conditions, however, the reduced co-enzyme nicotinamide adenine dinucleotide (NAD) produced in the oxidation of glyceraldehyde phosphate is re-oxidized through the flavoprotein-cytochrome system with the formation of 3 high energy bonds. Thus, the complete oxidation of one molecule of glucose to pyruvate results in a net gain of 8 ATP molecules. Further oxidation of pyruvate to $CO_2$ and water yields a further 15 molecules of ATP, i.e. a further 30 molecules per 1 molecule of glucose thus giving a total of 38 molecules of ATP formed in the complete oxidative process. The ATP produced by the tricarboxylic cycle are made by the reoxidation of reduced NAD, NADP and FAD (Flavine adenine dinucleotide) by the flavoprotein-cytochrome system, but ATP is also produced by reaction of ADP with GTP (Guanosine triphosphate) formed in the conversion of succinyl CoA to succinate.

Under normal conditions, the production of lactate is small (6 $\mu$mol per g brain per h), but under conditions of anaerobiosis or during convulsions, this can increase to as much as 400 $\mu$mol per g brain per h.

Anaerobic metabolism of glucose, yielding as it does a mere 2 molecules of ATP, cannot supply the energy requirements of normal cerebral function, and as a consequence, the brain is very dependent on the

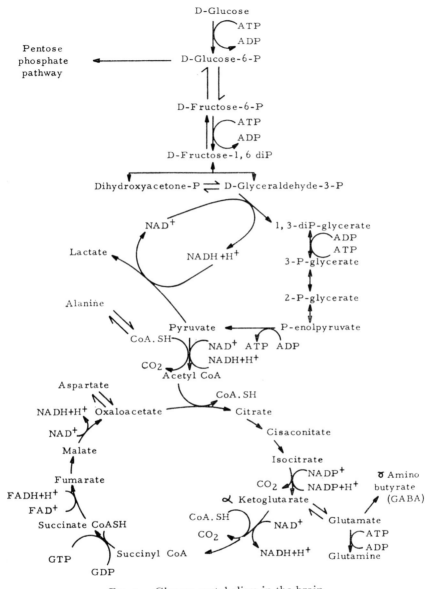

FIG. 1. Glucose metabolism in the brain.

efficient working of the tricarboxylic cycle. This dependence is reflected in the neurological dysfunctions which ensue on interference with its normal operation. Deficiency in thiamine, a co-factor in the conversion of pyruvate to acetyl CoA, has profound effects on the central nervous system as does niacin deficiency.

The metabolism of certain glucose metabolites is closely related to that of the glutamic acid group of amino acids. This group, glutamate, aspartate and gamma-aminobutyrate (GABA) have a special role in the CNS and account for 75 per cent of the free amino acids in the brain. They are found primarily in the grey matter associated with neuronal mitochondria. GABA is only found in nervous tissue and is believed to be a regulator of neuronal activity. Glutamate, by its energy dependent conversion to glutamine plays an important role in the detoxication of ammonia in the brain.

Aspartate and glutamate are glycogenic being readily and reversibly converted into oxaloacetate and $\alpha$ ketoglutarate by transamination reactions. These reactions may aid in regulating the concentration of metabolites entering the Krebs cycle. Another possible regulator of the Krebs cycle in the CNS is the metabolic sequence known as the 'GABA shunt' shown in Figure 2. This is a bypass around the citric acid cycle

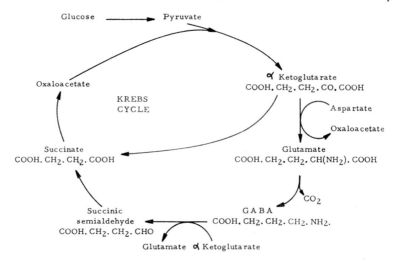

FIG. 2.   The GABA shunt.

from $\alpha$ ketoglutarate to succinate and is not found in other tissues since the enzyme catalysing the decarboxylation of glutamate to GABA is peculiar to the C.N.S. This enzyme, glutamate decarboxylase, like the transaminase enzyme, requires vitamin $B_6$ phosphate (pyridoxal phosphate) as a co-factor. The GABA shunt has been shown to take approximately 10 per cent of the total glucose turnover in guinea pig cortex.

The importance of these interrelationships between the dicarboxylic acids and glucose metabolism is emphasized by the deleterious effects resulting from vitamin $B_6$ deficiency. During $B_6$ deficiency, glutamate decarboxylase and transaminases are inhibited and seizures occur. Administration of pyridoxine antagonists like isoniazid and deoxypyridoxine have a similar effect. These induced seizures may be alleviated by the administration of GABA, thus suggesting that the seizures are primarily due to the dysfunction of glutamate decarboxylase. It is also interesting to note that glutamic acid restores hypoglycemic patients in insulin coma to consciousness at a lower blood sugar level than when glucose alone was used.

## THE BIOGENIC AMINES

The biogenic amines in brain are now in their third decade of intensive investigation. The literature involving these substances is now enormous and yet, from many points of view, especially that of function, their role is still speculative.

The term 'biogenic amines' refers to three aromatic amines found in brain, 5-hydroxytryptamine (5HT), dopamine (DA) and noradrenaline (NA). 5HT was isolated and characterized in brain by Amin, Crawford and Gaddum (1954). These workers were examining brain for its content of a polypeptide, substance P, for which they were using bioassay procedures for its estimation. The substance they isolated did not give the characteristic response of substance P, and after much painstaking work, was identified as 5HT. In the same laboratories, Vogt isolated NA from brain. Dopamine, on the other hand, was described by the group of Swedish workers headed by Carlsson.

Initial studies showed that these amines have fairly characteristic distributions. They were present mostly in central structures of brain, being low in neocortex. 5HT seemed to be particularly associated with brain stem and limbic system, NA with brain stem and hypothalamus, whilst DA was found mostly in the striatum. It remained for the Swedish workers to develop histochemical fluorescence methods to detail the cellular distribution of these amines. It was found that if the sections of brain were exposed to formaldehyde gas, the biogenic amines formed fluorescence complexes which could be examined with a microscope which used fluorescent light to illuminate the sections. The amines were then located in fine neuronal systems which were ubiquitously distributed in brain but whose cell bodies lay in central structures. A particular example was the 5HT-containing raphe nuclei found in the midbrain, whose cell bodies send axons both upwards to the cortex via a bundle of fibres in the lateral hypothalamus, the medial forebrain bundle, and downwards to the spinal cord. Similarly, dopamine neuron cell bodies lie in the substantia nigra and their terminals end particularly densely in the caudate nucleus.

### BIOSYNTHESIS

All three amines have very similar biosynthetic systems, all arising from amino acids and finally being decarboxylated to form amines.

## 5-hydroxytryptamine

The precursor amino acid of 5HT is tryptophan, a normal constituent of diet. Usually the major portion of this amino acid in the body is metabolized to other compounds such as kynurenine. Only one per cent of tryptophan forms 5HT, and of this, a large proportion is in the enterochromaffin cells of the gut. In brain, tryptophan is actively transported across the blood-brain barrier. The first enzymic step is that of 5-hydroxylation to another amino acid, 5-hydroxytryptophan (5HTP), (Fig. 3). This is the controlling enzyme in the synthesis of 5HT (see below) but is not saturated in brain, hence a large dose of tryptophan will lead to

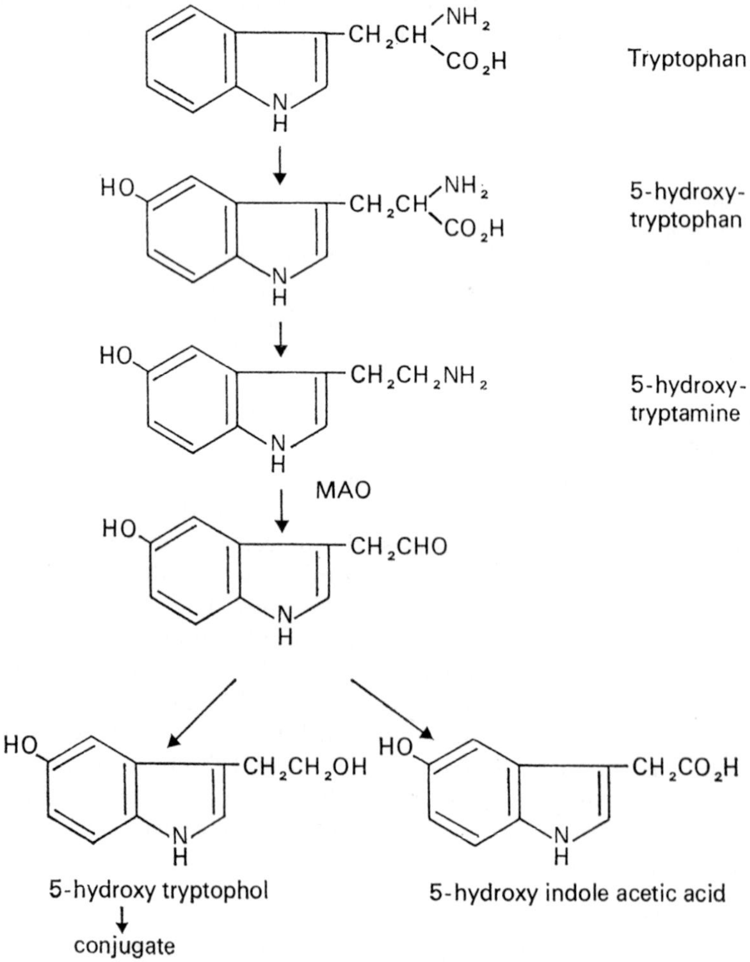

FIG. 3. 5HT metabolism in brain.

further formation of 5HT. The 5HTP produced is then decarboxylated to form 5HT. This appears to be taken up into storage particles where it is maintained against a concentration gradient probably complexed with ATP. It is envisaged that some of the 5HT leaks out into the cell, on to mitochondrial monoamine oxidase. This enzyme is responsible for the breakdown to the aldehyde, 5-hydroxyindole acetaldehyde. Here, theoretically, the pathway may divide with the formation of either 5-hydroxytryptophol or 5-hydroxyindolacetic acid (5HIAA). In brain, very little of the former exists, although it has been shown to occur in liver and its production to be increased with ethyl alcohol. 5HIAA is then the end product of 5HT metabolism in brain. Unlike NA, this is the only end product, and the 5HT which is released on nerve stimulation must also be broken down by oxidative deamination.

Monoamine oxidase itself is of some interest. There appear to be several isoenzymes which differ in their substrate specificity, and it has been shown (Collins et al., 1970), for example, that the iso-enzyme which has a high specificity for dopamine is found predominantly in the striatum, the region of brain particularly rich in that amine.

As has been pointed out, the end product of 5HT metabolism is 5HIAA. Methods for the determination of the turnover of 5HT (or indeed any of the biogenic amines) in brain in man are being sought. Urinary 5HIAA is unfortunately not representative, since it is also derived from 5HT metabolized in the gut. Ventricular and cisternal C.S.F. 5HIAA levels have been shown to mirror the concentration of this metabolite in brain and hence examination of lumbar C.S.F. in man for this end product has been performed in depressive illness. The concentration of 5HIAA has been found to be low in depression, and it has been concluded that 5HT turnover or release is low and possibly causative in this illness. One of the problems is that there is a gradient in the concentration of this metabolite from ventricle to lumbar C.S.F., presumably by comparison with animal experiments, because of an active transport mechanism to remove this metabolite, located in the choroid plexus of the 4th ventricle. Secondly, the concentration of 5HIAA in lumbar C.S.F. rises with age. At this stage, one cannot determine whether the changes reported in amine metabolism in this illness are primary and causing the illness or secondary to other changes which themselves precipitate depression.

*Dopamine*

Tyrosine is the starting material for the synthesis of both dopamine and NA. The first step is the formation of dihydroxyphenylalanine (DOPA) by the enzyme tyrosine hydroxylase which is present in the cytoplasm of the neuron (Fig. 4). DOPA is then decarboxylated, again by a soluble enzyme, dopa decarboxylase, to dopamine which is, like 5HT, taken into storage particles. DOPA is, of course, given therapeutically in the treatment of Parkinsonism, a disease in which there is cellular death of dopaminergic and probably other neurons in the striatum. It should be pointed out that DOPA, normally found intraneuronally, may when given systemically penetrate other than dopaminergic neurons. 5HT for example has been found to fall, in brain presumably by displacement, on this treatment. Dopamine from DOPA

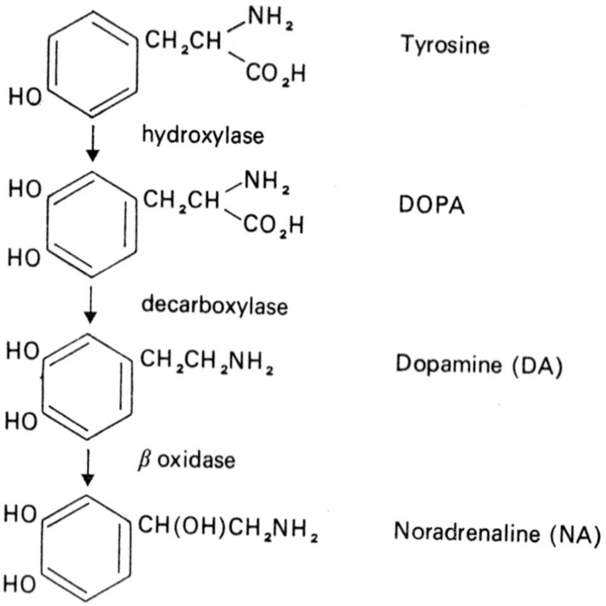

FIG. 4.    Synthesis of noradrenaline and dopamine.

can also be produced in capillary walls where decarboxylase is present. Hence DOPA administration may be regarded as 'unphysiological' and may account for a number of side-effects. Breakdown is either by oxidative deamination to dihydroxyphenylacetic acid or with methylation to 3-methoxy-tyramine and then deamination to homo vanillic acid.

*Noradrenaline*

Synthesis as far as dopamine is as described above. The difference is that the storage particles also contain the enzyme dopamine β oxidase and here β hydroxylation of dopamine to NA occurs (Fig. 4). The NA is stored as a catecholamine-ATP-chromogranin (a specific protein) complex.

Breakdown again intraneuronally is by oxidative deamination, and on release, methylation by COMT (Catechol O-methyl transferase) to form normetanephrine (Fig. 5). The amine is then deaminated to the aldehyde and thence, not to the acid VMA (Vanillyl mandelic acid) as in the peripheral sympathetic nervous system, but to the alcohol 3-methoxy-4-hydroxyphenylglycol (MHPG). Similarly, the non-methylated alcohol is formed, 3,4-dihydroxyphenylglycol (DHPG). At this point, conjugation occurs—at least in the rat brain—to the ethereal sulphate. This is presumably a detoxication mechanism perhaps related

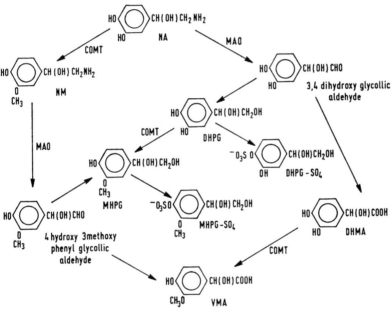

FIG. 5.    Breakdown pathways of noradrenaline in brain.

to forming a metabolite capable of being actively transported from brain. Because the glycols are the major end products of NA metabolism in brain, their concentration in urine has been used by various workers (Maas and Landis, 1968) as an index of NA metabolism in brain. Low levels of this metabolite have been reported in the urine of patients suffering from depressive illness, and this has been put forward as evidence for the role of noradrenaline in this syndrome.

RELEASE OF AMINES

Much of the work that has been done on control of biogenic amine synthesis has been done on the peripheral sympathetic neuron, and the findings have been extrapolated to brain often with little experimental justification.

As has been pointed out, NA is synthesized in vesicles which contain dopamine $\beta$ oxidase and also some storage particles. The vesicles are transported down the axon by axoplasmic flow at the rate of about 120 mm per day (Dahlström and Haggendal, 1966). Even so, Levett has pointed out that this is insufficiently fast to account for the turnover and release of NA and that this axoplasmic flow is more concerned with the transport of machinery for the formation of the amine than its gross flow. It has been suggested that the contents of vesicles are released on nerve stimulation by exocytosis. Certainly the perfusate from stimulated peripheral adrenergic nerve contains chromogranin and dopamine $\beta$ oxidase in similar proportions to that found in the vesicles. These vesicles may return to the nerve terminal cytoplasm still containing dopamine $\beta$ oxidase to continue the synthesis of NA.

It is important for nerve conduction that the neurotransmitter is rapidly inactivated on release. This is achieved firstly by enzymic means, mainly COMT in the case of NA, and also by re-uptake into the nerve terminal followed probably by active transport into the vesicles for re-release. It has been found that newly synthesized NA is preferentially released on nerve stimulation. Similar work also suggests two pools of NA, one large and with a relatively slow turnover, and one small and highly labile which is preferentially released on nerve stimulation.

CONTROL MECHANISMS

In spite of large changes in the functional state of the neuron, the level of the amines tends to remain constant and it is postulated that rapid changes in synthesis must take place to keep up with the change in utilization. Control in biochemical systems is often exerted upon the enzyme which limits the synthesis of any particular product: in the case of 5HT formation, the tryptophan-5-hydroxylase; in the case of DA and NA, tyrosine hydroxylase. Typically, one of the products of the reaction inhibits the enzyme at this point, and this is well illustrated by the inhibition of tyrosine hydroxylase by NA. This may be by way of competition between NA and pteridine co-factor for the reduced enzyme. It is presumed that NA in a small compartment is released on nerve stimulation, freeing the enzyme from inhibition and promoting synthesis. Similar increases in synthesis of 5HT have been demonstrated on stimulation of the perikarya of the 5HT neurons in the raphe nucleus, although the mechanism of this increase in synthesis is unknown. Longer-term effects of stimulation (24–48 hours) have been shown in catecholamine synthesis in the adrenal medulla which are blocked by inhibitors of protein synthesis, although the mechanisms involved are as yet unknown; of importance to the psychiatrist is the increased turnover of NA in brain on E.C.T. and on chronic dosage with tricyclic anti-depressants, again by unknown mechanisms.

CYCLIC AMP

This substance formed by adenyl cyclase from ATP has many functions. In general, it seems to behave as a 'second messenger' for hormonal activation of enzymic systems. In particular, it may mediate the $\beta$-effects of NA receptor stimulation. In brain, the iontophoretic application of this compound has been found to mimic in all respects the similar application of NA on certain cells in the cerebellum, and it may not be just fortuitous that the brain has particularly high adenyl cyclase activity, and the cerebellum the highest levels of cyclic AMP.

## OTHER POSSIBLE CENTRAL SYNAPTIC TRANSMITTERS

When examining the evidence for a substance being a neurotransmitter, there are several criteria which can be applied to test the hypothesis. If one or more of these cannot be fulfilled, it does not necessarily mean that the substance is not a transmitter, but obviously the more of them that can be satisfied, the stronger the evidence for the compound in question. Some of these criteria are (1) that the substance has a non-uniform distribution in the brain; (2) that it is present in nerve terminals; (3) that there are enzymes for its synthesis; (4) there should be a means of rapid inactivation, e.g. re-uptake or enzymic breakdown; (5) it should be released by nervous stimulation; and (6) when it is applied to the postsynaptic cell it should exactly reproduce the effect of presynaptic stimulation, i.e. it should mimic the natural transmitter. Probably the last of these is the most important, though reasons can be advanced why each of them might not be fulfilled under certain circumstances. Most of these criteria have been found to be true of *acetylcholine* (ACh) and *gamma-amino-butyric acid* (GABA) in the brain, where GABA is thought to be an inhibitory transmitter and ACh possibly both excitatory and inhibitory, depending on its site of release.

ACh is the transmitter at the neuromuscular junction and at the autonomic ganglion. It is also released from the recurrent collaterals of motoneuron axons which synapse with the Renshaw cells in the spinal cord: the Renshaw cells are short inhibitory interneurons which synapse with the original motoneuron innervating them, thus tending to inhibit repetitive discharges. ACh occurs in considerable quantities in the brain, though its distribution makes it apparent that only a fraction of the neurons could be cholinergic. The highest concentrations are found in the thalamus, caudate nucleus, hippocampus and cerebral cortex. It is synthesized by the enzyme choline acetylase and degraded by acetylcholine esterase. Choline acetylase shows a regional distribution which parallels that of ACh, though the distribution of acetylcholine esterase does not follow so closely; in particular, this enzyme is present in moderately high levels in the cerebellum, which contains little ACh or choline acetylase. The subcellular fractionation studies of de Robertis and of Whittaker have shown ACh, choline acetylase and acetylcholine esterase to be present largely in the nerve terminals. The ACh occurs in membrane-bound vesicles, choline acetylase is a soluble enzyme in the cytoplasm, and acetylcholine esterase is membrane-bound, probably being largely present in the postsynaptic membrane, which becomes attached to the nerve terminal when the brain is homogenized. Acetylcholine esterase has been found to occur along the axons of cholinergic neurons, and by a selective staining technique for this enzyme, Lewis and Shute have been able to trace the course of various cholinergic pathways in the brain. The most important of these are the projections ascending from the reticular formation in the brainstem to many parts of the brain, including the thalamus, hypothalamus, cerebellum, hippocampus, basal ganglia and cerebral cortex. Fibres also project to the cortex from the hippocampus and from the thalamus, and there are short cholinergic fibres within the cortex.

Cells can be found in most parts of the brain which are excited by ACh applied locally by micro-iontophoresis.* Krnjevic has found that 15 to 25 per cent of the neurons of the rat cerebral cortex are excited by ACh, these cells being concentrated mainly in the sensorimotor area, and mainly between 0·8 and 1·3 mm below the surface. In particular, the pyramidal cells are generally excited by ACh, though they are probably not cholinergic themselves as they contain little ACh or choline acetylase. In the cerebellum, the Purkinje cells respond to ACh, and are also known to be excited by the 'parallel fibres' from the granule cells, which stain for acetylcholine esterase; thus the granule cells are probably cholinergic, and the Purkinje cells cholinoceptive.

In the Renshaw cells in the spinal cord, the ACh receptors are of the nicotinic type like the neuromuscular junction, being excited by nicotine and tetramethyl ammonium, and blocked by curare. The receptors in cortical cells, however, are predominantly muscarinic, being excited by muscarine and blocked by atropine. The type of receptor found at intermediate levels of the C.N.S. is mixed muscarinic-nicotinic, probably due to there being some of each type.

Cortical neurons sensitive to ACh can also be fired by stimulation of the RF, and activation of them by either of these means can be blocked by atropine. Cells have also been found in the brain (including the cortex) which are depressed by ACh, though it should be remembered that this type of response is markedly dependent on the type of anaesthetic being used.

*Micro-iontophoresis is described in Chapter XVI, Vol. I.

It is possible to demonstrate a spontaneous release of ACh from the cerebral cortex. This was shown by Mitchell, who placed small cylinders containing an acetylcholine esterase inhibitor solution on the surface of the cortex ('cortical cups'). The rate of release is reduced, the deeper the anaesthesia, and is increased by convulsants: it is roughly proportional to the electrical activity of the cortex. Release is completely abolished by the anaesthetic chloralose. If the animal's visual system is stimulated by a flashing light, the ACh output from the visual cortex rises by about three times, and there is also a smaller increase over the rest of the cortex. Making sections in appropriate parts of the brain shows that the increased release from the visual cortex is due to a cholinergic pathway from the lateral geniculate body (the thalamic relay of the visual tract) to this part of the cortex, and the widespread release is due to fibres ascending from the RF to all parts of the cortex, the RF being activated by the sensory input. This widespread release of ACh can also be evoked by direct electrical stimulation of the RF. ACh release can also be shown in deep brain structures by local perfusion of them using the 'push–pull cannula', a device consisting of two narrow concentric tubes.

Thus, overall, there is good evidence that ACh is a transmitter in the brain, cholinergic neurons being important in the ascending reticular activating system, and also in some of the connections of the specific sensory pathways.

Neurons may receive inhibitory as well as excitatory inputs, and there are now two substances known to be inhibitory neurotransmitters: GABA in the cortex and glycine in the spinal cord.

GABA, formerly known as substance i, has been known for some time to be an inhibitory transmitter at the crustacean neuromuscular junction, which receives both excitatory and inhibitory inputs. In mammalian tissues, it occurs only in the C.N.S., and its synthesis and degradation are linked to the energy metabolism of the neuron (see above under 'Energy Metabolism'). It is one of the most common amino acids in the brain, being present in much higher concentrations than other postulated transmitter substances: the mean level of GABA is around 100 μg per g; that of ACh one to two μg per g, and noradrenaline under one μg per g. GABA does not have a striking regional distribution, but is present in particularly high concentrations in the superficial layers of the cerebral cortex, and in the layer of the cerebellar cortex containing the Purkinje cells. The latter is particularly interesting in view of the known inhibitory function of these cells. At the subcellular level, at least 40 per cent is present in nerve terminals, though it has not yet been demonstrated in 'storage vesicles' as have ACh and noradrenaline.

As with ACh, GABA is released spontaneously from the cortex, and this release is increased by electrical stimulation either locally or of areas

M

projecting to the cortex; Jasper has reported that the spontaneous release is higher during sleep than when the animal is awake.

Probably the most convincing evidence for GABA being an inhibitory transmitter in the cortex has been produced by Krnjevic, who applied it iontophoretically to cortical neurons while recording the membrane potential with an intracellular microelectrode. He showed that the changes in membrane potential and conductance caused by GABA were identical with the changes produced by stimulating inhibitory inputs to these cells. In addition to this, Curtis has found a specific antagonist, bicuculline, a convulsant which blocks both natural inhibition and the effect of applied GABA. Similar evidence has shown that GABA is the inhibitory transmitter at the synapse of the cerebellar Purkinje cells and Deiters neurons, which lie below the fourth ventricle.

Inhibitory synapses are also present in the spinal cord, for example, the synapse of the Renshaw cell on the motoneuron. There are good reasons, however, for believing that GABA is not the inhibitory transmitter here, even though it is present in the cord and is able to depress the firing of spinal neurons. Firstly, it does not hyperpolarize motoneurons in a way characteristic of natural inhibition, and secondly, its action is not blocked by the convulsant strychnine, which does block natural inhibition. The true inhibitory transmitter in the cord is thought to be *glycine*, which is present in high concentrations, particularly in the grey matter. Glycine exactly mimics the effects of the natural transmitter on the cell membrane, and it is also antagonized by strychnine. It is interesting to note that tetanus toxin, which like strychnine blocks spinal inhibitory mechanisms, does not antagonize glycine applied to motoneurons, and is therefore thought to act by preventing the release of the glycine from the inhibitory nerve terminals.

A final mention should be made of glutamic acid as a possible transmitter. Known cholinergic and monoamine-containing neurons can only account for a fraction of the nerve cells in the brain, and there must be other excitatory transmitters present. Glutamic acid is present in all parts of the brain in high concentrations, and it has the property of exciting nearly all the neurons so far tested. At the moment, there is little other evidence for its being a transmitter, though it could well be acting as a general modulator of neuronal activity rather than being specifically released from nerve endings.

### RELATION OF NEUROTRANSMITTERS TO EPILEPSY

There is a good deal of evidence for malfunctions in both cholinergic and GABA-containing systems being causative factors in epilepsy. Much of the evidence is circumstantial, but derangements in these systems serve as useful models in the investigation of the disease.

Inhibitors of acetylcholine esterase lead to a build-up of ACh, and thus there will be increased activity at synapses where ACh is a transmitter. Potent inhibitors, such as the organophosphorus nerve gases, cause convulsions in experimental animals and in man. There are some alterations of ACh metabolism in clinical epilepsy: it has been reported that ACh is present in the C.S.F. of epileptics, whereas it is absent in the C.S.F. of non-epileptic controls.

Convulsions occur during severe dietary deficiency of vitamin $B_6$ (pyridoxal) and also in the rare disease of vitamin $B_6$ dependency, which is a genetically-determined biochemical defect, the precise nature of which is unknown. Pyridoxal phosphate is an essential co-factor for both the enzyme which synthesizes GABA and the enzyme which catabolizes it, and it has been suggested that some types of convulsions could be due to defects in inhibitory mechanisms which are mediated through this transmitter. Seizures are induced by thiosemicarbazide, a drug which inactivates pyridoxal phosphate and reduces GABA levels, apparently having a greater effect on the GABA-synthesizing enzyme than on the enzyme which degrades it. However, thiosemicarbazide can still induce seizures when brain GABA levels are elevated above normal by selective inhibitors of its degradation. Also clinical epilepsy is usually unaffected by massive doses of pyridoxal. Hence the evidence for an involvement of GABA metabolism in the etiology of clinical epilepsy is far from conclusive, but further work in this direction could well be valuable. The physico-chemical basis of epilepsy is discussed by Jasper, Ward and Pope (1969).

## THE NUCLEIC ACIDS

The genetic information of a cell is stored in its nucleus in the form of deoxyribonucleic acid (DNA). These extremely large molecules, whose molecular weights can be of the order of $10^8$, are basically chains of molecules of deoxyribose (a pentose sugar), the molecules being linked by phosphate groups. Each deoxyribose carries one of four cyclic bases; these are *adenine* and *guanine* which belong to the class of compounds known as purines; and *cytosine* and *thymine* which belong to the pyrimidine group. The basic repeating unit of deoxyribose and one of these bases is called a *nucleoside*, and a nucleoside with an attached phosphate group is a *nucleotide*. DNA always contains equal amounts of adenine and thymine, and of guanine and cytosine. The well-known X-ray diffraction work of Watson, Crick and Wilkins has shown the structure of DNA to be a double helix, that is, two chains of nucleotides twisted together. In the centre of the helix, bases from opposite chains 'pair up', being held together by hydrogen bonding, and these weak attractive forces serve to hold the two chains together. The manner of pairing up is quite specific: adenine always pairs with thymine, and guanine with cytosine; thus a purine always pairs up with a pyrimidine. This explains why equal amounts of adenine and thymine, and of guanine and cytosine are always found.

The information stored in the DNA by means of the order of its bases is made use of via copying sections of it into a similar molecule, ribonucleic acid (RNA). RNA consists of a *single* strand of nucleotides, and the sugar it contains is ribose rather than deoxyribose. Three of the bases of RNA are the same as in DNA, but thymine is replaced here by *uracil*, another pyrimidine. By means of the complementary base pairing outlined above, one strand of the DNA is transcribed into RNA by means of the enzyme RNA polymerase. Unlike DNA, which is stable in the non-dividing cell, RNA is being continually synthesized and degraded. The synthesis of the RNA can be regulated according to the needs of the cell (see below).

Once the genetic information in the DNA has been copied into RNA, it can be expressed by translation of the code into protein.

## PROTEIN SYNTHESIS

### I. THE MECHANISM OF PROTEIN SYNTHESIS (Fig. 6)

Most of the knowledge of the mechanism by which proteins are assembled has come from work on bacterial systems, particularly the bacterium *E. Coli.*, although much of the information now also appears to be true of mammalian cells.

The order of the amino acids in a protein is specified by the order of the nucleotides in the DNA; as described earlier, one strand of the DNA is copied into RNA, which is then translated into protein. There are three different types of RNA: messenger RNA (mRNA), ribosomal RNA (rRNA), and transfer or soluble RNA (t or sRNA). Messenger RNA has a high molecular weight (up to several million), and conveys genetic information from DNA in the cell nucleus to the protein synthesizing machinery; it represents less than 5 per cent of the total cellular RNA. Ribosomal RNA, which constitutes up to 80 per cent of the cellular RNA, is also of high molecular weight (around a million) and is found combined with protein in the *ribosomes*, small particles 10 to 20 $m\mu$ in diameter which occur free in the cell cytoplasm or attached to the endoplasmic reticulum. The third type, transfer RNA, is a relatively small molecule of about 80 nucleotides, and acts as a carrier for amino acids in the assembly of protein.

Each amino acid in a protein is coded for by three nucleotides in the mRNA. As there are four different nucleotides, there are 64 ($4^3$) possible triplet codes ('codons'), and in *E. Coli*, 61 of these have been assigned to specific amino acids; thus most of the 20 common amino acids are coded for by more than one codon. The amino acids are assembled into the correct order for the formation of a protein by means of tRNA molecules. These carry an amino acid at one end of the molecule, and at one point along the nucleotide sequence is an 'anticodon', a triplet of nucleotides which is complementary to the codon for the amino acid which is attached to that tRNA. The anticodon pairs up specifically with the codon in the mRNA, in the same way that the two strands of DNA bind together. Thus an amino acid is directed to the appropriate place along the messenger. The understanding of this mechanism is largely due to Crick and is known as his 'Adaptor Hypothesis'. It might be expected that there would be 61 different tRNA molecules as there are 61 codons specifying amino acids; in fact there are less, though the exact number is unknown. This is accounted for by Crick's 'Wobble Hypothesis', which allows some flexibility in the tRNA molecule in the third base of its anticodon, permitting one anticodon to pair up with two or even three different codons.

The first step then is the pairing up of tRNA molecules with their appropriate amino acids; this is done by the aminoacyl tRNA synthetases, enzymes specific for both the amino acids *and* their respective tRNA's: thus there are at least 20 of these enzymes. The enzyme uses one molecule of ATP to form a high energy acyl bond between the amino acid and the tRNA, producing an 'aminoacyl-tRNA complex'. The job of linking up the amino acids into a protein is performed by the ribosomes, which bring together aminoacyl-tRNA complexes and the mRNA in the correct conformation, and form the peptide bonds.

The ribosome is composed of two unequal subunits; the smaller subunit has a binding capacity for mRNA, and the larger subunit is able to bind two tRNA molecules: the two tRNA locations are known as the 'A' and the 'P' sites.

Figure 6 shows the actual mechanism by which the amino acids are linked up. A tRNA molecule carrying the growing peptide chain (initially a single amino acid) occupies the P site in the ribosome, while in the A site is a tRNA carrying the next amino acid to be added. An enzyme contained within the ribosome catalyzes the transfer of the peptide chain from the tRNA in the P site onto the adjacent amino acid, thus elongating the chain by one unit. The tRNA leaves the P site, and the ribosome moves one codon's length along the mRNA so that the tRNA bearing the peptide now occupies the P site; the next aminoacyl tRNA complex can now enter the A site, and the process is repeated. How the ribosome is able to move along the messenger is unknown, though it involves the hydrolysis of GTP (Guanosine triphosphate: a high-energy phosphate compound similar to ATP) as an energy source. The process is remarkably fast in bacteria, the synthesis of large proteins taking only seconds, though it is rather slower in mammalian cells. More than one ribosome at a time can translate protein from a strand of mRNA: in electron micrographs several (typically around 5) can often be seen 'strung' along the messenger. This structure is known as a 'polysome'.

### 2. THE ACTION OF ANTIBIOTICS

One important respect in which bacterial and mammalian protein synthesis differs is in the ribosomes, which are smaller in bacteria. When

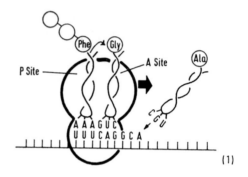

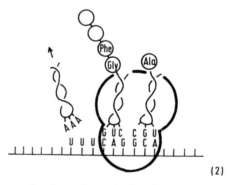

Fig. 6.  The mechanism of synthesis of protein molecules by the ribosome.

subject to centrifugation, bacterial ribosomes sediment at a rate of 70 S (Svedberg units), and mammalian ribosomes at 80 S. The ribosome is the site of action of many antibiotics which are selectively toxic towards bacteria, having little effect on protein synthesis in mammalian cells.

Chloramphenicol and erythromycin are two antibiotics which act on the larger ribosomal subunit, preventing peptide bond formation. On the other hand, streptomycin binds to the smaller subunit, and acts by causing misreading of the codons of the messenger: thus non-functional proteins containing 'wrong' amino acids are produced.

Although these drugs are without effect on protein synthesis in the cytoplasm of mammalian cells, the mitochondria, which produce some of their own proteins autonomously, contain bacterial-type ribosomes which may be susceptible. This may be why some antibiotics have toxic effects, for example the aplastic anemia associated with chloramphenicol.

### 3. CONTROL OF PROTEIN SYNTHESIS

Cells are able to control the synthesis of individual proteins, this being particularly apparent in the case of certain inducible enzymes, that is, enzymes whose levels are sensitive to the amount of some substance (the inducer) in the cell. Control is possible at two points: at the transcription of DNA into mRNA, and at the translation of mRNA into protein. Important questions related to control are how the correct points on the messenger for initiation and termination are selected. Again, most of the current knowledge is of bacterial systems, comparatively little being known of the system in mammalian cells.

A well-known model for the regulation of mRNA synthesis is shown in Figure 7a and is due largely to Jacob and Monod's work on the induction of β-galactosidase and related enzymes by lactose in *E. Coli*.

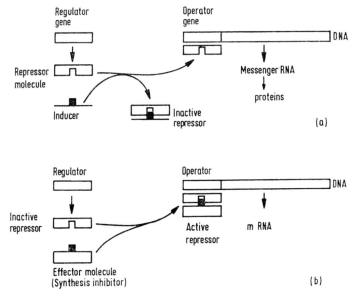

FIG. 7.  Models for the regulation of RNA synthesis.

A 'regulator gene' on the DNA codes for a repressor molecule, and this acts on an 'operator gene' which is closely linked to the genes coding for the proteins in question, and which in some way controls the transcription to mRNA (a 'gene' is a hypothetical section of the DNA molecule which is supposed to have a particular function). The substance which induces the protein synthesis combines with the repressor, rendering it inactive. A similar mechanism for *repression* of protein synthesis could be envisaged, where the regulator gene codes for an inactive repressor molecule and this inactive repressor then combines with the effector molecule to produce an active repressor (Fig. 7b). This mechanism of repression of protein synthesis appears to apply in *E. Coli* to the ten enzymes involved in histidine biosynthesis, where histidine exerts end-product inhibition by reducing the production of these enzymes.

A protein has been isolated from *E. Coli* which has many properties of a repressor molecule; it is fairly large, with a molecular weight of about 30,000 (Ptashne and Gilbert, 1970). How this repressor molecule acts is unknown, but the action may in some way involve the histones and protamines, basic proteins found combined with DNA. These proteins may normally mask the DNA, preventing its transcription.

How the correct starting point on the messenger is selected is also unknown, there being no specific triplet code to indicate this. On the other hand, the way in which the end of the protein is marked is fairly clear, this being by any one of the three triplets which are not assigned to any amino acid.

In mammals, hormones such as growth hormone and insulin stimulate protein synthesis, whereas adrenocortical hormones reduce it. There is evidence that the hormones may be affecting the synthetic activity of the ribosome itself. It is possible to set up a cell-free system which will synthesize protein *in vitro*, consisting of soluble cell extract and purified ribosomes. Such a system will synthesize protein faster if the ribosomes are prepared from animals which have been treated with, for example, growth hormone. However, no stimulation is observed if the ribosomes are prepared from untreated animals and the hormone added to the *in vitro* system; thus the effect is not a direct one.

For a more detailed account of the mechanism and control of protein synthesis, the reader is referred to Mahler and Cordes (1966).

### 4. FACTORS ALTERING RATES OF PROTEIN SYNTHESIS IN THE NERVOUS SYSTEM

Protein synthesis in nerve can be affected in a variety of ways. The changes in rates of synthesis may be quite large, for example when a peripheral nerve is sectioned, the axon begins to grow, and protein synthesis in the cell body rises by two to three times, though the control mechanism for this is unknown.

The electrical activity of a nerve can modify its rate of protein synthesis. In general, there is no marked rise in overall synthesis when the central nervous system is stimulated. However, the levels of certain proteins may be altered, for example tyrosine hydroxylase synthesis rises both in the brain following E.C.T. and in peripheral sympathetic nerves on chronic stimulation. As described in the section on the Functional Role of RNA and Protein, investigations of the effects of a variety of physiological stimuli on brain protein synthesis in experimental animals have given conflicting results.

Various psychotropic drugs such as chlorpromazine and L.S.D. have been reported to affect protein synthesis in brain, but in no case has any direct effect on the synthesizing machinery been found. The changes seen were probably indirect ones, perhaps through alterations in energy metabolism.

On the other hand, the stimulation of brain protein synthesis by thyroid hormone, growth hormone, etc., may be a more direct effect (see above).

## THE FUNCTIONAL ROLE OF BRAIN RNA AND PROTEIN

### INTRODUCTION

The relationship between RNA, protein metabolism and brain function, in particular the possibility of their involvement in the processes of learning and memory, have been of widespread interest and intense investigation in the last decade.

The brain has a high content of RNA. Neurones contain between 50–2000 $\mu\mu$g RNA per cell and are among the most active producers of nucleic acid in the body, comparable in this respect to certain actively secreting cells, e.g. the exocrine cells of the pancreas. As in other cells, RNA is synthesized in the nucleus and is found in both nucleus and cytoplasm. The nuclear RNA is situated in the nucleoli, which are a prominent feature of neuronal nuclei, and accounts for approximately one-fifth of the total RNA. The remaining RNA is found as ribonucleoprotein particles (ribosomes) situated in the endoplasmic reticulum. These particles are intensely stained by basic dyes and constitute the Nissl substance observed under the microscope. The glial cells have, on average, a far lower content of RNA (approximately 80 $\mu\mu$g per cell).

Proteins constitute 40 per cent of the dry weight of the whole brain, and most classes of proteins found in other tissues are also found in cerebral tissue. In addition, certain acidic proteins specific to the brain have been isolated and their significance will be discussed later. The brain has a very active protein metabolism which is curious since, unlike the pancreas or liver, the brain is not an organ which secretes protein to the outside. Although some nerve cells have a neurosecretory function, the bulk of the protein synthesized is utilized in the brain itself.

Neither the content nor rate of synthesis of brain RNA and protein remains constant in the course of development. The RNA and protein content of most areas of the developing rabbit brain have been found to increase rapidly from day one to the tenth day, and the overall rate of protein synthesis is generally greater in young animals than in adults. The incorporation of labelled uridine into brain RNA is more rapid in developing rats than in adult rats and it has been shown that RNA polymerase activity is higher in immature rat brain than in adult brain.

## RNA AND PROTEIN METABOLISM AND ALTERATION IN FUNCTIONAL STATES

All living cells are capable of adapting to new environmental conditions by gene activation leading to the production of new RNA and protein molecules. Examples of this are provided by processes of differentiation and development, e.g. in bacterial cultures exposed to a new substrate, and in the response of some cells to hormones. The possibility of gene activation being involved in nervous and mental processes has been studied by numerous workers and the plethora of data obtained, although in some cases contradictory, would suggest that the rate of synthesis of RNA and protein is, to some measure, dependent on the functional state of the nervous tissue. Whether this relationship is a direct or indirect one remains to be demonstrated.

Bennett, Krech and Rosenweig (1964) found that rats reared in conditions of environmental complexity and constant exposure to behaviour stimulation had an increased cortical weight, protein content and cholinesterase activity compared with rats kept in isolation in a restricted environment and subjected to minimal behavioural stimulation.

Hydén and his collaborators, using microtechniques involving the isolation of individual neurones and glia from the Deiters nucleus (which is concerned with balance) of the rabbit have shown that various types of physiological stimulation result in increased neuronal RNA and protein content, while the RNA and enzymic content of the glia are simultaneously reduced. The base composition of the RNA remained unchanged (see Hydén, 1967).

Generally, stimuli of moderate intensity have been found to increase the turnover of RNA of cells in specific areas of brain. Olfactory stimulation of fish has been shown to increase brain nuclear RNA and, in some cases, to alter the base composition. Auditory stimulation of dogs increased the RNA content in the area of the brain associated with the reception of auditory stimuli. Visual stimulation has been found to increase RNA turnover in the visual cortex and to increase the rate of transfer of RNA from the nucleus to the cytoplasm. However, if the levels of auditory and visual stimulation are raised sufficiently, a decrease in net RNA synthesis occurs. Indeed, intense stimulation of cortical tissue almost invariably results in a fall in RNA content. Orrego (1967) stimulated brain slices electrically and observed a 40 per cent fall in RNA synthesis. Convulsions induced electrically or by metrazol or insulin reduce brain RNA, and intense motor activity has the same effect. The reduction in brain RNA consequent upon intense stimulation may well be due to a decreased availability of nucleoside triphosphates, due to the high activity of ion active transport system, which require ATP.

A valid criticism of a great deal of the work done in this field is that in only a small number of studies have measurements of electrophysiological activity been made in the same nerve cells that were later subjected to biochemical analysis. Recent work performed independently by Peterson and Kernell (1970) and Berry (1969) on the giant neurone in the abdominal ganglia of *Aplysia californica* has demonstrated that prolonged electrical stimulation of ganglionic nerves, strong enough to elicit postsynaptic spikes in these giant neurones, produced an almost 100 per cent increase in the uptake of labelled nucleosides into nuclear and cytoplasmic RNA. It appeared that synaptic activation was required for this increase and mere spike activity had no effect. This would explain some of the contradictions in the literature. This work convincingly showed a relationship between electrical activity and RNA metabolism in nervous tissue but the mechanism whereby these two processes are linked remains as yet unknown.

There is abundant evidence that axoplasm generated in the cell body of the neurone travels down the axon at a rate of up to 400 mm per day. This evidence has been obtained autoradiographically using $^3$H leucine and $^{32}$P, and also by constricting nerve fibres and measuring the rate of accumulation of material there. RNA has also been shown to travel down the axon and this transported RNA is believed to be the origin of at least some of the axonal RNA, although there is some evidence for axonal RNA synthesis independent of the perikaryon. Stimulation increases the rate of generation and flow of axoplasm. For a general review of this subject see Talwar (1969).

LEARNING AND MEMORY

The experiments described in previous paragraphs relate only to the relationship of RNA and protein metabolism to non-specific alterations in functional state. However, the fact that nucleic acids and proteins are known to have the ability of encoding the genetic and immunological 'memory' has led many investigators to explore the possibility that RNA and protein are involved in information storage in the brain. This analogy between genetic and immunological memory and the memory process in the brain, although of questionable validity, has stimulated a vast quantity of research and a number of hypotheses have been formulated regarding the possible chemical nature of the engram.

Two types of memory have been distinguished. There is an initial period between the registering of the sensory stimuli and their fixation as an engram. This period is known as short-term memory and is of variable duration. During this period, the record is very labile and is easily abolished by such agents as anoxia, concussion, electroshock and anaesthesia. There is evidence that the short-term memory is an electrical phenomenon residing in the cortex and hippocampus. At some stage, the electrical events are consolidated into a more durable form known as long-term memory. It is highly likely that the long-term memory has a structural basis since it is resistant to such treatments as electroconvulsive shock, epileptic fits, anaesthetics and a variety of psychopharmacological agents known to alter the electrical response of the brain. The possibility that this 'structural basis' involves RNA and protein has been examined by experiments which fall into three main categories: those involving the use of drugs and metabolic inhibitors of RNA and protein metabolism, those in which an attempt is made to correlate changes in RNA and protein metabolism with a specific learning situation, and those in which a chemical extract from a trained animal is transferred to an untrained animal in an attempt to transfer memory of a learned task.

### THE USE OF METABOLIC AGENTS

Some inhibitors of RNA and protein synthesis have been found to interfere with the learning process, although some of the effects have been difficult to interpret. It was found that 8-azaguanidine, a substance known to interfere with RNA synthesis, prevented rats from learning a new maze but did not affect their performance in a previously learned maze. Barondes and Jarvik (1964) used Actinomycin D, an inhibitor of messenger RNA synthesis, and found that mice whose RNA synthesis was inhibited as much as 83 per cent were still able to learn and remember as well as controls in a simple passive avoidance conditioning situation.

Agranoff, Barondes and Flexner have used goldfish and mice and inhibited brain protein synthesis by injecting puromycin, cycloheximide or acetoxycycloheximide in the temporal lobe and hippocampus of the mouse or in the tectal part of the goldfish. These inhibitors have different modes of action. Acetoxycycloheximide, which delays the appearance of messenger RNA, was found to delay the appearance of an engram, whereas puromycin, which destroys the messenger permanently, abolishes the engram. It was concluded from experiments of this kind that protein synthesis is required for the establishment of the long-term memory.

Agents stimulating RNA and protein metabolism have been used to a lesser degree. Magnesium pemoline is believed to increase brain RNA polymerase activity and it has been reported to cause an enhancement of learning in a conditioned avoidance response. However, Smith failed to demonstrate a facilitation of learning and memory in human beings using this compound.

Hydén and his co-workers have studied the effect of learning situations on RNA metabolism using micromethods for separating individual neurones and glia. They trained rats to balance on a wire angled at 45 degrees to obtain food, and found that the trained rats showed a significant increase in the nuclear RNA of both neurones and glia, and also a significant change in the base ratio. Physiological stimulation not involving a learning situation did not alter the base composition. In later experiments a learning situation involving the transfer of 'handedness' was used and the RNA from cortical layers 5 and 6 were analyzed. Again they found that the RNA content on the experimental side of the brain was increased, and there was also a change in the base ratio. Although Hydén initially considered that base ratio changes only occurred in learning situations, subsequent experiments on cerebellar Purkinje cells have shown that in some cases base ratios can be altered by just passive stimulation alone.

In 1965 Moore and McGregor discovered a brain-specific soluble protein known as S 100, so called because of its solubility in saturated ammonium sulphate. This is an acidic protein containing 30 per cent glutamic acid and constitutes 0·1 per cent of the total brain proteins. This protein has been the subject of some elegant work by Hydén and Lange (1970) who observed that the amount of S 100 in the pyramidal nerve cells of the hippocampus increased during the learning of transfer of handedness in rats. That this increase was due to learning and not merely due to the sustained motor and sensory activity was convincingly demonstrated by the use of an antiserum against S 100. Intraventricular injection of S 100 antisera during the course of training prevented the rats from learning but did not affect motor function in the animals. These experiments were the first aimed at correlating specific brain protein components to learning processes in mammals.

The classic experiments of Avery *et al.* on the transformation of genetic characteristics by transfer of DNA from one organism to another were partly responsible for the acceptance of the view that DNA was the encoder of genetic information. This work has been used as a basis of several attempts to transfer a learned skill from one animal to another.

The initial work was performed on planaria, where the feeding of trained planaria to untrained ones was reported to result in a transfer of learned experience. However, reports of this kind have aroused considerable controversy and the results are considered by many to be of doubtful validity. Several groups of workers have claimed to be able to transfer learned responses in rats by injecting a phenol-extracted preparation of RNA from trained animals into the brains of untrained animals. However, the failure of attempts to reproduce these results has led to the suggestion that the transfer factor may be a contaminant of the RNA extract and not RNA itself. Ungar considers that the transfer factor may be a low molecular weight peptide and recently a peptide 'Scotophobin' has been isolated that is believed to be associated with dark avoidance (Ungar, Desiderio and Parr, 1971).

HORMONE EFFECTS

As part of the learning process, the pituitary-adrenal system appears to play an essential role in conditioned avoidance behaviour. Hypophysectomy impairs the acquisition of a conditioned avoidance response and it has been shown that peptide fragments of the ACTH molecule can restore the response performance of the hypophysectomized rat, without producing other metabolic or systemic effects.

At the present time, there is insufficient evidence to conclude that the engram is coded at the molecular level. Although it is well established that long-term memory has a structural basis, there are a number of hypotheses put forward in which it is postulated that the short-term memory is consolidated by the establishment of new synaptic junctions. However, since the establishment of these new junctions will require new RNA and protein synthesis, the changes observed in RNA and protein during the learning process could be explained without postulating that they represented the engram coded in a chemical form.

The biochemical aspects of memory have been discussed in detail by Richter (1966) and Rose (1968).

CLINICAL STUDIES

Hydén and Lange (1966) examined biopsy material from the Globus Pallidus of patients suffering from Parkinsonism and found a highly aberrant RNA in the glia at a very early stage of the disease. The RNA had a decreased guanine and uracil content but an increased adenine content. This biochemical error in the glia was found to persist for the duration of the illness. Initially the neuronal RNA was found to be less changed, but later in the development of the disease, from the time the overt clinical symptoms appeared, similar changes were apparent in the neuronal RNA too. The amount of RNA per nerve cell and glia were increased from 116 $\mu\mu$g to 145 $\mu\mu$g RNA per cell (neurons) and 17 to

34 $\mu\mu$g RNA per cell (glia). Hydén and Lange suggest that Parkinson's disease is caused by factors in the environment such as infections initiating the release of undesirable genomic activities which lead to a biochemical error in the glia. An alternative suggestion, but one for which there is no experimental evidence, is that the altered RNA was a reflection of a virus infection.

Engel and Morrell (1970) have made a study of RNA metabolism in epileptogenic tissue and found neurones with increased RNA staining properties but decreased incorporation of RNA precursors.

In man, a change occurs during the lifetime in the RNA content of neurones. The RNA content increases up to the age of forty, remains approximately constant for the next two decades, and after the age of sixty, falls rapidly. Cameron *et al.* (1963), reported that treatment of presenile and senile psychotic patients with doses of 100 g yeast RNA per day administered orally or intravenously improved their score in intelligence tests. However, since it is unlikely that RNA administered in this way arrives intact in the brain, the validity of this effect is open to question.

Protein synthesis in the brain is markedly dependent on thyroid hormone in the infant (although not in the adult) and thyroid deficiency in infancy leads to abnormal brain development and cretinism.

Alterations in brain protein levels have been reported in various pathological states. Some esterases have been found to be reduced or absent in the white matter in cases of multiple sclerosis, and changes in soluble protein levels have been described in idiopathic epilepsy. There have also been various reports of alterations in protein composition or turnover in mental disease, though none of them has been substantiated: they may well have been artefacts of poorly controlled diets or variations in locomotor activity.

Heath and co-workers have claimed to have isolated a protein fraction ('taraxein') from the serum of schizophrenic patients which has characteristic effects on experimental animals. This and similar findings from other laboratories have not been reliably reproduced however, and the existence of specific proteins in the serum of mental patients is doubtful.

A full account of factors altering cerebral protein metabolism can be found in the reviews by Lajtha (1964) and Jakoubek and Semiginovsky (1970).

## INBORN ERRORS IN METABOLISM

The term 'inborn error in metabolism', now taken to mean a genetically determined defect in an enzyme or in an enzyme-like carrier, was first coined by Garrod in 1908. A genetic mutation altering the DNA code results in the production of a modified enzyme protein molecule.

Depending on the nature of this modification the mutation may cause a decrease in, or total loss of, catalytic activity. In far rarer cases there is an increase in enzyme activity, e.g. in acute intermittent porphyria, hepatic delta-amino laevulinic acid synthetase, a key enzyme in the formation of porphyrine, is increased several-fold.

Mutations can also affect circulating proteins and structural proteins. The formation in man of abnormal haemoglobin molecules having a slightly altered amino acid sequence is an example of this type of mutation. Some of these abnormal haemoglobins are of little clinical significance in that they do not produce symptoms. Homozygous inheritance of the abnormal haemoglobin, haemoglobin 'S', causes the disease known as sickle cell anaemia. Here the abnormal haemoglobin crystalizes at the lowered concentration of oxygen in capillary blood, and changes the shape of the red cells (sickle cells). This increases the viscosity of the blood and results in capillary thrombosis. Heterozygous inheritance of the traits results in about 25 per cent of the haemoglobin being abnormal, and this is insufficient to cause sickling. This condition is known as the sickle cell trait. Wilson's disease is associated with an inherited defect in the circulating copper-carrying protein caeruloplasmin.

Most inborn errors or 'molecular diseases' as Pauling termed them are, however, associated with intracellular enzymatic defects or in cell membrane transport. It must be emphasized that although some of these errors have clinical effects, some may have no clinical manifestations whatsoever. Some of the clinical effects produced are often harmless, e.g. Pentosuria, but some have very serious consequences. Many inborn errors of metabolism, especially those of amino acids, cause neurological disorders. Primary inborn errors of metabolism are known for nearly all the amino acids with the exception of the dicarboxylic acids aspartate and glutamate.

CLASSIFICATION OF METABOLIC 'ERRORS'

Figure 8 shows a typical enzyme mediated reaction sequence in which A, B, C and D are the substrates and products of the main pathway and X and Y are the products of a minor pathway. The consequence of an enzymatic defect will depend on the position of the enzyme in the reaction sequence.

A defect in a permease enzyme, i.e. an enzyme affecting the entry of substrate into the cell, will result in there being insufficient intracellular A to saturate the enzyme ab thus causing a deficiency in B, C and D. Such a defect occurs in Hartnup's disease where the neutral amino acids are inefficiently reabsorbed in the renal tubules and jejunum. In this disease, there is a gross aminoaciduria involving all the neutral amino acids. Aspartate, glutamate, proline, methionine and cysteine are unaffected since they utilize a different transport carrier. A prominent feature of Hartnup's disease is the abnormally high excretion of certain indoles, in particular indoxysulphate and indolyl-3-acetic acid which are breakdown products of tryptophan by the intestinal bacteria. The reason for this is that since less tryptophan is absorbed in the gut, more is available to the intestinal bacteria.

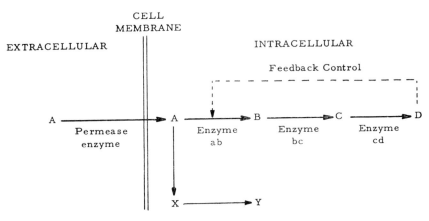

FIG. 8.   A typical metabolic pathway.

Normally, approximately 50 per cent of the daily nicotinamide requirement in the adult is supplied by the metabolism of tryptophan by the Kynurenine pathway; in Hartnup's disease, there is insufficient tryptophan to saturate this enzyme system and, as a result, the clinical symptoms of this disease resemble in many respects those of classical Pellegra (nicotinamide deficiency). The symptoms unlike those of most 'molecular diseases' tend to be intermittent with spontaneous remission. The most frequent symptoms are a light sensitive dermatitis and cerebellar ataxia and, in some cases, mental retardation.

A defect in the enzymes ab, bc and cd can lead to the extracellular and intracellular accumulation of the immediate or remote precursors of the reaction. In Von Gierke's disease, the absence of Glucose-6-phosphatase, the enzyme which initiates the process of glycolysis, leads to the abnormal deposition of glycogen in the liver. In the condition known as homocystinuria, there is a defect in methionine metabolism (Fig. 9), a virtual absence of cystathionine synthetase, which results in an accumulation of precursor homocystine in the plasma and urine and high methionine levels in the blood. Cystathionine is a normal constituent of human brain and is completely absent in patients with homocystinuria. Homocystinurics suffer from a number of skeletal abnormalities, cardiovascular disease and emotional instability. Mental retardation is not an invariable feature of the disease. Unlike Hartnup's disease, homocystinuria is a relatively common occurrence and is after phenylketonuria, the most common inborn error of amino acid metabolism. A survey carried out in Northern Ireland in 1965 of 2920 mentally retarded patients revealed 10 cases of homocystinuria and 69 cases of phenylketonuria.

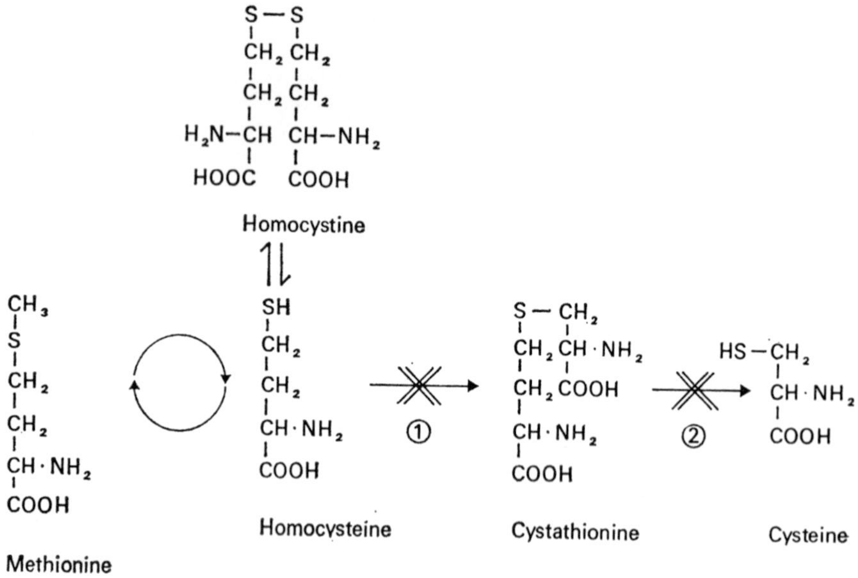

$$
\begin{array}{cc}
\text{S} & \text{S} \\
| & | \\
\text{CH}_2 & \text{CH}_2 \\
| & | \\
\text{CH}_2 & \text{CH}_2 \\
| & | \\
\text{H}_2\text{N--CH} & \text{CH--NH}_2 \\
| & | \\
\text{HOOC} & \text{COOH}
\end{array}
$$

Homocystine

$\uparrow\downarrow$

Methionine: $CH_3$ — S — $CH_2$ — $CH_2$ — $CH\cdot NH_2$ — COOH

Homocysteine: SH — $CH_2$ — $CH_2$ — $CH\cdot NH_2$ — COOH

① 

Cystathionine: S — $CH_2$ — $CH_2\cdot CH\cdot NH_2$ / $CH_2\text{COOH}$ — $CH\cdot NH_2$ — COOH

②

Cysteine: HS — $CH_2$ — $CH\cdot NH_2$ — COOH

FIG. 9.  Inborn errors of metabolism of sulphur-containing amino acids. (1) Homocystinuria; (2) Cystathioninuria.

There are three inborn errors of metabolism affecting the Krebs–Henseleit cycle for the conversion of ammonia to urea: hyperammonaemia, citrullinaemia and arginosuccinic aciduria (Fig. 10). In these diseases metabolic blocks occur at carbamyl phosphate synthetase or ornithine transcarbamylase: arginosuccinate synthetase and arginosuccinase respectively. All three conditions are characterized by ammonia intoxication with consequent mental retardation, cerebellar ataxia, poor muscular co-ordination and, occasionally, convulsions. All these conditions, especially the first two, are rare.

If the metabolism of the substrate A to product D is prevented by a metabolic block, the concentration of A will rise and conversion to X and Y by a minor pathway may occur. Under normal conditions, glycine is broken down via glyoxylic acid and formic acid to $CO_2$. In hyperoxaluria, however, the enzyme decarboxylating glyoxylic acid to formic acid is absent and instead the glyoxylic acid is converted to oxalic acid which subsequently appears in the urine. Similarly, histidine normally metabolized via urocanic acid to glutamic acid is transaminated to imidazole pyruvic acid in histidinaemia. This disease is due to lack of the enzyme histidase, and its symptoms include cerebral dysfunction.

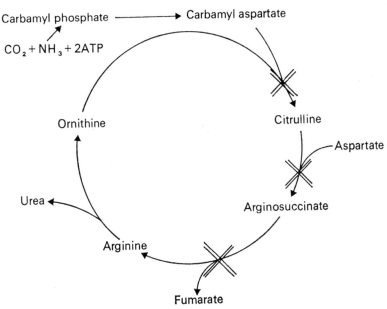

FIG. 10.   Inborn errors affecting the Krebs–Henseleit cycle.
(1) Hyperammonaemia; (2) Citrullinaemia; (3) Arginosuccinic aciduria.

The most important instance of alternate pathway utilization, from a neurological point of view, is provided by phenylketonuria in which there is a lack of phenylalanine hydroxylase (Fig. 11). This enzyme is responsible for converting phenylalanine to tyrosine and in its absence phenylalanine is metabolized by means of a number of pathways not utilized under normal conditions. The blood level of phenylalanine rises from a normal value of 1–4 mg per 100 ml to 15–63 mg per 100 ml and the level in the urine increases from 30 mg per day to 300–1000 mg per day. At present in the urine are a number of metabolites of phenylalanine. Phenylalanine is deaminated to phenylpyruvic acid and acetylated to N-acetyl phenylalanine. Some of the phenylpyruvic acid is excreted in the urine but some is converted to σ-hydroxyphenylacetic acid, phenylacetic acid and phenylacetylglutamine, all of which appear in appreciable amounts in the urine. σ-hydroxyphenylacetic acid is the most prominent being excreted in quantities of 100–400 mg per g creatinine.

There is evidence that there is an interrelationship between phenyl-alanine and tryptophan metabolism. Abnormal indole derivatives are found in the urine of phenylketonurics and certain metabolites of phenylalanine have been shown to inhibit 5-hydroxytryptophan decarb-oxylase, the enzyme responsible for converting 5-hydroxytryptophan to 5HT. Renson showed that liver phenylalanine hydroxylase is also re-sponsible for hydroxylating tryptophan to 5-hydroxytryptophan and that phenylalanine is a potent inhibitor of tryptophan hydroxylation.

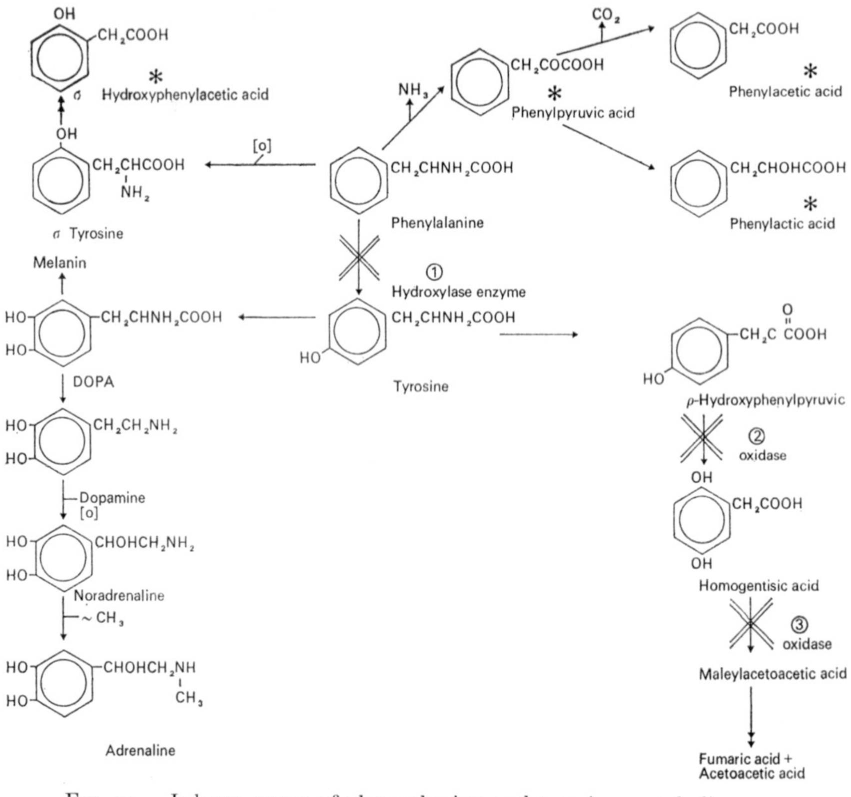

OH
—CH$_2$COOH
*
o Hydroxyphenylacetic acid

OH
CH$_2$CHCOOH
NH$_2$
[o]
o Tyrosine

Melanin

HO—CH$_2$CHNH$_2$COOH
HO—
DOPA

HO—CH$_2$CH$_2$NH$_2$
HO—
Dopamine
[o]

HO—CHOHCH$_2$NH$_2$
HO—
Noradrenaline
~ CH$_3$

HO—CHOHCH$_2$NH
HO—      CH$_3$
Adrenaline

CO$_2$
CH$_2$COCOOH
NH$_3$
*
Phenylpyruvic acid

CH$_2$CHNH$_2$COOH
Phenylalanine

① Hydroxylase enzyme
CH$_2$CHNH$_2$COOH
HO
Tyrosine

CH$_2$COOH
*
Phenylacetic acid

CH$_2$CHOHCOOH
*
Phenylactic acid

O
—CH$_2$C COOH
HO
p-Hydroxyphenylpyruvic

② oxidase

OH
CH$_2$COOH
OH
Homogentisic acid

③ oxidase
Maleylacetoacetic acid

Fumaric acid +
Acetoacetic acid

FIG. 11.    Inborn errors of phenyalanine and tyrosine metabolism.
(1) Phenylketonuria; (2) Tyrosinosis; (3) Alcaptonuria.

* Metabolites excreted in phenylketonuria.

The profound impairment of mental function which is a prominent feature of phenylketonuria may be due partly to 5HT deficiency. Phenylalanine is also known to inhibit the uptake of tyrosine by brain cells and to reduce the synthesis of adrenaline and noradrenaline by inhibiting DOPA decarboxylase. The mental performance of phenyl-ketonuric children can only be maintained if they are kept on a diet low in phenylalanine.

Two other congenital diseases of phenylalanine and tyrosine met-abolism, alcaptonuria and tyrosinosis, are far rarer. In the former, the urine darkens on exposure to air due to the formation of an oxidized product of homogentisic acid. Deposits of this substance in the cartilage often causes osteoarthritis in later life. In tyrosinosis $p$-hydroxyphenyl-pyruvic acid is excreted in large amounts.

Alternative pathway utilization is seen also in ketoaciduria, a disease in which the enzyme responsible for decarboxylating the $\alpha$-keto acids valine, leucine and isoleucine are absent. As a consequence, a number of abnormal metabolites of these acids appear in the urine giving it a characteristic 'maple syrup' odour—hence the alternative name 'maple syrup disease'.

If the product D of the pathway A $\rightarrow$ D is physiologically active, any block in the reaction sequence leading to D will have a marked clinical effect. There are a number of inborn enzymic defects which occur in the biosynthetic pathway leading to formation of thyroxine in the thyroid gland. In each case, the impaired synthesis of thyroxine results in goitrous cretinism. In addition, the final product of a biosynthetic pathway is often important for the regulation of the pathway by what Umbarger termed end product or feedback inhibition. Thus in goitrous cretinism the release of TSH is not impeded by the usual servo regulator, thy-roxine, and hyperplasia of the target gland results. In the Lesch-Nyhan syndrome, there is a failure to regulate the *de novo* synthesis of uric acid due to a specific defect in hypoxanthine guanine phosphoribosyl transferase.

Although the mutations responsible for these inborn errors of meta-bolism are present from the early stages in embryonic development, the clinical effects, if any, may not appear for many years. The osteo-arthritis caused by alcaptonuria is not usually evident until after the age of thirty and the overt clinical effects of intermittent porphyria on the autonomic nervous system do not manifest themselves before puberty.

For further reading in this field the reader is referred to Bondy and Rosenberg (1969).

## REFERENCES

AMIN, A. J., CRAWFORD, T. B. B. & GADDUM, J. H. (1954)   The distribution of substance P and 5-hydroxytryptamine in the central nervous system of the dog. *Journal of Physiology*, **126,** 596.

BARONDES, S. H. & JARVIK, M. E. (1964)   The influence of Actinomycin-D on brain RNA synthesis and on memory. *Journal of Neurochemistry*, **11,** 187.

BENNET, E. L., KRECH, D. & ROSENZWEIG, M. R. (1964)  Reliability and regional specificity of cerebral effects of environmental complexity and training. *Journal of Comparative and Physiological Psychology*, **57**, 440.

BERRY, R. W. (1969)  Ribonucleic acid metabolism of a single neuron: correlation with electrical activity. *Science*, **166**, 1021.

BONDY, P. K. & ROSENBERG, L. E. (eds.) (1969)  *Duncan's Diseases of Metabolism*. 6th Edn. W. B. Saunders & Co.

CAMERON, D. E., SVED, S., SOLYOM, L., WAINRIB, B. & BARIK, H. (1963)  Effects of RNA on memory defect in the aged. *American Journal of Psychiatry*, **120**, 320.

COLLINS, G. G. S., SANDLER, M., WILLIAMS, E. D. & YOUDIM, M. B. H. (1970)  Multiple forms of human brain mitochondrial monoamine oxidase. *Nature*, **225**, 817.

DAHLSTRÖM, A. & HAGGENDAL, J. (1966)  Studies on the transport and life span of amine storage granules in a peripheral adrenergic neuron system. *Acta physiologica Scandinavica*, **67**, 278.

ENGEL, J. Jr. & MORRELL, F. (1970)  Turnover of RNA in normal and secondarily epileptogenic rabbit cortex. *Experimental Neurology*, **26**, 221.

HYDÉN, H. & LANGE, P. (1966)  A genic stimulation with production of adenine-uracil rich RNA in neurons and glia in learning. *Die Naturwissenschaften*, **3**, 64.

HYDÉN, H. (1967)  Behaviour, neurol function and RNA. In *Progress in Nucleic Acid Research*. Edited by J. N. Davidson & W. E. Cohen, vol. 6, p. 187. New York: Academic Press.

HYDÉN, H. & LANGE, P. (1970)  Correlation of the S100 brain protein with behaviour. *Experimental Cell Research*, **62**, 125.

JAKOUBEK, B. & SEMIGINOVSKY, B. (1970)  The effect of increased functional activity on the protein metabolism of the nervous system. *International Review of Neurobiology*, **13**, 255.

JASPER, H. H., WARD, A. A. & POPE, A. (eds.) (1969)  *Basic Mechanisms of the Epilepsies*. London: J. A. Churchill.

LAJTHA, A. (1964)  Alteration and Pathology of Cerebral Protein Metabolism. *International Review of Neurobiology*, **7**, 1.

MAAS, J. W. & LANDIS, D. H. (1968)  In vivo studies of the metabolism of norepinephrine in the central nervous system. *Journal of Pharmacology and Experimental Theropeutics*, **163**, 147.

MAHLER, H. R. & CORDES, E. H. (1966)  *Biological Chemistry*, p. 752. London: Harper and Row.

MOORE, B. W. & McGREGOR, D. (1965)  Chromatographic and electrophoretic fractionation of soluble proteins of brain and liver. *Journal of Biological Chemistry*, **240**, 1647.

ORREGO, F. (1967)  Synthesis of RNA in normal and electrically stimulated brain cortex slices *in vitro*. *Journal of Neurochemistry*, **14**, 851.

PETERSON, R. P. & KERNELL, D. (1970)  Effects of nerve stimulation on the metabolism of Ribonucleic acid in a Molluscan giant neurone. *Journal of Neurochemistry*, **17**, 1075.

PTASHNE, M. & GILBERT, W. (1970)  Genetic repressors. *Scientific American*, June, 1970.

RICHTER, D. (1966)  Biochemical Aspects of Memory. In *Aspects of Learning and Memory*. Edited by D. Richter, p. 73. London: Heinemann.

ROSE, S. P. R. (1968)  Biochemical aspects of memory mechanisms. In *Applied Neurochemistry*. Edited by A. N. Davison and J. Dobbing, p. 356. Oxford and Edinburgh: Blackwell Scientific Publications.

TALWAR, G. P. (1969) Brain RNA. In *Biological Basis of Medicine*. Edited by E. E. Bittar & N. Bittar, vol. 5. London: Academic Press.

UNGAR, G., DESIDERIO, D. M. & PARR, M. (1971) Evidence for molecular coding of information in the nervous system. Abstr. 3rd Int. Meeting of Int. Soc. for Neurochem, p. 69.

Chapter XVI

# PHARMACOLOGY OF DRUGS OF IMPORTANCE IN PSYCHIATRY

## M. H. T. Roberts

### Introduction

The complexity of the biochemistry, anatomy and physiology of the nervous system is poorly understood, but even less is known about the nature of the delicate balance between the various chemical or physiological systems which give rise to the normal functioning of nervous tissue. The action of a drug on one system may be well known, but all too often its actions on other systems have not been studied, and nothing is therefore known of the modification of the balance of influences within the brain. The therapeutic value of a drug depends primarily upon the successful adjustment of this balance. A clear understanding of a drug's action is unlikely therefore to emerge from a detailed description of its effects upon one aspect of cell metabolism or one type of receptor or uptake mechanism. Regrettably, the restrictions of present-day knowledge force an emphasis upon only one or two actions of most drugs, which may prove to be misleading, as continued investigation reveals new properties and central actions.

The pharmacology of a drug can be presented from many different viewpoints: clinical efficacy, behavioural effects, local or widespread effects upon physiology and biochemistry or drug interactions *in vivo* or *in vitro*. All these aspects are discussed, but the central theme is the effect of drugs at the level of the single cell. Only by a knowledge at this level of the physiological or biochemical effects, can a real understanding emerge of the basic actions of a drug.

### Principles and Methods of Investigation

#### MECHANISMS BY WHICH DRUGS MAY INFLUENCE THE ACTIVITY OF NERVE CELLS

Drugs which are useful in Psychiatry alter the behaviour of patients by influencing the activity of various neuronal systems. A neuronal system functions by integrating the activity of individual neurones. This is why a study of psychotherapeutic drugs should be based on the investigation of drug action at the neuronal level.

The integrative and transmitting functions of nerve cells may be modified by the action of a drug upon the synaptic mechanism, the conducting membranes or the metabolic processes of synthesis and energy production. Although conduction in the soma or axon, or transmission at the synapse must always be involved in the modification of behaviour, this may be a direct or indirect effect of the drug.

*Energy Producing and Storing Mechanisms*

Energy metabolism is probably the most important process underlying all aspects of brain function. Drugs which modify this process may be expected to have very general but profound effects upon behaviour which may be of considerable therapeutic value. Energy production and storage will not be discussed here, as it has been well covered in Chapter XV, Volume I; also see D. F. Horrobin (1968).

*The Nerve Cell Membrane*

The cell membrane is a complex and highly organized structure through which substrates and drugs must pass. The membrane of nerve cells possesses the fundamental property of excitability which, if modified by drugs, results in an immediate and profound change in brain function.

Physico-chemical studies of the cell membrane reveal it to be a bimolecular layer of lipid molecules surrounded on the inside and outside of the cell by protein layers. Lipid soluble substances are able to pass this barrier with relative ease, but inorganic ions do so less easily. The nerve cell membrane contains high concentrations of phospholipids. All phospholipids contain phosphorus in a hydrophilic polar group which contacts the aqueous cell contents and the extracellular medium. The passage of inorganic ions through this lipid barrier is not understood, but an adequate hypothesis is the existence of aqueous channels through the lipid barrier. The ability of these channels to alter in diameter explains the changes in permeability of the neuronal membrane to cations and anions during generation of the action potential. The active transport of some ions across cell membranes involves the utilization of energy. Adenosine phosphatase, which liberates energy and a phosphate ion from adenosine triphosphate, is concentrated in nerve cell membranes. Active transport accounts for three important processes in nervous tissue: (1) the acceleration of the inward diffusion of nutrients, etc., (2) the active creation of a low sodium concentration inside the cell, subsequently maintained passively, and (3) the active accumulation of potassium ions inside the cell.

In general, the functioning of nerve cell membranes is not well understood, but certain drugs can be shown to have effects on the processes outlined above, which in time may come to be increasingly recognized as important sites for the action of therapeutic drugs.

*Synaptic Transmission*

The transmission of electrical impulses across the synaptic cleft in man and other mammals usually involves the release of a neurochemical. Invertebrates have been shown to possess tight junctions between cells across which electrical coupling, and not chemical release, accounts for transmission. It is quite possible that such ephaptic transmission occurs in man, but very little is known about the action of drugs on this process.

Figure 1 summarizes the general processes of chemical transmission in schematic form. The noradrenergic nerve terminal has been chosen as an example:

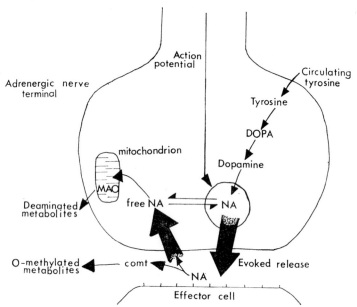

Fig. 1.   Schematic diagram of the synthesis and metabolism of transmitters in the adrenergic nerve terminal. NA = noradrenaline; MAO = monoamine oxidase; comt = catechol-o-methyl transferase.

Drugs may affect almost any of the processes associated with transmission, and will often influence several. The most important are:

*Conduction Along the Axon*

Drugs may stabilize the membrane, maintain its polarization and inhibit conduction of the action potential towards the terminal. Typically, the local anaesthetics have this effect.

*Inhibition or Acceleration of Transmitter Synthesis*

Two primary processes may be affected: (1) the transport of precursors into the cell, and (2) the action of enzymes synthesizing the transmitter.

## *Storage and Release of the Transmitter*

This consists of (1) active transport into the storage particles, (2) availability of binding sites in the store, and (3) release from the store and from the terminal. Drugs such as reserpine block transport of amines into store and false transmitters may occupy the stores. Both cause an apparent release of transmitter from the stores and reduce the availability of the transmitter.

## *Inactivation of the Transmitter*

Two general processes are included under this heading: (1) the purely intracellular catabolism of transmitter produced in excess of requirement and available store (catecholamines and 5HT), and (2) the rapid inactivation of transmitter released into the extracellular synaptic cleft: (a) the rapid re-uptake of transmitter into the nerve terminal (catecholamines and 5HT), and (b) extracellular degradation of the released transmitter (catecholamines and acetylcholine).

Drugs may specifically inhibit the intracellular enzymic destruction of transmitter causing 'spill over', i.e. the nonevoked release of transmitter into the synaptic cleft. These drugs also potentiate transmission due to the increased amount of transmitter released. Potentiation of transmission is also caused by drugs which block re-uptake into the terminal, for although the amount of transmitter released is not affected, its stay in the synaptic cleft is extended.

## *The Postsynaptic Receptors*

A wide range of drug actions may occur: (1) agonistic action. A drug may occupy the receptors eliciting the same response as the transmitter, (2) a weak agonist may occupy the receptors and reduce their availability to the more effective transmitter, thus directly interfering with transmission, and (3) an antagonist is usually ineffective in eliciting the postsynaptic response, but may compete with the transmitter for occupancy of the receptors. Usually, this type of antagonist has a molecular structure resembling the transmitter. Non-competitive antagonism occurs when the antagonist/receptor interaction is less easily reversible than the transmitter/receptor interaction. Some drugs inhibit the membrane response to the transmitter or interfere with all types of membrane receptor. These non-specific drugs are not termed antagonists.

### IDENTIFICATION OF CENTRAL SYNAPTIC TRANSMITTERS

The clear identification of a substance as a neurochemical transmitter is much more difficult in the brain than in the periphery. The criteria for identification of a substance as a neurotransmitter in brain are generally accepted to be:

1. *Presence and location:* (1) the substance or enzymes for its synthesis should be present and should probably predominate in the nerve endings rather than in the nerve cell bodies, and (2) the substance should probably be associated with a vesicular fraction and be present mainly in a 'bound' state.

2. *Release:* (1) stimulation of an appropriate nervous pathway should cause the substance to be released in a pharmacologically identifiable form, (2) when synthesis of new transmitter substance is prevented and the nerve is stimulated, histochemical evidence of transmitter depletion in the nerve terminals might be acceptable as evidence of release.

3. *Identity of action:* The application of the potential transmitter to the postsynaptic cell should reproduce the effects of nerve stimulation: (1) qualitatively, so that cell activity changes in the same direction, and (2) quantitatively, with regard to conductance changes in the post-synaptic membrane and in the amount of substance required to mimic nerve stimulation.

In the periphery, acetylcholine and noradrenaline are well established as transmitters, but in the central nervous system a much larger number of substances may have this function. The most important are acetylcholine, noradrenaline, 5-hydroxytryptamine, dopamine and histamine, but the amino acids glutamate, gamma amino butyric acid and glycine have recently been shown to be possible neurotransmitters.

The following is merely a brief summary of the extent to which the above criteria have been fulfilled for the biogenic amines. Acetylcholine, gamma amino butyric acid, glycine, L-glutamate and the role of cyclic AMP have been discussed in particular detail in Chapter XV.

NORADRENALINE

Noradrenaline occurs widely throughout the central nervous system. Using the histochemical fluorescence technique Dählstrom and Fuxe (1964) showed that the amine was contained mostly in nerve terminals which had a similar appearance to peripheral sympathetic nerve terminals. The only cell bodies containing noradrenaline lay in the lateral mesencephalon and pons.

No experiments demonstrating the release of noradrenaline from intact brain in response to electrical stimulation have been made, but radioactively labelled noradrenaline appears in the supernatant when slices of brain are stimulated. The local application of noradrenaline to cerebral neurones excites some cells and depresses others. Antagonists of noradrenaline prevent the excitation more frequently than the inhibition of cells, throwing doubt upon the specificity of the inhibitory receptor. It is not known if any of these receptors are subsynaptic. In the olfactory bulb of the rabbit, however, noradrenergic antagonists inhibit the depressant effects of both nerve stimulation and noradrenaline, but

it has not proved possible to visualize by microfluorescence the noradrenaline-containing nerve terminals. It may be noted in summary
that noradrenaline is probably a central neurotransmitter, but evidence
regarding its release from terminals and the subsynaptic nature of the
receptors on cells is incomplete.

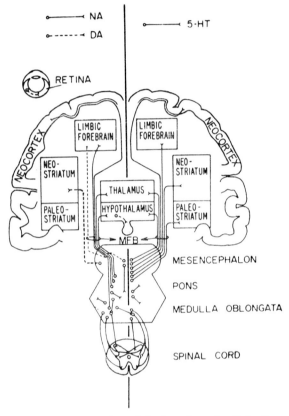

FIG. 2. Schematic representation of the location of cell bodies and fibre
tracts containing the biogenic amines in mammalian brain. NA =
noradrenaline; DA = dopamine; 5HT = 5-hydroxyptrytamine; MFB =
medial forebrain bundle.

DOPAMINE

Although dopamine is the precursor of noradrenaline, fluorescence
microscopy and chemical analysis demonstrated two systems of cells in
the brain, one containing dopamine, the other noradrenaline. The cell
bodies of the dopamine system lay in the substantia nigra and the terminals in the corpus striatum. The corpus striatum which contains little
noradrenaline is however rich in dopamine-$\beta$-hydroxylase which
converts dopamine to noradrenaline. Before a neurotransmitter function

for dopamine could be claimed it was necessary to demonstrate that dopamine itself was released by nerve stimulation. This has proved to to be extremely difficult but Vogt has shown that homovanillic acid (HVA) may be collected after stimulation of substantia nigra. HVA is not a metabolite of noradrenaline.

Although dopamine is very much less active over a wide range of pharmacological tests than the other amines, local application excites some cerebral neurones and depresses others. It is not known if these responses result from activation of specific receptors or if the dopamine is converted to another compound before eliciting the response.

It must be concluded that the evidence supporting a neurotransmitter role for dopamine is very incomplete.

### 5-HYDROXYTRYPTAMINE

Seventy per cent of the brain content of 5HT occurs in the synaptosomal fraction of brain homogenates, mostly in synaptic vesicles.

5HT is released from mouse spinal cord and stimulation of the nucleus raphe releases 5HT from the cortex and increases its rate of turnover in the hypothalamus, midbrain and medulla. It is not clear whether this latter effect is due to the release and subsequent degradation of 5HT, or due to a direct action of the electrical stimulation on the biosynthesis. It is therefore not certain that 5HT is released from nerve terminals as a transmitter.

Receptors for 5HT have been identified on neurones in the cortex, hippocampus, amygdala, midbrain and medulla. Local application of 5HT elicits excitatory and depressant responses. Antagonists of 5HT selectively and reversibly prevent the excitatory responses, but are less effective on the depressant responses. This suggests that depression of cell activity might result from a nonspecific action of the amine. There is no evidence that the responses to exogenously applied 5HT result from activation of postsynaptic receptors, and conclusive experiments to demonstrate the effect of 5HT antagonists on neurotransmission have not been conducted. The evidence supporting the proposal that 5HT is a central nervous system transmitter remains incomplete.

### The Absorption, Distribution and Excretion of Drugs

There are many factors which influence the entry of drugs into brain tissue but only the more important may be discussed here. These are the route of administration, absorption from the site of administration, the blood–brain barrier and excretion.

### ROUTE OF ADMINISTRATION AND ABSORPTION

Oral administration is the safest and most common route but is probably the least easily controlled. The plasma concentration of the drug will vary both within and between subjects so that conclusions regarding the effectiveness of an orally administered dose require a very large number of observations—a factor not always taken into account when designing drug trials.

Absorption from the gut depends largely upon the solubility of the drug in lipids and water. The cell membrane is partly lipid in composition and passage through the intestinal mucous membranes will be facilitated by lipid solubility. Highly ionized drugs are poorly absorbed from the intestine due probably to electrostatic binding to or repulsion from the mucosal membranes. Absorption is therefore influenced by the proportion of drug dissociated into charged ions at the pH of the intestine, i.e. the pK value.

Chemically unstable drugs may be broken down by the action of intestinal enzymes and the differing pH of the gastro-intestinal tract. Dilution of the drug by the contents of the gut will also significantly affect absorption. These factors and the failure of patients to adhere to the dosage and times advised by the physician make the oral administration of drugs uncertain. Intravenous injection of drugs usually gives rise to an extremely rapid response. Dilution of the drug by the bloodstream prevents the irritation of tissues at the point of injection and yet dilution is not a highly variable factor giving rise to large differences in response. Drugs may be degraded by enzymes in the blood or peripheral organs before reaching the brain, but a higher proportion of drug reaches brain tissues when this route is used than by any other except direct intracarotid injection. This latter is often used in the laboratory to reduce the destruction of drugs by the blood. Experimental administration of acetylcholine and 5HT for example are ineffective unless given in massive doses in spite of the considerable sensitivity of tissues to them. Similarly, L-DOPA is predominantly metabolized by the liver dopa decarboxylase and must be administered in large amounts before any central effects are detected.

Intramuscular injection is frequently used and gives high plasma levels of a drug fairly quickly. Often drugs are given intramuscularly in oily solutions to increase the time of absorption and prolong the action of the drug. The disadvantages of injection may be summarized as: the need for strict asepsis, the occurrence of an intravascular injection when this is not intended, pain, and the difficulty of self-administration. Parenteral routes are not as safe as oral medication.

DISTRIBUTION OF DRUGS

After a drug has been absorbed or injected into the bloodstream it must enter or pass through the various body fluid compartments—plasma, extracellular and intracellular fluids. Some drugs cannot pass cell membranes and are therefore restricted in their distribution. Passive and active processes are involved in the transport across cell membranes. The passive process involves either the passage of drug ions through aqueous pores in the membrane or their solution in the lipid membrane. Lipid soluble drugs which passively diffuse through the membrane do so at a rate which is directly proportional to the concentration gradient across the membrane and the lipid: water partition coefficient of the drug. The more lipid-soluble the drug, the faster it penetrates the cell. The passage of ions through pores may be seen as a filtration process due to the very small size, 4 Angstrom units (0·4 nm), of the pores. Substances with a molecular weight in excess of 200 do not pass through these pores and will only penetrate the cell through the lipid membrane or by an active process.

Active transport processes differ from passive processes in that they exhibit selectivity, can be saturated, and require energy. The process is thought to be mediated by carriers within the membrane that form a complex with the drug on the outside of the membrane, diffuse across to the inner surface and release the drug inside the cell.

The entrance of drugs into the C.N.S. and into cerebrospinal fluid is a special aspect of cellular penetration which follows the same general principles as for transfer into cells. The so-called blood–brain barrier is not a physical entity but exists at different places for different drugs. Access to the extracellular fluid of brain is restricted either at the capillary endothelial cells or at the membranes of the glial cell processes which surround the capillaries. For some drugs the activity of enzymes in these membranes prevents entry to brain and for others powerful inactivation or uptake into stores in various peripheral organs prevent accumulation in brain.

The entry of drugs into the cerebrospinal fluid is largely via the chorioid plexus, but the exit of drugs and the metabolites of drugs, is through the arachnoid villi. This occurs by bulk fluid flow and molecules are excreted regardless of lipid solubility and ionization. Specialized active transport mechanisms for the removal of drugs from the C.S.F. also exist.

Drugs may be stored in many areas of the body where special accumulation mechanisms exist. The stores are in equilibrium with the unbound drug in the plasma and as the free drug is metabolized more is released from the store maintaining the plasma level. Plasma proteins and tissue fat are the most important of these stores although, within cells, proteins, phospholipids and nucleoproteins also bind drugs. Drugs do not usually accumulate in the cerebrospinal fluid.

EXCRETION OF DRUGS

The kidney is the most important organ for the excretion of drugs. The lung, biliary system of the liver, salivary and sweat glands also excrete drugs to a small extent and may occasionally be important. The rate of drug excretion is often proportional to the rate of absorption because lipid soluble, non-polar molecules are reabsorbed by the epithelial cells of the excretory organs. Many drugs which are highly lipid soluble are therefore metabolized to lipid insoluble or ionized metabolites before excretion. Occasionally these metabolites are more pharmacologically active than the compound injected. Modification of the rate of metabolism of drugs is sometimes a useful method for prolonging drug action. Alternatively, accelerating the excretion is of value in cases of overdosage.

THE METHODS USED FOR THE STUDY OF DRUG ACTION IN BRAIN

The methods used to study the central actions of psychoactive drugs fall into three arbitrary divisions: behavioural, neuropharmacological and biochemical studies. The principles and techniques used in behavioural and biochemical studies have been fully covered in Chapters IX and XV of this volume and will not be repeated here. Toxicological studies are also of profound importance but are outside the scope of this chapter.

The relative lack of knowledge concerning the central actions of drugs relates clearly to the inadequacy of the available techniques. The brain is very difficult to study because:

1. It is inaccessible.

2. It is very sensitive to surgical interference and anoxia.

3. Neuronal isolation of any particular region is at least difficult and usually impossible.

4. The blood–brain barrier resists the penetration of many drugs.

5. The high metabolic rate of the brain reduces the value of post-mortem study of tissue concentration of drugs or substrates.

6. The *in vivo* functioning of organized neurones, neuronal systems or biochemical pathways probably differs significantly from that of brain homogenates or cell cultures which are studied *in vitro*.

PHYSIOLOGICAL AND NEUROPHARMACOLOGICAL STUDIES

Experimental investigation of the effects of drugs on physiological responses of the central nervous system have utilized a wide range of techniques. Considerable variation exists both in the type of response recorded and in the methods of applying the drugs. Among the earlier phenomena to be studied, but probably the least well understood, is the electroencephalogram (E.E.G.). Recordings may be taken from the scalp of human volunteers or patients or from wire electrodes placed into contact with the cortex or subcortical nuclei of animals. Often these studies have involved the observation of gross changes in appearance of the E.E.G. following injection of drugs but, increasingly, modern computing methods enable detailed analysis of the relative occurrence of different frequency components within the E.E.G., before and after drug injection. Correlation of the rhythms recorded from different areas of the brain may suggest regional rather than generalized effects of a drug.

These techniques have demonstrated that barbiturates slow and synchronize E.E.G. waveforms and amphetamine increases the frequency and desynchronizes the E.E.G. Gross observation of the subject confirms that these effects on the E.E.G. are paralleled by the anticipated changes in behaviour. However, atropine slows and physostigmine increases the frequency of the E.E.G., and yet the behavioural effects of these drugs are not very marked. It is necessary therefore to observe the E.E.G. simultaneously with other physiological, biochemical or behavioural measures of response to drugs. One technique illustrating how this is done is the observation of sleep duration, depth of sleep and frequency of occurrence of 'rapid eye movement' sleep whilst recording the E.E.G. These methods have proved to be extremely sensitive.

The recording of evoked potentials from scalp, cortical or subcortical electrodes has proved of value in assessment of drug action. These potentials may be evoked by stimulation of peripheral receptors—click, flash, touch, etc., or by electrical stimulation of structures within the brain. If a drug acts upon sensory or associated pathways these tests identify its action. Drug effects on conduction between two non-sensory nuclei in the brain may also be detected. A good example of the use of such a technique is the study of cortical evoked potentials following systematic administration of LSD and chlorpromazine (Bradley and Key, 1958). The two drugs exhibited opposite effects on all the measures recorded but it was shown that both acted at the same level within the brain. Potentials evoked from the periphery ascend towards the cortex along two routes: (1) the primary sensory pathways and (2) enter the reticular formation along collaterals from the primary sensory paths and ascend through the nonspecific thalamic nuclei. Although both drugs affected the peripherally evoked cortical potentials neither drug changed the potentials evoked from either stimulating the primary pathways or the reticular formation. It was concluded that both drugs had effects related to the collateral inflow of sensory information to the reticular formation from the main sensory paths. Other experiments using behavioural and lesioning techniques have tended to confirm these findings.

All the techniques referred to above used macroelectrodes which recorded the synchronous activity from a few cubic millimeters or more of tissue. Similar studies with tungsten or glass microelectrodes have proved particularly valuable as information is gained concerning the response of single cells to drugs. Two important aspects of the drug's action may be studied. Firstly, although it may be known that the drug causes excitation, this may result from a direct excitation of the cells or from the inhibition of inhibitory cells. These effects may be differentiated by the use of microelectrodes. Secondly, different cell types will exist within an anatomical area or nucleus and microelectrode studies will demonstrate the action of a drug upon each of the different cell types. In this way, functional rather than anatomical systems may be studied.

Pharmacological classification of chemical receptors on the membranes of neurones is also possible. The technique of microiontophoresis of drugs from multibarrelled micropipettes is used. Five glass tubes are drawn to a single fine point of 5 $\mu$m diameter. Ionized drug solutions are placed into these tubes and the application of currents of approximately $10^{-8}$ A ejects the drug ions from one or more of these barrels. When inserted into the brain, changes may be recorded in the rate of action potential production by nearby neurones when each of the drugs is ejected into its environment. With this technique it is possible to observe the potentiation of the excitatory and inhibitory effects of noradrenaline by the antidepressant drugs and to study what other neurochemical systems may be affected by the antidepressants. The amount of drug released during each application is so small that metabolism and diffusion away from the cell is rapid and repeated applications may be made enabling the detailed pharmacological study of the receptors involved. This is not possible with most other *in vivo* techniques as drugs usually require many hours for complete cessation of their pharmacological effects.

Drugs are applied by other novel routes which are sometimes used for behavioural and biochemical studies as well as physiological work. Direct application of drugs to both the inner and outer surfaces of the brain involves diffusion of the drug into the tissues. These routes avoid the blood–brain barrier but it is never clear how much drug successfully penetrates the enzymic and physical barriers in the tissue and dosage is therefore difficult to control. Not only may drugs diffuse into brain from cerebrospinal fluid, but metabolites of neurotransmitters may diffuse into C.S.F. from brain. It is possible to obtain C.S.F. from man by lumbar puncture and this fluid, which is in intimate contact with the brain, provides more rapid, precise and easily obtained information concerning the effects of drugs on the central nervous system of man than is available in other ways. Drug induced changes in metabolism may be detected and the rise and fall in the concentration of drug may be accurately followed providing the dynamic aspects of the brain–C.S.F. equilibrium is understood.

The push-pull cannula provides a method for perfusing subcortical nuclei with drug solutions. It consists of two steel tubes placed one inside the other. Fluid forced down the inner is syphoned up the outer. Thus a small ventricle is created and drugs or metabolites diffuse into this ventricle and are collected with the perfusate. Changes in the concentration of metabolites following drug application indicate the effects of the drug on the perfused nucleus. The limiting factor with this technique is the massive degree of tissue damage and the doubt which must exist regarding the continued normal functioning of the nucleus. This indeed is the major problem with all surgical investigations of the brain. Spreading depression, oedema, circulatory disturbances and also anaesthetic agents all significantly change the functioning of brain and make investigations of it by physical techniques very difficult.

## SYSTEMATIC DESCRIPTION OF DRUGS OF IMPORTANCE IN PSYCHIATRY

The classification of psychoactive drugs has been discussed intensively for the past two decades and a number of classification systems proposed but none universally accepted. A World Health Organization Group (1969) used the following classification and definition according to the clinical efficacy of the compounds:

### Psychotropic Drug

A drug that acts upon psychic function, behaviour or experience.

### Neuroleptic

Drugs with therapeutic effects on psychoses and other types of psychiatric disorders. Also known as antipsychotics, ataractics or major tranquillizers.

### Anxiolytic Sedative

Drugs which reduce pathological anxiety, tension and agitation without therapeutic effects on disturbed cognitive or perceptual processes. Formerly known as minor tranquillizers.

### Antidepressant

Drugs effective in the treatment of pathological depressive states. Also called psychic energizers or thymoleptics.

### Psychostimulant

Drugs that increase the level of alertness and/or motivation.

### Psychodysleptic

Drugs producing abnormal mental phenomena particularly in the cognitive and perceptual spheres. Also known as hallucinogens, psychotomimetics and in some cases psychedelics.

Although this classification is presently the most practical and useful it is probable that a relationship between clinical efficacy, molecular structure and pharmacological activity will emerge eventually and enable a system of classification which takes all these factors into account.

This classification and the following discussion of drug action is restricted to those drugs of particular importance in psychiatry; for further reading see Passmore and Robson (1970) and Goodman and Gilman (1968).

Clearly this chapter can only deal with the main groups of drugs used for psychiatric patients. The following categories are not covered:

1. Drugs which although they are very important in psychiatry are widely used in general medicine and are not exclusively used in psychiatric practice, e.g. barbiturates and amphetamines.

2. Very new drugs of uncertain clinical value but immense theoretical interest, e.g. tryptophan and L-DOPA.

3. Drugs frequently used by the psychiatrist which do not directly influence behaviour, e.g. disulfiram and the vitamins.

## NEUROLEPTICS

For many years psychoses have been treated with several types of sedative. Invariably these drugs impaired the attention span and performance of routine tasks and caused increased ataxia and somnolence. The neuroleptics do not possess these unwanted side effects to the same degree and their central actions appear to be quite different. Nevertheless the description by Delay of the effects of chronic administration of chlorpromazine on patients indicates that although at first sight the patient presents a normal appearance and is able to read and play cards, he does not speak spontaneously very much, does not take the initiative, and responses to external stimuli appear to be 'damped down'. (Wikler, 1957). Thus, the clinical advantage of the neuroleptics over the sedatives may be described as the induction of sedation in psychotic patients without causing the patient to sleep. Experimental investigation of the central effects of these drugs is complicated by the difficulty in producing 'psychoses' in animals and the subjective nature of the therapeutic effect. However, certain biochemical, behavioural and physiological effects of the drugs can be related to the drug's action in man and some tentative hypotheses advanced concerning their mode of action.

### THE RAUWOLFIA ALKALOIDS

The rauwolfia alkaloids had been used for centuries in India to treat insanity but were not used in the west until 1946 when they were introduced for the treatment of hypertension. Reserpine was isolated in 1952 from extracts of the root and in 1954 Kline reported its value as a neuroleptic. It is probable that nearly all the pharmacological activity of the powdered root and extract is associated with reserpine and only this compound will be discussed. Although modern medicine has replaced reserpine with more potent and less toxic antihypertensives and neuroleptics, it remains an important drug to the experimenter and the student of the amine hypothesis of depression.

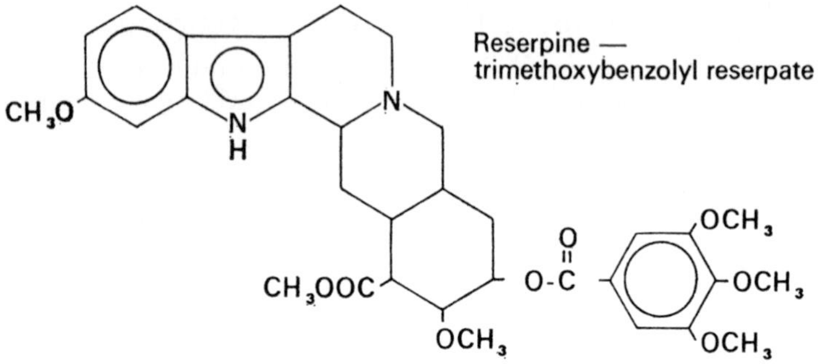

FIG. 3.

## Metabolism

Reserpine is not concentrated by the brain. Only 0·03 per cent of the total dose (100 μg kg s.c. in rats) of $^3$H reserpine appears in brain 30 min later and progressively falls to a minute 0·008 μg per g after 2 h. This concentration is maintained for 48 h. The maximum pharmacological effects of the drug are seen 6 h after injection, however, and remain for 48 h. The concentration and elimination of reserpine from brain has a time course which is rather different from the time course of the behavioural effects of the drug. An esterase located predominantly in the liver and intestinal mucosa degrades reserpine to reserpate and trimethoxybenzoate. Both metabolites are pharmacologically inactive and several studies have shown there is no correlation between the rate of metabolism and the effectiveness of the drug on behaviour. Some other explanation is required for the delayed onset and long duration of the behavioural effects.

## The Depletion of Brain Amines

Biochemical assay of brain homogenates and application of the technique of histochemical fluorescence have shown that in brain and other tissues, the concentration of 5HT, NA, dopamine and histamine are reduced following reserpine administration. The concentration of Ach is unaffected. In man and other animals, a rise in the 5HIAA and homovanillic acid content of urine precedes the reduction in concentration of brain amines. Increased excretion of the metabolites of noradrenaline probably also occurs but they are not easily detected. Studies with human platelets and more recently with homogenates and slices of animal brain have shown that reserpine treatment reduces the ability of these tissues to concentrate radioactively labelled 5HT, NA and dopamine.

This evidence has given rise to the following postulate of the action of reserpine:

1. Reserpine blocks the uptake of amines into neuronal storage sites. Presumably this blockage occurs during the period immediately following the injection and is maintained by the minute traces of drug which are still detectable in brain 48 h after a single injection.

2. A dynamic equilibrium between free and bound (stored) amine is postulated and reserpine, by blocking one of the balanced processes, causes the amine to leave the storage sites.

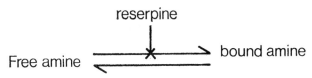

3. The free amine is degraded into acid metabolites which are eliminated in the urine. Newly formed amine will not be protected from enzymes by uptake into stores and is therefore broken down immediately

Inhibitors of monoamine oxidase which prevent the destruction of NA and 5HT, reverse the behavioural effects of reserpine and prevent the reduction of brain levels of the monoamines. Presumably, this indicates that if the enzymic destruction of amine is prevented, the high cytoplasmic concentration of the amine which rapidly results competes against the depleting action of reserpine on the stores and adequate neurotransmission occurs. The observation strongly supports the postulate that the tranquillizing effects of reserpine result from the depression of brain amine levels. It is very difficult to demonstrate whether the tranquillizing effects of reserpine relate more to NA or 5HT. Brodie and co-workers suggest that the depression of 5HT is the most relevant because:

1. The depletion of brain levels of NA and dopamine by other drugs does not cause sedation.

2. Analogues of reserpine affect NA and 5HT levels in the brain for different periods of time. The time course of the sedation usually follows that for 5HT and not NA.

3. Exposure to cold can depress brain levels of NA without affecting 5HT and no sedation occurs.

Carlsson and co-workers have suggested that the depletion of NA causes the sedation because administration of 3,4-dihydroxphenyl-alanine (DOPA—a precursor of NA) prevents the behavioural effects of reserpine, while administration of 5-hydroxytryptophan (a precursor of 5HT) does not. It remains unclear therefore whether the depletion of NA or 5HT gives rise to the behavioural effects of reserpine administration. It should be noted that chlorpromazine which has very similar behavioural effects does not depress brain levels of the amines at all.

*Peripheral and Central Pharmacology*

Reserpine was originally used as an antihypertensive agent. A transient elevation of blood pressure is rapidly followed by hypotension and bradycardia lasting for several days. These effects correlate well with the predicted actions of reserpine on noradrenaline stores of postganglionic sympathetic nerves. The noradrenaline is released from the storage granules by reserpine and although most is destroyed by mitochondrial monoamine oxidase some diffuses out of the cell onto receptors. Subsequently, when the stores are depleted of NA, sympathetic transmission is very much reduced and there is less smooth muscle tone in the arterioles. This is an incomplete explanation of the action of reserpine however, for the full hypotensive effects do not appear in the spinal animal. The medulla and midbrain must be intact and even decorticate animals do not react fully. This complex central action is not fully understood, but it is suggested that reduction of the activity in the amine-containing central pathways depresses the central sympathetic centres in the hypothalamus. Similar hypothalamic effects on endocrine secretion may account for the occurrence of lactation and inhibition of menstruation which can occur with reserpine.

The action of reserpine in reducing central and peripheral sympathetic activity gives rise to pupillary contraction, ptosis, bradycardia, increased gastric secretion and nasal congestion. The increased motility of the gut may be related to the local release of 5HT or to the cholinergic effects of reserpine.

Reserpine has little effect on the E.E.G. The slight reduction in frequency and increase in amplitude parallels the tendency of the subject to sleep. Convulsive activity is suppressed by high doses of reserpine but moderate doses may induce seizures. In experimental animals reserpine has been shown to increase the potency of convulsants which act on the brain and to potentiate electro-shock seizures. Dysrhythmia of the E.E.G. may occur in patients following chronic administration.

Detailed electrophysiological investigation of the effects of reserpine has not taken place as it has with chlorpromazine, but it appears that the two drugs may have quite different effects upon the reticular formation, chlorpromazine decreasing and reserpine increasing its activity.

Laboratory animals are often excited transiently after injection of reserpine but after 60 min become placid and unaggressive, remaining so for up to 48 h after a single dose. During this period a catatonia-like state may be induced. Indifference to environmental stimuli and a tendency to sleep occurs. However the animal may be easily aroused and ataxia and disequilibrium does not occur. Inhibition of conditioned response is probably due to the indifference to sensory stimulation and tests involving powerful stimuli are less easily inhibited by reserpine.

Although Barsa and Kline (1955) reported favourably on the use of reserpine in chronic schizophrenia it has now been replaced by the phenothiazines and butyrophenones.

### THE PHENOTHIAZINES

The dye methylene blue is one of this group of compounds and early this century many phenothiazines were synthesized in an attempt to find new dyes. A phenothiazine was used as a veterinary antihelminthic and other members of the series were investigated for pharmacological

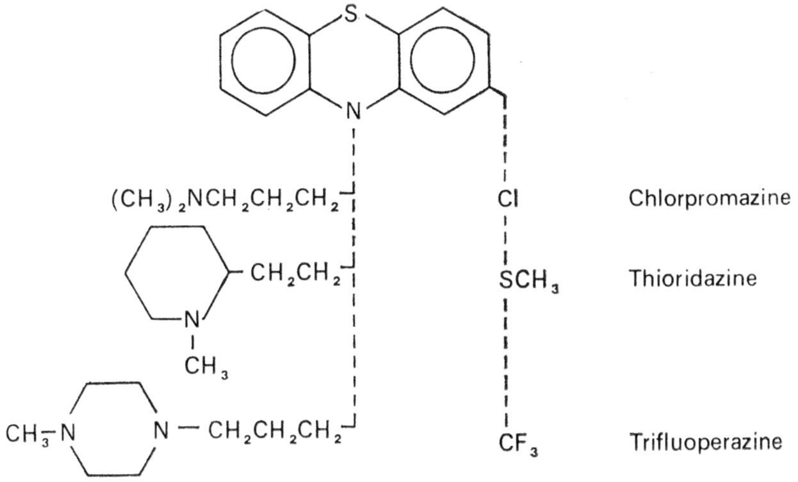

FIG. 4.

properties. Promethazine was found to have sedative properties and in 1950 Charpentier *et al.* synthesized chlorpromazine. The drug was used at first to potentiate anaesthesia but Delay and Deniker (1953) reported its value in the control of violent excitement. Its use as a neuroleptic rapidly spread.

Chlorpromazine remains the most widely used of the phenothiazine neuroleptics and will be described as the prototype drug of this series.

*Metabolism*

Chlorpromazine is rapidly absorbed following oral administration; maximum serum concentrations occur after 30 min.

Concentrations in the brain vary considerably depending upon the dose and route of administration but the midbrain, pons and medulla usually achieve the highest concentrations. Only 1 per cent is excreted as unchanged chlorpromazine, the rest as metabolites, of which there are a very large number. The principal processes of degradation involve sulphoxidation, hydroxylation, desmethylation and N-oxidation. The metabolites of chlorpromazine are in general less pharmacologically active than the drug itself but they are retained by the body for very long periods. Metabolites have been detected in the urine up to twelve months after a course of chlorpromazine.

*Peripheral Actions*

On peripheral structures chlorpromazine exhibits a strong antagonism to adrenaline and noradrenaline but only moderately antagonizes 5HT. Weak anticholinergic and antihistaminic properties are seen on isolated tissues.

Chlorpromazine causes hypotension and tachycardia. This is only partially caused by the blockade of peripheral alpha-adrenergic receptors and is primarily due to the central effects of chlorpromazine. Tolerance to these effects develops so that after several weeks hypotention is no longer produced even with high doses. The metabolic effects of adrenaline (e.g. hyperglycaemia) are not antagonized by chlorpromazine.

*Central Actions*

Biochemical studies *in vitro* have shown that chlorpromazine can uncouple oxidative phosphorylation in brain tissue and can inhibit ATPase activity. Usually, however, the concentrations of chlorpromazine required to achieve this are far in excess of those obtained by therapeutic doses. A reduction of the permeability of cellular membranes to $Na^+$, $K^+$ and $PO_4^{2-}$ may indicate the mechanisms by which chlorpromazine exerts some of its central effects. For example, the permeability of monoamine storage granules is affected and the ratio of free to bound 5HT increases. Again however it seems that the doses required for this action exceed those used clinically.

The central effects of chlorpromazine may be detected at all levels within the cerebro-spinal axis. The electrocorticogram shows increased synchronization and a shift towards the delta frequencies. These signs parallel the tendency towards drowsiness and disappear after a few weeks when tolerance to the sedative effects of chlorpromazine develops. Several studies indicate that these effects are not due to a direct action of chlorpromazine on the cortex. The cortical-evoked response to peripheral stimulation is modified, however, but this results from the action of chlorpromazine on lower centres. Little effect of chlorpromazine is seen on the physiology of the thalamus. Chlorpromazine, like haloperidol, blocks the behavioural effects of stimulation of the nigro-striatal pathway which contains dopamine. On the basis of this observation it has been claimed that chlorpromazine antagonizes the dopamine receptors on striate neurones. In this way dopaminergic transmission may be blocked. Reserpine, which depletes nerve terminals of dopamine would also block transmission and does in fact elicit parkinsonian symptoms. Hypothalamic outflow seems to be reduced in that temperature regulatory mechanisms are disturbed and a tendency towards poikilothermy is seen. Urinary levels of gonadotrophins, oestrogens and progestins are reduced and ovulation and the oestrus cycle may be depressed. Pseudo pregnancy and lactation may be induced. The limbic system does not seem to be markedly affected by chlorpromazine except at very high doses. Changes can be seen in the electrical activity of the hippocampus following clinical doses but this is probably secondary to the action of chlorpromazine on the reticular formation.

The tranquillizing action of chlorpromazine has been related by several authors to its action on the brain stem reticular formation. The proposals of Bradley (1968) are very well documented. He has observed that potentials in the cortex following direct stimulation of the reticular formation are not influenced by chlorpromazine, but are depressed by barbiturate. He concludes that chlorpromazine has little direct depressant effect on the reticular formation of the type seen with barbiturates. Potentials recorded in the reticular formation following peripheral stimulation, are considerably reduced by chlorpromazine, however. Bradley concludes that chlorpromazine has an action related to the inflow of sensory information to the reticular formation. The lack of effect of chlorpromazine on conduction in primary afferent pathways accounts for the ability of subjects to respond to stimuli but the tendency for an increased intensity of stimulation to be required after chlorpromazine may be related to the reduced effect of the stimulus on the arousal mechanisms of the brain stem.

At the level of single cells in the brain stem, chlorpromazine has been shown to antagonize the excitatory effects of noradrenaline. It is not known what role noradrenergic transmission has in the functioning of the reticular formation.

Chlorpromazine reduces motor activity and responsiveness to external stimuli without reducing motor power or coordination. At moderate doses (2·5 mg per kg) responses to conditioned stimuli are abolished but unconditioned responses still occur and feeding and social behaviour is facilitated.

In general, psychological tests in man have demonstrated quantitative but not qualitative differences between chlorpromazine and barbiturates. This is probably because these tests mostly follow single doses of the drugs and the tranquillizing effects of chlorpromazine only emerge clearly after the initial soporific effects have declined.

Chlorpromazine is used clinically to control states of excitement, e.g. in mania, agitated depression, schizophrenia and delirium. It is also used occasionally to treat anxiety (see Chapters X, XII and XV, Vol. II). Phenothiazines have also been used to potentiate anaesthesia and in the management of intractable pain, migraine and emesis. Their use is liable to be restricted by the occurrence of several adverse reactions. Excessive drowsiness usually declines as tolerance develops to the earlier sedative effects but vivid dreaming may be exceptionally distressing. Extrapyramidal effects ranging from akinesia to dystonic reactions and the full symptoms of Parkinsonism may occur. These are less frequent with thioridazine which is also less sedative than chlorpromazine. Autonomic effects such as hypotension and reflex tachycardia usually decline with continued treatment as do the anticholinergic effects of blurred vision, dryness of the mouth, urinary retention and constipation. For other adverse reactions which are less frequently seen, refer to Chapter XV, Volume II.

BUTYROPHENONES

Haloperidol is the prototype of this group of drugs being introduced by Janssen in 1958. Triperidol soon followed differing from haloperidol only by the substitution of a $CF_3$ group for the chlorine on the phenyl ring.

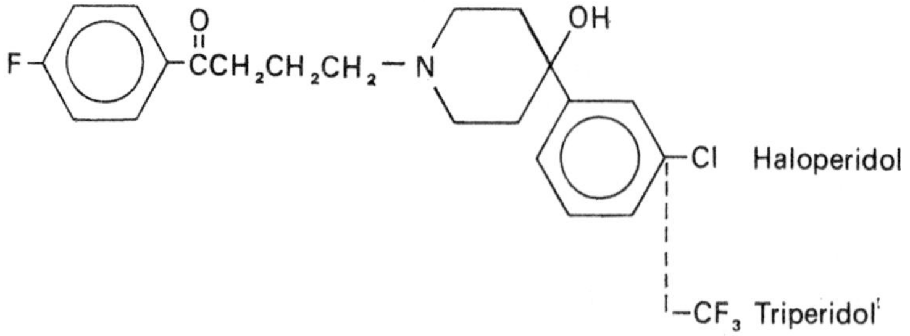

FIG. 5.

The similarity between the pharmacological and behavioural effects of the butyrophenones and phenothiazines is marked (Janssen, 1962). Their actions include taming of animals, the inhibition of psychomotor activity and potentiation of the effects of barbiturates. In animals catalepsy is seen and spontaneous activity and conditioned avoidance is inhibited. The butyrophenones differ from chlorpromazine in that they do not affect the convulsive threshold in animals and have only weak antihistamine and antiadrenergic activity. Little or no effect of the butyrophenones can be seen on the sympathetic or parasympathetic functions of the peripheral nervous system. In cats, dogs and rabbits haloperidol causes only a small though prolonged fall in blood pressure.

A marked central effect of haloperidol, like that of chlorpromazine, is the elicitation of extrapyramidal symptoms. Parkinsonism is believed to be caused by a malfunction of dopamine systems in the brain and it has been suggested that the butyrophenones antagonize dopamine. Supporting evidence for an action of haloperidol upon dopamine transmission has come from some particularly interesting animal experiments. If a unilateral lesion is placed in the caudate nucleus of a rat it exhibits a tendency when walking to rotate towards the operated side. It is believed that this postural and taxic asymmetry is due to the interruption of nigrostriatal dopaminergic transmission upon one side. Stimulation of the substantia nigra, which increases release of dopamine in the unoperated caudate nucleus, elicits rapid rotation of the animal towards the lesioned side. Administration of haloperidol blocks this rotation presumably due to antagonism towards the effects of the released dopamine.

Although early reports of the clinical efficacy of the butyrophenones were very enthusiastic, some controlled trials have displayed no real advantage of the drugs over the phenothiazines (Okasha and Tewfik, 1964).

There remains no doubt however that in some patients the butyrophenones are more effective than the phenothazines. In view of the fact that over 80 per cent of treated patients display extrapyramidal effects it has been concluded that the butyrophenones are most useful for the treatment of psychotic patients who tolerate phenothiazines poorly.

## ANXIOLYTIC SEDATIVES

In contrast to the neuroleptic agents the anxiolytic sedatives are not effective in the treatment of psychoses. They exert little effect on the autonomic nervous system and produce few extrapyramidal signs. They are distinguished by their anticonvulsant properties and their depressant effects on spinal reflex activity. The most widely used representatives of this class of compounds are meprobamate, chlordiazepoxide (librium), and diazepam (valium). The last two compounds are members of the benzodiazepine series.

### BENZODIAZEPINES

The pharmacology of the benzodiazepines has been reviewed in detail by Zbinden and Randall (1967). The majority of pharmaco-

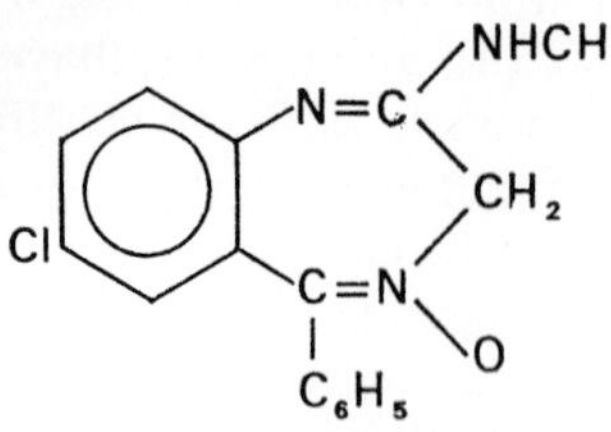

Chlordiazepoxide (Librium)

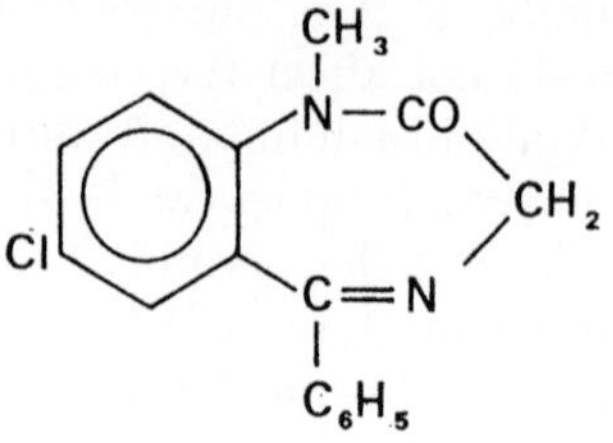

Diazepam (Valium)

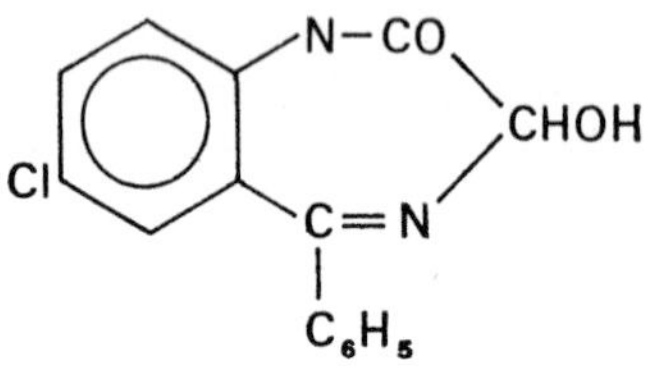

Oxazepam (Serenid)

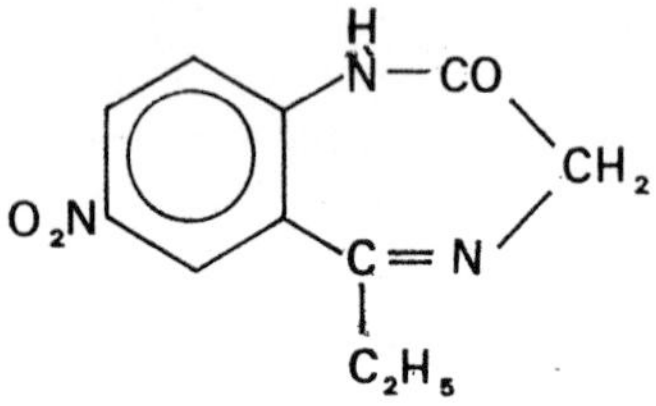

Nitrazepam (Mogadon)

FIG. 6.

logical studies have been made on chlordiazepoxide and it is this drug which is primarily discussed here.

Chlordiazepoxide is readily absorbed from the gut and peak concentrations are found in the plasma 1-2 hours after oral administration. It is widely distributed throughout the body, including the brain. Excretion of the drug and its metabolites continues for approximately a week after a single injection. In man metabolic degradation produces a lactam derivative which may be excreted as such or further degraded to an amino acid.

Electrophysiological studies have indicated that the effects of benzodiazepines on the activity of the limbic system are marked. Spontaneous activity in the hippocampus is reduced and the evoked response in the hippocampus to stimulation of the amygdala is also depressed. The frequency spectrum of the electrocorticogram is slowed by the benzodiazepines, presumably due to an effect on subcortical structures. The thresholds for eliciting paroxysmal discharge in the cortex and elsewhere are increased and behavioural as well as electrophysiological responses to stimulation are reduced by chlordiazepoxide. In particular the behavioural and electrocortical arousal response to stimulation of the mesencephalic reticular formation is reduced. The autonomic responses elicited by stimulation of the hypothalamus are also reduced by chlordiazepoxide. It must be remembered however that this drug stimulates the appetite.

The disruption of coordinated motor movement probably results from the marked muscle relaxant properties of these compounds. Polysynaptic reflexes are depressed due to an action on supra spinal and spinal control mechanisms. Recent evidence suggests this is due in part to a prolongation of presynaptic inhibition in the spinal cord.

On peripheral structures the benzodiazepines do not specifically antagonize acetylcholine, histamine, the catecholamines or 5HT. They are also without a specific action on peripheral autonomic neurones.

The selective effects of the benzodiazepines on behaviour are much greater than those of meprobamate. The taming effect on monkeys is very marked and isolation-induced fighting in mice is reduced by doses which do not impair locomotor activity. Conditioned avoidance responding is disrupted without impairment of the escape responses. In this, the benzodiazepines resemble chlorpromazine and contrast with meprobamate which resembles barbiturates.

Although the effects outlined above may occur with doses which do not reduce motor activity, sedation remains the principle unwanted effect of the benzodiazepines. Lethargy and ataxia may be related to the muscle relaxant effects of these drugs. Like the barbiturates hyperexcitability and irritability may occur with small doses. Stimulation of the appetite may give rise to an unwanted weight gain. Habituation and drug dependence can occur. Withdrawal symptoms include seizures, coma, aggravation of psychoses, insomnia and excitation.

### Antidepressants

In the late 1950's several drugs used in other branches of medicine were observed to elevate the mood of depressed patients. Clinical trials confirmed this effect, and subsequent pharmacological investigations demonstrated that they all tended to increase brain levels of the monoamines in a manner likely to potentiate monoamine actions in the brain. Although there is no conclusive proof that mood elevation results directly from the potentiation of monoamine effects, this is considered to be very likely. The outline of monoamine metabolism in Chapter XV, Vol. I, indicates two processes leading to the degradation of the monoamine which has been released into the synaptic cleft. Firstly, it is actively transported across the membrane into the axon terminal, and secondly, the mitochondrial monoamine oxidase converts it to the acid metabolite. The alternative process of methylation by catechol-o-methyltransferase inactivates the smaller proportion of released catecholamine. The antidepressant drugs have been shown either to block the uptake of monoamine into the axon terminal (the tricyclic antidepressants) or to inhibit enzymic degradation of the monoamines (the monoamine oxidase inhibitors—MAO inhibitors). The pharmacology of these two groups of drugs differs markedly, and they are discussed separately.

MONOAMINE OXIDASE INHIBITORS (MAO INHIBITORS)

The clinical use of these drugs has declined markedly in recent years, due to the occurrence of severe side-effects, and the greater efficacy of the tricyclic antidepressants. Interest in their pharmacology is maintained however by the role, which they share with reserpine, in giving rise to the monoamine theory of affective disorders. This theory proposes in part that depression may result from the reduction of monoamine concentrations in the brain, and that elevation of monoamine levels may counteract the symptoms of depressive illness. It must be remembered, however, that the monoamine oxidase inhibitors have pharmacological actions on other enzymes and metabolic systems.

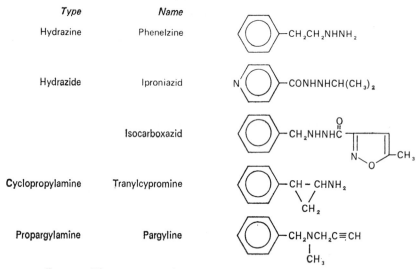

| Type | Name |
|------|------|
| Hydrazine | Phenelzine |
| Hydrazide | Iproniazid |
| | Isocarboxazid |
| Cyclopropylamine | Tranylcypromine |
| Propargylamine | Pargyline |

FIG. 7.    The structure of some Monoamine Oxidase Inhibitors.

*The Significance of Monoamine Oxidase (MAO)*

This enzyme has been fully discussed in Chapter XV. It is widely distributed in the body, functioning in the first stage of one route of the enzymic degradation of tyramine, tryptamine, noradrenaline, adrenaline, dopamine and 5-hydroxytryptamine. Inhibition of monoamine oxidase will lead to accumulation of amines in the tissues, but it should not be assumed that the physiological effects of released amines are always prolonged; firstly, because it is yet far from certain that any of these amines function as neurotransmitter substances in brain, and secondly, because other enzymatic and active uptake processes are present in some tissues which result in rapid inactivation of the amines. It is now considered that the main role of MAO is the destruction of excess amounts of unbound amine within the cell. Active re-uptake or in the case of the catecholamines catechol-o-methyltransferase, accomplishes the inactivation of released amines. Of course, following uptake, the amine may then be destroyed by monoamine oxidase.

The small proportion of intracellular amine which is present in an unbound form in the cytoplasm is in equilibrium with the firmly bound intragranular amine. Inhibition of monoamine oxidase leads to an increase in unbound amine which in turn leads to an increased concentration of intragranular amine. The potentiation of some physiological responses in the central nervous system by monoamine oxidase inhibitors may result, therefore, from a leakage of amine onto the subsynaptic receptors.

There is considerable evidence that in peripheral sympathetic nerves monoamine oxidase inhibition may, on occasion, reduce the effects of stimulation due to the formation of a false transmitter. Normally, tyrosine is decarboxylated to tyramine which is rapidly destroyed by monoamine oxidase. Following inhibition of this enzyme, tyramine accumulates and is converted to octopamine by dopamine $\beta$-hydroxylase. Octopamine is stored in adrenergic granules and is released by nerve stimulation, but is only a very weak adrenergic agonist. A significant reduction of the sympathetic response may therefore result.

## Pharmacology of Monoamine Oxidase Inhibitors

The accessibility of the peripheral autonomic system to experimental study has resulted in the accumulation of many facts about the peripheral actions of MAO inhibitors. The assumption that similar effects occur in the central nervous system is not always valid, however, and care must be exercised in extrapolating from peripheral to central systems.

### Peripheral Pharmacology

Administration of MAO inhibitors elevates the catecholamine content of the heart and the 5HT content of blood platelets. Although there are species differences, noradrenaline is not elevated to the same extent as 5HT, possibly due to the displacement of noradrenaline from stores by octopamine. These changes in tissue concentration are to some extent parallelled by changes in the excretion pattern of the amines and metabolites. The tryptamine, tyramine, 5HT, noradrenaline and normetanephrine content of urine is elevated, and the excretion of the corresponding acids is depressed. The excretion of acid metabolites is not used as an index of enzyme inhibition, as it is a less sensitive measure, and the hydrazine group of drugs inhibits the secretion by the kidney tubules of some acid metabolites.

Chronic administration of MAO inhibitors usually leads to some reduction of blood pressure which may occasionally be severe. This response is the opposite of that to be expected from the elevation of amine levels, and probably results from the release of octopamine as a false transmitter. It has been suggested that other pharmacological properties of these drugs, i.e. blockade of superior cervical ganglia and elevation of histamine levels, were responsible for hypotension, but this only occurs with doses much higher than those used clinically.

A particular danger associated with the clinical use of the mono-amine oxidase inhibitors is the occurrence of hypertensive crises. They occurred most frequently when tranylcypromine was used, due to the sympathomimetic action of these drugs in liberating noradrenaline from nerve terminals. Similar crises may also occur, however, if any of the MAO inhibitors are given in combination with sympathomimetic agents or the tricyclic antidepressants. Either drug will increase the concentration of amine at receptors and following MAO inhibition this concentration may cause severe hypertension. Sympathomimetic agents in food, e.g. tyramine in cheese, may have a similar action. Normally, dietary amines are inactivated in the liver by MAO, but following inhibition of this enzyme, they enter the circulation. The resulting hypertension may be severe, and deaths have been reported.

The MAO inhibitors also have marked effects upon carbohydrate metabolism. Blood levels of pyruvic and lactic acid are raised, presumably in response to the increased concentration of circulating amines, but the precise mechanisms are unknown. Insulin hypoglycaemia is potentiated by the MAO inhibitors, which should therefore be used with caution in patients receiving insulin. Sympathetic discharge causes the release of adrenaline which elevates blood sugar levels. MAO inhibitors would be expected therefore to cause hyperglycaemia by potentiating the sympathetic discharge. That potentiation of the hypoglycaemic action of insulin occurs is a situation analogous to the hypotension caused by these drugs.

Not all peripheral actions of the MAO inhibitors result from inhibition of MAO. The hydrazine groups in particular are effective inhibitors of other enzymes, e.g. diamine oxidase, liver microsomal enzymes and enzymes with pyridoxal-5-phosphate as a co-factor. Inhibition of enzymes in the liver which break down the morphine-like analgesics and the general anaesthetics gives the possibility of a dangerous potentiation of these drug effects.

*Central Pharmacology*

Little is known about the effects of MAO inhibitors on central synaptic transmission and there are no gross changes in the E.E.G. Although tranylcypromine may cause slight desynchronization of the E.E.G., this effect is probably related to the amphetamine-like properties of this drug. Locomotor activity of animals is increased by the MAO inhibitors, an effect probably related to elevation of brain catecholamine levels. In the dog and cat, locomotor activity is unaffected by MAO inhibitors, and in these species brain levels of only 5HT and dopamine are elevated. In the rabbit, rat and mouse, where all three amine levels are elevated, activity is increased. Of all the MAO inhibitors, the harmala alkaloids elevate brain amine levels most quickly, the rise lasting only a few hours. Following administration of the hydrazines, a slow rise in amine levels is maintained for several days.

The central effects of amine precursors are potentiated by pretreatment with MAO inhibitors, and the sedative effects of reserpine are prevented. Following reserpine and MAO inhibition, it is believed that the amine which is displaced from the storage granules is no longer degraded by MAO. Accumulation of amine occurs instead of depletion as after reserpine alone because unlike the non-ionized metabolites the free amine cannot easily pass the cell membrane and it therefore accumulates.

Central sympathomimetic effects are seen with tranylcypromine and the hydrazines due to the direct liberation of catecholamines by these drugs. All MAO inhibitors will potentiate the central, as well as the peripheral effects of sympathomimetic agents giving increased excitation and hyperthermia. These effects were discussed in the peripheral pharmacology section, as was the potentiation of barbiturates and narcotics.

In summary it may be noted that many of the effects of MAO inhibitors are adequately explained by a knowledge of their action on monoamine oxidase. The drugs also possess actions apparently quite unrelated to effects on this enzyme, however, and the relationship between these actions and their therapeutic effects is not clear. It should be noted that MAO inhibitors were used to treat both depressive illnesses and hypertension; in the first case, improvement may be related to elevation of amine levels in brain, and in the case of hypertension, to a reduced effectiveness of amine transmission. It is quite possible that actions on other systems may be proved important in the future.

### THE AMINE UPTAKE INHIBITORS

This group of antidepressant drugs is often referred to as the tricyclic drugs, from the appearance of their chemical structure. They are also referred to as thymoleptics. Imipramine was synthesized in 1954 and due to its resemblance to chlorpromazine was tested for tranquillizing potency, but found to worsen the symptoms of chronic schizophrenic patients. Subsequent tests showed its antidepressant potency. The chemical structure of the major compounds in the series is shown in Figure 8.

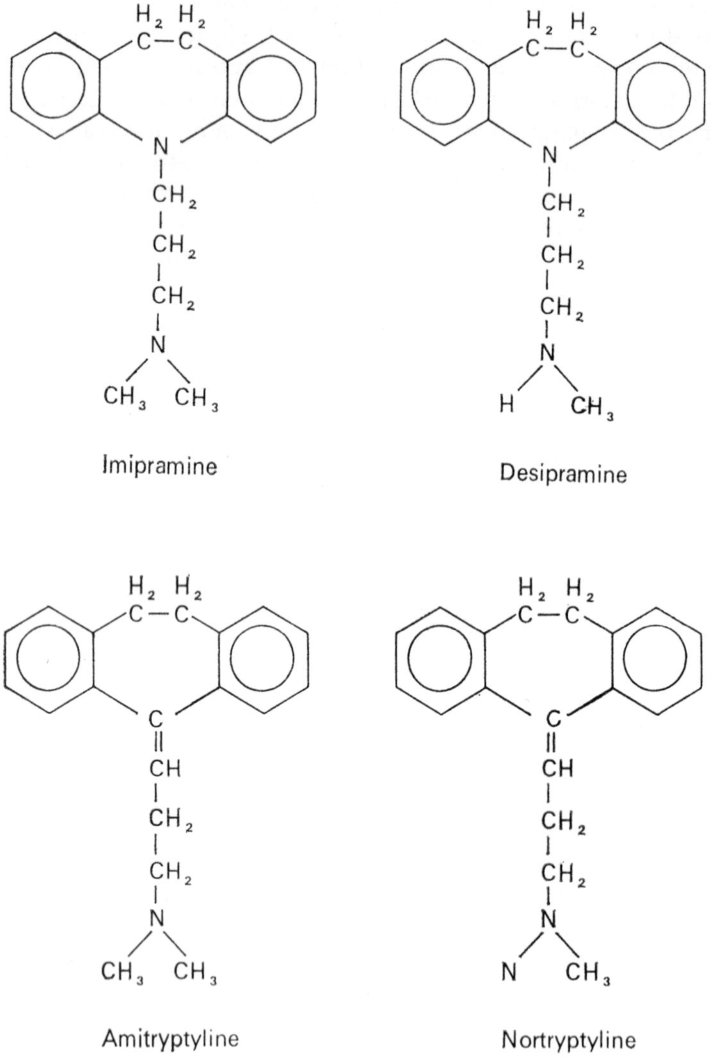

Imipramine

Desipramine

Amitryptyline

Nortryptyline

Fig. 8.

These drugs are rapidly absorbed after systemic or oral administration and are widely distributed through the tissues. In the brain the greatest concentrations are achieved in the cerebrum and midbrain.

The most important routes of metabolism are hydroxylation and demethylation with the liver microsomal enzymes probably playing the most important role. It has been demonstrated that some imipramine is demethylated to the possibly more potent desmethylimipramine prior to further breakdown (Sulser, Watts and Brodie, 1962). The extent to which formation of desipramine is responsible for the therapeutic effect of imipramine is not clear.

*Postulated Basis of Therapeutic Action*

Chapter XV discusses the mechanisms of amine inactivation in some detail. It must of course be remembered that it is not yet certain that 5HT, noradrenaline and dopamine function as neurotransmitters in brain. As indicated in the section on monoamine oxidase inhibitors, several mechanisms have been clearly demonstrated in brain tissue which are likely to inactivate amines released by nervous activity. The first step in the process is the active re-uptake of amine into cells, and is followed by either the rebinding of amine into stores or degradation by MAO. These processes have been thoroughly studied in peripheral organs, but, in the brain, uptake of 5HT or catecholamines following intravenous infusion is prevented by the blood–brain barrier. Amine uptake by brain is therefore studied following injection into the ventricles, or *in vitro* by immersing brain slices in an amine solution. Techniques of radioactive labelling of the amine are usual. The considerable concentration of amines into brain tissue which has been demonstrated by these techniques can be powerfully inhibited by small concentrations of tricyclic drug.

In peripheral organs the physiological response to stimulation of sympathetic nerves is augmented by the tricyclics and the response of brain cells to exogenous application of amine is also increased. A cause–effect relationship is presumed to exist between the potentiation of amine responses which are believed to result from the increased stay of the transmitter in the region of the synapse following its release from the preterminal. The tricyclics have only a very slight effect on the uptake of amines in the storage granules, and therefore do not influence the synthesis of amines.

Acceptance of the postulates outlined above should be tempered by a knowledge of the other pharmacological properties of these drugs which are discussed later. These properties are often very marked and have not been investigated to the same extent as the central effects on amine uptake, but may nevertheless be involved in the therapeutic effects of these drugs.

*Peripheral Pharmacology*

The peripheral actions of the tricyclic antidepressants may be summarized as the potentiation, or at higher doses, antagonism to sympathetic responses and marked anticholinergic and antihistamine effects. Many effects of exogenous 5HT administration are potentiated by low doses of tricyclics, but others are antagonized, usually by high doses. In most of these actions, the tricyclics resemble the phenothiazines, for although not all these actions are major aspects of phenothiazine pharmacology, under suitable conditions they can be seen.

The potentiation of noradrenergic responses can result from the inhibition of uptake mechanisms and has been demonstrated in a wide range of organs and species. The uptake of noradrenaline is inhibited by many other drugs including the antihistamines; the phenothiazine derivatives; adrenergic blocking agents; the monoamine oxidase inhibitors harmine, phenelzine and tranylcypromine; cocaine; and many sympathomimetic amines. Obviously those drugs which possess other potent actions such as receptor blockade (phenothiazines and adrenergic antagonists) or transmitter release (sympathomimetic agents) will not give rise to a simple potentiation of sympathetic responses. Equally, the tricyclic drugs themselves have other potent actions which frequently mask the potentiation of adrenergic responses.

The antagonism of sympathetic responses usually occurs with larger doses of tricyclics. Although originally thought to result from the blockade of noradrenaline release, a direct postsynaptic antagonism is more likely because the effects of exogenously applied noradrenaline may also be blocked. The effects of the indirectly acting amines, tyramine and amphetamine, are also diminished by the tricyclics, but the mechanism of action may be both inhibition of the uptake process and postsynaptic blockade.

The peripheral effects of exogenously applied serotonin are also potentiated by low doses of tricyclics and reduced by higher doses. Uptake of serotonin by nerve cells is believed to be a principal method of inactivation in the C.N.S., and the tricyclics have been shown to block this uptake into blood platelets. In general, effects on peripheral responses to serotonin are much weaker than effects on noradrenergic systems.

The anticholinergic activity of the tricyclics *in vitro* was initially reported to be weak, but later studies on the antagonism of the hypotensive response to acetylcholine *in vivo* demonstrated a distinct anticholinergic action. This is to be expected from the frequent occurrence of marked cholinolytic side-effects following antidepressant therapy. It is likely, however, that many of these effects result from a reduced central parasympathetic outflow, because in peripheral systems the cholinolytic potency of imipramine has only a weak cholinolytic effect.

The tricyclic antidepressants also possess substantial antihistaminic properties in peripheral systems.

*Central Pharmacology*

The tricyclic drugs have been shown to have effects on the C.N.S. which are similar to their peripheral actions. Thus, uptake of noradrenaline and 5HT is inhibited and the potentiation of responses to these amines occurs with low doses of tricyclics, and inhibition occurs with high doses. Anticholinergic and antihistaminic actions have also been reported. Attempts have been made to relate the actions on cholinergic and histamine systems to the therapeutic efficacy of the drugs, but little support for these postulates has been obtained. Rating the antihistamine potency of the tricyclics against their potency as antidepressants seems to give an inverse correlation. Similar studies rating cholinolytic activity against clinical efficacy have failed to show any correlation. The central and peripheral potencies of drugs are often very different, however, and the above studies usually used peripheral potency as the measure of antagonistic actions. In any case, it is very likely that antidepressant activity results from an action on several systems of the brain, and knowledge of the drugs' potency on any one system may not allow prediction of antidepressant potency. This would be derived only from knowledge of its action on all relevant systems.

There can be little doubt of the relevance of an action on monoamine systems to the relief of depression, even though a direct correlation between uptake blockade, response potentiation and clinical efficacy is not always clear. Many of the behavioural and pharmacological effects of reserpine are prevented by the tricyclics, which do not directly interfere with the depletion of amine stores by reserpine. Their action is probably, therefore, to potentiate amine transmission, and counteract its reduction by reserpine. Some of the actions of reserpine (e.g. hypothermia) are also reduced by chlorpromazine, so the antagonism of reserpine is not specific to tricyclics. The potentiation of the central effects of amphetamine by the tricyclics does not occur with chlorpromazine, and this is considered a fairly specific effect of the tricyclics. Unfortunately, the complexity of amphetamine action (NA release, MAO inhibition and uptake blockade) is such that the mechanism is not clear.

The relative importance of effects on NA and 5HT systems is not clear. Responses to both NA and 5HT are usually affected by the tricyclics. The shortage of clear data on the comparative relevance of the two amines is due to the blood–brain barrier preventing *in vivo* uptake studies and the difficulty in eliciting clear serotonin responses from brain tissue. However, tryptophan and 5HTP administered in combination with MAO inhibitors to depressed patients elicited favourable results suggesting the relevance of the modification of 5HT systems to the treatment of depression.

Most of the described pharmacological effects of the tricyclics have a fairly rapid onset. It is well known, however, that their therapeutic effects are delayed in onset for approximately 10 days. Many theories, but few facts, have tried to reconcile these differences. The delay has been variously attributed to:

1. The delayed onset of an unknown pharmacological effect of the drugs.

2. An immediate action upon amine storage granules in the cell bodies which may take 10 days to reach the synaptic terminals by axoplasmic flow.

3. The slow development of tachyphylaxis to some of the drugs' effects may slowly change the overall pattern of the drugs' central action.

Experimental evidence is insufficient to differentiate between these and other possibilities.

### THE PSYCHODYSLEPTICS

Drugs producing bizarre or heightened psychological effects are among the oldest known, being used by ancient civilizations and primitive tribes in religious ceremonies. Many drugs will elicit hallucinations and bizarre behaviour, but mostly do so with very high, toxic doses. The psychodysleptics seem to have their effects without marked side-effects. Opium and hashish are among the best known psychoactive plant products of the old world, with mescaline, psilocybin and bufotenine from the new world. Synthetic psychodysleptics are LSD (lysergic acid diethylamide), piperidyl benzylates and phencyclidines. Although many of these drugs have a remarkable resemblance to each other, and to NA, 5HT or dopamine, this is not true of the piperidyl benzylates and phencyclidine. The pharmacology of the drugs resembling the biogenic amines reveals no clear common basis of action, and each must therefore be discussed separately.

#### MESCALINE

The structure of mescaline has been shown twice in Figure 9 in order to underline the similarity to both noradrenaline and dopamine, and also to the indole nucleus of serotonin. It has been suggested that the right-hand configuration is preferred, but the structure in tissue solution is quite unknown. Mescaline exerts marked effects on both catecholamine and indolealkylamine systems in animals and man, and no clear conclusions can be made regarding a discrete action of mescaline in relation to any of these systems.

Moderate doses of mescaline have no direct effect on the blood pressure of dogs, but inhibit the pressor effect of adrenaline. However, the response of the cat nictitating membrane to adrenaline is potentiated

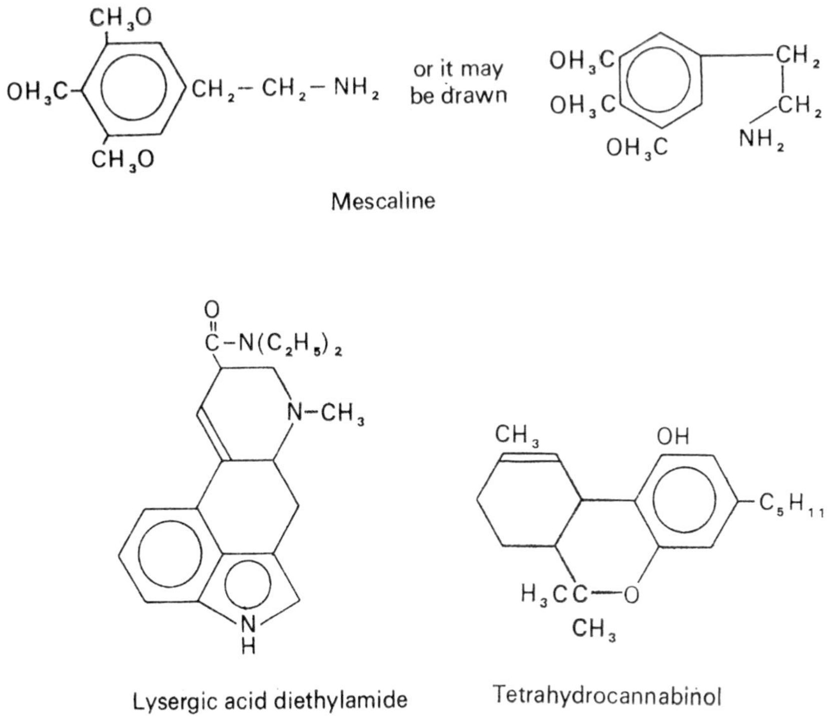

CH$_3$O

OH$_3$C—⟨benzene ring⟩—CH$_2$—CH$_2$—NH$_2$

CH$_3$O

or it may
be drawn

OH$_3$C—⟨benzene ring⟩—CH$_2$
OH$_3$C                        CH$_2$
OH$_3$C            NH$_2$

Mescaline

⟨structure⟩
$\overset{O}{\overset{\|}{C}}$—N(C$_2$H$_5$)$_2$

N—CH$_3$

N
H

Lysergic acid diethylamide

CH$_3$            OH

⟨structure⟩—C$_5$H$_{11}$

H$_3$CC—O
CH$_3$

Tetrahydrocannabinol

FIG. 9.    Structural formulae.

by small doses of mescaline. Similarly, antagonism and potentiation of
the effects of serotonin have been reported. These effects are dependent
on the dose, the species and the organ studied; even excision of the
organ often changes the effect of mescaline. It must be concluded that
peripheral studies of the actions of mescaline have not contributed
significantly to an understanding of its pharmacology.

Studies in the central nervous system have proved to be equally confusing. The alpha content of the E.E.G. is reduced and low voltage fast
activity is increased due possibly to a direct action on the medullary
brain stem. These effects in man and animals are counteracted by
chlorpromazine and barbiturates. Although many of the effects elicited
by mescaline are very similar to those of LSD, mescaline does not show
a specific and potent antagonism of biogenic amines as does LSD.
Furthermore mescaline when applied directly onto single neurones of
the cortex is an agonist of noradrenaline. Many other drugs have sympathomimetic effects, but do not cause bizarre or psychotic behaviour,
and it has been suggested that a metabolite of mescaline may be respon-

sible for its psychotomimetic effects. This possibility is extremely attractive due to:

1. Two to three hours' incubation of brain slices with mescaline is necessary before several of its biochemical actions occur.
2. Hallucinations occur two to three hours after blood and brain levels of mescaline have declined due to its incorporation into liver proteins.
3. Uterine contractions are stimulated only *in vivo* not *in vitro*.

However, no knowledge exists concerning the nature of this metabolite which has been variously postulated to be demethylated mescaline, an indolic compound, an alcohol or an aldehyde.

Snyder and Merril (1965) made molecular orbital calculations for a variety of hallucinogenic and structurally similar non-hallucinogenic analogues in the phenylethylamine, amphetamine and tryptamine series, as well as for LSD. They observed a close correlation between the energy of the highest filled molecular orbital of the compounds, an index of electron donation, and their hallucinogenic potency. At present little can be added in confirmation or otherwise of the relevance of this correlation.

The present state of knowledge concerning the pharmacology of this fascinating drug is most unsatisfactory from the viewpoint of those who believe that the behaviour elicited by mescaline resembles a true psychosis sufficiently to merit interest. Although no one doubts that considerable differences exist between schizophrenia and the mescaline experience, the similarities are obvious (Osmond and Smythies, 1952). Furthermore, repeated doses of mescaline give rise to marked tachyphylaxis of the response. Cross-tachyphylaxis between mescaline, psilocybin and LSD occurs and much higher doses of these drugs are required to elicit a response from schizophrenics. These phenomena are discussed at length by Hoffer and Osmond (1967).

LYSERGIC ACID DIETHYLAMIDE (LSD)

This compound was synthesized by Hoffman in 1943, who accidentally inhaled the dust and experienced vivid psychological changes and hallucinations. Subsequently, it was found that the psychotomimetic properties of ergot, ololiuqui and morning glory were due to very similar compounds, the most potent being lysergic acid amide with one-tenth the hallucinogenic potency of LSD. The effective dose of LSD is approximately 1 $\mu$g per kg in humans, and very few measures of animal behaviour or tissue pharmacology show any effect of LSD at this dose. This observation reveals the problem underlying the study of LSD, for although its pharmacology is well known, the doses required are usually much greater than those which cause hallucinations.

LSD is very rapidly absorbed and distributed to the tissues. The highest concentrations are in gut and liver, the lowest in brain (0·0003 $\mu$g per g). LSD contracts the isolated uterus, and constricts peripheral blood vessels. Central effects include the potentiation of the pressor response to adrenaline and the elevation of body temperature. In human volunteers, the pupil is dilated, and this response has been found to be an excellent measure of the intensity of the psychological experience.

The E.E.G. is activated by LSD. If the brain is sectioned just anterior to the brain-stem reticular formation, LSD no longer has this effect. A lesion just posterior to the reticular formation leaves the LSD effect unimpaired. Studies of the threshold to direct electrical stimulation of the brain stem show that LSD does not itself stimulate the reticular formation. It is therefore proposed that LSD acts in relation to the collateral input to the reticular formation by increasing the inflow of sensory information. This proposal is in agreement with observations of increased stimulus generalization, difficulty in concentrating, and theories of the neural bases of hallucination.

Peripheral and central studies of LSD action show it to be a powerful antagonist of 5HT. Woolley (1962) amplified Gaddum's suggestion that this may be the basis of the hallucinatory action of LSD. This thesis was very attractive, due to the weight of evidence linking 5HT to mental disease, and to the fact that many hallucinogens contain an indole nucleus. However many other antagonists of 5HT are now known, and they do not all cause hallucinations, and several hallucinogens do not appear to antagonize 5HT.

Among other actions of LSD which may form the basis of hallucinatory activity is its action on tissue cultured oligodendroglia. Less than 1 $\mu$g per litre concentration causes changes in contractile rhythms, dispersion of granules, and elicits irregular movement of the nucleus. The underlying biochemical changes in these cells are not known, but glucose oxidation is inhibited, as are many enzymes, and the transport of substrates into brain is markedly affected. It has been proposed that the accelerated penetration of toxic substances into brain from blood may be the basis of LSD-evoked hallucinations, but this has proved very difficult to confirm.

The actions of LSD in antagonizing histamine, noradrenaline and cholinesterase have all been proposed as the basis of its hallucinatory actions. However, somewhat higher doses are required than those which block serotonin, and specific antagonists of these substances tend not to be hallucinogens. It can only be concluded at this time that the psychological effects of LSD are probably caused by a combination of effects on several biochemical and physiological systems of the brain.

HALLUCINOGENS STRUCTURALLY RELATED TO TRYPTOPHAN

These compounds can all be synthesized from the tryptophan nucleus, although it is not clear whether such a synthesis occurs *in vivo*. It is theoretically possible that the formation of one of these compounds due to a metabolic malfunction, underlies the schizophrenic psychosis. Well known hallucinogens exhibiting some structural similarity to tryptamine are psilocin, bufotenine, diethyl- and dimethyltryptamine. The methylation of tryptamine and some of its metabolites may be accelerated by administering L-methionine, a methyl donor. There is some evidence that administration of this compound to some schizophrenics causes an acute psychosis. The *in vivo* formation of hallucinogenic metabolites of tryptamine following methionine administration has not been demonstrated, however.

TETRAHYDROCANNABINOL

Tetrahydrocannabinol is the principal constituent of cannabis, also known as hashish and marihuana, which has been in use for centuries. It is believed to be a nonaddictive drug which does not give rise to serious or prolonged mental illness or personality deterioration, but social factors cause it to be a transition drug in the pathway from the amphetamines to heroin and cocaine addiction. Subjectively, dreams or dream images are characteristic responses to cannabis with elementary hallucinations being rare.

The motor effects of cannabis are restricted to fine movements involving complex reflex actions. Anaesthesia is potentiated, and body temperature lowered. These effects are mostly central in origin, and in animals are abolished by lesions in the region of the midbrain and medullary reticular formation. Slight antagonism of cannabis extracts to ACh, 5HT and adrenaline *in vitro* have been observed, but it is uncertain if this has any relevance to the subjective effects of cannabis. A considerable elevation of brain 5HT has been observed in the rat following cannabis, but this has not been confirmed by several other workers.

The mode of action of cannabis is not understood. It is known, however, that cross-tolerance, which is easily seen between the indole hallucinogens and mescaline does not extend to cannabis, and on this basis it is suggested that a different mechanism of action is likely.

REFERENCES

BARSA, J. A. & KLINE, N. S. (1955) Treatment of 200 disturbed psychotics with reserpine. *Journal of the American Medical Association*, **158**, 110–113.
BRADLEY, P. B. & KEY, B. J. (1958) The effects of drugs on arousal responses produced by electrical stimulation of the reticular formation of the brain. *Electroencephalography and Clinical Neurophysiology*, **10**, 97–110.

BRADLEY, P. B. (1968) Synaptic transmission in the central nervous system and its relevance for drug action. *International Review of Neurobiology*, **11**, 1–56.

DAHLSTROM, A. & FUXE, K. (1964) Evidence for the existence of monoamine-containing neurones in the central nervous system. I. Demonstration of monoamines in the cell bodies of brain stem neurones. *Acta physiologica scandinavica*, **62**, Suppl. 232: 1–55.

DELAY, J. & DENIKER, P. (1953) Neuroplegics in psychiatric therapy. *Therapie*, **8**, 347–364.

GOODMAN, L. S. & GILMAN, A. (1968) *The Pharmacological Basis of Therapeutics*. 3rd edn. London: Macmillan.

HOFFER, A. & OSMOND, H. (1967) *The Hallucinogens*. London: Academic Press.

HORROBIN, D. F. (1968) *Medical Physiology and Biochemistry*. London: Arnold.

JANSSEN, P. A. (1962) Comparative pharmacological data on 6 new basic 4'-fluorobutyrophenone derivatives: haloperidol, haloanisone, triperidol, methylperidide, haloperidide and dipiperone. *Arzneimittelforsch*, **11**, 923–938.

OKASHA, A. & TEWFIK, G. I. (1964) Haloperidol: a controlled clinical trial in chronic disturbed psychotic patients. *British Journal of Psychiatry*, **110**, 56–60.

OSMOND, H. & SMYTHIES, J. R. (1952) Schizophrenia: A New Approach. *Journal of Mental Science*, **98**, 309–315.

PASSMORE, R. & ROBSON, J. S. (1970) *A Companion to Medical Studies*. 2nd edn. Edinburgh: Blackwell.

SNYDER, S. H. & MERRIL, C. R. (1965) A relationship between the hallucinogenic activity of drugs and their electronic configuration. *Proceedings of the National Academy of Sciences of the U.S.A.* **54**, 258–266.

SULSER, F., WATTS, J. & BRODIE, B. B. (1962) On the mechanism of antidepressant action of imipramine drugs. *Annals of the New York Academy of Sciences*, **96**, 279–288.

WIKLER, A. (1957) *The Relation of Psychiatry to Pharmacology*. Baltimore: Williams and Wilkins.

WOOLLEY, D. W. (1962) *The Biochemical Basis of Psychoses*. New York: Wiley.

WORLD HEALTH ORGANISATION (1969) Research in Psychopharmacology. *International Journal of Psychiatry*, **7**, 259–285.

ZBINDEN, G. & RANDALL, L. O. (1967) Pharmacology of Benzodiazepines: Laboratory and Clinical Correlation. In *Advances in Pharmacology*, 5. Edited by S. Garattine & P. A. Shore, New York: Academic Press.

## ACKNOWLEDGMENTS

Figure 1 was modified from Gaddum's Pharmacology 6th Edition by A. S. V. Burgen & J. F. Mitchell, Oxford University Press, London, 1968.

Figure 2 was taken from N.-E. Anden, A. Dahlström, K. Fuxe, K. Larsson, L. Olsen, U. Ungerstedt, *Acta physiologica scandinavica*, **67**, 313–326, 1966.

# Chapter XVII

# NORMAL AND ALTERED CONSCIOUSNESS: A CONTRIBUTION FROM ELECTROENCEPHALOGRAPHIC STUDIES

## Ian Oswald

### INTRODUCTION

The psychiatric and neurological literature contains phrases like 'altered consciousness' and 'diminution of the sensorium'. What do these phrases mean? They imply altered subjective and wholly personal experience. Yet they are generally applied when the patient's spontaneous behaviour, or responses to his environment, differ from those which the observer would expect of a healthy man under such circumstances. The differences remind the observer of his own experiences of dreams and of similarly inappropriate behaviour by patients known to have 'organic' disorder of the brain, such as injury, or abnormal chemical environment. The observer empathetically feels that the patient's awareness of reality is disordered.

The normal ability to display anticipation, to respond in smooth sequences to successive events, to relate together a complex body of past and present information, and subsequently to show evidence of memory (or later behaviour adjusted to such information as may, at the earlier time, have been newly available) are changed, and generally in the direction of diminution. One must consider not just the sustained capacity for response but also the degree to which a short-lived change can be evoked. The drugged patient may be continuously drowsy and only briefly capable of poor-quality responses to strong stimulation. A normal person can spend a long time in drowsiness but does not then need very powerful stimulation to rouse him to a sustained higher level of capability. The former remains in a state of 'clouded consciousness', whereas the second achieves and sustains normal consciousness. There are, of course, some states of altered consciousness to which terms like 'clouding' or 'diminution of the sensorium' are not customarily applied, namely, where the individual's report and behaviour seem to indicate an enhanced awareness and capability, as may temporarily occur after moderate doses of amphetamine.

### LEVELS OF VIGILANCE

The term *vigilance* has often been used to indicate that there are overall states of the organism that may vary in a graded way. A healthy person in a state of normal wakefulness is said to manifest a high level of vigilance, apparent both in his physical activity and in his evident mental capabilities. Someone who is asleep is said to manifest a low degree of vigilance, so that if you tickle his face with a feather his physical responses may be clumsy and ill-directed and his mental awareness of the nature of the stimulus may seem to have been slight. The concept of vigilance implies a continuum of ascending 'levels'. A healthy person may be intensely alert, calmly reflective, in idle reverie, frankly drowsy, sleeping yet easily rousable, or sleeping so profoundly that, though you shout and pull his hair, it is only with the greatest difficulty that he can be made to respond. All these conditions represent different levels of vigilance, different global states of reactivity, and make possible different degrees of consciousness. It is important to remember when reading psychology texts that modern psychology has found it convenient to ignore the concept of differing states, so that studies of learning, memory and perception carry only an implicit assumption that the individuals studied were in a uniform state of alert wakefulness.

## The Brain-stem Reticular Formation

In the 1950s it became possible to relate the concept of global states of vigilance to neurophysiological knowledge, for at this time there matured the concept of the activating reticular formation of the brain-stem. It really had older roots: thirty years earlier von Economo had observed many cases of encephalitis lethargica and attributed the inertia and altered consciousness in these patients to a disturbance of sleep function brought about by inflammation within the central brain-stem, particularly the periventricular grey matter, the hypothalamus, and parts of the mid-brain. The neurosurgeon Cairns (1952) drew attention to the fact that, whereas lesions of the upper cervical spinal cord did not cause disturbance of consciousness, similar lesions in the mesencephalon and diencephalon frequently provoked a state resembling persistent sleepiness. Damage to the cerebral cortex, of itself, does not usually result in coma, yet coma may follow if, as may happen, the mid-brain is subjected to compression at the tentorial opening by herniation of temporal lobe. Drowsiness, passing into coma, also frequently results from mid-brain compression, while the cortex remains undisturbed, in cases of haemorrhage within the posterior fossa (Jefferson and Johnson, 1950). It was found that experimental concussion in monkeys caused impairment of function especially in the brain-stem reticular formation (Folz and Schmidt, 1956) and some cases of human unconsciousness caused by head injuries have electroencephalograms (E.E.G.s) similar to those of sleep (Chatrian, White and Daly, 1963).

Against this neurological background were set the laboratory findings of Bremer (1935) who described how, when a cut was made through the lower medulla of the cat brain to produce the *encéphale isolé* preparation, it showed periods of apparent sleep that alternated with periods of apparent wakefulness as manifested by, among other things, the E.E.G. and the size of the pupils. On the other hand a cut through the upper mid-brain, producing the *cerveau isolé*, led to a preparation manifesting signs as of continuous sleep. Understanding of these experiments became possible following the work of Moruzzi and Magoun (1949), who showed that electrical stimulation of the central grey matter, or reticular formation, of the already sleeping *encéphale isolé* caused the abrupt appearance of signs of wakefulness. So arrived the concept of the brain-stem reticular activating system, of a central core within the brain-stem from which non-specific impulses ascended to the cortex and descended to the spinal cord. They were 'non-specific' because they did not convey information of a specific sensory kind. Instead they tended, as it were, to activate the cortex or the spinal cord. When the ascending flow of non-specific impulses increased, cortical vigilance was raised, cortical activity was facilitated and the organism was enabled efficiently to deal with life events; it was awake. When the flow declined then the animal's capability declined; it was drowsy, and further decline represented a state of sleep, or even lower vigilance. The intensity of the flow upward and downward from the reticular formation depended upon the degree of excitement of the latter and this was believed to be increased by impulses arriving from all sensory paths, and flowing into it through 'collateral afferents' which branched off from the classical sensory routes. The reticular formation could also be excited by carbon dioxide, by amphetamine, by various bodily metabolites, or by some corticofugal impulses. Conversely its activity could be damped down by other impulses from the cortex or from the blood pressure receptors, or by such drugs as barbiturates or ether. So the level of vigilance, or the degree of consciousness in the intact animal, came to be seen as paralleling the intensity of upward and downward flow of impulses from the reticular formation. Both were graded along a continuum.

However, consciousness and wakefulness are not the same thing. An animal can have its cortex removed and still show a 24-hour rhythm of sleep alternating with behavioural wakefulness. Yet we would hesitate to think of such an animal as conscious. In other words, the concept of the vigilance of any part of the central nervous system must include consideration of local conditions. We may think of our consciousness as dependent upon the cortex itself and that the vigilance of the cortex may be impaired through lack of ascending activating reticular formation impulses, but it might also be impaired because of local oedema, or local abnormality of electrolyte environment, or suboptimal level of, for example, thyroid hormone. The latter two conditions would be presumed to affect not merely the cortex but also the brain-stem reticular formation itself, as would be expected of barbiturate drugs.

Drug-induced loss of consciousness, or anaesthesia, became understandable in terms of the reticular formation. A sudden stimulus to a sensory nerve, say an electric shock to the sciatic nerve, is followed by a brief electrical *evoked potential* that can be recorded, using appropriate apparatus, higher up the nerve, then in the spinal cord at a later moment, and then in the brain. In the brain it can be recorded from both the reticular formation and the cerebral cortex. When ether or barbiturates are administered in anaesthetic doses the evoked potential in the cortex is very little changed, but the evoked potential in the reticular formation is greatly decreased (Arduini and Arduini, 1954). Consequently the state of anaesthesia induced by these agents can be conceptualized as one resulting mainly from a damping down of the reticular formation and a loss of ascending activating impulses to the cortex, with the consequence that although the information from the sensory nerve reaches the cortex, the cortex cannot handle the information in a normal and efficient way, such as would lead to consciousness, or awareness, of the stimulus. It is possible in the same way to understand how anxiety can impede induction of anaesthesia, by reason of counteracting reticular formation excitation (presumably by corticofugal signals).

## THE E.E.G.

The electroencephalogram, or E.E.G., is a useful tool for the study of states of consciousness. It tells us about the fluctuations of spontaneous brain potentials recordable from the scalp. The E.E.G. machine is really just a highly sensitive voltmeter with ink running out from the tip of the pointer so that a written trace appears on paper dragged at a steady speed below it. Usually 8 to 16 such traces are written simultaneously to allow moment-to-moment comparison of potential fluctuations over different areas of the scalp. The healthy human, awake but relaxed with eyes closed, usually manifests an *alpha* rhythm, at about 10 c per sec, over the back of the head. There are individual variations in voltage and in some quite healthy people one does not see much alpha rhythm. In those in whom it is present, it can be made abruptly to disappear when vigilance is raised, through opening the eyes or intense concentration upon mental arithmetic. When someone becomes very bored or drowsy, even with the eyes open, the alpha rhythm will return but then, a drowsiness increases, the alpha rhythm is lost and a low voltage E.E.G. takes its place (Fig. 1). As the minutes pass and he falls well and truly asleep, even larger and slower waves appear in the E.E.G.

O

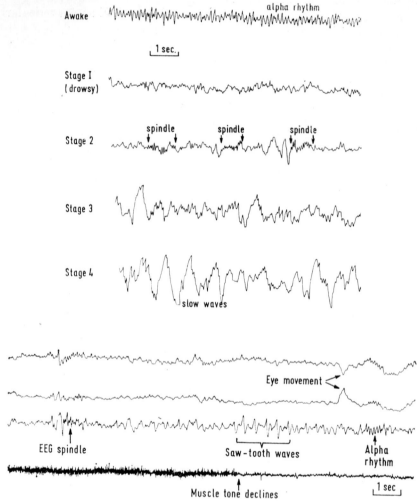

FIG. 1.  The stages of sleep. The upper part of the figure shows the
E.E.G. alpha rhythm in wakefulness, the irregular small slow waves of
Stage 1 sleep or drowsiness, the 'spindles' of Stage 2 sleep (they persist
into Stages 3 and 4) and the large slow E.E.G. waves of Stages 3 and 4.
This sequence from wakefulness through Stage 1 to Stage 4 usually occurs
in the first quarter-hour after falling asleep at night.

The lower portion of the figure shows a typical transition into paradoxical sleep. The top two channels derive from electrode placements
above and below the outer canthi, the third channel shows the parietal
E.E.G. and at the bottom is the submental electromyogram. The
transition into paradoxical sleep is accompanied by abrupt loss of muscle
tone, and a changed E.E.G. in which, instead of repeated 'spindles',
saw-tooth waves and a little alpha rhythm are now present, together
with occasional rapid eye movements.

together with *sleep spindles* (Fig. 1) and after a further period the whole E.E.G. is dominated by very large slow waves at about 1 or 2 c per sec. These changes are designated as Stages 1 to 4.

When the very large slow waves are present in the E.E.G. of sleep we call it Stage 4 and this is a time during which it is much more difficult to awaken the individual than when he is in Stage 2 sleep, with just the occasional big slow waves and the sleep spindles. There is in fact a broad relation between the presence of slow waves in the E.E.G., cortical inefficiency and impaired responsiveness. Large slow waves may, for example, be present in the cortex as a result of impairment in

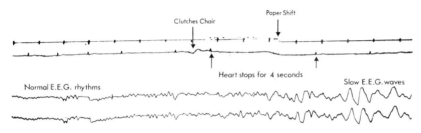

FIG. 2. An emotional swoon or faint causing slow waves in E.E.G. The time-marker at the top indicates seconds and below this is the EKG with the QRS complexes easily visible. The bottom two channels are of frontal E.E.G. The record is from a young man, very anxious in the recording situation, and sitting up in a chair. To the left, normal E.E.G. rhythms are present and the heart rate is about 50 per min but then there is a two-second delay between successive heart-beats, he clutches the arms of the chair and causes movement artifact, then his heart stops for four seconds, followed by a delay of another two seconds before the next heart beat. Just after this he collapsed and fell forwards.

Note that, as his heart slows, diminishing the brain's blood supply, large slow waves appear in the E.E.G. to the right-hand side of the illustration.

the local oxygen supply. This can be caused by anoxaemia, by vaso-constriction, or by fall of blood pressure. Figure 2 illustrates the changes associated with an ordinary emotional swoon or faint. Equally large slow waves can be found in coma, such as may follow overdose of hypnotic drugs or result from low blood sugar, in severe vitamin $B_{12}$ deficiency, hypothyroidism, low blood potassium level, or oedema from a space-occupying lesion. Lower voltage slow waves of 4 to 6 c per sec are found in deliria. Large slow waves coupled with sudden high frequency waves called *spikes* are characteristic of epilepsy. In the epileptic the actual seizure is accompanied by a *paroxysm* of these abnormal electrical waves which may last for several seconds or several minutes (Fig. 3). In cases of *centrencephalic epilepsy* the abnormal electrical waves

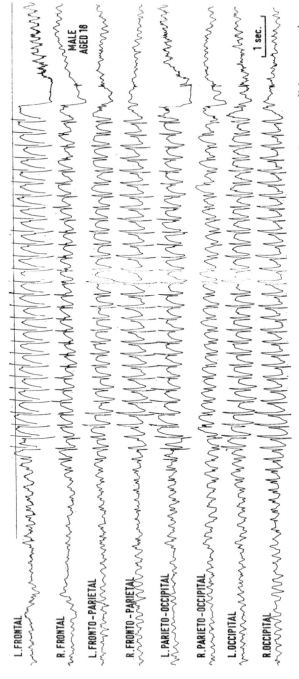

FIG. 3. An E.E.G. spike-and-wave paroxysm in a youth of 18. Although these bilateral electrical abnormalities occurred every couple of minutes during recording, he had convulsions only at intervals separated by months.

Note that large slow waves are present, as in other states of impaired consciousness, but here alternate with high voltage fast spikes. In its onset the paroxysm can be seen to build up for an initial couple of seconds but to be abrupt in offset. The subsequent E.E.G. rhythms remain rather slower than normal. Consciousness is impaired (see text) during such paroxysms even in the absence of any motor seizure.

are present simultaneously and symmetrically on both sides of the brain and commonly there is visible an alternation between high voltage slow waves and high voltage single spikes once every third of a second. Many such discharges are accompanied by a grand mal seizure, but in others the casual observer may notice nothing wrong with the patient, or perhaps only a brief hesitation and a far-away appearance on his face. In focal epilepsy the abnormal electrical rhythms may appear to affect one part of the brain alone or, originating in one part of the brain, may then spread in the course of a few seconds to involve other parts of the brain. Slowed E.E.G. rhythms can persist for minutes after a convulsion, and are associated with impaired consciousness and subsequent amnesia (post-ictal automatism).

It is important to realize that when a motor convulsion does not occur in such patients (or indeed may never have occurred in their lives) at the times when the abnormal electrical discharges are present, whether they be generalized over the whole head, or simply focal in one part of the brain alone, an alteration in consciousness should be presumed. In the case of focal epilepsy this may not be simply a change in the general efficiency of thinking and awareness, but there may be some positive abnormality such as olfactory, gustatory, visual, or auditory hallucination, or a mood change of fear or depression.

It is not easy to catch enough brief periods of abnormal rhythm in the E.E.G. of most epileptic patients to make an intensive study of the associated alterations of consciousness, but a few patients with generalized and symmetrical abnormalities have them with sufficient frequency to make possible studies that relate their performance at any one moment to the electrical rhythms. In cases of petit mal, that is to say of centrencephalic epilepsy where there is merely a clinically evident impairment of consciousness, with a vacant gaze but no convulsion, some patients can reply to simple questions while the abnormal rhythms are present. Some who can do this are quite unable to reply to more complex questions, but yet may do so when the abnormal rhythms have just ceased. In other words they may retain a memory of the questions put to them. If such people have been asked to pay continuous attention to something such as a source of intermittent stimuli requiring responses from them, it is possible to plot a graph, as in Figure 4, which indicates how, although performance may not be wholly lost, it is much impaired from early in the centrencephalic paroxysm and returns gradually towards the end of the paroxysm.

OVER-BREATHING

In routine clinical E.E.G. examination it is customary to ask patients to *over-breathe* for three minutes. The reason is that over-breathing causes a reduction in cerebral blood flow and when this happens epileptic-type

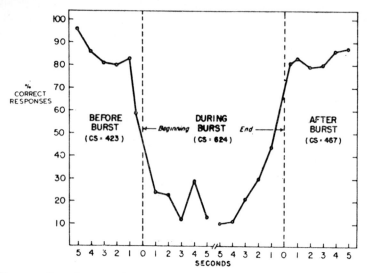

FIG. 4.  Impairment of responsiveness during E.E.G., wave-and-spike paroxysms or bursts. Patients engaged on a task requiring attention make fewer correct responses during the time of the abnormal E.E.G. waves. Notice that performance improves during the five seconds just before the end of a paroxysm (from Mirsky and Van Buren, 1965).

paroxysms are more likely to occur in the brain and be seen in the E.E.G.

It is important for the psychiatrist to remember that over-breathing, or hyperventilation, is an invariable response to anxiety. It can be understood as part of an emergency reaction but, in our civilized life, primitive emotions may not always be accompanied by physical activity of such violence as would match the hyperventilation, and in consequence the degree of hyperventilation is usually disproportionately great. In some people the degree of disproportion is extreme and this is always so in what is commonly termed a 'panic attack'. It should be remembered that if a young adult breathes at the normal rate, but to maximum depth, he will over-breathe to such an extent as to cause, on average, a reduction in his cerebral blood flow of about one-third and in some individuals this may amount to one-half (Kety and Schmidt, 1946). The effect is greater if the individual is erect rather than recumbent. Hyperventilation causes a reduction in the partial pressure of carbon dioxide, a vasodilator substance that normally helps to keep open the arterioles. In addition there is evidence that there are vasodilator impulses to the cerebral arterioles and that, when the carbon dioxide in the blood falls, the flow of impulses is reduced in those parasympathetic nerves that emerge with the 7th nerve and, from the geniculate ganglion, pass in the greater superficial petrosal nerve to join the carotid plexus.

Many patients who are brought to hospital in a state of panic can be observed to be hyperventilating to a considerable degree, respiration often being deep and sighing rather than very rapid. If it were possible to do an immediate E.E.G. with such people it would be found that there was a considerable slowing of the rhythms, sometimes (especially in the under 25s) amounting to the predominance of very large slow waves similar to those seen in Figure 2. If, when one sees a patient in a panic attack, one remembers this, and also that his cerebral blood flow is greatly reduced, one may the more readily understand why he seems impervious to reassurance and is so lacking in insight. His brain is not functioning properly owing to lack of oxygen, and afterwards there may be a degree of amnesia, so that he may then describe the whole episode as a "black-out".

In clinical practice hyperventilation attacks are more common among young adults or adolescents, but will occur at any age, are often accompanied by feelings of pins and needles in the hands and feet and around the mouth, and the change of pH in the blood causes a reduction of ionized calcium in the blood so that *tetany* results, with carpopedal spasm, that the patient feels most in the hands. He or she notices that the hands are stiff and cannot be moved into their normal position, and so becomes even more terrified. The raised anxiety causes an increase in general muscle tone, including the muscle tone of the thoracic cage and the patient feels unable to breathe. So he fights even harder for breath and feels even more frightened. As soon as the plasma carbon dioxide can be raised again, the mental state returns to whatever it has more generally been, and much of the anxiety subsides. The return can be achieved by very firm instructions to hold the breath, to breathe once, to hold the breath, to breathe once, to hold the breath and so on: or by re-breathing from a paper bag.

## VARIOUS STATES OF CONSCIOUSNESS

### DREAMS

There are many different states in which cortical vigilance is impaired yet not sufficiently to prevent an active mental life. Some of these states are normal and some are pathological. Naturally-occurring dreams have long excited the interest of psychiatrists and intrigued them because of the resemblances between the quality of thinking and that found in schizophrenia. Dreams are fragments of a fantasy life, just as are day-dreams, although in the case of the latter there is usually present sufficient environmental stimulation, and cerebral vigilance is high enough, to enable the individual to keep at least within easy call of reality. Day-dreams on retiring to bed tend to lose their status and become dreams. Man is an especially visual animal and it is not surprising that his fantasy life should reflect real life and that descriptions of dreams should emphasize visual experiences. However, like real life, the life of fantasy includes experiences of all other sensory modes and, far from being a sort of spectator-experience of sundry images, is a fantasy *life* experience. Thus the man that has been blind from birth will never *see* anything in his dreams, but will have dreams in which he goes from place to place, talks to his friends, feels things, hears things and experiences moods and emotions as he goes around.

Freud regarded his original writings on the subject of dreams as the high point of his life's work but since the early 1960s there has been a great increase in the study of dreams, through advances made in the laboratory. In the last few years many previous statements have been made obsolete and old preconceptions swept away. The really outstanding new departure has been the realization that a large proportion of the night is spent in dreaming, and that individual dreams last much longer than had generally been supposed. In fact we may now say with some confidence that some sort of mental life probably continues throughout the whole of sleep.

Sleep may be divided into two kinds, which we may call *orthodox sleep*, having E.E.G. spindles and large slow waves, and *paradoxical sleep*, having no spindles and an absence of very large slow E.E.G. waves (Oswald, 1970). Paradoxical sleep in man is characterized mainly by E.E.G. waves at 4–6 c per sec, with a little alpha rhythm and occasional bursts of 'saw-tooth' waves at 2–3 c per sec (Fig. 1). Paradoxical sleep thus has an E.E.G. that does not differ greatly from that of drowsiness, or Stage 1 sleep, and is thus not far different from the E.E.G. of fully conscious life. Many workers who have conducted their research with animals have referred to it as 'activated' sleep, implying that cerebral vigilance was fairly high. It would therefore not be surprising if mental life were active during this time. The two kinds of sleep alternate about every hour and a half and paradoxical sleep occupies only 20–25 per cent of the time.

Paradoxical sleep is accompanied by intermittent bursts of jerky, rapid eye movements and is often called rapid eye movement or REM sleep. When people are awakened from one of these periods and asked what was passing through their mind, they are able to recall fairly detailed mental life on about 80 per cent of occasions and tend to characterize it as dreaming because of its adventurous and colourful or even bizarre features. When awakened from the other kind of sleep, orthodox, or NREM sleep, they more often report having just been 'thinking' and usually describe more mundane mental life, filled with day residues. There is now evidence that, as mental life progresses in the intervals between the eye movements, it is as mundane as during orthodox sleep, but that, at the precise moment of the eye movements (which are associated in time with the 'saw-tooth' E.E.G. waves), a psychotic flavour, or qualitative daftness, is injected momentarily into the dream and gives it its unique and schizophrenia-like quality (Molinari and Foulkes, 1969).

Paradoxical sleep is also accompanied by abolition of muscle tone throughout most of the skeletal muscles, and loss of most stretch reflexes, so that the individual is paralyzed. The dreamer becomes aware of his paralysis only when, in his nightmare, perhaps being swept towards some terrible disaster, he struggles to escape, and finds himself momentarily unable to move. Each period of paradoxical sleep is also associated with penile erection, or increased vaginal blood flow, except that penile erection is reduced where dream anxiety-content is high (Karacan et al., 1966). It is only one of many links between sexual function and paradoxical sleep, that suggest that Freud was right in linking dreaming and sexuality.

Freud regarded the dream as a protector of sleep and it does seem that he was not far from the truth. External sensory stimuli still reach the brain during paradoxical sleep but they tend to become incorporated into the dream in disguised form. The disguise may be in the form of some assonant representation, such as the spoken name, 'Robert', being accompanied by a dream about a rabbit, or the representation may be purely symbolic (Berger, 1963).

Paradoxical sleep recurs about 5 times in the average night and lasts about 20 minutes each time. Not only does it have duration, it also has intensity, and one measure of the intensity is the profusion of rapid eye movements per unit time. The more profuse the eye movements, the more active or vivid the dream experience. Hypnotic drugs reduce the intensity, and cause both fewer eye movements and less perceptually bizarre or active dreams.

DELIRIUM

The similarities between dream-thinking and schizophrenic thinking led to hopes that there would be some clear relationship between paradoxical sleep and schizophrenia. It has not, thus far, proved to be the case. However, studies of paradoxical sleep and dreams have thrown light on some deliria, namely those that occur when alcohol, barbiturates or other hypnotics have been withdrawn. Understanding of delirium tremens may be assisted if we consider some effects of alcohol, or of hypnotic drugs that also induce dependence. Continued use results in hepatic enzyme induction, which may, in turn, lead to decreased duration in the effect of either the alcohol or the hypnotic, but cannot explain the decreased sensitivity that we call *tolerance*, that follows upon repeated exposure. Tolerance must be attributed to the brain. Just as the use of alcohol, or hypnotic drugs, brings about compensatory adjustments in the liver cells, so also compensatory modifications to the brain's neuronal machinery can be inferred. They must be such as to counteract the drug's effects on the neurone, so allowing tolerance to develop. The compensatory modifications in the brain will themselves then cause symptoms and signs if left unopposed by the presence of the drug. So in the brain we should look for tolerance mechanisms and also the mechanisms of *dependence*. We may consider what such agents do to anxiety, to convulsion-threshold, to paradoxical sleep and dreaming, to restlessness and to sleep duration. The easiest of these to measure is the duration of paradoxical sleep and this is portrayed in Figure 5.

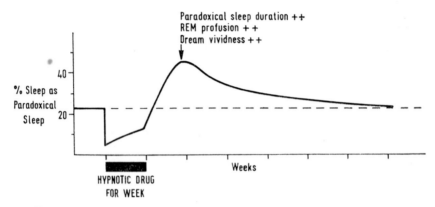

Fig. 5.   When an hypnotic drug is taken sleep is altered, and, among other things, the proportion spent as paradoxical sleep is reduced. Continued administration leads to tolerance and a reduced effect. It is not the drug that has changed, but the brain. The neuronal modifications persist after the drug is withdrawn and cause rebound abnormalities opposite in kind to those initially caused by the drug. The slow but inevitable turnover of neuronal protein is believed to underly the gradual return to normal after drug withdrawal, through slow elimination of the drug-instituted neuronal modifications. Compare with Figure 6.

Barbiturates and alcohol cause a reduction of paradoxical sleep. The brain adjusts to these agents, so that, when they are withdrawn, the modifications that have come into being to counteract the foreign agents, now cause an abnormally great amount of paradoxical sleep, which is also increased in intensity. Barbiturates and alcohol reduce anxiety. The brain adjusts to them, and when they are stopped the patient is similarly left more anxious than before they started: raised anxiety and vivid dreams give rise to nightmares. Barbiturates and alcohol reduce the liability to convulsions, but when they are withdrawn after the brain has adjusted to them, the patient is left for a period with an increased liability to fits. Barbiturates and alcohol tend to cause inertia and will reduce intra-sleep restlessness. The brain adjusts to them so that, when they are stopped, restlessness, including intra-sleep restlessness, is greatly increased. They prolong the sleep period but, after a couple of months of administration, sleep duration has returned to baseline durations. When the alcohol or hypnotic drug is stopped, insomnia results.

If we take all these features together, we can see that the withdrawal of either alcohol or hypnotic drugs, at its most extreme represents the picture of delirium tremens, with insomnia and restlessness, heightened anxiety and heightened dream-experiences, often of a terrifying nature, that intrude even into wakefulness.

The normal person has a delay of about an hour's orthodox sleep between wakefulness and the dreaming or paradoxical sleep, but withdrawal of an hypnotic causes the paradoxical sleep to come on at the very onset of sleep, and the delirium tremens patient flits rapidly between having a waking brain and having paradoxical sleep which keeps intruding into his wakefulness. In other words he has a brain state especially geared to dreaming or fantasy thinking.

Although we may thus gain some understanding of drug-withdrawal delirium in terms of paradoxical sleep, different mechanisms must be recognized as operating in the case of other deliria, although in these also one may see evidence of a continual spontaneous flitting between different levels of vigilance, especially a sagging, as it were, of the level of vigilance very soon after it has been raised by deliberate stimulation. In the delirium that may occur in acute chest infections (especially in those with chronic bronchitis and emphysema), acute heart failure, severe anaemia, or certain drug intoxications, as in poisoning from hyoscine (antimotion sickness pills) or after overdose of tricyclic drugs, the delirium, with its disorientation, hallucinations, inability to sustain attention, impairment of memory and often paranoid ideas, is accompanied by varying degrees of slow waves in the E.E.G. At rest the slow waves may be almost continuous, but an alerting stimulus may cause their transitory diminution. The state of vigilance is low and reactivity impaired.

The presence of E.E.G. slow waves in such patients appears to be universal (Romano and Engel, 1944; Laidlaw and Read, 1961). While only one variety of delirium is especially associated with paradoxical sleep, we can liken any of the deliria to dreaming. In the early work on paradoxical sleep there grew up a false belief that dreaming was confined to that state. In fact dreaming occurs, even if less colourfully, in all other states of reduced vigilance that are compatible with mental life, and in all these states the capacity to form engrams or stable memory-traces is impaired. Hypnagogic hallucinations of drowsiness (Oswald, 1962), namely brief dreamlets containing visual, auditory, or other sensory experiences lead into organized dream adventures, as the individual passes at sleep onset from Stage 1 sleep into Stage 2 sleep.

PERCEPTUAL ISOLATION

The presence of impaired cortical efficiency, with E.E.G. slow waves, seems always to be accompanied by thinking divorced from reality. In the case of ordinary drowsiness we might suppose that this is partly because the sensory inflow that defines reality has been reduced. We go to bed in a quiet and comfortable room with uniformity of our surroundings. Monotony promotes sleep, just as novelty keeps us wide awake.

Experiments in extreme monotony have been carried out during the past 20 years, into what is known as 'sensory deprivation' or 'perceptual isolation'. It has generally been effected by putting gloves on the hands to reduce tactile information, together with continuous masking 'white' noise (like the sound of a waterfall), ground-glass goggles on the eyes, and with various restrictions of movement. The reported effects of this have varied with different individuals, partly according to their expectations. However, hypnagogic hallucinations are frequently described by people who remain under these circumstances for long periods, together with feelings of unreality and difficulty in thinking.

After several days of confinement and then subsequent release, visual perception can be briefly abnormal and there may be a lack of volition for several days. Zubek, Welch and Saunders (1963), kept subjects under conditions of perceptual isolation for 14 days and noted a gradual slowing of the E.E.G. rhythms, which persisted for more than a week after release.

The abnormalities of cerebral function and associated psychological changes in this last experiment are obviously relevant to prisoners kept in solitary confinement and subsequently interrogated and led into false confessions. Their situation is, however, more complex. Many would be suffering also from sleep deprivation: many authors have described how prisoners awaiting interrogation are deliberately kept awake by their guards. Sleep deprivation is another cause of reduced cerebral vigilance and severely sleep-deprived people are liable to hallucinatory experiences, paranoid delusions, and an incapacity to relate present reality to facts learned in the past. Prisoners would also have been subjected to recurring episodes of fear. Throughout the whole of the animal kingdom intense fear, especially when coupled with imposed limitation of action, results in a trance state variously called 'animal hypnosis', 'the sham-death reflex', 'experimental catatonia', or the 'still reaction'. The electrophysiological picture resembles that of sleep (Oswald, 1962). It was a state familiar to Pavlov who wrote of 'transmarginal inhibition' in the cortex, a concept that has been drawn upon extensively by Sargant (1957, 1969) in discussing the states of unreality or exaltation, with or without visions, that follow upon intense emotional excitement, often accompanied by loud and rhythmic drumming, or other sensory stimulation, and leading to religious or political conversion, namely a renunciation of old ways and an acceptance of new ideas. We may therefore suppose that, in the case of political prisoners who, under conditions of prolonged confinement and interrogation, sign false confessions, there may be operative the effects of perceptual isolation, sleep deprivation, 'transmarginal inhibition' and such factors as low blood sugar from starvation, or electrolyte disturbance owing to diarrhoea, all of which would act to lower cerebral vigilance, produce slowing of the E.E.G., and impaired thinking and grasp of events.

TRANCE STATES

There are other forms of trance in which consciousness is held to be altered. In some cultures these are attained partly through the use of drugs, but in a number of oriental countries various meditative states are attained by concentration and practice alone. In those practised by Zen monks (Kasamatsu and Hirai, 1966), once the meditation is under way, opening of the eyes can be without effect on established alpha rhythm. In other instances, including transcendental meditation, periods of slowing of the E.E.G. waves occur, but these are slight according to Wallace (1970), who reports decrease in whole-body oxygen consumption, as much as 20 per cent, without other than slight slowing in the E.E.G. Reduction of oxygen consumption occurs also in sleep, but only in the presence of very much more profound E.E.G. changes, with the loss of awareness that we all associate with sleep. It would seem therefore that in such states as transcendental meditation, the individual may be able to meditate inwardly in an intense manner while relatively out of touch with reality and with his body in a state of relaxation comparable to that prevailing during sleep.

The more common trance state in Western countries is the hypnotic trance. It is induced by verbal suggestions, with or without a variety of other more or less impressive environmental manoeuvres that suggest omnipotence on the part of the hypnotist. Although many hypnotists use phrases like, 'you are going to sleep', in fact the hypnotic trance is not a state of sleep and it is quite unnecessary to use the word when inducing the trance. The individual does not lose consciousness, he remains aware of the world, unless the hypnotist suggests anaesthesia for some particular modality, but he does not respond to the world in the normal way. His responses become restricted to those that the hypnotist suggests. He remains awake and his physiology is in every way that of the awake person, though there is some evidence that, with suggested anaesthesia or analgesia, there may be reduction in electrical potentials evoked in the brain by a stimulus (Levy and Behrman, 1970).

In much of the foregoing discussion attention has been drawn to changes in the E.E.G. that accompany states of altered consciousness, and these changes have been those associated with lowered vigilance. However we may assume that there is an optimum level of vigilance and that impairment of consciousness will result if vigilance is raised to excessively high levels. As already mentioned, when this is brought about through fear, a reaction may follow, with the individual passing into a state resembling sleep (transmarginal inhibition). However, there are drugs that will raise cerebral vigilance, make E.E.G. rhythms faster and which have in addition their own more specific actions on restricted cerebral functions. Examples are dexamphetamine and LSD (lysergic acid diethylamide).

### DRUGS AND ALTERED CONSCIOUSNESS

Dexamphetamine derivatives can produce a sense of exaltation (Jonsson, 1969). Prolonged use leads to dependence, with inertia, feelings of impaired mental powers, and mood depression as withdrawal features (Fig. 6). The effect of intravenous injection of methamphetamine has been referred to as a 'whole-body orgasm'. The user is filled with feelings of well-being, energy, confidence and power, coupled with inability to sleep and anorexia, which, in the long term, leads to malnutrition. Acute psychoses resembling schizophrenia, but with rather more visual hallucinatory features, have been observed by many. These are not due to the induced sleep-deprivation alone, since the administration of dexamphetamine to persons not previously receiving the drug will produce paranoid psychoses within 24 hours in those who have received doses of the order of 500 mg (Griffith et al., 1970). In the case of LSD, differing effects are caused in different people, including fear or panic in some. Others report transcendental experiences with freedom from anxiety. The more specific effects of the drug are visual, with distortions of colour intensity and of movement, or even frank hallucinations. Overall there is a sense of intense awareness (Freedman, 1968).

Dexamphetamine, LSD and similar drugs alter the perception of time, so that a short period of clock time seems of much longer duration both subjectively and on testing (Fischer, Griffin and Liss, 1962). Lengthening of perceived time may account for the reputation that cannabis is an aphrodisiac. It is described as enhancing the intensity of sensory experience (Weil, Zinberg and Nelsen, 1968) and if pleasurable experiences are made to seem lengthier, its reputation may be explicable. It should be noted that states of lowered vigilance, brought about by quinalbarbitone 200 mg by day, or by perceptual isolation (previously discussed), also alter the perception of time, but in the opposite direction, so that a long period of clock time seems of short duration both subjectively and on testing (Goldstone, Boardman and Lhamon, 1958; Banks and Cappon, 1962; Vernon and McGill, 1963).

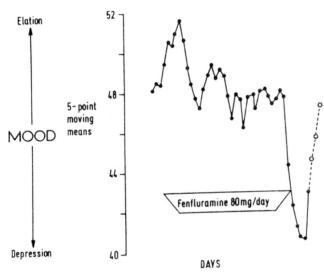

Fig. 6. Amphetamine derivatives can alter mood and subjectively-experienced powers of concentration. After use of fenfluramine as a slimming drug for 28 days, withdrawal depression of mood occurred and was accompanied by self-ratings of impaired powers of concentration. (Reproduced, with permission, from Oswald et al., 1971). Compare with Figure 5.

Drugs that alter consciousness are associated not only with misperception of one's true state of efficiency, but also objectively alter efficiency on certain tasks. Dexamphetamine will improve skilled performance (Kornetsky et al., 1959). On the other hand hypnotic drugs, such as barbiturates and nitrazepam, will lead to an impairment of skilled performance that is still present more than 12 hours after a clinical dose (Malpas, et al., 1970). Alcohol will, of course, do the same and is capable of interaction with other drugs, so that, for example, the ingestion of alcohol concomitantly with a drug such as amitriptyline leads to much greater impairment of performance on tasks that require the subject to remain constantly aware of potentially important stimuli (Landauer, Milner and Patman, 1969).

## REFERENCES

ARDUINI, A. & ARDUINI, M. G. (1954)    Effect of drugs and metabolic alterations on brain stem arousal mechanisms. *Journal of Pharmacology and Experimental Therapeutics*, **110**, 68–70.

BANKS, R. & CAPPON, D. (1962)    Effects of reduced sensory input on time perception. *Perceptual and Motor Skills*, **14**, 74.

BERGER, R. J. (1963)    Experimental modification of dream content by meaningful verbal stimuli. *British Journal of Psychiatry*, **109**, 722–740.

BREMER, F. (1935)    Cerveau isolé et physiologie du sommeil. *Compte rendu de la Société de biologie. Paris*, **118**, 1235–1241.

CAIRNS, H. (1952)    Disturbance of consciousness with lesions of the brain-stem and diencephalon. *Brain*, **75**, 109–146.

CHATRIAN, G. E., WHITE, L. E. & DALY, D. (1963)    Electroencephalographic patterns resembling those of sleep in certain comatose states after injuries to the head. *Electroencephalography and Clinical Neurophysiology*, **55**, 272–280.

FISCHER, R., GRIFFIN, F. & LISS, L. (1962)    Biological aspects of time in relation to (model) psychoses. *Annals of the New York Academy of Sciences*, **96**, 44–65.

FOLZ, E. L. & SCHMIDT, R. P. (1956).    The role of the reticular formation in the coma of head injury. *Journal of Neurosurgery*, **13**, 145–154.

Freedman, D. X. (1968)    On the use and abuse of LSD. *Archives of General Psychiatry*, **18**, 330–347.

GOLDSTONE, S., BOARDMAN, W. K. & LHAMON, W. T. (1958)    Effect of quinalbarbitone, dextro-amphetamine and placebo on apparent time. *British Journal of Psychology*, **49**, 324–328.

GRIFFITH, J. D., CAVANAUGH, J. H., HELD, J. & OATES, J. A. (1970) In *Amphetamines and Related Compounds*, p. 897. Edited by E. Costa and S. Garattini. New York: Raven Press.

JEFFERSON, G. & JOHNSON, R. T. (1950)    The cause of loss of consciousness in posterior fossa compression. *Folia psychiatrica, neurologica et neurochirurgica neerlandica*, **53**, 306–319.

JONSSON, C. O. (1969)    In *Abuse of Central Stimulants*, p. 71. Edited by F. Sjöqvist & M. Tottie. Stockholm: Almqvist and Wiksell.

KARACAN, I., GOODENOUGH, D. R., SHAPIRO, A. & STARKER, S. (1966)    Erection cycle during sleep in relation to dream anxiety. *Archives of General Psychiatry*, **15**, 183–189.

KASAMATSU, A. & HIRAI, T. (1966)    An electroencephalographic study on the Zen meditation (Zazen). *Folia psychiatrica et neurologica japonica*, **20**, 315–336.

KETY, S. S. & SCHMIDT, C. F. (1946)    The effects of active and passive hyperventilation on cerebral blood flow, cerebral oxygen consumption, cardiac output and blood pressure of normal young men. *Journal of Clinical Investigation*, **25**, 107–119.

KORNETSKY, C., MIRSKY, A. F., KESSLER, E. K. & DORFF, J. E. (1959)    The effects of dextro-amphetamine on behavioural deficits produced by sleep loss in humans. *Journal of Pharmacology and Experimental Therapeutics*, **127**, 46–50.

LAIDLAW, J. & READ, A. E. (1961)    The electroencephalographic diagnosis of manifest and latent 'delirium' with particular reference to that complicating hepatic cirrhosis. *Journal of Neurology, Neurosurgery and Psychiatry*, **24**, 58–70.

LANDAUER, A. A., MILNER, G. & PATMAN, J. (1969)    Alcohol and amitriptyline effects on skills related to driving behaviour. *Science*, **163**, 1467–1468.

Levy, R. & Behrman, J. (1970)   Cortical evoked responses in hysterical hemi-anaesthesia. *Electroencephalography and Clinical Neurophysiology*, **29,** 400–402.

Malpas, A., Rowan, A. J., Joyce, C. R. B. & Scott, D. F. (1970)   Persistent behavioural and electroencephalographic changes after single doses of nitrazepam and amylobarbitone sodium. *British Medical Journal*, **2,** 762–764.

Mirsky, A. F. & Van Buren, J. M. (1965)   On the nature of the 'absence' in centrencephalic epilepsy: a study of some behavioural, electroencephalographic and autonomic factors. *Electroencephalography and Clinical Neurophysiology*, **18,** 334–348.

Molinari, S. & Foulkes, D. (1969)   Tonic and phasic events during sleep: psychological correlates and implications. *Perceptual and Motor Skills*, **29,** 343–368.

Moruzzi, G. & Magoun, H. W. (1949)   Brain stem reticular formation and activation of the EEG. *Electroencephalography and Clinical Neurophysiology*, **1,** 455–473.

Oswald, I. (1962)   *Sleeping and Waking*. Amsterdam: Elsevier.

Oswald, I. (1970)   *Sleep*. London: Penguin Books.

Oswald, I., Lewis, S. A., Dunleavy, D. L. F., Brezinova, V. & Briggs, M. (1971)   Fenfluramine and imipramine: drugs of dependence though not of abuse. *British Medical Journal*, Vol. 3, 70–73.

Romano, J. & Engel, G. L. (1944)   Delirium. *Archives of Neurology and Psychiatry*, **51,** 356–377.

Sargant, W. (1957)   *Battle for the Mind*. London: Heinneman.

Sargant, W. (1969)   The physiology of faith. *British Journal of Psychiatry*, **115,** 505–518.

Vernon, J. A. & McGill, T. E. (1963)   Time estimations during sensory deprivation. *Journal of General Psychology*, **69,** 11–18.

Wallace, R. K. (1970)   Physiological effects of transcendental meditation. *Science*, **167,** 1751–1754.

Weil, A. T., Zinberg, N. E. & Nelsen, J. M. (1968)   Clinical and psychological effects of marihuana in man. *Science*, **162,** 1234–1242.

Zubek, J. P., Welch, G. & Saunders, M. G. (1963)   Electroencephalographic changes during and after 14 days of perceptual deprivation. *Science*, **139,** 490–492.

## Chapter XVIII

# GENETIC ASPECTS OF MENTAL DISORDER

## N. Kreitman and R. Clayton

### INTRODUCTION

The study of the genetic aspects of mental disorder is often relatively neglected by psychiatrists. This lack of enthusiasm appears to have two main causes. Firstly, it is assumed, wrongly, that to demonstrate that genetic factors are of major importance for a particular illness is tantamount to renouncing hope of cure: in fact the precise opposite may be nearer the truth. Secondly, there may be a reluctance to introduce concepts and knowledge from a branch of medicine which is not easily integrated with considerations of social and psychological factors. Such a refusal to enlarge the framework of thinking can only be termed obscurantist. Moreover, it is likely that the importance of genetics will increase as psychiatry develops. In neurology, for example, important nosological distinctions have been possible through the combined use of clinical observation and genetic studies. To date, it is not easy to point to any such examples from the field of psychiatry, but undoubtedly nosological clarification, when ultimately achieved, will owe a good deal to the contribution of the geneticist.

Meanwhile genetic studies should not be neglected by the clinician, not only because of their contribution to our understanding of particular psychiatric disorders, but also because they provide a way of thinking about aetiology which has widespread applications to the whole field of psychiatry.

Shortly after Freud began publishing findings on the relationship between abnormal behaviour patterns and early experiences, Mendel's laws of inheritance were rediscovered and Garrod, between 1902 and 1908, published a series of papers on the genetics of biochemical abnormalities in man. He saw quite clearly that he had but uncovered the tip of an iceberg and that a wealth of genetically determined biochemical variation must exist in the human population, and that this in turn would rest on the genetic control of the enzymic constitution of the body. The lack of interest of his colleagues induced him to turn his researches elsewhere, and although sporadic analyses appeared in the literature it is essentially only in the last 10 to 15 years that the biochemical genetics of man has become a serious study. We know today of some 80 to 100 genetically transmitted biochemical lesions. Among these are some which result in mental defect, the recognition of which has permitted us to distinguish a number of separate entities from the vast amorphous population of the mentally subnormal. It has also led to the conclusion that there are many different genetic lesions which may lead to a similar condition. At the same time that Garrod made his pioneering investigations, Pearson, and later Johansen, were devising methods to estimate the genetic transmission of characteristics which appear to vary continuously, or to be so complex that there were no clearly defined sub-groups in the population. The method for this statistical assay of heritability of continuously varying or highly complex conditions has also been developed in recent years, in part stimulated by work on animals and plants of economic importance and in part from the researches of statisticians. More recently, medical epidemiologists have contributed by refining the criteria of population sampling and measurement.

## The Interrelationship of Genotype and Environment

All the responses of an organism, developmental and otherwise, are implicit in its genotype, which is defined as the sum total of its genes. But no organism can be conceived of as without an external environment, which must include other individuals of the same species, nor can any particular characteristic be conceived of except in the context of internal environment. Neither can we now conceive of an organism as a tabula rasa, its final conformation being a product of the environment alone.

There is no such thing as an absolutely stable environment. Every biological entity from the moment of conception must function in a changing universe. There is always a certain range of environmental conditions within which an organism is viable, but beyond the limits of which it becomes malfunctional or dies. This range of conditions may be described in quantitative or qualitative terms. The degree of variation in the environmental conditions which can be tolerated will depend on the genetic constitution of the individual. Thus, individuals of a particular genotype may not be able to function except within very narrow environmental limits, while others may not achieve normality under any known conditions. All intracellular biochemical reactions are controlled by enzymes, and the structure and properties of all enzymes are under the control of specific genes. Thus the statement that extremes of environment lead to cell death or dysfunction can be taken as meaning that the limits of tolerance have been passed within which the gene-controlled reactions can take place. When it is said that a particular substance in a given concentration is poisonous for a particular species, this statement can be interpreted as meaning that very few or no individuals possess the genetic equipment to metabolize the substance, and hence such genetic differences as may exist between one individual and another are of minimal relevance to the outcome. In such circumstances it is customary to speak of the cause of death or disorder ( in this instance poisoning) as environmental in origin.

On the other hand, it is equally possible that in lesser concentrations of the toxic substance only certain members of the species will be affected. These will be those whose genetic constitution is relatively defective, and if the substance in question is one which is part of the environment of most members of the species, conventional language ascribes death in such cases to genetic causes.

These concepts of environmental and genetic contribution to the development of dysfunction or to death can be restated in terms of *variation* in the population. Where there is evidence that a large number of individuals share identical environments and have done so since birth yet only a proportion develop an illness, then the variation between individuals with respect to illness can theoretically be accounted for in terms of differences in the genetic constitutions of the members of the group. In these circumstances one can speak of genetic variation as a cause of illness, provided that it is never forgotten that such a statement is only true for a given environment. In a different environment, in which the relevant factor is missing, there would be no illness and genetic predisposition to abnormal reactions would remain unknown, or if known, of no practical importance.

Conversely, if it is first established that a group of individuals are genetically similar—a situation which can readily be achieved in the laboratory, though one which is often difficult to establish in human situations—then differences in individuals in respect of illness can usually be accounted for in terms of variation in their environment. In these circumstances it is environmental variation which can be incriminated but only in the setting of a given genetic constitution. Other species of organisms, for example, may be perfectly resistant to the environmental agent, and in this case its noxious effect would be simply non-existent.

It is, of course, also possible for both environmental and genetic variation to be important in the aetiology of a given disorder, and this mixed causation is very common in human illnesses of many kinds. But even in the 'pure' cases of either environmental or genetic variance being responsible for the development of a disorder in certain members of a population, it is evident that the geneticist is, in principle, as much concerned with environments as he is with genes. The 'nature-nurture' controversies of the older literature require to be carefully restated in these more comprehensive terms if they are to retain any meaning whatsoever.

The relative contribution of the genotype and of the environment, and the particular aspects of either which contribute to the manifestation of any particular characteristic, may not be the same in individuals who are superficially alike. There are some five or six genetically different and independent forms of goitrous cretinism. One of these is a defect in the iodine pump, another is a defect in organic iodification, yet another a defect in the coupling of the iodotyrosine; others again involve failures in the deiodinating enzymes. Although goitrous cretinism is the end result of any one of these defects, the response to the different possible forms of treatment will depend on the specific nature of the lesion. It is worth pointing out here that even a genetically entirely normal individual will be indistinguishable from any one of these if there is no iodine in the diet.

The model of illness or dysfunction outlined in this section is best illustrated at the cellular level. In clinical practice it is usually a physiological system which is considered important. In psychiatry this usually means the central nervous, endocrine or metabolic systems. The model remains equally valid when transposed from cellular to a system level but requires some elaboration. Thus it will be evident that the failure of a group of cells will be manifest not only in their dysfunction within the system of which they are part, but also as a wide range of secondary effects, some reflecting compensatory activity, and some as the breakdown of secondary systems. It is perhaps useful to distinguish aetiology as the essential or primary cause from the processes which follow the aetiological disruption of function and culminate in the manifest disorder. This division between aetiology and pathology is carefully maintained in some branches of general medicine, and psychiatrists would do well to follow the example.

## GENE ACTION

We define a *gene* as the determinant of the characteristic of the organism transmitted from parent to offspring. These determinants are composed of deoxyribose nucleic acid (DNA) and are carried on the *chromosomes*, which are found in pairs in the nucleus of every cell. In man there are 23 such pairs; each gene is located at a particular point on a given chromosome, and one copy of each gene in an individual in derived from each parent. However, a gene exists in many forms which are produced by *mutation*. Corresponding genes on chromosome pairs are known as *alleles*. If each parent has contributed an identical gene at a given locus the offspring is *homozygous* for this gene. If they are not identical in their structure (i.e. in the information which they convey) the individual is a *heterozygote*. A gene detectable only in homozygous form is known as a *recessive* and one whose presence can be detected in a single dose is *dominant*.

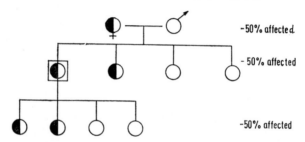

FIG. 1. Dominant transmission, one parent affected. The diagram is applicable to conditions which are viable and do not prevent procreation. (If the condition is lethal or infertile each case is a new mutation.) The hepatic porphyrias follow this pattern of transmission as does Huntington's chorea. The variable late age of onset in Huntington's does not affect the basic transmission pattern.

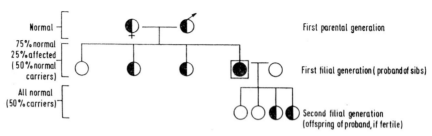

FIG. 2. A square indicates the proband.

Recessive transmission, both parents heterozygous in the first parental generation. Such a mating, if involving a rare allele, is more likely to occur if the parents are descended from a common ancestor who carried the gene in question; hence such pedigrees contain an excess of first degree cousins compared to the general population.

The frequency of affected individuals, normal or heterozygotes in the first filial generation (siblings of proband) is shown. The likely frequency of heterozygotes in the second filial generation (probands' offspring) is shown for genes not materially affecting viability and fertility (e.g. alcaptonuria) and is irrelevant for lethal or semi-lethal conditions like maple syrup urine disease, galactosemia etc.

The sum total of all of the genes of an individual is known as the *genotype* of that individual. The function and appearance of the individual carrying a given genotype is known as its *phenotype*. The phenotype is the resultant of the interaction of the genes with each other and with the environment, both internal and external.

The necessary interaction of genotype with environment was first recognized by Fisher in 1918. Some genes may produce phenotypic effects which are so severe that they can be detected no matter what the environment; others produce effects at the cellular and tissue level which are smaller than the effects of environmental fluctuations.

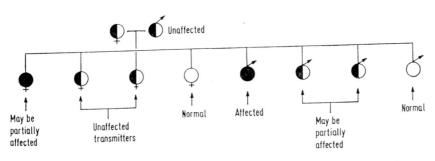

FIG. 3.   Sex limited genes (usually affecting secondary sexual characters). Such genes are transmitted normally, but the phenotype is affected by the sex hormones. Baldness is an example; conditions requiring oestrogens for expression will obviously reverse the sex distribution of phenotypes.

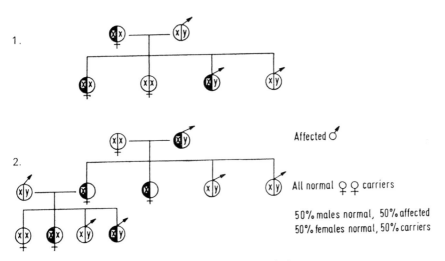

FIG. 4.   Sex-linked transmission.

1.   Viable or almost normal female heterozygote, severely abnormal, infertile or poorly viable male, e.g. Hurler's syndrome, Lesch–Nyhan syndrome. Transmission is by normal male marrying a heterozygous female. Half the offspring of either sex carry the affected chromosome. Of these, the males are ill, the females carriers.

2.   Male affected but fertile, normal or almost normal female, e.g. colour blindness. The male progeny are normal. The females are carriers and their sons will be affected, their daughters normal.

Note: Random inactivation of an X chromosome in female cells will cause effective cellular mosaicism in heterozygous females (Lyon effect).

Nevertheless it is impossible to consider genotype without environment, although their relative contributions can be described and measured for any aspect of the phenotype. If we have insufficient information to recognize co-operating relevant genes because their individual effect on the phenotype at the morphological or functional level is smaller than the environmental fluctuations, then the only course open may be to calculate *heritabilities* (a measure of the size of the genetic contribution) and come to the conclusion that the character is *multigenic* (i.e. controlled by the co-operation of many different genes). If we have specific information about the biochemical changes caused by any of these *mutants*, irrespective of the size of the contribution made by such biochemical changes to the functions, morphology or development, then the problem may be stated in entirely specific terms.

The primary action of a gene is to code for a specific protein. The gene itself is composed of deoxyribose nucleic acid (DNA), which specifies a strand of messenger ribose nucleic acid (mRNA) which in turn determines the amino acid sequence of a specific peptide chain. This peptide chain may be a simple enzyme; it may form part of a multi-chain enzyme, or it may be a structural protein. The specific properties of a protein depend on its three dimensional shape, and this is derived from the amino acid sequence.

Mutant proteins are due to amino acid substitutions which may occur at different points in the sequence as a result of a mutation in the DNA which specifies that protein. Some amino acid substitutions are without noticeable effect on the function of a protein; others may modify it in some way, for example if it is an enzyme its efficiency may be impaired.

The possession of a mutant protein may come to affect the physiology of the cells in which it is synthesized. Should the cell be modified in any way as a result of the possession of the variant protein it may in its turn come to affect the functioning of the tissues of which it forms a part. Stemming from this there may be a cascade of tertiary consequences which in their turn will depend upon the relationships, both developmental and functional, of the affected tissues, to the whole of the organism.

Many enzymes have an efficiency relative to the task to be performed which is almost or entirely adequate even if only half of the amount of normal enzyme is present. Thus in an individual heterozygous for a mutant and a normal enzyme it may not be possible to distinguish the heterozygote from the normal if we look merely for the physical or physiological consequences of the possession or mutant enzyme, and the variant can be observed only when homozygous.

However, if there are other genetic defects also affecting the same cells or tissues there may be a latent weakness present, so that the accumulated instabilities of the organ may be such that trivial environmental changes such as temperature, growth rate, dependence on nutritional level and so on may make all the difference between a heterozygote which is apparently normal and a heterozygote which is abnormal or almost as abnormal as a mutant homozygote. Similarly many heterozygotes who have half of their quantity of a given enzyme in abnormal form are apparently physiologically normal given an average substrate level, or work load. If the substrate level is raised by being pumped in abnormally from the environment, then the capacity of the reduced amount of the normal enzyme in the heterozygote to process this is incommensurate with the load. Thus intermediary metabolites accumulate and the phenotype of the heterozygote is no longer normal. At the biochemical level, then, the gene effect has now become dominant under these conditions. Nevertheless a partial elevation of intermediary metabolites may not produce the clinical effects associated with the even greater accumulation of intermediary metabolites in homozygotes and at the level of functioning of the individual the gene may still be recessive.

A test of this kind can distinguish the homozygous normal person from the heterozygous for many diseases, for example phenylketonuria (see below). The heterozygote is clinically normal but may be detected by feeding excess phenylalanine, which they can process only very slowly.

In those instances where we have the technique available to recognize a given specific protein which is the primary coded gene product we can detect the many variant (genetically allelic) forms which may exist in a population. If each parent has donated a different allele to the offspring, both types of proteins specified will be made together. In such a case there are two regular findings: firstly, that both products in the heterozygote may be recognized simultaneously as being present, and secondly, that environmental fluctuations have little, if any, effects on the presence of these gene products. If however we focus our attention on the morphology and function of the mutant individual we find first that we are frequently able to detect only one of the two alleles present; thus at this level we can talk of dominance and recessiveness; and secondly that it is at this level that interaction with the environment may, under appropriate circumstances, bring about very considerable changes in the expression of the mutant and even in our recognition of its presence.

A few simple examples may illustrate these points.

1. *Dominance-recessiveness and levels of the phenotype.* Sickle-cell anaemia, as shown in Figure 5, is a disease which in the homozygous recessive presents a multiplicity of symptoms which may involve several systems, all of which can be shown to be due to two abnormal properties of the red cells—their abnormal fragility and abnormal shape causing

clumping in the capillaries. Neither of these features is present in the heterozygote. The abnormal properties of the homozygous red cell are due to an abnormal haemoglobin; both normal and abnormal haemoglobin are present together in the red cell of the heterozygote. Thus at the biochemical level there is no dominance or recessiveness. The heterozygous red cell may show transient and minor anomalies in conditions of reduced oxygen tension. Thus the gene may be regarded as intermediate in expression under these conditions.

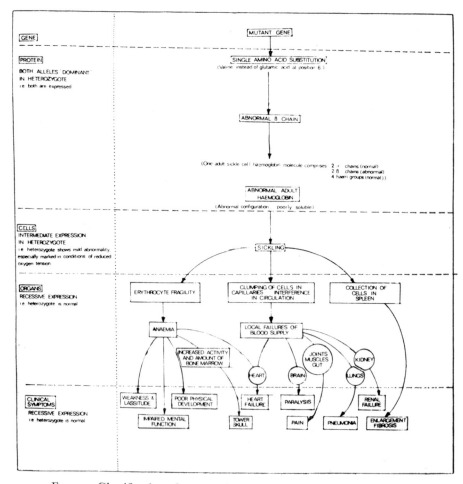

FIG. 5. Classification of a gene effect as dominant or recessive depends on the criterion of recognition (e.g. biochemical vs. morphological) and the level at which the gene-determined disturbance is being recognized (e.g. the gene-specified protein product, the cell containing it, the tissues in which the cells take part, the whole functioning organism).

Example: sickle-cell anaemia.

2. *Gene expression and environment.* Some genes are known in *Drosophila* which are dominant in one environment and recessive in another. In the New Zealand Southdown sheep there is a segregating genetic difference which affects xanthophyllase in these animals. Those individuals which do not possess the effective enzyme are unable to break down the xanthophyll from fresh green food. Xanthophyll acts as a photosensitizer in those parts of the animal which are exposed to sunlight. Thus only animals which are homozygous for the mutant form of the enzyme, which have fed on fresh green-stuffs and which are exposed to sunlight will develop lesions in the exposed areas of skin of the face. Animals which are genetically identical but which although fed on green-stuffs are kept out of sunlight appear normal, as do those which are allowed into the sun but are fed on stored food products. Clearly two environmental factors are required to co-operate together to produce a phenotypic discrimination of the homozygous mutant from the normal individual. Nevertheless methods of protein assay can determine a mutant individual regardless of the environment in which it is exposed.

3. *Gene expression and the residual genotype.* The genetic background may affect the dominance or recessiveness of a gene and the relationship between heterozygotes and homozygotes. There is a series of alleles affecting coat colour in guinea pigs. A heterozygote between any two alleles may be intermediate in expression to either homozygote, or produce an increased effect as compared with either homozygote, or a decreased effect as compared with either homozygote, according to the residual genetic background involving other loci which also affect the coat colour production system. Alleles which produce a high contribution to total melanin formation in many genetic backgrounds may produce an exceptionally low one if some alleles at other loci are changed.

### Gene Expression, Penetrance and Expressivity

We may now define *penetrance* as the percentage of the individuals with particular genotype which manifest the change in functioning or physiology which this genotype is able to bring about. Thus if the environment and the residual genotype are such as to favour developmental or functional instability, 100 per cent penetrance may occur, whilst if the conditions favour the restoration of homeostasis, penetrance may be very low or even drop to zero. *Expressivity* on the other hand is a description of the range and degree of severity of the changes in structure or function brought about by the mutant. It too is subject to alteration by the residual genotype and by environmental conditions.

The same environmental stress may produce different effects on different genes affecting the same developmental system. Thus in

*Drosophila* growth at high temperature increases the penetrance and expressivity of genes which diminish wing development and favour balancers, while penetrance and expressivity are decreased by the same environmental conditions in a different gene which produce an increased wing development and diminished balancers.

### SIMILAR PHENOTYPES BUT DIFFERENT GENOTYPES

It is important to appreciate that at the clinical level of description a given phenotype may be due to quite different genetic causes in different individuals. There are two ways in which distinct genotypes may come to have similar phenotypic expression. One is if there are several sequential steps, each solely devoted to the elaboration of a particular end product in a sequence; the example of goitrous cretinism already referred to is one such instance. Here a sequence of reactions requires to be completed in order to produce normal thyroid hormone. Genetic defects anywhere along the chain will result in thyroxin deficiency, manifested as goitrous cretinism.

Mimic phenotypes may also be produced in another manner. During development tissues come to affect one another and these interactions determine their subsequent developmental pathways. Genetically determined malformations affecting any of these interactions may produce a similar end result. Thus there are almost 30 different genotypes which result in absence or destruction of the labyrinth in the mouse. Some of these are produced by defective development and some of them are associated with degenerative processes. The morphology, ontogeny and developmental and cellular inter-relationships and the chronology of events may serve to distinguish them, as do the genetics. The behavioural result, however, of all of these mutants is deafness, head-shaking and circling movements.

In addition to full mimicry, partial overlaps of phenotypes may also occur but the distinction between the genetic bases is usually evident from consideration of the whole clinical picture.

We may summarize in the following way:

1. Similar phenotypes may not be the same genetically or respond in the same way to a specified environmental change.

2. Given genes may make a contribution to the phenotype that varies with the environment and the residual genotype; at the level of the complex syndrome, penetrance below 100 per cent and varied expression of a genotype may occur for certain conditions. (This should not be used as a routine excuse to explain away a discrepancy from an ideal model.)

3. The presence of a genetic condition, if its presence is undetectable except under specific conditions, may nevertheless be demonstrated

regularly if a biochemical assay is used rather than an assay depending on morphology, behaviour or physiology.

## Sources of Evidence in Psychiatric Disorders

### 1. *Familial Clustering*

It is often assumed that demonstration of familial clustering of illness (termed segregation) constitutes evidence for the importance of genetic factors in aetiology, and that the more clear-cut such clustering the stronger the evidence. This of course is not the case. Among the families of doctors will be found a higher proportion of other medical practitioners than in the population at large, yet no one proposes a genetic basis for this phenomenon, which is an example of cultural rather than genetic transmission. It is true that the discovery of a classical Mendelian ratio for a behavioural syndrome lends some weight to a genetic aetiology, but all that can be said with certainty is that failure to demonstrate familial segregation after careful investigation is evidence against a genetic basis for a characteristic. Even this negative test cannot be applied if the characteristic in question is universally distributed throughout the population, in which case clustering is impossible *a priori*.

### 2. *Twin Studies*

Twin studies have played a prominent part in psychiatric genetics as they offer one of the nearest approaches to an experimental investigation in the human situation.

Twins are of two kinds, identical or monozygotic (MZ) and fraternal or dizygotic (DZ). Identical twins are formed by the division of a fertilized ovum or zygote into two identical cells which separate completely and from each of which a foetus then develops. The two resulting individuals are therefore of identical genotype. Further, the environment in which monozygotic twins are raised is also closely similar. The two individuals are of course of identical age and sex, are raised in the same family, will usually elicit very similar responses from teachers and others (if only because they are often difficult to tell apart) and so forth. Thus the within-pair variation with respect to genotype is zero, and for environmental variables it is also extremely limited.

In contrast dizygotic twins are derived from two separate zygotes, as the name implies. Genotypically they are no more alike than siblings. Like the monozygotic variety they are of identical age, have the same parents, and if attention is confined to same sex dizygotic twins, they can be considered to share a common environment. In other words, within each pair there is a substantial degree of genotypic variation but little or no environmental variation.

If a series of twins in whom at least one member has the illness under study (the probands) can be examined, the frequency with which the second twin or co-twin is similarly affected can be ascertained; this frequency, termed the concordance rate, can be described in different ways. If there is no difference in concordance rates between MZ and DZ twins genetic contributions to a disorder can be largely discounted, since the frequency of illness in those with the same genotype as the probands is no greater than those who are genetically distinct. If, on the other hand, concordance rates are higher in the monozygotic than in the dizygotic twins, then a genetic contribution to the illness can be deduced, since in this instance individuals of the same genotype as the probands show more illness than those whose genetic composition is different.

The argument on which the method of comparing monozygotic and dizygotic pairs is based assumes a constant environment for the two members of each twinship; it does not of course necessarily imply that all the twin pairs in the series are drawn from one common environment.

## SOME PROBLEMS OF TWIN METHODS

The orthodox variety of twin studies, based on comparison of concordance in monozygotic and dizygotic pairs, has been subject to a number of criticisms. These and the concensus of current thought about their validity can be summarized as follows.

### 1. *The Relationship of Twins*

All twins have a relationship with their co-twins which non-twins cannot have. They tend to be very closely involved with each other, in a manner which has often been dramatized by fictional writers, and to identify with each other (in the psychoanalytic sense) especially if they are monozygotic twins. Conceivably this special relationship might itself be conducive to mental illness, particularly schizophrenia. If so, it follows that data from twins have only limited application to patients in general, and further that monozygotic pairs might show higher concordance than dizygotic pairs for reasons other than their greater genotypic similarity.

If the twin relationship itself conduces to illness, or if co-twins developed illness by an identification mechanism, it would follow that mental disorders would be commoner in twins than in singletons. Apart from one early study, all recent investigations have failed to confirm this prediction. More directly it has been shown that twins who separate before either one falls ill tend to have concordance rates only marginally lower than those who remain in touch with each other. There are also a number of clinical studies in which very close identification has been described for pairs who nevertheless remain discordant for illness.

There is thus no evidence that identification mechanisms are important in explaining concordance rates, though it is difficult to exclude a
marginal contribution from this source.

## 2. Sampling Problems

In order to generalize the findings from a sample to the population
from which it is drawn, it is clearly necessary for the group which has
been studied to represent the population in an unbiased manner. This
principle has only been fully appreciated in twin studies relatively
recently. Many of the earlier classical investigations had obtained data
by scrutiny of hospital populations which are, of course, heavily biased
towards the chronic and the severely ill. While drawing attention to
this, Rosenthal (1961a, 1961b) also pointed out in connection with
schizophrenia that concordance rates were appreciably higher for probands who were seriously ill than for those with less severe forms of
illness. Moreover, concordant pairs are more likely to be admitted to
hospital since families have greater difficulty in coping with two sick
members than one. Once in hospital concordant pairs are also likely
to excite more interest and to be more easily traced than discordant
twins, with further bias to the sample.

These cogent objections can be met by conducting surveys (a) by
using serial admissions to hospital rather than resident populations as
the source of data, or better still (b) by ascertaining all the twin pairs
born in an area and then following them up in order to investigate the
pairs which produce at least one sick member. The latter approach is
the ideal, but needless to say is difficult to achieve.

The question of how far sampling problems affect the interpretation
to be placed on the various studies in the literature will be taken up
again in connection with particular disorders.

## 3. The Description of Concordance

There are two ways of estimating concordance. First they can be
described by considering each *proband* and then determining the percentage in the series where the co-twin is also ill. If the co-twin has also
been independently ascertained he becomes a proband in his own right,
and the twinship is then considered to yield two probands each with a
sick co-twin. Alternatively one can consider *twinships* and determine the
percentage of pairs which are concordant. The effect of these different
methods is illustrated in the following table.

| | Number of pairs | Concordant pairs | Discordant pairs | Pairwise concordance | Proband concordance |
|---|---|---|---|---|---|
| MZ | 100 | 50 | 50 | 50% | 67% |
| DZ | 180 | 20 | 160 | 11% | 20% |

Each method is legitimate but the proband method gives higher numerical values for concordance. While this rarely affects the interpretation of, say, monozygotic as against dizygotic rates, the high figures tend to convey to the uncritical an impression that genetic factors are particularly important; for example, Kallmann's much quoted figure of 84 per cent concordance for schizophrenia in monozygotic pairs was taken to mean that the genetic contribution to schizophrenia was overwhelmingly important. The pairwise method yields figures of lower magnitude. The important point here is not the specious aura of conviction that attaches to higher numbers, but the need for considering carefully which convention has been used when collating findings from different studies.

A more important criticism is the method of age-correction employed by various authors. Most authorities have collected series in which not all the twins have yet passed the upper age limit of manifestation of illness. Thus some pairs, who at the time of observation are discordant, may be expected to become concordant in due course. The estimates of final concordance have usually been based on the Weinberg method, which assumes the risk of illness to be equally spread over the possible age range of manifestation. Evidence suggests, however, that concordant twins usually fall ill within a few years of each other. Correction by the Weinberg method therefore gives estimates which are too high and in some instances, as with manic depressive psychosis, are patently absurd (for example over 100 per cent).

Any reported concordance values must therefore be interpreted with respect to any age corrections that have been carried out. The more modern tendency is to dispense with such adjustments to the basic data altogether.

### 4. *Other Problems*

In the past both the clinical diagnosis of each twin and their zygosity relationship (MZ or DZ) was made by the same observer, the latter determination being influenced by such criteria as similarity of appearance. Each type of assessment could thus be biased by the other. Modern serological techniques enable zygosity to be determined with near-certainty and without the examiner's knowledge until after the clinical assessment is complete. These advances have only partly solved the problem of bias, however, since the traditional method of visual judgement has been found to be surprisingly good, and the examiner can scarcely avoid such a major clue to zygosity.

The geographical area in which studies have been carried out is another source of difficulty. As will be documented later in connection with schizophrenia, the more recent twin studies have largely derived from Scandinavian countries. They meet the methodological desiderata more closely than earlier investigations conducted in other parts of the world and in general they have reported much lower concordance rates. However, genetic studies of all kinds from Scandinavia have generally yielded lower figures than those from elsewhere. It is not clear, therefore, if the more recent work with its relatively low concordance values reflects a truer picture by virtue of methodological superiority or simply points to a difference between Scandinavian populations and the rest of the Western world with respect to genetic susceptibility, particularly to schizophrenia.

Lastly, the cogent problem of diagnostic disparity must be raised. It appears very probable that disorders currently labelled in psychiatry as a single entity include a mixture of different subgroups. This is particularly true of the psychoses, which are almost certainly heterogenous but in which the diagnostic reliability of the subgroups is low. If experience with other branches of medical genetics is any guide, it is highly probable that these sub-varieties will be found to show different genetic patterns of transmission. Meanwhile it is often difficult to interpret the data to hand. The additional problems of comparing the results of different investigators, each using their own criteria, scarcely needs underlining. Problems of diagnostic variability are serious handicaps in all branches of psychiatric research and in genetics no less than elsewhere.

OTHER TWIN METHODS

The classical techniques of comparing monozygotic and dizygotic concordance rates is by no means the only use that can be made of twin data. One variation that shows considerable promise is based on monozygotic pairs only. In any discordant monozygotic pair, it is argued, there must be some difference in the environments of the two individuals to account for their different outcomes, since genotypic variation is ruled out. Hence detailed comparisons of the histories of the twins from conception onwards may yield clues to environmental causation. The histories to be studied extend from the moment of conception onwards and not simply from birth. Indeed, intra-uterine differences, for example of placental blood supply, may be of considerable importance.

Another approach again using monozygotic pairs might be to focus upon pairs separated at birth and to contrast pairs which are concordant and pairs which are discordant with respect to their history and current environment. In this kind of study environmental variation is to some degree built in and it is the development of illness which is the dependent or outcome variable. Unfortunately the method remains largely theoretical at present as monozygotic twins containing at least one member who is psychiatrically ill and whose separation dates from early infancy are extremely rare and no systematic series has ever been collected. There are nevertheless reports of early-separated monozygotic pairs which furnish evidence of considerable if anecdotal interest.

ADOPTION STUDIES

Reference has already been made to the phenomenon of cultural transmission, or more accurately, of familial transmission of behaviour through influence and example rather than by genetic means. In recent years the possibility of various pathological patterns of interaction in families conducing to the development of illness has received a good deal of attention. Suggestions have been made that disordered familial relationships might in themselves be enough to predispose to psychiatric illness, quite apart from any genetic factors. Given simple geneological data it is not possible as a rule to deduce with any certainty whether the transmission from one generation to the next is best explained by one or other or a combination of both processes, though much may be inferred from such evidence as the proportions affected in each generation.

One approach to this difficulty is by studying individuals whose genetic equipment does not derive from the families in which they are raised, namely adoptees. In theory two methods are possible. One is to consider the families of probands which contain an adopted individual and to determine whether adopted members and non-adopted members (other than the patient) manifest illness in the same or different proportions. If, for example, the proportion of true siblings and of adopted siblings manifesting a disorder is the same, then some kind of cultural transmission is much more probable than a somatic or genetic one. However, there are numerous practical difficulties about such an approach.

An alternative method is to consider the psychiatric outcome of children whose parents are known to have suffered from a specified illness and whose offspring have been adopted into normal families in infancy. If the proportion of children who subsequently display the illness is the same as the proportion of children affected in intact families containing a sick parent then, subject to certain reservations, a genetic basis can be deduced. Studies of this type face considerable difficulties; nevertheless they have been successful in two important investigations relating to schizophrenia.

BIOCHEMICAL TECHNIQUES

Various methods mentioned so far are primarily of value in investigating whether genetic factors are of major importance in the aetiology of an illness (in the sense outlined in the introduction). If the evidence favours an affirmative interpretation, the next problem is the determination of the pattern of transmission. Here attention should be drawn to a method which can be used to ascertain whether an apparently healthy individual may be a 'carrier', that is to say a heterozygote for a recessive gene.

Such an individual appears clinically normal within the usual range of environments. But with laboratory animals under experimental conditions, quite minor changes in temperature or nutritional supplies may make the abnormality manifest. In the human situation the imposition of a specific stress, which a normal individual can readily deal with, may in the heterozygote lead to detectable abnormalities. Thus heterozygotes for sickle-cell haemoglobinaemia may show sickling of red blood cells under conditions of reduced oxygen tension, while administration of phenylalanine to heterozygotes for phenylketonuria will lead to delayed metabolism of the amino acid and the accumulation of intermediate metabolites. Under test conditions the 'recessive' character of the gene has been temporarily changed to a 'dominant' one. Specific tests are of course only possible when the function of the gene in question is clearly understood (see Table 3) but are likely to be increasingly useful as biochemical knowledge of gene effects becomes more extensive.

In some diseases (see Table 3) the heterozygote may be detected by minor histological abnormalities although the organs are macroscopically normal.

## GENETICS OF SPECIFIC DISORDERS

### SCHIZOPHRENIA

Schizophrenia has attracted more genetic investigation than any other psychiatric condition. So far this effort has been rewarded by an impressive accumulation of data rather than by an increased understanding.

There have been a considerable number of twin studies in schizophrenia, dating from Kallmann's classic work (1938, 1953). (See Table 1.) The variation in concordance rates obtained by various authors for monozygotic twins ranges from zero to 84 per cent. Some reasons for this variability have been described in the section on techniques of genetic investigation. They include selection from biased populations containing an excess of severe and chronic cases, the selective notification of concordant pairs, inappropriate statistical corrections for age effects,* diagnostic bias in concordant pairs, differences in diagnostic concepts and perhaps also dubious zygosity diagnoses in a few instances. It may also be noted that apart from Inouye's study most of the later investigations have reported lower values than the earlier ones. Since

* These have in fact been eliminated on Table 1.

TABLE I

*Concordance for Schizophrenia in Monozygotic and Dizygotic Twins*

| Investigator | Year | MZ% | DZ% |
|---|---|---|---|
| Luxemberger | 1928 | 59–76 | 0 |
| Rosanoff, *et al.* | 1934 | 61 | 10 |
| Euen Moller | 1941 | 0–71 | 8–17 |
| Kallmann | 1946 | 69 | 10 |
| Slater | 1953 | 65 | 11 |
| Inouye | 1961 | 36–60 | 6–12 |
| Tienari | 1963 | 0 | 5–14 |
| Kringlen | 1964 | 25 | 16 |
| Harvald and Hauge | 1965 | 29 | 6 |
| Gottesman and Shields | 1966 | 42 | 9 |
| Kringlen | 1967 | 25–38 | 8–12 |

Pairwise concordance, uncorrected for age. Where a range is shown the second figure indicates the effect of including border-line cases (after Kringlen, 1967).

these more recent studies are in general less contaminated by technical defects the lower concordance rates they report are clearly to be preferred (although they may not be wholly representative, being based largely on Scandinavian populations). At the same time it will be seen that almost every investigator has reported substantially higher concordance for monozygotic than for dizygotic twins. It must therefore be deduced that there is a major genetic component in the aetiology of schizophrenia, even though the magnitude of that component is less overwhelming than was formally supposed and that environmental contributions are also clearly important.

Studies of discordant monozygotic pairs have been directed to the nature of these environmental agents. Tienari (1963, 1966) commented that frequently the sick member of the pair was the one who had shown more psychological dependency and passivity and had had more physical illness than the healthy twin. Pollin and Stabenau (1968) reporting in detail on 15 discordant monozygotic twins drew attention to the lower birth weight of the probands in 12 of these pairs, and a frequent history of difficulty at delivery or other peri-natal traumata. They are careful to point out, however, that the sicklier of the two twins was also the one who elicited the greater maternal anxiety, which might thus represent an additional aetiological component of their illness. Nevertheless, other investigators, notably Slater (1953), have failed to find an excess of prematurity in the ill members of discordant monozygotic pairs.

Another line of enquiry and one of great interest concerns the range of characteristics of the co-twins of schizophrenics. Any phenotypic characteristics common to both the probands and the co-twins might be plausibly ascribed to their genotypic similarity. Some of the co-twins are of course schizophrenics. In some of the other cases they appear to be schizoid though not psychotic. This tempts the speculation that it is the schizoid characteristic which is transmitted genetically—but unfortunately for this view the co-twin may display only minor neurotic illness or indeed be perfectly normal. Kringlen (1967) has made a special study of the personalities of co-twins and reports that any form of illness or none at all might be encountered. Heston (1966) has even suegested, using a different experimental design, that the genotype might confer specially valued characteristics such as creativity and artistic gifts, though these speculations have not been widely accepted.

*Adoptive Studies*

Heston (1966) succeeded in following up a group of 50 children born to schizophrenic mothers and adopted into normal families in infancy. He found that 14 per cent of the adoptees developed schizophrenia, a proportion identical with that to be expected had they been reared with their schizophrenic mothers. None of the control group of adoptees born to normal mothers developed the illness nor were any of the children of the adopting families themselves affected. Corroborative findings have been reported by a group of other workers (Kety, *et al.*, 1968). Studies of this kind lend considerable emphasis to the importance of somatic as against cultural familial transmission.

*Segregation in Families*

The nosological status of a clinically atypical condition can be materially clarified if it is found to be genetically linked with some more typical form of the disorder. Indeed, even for typical cases a classification will be much strengthened if genetic evidence is forthcoming to support its validity. A number of studies have been directed to the genetic basis of the two major Kraepelinian psychoses, schizophrenia and manic depressive psychosis. In general they suggest that there is a pronounced tendency towards familial segregation. Some authors, however, have pointed out that there is nevertheless an appreciable degree of heterogeneity; thus although most of the psychotic relatives of a schizophrenic are likely to suffer the same disorder themselves, manic depressive psychosis will also be represented in a proportion which, although lower than that for schizophrenia, is higher than would be expected from general population estimates. Manic depressive psychoses tend to 'breed true' more often than schizophrenia but also show some heterogeneity. Odegard (1963) suggests that the degree of genetic specificity for *type* of psychosis is relatively low, but the question remains an open one.

Attempts to improve the classification of atypical psychoses by means of the clinico-genetic approach have not been outstandingly successful. It appears that atypical psychoses often occur in similar guise in other psychotic family members, suggesting that from the genetic viewpoint they should not be amalgamated into either of the two main groups.

## Late Onset Schizophrenia

It has been established that the schizophrenia-like illnesses of middle and later life, including paraphrenia and late paranoid states, tend to display not only an incomplete clinical picture of the psychosis but also to have a lower incidence of schizophrenic illnesses in first degree relatives than is found with younger patients. This observation has led to the suggestion of a quantitative aspect to the transmission process such that individuals with multiple deviant genes will break down under the early stresses of life, while those with fewer such genes will become ill only in consequence of cumulative stresses or the eventual failure of protective mechanisms, whether biological or psychological in kind (Post, 1967). It is also possible, however, that a number of different specific genes with different age-of-onset effects are involved, forming a series which is only superficially a continuum.

## The Pattern of Transmission

When considering clinically-derived entities of unknown aetiology such as schizophrenia, the clinical geneticist can only make inferences from the phenotypic to the genotypic level and the kinds of concepts he employs reflect the degree of refinement of his material.

Schizophrenia does not follow any of the classical Mendelian patterns. At various times a wide range of theories have been presented by different authorities, including dominance with low penetrance of the gene, recessivity, and models requiring two and three genes. None of these has proved satisfactory; in particular theories invoking limited penetrance have encountered strong opposition in the absence of any direct evidence.

The current concensus is, however, increasingly towards the adoption of a polygenic model, the evidence for which has been ably reviewed by Shields (1968). On this view the genetic predisposition to schizophrenia is continuously distributed throughout the population. In the face of somatic or environmental stress, the nature of which has yet to be clarified, individuals with genetic loadings high enough to reach a critical threshold then display a qualitative change in psychological function which is clinically described as schizophrenia.

The known facts on the prevalence of schizophrenia in the various degrees of kinship of schizophrenic patients and the data on late onset illness are better accommodated in this model than any other, although the fit is still not perfect. It must be emphasized, however, that schizophrenia is almost certainly not a homogenous entity and it is perfectly credible that different variants of the disorder may be connected with different genes having differing modes of transmission. (See also section on mental defect.)

MANIC DEPRESSIVE PSYCHOSES AND ALLIED CONDITIONS

## Twin Studies

Studies of affective disorders in twins have been relatively fewer than those with schizrenia despite the fact that the higher prevalence of manic depressive psychosis should make the task of collecting samples less difficult. There has also been rather less critical discussion of the subject and only one investigation to date has been based on population surveys (Harvald and Hauge, 1965).

The results of the main twin studies are summarized in Table 2. It can be seen that more recent investigators report lower monozygotic concordance rates than those from earlier years, and that Kallmann's estimates are outstandingly high.

TABLE 2

Concordance for Manic Depressive Psychosis in Monozygotic and Dizygotic Twins

| Investigator | Year | MZ% | DZ% |
|---|---|---|---|
| Luxemberger | 1928 | 75 | 0 |
| Rosanoff et al. | 1935 | 70 | 16 |
| Kallmann | 1950 | 96 | 26 |
| Slater | 1953 | 50 | 23 |
| la Fonseca | 1959 | 75 | 39 |
| Harvald and Hauge | 1963 | 60 | 5 |
| Kringlen | 1967 | 33 | 0 |

Pairwise concordance (after Kringlen, 1967).

The relationship between the severity of illness in the probands and the prevalence of illness in the co-twins has not been worked out in detail but it seems likely that there is in fact a positive relationship. Since manic depressive psychoses are often treated without in-patient admission, and since all twin studies to date have used admission as the criterion of illness, it is evident that the available estimates of concordance require cautious interpretation. Nevertheless, it can be seen that all investigators report substantially higher concordance for monozygotic than dizygotic twins and there can be little doubt that genetic factors are of major importance in the aetiology of the illness for those patients included in these studies.

Little is established about the factors determining which twin of a discordant monozygotic pair will develop the psychosis. The relationship between the twins itself does not seem to be critical, since twins reared apart show similar concordance rates to those brought up together (Price, 1968). There has been considerable speculation about the personality characteristics of the healthy co-twin. Kallmann, and later Slater, reported that a very high proportion of such healthy co-twins showed a markedly cyclothymic personality, though with mood swings short of psychosis, and it has been suggested that it is primarily the cyclothymic characteristic which is transmitted from one generation to the next.

## Familial Segregation in the Sub-groups of Affective Disorder

Many investigators have studied somewhat heterogenous clinical conditions subsumed under the broad title of 'manic depressive psychosis' in the Kraepelinian scheme, including single and recurrent depressive illnesses, involutional depression, isolated manic episodes and manic depressive alternation. Using mixed groups of this kind it has been shown that certain symptoms tend to cluster selectively within families; these include elation, retardation, anxiety and hypochondriasis. Age at onset of first attack has also been shown to have a positive though low correlation of about 0·3 between pairs of affected first degree relatives. Such clustering suggests the possibility of genetically distinct syndromes and in recent years interest has been revived in the sub-groups of affective disorder, and in particular in the manic depressive syndrome or bipolar psychosis, as compared with recurrent depressive episodes without mania, or unipolar psychosis. Starting with groups of probands who could be clearly diagnosed as having one or the other of these disorders, Perris (1966) reported that the genetics of the two forms can also be differentiated; manic depressive probands show a familial incidence of about 10 per cent in first degree relatives of bipolar cases but no excess of the unipolar form, while among affected relatives the sex ratio was approximately unity; unipolar probands had an excess of unipolar but not of bipolar psychosis in their families, and among the affected individuals females outnumbered males. The preponderance of females was particularly marked among the affected kin of the female probands. Winokur and Clayton (1967) reported similar results.

This work is of great interest, though it must be borne in mind that studies by other investigators (Stendstedt, 1952; Angst, 1966) have reported series which do not replicate all Perris's findings. On the other hand the diagnostic criteria of these other workers were less extreme than his. At present all that can be said is that the hope of distinguishing genetically distinct sub-groups of the affective disorders remains a reasonable one.

Another division of considerable interest hinges on the differential antidepressant drug effects displayed by some patients with psychotic depression. Pare and Mack (1971) have claimed that if patients with an endogenous depression show a selective response to either the monoamine oxidase inhibitors or the tricyclic group of drugs then affected relatives are likely to respond similarly. If confirmed, this observation would open the way for more extensive pharmacogenetic investigations of the affective disorders as a whole.

At the clinical level it is not at present possible to distinguish between these variants of affective disorder. The syndrome presented by a patient with a bipolar psychosis who is in a depressive phase is identical to that of the psychotic with recurrent depression. There are of course many other examples in medicine of phenotypic identity despite genotypic diversity.

## Late Onset Depressions

Involutional melancholia and late onset depression have been usually regarded as part of the group of affective disorders. One consideration which influenced Kraepelin's inclusion of involutional melancholia within the manic depressive group was that the affected relatives of involutional probands displayed typical manic depressive or recurrent depressive syndromes. It has been shown however (Kay, 1959; Hopkinson, 1964) that late onset cases have fewer affected relatives than early onset cases, and as with schizophrenia it has been argued that the genetic contribution to the aetiology of late onset cases is probably relatively minor. It may also be less specific in that relatives of involutional melancholics are clinically somewhat heterogenous.

Finally it may be mentioned that attempts to distinguish reactive depression from other neurotic illnesses or from endogenous depression on genetic grounds have proved inconclusive.

## Mode of Transmission

In so far as it is still legitimate to consider Kraepelin's group of manic depressive psychoses as a single entity two theories have been proposed to cover the data as it stands at present. An autosomal dominant gene has been advocated on the grounds of equal likelihood of transmission by either parent, the absence of increased consanguinity among the probands' parents, and the absence of demonstrable sex linkage. However, any major gene would have to be one with fairly low penetrance and it has sometimes been assumed that the expressivity of the gene is itself controlled by other modifier genes. Such a formulation comes close to the alternative theory of polygenic transmission. A critical decision between these two views is not easy on existing data or indeed on any that is likely to be readily obtained. However, it has been indicated already that the whole question may well be unprofitable if the genetic heterogeneity of the affective psychoses is confirmed in which case quite different modes of transmission may be anticipated for the different sub-groups.

Perhaps it may be added that the question of sex limitation in the affective psychoses has been frequently raised but still remains sub-judice.

NEUROSIS AND PERSONALITY DISORDERS

The personalities of normal individuals whose lives are led in environments which contain no markedly unusual features display a certain amount of variation along a number of different parameters. An individual who falls outside the central range of the distribution is judged to be deviant, and may also be classified as psychiatrically ill. Speaking very generally, such a person will be classified as having a personality disorder if his pattern of behaviour is a stable one which causes distress to himself or others, and as a neurotic if it is transient and is associated with subjective discomfort (Foulds, 1965).

In both instances, since extremes of a normal range of behaviour are an issue, the distinction between normality and abnormality is bound to be somewhat arbitrary. Moreover, since such deviations can occur with respect to a large number of dimensions of behaviour which themselves will often be correlated, it is evident that a distinction between the various sub-groups of the neuroses, and between them and the personality disorders, must always be difficult to draw.

Hence it is impossible to discuss the genetic aspects of neurosis and personality deviation without at the same time mentioning what little has been established regarding normal personalities. The relatively greater availability of normal subjects than of special categories of patients has made it possible to utilize a group of subjects of great theoretical relevance but of practical rarity, namely, monozygotic twins brought up apart. Four such studies have been conducted, three using volunteers and with control data from pairs raised together (Newman, Freeman and Holzinger, 1937; Shields, 1962; Wilde, 1964) while the fourth lacks control data but is based on a twin sample derived from birth registers (Juel-Nielsen, 1965).

In these and in orthodox studies of monozygotic and dizygotic twins, intelligence has been consistently found to be one of the characteristics more highly correlated in monozygotic than in dizygotic twins, and particularly in those reared together; however, even the monozygotic pairs reared apart still tend to have higher concordance than dizygotic twins. The conclusions to be drawn regarding the heritability of intelligence, and its importance in relation to education, is a somewhat polemical issue which hinges chiefly on just what is measured by available intelligence tests. Here it may simply be noted that these tests are generally constructed with reference to a Gaussian distribution and, in so far as they are valid, indicate that the genetic contribution to intelligence must be of a polygenic kind. This may not be true of all mental abilities, however, nor is the profound importance of education to be overlooked. The interested reader is referred to specialist texts (e.g. Butcher, 1968).

Neuroticism defined by Eysenck (1959) as a personality dimension of susceptibility to neurotic breakdown is more closely correlated in monozygotic twins (Eysenck and Prell, 1951; and Wilde, 1964). In a detailed psychometric study of normal adolescent twins, Gottesman (1963) showed that the variance on social introversion, as measured by the M.M.P.I. also owed more to genetic than environmental sources. Moreover, it is possible that the magnitude of the genetic contribution is masked by a 'polarizing' process in monozygotic twins brought up together; Shields (1962) showed that the correlation for introversion was lower in monozygotic pairs who had grown up in the same household than in those reared apart (though still substantially higher than in dyzygotic twins) and Wilde (1964) provided some confirmation for this finding. Cattell and Malteno (1940) suspected a similar masking effect from tests of verbal fluency.

But at the clinical or descriptive level of personality profiles, based on the life stories of twin pairs, few general conclusions can be drawn. Investigators have commented on striking similarities and dissimilarities equally, according to which aspect of a particular pair was under discussion and often with respect to characteristics to appear to be idiosyncratic for a given couple. It is difficult to progress beyond basic platitudes regarding the importance of both genetic and environmental influences in personality formation, but it does seem that most clinicians are inclined to underestimate the weight of data regarding the genetic determinance of the normal personality, notwithstanding Freud's own observations to the contrary.

*Neurosis*

Of the various neurotic syndromes it is perhaps the obsessional variety which comes closest to being a discrete clinical entity. Brown (1942) found a 7 per cent incidence among the first degree relatives of obsessional neurotics with the same illness. Lewis (1936) reported that over a third of such relatives had obsessional traits but did not indicate how many were considered to be clinically ill. It is possible that being raised by parents of an obsessional disposition may conduce the offspring to the development of obsessional illness in later life but the relation between obsessional traits and symptoms is not at all straightforward: not all obsessional neurotics show premorbid obsessive personalities and few people with obsessional traits progress to a neurosis.

Claims for the genetic specificity of other neurotic syndromes must be treated with some reserve. Anxiety reactions have been shown to occur more commonly in monozygotic co-twins of anxious probands than might be expected in the general population (Slater and Shields, 1967). But a series by Parker (1964) showed little difference in concordance rates between monozygotic and dizygotic twins if specific syndromes of neurosis, psychosomatic illness and personality disorder are considered; indeed, even if no distinction is drawn between these syndromes there is no real evidence of monozygotic/dizygotic difference (Slater, 1953).

On the other hand, family studies with anxiety, depressive, hysterical and obsessional neurotics show that first degree relatives of such patients themselves have a raised prevalence of neurosis and those who are ill tend to have the same disorder as the probands; this seems to be most evident for anxiety states and least so for hysteria (Slater, 1961). Nevertheless, there is considerable overlap between the types of neurosis found in such families (Brown, 1942).

At present, then, the evidence is somewhat paradoxical, pointing on the one hand to important genetic determinance of neuroticism within the normal range, but to the prepotent influence of family environment in clinical illness.

*Personality Disorders*

Much of the early work on the genetic aspects of personality disorder was concerned with criminality. Lange's study (1931), one of the first to apply twin methods to psychiatry, led him to conclude that criminal behaviour was almost totally determined by an innate predisposition. Rosanoff, Hardy and Plesset (1941) reported on a larger twin series including both adult criminals and juvenile delinquents. For the former group among males the MZ and DZ concordance rates were 66 per cent and 14 per cent respectively. Interestingly there was practically no difference between the rates for the different types of twins among juvenile delinquents, implying that psychosocial stresses are probably of major importance in the latter. In a balanced overview of the 'aetiology' of criminal behaviour these authors point to the role of cerebral injury and of alcoholism as of major importance but conclude that genetic determinants are nevertheless of considerable significance.

Little further work seems to have been done on the theme presumably because few psychiatrists today would consider 'criminality' as an appropriate unit of behaviour, and attention has focused rather on the social and cultural determinants of deviance. Yet one major component of sociopathy which cannot be ignored is the individual's own ability to learn and adhere to group norms, that is to say his social conditionability. Eysenck (1964) has claimed that his extraversion factor is a measure of the ease with which an individual acquires and retains conditioned responses, and criminals have abnormally high E scores. The genetic transmission of criminal propensities is thus largely identical to that of extraversion according to this theory. In so far as criminal behaviour is viewed as a failure to learn normally accepted standards of conduct this theory would help explain why certain individuals rather than others come to show criminal behaviour; they can also be extended to account for the effects of brain injury and other forms of cerebral damage. It would not, however, provide an adequate explanation for criminals who come from subgroups in the population where law breaking is the usual pattern.

Alcoholism has long been known to cluster in families but there is little agreement as to what inferences should be drawn from this fact; thus a recent authoritative review stated 'genetic inheritance of alcoholism has not been demonstrated' (Kessel and Walton, 1967). Certainly there is no concensus as to what biochemical abnormality, if any, might be aetiologically responsible for, as distinct from secondary to, alcohol addiction. Yet two lines of enquiry suggest that genetic influences may be of some importance. One is derived from behavioural genetics and discussed more fully below. It has proved possible to breed strains of mice with a preference for alcohol rather than water under certain experimental conditions, and these animals have high levels of liver alcohol and aldehyde dehydrogenases. How relevant these findings are to addiction in man is debatable. Secondly there is work on twins which in general reports not only a higher monozygotic than dizygotic concordance rate, but also that the degree of concordance within monozygotic pairs varies with the severity of addiction in the proband (Kaij, 1960). If confirmed, this evidence would have to be taken very seriously.

Twin studies of homosexuality have been seriously hampered by selection biases, since most homosexuals presenting to psychiatrists are atypical by virtue of suffering from a psychiatric illness in addition to their sexual deviance. This was clearly shown by Kallmann's study (1952) which reported an astonishing 100 per cent concordance in male MZ twins, but the probands mostly consisted of mental defectives and psychopaths who happened also to be homosexuals. The problem of contaminated groups has still not been satisfactorily overcome, but more recent and less severely biased investigations have quoted much lower values: for example Heston and Shields (1968) found approximately 50 per cent MZ and 14 per cent DZ concordance; detailed case studies pointed to the importance of environmental determinants in addition to the undoubted genetic predisposition. There is no evidence that twins are more likely to be homosexual than non-twins.

MENTAL DEFECT

If we now turn to the problem of mental defect it is plain that calculations of heritability on the one hand and the distribution curve of defects in the population on the other both lead to the conclusion that it is multigenically determined, i.e. a very large (unknown) number of genes co-operate together in various (unknown) combinations. On the other hand very many of the known biochemical mutants in man have marked effects on mental function and a number of them directly cause mental defect. These specified diseases may then be separated from those which can be measured only as contributing to the sum of multigenic causality, and in certain cases specific and accurate therapies may be developed (Holman, 1970). Thus where we are unable to specify the contribution of individual genes the only practical as distinct from theoretical use we can make of genetics is that of establishing heritabilities and therefore risks in genetic counselling. On the other hand in those increasing number of instances where the specific biochemical lesion has been isolated and recognized the counselling can be more specific while the possibility of treatment is opened up.

The numbers of genetically determined biochemical lesions associated with mental defect or abberant behaviour are constantly being added to by new reports in the literature (see Menkes and Migeon, 1966; Hsia et al., 1968; McKusick, 1970); nevertheless many of the diseases described below are very rare. They are, however, described because they afford some insight into the problem of the genetic contribution to the intellect and psychology of the individual. The rarity of a pathological condition does not mean that the genetic control of a particular function occurs but exceptionally. On the contrary, one must always remember that the discovery of a mutant is in fact the discovery of a genetically controlled function, which is recognized because the effect of the mutant is sufficiently striking to attract the attention of the clinician. We must expect that the locus now designated by a newly developed biochemical assay will have many alleles, since this is found for loci which have been studied for longer periods in more favourable organisms. Allelic series show a wide range of efficiencies of the function they control and therefore of genetic potential and response in the population.

The rarity of the abnormal phenotypic condition is probably due to one of the following situations. (1) Most of the other alleles at this locus are less severe in effect, do not cause recognizable clinical effects, but are part of the range of the 'normal'. (2) We are still relying on gross symptoms for the recognition of a difference, yet a biochemical evaluation may bring to light individuals who are genetically abnormal but, because of other factors, are conditionally behaviourally acceptable: that is, the condition is incompletely penetrant. Biochemical evaluation may also demonstrate the existence of other alleles of the series which make a smaller or a latent contribution to abnormality. (3) The condition has only recently been discriminated by a biochemical technique and few studies have yet been made on large populations, using this technique. (4) If it is dominant, then the selection pressure against it is so high that each case is virtually a new recurrence of the mutation. (5) If it is recessive, then selection against homozygotes is total and partial against heterozygotes.

Phenylketonuria accounts for 1 per cent of the inmates of mental institutions. There are 30 to 40 other conditions described today which lead to mental defect; most can be distinguished from one another only by biochemical screening. If their average frequency in the population is similar to that of phenylketonuria, then it could be that appropriate screening tests could even now assign the causation of a significant proportion of mental defectives to specific biochemical lesions.

*Phenylketonuria*

Phenylketonuria is a recessive autosomal defect associated with mental deficiency, with an incidence of about 4 in $10^5$. It was first described by Følling in 1934 and the genetic basis established by Jervis (1939) who elucidated the metabolic defect (1947) and the enzyme responsible (1953). Useful reviews are by Knox (1966), and Hsia (1970). The majority of patients are idiots, a smaller percentage are imbeciles and there are rare individuals with relatively slight intellectual impairment (see Fig. 6). Most phenylketonurics tend to be lighter in colour than their sibs and the majority have blue eyes and blonde hair. About half of the affected individuals show a greater or lesser degree of microcephaly. About three-quarters of the patients have abnormal E.G.G. patterns usually of the petit mal variety.

The striking biochemical characteristics of these patients is the excretion of phenyl pyruvic acid in the urine and an elevation of phenylalanine in the plasma to 30 times the level of normals. Jervis was able to show that phenyl alanine hydroxylase, the enzyme system catalyzing the oxidation of phenylalanine to tryosine, is affected. This system comprises two enzymes in the liver, a labile enzyme, and a stable enzyme which acts as a co-factor. In patients with phenylketonuria the second enzyme, or co-factor, is entirely normal but there is a deficiency in the labile enzyme.

Studies with $C14$ labelled L phenylalanine show that very little of the phenylalanine in the mutant is converted to tyrosine. The excess phenylalanine is converted to phenylpyruvic acid and thence to phenyl-

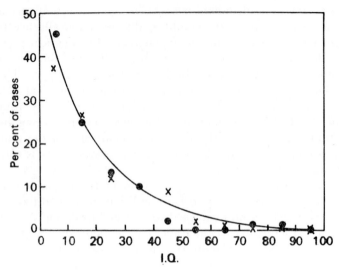

FIG. 6.   Frequency distribution of I.Q.s among two series of patients with phenylketonuria (a total of 434 individuals) from Knox (1966).

lactic acid, phenylacetic acid and phenyl acetyl glutamine. These are all excreted in the urine, which also contains *o. hydroxyphenylacetic acid, m. hydroxyphenylacetic acid* and indole products from trypto-phane and tyrosine. The excess phenylalanine inhibits tyrosine meta-bolism both *in vitro* and *in vivo* and this must account for the decreased production of melanin and the generally light pigmentation observed. The blood adrenaline level is exceptionally low and the production of thyroglobulin is affected. These effects may be understood with refer-ence to Figure 7.

There is also an effect on a separate metabolic pathway, that of trypto-phane metabolism. There is marked decrease of 5-hydroxytryptamine (serotonin) in the blood and brain, and an excess production of the indole derivatives of tryptophane and tyrosine; and these effects may be produced in experimental animals by loading them with phenylalanine in excess. The interference with tryptophane conversion can be shown to occur in *in vitro* systems although the amount of phenyl alanine re-quired is in vast excess. It has been suggested that the serotonin level is related to the observed delay of myelin formation.

In summary, the main points to note are (a) that the primary defect lies in the absence of one enzyme only, but that (b) the metabolic con-sequences may be complex, including (i) the excretion of numerous compounds derived from substances accumulated as a result of the block (ii) deficiencies in compounds which are not synthesized in con-sequence of the block, and (iii) that abnormal concentrations of some

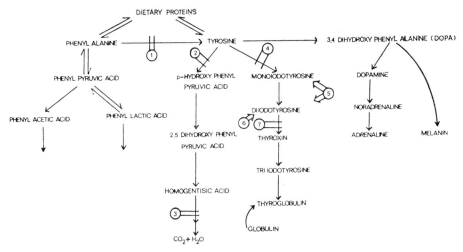

FIG. 7. Arrows indicate enzyme controlled reactions. =O or ⇐O indicates the site of a genetic block; that is, the reaction does not proceed in the genetic absence of the relevant enzyme.

Genetic blocks: (1) phenylketonuria (2) tyrosinosis (3) alcaptonuria.

These diseases are not similar, because the metabolic blocks are placed in a branching network, and the consequences of each block are different.

The effect of the enzyme defect in phenylketonuria on pigmentation, adrenalin and thyroglobulin levels and the metabolites excreted can be understood from this flow sheet (see text). The excretion of indoles and interference with serotin synthesis from 5-hydroxytryptophane are due to interference with an independent metabolic sequence by some PKU metabolites (phenyl acetic, phenyl lactic and phenyl pyruvic acids). Genetic blocks (4), (5), (6), (7). These are some of the genetically and biochemically distinct goitrous cretinisms. These all have the same end-effect—no thyroglobulin—and they are therefore similar phenotypically.

of these metabolites, in this case phenylalanine, may interfere with other biochemical pathways.

Recently several conditions have been identified in humans and in mice which show elevated levels of phenylalanine in blood. Some rare individuals with high phenylalanine concentrations but no mental defect may represent a disorder other than classical phenylketonuria.

Heterozygotes are normal in intelligence, pigmentation, and their excretory pattern, but may be distinguished by the persistence of high phenylalanine levels and level of phenyl pyruvic acid excretion in the urine after a loading test.

It is claimed that the incidence of mental instability is higher in heterozygotes than in a control population. Two studies on the incidence of mental disease in the families of phenylketonurics found that the incidence of psychoses was higher than expectation, although the figures were barely significant; the discrepancy was most marked in those over 45 years of age.

It is rare that phenylketonuric women become pregnant but genetically normal children born to such mothers may show the characteristic pattern of phenylketonuria indicating that the high level of circulating phenylalanine in the mother is injurious to the developing foetus.

Rats fed with excessive phenylalanine show retardation of learning ability, and mental deficiency has been produced in monkeys fed as infants over a long period with excessive phenylalanine. Nevertheless, no direct correlation has yet been demonstrated between the I.Q. and the level of any of the metabolites in urine or plasma or cerebro spinal fluid and any of the substances mentioned.

Low phenylalanine diet abolishes most of the biochemical abnormalities detected and affects many of the clinical signs including pigmentation and the E.E.G. If phenylalanine is restored to the diet all these abnormalities return, and may be intensified if large doses of phenylalanine are given. With a low phenylalanine diet the excretion of all the substances derived from phenylalanine decreases to normal levels. The serotonin level rises although the amount of 5-hydroxyindole acetic acid in the urine is unaffected. The abnormal components in the $\beta$ globulins in plasma disappear.

Low phenylalanine diet prevents the intellectual impairment if given for the first few years of life, after which time changes are evidently irreversible. The effect on I.Q. may be seen in Figure 8. The treatment to be effective must be initiated in the first few weeks of life.

Phenylketonuria has been described in some detail because it illustrates the complexity of the metabolic changes which may be caused by a single gene. Numerous other such diseases have been elucidated in recent years, and some of these are summarized in Table 3. The table also includes some diseases referred to in subsequent sections.


BIOCHEMICAL GENETICS OF BEHAVIOURAL CHANGES

THE PORPHYRIAS

The biosynthesis of haem involves the production of a number of porphyrins in the intermediary stages. Several genetic lesions of porphyrin metabolism are known. These may be divided into two classes, hepatic and erythrocytic. The wide range of symptoms associated with the hepatic form include psychoses and emotional disturbances. In the hepatic porphyrias the red cells are not affected, but porphyrins are accumulated in the liver and are excreted in the urine and faeces (Dean, 1969).

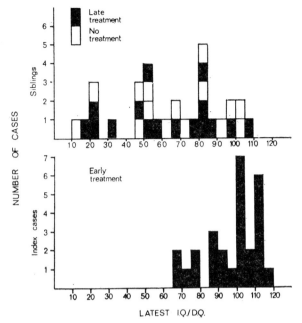

Fig. 8. Comparison of I.Q./D.Q. of matched pairs of siblings treated late or untreated (top row) or treated early by low phenylalanine diet (bottom row). After Berman, Waisman and Graham, 1966.

1. *Intermittent Acute Porphyria* (Swedish porphyria, pyrolloporphyria)

Transmission is by a dominant gene. There is no photosensitivity of the skin and little excretion of porphyrin in faeces, but the urine shows the classical port-wine colouration. Gastrointestinal disorders of varying degrees of severity include colicky abdominal pain, constipation and vomiting, the attacks lasting a few days to several months. The neurological manifestations may involve cranial nerves, cerebral function, the autonomic nervous system (producing symptoms which may include hypertension) and peripheral nerves. The peripheral neuropathy is associated with pain in the limbs, weakness or flaccid paralyses. The bulbar symptoms include difficulty in swallowing, aspiration and vocal cord control. 'Hysterical' symptoms are the most frequent psychic changes described. Patients may complain of dyspepsia or be described as nervous for many years before the first acute attack. Instances are recorded in which acute porphyria has been diagnosed as schizophrenia or as a depressive condition as was long believed about King George III. Affected individuals present symptoms intermittently and to varying degrees. The symptoms usually appear after puberty, and women are particularly liable to some symptoms in the pre-menstrual period and during pregnancy. The pedigrees contain individuals who are largely

TABLE 3

*Diseases Associated with Mental Deficiency or Psychiatric Symptoms*

A. *Defects in Amino acid Metabolism*

| Disease | Enzyme involved, metabolic effect | Effect on brain etc. | Other systems | Detection of heterozygote and/or foetus | Remarks |
|---|---|---|---|---|---|
| Phenylketonuria (PKU) Autosomal recessive | Absence of phenylalanine hydroxylase Changes in metabolic pattern (See text) Pyridoxylidene β phenylethylene in brain and urine PKU mice and urine of human PKU is neurotoxic in mice | Usually severe mental retardation, tantrums, seizures, exaggerated anxiety reflexes (see text) | Pigmentation, reduced growth rate, microcephaly etc. (see text) | Heterozygote detected by Loading test | Low phenylalanine diet treatment |
| Other conditions with some similarities to PKU | High plasma phenylalanine levels | Severe effects of PKU absent Normal or possibly slightly reduced I.Q. | | | Some are probably allelic to PKU |
| Hartnup's disease Autosomal recessive | Impaired tryphotophane absorption in gut and reabsorption in kidney tubule Indolylacetic monoamino and carboxylic acids excreted Reduced kynurenin and nicotinamide | Ataxia, choreiform, movements, mental retardation in about ¼ cases Psychiatric symptoms. Emotional instability, delusions, hallucinations | Pellegra-like rash | Some skin Photosensitivity in heterozygote | Nicotinamide treatment |

| Disorder / Inheritance | Biochemical defect | Clinical features | Physical signs | Detection / heterozygote | Comments |
|---|---|---|---|---|---|
| Homocystinuria Autosomal recessive | Deficiency of cystathione synthetase; Brain cystathione low; Homocystine excreted; Serum homocystine and methionine low | Variable mental retardation, seizures, (paraplegia progressive?) | Skin mottling; Lens dislocation; Cardiovasular and skeletal anomalies; Thromboses; Fine, sparse hair | Detectable in cultured cells including foetal cells; Heterozygote may have lower enzyme level | Schizophrenic relatives |
| Cystathionuria | Cystathionase deficiency; High cystathione in tissues including brain, body fluids and urine | Emotional disorder, mental defect in some cases | | Detectable on foetal cells; Heterozygote detected by methionine loading | Rare; Varying phenotypes, possibly different alleles |
| Maple-syrup urine disease Autosomal recessive | Deficiency branched chain keto acid decarboxylase; Oxidative decarboxylation of keto acids is blocked; Branched chain ketonuria (leucine, isoleucine, valine) | Vomiting, lethargy, convulsions, muscle hypertonicity, gross brain damage, die 1 week–1 year; If survive longer, spastic, low I.Q. | | Detectable on cultured cells including foetal cells; Low enzyme activity in heterozygous leucocytes | Reduced branched chain amino acids in diet may help |
| Intermittent branched chain ketonuria | Reduced branched chain keto acid decarboxylase | Less severe than MSU disease above; Episodes of encephalopathy possibly precipitated by high protein diet infections | | | Possibly allelic to MSU disease |

TABLE 3—*Continued*

| Disease | Enzyme involved, metabolic effect | Effect on brain etc. | Other systems | Detection of heterozygote and/or foetus | Remarks |
|---|---|---|---|---|---|
| Enzyme deficiency methemoglobin-aemia recessive | Deficiency of diphosphopyridine nucleotide enzyme Met Hb not reduced | Mental defect | | Heterozygote detectable | |
| Histidinaema | Histidase deficiency Histidase not converted to urocaic acid, high blood histidine, excretion of histidine and imidazol metabolites | Speech retarded and slurred in younger cases I.Q. low in some cases Cerebellar ataxia Short auditory memory | | Histidine loading Detectable in skin biopsies | |
| Goitrous cretinism 1 | Iodotyrosine deiodinase deficiency | Mental defect | Severe hypothyroidism and goitre | | |
| Goitrous cretinism 5–6 other different forms | Identified and different enzymes involved in each disease | Mental defect | Severe hypothyroidism and goitre | | |

Other disease of amino acid metabolism causing mental deficiency include hypervalinemia, proline oxidase deficiency, hydroxyproline oxidase deficiency, orotic acid uria, lysine intolerance, hyperglycinuria with hyperglycinemia, citrullinemia, hyperammonemia (2 different forms), arginosuccinic acid uria, hyperprolinemia A and B, argininemia, methylmalonic acid uria, hyperlysinemia, isovaleric acid uria.

References to possible dietary treatments for some of these diseases are given by Holman (1970) and Berman, Waisman and Graham (1966).

B. *Errors of Carbohydrate Metabolism and the Storage Diseases:*
*Mucopolysaccharidoses, Mucolipidoses, Sphingolipidoses.*

| Diseases | Enzyme affected, metabolic effect | Effect on brain etc. | Other systems | Detection of heterozygote and/or foetus | Remarks |
|---|---|---|---|---|---|
| Galactosaemia Autosomal recessive | Absence of galactose I phosphate uridyl transferase Galactose I phosphate in tissues, high brain galactitol, Galactose, amino acids and albumin excreted, elevated blood galactose | Mental retardation | Hepatospleno-megaly, cirrhosis, jaundice, cataracts, nutritional failure | Enzyme level usually inter-mediate in heterozygote Detectable in cultured cells including foetal cells | Prompt treat-ment by galac-tose-free diet necessary or damage permanent Mental retarda-tion persists Other genetic forms of the condition may exist |
| Hurler syndrome Autosomal recessive | Abnormal mucopolysaccharide accumulation and excretion | Severe mental retardation Rapid deterioration | Connective tissue Gargoylism, skeletal dys-plasia, corneal clouding, cardiopathy | Metachromatic granules in cultured skin fibroblasts Heterozygous and homozygous foetal cells pos-sibly distingui-shed by $S^{35}$ incorporation | Both Hunter and Hurler cells in mixed tissue culture can grow normally: i.e. they each supple-ment the other metabolically |

TABLE 3—*Continued*

| Disease | Enzyme affected, metabolic effect | Effect on brain etc. | Other systems | Detection of heterozygote and/or foetus | Remarks |
|---|---|---|---|---|---|
| Hunter syndrome X-linked recessive | Abnormal mucopolysaccharide accumulation and excretion | Mental defect less severe and slower progress than Hurler | Connective tissue Similar in appearance to Hurler | Detectable in cultured cells Heterozygous ♀♀ have both normal and abnormal cells Metachromatic granules in cultured fibroblasts | Both Hunter and Hurler cells in mixed tissue culture can grow normally; i.e. they each supplement the other metabolically |
| Tay-Sachs disease (amaurotic idiocy) Autosomal recessive | Absence of hexosaminidase A Accumulation of monosialo ceramide trihexoside (Tay–Sachs ganglioside) | Spasticity and convulsions by 4–6 months, severe mental deterioration, hyperacuisis, bursts of laughter | Enlarged head, Blindness, red spot on macula, muscular weakness, die by 2½–3½ years | Diagnosed in 15 and 20 week foetus | More frequent in Jewish populations |
| Gaucher's disease 1. (infantile) Autosomal recessive | Absence of glucocerebrosidase Accumulation of cerebrosides and phosphatides | Mental defect | Hepatosplenomegaly | | Metachromatic granules in cultured cells |

| | | Mental deterioration | Hepatospleno-megaly | An adult form also exists |
|---|---|---|---|---|
| 2. Juvenile Gaucher's Autosomal recessive | Reduced glucocerebrosidase activity | | | An adult form also exists |
| Nieman–Pick disease | Sphingomyelinase deficiency Accumulation of sphingomyelin | Severe and progressive degeneration of CNS Myoclonic seizures, cachexia | Organomegaly foam cells Red spot on macula Die 5 months–6 years | 3–4 distinct sub-types with different tissue enzyme levels Detectable in cultured cells |
| Metachromatic leucodystrophy Autosomal recessive | Absence of arylsulphatase A (sulphatide sulphatase) Accumulation of sulphatides, metachromatic substances in urine | Weakness ataxia Paralysis mental defect | Acid glycolipids in tissue | Detectable in tissue culture |
| 1. Infantile 2. Late infantile 3. Juvenile 4. Late onset form | Reduced enzyme levels probably account for other forms. Otherwise as infantile | 2. Cerebellar signs 3–4 years 3. Onset at 3–10 years Loss of emotional control, irritability, personality changes, then mental deterioration. Die by about 15 years 4. Late onset similarly characterized by mental and emotional instability and deterioration | | Juvenile and adult forms are usually misdiagnosed as a psychiatric problem |

Other defects of carbohydrate metabolism and storage diseases (generally but not exclusively affecting mucopolysaccharides, glycolipids or mucolipids) which lead to mental defect include: fucosidosis, mannosidosis, lactosyl ceramidosis, lipomucopolysaccharidosis, sulphatidosis, triose phosphate isomerase deficiency Pompe's, von Gierkes, Sanfilippo's, Morquio's, Scheie's and Krabbe's diseases, generalized gangliosidosis 1, and 2, cephalin lipidosis. I cell disease, sea blue histiocyte syndrome, etc. Important reviews are given by Brady (1970), McKusick (1969), Spranger and Wiedemann (1970).

TABLE 3—*Continued*

C. *Miscellaneous Diseases*

| Disease | Enzyme involved, metabolic effect | Effect on brain etc. | Other systems | Detection of heterozygote and/or foetus | Remarks |
|---|---|---|---|---|---|
| Lesch Nyhan syndrome Sex linked recessive | Absence of hypoxanthine-guanine phosphoribosyl transferase (HGPRT) Hyperuricaemia | Choreoathetosis, spasticity Aggressive behaviour. Self mutilation, mental retardation (see text) | Gouty tophi (see text) | Detectable on cultured cells, including foetal cells. Heterozygous ♀♀ have both normal and deficient cells in some tissues | |
| Hyperuricaemia Sex linked recessive | Low levels of hypoxanthine-guanine phosphoribosyl transferase Hyperuricaemia | Normal | Gouty tophi | | Probably allelic to HGPRT deficiency |
| Porphyria 1 (variegate) autosomal dominant Porphyria 2 (intermittent) autosomal dominant Porphyria 3 (coproporphyria) autosomal dominant | Excretion of porphyrins (see text) | Behavioural and neurological changes precipitated by various drugs and oestrogens (see text) | Liver porphyrin synthesis Photosensitization may occur | | Latent condition of these porphyrias can produce psychiatric symptoms |

| | | | | |
|---|---|---|---|---|
| Wilson's disease Autosomal recessive | Ceruloplasmin deficiency | Degeneration of basal ganglia, spasticity, rigidity and tremors (dysarthria, disphagia are final changes) May be preceded by personality and behaviour changes, schizophreniform symptoms, 'emotionalism' | Cirrhosis grey-green-brown ring in limbus of cornea Copper in tissues | Rate of $Cu^{64}$ incorporation to ceruloplasmin | Treatment by B.A.L. and penicillamine No Cu-rich food Patients have been given (*inappropriately*) psychiatric treatment |
| Periodic paralysis Autosomal dominant (some families incomplete penetrance?) | Corticosteroids | Migraine, paralytic effects follow illness, epileptiform seizures. Feelings of apprehension and excitability Resembles hysteria. Attacks induced by excitement, anger, anxiety, exertion, menstruation, cold, infections, trauma, alcohol, carbohydrate-rich diet | | | Administer potassium salts |

or entirely symptom-free, but in whom attacks may be precipitated by various drugs, including barbiturates, sulphonamides, griseofulvin and oestrogens. High levels of anino-levulinic acid (ALA) are found, and the liver has an increased ALA-synthetase activity.

## 2. *Variagate Porphyria* (South African Porphyria)

This too is due to a dominant gene and latent cases are again frequent. There is excretion of porphyrin in the faeces and deposits in the liver, and during the acute attacks porphyrin is also found in the urine. The symptoms include photosensitivity, excessive response of the exposed skin to trauma, sometimes excess pigmentation and hypertrichosis, abdominal pains and neurologic symptoms. In attacks, 32 per cent of patients have a confusional state, 23 per cent show abnormal behaviour and 12 per cent epileptic seizures. Again the expression is variable in different individuals and women are particularly vulnerable to attacks during pregnancy and menstruation. Attacks are precipitated or the illness made more acute by administration of barbiturates, sulphonam- ides, ethanol or general anaesthetics. Typically there is abdominal and muscular pain and weakness, vomiting and tachycardia. Emotional disturbance and depression is very frequent and there may be halluci- nations. Severe depression may follow an acute attack.

Cases of porphyria associated with alcoholism, Sedormid (apronal) administration and ingestion of the fungicide hexachlorbenzene have been reported. The genetic basis of these is unclear.

The significance to psychiatry of findings in the porphyrias may be outlined as follows: that the emotional and irrational responses and bizarre behaviour which are frequently manifested by individuals with either genetic or acquired porphyria can occur in marked form during acute episodes but may also to some extent be present in the absence of the more severe physical symptoms. One can make the very general and reasonable assumption that porphyrias (as in the case of other human genetic diseases) represent the severely affected and hence recognizable alleles in a population which has many alleles of varying effectiveness at the same locus. These markedly abnormal genes can be taken as extreme representatives of some of the presumably large number whose biochemical effects include a potentiating contribution to psychic instability. The conversion of latent forms of porphyria into overt crises as a result of a number of environmental insults exemplifies the relationship between environment and genotype in the production of the phenotype.

### DISORDERS OF PURINE METABOLISM—THE LESCH-NYHAN SYNDROME

The first report on this disease was published in 1964 and a fuller report made in 1968 (Nyhan, 1968). It is a sex-linked recessive and is characterized by developmental retardation, spastic cerebral palsy, choreoathetosis and aggressive behaviour, including verbal and physical aggression against others and self-mutilation. The children showing aggressive behaviour may swear, punch people and bite them. Their auto-mutilation most typically takes the form of biting the fingers or lower lip leading to progressive destruction. This behaviour is evidently compulsive and it is reported that the children feel pain and are terrified of their activity. Nyhan reports that in spite of the low I.Q.'s measurable for these children they appear to be alert, and interested in the events in the ward, show a sense of humour and are very affectionate. Aggressive behaviour to others appears to be equally compulsive and is usually followed by apology. Although the children are retarded and may have severe speech difficulties some of them give interesting answers when asked why they bite themselves, e.g. 'Because I can't help it', 'I do it when I get mad', 'My uric acid is too high'. Intelligible answers are however not usually possible from these children.

All these patients have a deficiency of hypoxanthine-guanine phosphoribosyl transferase (HG-PRTase), synthesize purines excessively and are hyperuricaemic. Many develop gouty arthritis and uric acid tophi but this is not an essential feature. Similarly, males in some kindreds have been reported who have very low levels of HG-PRTase and are hyperuricaemic, have gouty arthritis, but are not aggressive or self-mutilating. This is probably an allelic condition.

This disease, being a sex-linked recessive, affects males as expected. The Lyon hypothesis postulates that females heterozygous for an X chromosome borne mutation will have cells in which the expression of one or other allele is mutually exclusive due to an inactivation of one of the two X chromosomes at random. Heterozygotes may be detected by cultivating skin fibroblasts which show the Lyon effect, that is, the cell population contains cells with the normal level of enzyme and cells in which the enzyme is absent. Should inactivation of the chromosome bearing the normal allele occur early, individual females may come to have the majority of their cells bearing the deficient allele; and in fact Nyhan reports that some female relatives are obviously aggressive and some may even self-mutilate.

The presence of a defective foetus can probably be reliably determined as it has been shown that levels of HG-PRTase may be measured in cells from the amniotic fluid, and enzyme deficient cells were found from a foetus at genetic risk. The reality of the relationship between the behaviour and the biochemistry is illustrated by the production of phenocopies in rats, by feeding them with excessively high doses ($LD_{50}$) of caffeine or theophylline, which are both methylated xanthines (purines). Caffeine causes them to mutilate their own paws and theophylline causes self-mutilation around the mouth. Aggressive behaviour to other rats is possibly evoked by caffeine.

INHERITANCE OF ALCOHOL PREFERENCE

Numerous experiments with rats and mice indicate that strains may differ from each other in preference for dilute alcohol solutions or water. Thus one particular strain of mice prefer alcohol and another avoids it, while the hybrid between them shows intermediate behaviour. This clearly indicates a genetic contribution to the behaviour which itself is of course learned. In rats, selection can increase the number showing preference for alcohol although variability within the strains persists, suggesting a large environmental component. In genetically mixed mouse populations the heritability of alcohol preference is very low. This suggests that the behavioural aspect of the genetic contribution may be overwhelmed by the residual genotype in normal conditions, as well as by environmental factors.

Correlation of alcohol preference with other characteristics is suggested by the behaviour of two strains of rats previously selected for emotional reactivity or non-reactivity. The non-reactive animals had a higher preference for alcohol and a higher total intake.

Two enzymes concerned with alcohol metabolism have been studied in mice, namely alcohol dehydrogenase (genetic variants of which have been found in various organisms including *Drosophila* and man) and aldehydehydrogenase. In both drinking and teetotal mouse strains, alcohol dehydrogenase levels rise following forced alcohol consumption and drop to base value in about four weeks. However there are differences between the strains; thus alcohol dehydrogenase activity is 30 per cent higher and aldehydedehydrogenase is 300 per cent higher in C57 black (topers) than in DBA (teetotalers). The $F_1$ is intermediate for enzyme levels and for alcohol preference. Levels of acetaldehyde in the blood after injection of alcohol is slightly higher in DBA than in C57 black, so that the avoidance of alcohol by DBA mice may be due to sensations related to those following antabuse and alcohol ingestion in man. Female rats have been shown to metabolize alcohol more efficiently than males (Sheppard *et al.*, 1968).

Although it would appear that all these findings are likely to have some relevance for the understanding of alcoholism in man it would be premature to say in what way they should be interpreted, but genetic differences in metabolism may be found (Vesell *et al.*, 1971).

PHARMOCOGENETICS

Numerous genetically determined drug idiosyncrasies are known (Evans, 1969); these are of interest for three reasons. The first is that they denote the general reservoir of genetic variability in the population which remains unknown until some specific test is used as discriminant. Any stress or test which causes a subgroup of a population to behave in a different way from the remainder, such as a loading test (see Biochemical Genetics) or the metabolism of a specific drug, will expose genetic diversity that has been invisible under normal conditions. Secondly, the recognition of genetic variants holds out hope for useful discrimination with respect to suitability for treatment or liability to risk with specified drugs; and individuals with a latent instability which may contribute to manifest breakdown under particular environmental stress may also be recognized (see porphyria). Finally, the discovery of metabolic singularities serves to discriminate between clinically homogeneous but genetically diverse diseases. For example, until the three separate subtypes of cystinuria were elucidated biochemically, the genetic basis of tranmission was not understood. In the same way gargoyle-like facies, usually with severe mental defect, is now known to include some 16 different disease entities. It may therefore be hoped that useful subdivision of conditions such as schizophrenia or endogenous depression might be made, not in terms of behavioural patterns, but in terms of underlying biochemical diversity as evidenced by responses to drugs with an effect on nervous function.

The few examples described below are those involving (1) drugs in use in clinical psychiatric practice (2) drugs of general use that the psychiatrist may have occasion to use and idiosyncratic responses to which might occur.

### 1. *Phenothiazine*

Administration of phenothiazine distinguishes two kinds of individuals, those that incur symptoms of Parkinsonism after administration of *small* doses, and whose relatives have four times the incidence of paralysis agitans than a control population, and those individuals in which administration has no effect and whose relatives have a low incidence of paralysis agitans.

### 2. *Pseudocholinesterase Deficiency*

Patients whose muscle relaxation and apnoea following administration of suxamethonium persists for two or three hours instead of the usual two minutes were found to have low levels of serum pseudocholinesterase. Heterozygotes show an intermediate level of sensitivity. Recent studies show that there are two separate loci concerned: four alleles of locus EI have been discovered so far, and two of E2. These make possible 30 different genotypic combinations between them, and the phenotypes manifest a very wide range of esterase activity, some individuals being normal, some sensitive to the drug, while some suffer from prolonged paralysis.

### 3. *Phenelzine Metabolism*

Phenelzine is an M.A.O.I. which may produce severe side-effects in some individuals. These have an inefficient acetylation mechanism and metabolize the drug slowly; the same or a related system affects isoniazid and sulphonamide metabolism. The slow metabolizers of phenelzine were first recognized by their slow isoniazid inactivation rate, which is associated with the risk of peripheral neuritis.

4. The familial nature of the different response to M.A.O.I. and tricyclic drugs has already been described (see Affective Disorders).

5. Diphenylhydantoin, used in the treatment of epilepsy, is toxic to those that cannot hydroxylate it.

6. A genetic inability to de-ethylate phenacetin is known.

7. The response to salicylate appears to be polygenic.

8. The dramatic reaction of individuals with hepatic porphyria to barbiturates, anaesthetics, oestrogens and androgens has been already described (see p. 439).

## QUANTITATIVE GENETICS OF BEHAVIOUR

Numerous studies have been made of the genetic determination of behaviour patterns, especially in mice and rats (reviewed by McClearn, 1970; Lindzey *et al.*, 1971). The majority of these studies are based on behavioural features which may be quantified, but interpretation of which may not however be unequivocal: thus the rate of defaecation in mice under various conditions is generally interpreted as a measure of emotionality; the frequency with which mice will leave a lighted area to enter into a dark small area, or will leave a dark area to enter into a lighted area is frequently interpreted as a measure of timidity; while the degree of movement of mice in an open space, and the area covered, is frequently interpreted as a measure of investigative or exploratory capacity. Speed of learning tasks, and memory retention, aggressiveness and tameness, have also been measured, and in addition a number of abnormal behaviour patterns such as seizures when subject to auditory stimuli. In a few cases the patterns of inheritance have turned out to be surprisingly simple and straightforward, but in the majority of cases what have been obtained are heritability estimates, often very high and implying a polygenic basis, rather than evidence of clearly segregating differences. A number of single gene differences have been found to have pleiotropic effects on behaviour.

A detailed review of these data is beyond the present scope. Nevertheless these observations are mentioned since whatever comparisons may be made with humans, the demonstration of a genetic basis for complex forms of behaviour will become of increasing relevance in clinical psychiatry.

## Chromosomal Abnormalities

During cell division, either of the germ cells or of the somatic cells, errors may occur in the structure or composition of the chromosomes. If a somatic cell is modified the number of abnormal cells derived from it may not be large. The person affected is termed mosaic; this condition will not be further discussed. If a germ cell is abnormal the progeny are affected: some of the types of abnormal individuals so produced are described in this section.

Changes in chromosomes may be in *number*, in that some are represented in more than two copies or some may be missing, or of *structure*, in that chromosomes may be damaged by losing a portion, or they may have a part of a chromosome from a different pair fused to them (translocation). Other possible anomalies include inversions, when a segment of chromosome is broken off and reinserted in the reverse orientation to its original one. Disorders may involve sex chromosomes or autosomes.

Chromosomal abnormalities of some kind occur in about 7 per cent of all conceptions but the great majority of the abnormal zygotes abort spontaneously and chromosomal errors are found in only about 0·5 per cent of live births. There is, however, considerable variation in the abortion rates of the different types of chromosome anomalies. About 40 per cent of all spontaneous abortions are associated with chromosomal defect.

Several chromosomal aberrations occur more frequently in the offspring of older mothers, including Mongolism (but see below), Edward's and Pätau's syndromes, XXX and XXY, but not XO or XYY.

Chromosomes are classified into lettered groups from A to G by overall size and appearance, and also numbered from 1 to 23 plus the sex chromosomes X and Y.

### AUTOSOMAL DEFECTS

Three syndromes characterized by an extra chromosome (trisomy) have been well studied. These are Down's syndrome, and Pätau's and Edward's syndromes. Down's syndrome, trisomy 21, gives rise to Mongolism. This is characterized by low I.Q., lowered viability, absence of the palmar crease, an epicanthic fold, a trident hand and a friendly personality. They have a 15 times increased risk of leukaemia.

The frequency of Mongolism among all live births increases in a curvilinear relationship with the age of the mother at the time of parturition. Up to about the age of 30 the risk of a Mongol birth is

Q

somewhat less than 1 in a 1000. Between 35 and 39 it is in the order of 3·5 to 4 per 1000, while between 40 and 44 it increases to 10 to 15 per 1000. A mother who produces a Mongol due to trisomy 21 is at no greater risk for producing a second child similarly affected than any other woman of comparable age.

However, Mongolism can also be due to another form of chromosomal defect which usually involves chromosome 21 but represents a translocation between that chromosome and some other, usually 14, 15 or 22. This form of Mongolism, which is much less common, is not related to the maternal age at birth and moreover tends to have a raised familial incidence. A mother who produces a Mongol due to translocation is therefore at high risk of producing a second such child. Since the two forms of Mongolism are clinically indistinguishable, accurate advice can only be given after detailed chromosomal analysis of the child and both parents. In the absence of such facilities the mother's age may be taken as an approximate guide to the aetiology of the Mongolism in the child and it has been estimated that mothers below the age of 25 who produce a Mongol have 50 times the risk of other mothers of comparable age of producing a second such infant; between 25 and 34 the risk drops to about a five times excess, while above 35 there is virtually none.

Patäu's syndrome also shows developmental retardation and mental defect and there are also numerous morphological abnormalities including face, hands, feet, C.N.S. and internal organs. It probably involves chromosome 13. Its frequency is estimated at 1 in 7,600 live births. Edward's syndrome is trisomy 18. The estimated frequencies range from 1 in 3,500 to 1 in 6,700. The mental defect is severe and there are other neurological effects and morphological anomalies involving skull and fingers. Almost all of them die before one year; most of them before three months. Other chromosomal anomalies exist which may overlap in appearance with these three.

Deletions and duplications of part of the material of a chromosome may occur and may produce anomalous development and reduced I.Q. A few are described briefly here. (1) The cri-du-chat syndrome is due to a deletion of the short arm of a B group chromosome (5?). There is developmental retardation, a cry resembling that of a kitten, moderate microcephaly with a round face, epicanthus and palpebral fissures which slant down and outwards, and prominent corneas. (2) Individuals with deletion of a short arm of an E group chromosome (7 or 8) are usually feeble-minded, have occular anomalies, small jaw, a flat nose bridge and large auricles. (3) Deletion of the longer arm of an E group chromosome (18?) is associated with nasomaxillary hypoplasia and many other morphological changes. They are microcephalic imbeciles. A fuller description of some of these conditions is given by Polani (1969).

SEX CHROMOSOME ABNORMALITIES

Anomalies of the X or Y chromosomes (sex chromosomes) affect the development of the gonads and secondary sexual characters. There may be other developmental features. Loss of an X or Y or the addition of extra ones may occur and structural anomalies have been reported. Only a few of the possible anomalies are described here (Court Brown, 1969).

A Y chromosome has physically masculinizing properties and the addition of a large number of X chromosomes tends to reduce the I.Q. Although not all of the types of sex chromosome anomaly cause mental subnormality most cause gonadal or genital dysgenesis, with associated infertility, and this in itself may not be without psychiatric effect.

Many of the individuals with composition XXY are discovered after referral from endocrinological clinics. XXY individuals manifest Kleinefelter's syndrome. These males may develop normally until puberty when they develop hypogonadism. The face hair is diminished or may be absent, the body hair is feminized and gynaecomastia may occur. From the psychological viewpoint one of the most contant characteristics is a low average I.Q., albeit with a considerable variation (up to normal) about this low mean. As personalities many cases show psychosexual infantilism and in a few instances paedophilic practices may develop which lead the patient into legal difficulties. In addition a variety of other psychiatric features have been ascribed to these patients including conversion hysterical symptoms, severe psychoneuroses and paranoid reactions. Earlier reports of a specific association with schizophrenia are probably unfounded.

The best known sex chromosome anomaly besides Kleinefelter's is Turner's syndrome whose composition is XO. These women have short stature, neck webbing and ovarian dysgenesis. At birth they have a higher mortality than normal due to associated cardiovascular malformations. The intelligence is unaffected, though they are reported to have a relative inability to recognize spatial relationships (Money, 1968).

High grade abnormality is often associated with chromosome anomalies especially XXY, XXXY and mosaics. Severe abnormality is found in XXX, XXXX, XXXXX, XXXY and XXXXY. These are all very rare.

There is evidence that XXYY have a low I.Q. and may be violent, while evidence has also been presented that some of the XYY's are above average both in height and in psychopathy. About 1 in 700 newborn males are XYY and the percentage of such individuals in the population of tall, criminally insane men shows a twentyfold increased probability of being XYY compared to the population at large (Jacobs, et al., 1971).

It is difficult to estimate how commonly sex chromosome anomalies occur among psychiatric patients. It is thought that approximately 1·2 per cent of mental defectives and between 0·5 and 0·7 per cent of other psychiatric patients may fall into this category. Similarly is it not clear whether the chromosomal imbalance itself leads directly to psychiatric symptoms as an essential part of the syndrome, or to what extent the clinical picture is due to the realization by these individuals of their difference in physique and capacity from the normal. All individuals with sex chromosome anomalies are infertile.

The outlook for individuals with chromosomal defects is unlike that for individuals with a disadvantageous allele for a given locus, since large numbers of loci are carried on each chromosome and a curative therapy based on aetiology seems impossible. It may be that some alleviation of secondary sexual effects might be obtained in certain cases of sex chromosomal defects.

## GENETIC COUNSELLING

Occasionally a couple may seek advice of the psychiatrist on the likelihood of a child developing an illness known to occur in the family. Often such advice is sought before a child has been conceived.

The example classically used to illustrate the principles to be applied in this situation is that of Huntington's chorea. This disorder follows an autosomal dominant transmission pattern, although the number of patients manifesting the disease is only 70 per cent of the number to be expected on theoretical grounds. The age of onset may be at any point in life and for present purposes it may be taken that each decade represents a period of equal risk.

If the parent has not himself or herself manifested any features of the disease—which is often the case when genetic advice is sought—the first step is to calculate the likelihood that they will yet do so. Assuming that one of the enquirer's own parents has Huntington's chorea then *at his birth* there was a 0·5 probability that the subject was destined to manifest the illness himself at some time in his life. The subject has, however, remained free of symptoms up to the time of consultation. He has thus already passed a proportion of the period at risk and his likelihood of being genotypically positive for the disease is that much reduced. This point may be put in another way: if the subject is genotypically positive he will at some point in his life manifest the illness, but since after an appreciable period has elapsed he is still healthy it is relatively less likely that he is going to show the disorder at all. For a subject aged 40 years, four sevenths or 57 per cent of his life span (of 70 years) has already passed, leaving 43 per cent to go. In more formal terms, the probability that he will yet develop the illness is 0·43 times the probability that he will ever get the disease at all, i.e. $0.43 \times 0.5 = 0.22$.

Were the subject genotypically positive then half his children would be similarly affected. Any given child, such as the one yet to be conceived, would then have a fifty-fifty chance, or a probability of $0.5$, of also developing the illness. The likelihood of the subject producing an affected child is thus $0.5$ times his own likelihood of being genetically positive, i.e. $0.22 \times 0.5$ which is $0.11$ (for any *one* child). This estimate in the situation just outlined is in fact rather too high, the disease manifestation being less than 100 per cent. However, as there is no evidence as to why the disorder does not show full penetrance it is probably advisable to work on the theoretical basis of Mendelian ratios for counselling purposes.

The same principles can be applied to any other disorder for which adequate data are available, bearing in mind that the risk for any combination of events such as that both the individual and his offspring will have a genetic lesion, is always the product and not the sum of their individual probabilities.

All such estimates can only represent a statement of likelihood on the basis of which the prospective parents must act as they see fit. They give small comfort of course to parents who in consequence remain childless all their lives, or who are unfortunate enough to produce a child who develops a serious genetically based illness despite the low probability of such a misfortune occurring. It would be far more satisfactory if a definite statement could be made regarding a particular foetus and this is now possible for certain disorders. By the technique of amniocentesis a sample of foetal cells can be obtained from the liquor amnii, and after tissue culture and appropriate testing it is possible to state with near certainty whether or not a given foetus will develop the disorder in question. The technique is at present applicable only to two classes of disorder, namely certain specific biochemical anomalies likely to be associated with mental defect, and chromosome abnormalities including translocations and sex chromosome anomalies. Special centres are envisaged for the near future in which expertise in medical genetics and obstetric skills for amniocentresis investigations will be combined.

Most foetuses with severe genetic defects abort spontaneously. For those that do not, induced abortion can be performed under the special provisions of the Abortion Act covering such contingencies. The parents may then try again to produce a normal foetus in the reasonable expectation that eventually they will succeed (Friedmann, 1971).

It need scarcely be added that considerable tact and sensitivity are required when discussing these issues with parents, both prospective and actual. It is the psychiatrist's duty to present the facts in a sympathetic and comprehensible way and to ensure as far as he can that the final decision is the parents' and not his own. Undoubtedly ethical problems do arise in this kind of work, but they require for the most part to be resolved by the parents rather than by the physician.

## CONCLUSION

Biochemical and clinical genetic investigations are easier to carry out if there are already signposts to relevant and profitable lines of investigation such as a histological abnormality, or a deposit of abnormal material, or an obvious and fairly constant modification of blood or urine: such conditions are a hopeful starting point for discriminant analysis. Thus gargoylism is phenotypically striking, and histochemical peculiarities are observable. While four biochemically different types of genetic gargoylism were listed in a review article in 1965, the latest count (1971) is 16, (10 mucolipidoses and six mucopolysaccharidoses). An apparent absence of such clear pointers may be one of the reasons for the resistance, so far, of some conditions, such as schizophrenia, to attempts to analyse them usefully.

If some generalized syndrome comprises a number of different disease conditions, and if the syndromes are conditional upon a specific concatenation of genetic circumstances, these cases would be rather resistant to analysis. In any case, function—although it may ultimately be based on structure (whether gross or ultrastructural or biochemical)— is always more difficult to describe than structure, and psychiatric function is perhaps more difficult still. The longer the causal chain from genetic lesion to pleiotropic pattern, the more environmental stresses or life experiences may 'confuse' the picture from the viewpoint of the geneticist.

However, it seems unrealistic to suppose that the heritable component of any condition should be based upon exceptional or uniquely obscure kinds of genes and gene mechanisms. The whole of the history of human biochemical genetics and indeed of genetics in general can only be conducive to optimism for the future.

## REFERENCES

ANGST, J. (1966)   *Zur Ätiologie und Nosologie Endogener Depressiver Psychosen.* Berlin.

BERMAN, P. W., WAISMAN, H. A. & GRAHAM, S. K. (1966)   Intelligence in treated phenylketonuric children: a development study. *Child Development*, **37**, 731–747. (See Fig. 8.)

BRADY, R. O. (1970)   Cerebrolipidoses. *Annual Review of Medicine*, **21**, 317–334. (See Table 3B.)

COURT BROWN, W. M. (1969)   Sex chromosome aneuploidy in man and its frequency with special reference to mental abnormality and criminal behaviour. *International Review of Experimental Pathology*, **7**, 31–97.

BROWN, F. (1942)   Heredity in the psychoneuroses. *Proceedings of the Royal Society of Medicine*, **35**, 785–790.

BUTCHER, H. J. (1968) *Human Intelligence: Its Nature and Assessment.* London: Methven.

CATTELL, R. B. & MALTENO, E. (1940) Contributions concerning mental inheritance. II. Temperament. *Journal of Genetic Psychology,* **57,** 31–47.

DEAN, G. (1969) The Porphyrias. *British Medical Bulletin,* **25,** 48–51.

EVANS, D. A. P. (1969) Genetic factors in drug therapy. *Scientific Basis of Medicine. Annual Reviews,* 166–182.

EYSENCK, H. (1959) *Manual of the Maudsley Personality Inventory.* London.

EYSENCK, H. (1964) *Crime and Personality.* London: Routledge & Kegan Paul.

EYSENCK, H. & PRELL, D. (1951) The inheritance of neuroticism: an experimental study. *Journal of Mental Science,* **97,** 441–465.

FØLLING, A. (1934) Uber Ausscheidung von Phenylbrenztraubensaure in den Harn Als Stoffwechselanomalie in Verbindung mit Inbezilltiat. *Zeitschrift für physikalische Chemie,* **227,** 169.

FOULDS, G. A. (1965) in collaboration with T. Caine. *Personality and Personal Illness.* London: Tavistock Publications.

FRIEDMANN, T. (1971) Prenatal diagnosis of genetic disease. *Scientific American,* **225** (5) 34–42.

GOTTESMAN, I. (1963) Heritability of personality: a demonstration. *Psychological Monographs.* Edited by G. Gimble. No. 572, **77** (9) 1–21.

HARVALD, B. & HAUGE, M. (1965) Hereditary factors elucidated by twin studies. In *Genetics and the Epidemiology of Chronic Diseases.* Edited by J. Neel, M. Shaw & W. Schell. O.S. Dept. Health Education and Welfare, Washington.

HESTON, L. (1966) Psychiatric disorder in foster home reared children of schizophrenic mothers. *British Journal of Psychiatry,* **112,** 819–825.

HESTON, L. & SHIELDS, J. (1968) Homosexuality in twins. *Archives of General Psychiatry,* **18,** 149–160.

HOLMAN, N. A. (1970) Dietary treatment of inborn errors of metabolism. *Annual Review of Medicine,* **21,** 335–356. (See Table 3A.)

HOPKINSON, G. (1964) A genetic study of affective illness in patients over 50. *British Journal of Psychiatry,* **110,** 244–254.

HSIA, D. YI-YUNG BERMAN, J. L., JUSTICE, P., NADLER, H. L. & O'FLYNN, M. E. (1968) Metabolic disorders associated with mental retardation. *Pediatric Clinics of North America,* **15,** 889–904.

HSIA, D. YI-YUNG (1970) Phenylketonuria and its variants. *Progress in Medical Genetics,* **7,** 29–68.

JACOBS, P. A., PRICE, W. H., RICHMOND, S. & RATCLIFFE, R. A. W. (1971) Chromosome surveys in penal institutions and approved schools. *Journal of Medical Genetics,* **8,** 49–58.

JERVIS, G. A. (1939) Genetics of phenylpyruvic oligophrenia. *Journal of Mental Science,* **85,** 719.

JERVIS, G. A. (1947) Studies of phenylpyruvic oligophrenia: the position of the metabolic error. *Journal of Biological Chemistry,* **169,** 651.

JERVIS, G. A. (1953) Phenylpyruvic oligophrenia: deficiency of phenyl alanine oxidizing system. *Proceedings of the Society for Experimental Biology and Medicine,* **82,** 514.

JUEL-NIELSEN, N. (1965) Individual and environment. *Acta psychiatrica et neurologica scandinavica, Supplement,* 183.

KAIJ, L. (1960) *Alcoholism in Twins: studies in the aetiology and sequels of abuse of alcohol.* Stockholm.

KALLMANN, F. J. (1938) *The Genetics of Schizophrenia.* New York: Norton.

KALLMAN, F. J. (1952) Comparative twin study on the genetic aspects of male homosexuality. *Journal of Nervous and Mental Diseases,* **115,** 278–283.

KALLMAN, F. J. (1953)   *Heredity in health and mental disorder.* New York.
KAY, D. (1959)   Observations on the natural history and genetics of old age psychosis: a Stockholm material. *Proceedings of the Royal Society of Medicine,* **52,** 791–794.
KESSEL, N. & WALTON, H. (1967)   *Alcoholism.* London: Penguin Books.
KETY, S., ROSENTHAL, D., WENDER, P. & SCHULSINGER, F. (1968)   The type and prevalence of mental illness in the biological and adoptive families of adopted schizophrenics. In *The Transmission of Schizophrenia.* Edited by S. Kety and D. Rosenthal. Pergamon Press.
KNOX, W. E. (1966)   Phenylketonuria. In *The Metabolic Basis of Inherited Disease.* Edited by J. B. Stanbury, J. B. Wyngaarden & D. S. Fredrickson. 2nd Edition, pp. 258–291. McGraw Hill, N. Y., London.
KRINGLEN, E. (1967)   *Heredity and Environment in the Functional Psychoses.* London: Heinemann.
LANGE, J. (1931)   *Crime as Destiny.* (tran. C. Haldane). London: Allen & Unwin.
LEWIS, A. (1935/36)   Problems of obsessional illness. *Proceedings of the Royal Society of Medicine,* **29,** 325–326.
LINDZEY, G., LOEHLIN, J., MANOSEVITZ, M. & THEISSEN, D. (1971)   Behavioural genetics. *Annual Review of Psychology,* **22,** 39–94.
McCLEARN, G. E. (1970)   Behavioural genetics. *Annual Review of Genetics,* **4,** 437–468.
McKUSICK, V. A. (1969)   The nosology of the mucopolysaccharidoses. *American Journal of Medicine,* **47,** 730–747. (See Table 3B.)
McKUSICK, V. A. (1970)   Human genetics. *Annual Review of Genetics,* **4,** 1–46.
MENKES, J. H. & MIGEON, B. K. (1966)   Biochemical and genetic aspects of mental retardation. *Annual Review of Medicine,* **17,** 407–430.
MONEY, J. (1968)   Cognitive deficits in Turner's Syndrome. In *Progress in Human Behaviour Genetics.* Edited by S. G. Vandenburg. Baltimore: John Hopkins Press.
NEWMAN, H., FREEMAN, F. & HOLZINGER, K. (1937)   *Twins: a study of heredity and environment.* Chicago, Ill.: Univ. Chicago Press.
NYHAN, W. L. (1968)   Clinical features of the Lesch–Nyhan Syndrome. Introduction—Clinical and genetic features (and) Summary of clinical features. In *Seminars on the Lesch–Nyhan Syndrome. Federation Proceedings,* **27** (4), 1027–1033 and 1034–1041.
ODEGARD, O. (1963)   The psychotic disease entities in the light of a genetic investigation. *Acta psychiatrica et neurologica scandinavica. Supplement,* 169, 39, 94–104.
PARE, C. & MACK, J. (1971)   Differentiation of two genetically specific types of depression by response to antidepressive drugs. *Journal of Medical Genetics,* **8,** 306–309.
PARKER, N. (1964)   Twins: a psychiatric study of a neurotic group. *Medical Journal of Australia,* **2,** 735–742.
PERRIS, C. (1966)   A study of bipolar (manic-depressive) and unipolar recurrent depressive psychoses. *Acta psychiatrica et neurologica scandinavica. Supplement,* 194. Copenhagen.
POLANI, P. E. (1969)   Autosomal imbalance and its syndrome, excluding Down's. *British Medical Bulletin,* **25,** 81–93.
POLLIN, W. & STABENAU, J. R. (1968)   Biological, psychological and historical differences in a series of monozygotic twins discordant for schizophrenia. In *The Transmission of Schizophrenia.* Edited by D. Rosenthal & S. Kety. Pergamon Press.

Post, F. (1967) The schizophrenic reaction-type in late life. *Proceedings of the Royal Society of Medicine*, **60**, 249–254.

Price, J. (1968) *The genetics of depressive disorder in recent development in affective disorders*. Edited by A. Coppen & A. Walk. Royal Medico-Psychol. Assoc., London.

Rosanoff, A., Hardy, L. & Plesset, I. (1941) The etiology of child behaviour difficulties, juvenile delinquency and adult criminality with special reference to their occurrence in twins. *Psychiatric Monographs*, No. 1. Calif.

Rosenthal, D. (1961*a*) Sex distribution and the severity of illness among samples of schizophrenic twins. *Journal of Psychiatric Research*, **1**, 26–36.

Rosenthal, D. (1961*b*) Problems of sampling and diagnosis in the major twin studies of schizophrenia. *Journal of Psychiatric Research*, **1**, 116–134.

Sheppard, J. R., Albersheim, P. & McClearn, G. E. (1968) Enzyme activities and alcohol preference in mice. *Biochemical Genetics*, **2**, 205–212.

Shields, J. (1962) *Monozygotic Twins Brought Up Apart and Brought Up Together*. London: Oxford University Press.

Shields, J. (1968) Summary of the genetic evidence. *Journal of Psychiatric Research*, **6**, (Suppl. 1) 95–126.

Slater, E. (1953) with assistance of Shields, J. Psychotic and neurotic illness in twins. *Medical Research Council Special Report*, 278, London: H.M.S.O.

Slater, E. (1961) 'Hysteria 311.' *Journal of Mental Science*, **107**, 359–381.

Slater, E. & Shields, J. (1967) Genetical aspects of anxiety. Ch. 9. In *Studies of anxiety*. Edited by M. Lader. World Psychiat. Assoc. and Roy. Medico. Psychol. Assoc. London.

Spranger, J. W. & Wiedemann, H. R. (1970) The genetic mucolipidoses: diagnosis and differential diagnosis. *Humangenetik*, **9**, 113. (See Table 3B.)

Stendstedt, A. (1952) A study in manic-depressive illness: clinical, social and genetic investigations. *Acta psychiatrica et neurologica scandinavica. Supplement* 79. Copenhagen.

Tienari, P. (1963) Psychiatric illness in identical twins. *Acta psychiatrica et neurologica scandinavica. Supplement* 171.

Tienari, P. (1966) On intrapair differences in male twins with special reference to dominance-submissiveness. *Acta psychiatrica et neurologica scandinavica. Supplement* 188.

Vesell, E. S., Page, J. C. & Passananti, G. T. (1971) Genetic and environmental factors affecting ethanol metabolism in man. *Clinical Pharmacology and Therapeutics*, **12**, 192–201.

Wilde, G. (1964) Inheritance of personality traits. *Acta psychologica*, **11**, 37–51.

Winokur, G. & Clayton, P. (1967) Family history studies. L. Two types of affective disorders separated according to genetic and clinical factors. *Recent Advances in Biological Psychiatry*, **9**, 35–50.

# Chapter XIX

# THE BIOLOGICAL ROOTS OF PERSONALITY

## Ian Oswald and Sula Wolff

### INTRODUCTION

Man is uniquely capable of profiting from his past experience and of making inferences about his future. Learning plays so important a part in his behaviour, compared with that of lower animals, that unlearned forces can be difficult to discern. It would, however, give us a false picture of man if we failed to see him in the light of comparative data and as a member of the Animal Kingdom. Man's personality is determined by heredity, by influences arising during intra-uterine life, by paranatal complications, by post-natal interference with normal brain development, as well as by learning during critical periods of early childhood and during maturation, through adolescence to maturity. He is, like lower animals, equipped with a number of innate behavioural responses liable to be released by certain sensory patterns and is, like other animals, swayed by his changing internal hormonal environment.

### HEREDITY

Professional breeders of dogs and horses are in no doubt that temperament is inherited, but in the case of Man, with his immense capacity for learning, anecdotal observations ('Isn't she like her mother?'), can be countered by the argument that the son is like his father because he grew up with him and learned peculiarities of behaviour from him. In other words, some means of isolating the genetic and the learned contributions to behaviour becomes necessary.

In animal studies this is comparatively simple. The experiments of Broadhurst (1960) offer an example. Starting with a group of rats of varying emotionality he bred, for emotional reactiveness and emotional nonreactiveness, through successive generations. The chosen index of emotional response was that of defaecation, since, when frightened, rats (and monkeys, and a proportion of humans), have a tendency to evacuate their bowels. Broadhurst placed rats individually in a special chamber where there was a very bright light and accompanying loud noise. At the end of two minutes he counted the number of faecal pellets that had been deposited. Rats who reacted by depositing numerous faecal pellets were mated with other rats who had responded similarly while in the frightening situation. On the other hand, individual rats who had dropped few or no pellets were mated with others who had dropped few or no pellets. The offspring were tested in like manner and then similarly mated according to their reactions. The procedure was continued until, after ten generations, two distinct strains of rats had been developed. One consistently dropped no faecal pellets when placed in the frightening situation, and the other consistently dropped numerous faecal pellets in the same circumstances.

It was then necessary to establish that this supposed response to emotion was a manifestation of an inherited trait and not simply one that had been learned from the parent rats. In order to test this, *cross-fostering* was carried out. Within a few hours of birth, half the litter from each one of a group of non-reactor mothers was swopped for half the litter of a similar number of reactor mothers. The young rats then grew up and were tested again in later life to see if rodent-style toilet training imparted by their mothers, whether genuine or foster, was responsible for their habits in later life. In fact the offspring responded in the frightening situation in accordance with the genetic strain from which they derived, and not in accordance with the manners of their adoptive mothers.

It could still be argued that while they were *in utero* some influence from a placid or an emotionally reactive mother crossed the placenta and affected their later personality. It was possible to test this by *cross-breeding*.

If an intra-uterine effect was paramount then the offspring of a cross between a reactive father and a non-reactive mother should be less reactive than the offspring of a cross between a non-reactive father and a reactive mother. No such effect was found, and consequently it was regarded as established that emotionality, as measured by defaecation under standard conditions, in these rats was inherited. The two strains of rats are known as the Maudsley reactive and non-reactive strains and have become widely used in research into behavioural genetics.

HUMAN GENETIC STUDIES

Deliberate genetic experiments are impossible in man and it is therefore necessary to turn to twins, namely, dizygotic (DZ) twins, who share certain genetic material and monozygotic (MZ) twins who share it all. Most important is the comparison of MZ twins reared together and MZ twins where each member of the pair had been reared separately. Newman, Freeman and Holzinger (1937), in the U.S.A., carried out a study of intelligence test performance in MZ twins who had been reared together and reared apart respectively. Their work demonstrated a close correlation between twin-pair members reared apart, and made possible the inference that heredity was the principal determinant of intelligence. It should be added, however, that environmental influences can play a modifying role in influencing behaviour in what are generally regarded as tests of intelligence. Douglas (1964) has described a follow-up study, over the course of many years, of all children born in England and Wales in one week of 1946. At the age of eight their performance on scholastic tests was measured. The same was done again when they were aged 11. In the interval those who had performed well at age eight, and who had been living in homes of high parental interest in school work, improved their performance by an average of an extra three per cent, whereas those who had started as equally above-average scholars at age eight, and had lived in homes where the parents took little interest in their school work, had fallen back by 6·4 per cent. Where 'streaming' had been carried out in the schools, children of *equal initial* performance ability had gained 8·8 percent if they had been fortunate enough to enter upper streams, but those children who had been put into the lower streams had lost 3·2 percent on average. Evidently environmental experience determines whether latent abilities are developed, or retarded.

Reliable tests of intelligence were developed earlier than tests of personality but even so reports appeared of MZ twins reared apart who showed remarkable resemblance in their adult lives. Cattell, Stice and Kristy (1957) carried out a factor analytic study of twin personality features and concluded that cyclothymia and 'exuberance' factors were more determined by heredity than were general neuroticism and somatic anxiety factors.

The most comprehensive study of twins is that of Shields (1962). Through the British Broadcasting Corporation he traced 44 adult pairs of MZ twins brought up apart (Sep), 44 pairs of MZ twins brought up together (Control) and 32 pairs of DZ twins brought up together (DZ). Those who had been brought up apart had in more than half the instances been separated from one another by the age of three months. Shields assessed the behavioural characteristics of the twins by personal interviews, by intelligence tests, and by self-rating questionnaires of extraversion–intraversion qualities.

As far as intelligence was concerned the MZ twins resembled one another more than the dizygotes. As a measure of resemblance of the one member of each twin pair to the other, Shields used 'intra-class correlation coefficients'. These were as follows for intelligence.

|  |  |
|---|---|
| MZ Control | + ·76 |
| MZ Sep | + ·77 |
| DZ | + ·51 |

Personality testing yielded some intriguing results. The measures of alikeness of the members of the twin pair to each other in the case of extraversion–intraversion, and of neuroticism were as follows:

| | Extraversion–intraversion | Neuroticism |
|---|---|---|
| MZ Control | + ·42 | + ·38 |
| MZ Sep | + ·61 | + ·53 |
| DZ | + ·17 | + ·11 |

In terms of both extraversion–intraversion and neuroticism, the MZ twins were more alike than the DZ twins, but the MZ twins who were separated from each other in early life were actually *more alike* in their adult personality than were those twins who had been reared together! The author attributed this finding to the twin relationship itself.

Although MZ twins may share the same genetic constitution they are in fact very rarely physically identical. One is nearly always bigger than the other, and, as we shall see in the later parts of this chapter, there are a great many other influences that can determine personality and bring about differences between twins. Consequently in the situation of sibling rivalry that inevitably is present in any family group, and certainly within a pair of twins, one twin will tend to have certain advantages over the other, and so one twin might tend always to take the initiative and the other to be more submissive, and so on. Just as when two trees of the same genetic stock grow close together they both become mis-shapen by reason of the presence of the other, whereas planted at a considerable distance would both grow to a full and rounded natural form, so it would seem, the twins brought up apart were better able to develop naturally and without distortion.

However, the control and the separated MZ twins all resembled each other in personality much more than the dizygote twins. In their little traits and habits, in their attitudes, and especially in their gestures and mannerisms, their sexual adjustment, and their rapport with an interviewer, the MZ twins were strikingly alike.

A different method of approach was adopted by Freedman and Keller (1963), whose studies concerned twenty pairs of twin babies, both MZ and DZ. The studies of behaviour were carried out before the zygocity had been determined and depended upon the fact that, in their first year of life, according to Piaget, infants do not take an interest in one another, or imitate one another. Experienced observers each month rated the degree of difference between each member of a twin pair, according to a number of agreed criteria. At the end of the study it was found that there were consistent differences, from month to month, much more often in the case of the DZ twins. If one member of the pair was more lively in one month, he would be more lively in the next month. On the other hand, among the MZ twins there was a low degree of consistency in the rating of behavioural difference. The MZ twins were so alike, it was difficult to demonstrate consistent differences between them.

BODY-BUILD AND PERSONALITY

Body-build must depend in part on life experiences, particularly upon nutrition, but it is commonly believed also to be greatly influenced by heredity. Various authors have suggested that body-build is linked both to personality and to predisposition towards specific mental illnesses. Kretschmer proposed that a cyclothymic personality was associated with a pyknic or thick-set body-build, but that schizoid and schizophrenic features were linked with a lean or asthenic build.

Sheldon, and later Parnell (1958), espoused related hypotheses, but the methods of measuring personality, or of reaching a diagnosis, and the methods of estimating or measuring body-build, did not meet criticisms made of test-retest or inter-observer reliability, nor of the fact that a change in diet could alter build. An independent attempt to confirm Parnell's reports was conducted by Fowlie (1962). Fowlie found test–retest reliability to be low, and in general failed to confirm Parnell's claims, in particular he failed to find any link between body-build and psychiatric diagnosis.

## Pre-natal Effects on Personality

We may recognize that, for those who grow up in an environment which is not grossly distorting, basic personality traits are primarily determined by genetic constitution. We might suppose genetic forces alone might operate during intra-uterine environment. However, even at that time, environmental forces can make a contribution.

In recent years we have seen the example of thalidomide, a foreign chemical interfering with the development of the foetal limbs. The central nervous system also has to develop *in utero* and it now seems possible that subtle effects upon its development could be exerted by naturally occurring chemicals, namely, hormones, and that if the concentration of some of these were abnormal, then the finer differentiation of the nervous system might be so affected as to cause some degree of personality distortion in the offspring.

It was proposed by Stott (1959) that 'pregnancy stress' of mothers could lead to 'unforthcomingness' of the subsequent child, namely, timidity, mousiness, and a lack of natural assertiveness. He was led to this conclusion after a study of backward children and by data gathered about their mothers' pregnancies from clinical records, and other retrospective sources. Stott's hypothesis was soon confirmed in rodents.

If mice live under crowded conditions, enlargement of their adrenal glands occur. Pregnant mice were crowded in cages by Keeley (1962), while control pregnant mice lived in relatively spacious circumstances. After the birth of their offspring, 50 per cent of each kind were cross-fostered. When the offspring were tested, near maturity, by recording the time which elapsed before a single mouse spontaneously would leave its cage to venture across an open space for food, the offspring of the crowded mice took very much longer before they dared to venture out. They were unforthcoming—and in other ways less active and slower to respond.

The role of adrenaline was tested by Thompson, Watson and Charlesworth (1962), using a large number of rats. Some of the groups of rats were injected with adrenaline in the first, second, or third 'trimesters' and others got saline. When their offspring had been born, and half cross-fostered, the eventual mature offspring were found to be less ready to venture forth from the shelter of the sides of a test chamber, if their mothers had been injected with adrenaline in the second or third 'trimesters'.

As might be expected the effects of this sort of procedure depend upon the genetic constitution of the animals and Joffe (1965), for example, has used groups of the Maudsley reactive and non-reactive rats (see page 463), and found that gestational stress, presumably releasing adrenaline, had an effect which varied according to the genetic constitution.

Adrenaline is not the only chemical that can cross the placenta from mother to foetus. Testosterone, which is present in small amounts in normal women, has been investigated in guinea pig pregnancies. If very small doses are injected between certain critical days of development, namely days 30 to 35 of the guinea pig pregnancy (Goy, Bridson and Young, 1964; Phoenix et al., 1959) the offspring show no macroscopic abnormalities, but when the females grow up and engage in sexual behaviour they are relatively unfeminine in what they do. They display feminine-style lordosis infrequently and mount like males in a way that no well-conducted lady guinea pig should. One must conclude that testosterone, or some metabolite, crossed the placenta and acted upon the developing central nervous system in a way that permanently affected the behavioural characteristics of the female guinea pig.

The brain of many animals, including man, is not fully mature at birth and finer differentiation continues in the first year. It has been demonstrated by many experimenters that induced abnormalities of hormonal environment just after birth can permanently affect the pattern of rodent sexual responsiveness in later life. Levine and Mullins (1964), for example, gave a single injection of 100 μg of oestradiol benzoate to female rats 96 hours after birth, and when these grew up they were wholly lacking in normal sexual receptivity. The same dose given to male rats 96 hours after birth led to adult rats unable to achieve intromission, although they mounted as frequently as normal animals.

The nature of the mounts was bizarre, and from the 'head, the side, or high up on the back of the receptive female'. The neonatal hormonal environment can affect more than just sexual behaviour in later life; for example, excess oestrogens at five days of age caused increased stress-induced defaecation in rats of both sexes, when they were 100 days old and also less grooming (Gray, Levine and Broadhurst, 1965).

It seems likely that the general principles of these findings apply to primates, including man. Goy (1968) established scales whereby the normal play of monkey infants could be scored. In some characteristics, such as rough-and-tumble play, or chasing, or mounting, the males normally scored much more highly than the females. However, when he had given small doses of testosterone to pregnant monkeys and allowed their female offspring to grow up to the age of two years, it was found that these experimental girl monkeys were half-way between the normal female and the normal male pattern in respect of their frequencies of mounting, chasing play, and rough-and-tumble play.

Deliberate experiments are not possible with humans but studies have been made of the behaviour of girl hermaphrodites (Money, 1970). Many of their mothers had been given progestin during early pregnancy (in an attempt to prevent abortion), while others were cases of hyper-adrenocortical hermaphroditism (caused by a recessive gene). These girls were characterized by having partial labial fusion and a large clitoris. As controls, Money used girls with Turner's syndrome, in which there is genetic absence of the gonads. He had thirty-seven patients in all, twenty-two of whom were the hermaphrodites and fifteen who suffered from Turner's syndrome. Both kinds of hermaphrodite were rated very high on tomboyishness, whereas girls with Turner's syndrome were rated low. The hermaphrodites had a relatively intense interest in outdoor athletic pursuits, were regarded as tom-boys by other children, they were interested in boys' toys, gave a low priority to marriage, and a high priority to wearing garments of a masculine kind.

At the present time we may only suspect that the developing brain of the human foetus could be influenced by an imbalance in the maternal hormones that reach it across the placenta and that, for example, excess as a result of anxiety, might permanently affect the personality characteristics of the child. We must also suspect that drugs, such as barbiturates or amphetamines, taken by the mother during her pregnancy, can affect the developing foetus, not to cause macroscopic abnormalities alone (Nelson and Forfar, 1971) but also in affecting the finer differentiation of the central nervous system so that the behaviour of the grown offspring will be influenced, as has been shown to be true of rats whose mothers received chlorpromazine or dexamphetamine (Clark, Gorman and Vernadakis, 1970).

## Congenital Modifications of Personality

Cerebral damage early in life is one cause of defect in personality development. Not only can some gross personality disorders be attributed to this, but lesser or minimal degrees of brain damage may be capable of subtler effects on the personality of a substantial section of the population, and probably play an especial role in the case of those who come in conflict with the law or who present in the psychiatric clinic. Central nervous system responses are graded, so that there may be presumed to be an unlimited range, from gross, to slight, to negligible, in the degree of brain damage, and the degree of effect on personality.

Stott (1966) argued that congenital defects, possibly of intra-uterine origin, play a substantial role in the kind of personality maladjustment that is expressed in delinquency, and he adduces evidence that multiple minor physical defects, including liability to such things as squint or infantile pneumonia, are especially frequent in those with minimal congenital brain defects. It has, of course, long been recognized by paediatricians that the brain-damaged or mentally defective child is especially liable to pneumonia.

### MALNUTRITION

In Stott's studies, backwardness in reading and arithmetic, together with personality maladjustment, were coupled with and attributed to a global type of congenital handicap. Low intelligence (as measured by formal tests) and maladjustment, manifest as delinquency, feature most markedly in lower social-class groups or in specific ethnic minorities. Hereditary inferiority, or lack of optimal psychological environment, are sometimes advanced as explanations, with political or racist fervour, but one feature, generally overlooked, is the possible role of under-nutrition.

Might poor nutrition of pregnant mothers and infants in poorer socio-economic groups impair the development of the brain *in utero*, and its continuing differentiation in the early months of life, so impairing potential for later intellectual and social skills? Starvation of the human mother causes reduced birth weight of the offspring, and in infant humans and infant rats there is normally a considerable amount of postnatal brain growth. Severe undernutrition of children in the first year of life is associated with reduced brain weight, less brain protein and RNA, and fewer brain cells in the cerebrum (Winick, Rosso and Waterlow, 1970). The same is true of infant rats (Dobbing, 1968), in whom there is also a slower maturation in the E.E.G. and in the brain amino-acid content, affecting most severely the phylogenetically younger parts of the brain (Mourek *et al.*, 1970)—and it is these phylo-

R

genetically younger areas which are often referred to as our 'higher centres'. The noradrenaline and dopamine content of the brain is also substantially lower in rats whose pregnant mothers had been fed a diet poor in protein (Shoemaker and Wurtman, 1971).

The adaptive or intelligent behaviour of young children who have suffered severe malnutrition has been reported to be impaired, and if the malnutrition occurred while the brain was still differentiating rapidly, namely, in the first six months of life, later treatment of the malnutrition failed to bring performance up to the level of control infants (Cravioto, Delicardie and Birch, 1966). A few years ago it was customary not to feed premature babies in the first few days of life. The deficiency of food, and need to burn what there was in order to keep warm, resulted in a permanent deficiency in brain growth compared with premature babies who, in more recent years, have been given adequate nourishment (Davies and Davis, 1970). In all it would appear that maternal or early infantile malnutrition can be another reason for failure of optimum development in intellect and personality.

Additional evidence that minor degrees of neural defect of early origin can be associated with subsequent subtle personality deviation is provided by a study, conducted in St. Louis, by a group at the Washington School of Medicine (Corah et al., 1965). The children had all been born in the same hospital in the same period, but 134 had been normal full-term newborns and 101 had been full-term newborns who, at the time, had been recorded as having shown signs of hypoxia.

Corah et al. successfully traced 235 of the children when they were seven years old. Neurological, psychological and psychiatric examinations were conducted throughout the whole of one day and without knowledge of the status at birth. Neurological examination failed to distinguish between those who had been hypoxic seven years before and those who had not. However, ratings by parents and by schoolteachers were used to obtain a Vineland Social Quotient. The distribution of scores for the two groups was different (see Fig. 1). Psychological assessment showed that those who had been hypoxic at birth were, at the age of seven, more often 'explosive', 'obtuse', or lacking in social sensitivity. They were more impulsive, more rigid, and were liable to a greater degree of distractability.

Psychiatrists who examined the children were asked to give an overall rating of 'organicity' and in doing this, the psychiatrists, who did not know the birth status, gave significantly higher scores to those who had been hypoxic at birth, indicating that clinicians are capable of detecting minor behavioural cues which are considered to be indicative of neurological deficit, even when these cues are not clearly specified.

It is important to note that Figure 1 suggests no all-or-none effect of minor cerebral damage, but that the hypoxic group were simply shifted to a lower range in the social maturity scale. There was no sharp division between frank pathology and more subtle personality modification.

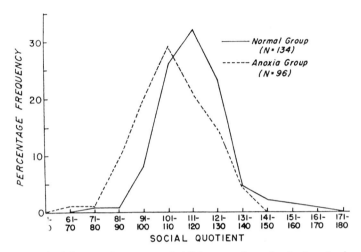

FIG. 1.    Social maturity scores of children aged 7 who had or had not been hypoxic at birth. The hypoxics are less mature but note that the distributions overlap, with no sharp divide to mark out a child who had earlier been hypoxic (from Corah *et al.*, 1965).

An even more striking illustration of relationships between personality maladjustment, multiple congenital handicaps, and family stress in early life, is provided in the studies of low birth-weight Edinburgh children by Drillien (1963; 1969), who followed them over a period of many years.

The 600 children in her study had been born between 1953 and 1955. One third had a birth weight of under 2000 grams. In the subsequent five years all children were seen at home by the same investigator on a minimum of seven occasions, and ratings of the parental relationship in the home, in terms of family stress, were made. The children were later assessed in their second year at school (Drillien, 1963) and again when they were 11 to 12 years old (Drillien, 1969).

Early in the study it became clear that children who had been of low birth weight frequently experienced difficulty at school in their intellectual capacity, and in their personality adjustment, as rated by schoolteachers. In the table below, taken from Drillien's data, mean scores on the Bristol Social Adjustment Guide (a high score implies maladjustment) are shown for those who had been under 2000 grams and who had been over 2500 grams at birth. This is related to whether or not there was family stress in the pre-school years and whether or not there were complications of birth. It will be seen that the children, when aged about seven years, were more maladjusted if they had been of low birth weight and that this was true irrespective of birth complications or family stress. However, where there had been family stress, a well-adjusted personality was less likely. Where there had been complications of birth, the situation was also bad, and where there had been

TABLE I

*Scores given by schoolteachers on the Bristol Social Adjustment Guide to children aged 7. Relation to birth weight, family stress in pre-school years, and complications of pregnancy and delivery (from Drillien, 1963). A higher score means poorer personality adjustment.*

|  | Birth weight under 2000 g Mean scores | P | Birth weight over 2500 G Mean scores | P |
|---|---|---|---|---|
| No stress |  |  |  |  |
| No complications | 6.4 |  | 4.9 |  |
|  |  | 0.05 |  | 0.001 |
| Complications | 10.5 |  | 8.2 |  |
| Stress |  |  |  |  |
| No complications | 13.1 |  | 7.5 |  |
|  |  | n.s. |  | 0.001 |
| Complications | 20.0 |  | 15.6 |  |
| No complications |  |  |  |  |
| No stress | 6.4 |  | 4.9 |  |
|  |  | 0.01 |  | 0.001 |
| Stress | 13.1 |  | 7.5 |  |
| Complications |  |  |  |  |
| No stress | 10.5 |  | 8.2 |  |
|  |  | 0.001 |  | n.s. |
| Stress | 20.0 |  | 15.6 |  |

family stress and complications at birth, the liability to maladjustment was greater still. Where family stress and complications of birth were combined with low birth weight, the mean score on the Social Adjustment Guide was 20 (the maximum), which indicates that the average child in these circumstances was severely maladjusted.

The children were reviewed again when aged 11 to 12. Those who had been of adequate birth weight scored more highly on group I.Q. tests than those who had been underweight. Boys were always worse affected by low birth weight than girls. At this later age the behavioural abnormalities, though causing less marked differences than at about the age of 7, were still apparent in the case of boys from average working class homes. Where the birth weight had been over 2500 grams, 54 percent were rated as well-adjusted and only 17 percent maladjusted, whereas in instances where the birth weight had been under 2000 grams, only 28 percent were scored as well-adjusted and 44 percent maladjusted. In the case of boys from the poorest homes, though there had been a difference in degree of maladjustment at age 7, it no longer revealed itself at the later age. This appeared not to be due to any improvement among those who had been of low birth weight, but to the deterioration of behaviour of the other boys from poor and underprivileged homes.

The low birth weight, in itself, may not have been the primary factor, even where its role was demonstrable, if the work on the early feeding of prematures, cited earlier, is born in mind.

Drillien's studies are of especial value in the illustration they provide of the several contributions of prenatal factors, paranatal complications, family stress in the early years, and social class handicaps. Any one factor can contribute to poorer personality development and where there is more than one adverse factor the effects are cumulative. There are not sharp divisions that enable one to say, 'This boy's personality is abnormal because . . .', rather one must say that personality is graded, and that in any one individual the personality may have been shaped for better or worse by many factors, each contributing, and each interacting with the others: from the child grows the man.

### The Animal Heritage

The foregoing discussion makes us realize that it would be artificial if someone's personality characteristics were attributed solely to inheritance, or thought of as being shaped only by prenatal or paranatal circumstances, and equally artificial if they were thought of as determined solely by features of upbringing. However, we incline to the belief that, for Man, upbringing is of greatest importance if only because, as physicians, we seek scope for preventive therapeutics and can look to the early and formative years as a time when the influence of parents and society could most yield benefits.

It is within a framework of a biological endowment, however, that the learning of social skills occurs. Humans, like animals, are endowed with specific innate responses waiting to be triggered off by certain complex sensory patterns. The mother rat will 'retrieve' any baby rats, or indeed baby kittens, in the vicinity, and if more and more are provided, she will pile them up and up into a great heap.

Apparently she is driven to this by the action of the hormone prolactin on the brain (it will elicit the behaviour even in virgin rats) so that when the pattern of sensory input has some of the characteristics of small infants, an inevitable response ensues. Because of the unlearned nature of these responses we think of them as instinctive. They are probably very frequent in humans too, yet so modified by learning that we often fail to recognize them.

The infant monkey or chimpanzee, when lonely or frightened will appear to 'comfort' itself by squatting on its haunches with head bowed, rocking backwards and forwards. The same behaviour is common among children of 18–24 months who, when put to bed and thereby separated from secure companionship, will quite often rock to and fro in similar manner, or else, when lying on their backs, roll the head and shoulders rhythmically from side to side, perhaps humming to the rhythm. It is a form of behaviour that can often be seen by day during a visit to a shelter for children abandoned by, or removed from, their parents, or in an institution for mentally-retarded children (where there is probably a severe staff shortage) or for blind or deaf children (Berkson and Davenport, 1962). These same conditions of deprivation of interesting stimulation and of companionship cause the same sort of rocking, and other stereotypes in young chimpanzees as well (Davenport and Menzel, 1963). Another apparent comfort-habit of childhood is thumb-sucking and this is just as true for the chimpanzee and the rhesus monkey. Although it is an unlearned response it interacts with learning. Infant monkeys who are reared in the absence of their mothers, and bottle-fed, more often suck their thumbs, toes or penises than similar monkeys who are cup-fed—but the latter direct their oral drive into more biting of their own bodies (Benjamin, 1961), and will in fact do so with especial vigour at times when a normally-reared monkey would direct its aggression outwards.

There are other examples of behaviour that we share with lower animals and that serve broader social functions. The phrase 'pecking order' is part of everyday language, but the 'dominance hierarchy' is a feature of life in more than just the fowl-yard. Primate species all appear to have hierarchical orders within their social groups, with a vigorous male at the top, and a consistent structuring below him, in which threatening grimaces or gestures, more often than physical violence, serve to rebuff challenges and to ensure priorities for food, mates or protection. A monkey reared without normal opportunities for social interaction during its early life has not learned to use its innate response tendencies appropriately, and is unable to enter into a consistent hierarchical relationship, so that it is difficult for him to become a group member (Mason, 1961).

The assertion of dominance, and the acknowledgement of submission, are maintained by innately-determined social signals. Submission can be signalled in most non-human primates by 'presenting' of the backside. We don't do it in quite the same way, but when one sees a dog signalling submission by lowering of the tail and hanging of the head, one recognizes something nearer to the human practice whereby submission is signalled by aversion of the eyes. 'Permission' for the other person to speak during a conversation is also signalled by this dropping of the eyes (Argyle, 1967).

Threat is conveyed by baboons and macaque monkeys through staring, sometimes with quick jerking of the head, down and then up, in the direction of the opponent, with ears laid back, and a pronounced raising of the eyebrows (Hall and De Vore, 1965). A little reflection allows one to realize that one has seen the same staring, eyebrows raised, with quick head-jerks, in man, 'Want a fight, huh?'.

It is probable that most human social signals are learned and vary with local customs, but we may infer from other primates that many facial expressions or bodily poses have an innately-determined significance for man too—in fact the smile of a baby, to be discussed later, is a human social signal that universally and immediately evokes stereotyped responses.

Male monkeys who have been reared in total isolation and who are then presented with a bright-bottomed female at her time of maximum sexual receptivity, appear puzzled and unable fully to take advantage of the situation, yet nevertheless have penile erections. Response to the complex visual stimulus offered by the female form is evidently innate. More subtle were the studies of Sackett (1966), who found that the pictures of another monkey infant, or of a threatening adult, released innate responses.

Sackett reared monkeys in total isolation for nine months. On one ground-glass wall of their cages could be projected colour pictures. The pictures included one of an adult monkey with a 'threat' facial expression, one of a frightened monkey, one of another infant monkey, and control pictures of laboratory apparatus, a sunset, and so on. Observers scored the amount of vocalization, and the amount of apparent play, or other disturbance, provoked by the presentation of the pictures for 2 minute periods at intervals over the nine months. The threat pictures were much the most disturbing and caused vocalization four times as often as the control pictures. Pictures of another infant gave the highest scores for play. A mechanism was present whereby the monkey could sometimes choose to project the slides himself and this made possible one of the most important findings. In the first two and a half months of life the 'threat' picture was treated no differently from the infant monkey picture, but between three and four months of age the threat picture provoked extreme vocalization and avoidance, yet by the sixth month was again treated no differently from the other.

We may interpret the observations in terms of an innate capacity to respond to facial expression and in terms of the *delayed appearance of a capacity for fear* in response to a specific facial-appearance stimulus, and later extinction of the fear response, when it had been learned that no harm followed the threat picture. The monkey matures more rapidly than the human and the delayed appearance of fear at 2·5–3 months parallels its appearance at about six months in the human, as will be discussed later. The delayed appearance is an example of a *critical period* phenomenon coming at a time of life determined by the maturation of the nervous system. Normally the fear response to a fellow-being develops only after an earlier critical period during which *attachment* to other fellow-beings has begun.

The early development of attachment responses has been most often studied in lower vertebrates, especially birds, and the term *imprinting* has been used to signify this form of early learning which can only fully take place within a limited time period after birth. It is a form of learning that occurs in the absence of conventional reward (food, warmth, etc.) and initially depends only on visual, auditory or gustatory contact (though it is later strengthened by reinforcement in the usual way). The 'imprinted' object (normally the mother, owing to her proximity) is assiduously followed by the 'attached' infant, if only with the eyes of the non-ambulant human, who cries and puts out other distress-signals if lost, and continues to do so until restored to the fold. A potentially interesting feature of the animal studies is that the general kind of object upon which the initial imprinting takes place is one that is favoured as an eventual sexual object, so that birds experimentally imprinted on humans may, when mature, attempt to copulate with humans.

## BIOLOGICAL ASPECTS OF HUMAN DEVELOPMENT

### SOCIAL RESPONSES IN INFANCY AND EARLY CHILDHOOD

The methods of animal ethologists have been applied with increasing success to the study of early childhood behaviour (Schaffer, 1971). Spitz and Wolf (1946) described *the infant's smiling response*. They found that at around six weeks of life, but not before, infants began to smile at a certain facial configuration which had the properties of regularly eliciting a social smile from the baby. At between six weeks and three months infants respond to a life-sized face with eyes, seen in full front view. Smiling is enhanced if the face is also moving. Masks, even unpleasant ones, can have the same effect. If the face is turned to present a profile to the baby, his smile fades and he no longer pays attention. The smiling response at this stage is undiscriminating, and occurs whatever the expression on the face presented to the infant. At around three months a change occurs. Infants no longer smile at any human face; they now smile selectively at familiar faces, for example at those of their mothers and fathers. Infants reared in institutions by multiple care-takers will not develop a discriminating smiling response if no one person becomes more familiar than another. The *differential smiling response* is one of the first signs of a specific attachment forming between the infant and his parents.

More recent research has focussed both on the antecedents of the baby's smile and on those attributes of human faces that make them into particularly attractive spectacles for young infants. Peter Wolff (1963) for example, found that eye-to-eye contact with other people is first made at around three and a half weeks of age. Before then the baby's gaze wanders without inducing a feeling of contact in the other person. Kagan and his colleagues (1966) found that four-month old infants smile significantly more at three-dimensional models of faces with regular features than they do at models on which eyes, nose and mouth are 'scrambled'.

The *separation reaction* is the next landmark in the sequence of social responses in infancy. Schaffer and Callender (1959) observed 76 children under one year of age during and after a brief hospital admission. All babies cried rather often and vocalized little while in hospital. Babies under seven months, however, responded to their unfamiliar nurses as positively as to their mothers, and when the mothers left after visiting time, the babies did not protest. On returning home they were at first rather quiet and preoccupied, staring at their environment, so that their mothers found it difficult to make social contact with them. This state lasted from a few hours up to three days, and was thought to be a reaction to the cessation of the sensory monotony experienced in hospital.

Babies over *seven months* behaved very differently both in hospital and on returning home. In hospital they protested vigorously each time their mothers left and they reacted with manifestations of anxiety when approached by strange nurses, who were not able to comfort them. Such reactions lasted from one to eight days and then they stopped. Children now cried less, babbled more and became more responsive to their unfamiliar caretakers. However, they continued to cling to their mothers and to cry when the mothers left. On returning home these older infants showed a syndrome of 'over-dependence', clinging to their mother, crying when she disappeared from view, and attempting to follow her wherever she went, at least with their eyes. This state lasted for about two weeks.

Fretting in response to transient domestic separations from familiar people (as when the mother temporarily leaves the baby alone in a room) has been used by Schaffer as an index of *social attachment* (Schaffer and Emerson, 1964). He found that attachment behaviour starts at about six to seven months. While the mother is usually the person to whom infants form their first and strongest attachments, this is not always so. Sometimes fathers, grandparents, or older siblings are chosen, although they do not undertake the major nurturing functions and although the baby sees less of them than of the mother. The first social attachment appears to depend on the capacity of the other person to provide optimum stimulation and interest for the infant. As in the rhesus monkey, it is not primarily related to feeding. The next social response to develop is the *fear of strangers* (Schaffer, 1966*a*), usually appearing as a transient phenomenon four weeks after the first evidence of specific social attachments. Schaffer found the intensity of specific attachments to reach a peak at around 41–44 weeks, to decline temporarily and then slowly to rise again. The decline coincided with the onset of crawling and walking, suggesting that the novelty of these new motor skills temporarily diverts the child's attention from the need for the familiar person's presence.

In summary, the infant undergoes three stages of early social behaviour:

1. An asocial stage in which he seeks optimum sensory stimulation from all aspects of his environment (up to 6–12 weeks);

2 A stage of indiscriminate attachment behaviour in which human beings are singled out as particularly satisfying objects (from about 3 to 7 months); and

3 A stage in which true social attachments to specific individuals are formed (in the third quarter of the first year of life).

There are, of course, marked individual differences in the rate of development of social, as of other responses in infancy. There are also individual differences in the quality of responses and in the ease with which they can be elicited. Some of these individual differences are genetically determined. Freedman (1965) has provided suggestive evidence that identical twins are more alike in their development of the social smile and the fear of strangers than are fraternal twins. Moreover, the age of onset of social responses is related to the child's intelligence as measured by developmental tests.

Thomas *et al.* (1963) also produced evidence for the constitutional basis of some aspects of behaviour in early childhood. In a longitudinal study of infants and young children they demonstrated that there are qualities of temperament which distinguish between children but remain relatively stable for each individual child, at least during his first three years.

The following temperamental attributes were delineated by these research workers: level of motor activity; sensitivity to stimuli (e.g. how readily the child woke at night in response to light and sound, whether small or big stimuli were needed to elicit responses from him in different situations during the day); intensity of response (e.g. whether, when he cried, he tended to cry softly or loudly, when amused he tended to smile or to laugh uproariously, when frustrated he merely sulked or had a temper outburst); rhythmicity of biological functions (the regularity of the child's patterns of sleeping, eating and elimination); predominant mood (whether happy or sad); adaptability (how often a child had to encounter the same new situation, such as being given a new food, being bathed, having his hair cut, before adapting to the situation); approach or withdrawal in the face of novel situations (e.g. the first spoonful of orange juice in infancy, the first haircut, meeting a stranger, entering nursery school for the first time); persistence; and distractibility. Because these qualitative aspects of behaviour could be observed soon after birth, and because they tended to remain stable at least during the early years of childhood, they were thought to have a constitutional basis.

The child's actual life experiences also contribute to the nature of his early social behaviour. The intensity of attachment, for example, is greater when the number of caretakers is low; the greater the number of people encountered by the infant in his daily life, the later the onset of his fear of strangers (Schaffer, 1966a).

Despite individual differences in the rate of development and in the quality of responses, differences depending both on genetic and on environmental variables, the sequence of social responses in infancy and early childhood, like the sequence of cognitive stages of development examined in Chapter IX, Vol. I, is fixed. It depends on a common genetic heritage which all human infants share.

BOWLBY'S BIOLOGICAL THEORY OF ATTACHMENT BEHAVIOUR

Bowlby (1969) has reviewed the studies of attachment behaviour in subhuman primates and in man. The behaviour of both mothers and young in these species results in the maintenance of proximity between them. Bowlby views these behaviour patterns in mothers and young as biologically adaptive to the ordinary, expectable environment (which Bowlby calls the 'environment of evolutionary adaptedness') and as fulfilling two main functions necessary for survival and propagation: protection of the young against predators and enabling the young to learn adaptive patterns of behaviour from their mothers by imitation. In human babies one of the most important components of early learning is language. We know that the early basis for language is acquired by imitation during the stage of life at which attachment behaviour is at its height (Lenneberg, 1967) and that children deprived of opportunities to form attachments to individual mother figures are in later life retarded in language development (Ainsworth, 1962; Tizard and Joseph, 1970). Bowlby suggests that behaviour patterns mediating attachment of young to adults are complementary to those mediating care of young by adults; that these behaviours are instinctive, depending on universally present, innate control systems which become effective at different stages of the life cycle; and that the sequence of their un-folding is environmentally stable to a high degree.

In human mother-child couples the maintenance of proximity is at first dependent entirely on the mother's behaviour. In the second half of the first year of life the infant takes on a more active role and his proximity-seeking is at its height in the second and third years of life. Thereafter it gradually decreases as the child becomes, and is allowed to become, more independent and ventures forth into the outside world. Bowlby regards affective and motivational aspects of proximity-seeking, such as the child's dependency needs and the mother's protective love of the baby, as inner, experiential counterparts rather than 'causes' of the behaviour patterns he discusses.

Attachment behaviour is the behavioural system most intensively studied so far. It is likely that in time as much will be known about other ubiquitous behavioural systems which, like attachment, are independent of culture and of individual parental attitudes. Attachment behaviour is the basis for the infant's earliest social interactions, which themselves show superadded characteristics depending on culture and on indivi-dual variations. The biological basis for later social interactions, such as the struggle for autonomy in the child's third year of life, and his erotic relationships with parents during the stage of primary identification between three and five years (the genital stage in psychoanalytic terms) has yet to be established.

THE VICISSITUDES OF THE CHILD'S EARLY SOCIAL RELATIONSHIPS

The clinical syndromes associated with early social and maternal deprivation will be discussed elsewhere (Chapter III, Vol. II). The subject has recently been well reviewed by Rutter (1972). Here it need only be said that personality development is impaired when there is interference between the biological control systems and the environ-mental stimuli necessary to activate them during the sensitive periods of an individual's development. Such interference can come from organic deficits in the individual, such as diffuse brain damage, blind-ness or deafness. Blind children, for example, develop specific attach-ments more slowly that sighted children, but their attachments are more intense and persist longer (Bowlby, 1969).

During the stage of indiscriminate social attachment, between three and six months, the essential environmental ingredient is not a con-tinuous parent figure but adequate social stimulation of all kinds. Schaffer (1966b) has shown that the developmental level of infants dropped significantly during a period in hospital between the ages of three and six months (as measured by a rise of measured intelligence on returning to their homes) while no drop occurred during a similar period in a baby-home where opportunities for social interactions were much greater. In both settings the infants were looked after by multiple caretakers. Schaffer also found that constitutionally active infants were protected against cognitive retardation during the period of social deprivation in hospital, while constitutionally inactive, placid babies, less able to seek out stimuli for themselves, suffered more. This study demonstrates that differences in the effects of deprivation cannot be accounted for by its duration and the age of the infant alone. Constitutional aspects of temperament also play a part.

Serious personality impairment is known to occur when, during the stage of specific social attachment, between six months and three years, infants are not given opportunities to form enduring relationships with a limited number of people. Children reared by many caretakers simultaneously, or exposed to repeated disruptions of their early attachments, show subsequent deficits in cognitive developments, especially in language, and in their capacity to form affectionate bonds with others (Ainsworth, 1962).

Adverse experiences in early childhood (especially during the first three stages of emotional development, see Chapter X, Vol. I) are important causes of behaviour disorders in childhood and of psychoneurotic illnesses and certain personality disorders in adult life. Bowlby's theoretical contribution to the work of developmental psychologists and ethologists, suggests that it may be fruitful to regard some of these disorders not only from a social and psychological point of view but also in biological terms as due to interferences, during sensitive periods of development, between innate biological control systems of behaviour and their environmental determinants.

COGNITIVE DEVELOPMENT

Affective and social development in childhood is paralleled by cognitive development. In fact, the child's intellectual level at each stage, that is how he perceives and reasons about the world and himself in relation to people, things and ideas, is one of the major determinants of his social and emotional development. Knowledge about cognitive processes in childhood is more advanced than knowledge about social behaviour because of the contributions of Jean Piaget to child psychology (Piaget, 1932, 1951, 1952). An outline of Piaget's stages of intellectual development is found in Chapter IX, Vol. I.

Piaget describes four factors contributing to the cognitive development of the child:

1. Maturation, that is organic, neurological maturation determined by innate biological factors;

2. Opportunities for the exercise of functions and for experiences of interactions with inanimate objects;

3. Opportunities for social interactions and learning from being taught; and

4. Internal, psychological, mechanisms for constructing successive, cognitive models (Piaget and Inhelder, 1970).

These inner mechanisms, or schemata as Piaget has called them, depend on interactions between the first three factors. Their development however, although varying in rate, is fixed, and Piaget has described a universally-present sequence of qualitatively different cognitive models characterizing the stages of personality development in childhood. Organic, maturational factors determine the maximum rate of development for the individual and his maximum adult level. Interactions with inanimate objects and with people affect the specific contents of a child's thinking. In addition, restriction of opportunities for such interaction can impede the rate of development and set limits to ultimate achievements. The sequence of transformation of cognitive models, however, like the sequence of social-emotional relationships, depends in addition on biologically determined and universally present potentialities.

## REFERENCES

AINSWORTH, M. D. (1962) The effects of maternal deprivation: a review of findings and controversy in the context of research strategy. In *Deprivation of Maternal Care: A Reassessment of its Effects*. Public Health Papers No. 14. Geneva, W.H.O.

ARGYLE, M. (1967) *The Psychology of Interpersonal Behaviour*. Hammondsworth, Middlesex. Penguin Books.

BENJAMIN, L. S. (1961) The effect of bottle and cup feeding on the non-nutritive sucking of the infant rhesus monkey. *Journal of Comparative and Physiological Psychology*, **54,** 230–237.

BERKSON, G. & DAVENPORT, R. K. (1962) Stereotyped movements of mental defectives. *American Journal of Mental Deficiency*, **66,** 849–852.

BOWLBY, J. (1969) *Attachment and Loss: Vol. I. Attachment*, the Hogarth Press and the Institute of Psycho-Analysis, London.

BROADHURST, P. L. (1960) In *Experiments in Personality*, Vol. I. Edited by H. J. Eysenck. London: Routledge and Kegan Paul.

CATTELL, R. B., STICE, G. F. & KRISTY, N. F. (1957) A first approximation to nature-nurture ratios for eleven primary personality factors in objective tests. *Journal of abnormal and social psychology*, **54,** 143–159.

CLARK, V. H., GORMAN, D. & VERNADAKIS, A. (1970) Effects of pre-natal administration of psychotropic drugs on behaviour of developing rats. *Developmental Psychobiology*, **3,** 225–235.

CORAH, N. L., ANTHONY, E. J., PAINTER, P., STERN, J. A. & THURSTON, D. (1965) Effects of perinatal anoxia after seven years. *Psychological Monographs*, **79,** No. 3.

CRAVIOTO, J., DELICARDIE, E. R. & BIRCH, H. G. (1966) Nutrition, growth and neurointegrative development: an experimental and ecologic study. *Pediatrics, Springfield*, **38,** 319–372.

DAVENPORT, R. K. & MENZEL, E. W. (1963) Stereotyped behaviour of the infant champanzee. *Archives of General Psychiatry*, **8,** 99–104.

DAVIES, P. A. & DAVIS, J. P. (1970) Very low birth weight and subsequent head growth. *Lancet*, **2**, 1216–1219.

DOBBING, J. (1968) In *Applied Neuro-Chemistry*. Edited by A. N. Davison & J. Dobbing. Oxford: Blackwell.

DOUGLAS, J. W. B. (1964) *The Home and the School*. London: MacGibbon and Kee.

DRILLIEN, C. M. (1963) Obstetric hazard, mental retardation and behaviour disturbance in primary school. *Developmental Medicine and Child Neurology*, **5**, 3–13.

DRILLIEN, C. M. (1969) School disposal and performance for children of different birth weight born 1953–1960. *Archives of Diseases in Childhood*, **44**, 562–570.

FOWLIE, H. C. (1962) The physique of female psychiatric patients. *Journal of Mental Science*, **108**, 594–603.

FREEDMAN, D. G. & KELLER, B. (1963) Inheritance of behaviour in infants. *Science*, **140**, 196–198.

FREEDMAN, D. G. (1965) Hereditary Control of early social behaviour. In *Determinants of Infant Behaviour*, Vol. III, Edited by B. M. Foss. Methuen, London.

GOY, R. W., BRIDSON, W. E. & YOUNG, W. C. (1964) Period of maximal susceptibility of the prenatal female guinea pig to masculinizing actions of testosterone proprionate. *Journal of Comparative and Physiological Psychology*, **57**, 166–174.

GOY, R. W. (1968) In *Endocrinology and Human Behaviour*, p. 12. Edited by R. P. Michael. London: Oxford University Press.

GRAY, J. A., LEVINE, S. & BROADHURST, P. L. (1965) Gonadal hormone injections in infancy and adult emotional behaviour. *Animal Behaviour*, **13**, 33–45.

HALL, K. R. L. & DEVORE, I. (1965) In *Primate Behaviour*, Edited by I. DeVore. p. 53, New York: Holt, Rinehart & Winston.

JOFFE, J. M. (1965) Genotype and prenatal and premating stress interact to affect adult behaviour in rats. *Science*, **150**, 1844–1845.

KAGAN, J., HENKER, B. A., HEN-TOV, A., LEVINE, J. & LEWIS, M. (1966) Infants' differential reactions to familiar and distorted faces. *Child Development*, **37**, 519–532.

KEELEY, K. (1962) Prenatal influence on behaviour of offspring of crowded mice. *Science*, **135**, 44–45.

LENNEBERG, E. H. (1967) *Biological Foundations of Language*, New York: Wiley.

LEVINE, S. & MULLINS, R. (1964) Estrogen administered neonatally affects adult sexual behaviour in male and female rats. *Science*, **144**, 185–187.

MASON, W. A. (1961) The effects of social restrictions on the behaviour of rhesus monkeys: III dominance tests. *Journal of Comparative and Physiological Psychology*, **54**, 694–699.

MONEY, J. (1970) Sexual dimorphism and homosexual gender identity, *Psychological Bulletin*, **74**, 425–440.

MOUREK, J., AGRAWAL, H. C., DAVIS, J. M. & HIMWICH, W. A. (1970) The effects of short-term starvation on amino acid content in rat brain during ontogeny. *Brain Research*, **19**, 229–237.

NELSON, M. M. & FORFAR, J. O. (1971) Associations between drugs administered during pregnancy and congenital abnormalities of the fetus. *British Medical Journal*, **1**, 523–527.

NEWMAN, H. H., FREEMAN, F. N. & HOLZINGER, K. J. (1937) *Twins: A Study of Heredity and Environment*. Chicago: University of Chicago Press.

PARNELL, R. W. (1958) *Behaviour and Physique*, London: Edward Arnold.

PHOENIX, C. H., GOY, R. W., GERALL, A. A. & YOUNG, W. C. (1959) Organizing action of parentally administered testosterone propionate on the tissues mediating mating behaviour in the female guinea pig. *Endocrinal*, **65**, 369–382.

PIAGET, J. (1932) *The Moral Judgement of the Child*. London: Routledge and Kegan Paul.

PIAGET, J. (1951) *The Child's Conception of the World*. London: Routledge and Kegan Paul,

PIAGET, J. (1952) *The Language and Thoughts of the Child*. London: Routledge and Kegan Paul,

PIAGET, J. & INHELDER, B. (1970) *The Psychology of the Child*. London: Routledge and Kegan Paul,

RUTTER, M. (1972) *Maternal Deprivation Reassessed*. London: Penguin Books.

SACKETT, G. P. (1966) Monkeys reared in isolation with pictures as visual input: evidence for an innate releasing mechanism. *Science*, **154**, 1468–1473.

SCHAFFER, H. R. & CALLENDER, W. M. (1959) Psychological effects of hospitalization in infancy. *Paediatrics*, **24**, 528–539.

SCHAFFER, H. R. & EMERSON, P. E. (1964) The Development of social attachments in infancy. *Monographs of the Society for Research in Child Development*, **29**, No. 2. (Serial No. 93).

SCHAFFER, H. R. (1966a) The onset of fear of strangers and the incongruity hypothesis. *Journal of Child Psychology and Psychiatry*, **7**, 95–106.

SCHAFFER, H. R. (1966b). Activity level as a constitutional determinant of infantile reaction to deprivation. *Child Development*, **37**, 595–602.

SCHAFFER, H. R. (1971) *The Growth of Sociability*. London: Penguin Books.

SHIELDS, J. (1962) *Monozygotic Twins*. London: Oxford University Press.

SHOEMAKER, W. J. & WURTMAN, R. J. (1971) Perinatal undernutrition: accumulation of catecholamines in rat brain. *Science*, **171**, 1017–1019.

SPITZ, R. A. & WOLFF, K. M. (1946) The smiling response; a contribution to the ontogenesis of social relations, *Genetic Psychology Monographs*, **34**, 57–125.

STOTT, D. H. (1959) Evidence for pre-natal impairment of temperament in mentally retarded children. *Vita humana*, **2**, 125–148.

STOTT, D. H. (1966) *Studies of Troublesome Children*. London: Tavistock Publications.

THOMAS, A., BIRCH, H. G., CHESS, S., HERTZIG, M. E. & KORN, S. (1963) *Behavioural Individuality in Early Childhood*. New York University Press.

THOMPSON, W. R., WATSON, T. & CHARLESWORTH, W. R. (1962) The effects of prenatal maternal stress on offspring behaviour in rats. *Psychological Monographs*, **76**, No. 38.

TIZARD, B. & JOSEPH, A. (1970) Cognitive development of young children in residential care: a study of children aged 24 months, *Journal of Child Psychology and Psychiatry*, **II**, 177–186.

WINICK, M., ROSSO, P. & WATERLOW, J. (1970) Cellular growth of cerebrum, cerebellum, and brain stem in normal and marasmic children. *Experimental Neurology*, **26**, 393–400.

WOLFF, P. H. (1963) Observations on the early development of smiling. In *Determinants of Infant Behaviour, Vol. II*. Edited by B. M. Foss. London: Methuen.

# INDEX

The Volume numbers are indicated by I and II

i

# NOTES

NOTES

NOTES